THE EVERLASTING GOSPEL

Charles H. Spurgeon

Solid Ground Christian Books

Other Related Titles from Solid Ground

In addition to the book *The Everlasting Gospel* which you hold in your hands, Solid Ground has published the following related titles:

THE GOSPEL FOR THE PEOPLE by Charles H. Spurgeon

Sixty Short Sermons, with a 34 page Sketch of Mr. Spurgeon's Life, and Fourteen Portraits and Engravings, with a Preface by Pastor Thomas Spurgeon. These Short Sermons were selected by Thomas Spurgeon (his son) from the Series with a view to their being used in Mission Halls, and other similar places. They are about half the length of the ordinary Sermons.

THE GOSPEL OF THE GRACE OF GOD by Thomas Spurgeon

This precious little volume was published in 1884 with the hearty approval of all those who heard the sermons preached by Thomas Spurgeon (son of Charles H. Spurgeon) during an illness of his father. The Publishers asked Charles to write a Preface to help the circulation of the work.

COMMENTING & COMMENTARIES by Charles H. Spurgeon

A Reference Guide to Buying the Best Books

"*Commenting and Commentaries* is a guide for buying and using Bible commentaries of many kinds, made entertaining by the pungent good humor of the author, Charles Haddon Spurgeon. It is an invaluable resource for ministers and theological students, as well as all Bible students, introducing them to the riches of the best of what has been written about the Bible in past generations. Let Commenting and Commentaries be your key to unlock the world of pre-twentieth-century evangelical Bible commentaries. You will find the key tried and true!" - Joel Beeke

FROM THE PULPIT TO THE PALM BRANCH

A Memorial to Charles H. Spurgeon

This impressive volume is a true celebration of the life of "The Prince of Preachers" with special focus on the last months of his life, his death and the twelve remarkable days which followed. This rare volume contains the very last addresses delivered by Spurgeon in the last month of his life.

"Many will be happy to know this long-unobtainable volume on Spurgeon is to be available again. I have collected such books for years but not yet owned this rare book. May the recovery of Spurgeon's memory lead many to the devotion to Christ which so marked his life!" - Rev. Iain H. Murray

THE EVERLASTING GOSPEL
OF
THE OLD AND NEW TESTAMENTS

CHARLES H. SPURGEON

SOLID GROUND CHRISTIAN BOOKS
BIRMINGHAM, ALABAMA USA

Solid Ground Christian Books
PO Box 660132
Vestavia Hills AL 35266
205-443-0311
mike.sgcb@gmail.com
www.solid-ground-books.com

THE EVERLASTING GOSPEL
of the Old & New Testaments
Charles Haddon Spurgeon (1834-1892)
Selected by General Sir Robert Phayre (1820-1897)

First published in 1897 by Passmore and Alabaster in London

First Solid Ground edition published in May 2013

Cover design by Borgo Design
Contact them at borgogirl@bellsouth.net

ISBN- 978-159925-2858

"THE EVERLASTING GOSPEL"

OF THE

OLD & NEW TESTAMENTS.

SERMONS PREACHED

BY

C. H. SPURGEON.

SELECTED BY

General Sir ROBERT PHAYRE, K.C.B.

"Ye were redeemed . . . with the precious blood of Christ, as of a lamb without blemish and without spot: who verily was foreordained before the foundation of the world, but was manifest in these last times for you, who by him do believe in God, that raised him up from the dead, and gave him glory; that your faith and hope might be in God. Seeing ye have purified your souls in obeying the truth through the Spirit unto unfeigned love of the brethren, see that ye love one another with a pure heart fervently: being born again, not of corruptible seed, but of incorruptible, by the word of God, which liveth and abideth for ever. For all flesh is as grass, and all the glory of man as the flower of grass. The grass withereth, and the flower thereof falleth away: but the word of the Lord endureth for ever. And this is the word which by the gospel is preached unto you."—1 PETER i. 18—25.

London:
PASSMORE & ALABASTER, PATERNOSTER BUILDINGS.

All rights reserved.

PUBLISHERS' NOTE.

ONLY a few days before SIR ROBERT PHAYRE received his Lord's summons, "Come up higher," he had completed the selection of Sermons here published, and given instructions for them to be bound in a volume for his own use. He had also chosen the title as printed on the present title-page, and the passage of Scripture which he wished to have inserted there as a kind of motto for the whole series of discourses. The gallant general was a regular reader and an ardent admirer of MR. SPURGEON's Sermons, and in his opinion the thirty-six here collected formed by themselves a most timely testimony against many of the prominent and pernicious errors and heresies of the present day. It is thought that many will wish to possess the volume compiled by this eminent Protestant and Evangelical leader so shortly before he went to join the beloved preacher in the presence of their Lord.

CONTENTS.

PAGE

FOUNDATION WORK.
"And the king commanded, and they brought great stones, costly stones, and hewed stones, to lay the foundation of the house."—1 Kings v. 17. 1

THE SERPENT'S SENTENCE.
"And the LORD God said unto the serpent, Because thou hast done this, thou art cursed above all cattle, and above every beast of the field; upon thy belly shalt thou go, and dust shalt thou eat all the days of thy life: and I will put enmity between thee and the woman, and between thy seed and her seed; it shall bruise thy head, and thou shalt bruise his heel."—Genesis iii. 14, 15. 13

CHRIST, THE CONQUEROR OF SATAN.
"And I will put enmity between thee and the woman, and between thy seed and her seed; it shall bruise thy head, and thou shalt bruise his heel."—Genesis iii. 15. 25

THE INCARNATION AND BIRTH OF CHRIST.
"But thou, Bethlehem Ephratah, though thou be little among the thousands of Judah, yet out of thee shall he come forth unto me that is to be ruler in Israel; whose goings forth have been from of old, from everlasting."—Micah v. 2. 37

"GOD WITH US."
"They shall call his name Emmanuel, which being interpreted is, God with us."—Matthew i. 23. 45

THE GREAT MYSTERY OF GODLINESS.
"And without controversy great is the mystery of godliness: God was manifest in the flesh, justified in the Spirit, seen of angels, preached unto the Gentiles, believed on in the world, received up into glory."—1 Timothy iii. 16. 57

THE HEXAPLA OF MYSTERY.
"And without controversy great is the mystery of godliness: God was manifest in the flesh, justified in the Spirit, seen of angels, preached unto the Gentiles, believed on in the world, received up into glory."—1 Timothy iii. 16. 69

THE MAN CHRIST JESUS.
"Now consider how great this man was."—Hebrews vii. 4. ... 81

FOUND BY JESUS, AND FINDING JESUS.
"The day following Jesus would go forth into Galilee, and findeth Philip, and saith unto him, Follow me. Now Philip was of Bethsaida, the city of Andrew and Peter. Philip findeth Nathanael, and saith unto him, We have found him, of whom Moses in the law, and the prophets, did write, Jesus of Nazareth, the son of Joseph."—John i. 43—45. 93

THE ESSENCE OF SIMPLICITY.
"Jesus heard that they had cast him out; and when he had found him, he said unto him, Dost thou believe on the Son of God? He answered and said, Who is he, Lord, that I might believe on him?"—John ix. 35, 36. 105

SALVATION BY WORKS, A CRIMINAL DOCTRINE.
"I do not frustrate the grace of God: for if righteousness come by the law, then Christ is dead in vain."—Galatians ii. 21. 117

THE GOSPEL OF THE GLORY OF CHRIST.
"The light of the glorious gospel of Christ."—2 Corinthians iv. 4. ... 129

THE COMMON SALVATION.
"The common salvation."—Jude 3. 141

NUMBER 1,500; OR, LIFTING UP THE BRAZEN SERPENT.
"And Moses made a serpent of brass, and put it upon a pole, and it came to pass, that if a serpent had bitten any man, when he beheld the serpent of brass, he lived."—Numbers xxi. 9. 153

THE BLOOD OF SPRINKLING.
"And to Jesus the mediator of the new covenant, and to the blood of sprinkling, that speaketh better things than that of Abel. See that ye refuse not him that speaketh. For if they escaped not who refused him that spake on earth, much more shall not we escape, if we turn away from him that speaketh from heaven."—Hebrews xii. 24, 25. 165

THE BLOOD OF SPRINKLING (Second Sermon).
"Ye are come .... to Jesus the mediator of the new covenant, and to the blood of sprinkling, that speaketh better things than that of Abel. See that ye refuse not him that speaketh."—Hebrews xii. 24, 25. 177

THE TEACHING OF THE FOOT-WASHING.
"Jesus knowing that the Father had given all things into his hands, and that he was come from God, and went to God; he riseth from supper, and laid aside his garments; and took a towel, and girded himself. After that he poureth water into a bason, and began to wash the disciples' feet, and to wipe them with the towel wherewith he was girded."—John xiii. 3—5. 189

JESUS, THE KING OF TRUTH.
"Pilate therefore said unto him, Art thou a king then? Jesus answered, Thou sayest that I am a king. To this end was I born, and for this cause came I into the world, that I should bear witness unto the truth. Every one that is of the truth heareth my voice."—John xviii. 37. 201

THE INDWELLING AND OUTFLOWING OF THE HOLY SPIRIT.
"He that believeth on me, as the scripture hath said, out of his belly shall flow rivers of living water. (But this spake he of the Spirit, which they that believe on him should receive: for the Holy Ghost was not yet given; because that Jesus was not yet glorified.)"—John vii. 38, 39.

"Nevertheless I tell you the truth; It is expedient for you that I go away: for if I go not away, the Comforter will not come unto you; but if I depart, I will send him unto you."—John xvi. 7. 213

CONTENTS.

THE HOLY SPIRIT'S CHIEF OFFICE.

"He shall glorify me: for he shall receive of mine, and shall shew it unto you. All things that the Father hath are mine: therefore said I, that he shall take of mine, and shall shew it unto you."—John xvi. 14, 15. ... 225

THE LEADING OF THE SPIRIT, THE SECRET TOKEN OF THE SONS OF GOD.

"As many as are led by the Spirit of God, they are the sons of God."—Romans viii. 14. ... 237

THE GREATEST EXHIBITION OF THE AGE.

"For as often as ye eat this bread, and drink this cup, ye do shew the Lord's death till he come."—1 Corinthians xi. 26. ... 249

THE WINNOWING FAN.

"Follow peace with all men, and holiness, without which no man shall see the Lord: looking diligently lest any man fail of the grace of God; lest any root of bitterness springing up trouble you, and thereby many be defiled."—Hebrews xii. 14, 15. ... 261

THE FAINTING WARRIOR.

"O wretched man that I am! who shall deliver me from the body of this death? I thank God, through Jesus Christ our Lord."—Romans vii. 24, 25. ... 273

ONWARD!

"Brethren, I count not myself to have apprehended: but this one thing I do, forgetting those things which are behind, and reaching forth unto those things which are before, I press toward the mark for the prize of the high calling of God in Christ Jesus."—Philippians iii. 13, 14. ... 281

THE CHILD OF LIGHT WALKING IN LIGHT.

"If we say that we have fellowship with him, and walk in darkness, we lie, and do not the truth: but if we walk in the light, as he is in the light, we have fellowship one with another, and the blood of Jesus Christ his Son cleanseth us from all sin."—1 John i. 6, 7. ... 293

WALKING IN THE LIGHT, AND WASHED IN THE BLOOD.

"But if we walk in the light, as he is in the light, we have fellowship one with another, and the blood of Jesus Christ his Son cleanseth us from all sin."—1 John i. 7. ... 305

THE ASCENSION AND THE SECOND ADVENT PRACTICALLY CONSIDERED.

"And while they looked stedfastly toward heaven as he went up, behold, two men stood by them in white apparel; which also said, Ye men of Galilee, why stand ye gazing up into heaven? this same Jesus, which is taken up from you into heaven, shall so come in like manner as ye have seen him go into heaven."—Acts i. 10, 11. ... 317

CONTENTS.

THE LAMB IN GLORY.

"And I beheld, and, lo, in the midst of the throne and of the four living creatures, and in the midst of the elders, stood a Lamb as it had been slain, having seven horns and seven eyes, which are the seven Spirits of God sent forth into all the earth. And he came and took the book out of the right hand of him that sat upon the throne."—Revelation v. 6, 7. 329

THE HEAVENLY SINGERS AND THEIR SONG.

"And when he had taken the book, the four beasts and four and twenty elders fell down before the Lamb, having every one of them harps, and golden vials full of odours, which are the prayers of saints. And they sung a new song, saying, Thou art worthy to take the book, and to open the seals thereof: for thou wast slain, and hast redeemed us to God by thy blood out of every kindred, and tongue, and people, and nation; and hast made us unto our God kings and priests: and we shall reign on the earth."—Revelation v. 8—10. 341

"THE MARRIAGE OF THE LAMB."

"Let us be glad and rejoice, and give honour to him: for the marriage of the Lamb is come, and his wife hath made herself ready. And to her was granted that she should be arrayed in fine linen, clean and white: for the fine linen is the righteousness of saints."—Revelation xix. 7, 8. 353

THE FOLLOWERS OF THE LAMB.

"These are they which follow the Lamb whithersoever he goeth. These were redeemed from among men, being the firstfruits unto God and to the Lamb. And in their mouth was found no guile: for they are without fault before the throne of God."—Revelation xiv. 4, 5. 365

A VOICE FROM HEAVEN.

"Here is the patience of the saints: here are they that keep the commandments of God, and the faith of Jesus. And I heard a voice from heaven saying unto me, Write, Blessed are the dead which die in the Lord from henceforth: Yea, saith the Spirit, that they may rest from their labours; and their works do follow them."—Revelation xiv. 12, 13. 377

THE BARRIER.

"And there shall in no wise enter into it any thing that defileth, neither whatsoever worketh abomination, or maketh a lie: but they which are written in the Lamb's book of life."—Revelation xxi. 27. 389

EARLY AND LATE; OR, HORÆ GRATIÆ.

"For the kingdom of heaven is like unto a man that is an householder, which went out early in the morning to hire labourers into his vineyard. . . . . And he went out about the third hour, and saw others standing idle in the market-place. . . . . Again he went out, about the sixth and ninth hour, and did likewise. And about the eleventh hour he went out, and found others standing idle, and saith unto them, Why stand ye here all the day idle?"—Matthew xx. 1, 3, 5, 6. 401

NUMBER 2,500; OR, ENTRANCE AND EXCLUSION.

"And they that were ready went in with him to the marriage: and the door was shut."—Matthew xxv. 10. 413

Metropolitan Tabernacle Pulpit.

FOUNDATION WORK.

A Sermon

DELIVERED ON LORD'S-DAY MORNING, JULY 7TH, 1889, BY

C. H. SPURGEON,

AT THE METROPOLITAN TABERNACLE, NEWINGTON.

"And the king commanded, and they brought great stones, costly stones, and hewed stones, to lay the foundation of the house."—1 Kings v. 17.

"THE king commanded": that is the beginning of all. Holy zeal waits for the king's orders. But as soon as the command was given there was neither pause nor hesitation; "the king commanded, and they brought." Oh, that it were always so in the church of God; that the King's command were at once followed by his people's obedience! That obedience was true to every detail: "The king commanded, and they brought great stones, costly stones, and hewed stones." They did not omit one particular, or deviate in the least degree. The advice of the Blessed Virgin to the servants at the marriage-feast is our advice to all workers—"Whatsoever he saith unto you, do it." Work done without the Lord's command may be nothing more than mere will-worship, unacceptable with the Lord. Where the word of a king is, there is power; and you may expect that power to go forth with you when you go forth under the guidance and authority of the divine command.

Solomon began to build the temple at the foundation. You smile, and wonder how he could have begun anywhere else. Ah, dear friends! I wish common-sense ruled people in religion as well as in building temples; for many brethren begin their building at the top. To baptize an unbeliever on the ground of a faith which does not yet exist, is laying the topstone before the foundation. To gather into church fellowship those who are not gathered to Christ, is attempting to pile on the roof before there are any walls. For any of you to make a profession of religion without being born again, is building the third story before there is any basement. How much we have in this world of hanging up houses in the air!—I mean, making professions without having anything upon which to base them. Begin with the foundation.

The foundation, in his case, had to be carried to a great height, because the area upon which the temple stood was on high above the

No. 2,094

valley. As there was not space enough on the mount, it was necessary to build up from the depth of the valley scores of feet in perpendicular height, to form a foundation upon which there would be sufficient space for the temple and its surroundings. Portions of the massive masonry which formed the foundation of the enlarged area remain, to be wondered at by all who gaze upon them. Solomon paid especial care to the foundation.

Very much of foundation work is out of sight, and the temptation is to pay but small attention to its finish. It was not so with Solomon. Although it was very much out of sight, the king took care that the underground portion of the temple should be worthy of the rest of the edifice: it was to be made of " great stones, costly stones, and hewed stones." Builders in these days would think it absurd to spend time and labour in the hewing of stones which would never be seen. Foundations may call for something firm and solid, but certainly for nothing costly, and hewn with care. Out of sight, out of mind; and therefore none will spend time and trouble upon it. Not so the wise king engaged in the service of God. He paid great attention to underground work; and "great stones, costly stones, and hewed stones" were brought at his command to form the foundation of the temple. He designed to make it all of a piece: it was to be as truly "magnifical" in its foundation as in its roof There was to be no poverty of material, no scamping of any portion of the work. It was for God, and it was to be built by the king of Israel; and it would neither honour God nor the king to have a bad foundation.

I want, dear friends, to urge that all our work for God should be done thoroughly, and especially that part of it which lies lowest, and is least observed of men. I shall first say, *this is God's method:* he builds all his works with good foundations; secondly, *this should be our method* in all work for God; and, thirdly, *this is a wise method.* Briefly upon each, as the Holy Ghost shall help me.

I. First, THIS IS GOD'S METHOD. Wherever you turn your eye upon the work of God, it is perfect. It will bear the keenest inspection. You may look at it from a distance with the telescope, or you may search into it with the microscope; but you shall find no imperfection. The Lord's work is perfect, not merely on the surface, but to its centre. If you cut deep, or if you pull it to pieces, dividing atom from atom, you shall see the wisdom of God in the minutest particle.

Observe *the work of creation.* God took care that even in the material universe there should be a grand foundation for his noble edifice. We have the story of the fitting up of the world, during the seven days, for the habitation of man; but we have not the history of the creation of the earth before that time. To prepare for the seven days' rapid furnishing of the earth for man, millions of years may have elapsed. The foundation was laid with great care. No limit can be set to the period preceding the making of man, if you only follow the Word of God in Genesis. "In the beginning"—that was a long, long while ago—"God created the heaven and the earth"; and during that process of creation it went through a great many stages; for God was determined that the house in which man should dwell should be thoroughly furnished for him. I cannot conduct you to the foundations of the earth; but I do ask you to go down with me into the cellar. Consider that vast deposit of salt for our comfort and health; and the mines of iron and other metals which lay the corner-stones of trade and commerce. Look at the store of coals laid up in the deep places for us. God would not send his child here in winter time, and put no coals in the cellar for him; but he took long ages to provide the world with that fuel which is necessary for a thousand useful purposes. Those metals which are the best treasures of the soil, are usually placed lowest by God. "In his hand are the deep places of the earth: the strength of the hills is his also." If ever science shall be able to investigate below the crust of the globe into its fiery caldron within, they will discover fresh wonders of God's power and wisdom. What benefit may be bestowed upon us even by the secret fires which burn and rage within the world's innermost heart, or what may be the blessing derived by us from these underlying fountains of water gathered in the deeps, we cannot estimate. Suffice it to see that God's creation is not only full of glory in its loftiest pinnacles, but also in its utmost depths. God is the Master-builder, and he layeth the foundation well.

The same is true of God's work called *Providence*. No event happens but he has planned it, and ordained that a multitude of other events should precede or follow it. The doings of Providence are threaded together, like pearls upon a string; there is a relation of this to that, and of that to another. God does not allow events to blow about like scattered leaves in autumn; neither are they the inventions of a trying moment, when he is driven to fresh expedients that his end may not be frustrated. Events dovetail the one into the other. Every fact is fitted and adapted to take its place in the design of the great Architect. Certain great principles underlie all history. One who had but little spiritual knowledge, yet confessed that "there is a power abroad which makes for righteousness": he could not help seeing that; and he might have seen more had he opened his eyes. There is, in the affairs of man, many a touch of God's own hand. History looks like a tangled skein; but when you and I shall see it disentangled, we shall wonder at the infinite wisdom and kindness and goodness of God. Behold, in all things everything is of him, and by him, and through him, to the praise of his glory. In God's government of the universe he makes sure of his foundation.

But we come into clearer light when we look at *the Lord's greatest work of redemption*. You and I are not saved haphazard. It is not as though God had saved us on the spur of the moment, as an afterthought which was not in his first intent. No; redemption plays an essential part in the purposes of the Lord. I delight to look back upon the Lord's redeeming thoughts before all time, and say of them, "These are ancient things." Long before the stars flew like sparks from the anvil of omnipotence, God had contrived the way for the redemption of his own. In the covenant council-chamber the divine Persons of the sacred Unity arranged the procedure of all-glorious grace; and to-day all things are wrought according to the purpose of his eternal will. The foundation of redemption was securely laid in the covenant of grace, of which the Lord Jesus is the foundation. Infinite love, infallible wisdom, immutable faithfulness: all these combined to lay a foundation which can never be moved.

Go a little further, dear friends, and come to the day in which the Lord provided an atonement for us, and thus laid an immovable foundation. It has been suggested that he might have saved us, if he willed, without a sacrifice, letting law and justice stand on one side. This is after the manner of the men of the day: the jerry-building of the hour scorns so mean a thing as a foundation. But God does not build in this vile fashion. God will have no flaw in the salvation of his people; and that there never might arise a question as to the justice of the divine act by which their iniquity is passed over, he has exacted a penalty at the hand of their Surety. Now the Lord justly forgives their transgression. Justice, vindicated by a glorious sacrifice, brings for a foundation " great stones, costly stones, and hewed stones." All the angels of God might search all heaven in vain to find a fit foundation-stone for the temple of grace; but when the Only-Begotten of the Father offered himself without spot unto God, it was seen that he was in all respects fit to be the foundation of man's redemption. He is a chief Corner-stone, elect, precious, able to bear all that can be laid upon him. What a wonder it was that God would yield him up to die, to be the basis of our hope! Talk of the great stones and costly stones of Solomon's Temple, they are not worthy to be mentioned in the same day as this chief Corner-stone, on which all the hopes of his elect are laid; for they behold in him the sacrifice for sin, the destroyer of evil, and the reconciler of the lost. Glory be to God! in resting upon Jesus we do not build on the sand, but on a rock. He is the foundation of God, which standeth sure. The whole temple of the church is sustained by him.

When you are rejoicing in your sonship, your union to Christ, your high privileges, your eternal glory, do not forget the less visible, but equally essential, foundation blessings of eternal personal election, the everlasting covenant, the unchanging purpose, and the infallible oath of God. Sing evermore of the love which from eternity was fixed upon you, and of the purpose settled and established concerning you; for these lie at the foundation of all the favours you enjoy. Solomon's foundations astonish beholders on earth; but those of God will fill angels with amazement throughout eternity.

Once more: while illustrating the truth that God's method is to lay a good foundation, I must beg you to think of the application of redemption to the heart of every one of the redeemed *in personal salvation.* Beloved, when God saved us, it was no superficial work: the building of his grace in our souls is no wooden shanty, but a building which hath foundations. Look back at the early dealings of God with you before you knew him: he says, "I girded thee, though thou hast not known me." Your experiences in your ungodly state were made to lay a foundation for the higher work of grace in your hearts. This was more fully seen in the operations of grace when God began to deal with you effectually. When he wrought in you conviction of sin, what an out-digging there was! With some of us the throwing out of the foundation lasted for years; and for myself, I began to think there never would be a trace of anything built up in my heart. What a trench was dug in my soul! Out went my supposed merits! What a heap of rubbish! Out went my knowledge, my good resolves, and my self-sufficiency! By-and-by, out went all my strength. When this out-digging was completed, the ditch was so deep that, when I went down into it, it seemed like my grave. Such a grief it was for me to know my own sinfulness, that it did not seem possible that this could help my upbuilding in comfort and salvation. Yet so it is, that if the Lord means to build high, he always digs deep; and if he means to give great grace, he gives deep consciousness of need of it. Our convictions of sin, though painful and humbling, are a needful part of edification in righteousness. Since then we have been the subjects of a great deal of secret, unseen, underground work. The Lord has spent upon us a world of care. My brother, you would not like to unveil those great searchings of heart of which you have been the subject. You have been honoured in public; and, if so, you have had many a whipping behind the door lest you should glory in your flesh. Whenever God has filled your boat with fish, and you have been more than ordinarily successful, that boat has begun to sink. Great mercies are great humblers of sincere souls. You have gone down in proportion as God has gone up with you. All those chastenings, humblings, and searchings of heart have been a private laying of foundations for higher things. Ay, and the Lord has done much more than this in his own unseen but effectual way. He has given instruction, and revelation, and sanctified fellowship, and these have been your own, and not another's. No one has seen what the Lord has wrought in you; but if it had not been for this, you could not have been built up in holiness and usefulness. Thank God, he works the greater wonders of his love in the dark, out of sight. Yet, as the foundation is the most important part of the building, so the secret, humbling processes of grace have a value second to none. Yes, my brethren; for the upbuilding of a temple for his indwelling, the Lord " brings great stones, costly stones, and hewed stones to lay the foundation of the house."

II. I want now to see that THIS MUST BE OUR METHOD. We must build after this fashion, and make sure of our foundations.

First, let it be so *in the building up of our own life*. Every man and woman here, but especially those who are young, have a life to build up. It is a great thing to begin by believing good solid doctrine. Some people have believed twenty different gospels in so many years; how many more they will believe before they get to their journey's end it would be difficult to predict. I thank God I never knew but one gospel; and I have been so perfectly satisfied with it, that I do not want to know any other. Constant change of creed is sure loss. If a tree has to be taken up two or three times a year, you will not need to build a very large loft in which to store the apples. When people are always shifting their doctrinal principles, they are not likely to bring forth much fruit to the glory of God. It is good to begin with a firm hold upon those great fundamental doctrines which the Lord has taught in his Word. Draw into their places in your belief, and in your experience, those " great stones, costly stones, and hewed stones" of sure revelation which lay the doctrinal foundation of the temple of faith.

It is a great blessing to have a deep, solid, inward experience. Beloved, never think that you have taken hold of a truth till it has taken hold of you. We do a great deal of flimsy work in religion, to our cost and injury. If much of our supposed experience were laid on the wall of our confidence, the first real stone that pressed on it would crumple it all up. We want things solid, vital, real— "great stones, costly stones, and hewed stones, to lay the foundation of the house."

Beloved, how much is done in private by every Christian who is really sanctified, in the matter of the mastering of sin. It is not fit, in cases of inward conflict, to open the door or the window, and bid everybody come and see. If you have the wild beast of sin to tackle, shut the door and have it out alone, God helping you. You will never attain to a holy life unless there are secret conflicts with sin. There must also be hidden communings with God. That grace which is Artesian is grace indeed. When you have tapped the deep that lieth under, up leaps the stream with an irresistible force, fresh from the very bowels of truth. I pray God to deliver us from the present superficialities of religion. Xavier is said to have made innumerable converts in India by going about with a little pot of water and a brush, and sprinkling them as he went along. If men do not in that way make converts now, I am afraid the work is not much deeper or more effectual. Unless men have new hearts, and right spirits, it is all in vain that they make new professions. We need to be baptized into the grace of God till every part of our old nature is buried with Christ, and the whole of our new nature is dyed in the colour of almighty love. God grant it may be so! Be thorough; be real, be intense. In your building up of character, look well to the foundation.

So it must be, next, *in the building up of a church*. Is that a church of God which is not founded on everlasting truth? There are numbers of hasty builders with wood, hay, and stubble; but these neither attend to foundation nor to material laid thereon. Splendid stuff for rapid construction is good, well-trussed hay! Bring a truss at a time. What a pile of building we will show in a day! You wanted a house, and we have built you one in a trice. The wall is three feet thick, and wonderfully warm. We have built a house in a day. In this way new sects and parties have been marshalled and called churches of Christ. Is this worth while? "Thus saith the Lord, shall it prosper?" For my part, although I would be zealous in the service of my Lord, I had rather, by the grace of God, "lay great stones, costly stones, and hewed stones" upon the solid, rocky old doctrines of the gospel, than gather the greatest crowd, without faith and life. The stones of the temple were so squared and polished that you could not get a knife in between them when they were placed side by side; the stones thus adjusted were like a solid, united mass. So let us build. "Slow work," say you. Yes, but it will be equally slow in coming down, and that is the thing we must care about: we build for eternity.

To maintain solid truth you need solid people. Vital godliness is therefore to be aimed at. Twenty thousand people, all merely professing faith, but having no energetic life, may not have grace enough among them to make twenty solid believers. Poor, sickly believers turn the church into an hospital, rather than a camp. Weak believers are poor stuff for building a church with. Alas! much has been done of late to promote the production of dwarfish Christians. The endeavour has been to increase breadth at the expense of depth. What would you think of those who should break the dams of our reservoirs to let the water spread over the country? The accident which did this in America has spread ruin throughout a great district. I fear that nothing but mischief can come of the present liberal *régime* which talks of universal fatherhood, and virtually breaks down the separating wall which is meant to guard the church of God. If, in order to spread our sea, we make it very shallow, and it breathes miasma and death over the plain, it will be a sorry exchange for life eternal. Oh, to have a church built up with the deep godliness of men who know the Lord in their very hearts, and will seek to follow the Lamb whithersoever he goeth! I look with great delight, although with much sorrow, upon our Society's church-building on the Congo. When we think of the many men who have died there, it has indeed been true already that "great stones, costly stones, and hewed stones" have been laid for a foundation. If God will enable his church to make such sacrifices, he means to build a fair palace for his glory. When the great demands of a work call for unusual consecration, and unknown donors drop large sums into the treasury of the church, then also is there hope of a grand upbuilding. When Christian men, for the truth's sake can part with friends, lose popularity, and involve themselves in loss, then are "great stones, costly stones, and hewed stones" being built into the foundation of the temple of the Lord.

This morning a large number of friends are present who have been attending the Sunday-school Convention. I welcome them heartily, and I wish to turn my subject towards them, by saying—Dear friends, *in the building up of character in others* we must mind that we do the foundation work well. Sunday-school teachers are those who do the foundation work; for they begin first with young hearts, while they are tender and susceptible. It is a most important thing that we have our children and young people well instructed in divine truth and soundly converted. If we tone down the gospel which we teach, under the notion of making it more suitable to children, we shall greatly err: we may make it more childish, but we shall not make it more fit for children, nor a more effective instrument for their salvation. The same gospel which is preached in this great Tabernacle to this crowd is preached downstairs in our Sunday-school, to the young; and if I thought it was not so, I should despair of seeing any conversions. The lads and lasses want just the same truths as the adults, only it should be stated in simpler language, with more of parable and illustration. Fundamental truths are as much connected with the salvation of a child as with the salvation of a full-grown man. Christ receives adults, but he also suffers little children to come to him. Let us always take good heed that our Sunday-school teaching is as solidly truthful as our instruction of the church.

But be it never forgotten that the major part of teaching will lie in example; and, therefore, the life of the teacher must be of the very best. It is wonderful how children copy the conduct of a beloved teacher: for good or for evil, the force of example over the imitative faculty of youth is very great. When their hearts are tender they are moulded for God and good things, as much by what they see in our character as by what they hear from our lips. Most of you have seen in the British Museum the Egyptian brick which bears the mark of a dog's foot upon it. When it was as yet soft mud, a dog, who was wandering through the brickfield, set his signature upon it, and there it stands—*Dog of Nilus: his mark*. Any casual word or foolish act may make a mark on a child's character as indelible as the dog's signature. This may be done when we are not intending it; how much more when with our heart's intent we write upon a loving mind! An unhallowed remark, or an ill-advised act, may start a soul upon the line of destruction. As the Japanese copyist was very careful to imitate the crack in the plate, and the flaw in the design, so shall we find young people peculiarly apt to follow our faults and infirmities. Oh, for holy teachers and preachers! Let us be such that we may dare to bid our disciples mark us, and have us for ensamples. How surely are the impressions of our early days retained when after-learning is forgotten! How easily may you who work upon the precious material of a young mind leave on it an undying record! I remember a man of God, who has now gone to his reward, who was the means of producing, under God, a library of useful lives. I do not mean books in paper, but books in boots. Many young men were decided for the Lord by his means, and became preachers, teachers, deacons, and other workers; and no one would wonder that it was so, if he knew the man who trained them. He was ready for every good word and work; but he gave special attention to his Bible-class, in which he set forth the gospel with clearness and zeal. Whenever any one of his young men left the country town in which he lived, he would be sure to have a parting interview. There was a wide-spreading oak down in the fields; and there he was wont to keep an early morning appointment with John, or Thomas, or William; and that appointment very much consisted of earnest pleadings with the Lord, that in going up to the great city the young man might be kept from sin, and made useful. Under that tree several decided for the Saviour. It was an impressive act, and left its influence; for many men came, in after years, to see the spot, made sacred by their teacher's prayers. We ought to be ingenious in our methods, and spare no pains to influence young people for their good. "Great stones, costly stones, and hewed stones" may be fitly used in such building as this. If the Lord by our means prepares but one soul for eternal bliss, we shall not have lived in vain.

But, beloved friends, one of the most important things about dealing with children is, that we teach them what we have well prepared. Their mental food must be carefully cooked. If ever a teacher goes to the class without preparing the lesson, the teaching is sure to be very poor work. Nobody sees you when you are preparing your lesson; nobody commends you for your diligent research. It is the public address which is noted; but the secret study is that to which the commendation really belongs. If this private preparation is neglected, it is a very serious omission. Indeed, bad work in places which are not looked at is a wretched order of things. Some time ago it fell to me, as executor, to arrange for the sale of the goods and effects in a house most elegantly furnished. Certain fine pictures were to go to Christy and Manson's. The drawing-room was expensively adorned, and the wall decorations were elaborate with a pattern in which gold stars were somewhat plentiful. When the paintings were taken down, I was not a little surprised to see that behind them the wall was bare of ornament, so that at no time could those pictures have been shifted without showing how the decoration had been stinted. The owner was rich; yet his tradesman must needs practise such pinching economy of a little gilding. I am afraid if we were to take down the pictures in some Sunday-school teachers and Christian ministers, there would be seen ugly patches of neglect. It should not be so, brethren, in the work of the Lord. It must not be so! Our power under God will lie very much in the heartiness of our private work. Years ago, when I was suffering from gouty rheumatism, a gentleman sought an interview, who was confident that he could cure me almost immediately. He was a marvellously positive quack, and before long he had informed me that he had in his exclusive possession a most astounding medicine. I do not know whether a smell of it would not have cured all the ills of humanity. No, he could not even hint what the medicine was; and I did not press the point, for I could not expect to be favoured with the golden secret; but I was indulged with some insight into the preparation of the miraculous drug. The professor said, "These pills are infallible in their effect, because they are so powerful. Their power does not lie in the mere ingredients, which are extremely simple; but their efficacy is the result of the careful preparation of the material by myself." Being a very healthy man, and full of life-force, the professor professed to work up these pills in such a way that he transferred to them the electric or biological energies of his own personality; and thus he infused health-power into the sick. I have never taken the aforesaid pills; but I have used their author's assertion as a lesson. I believe that if preachers and teachers work into their lessons the life of their souls, and the whole power of their minds, their teaching will be far more effectual for good than if they merely repeat good things, and put no heart into them. See to it that your heart and soul is worked into your teaching. Next time we are studying the Scripture lessons, let us think to ourselves, "This is foundation work. No one will know how I have worked at it; but the Lord, whom I serve, will take note of all that I do, and he will be pleased with conscientious foundation work." Brethren, we must put " good stones, costly stones, and hewed stones " into the unseen part of our edifice, that, as a whole, our work may be meet for the thrice-holy Lord.

III. My time fails me; but under my third head I must carefully, though briefly, set forth the reasons why this should be done. IT IS A WISE METHOD.

First, because *it is suitable for God.* You build your temple *for God,* and not for men: you should, therefore, make that part of the building good which will be seen *by him;* and as he sees it all, it must be all of the best. The Lord sees just as much the foundation as he does the top-stone: all things are naked and open to the eyes of him with whom we have to do. Even heathens recognized this. A Grecian sculptor had to prepare an image of a god, for one of the temples. He was working away with all his might at the back of the head, and at the hinder garments of the figure. One said to him, "Your work is needless, for that part of the figure is to be built into the wall." "But," said he, "the gods can see in the wall. This is for the gods, and not for men." Let us catch the spirit of the heathen artist, and do work for God in a manner fit for the Omniscient. It is meet that the foundation which is invisible should be perfected, if we expect the Invisible God to accept it; for, otherwise, if we spend our strength on what is seen by men, it will be pretty evident that we, after all, are working for the praise of man, and not for the glory of God.

Next, look well to the foundation that is out of sight, *for your own sake.* No builder can afford to be negligent over the unseen part of a building; for it would involve a serious injury to his character. The very act of scamping is mean and degrading, and lowers a man's tone. I do not care who he is, if he habitually trifles over that which is not seen, the habit will defile his sincerity in other respects, and lead him to practical hypocrisy in religious concerns. The bare idea that we need not do our best if we are not seen, is debasing to the soul. To-day many aim at doing things cheaply, getting through work as fast as possible, and making a great show for the money. Let us avoid this popular form of lying! Let us do every part of our work as beseemeth men who are elect of God, redeemed by precious blood, and called into fellowship with Christ by the Holy Ghost. What if a sham might pass current with other men, yet it must not be adopted by those who are of heaven-born race, and have a quickened conscience within their bosom. "Why," saith one, "nobody would respect you any the less if you did such work slightingly, for everybody else would do so." Listen: I should respect myself the less if I scamped my work, and I set a great value upon my own respect of myself. What if another esteems me? I am still wretched if I know that he is mistaken, and have not the approbation of my own conscience. A conscience void of offence, both towards God and towards men, is of more worth than the applause of nations.

Further, lay the foundation well, and look to that part which is out of sight, because in this way *you will secure the superstructure.* There was a bit of a flaw in the foundation, but nobody saw it; for the builder covered it up very quickly, and ran up the whole concern as quickly as possible. The walls were built, and built well. It seemed clear that the fault down below was of no consequence whatever; and as it had a little cheapened the underground construction, was it not so much the better? How long was this the case? Well, the next year nothing happened: a longer time passed away, and then an ugly crack came down the wall. Had there been an earthquake? No, there was no earthquake. Perhaps a cyclone had beaten upon the work? No, there was no cyclone: the weather was the same as usual. What was the cause of that gaping space which marred the beauty of the building, and threatened to bring it down? It was that blunder long ago: that underground neglect produced the terrible mischief above, which would involve a great expense, and perhaps render it needful to take all the building down. That which was out of sight did not always remain out of mind; it only needed time to produce a dangerous settlement. If certain men of our acquaintance had been soundly converted at the first, backsliding and apostasy would not have followed, to our shame and grief. If certain preachers had done their work in the church of God better in years now past, those sad departures from the truth, which now vex the saints, would not have occurred. If to-day you do not teach your children the gospel fully and clearly, the evil may not be seen in your present classes, nor possibly even in this generation: but children's children will bear the impress of the slight work done at this hour. Years may be needed for the development of the full result of a false doctrine.

Besides, dear friends, to lay a good foundation, on Solomon's part, was the way *to save himself from future fears*. Buildings which have to hold a crowd endure seasons of test and trial. Years ago, I was preaching in a building which was exceedingly crowded, and, to my apprehension, there was a continuous tremor. I grew so anxious that I said to a friend, who understood such matters, "Go downstairs and see whether this building is really safe; for it seems hardly able to bear the weight of this crowd." When he returned he looked anxious, but gave me no answer. The service ended quietly, and then he said, "I am so glad that everything has gone off safely. I do not think you should ever preach there again; for it is a very frail affair; but I thought that if I frightened you there would be more risk in a panic than in letting the service go on." Solomon had built with "great stones, costly stones, and hewed stones"; and therefore, when the vast multitudes came together around the temple, it never occurred to him to fear that the great weight of people might cause a subsidence of the foundation. Oh, no! he stood there, and prayed to God with collected mind, altogether undisturbed by any apprehension of possible disaster. He that builds well for eternity will escape a thousand fears. Doubts and fears are often born of a knowledge that something has been left undone, or has been done slightly, in the process of building upon Christ. Beloved members of this church, you that are often subject to doubts and fears, do you not think that these might be cured by a more real faith and truer dealings with God? Are you lax as to your private study of the Word, or negligent in your secret prayers? If so, I do not wonder that you have doubts. Here is a suggestion as to the way of curing and preventing them. Make your religion solid work: have no more of it in appearance than you have in reality. Get down to the rock every time. Do nothing with careless superficiality. If you pray, plead with your whole heart. If you hear the Word, put your very soul into it. "Sure work for eternity!" be this your motto. Specially look well to the underground and unseen parts of godliness; so shall your comfort be constant and joyful.

Beloved, lastly, do look well to the foundation, **and to the secret** part of your dealings with God, because *there is a fire coming which will try all things.* " Every man's work shall be made manifest: for the day shall declare it, because it shall be revealed by fire; and the fire shall try every man's work of what sort it is." No matter where we build, nor how we build, the fire will come upon all the works of man. The wood, hay, and stubble builders cry, "Do not bring any fire here! The proposal is horrible!" But in vain do they protest, for God has determined that the fire shall be. Now, even should you build the upper and visible part of your life with stone, it will not avail if the under portion is of hay. The fire will bring it all down. What a blaze! What a blaze! Stand far off, and see the smoke thereof go up like that of Sodom and Gomorrah. What is left? Only a handful of black ashes! Is this the whole remaining result of an entire life? Is this the substance of a life of notoriety, and publicity, and honour? How terrible! Yet if the foundation part of your life is of consumable material, that must be the bitter end. God be thanked, the man that builds on the rock Christ Jesus, and builds on him gold, silver, and precious stones, has no cause to fear the last conflagration. To-day he weeps, because he has built so little. "O Lord," saith he, "I wish I could have done a thousand times as much for thee!" But after the fire has gone through it and through it, and what is built remains, how thankful he will be! See how it shines amid the fire! The flames give it a glow and burnish never seen before. The rust and the tarnish are gone, and the whole fabric shines like the pure gold which it really is. Its precious stones are even more brilliant than before, and in nothing has the structure suffered loss. The Lord be praised! A life well grounded in Christ Jesus, made sound throughout by the power of the Spirit, will bear to be inspected of God, and even to be inspected by the envious eyes of men, who would fain find fault with it; and at last it will bear the trial of the judgment-day, and will be found to the praise and glory of God for ever and ever. Therefore, see to it that you lay the foundation of all your religion with "great stones, costly stones, and hewed stones," that so it may last for ever.

To those of you who are not converted, let this be the final word of my sermon: build on God's foundation, build on Christ, the sacrifice appointed of the Lord for the putting away of sin; and see to it that with sincere repentance, childlike faith, and gospel holiness, you build thereon "great stones, costly stones, and hewed stones," which shall lie firmly on the One Foundation, and never be removed therefrom, world without end. Amen.

PORTIONS OF SCRIPTURE READ BEFORE SERMON—Psalm xxxiv.; 1 Kings v. 13—18.

HYMNS FROM "OUR OWN HYMN BOOK"—34 (Version I.), 118 (Song II.), 732.

Metropolitan Tabernacle Pulpit.

THE SERPENT'S SENTENCE.

A Sermon

Delivered on Lord's-day Morning, September 21st, 1890, by

C. H. SPURGEON,

AT THE METROPOLITAN TABERNACLE, NEWINGTON.

"And the Lord God said unto the serpent, Because thou hast done this, thou art cursed above all cattle, and above every beast of the field; upon thy belly shalt thou go, and dust shalt thou eat all the days of thy life: and I will put enmity between thee and the woman, and between thy seed and her seed; it shall bruise thy head, and thou shalt bruise his heel."—Genesis iii. 14, 15.

Some master in Israel who wanted to help the memories of his hearers has said that the three things to be preached above everything else are the three R's—Ruin, Redemption, and Regeneration. He spake wisely and well. How will men seek salvation if they do not feel their ruin? Where is there salvation save in the atoning blood? What is salvation but being created anew unto holiness? It is a noteworthy fact that, in Holy Scripture, there are three third chapters which deal with these things in the fullest manner. The third of Genesis reveals Ruin; the third of Romans teaches Redemption; the third of John sets forth Regeneration. Will our young friends be so good as to read those chapters through with care, at home? It is also worthy of mention that not only do each of these chapters teach its own R, but that it also teaches the other two R's. In this third of Genesis we have not only Ruin, but we have the Redeemer in "the seed of the woman," and we have Regeneration in the expression, "I will put enmity between thee and the woman." God's regenerating power creates a hatred of evil in the chosen seed. The same you will find in the other chapters; for the third of the Romans contains a fearful description of the sin and ruin of men; and in the third of John, after you have read, "Ye must be born again," not far from it you find it written, "And as Moses lifted up the serpent in the wilderness, even so must the Son of man be lifted up, that whosoever believeth in him might not perish, but have eternal life." Believe any of these great truths, and the rest follow as a necessary consequence. May we be helped this morning to learn something with regard to Ruin, Redemption, and Regeneration, from the passage now before us!

I pray you, never regard that story of the serpent as a fable. It

No. 2,165.

is said, nowadays, that it is a mere allegory. Yet there is nothing in the Book to mark where history ends and parable begins: it all runs on as actual history; and as Bishop Horsley forcibly remarks, " If any part of this narrative be allegorical, no part is naked matter of fact." It seems to me that if there was only an allegorical serpent, there was an allegorical paradise, with allegorical rivers, and allegorical trees; and the men and women were both allegorical, and the chapter which speaks of their creation is an allegory; and the only thing that exists is an allegorical heaven and an allegorical earth. If the Book of Genesis be an allegory, it is an allegory all through; and you have an allegorical Abraham, with allegorical circumcision, an allegorical Jacob and an allegorical Judah; and it is not unfair to push the theory onward, and impute to Judah allegorical descendants called Jews. But if you borrow any money of this race, you will not find them allegorical when you have to pay. It is idle to call the narrative of the Fall a mere allegory; one had better say at once that he does not believe the Book. There is something sane about that declaration, although it be folly: but to say, " Oh, yes, it is a venerable volume, and worthy to be studied; but it is padded out with many an allegory," is to say something which confutes itself, if you come to look into it. The Book is intended to be real history, and it contains some portions which, by the consent of everybody, are real history; but Moses could not be an historian, and yet set mere fables before us as a part of his story. To write a jumble of allegory and of fact causes a man to lose the character of a reliable historian, and we had better repudiate him at once. There was a real serpent, as there was a real paradise; there was a real Adam and Eve, who stood at the head of our race, and they really sinned, and our race is really fallen. Believe this.

When Satan, "that old serpent, the Devil, and Satan"—as the Apocalypse calls him—determined to tempt Eve, in order that he might destroy the race in which God evidently took much delight, he could not appear to the woman as a spirit. Spirits are not to be discerned by the eye; since a pure spirit is a thing which none of the outward senses of human beings can apprehend. An immaterial spirit must be invisible; and therefore he must embody himself in some way or other before he can be seen. That Satan has power to enter into living bodies is clear, for he did so upon a very large scale with regard to men in the days of Christ. He and his legions were even compelled to enter into the bodies of swine rather than be cast into the deep. Being compelled to have an embodiment, the master evil spirit perceived the serpent to be at that time among the most subtle of all creatures; and therefore he entered into the serpent as feeling that he would be most at home in that animal. Out of the serpent he spoke to Eve, as though the serpent itself had spoken. There was an actual and material serpent, but the evil spirit who is known as " the old serpent" was there, possessing the natural serpent with all his masterly cunning. Cruelly determining to lead the human race into sin, that he might thus ruin it and triumph over God, the fallen angel did not hesitate to assume a reptile form. Well might Milton make him say—

> "O foul descent! that I, who erst contended
> With gods to sit the highest, am now constrain'd
> Into a beast; and, mix'd with bestial slime,
> This essence to incarnate, and imbrute,
> That to the height of deity aspired!"

Notice, carefully, that when the Lord comes to deal with the serpent, he does not question him as to his guilt, and the reason of it; and the reason is, perhaps, that the guilt of the arch-enemy was self-evident; or, better still, because the Lord had no design of mercy for him. He meant to make no covenant of grace for the devil or his angels; for he took not up angels, though he took up the seed of Abraham. In the infinite sovereignty of God he passed by the fallen angels, but he chose to raise fallen man. Those who cavil at the doctrine of election should answer this question: Why is it that God has left devils without hope, and yet has sent his Son to redeem mankind? Is not divine sovereignty manifested here? We can give no answer to the question, What is man that God thus visits him with distinguishing grace? save this—" He will have mercy on whom he will have mercy, and he will have compassion on whom he will have compassion." Intending, therefore, no forgiveness to this evil spirit, the Lord put no questions to him. His interrogation of our first parents was a sign of mercy. When God chides with a man's conscience, it is with the view of blessing him. Do I speak to any man here whose sense of sin is aroused, who is accused by the Word of God, who feels the Spirit of God working within him as a spirit of bondage? You may be hopeful because it is so. If God had meant to destroy you, he would have left you alone, even as he left the serpent without a word of expostulation, and he would have passed sentence upon you speedily. The very rebukes of God are tokens of his favour towards men. With the serpent, that is, with the evil spirit, God had no upbraidings, but dealt at once by way of doom.

He pronounced a sentence upon the serpent, which, while it was terrible to him, is most encouraging to us; and so far as our first parents understood it, it must have been a sun of light to their dark, depressed souls. For many a year this was the lone star of believing hearts: this gospel of the serpent's doom. Satan was their enemy; he had done them wrong. He was also God's enemy, and God would fight against him, and call them into his battle. He would raise up One who would suffer, but would win the victory—One whom he calls "the seed of the woman." By him Satan's head would be bruised; and in that very fact, the race of man would be unspeakably blest.

Last Sabbath morning I introduced to you Immanuel—God with us, born of a virgin. We are now running on the same lines, and again I would speak of our Lord Jesus as the woman's seed, and extol him as espousing our quarrel, and undoing the mischief which the old serpent has wrought us. In him his believing people shall bruise Satan under their feet shortly.

We will consider the whole passage, and draw from it seven lessons. As there are so many, I cannot dwell upon any one of them at length; but must give you hints of the wealth of meaning which lies within the words of these most instructive verses. With regard to our arch-enemy, we may here learn much.

First, notice THE INSTRUCTIVE FORM UNDER WHICH SATAN APPEARS. The text begins, "The Lord God said unto the serpent." Under the serpent form he beguiled the woman, and under that form he was condemned. He is a serpent still. He can go about among the weak and defenceless as a roaring lion seeking whom he may devour; but he is most at home as the embodiment of craft. The serpent was most *subtle*, and so is the evil one most cunning. You think you understand the ways of Satan; but you are mistaken. You have been tempted by him these thirty years, and you believe your experience can unravel all his plots. Ah, my brethren! he has been engaged in the work of tempting men for nearly six thousand years; and he is not only much older, but he is far more acute and more sagacious than you are. His ways are not easily found out; and though we are not ignorant of his devices, we know not which device he will next use. If we have successfully escaped his nets for forty years, the skilful fowler may even yet entangle us. We have need each day to cry, "Lead us not into temptation; but deliver us from evil." John writes of him in the Revelation as "that old serpent, called the Devil, and Satan, which deceiveth the whole world." He is more cunning than the wisest: how soon he entangled Solomon! He is stronger than the strongest: how fatally he overthrew Samson! Ay, and men after God's own heart, like David, have been led into most grievous sins by his seductions. We do not know where he now lurks, or from what quarter he will next shoot his arrows; but we may rest assured that he is always plotting mischief against the people of God, and he is working subtilely to effect their pollution. We may wisely enter into Paul's anxiety when he wrote to the Corinthians, "But I fear, lest by any means, as the serpent beguiled Eve through his subtilty, so your minds should be corrupted from the simplicity that is in Christ." From the evil machinations of the subtle one, may the Lord deliver us!

A serpent is very *insinuating*. It can enter where another creature could not. Ever so small an opening makes room for a serpent, and it winds itself in without noise. Satan is very insinuating; and as he entered Paradise, so can he penetrate into the most secret and sacred places. He creeps into the church, watch though we may. He creeps into houses though sanctified by devotion. Have you never found him intruding into your closet during your prayer? There may seem to be no loophole, and yet there he is, where he was least expected. Has he not wound himself into your families? Has he not crept into your hearts? How can we keep him out? We watch against his attacks from without; but, behold, he has found a lodging-place within! Subtle and insinuating is Satan: he is a serpent indeed!

And how *venomous!* What poison one fang of the old serpent will throw into our moral system! Look around, and see how many have been poisoned with the desire for strong drink, with lust, with avarice, with pride, with anger, with unbelief. Fiery serpents are among us, and many die of their venom. If we tolerate the least sin, it is a burning drop in the veins of the soul. One touch of the fangs of this serpent will work immeasurable sorrow, even if the soul be saved from death. It is only the power of God that keeps us from being destroyed by this viper. Had he his will, he is a spirit so malignant that no heir of heaven would survive. O God, keep thine own! Deliver us from the evil one!

In all probability the reptile called the serpent was a nobler creature before the Fall than now. The words of our text, so far as they literally concern the serpent, threaten that a change would be wrought in him. It has been a sort of speculative opinion that the creature either had wings, or was able to move without creeping upon the earth as it now does. Of that we know nothing; but assuredly the serpent is a hated thing, with which manhood is at war, and its form and habit typify all that is mean and cunning. There is nothing noble, nothing brave, nothing true about the idea of a serpent. Satan was among the first-born of the morning, a swift and shining servant of God; but he transgressed against his Sovereign and fell, and now he is nothing but a serpent—malignant, base, cunning, and untrue. He is fitly figured by "the wily snake." "He was a murderer from the beginning, and abode not in the truth, because there is no truth in him. When he speaketh a lie, he speaketh of his own: for he is a liar, and the father of it" (John viii. 44). He goes out to deceive the nations (Rev. xx. 8). He works signs and lying wonders (2 Thess. ii. 9). He lays snares, and takes men captive (2 Tim. ii. 26). Keep before your minds the form of a serpent, and remember that after this manner Satan will attack you. Only let me soften your fears with the sight of another serpent : the serpent of brass lifted upon a pole brought life to those whom evil serpents had injured. It seems to me a wonder of condescending grace that our Lord Jesus could allow himself to be symbolized by a form which had been assumed by the great enemy of souls. Yes, there was the brazen serpent lifted high upon a pole, and they that looked, though bitten by fiery serpents, lived. Even thus is Jesus on the cross the sure remedy for sin of every kind. Look out with all your eyes of caution for the old serpent, the devil; but at the same time look up with all your eyes of faith to him who was made a curse for us that we might live.

II. So much for the first lesson, now for the second. Observe THE MEMORABLE FACT AS TO SATAN'S CONDITION. "The Lord God said unto the serpent, Because thou hast done this, thou art cursed"; and the curse was made emphatic and superlative. He with whom we have to contend has the curse of God upon him even now. God has blessed his people, but he has cursed their great enemy. The curse of God blights and blasts, even as in the case of the fruitless fig-tree, which, beneath the sentence of the Lord Jesus, withered away. The curse of God has fallen upon that foul spirit who represents evil : it could not justly be otherwise. This is his shame and your strength. The next time you are fighting with Apollyon, here is a keen shaft to hurl at him. Tell him he is accursed of God; and what has he to do with those whom the Lord has blessed? He whom God blesses is blessed, but he whom God curses is cursed indeed. Upon all the power of sin and error, yea, upon Satan himself, who is the ringleader in evil things, the curse of God abideth; and this is prophetic of their overthrow. The truth shall conquer, holiness shall overcome. Falsehood and wrong bear the brand of Cain upon their brow, and they shall wither from the root.

Satan was cursed with reference to us. Our fall has brought him no gain, but an increase of divine displeasure, of disappointment, and envy. He was under God's wrath before, but now the Lord saith concerning him, "Thou art cursed above all cattle, and above every beast of the field." Though there cometh pain and groaning upon all the lower creation through man's sin, there shall come upon the old serpent a far more exceeding measure of the curse, because he has dared to lead into revolt the race of man. Who will willingly be the slave of a tyrant whom the Lord has cursed?

Not only Satan, but every form of sin, is under the curse. The tempter would make you think that some shapes of sin are blessed; but this is false. All sin has a curse attached to it. Keep far from it. Is it false doctrine? It is accursed. Is it living in wantonness and carnal pleasure? It is accursed. Touch it not. You cannot do wrong without defiling yourself with that which God has cursed. You may imagine that you will gain many good things by yielding a little to sin; but this is a lie of the adversary: evil is loss and ruin. The curse which God pronounced on the serpent is pronounced on the whole of his seed, and everything that is impure, untruthful, and unholy lies under the ban of God.

Brethren, if for Christ's sake we should suffer poverty, or reproach, or slander, or even death, there would be a blessing in it all; but if by means of doing evil we should rise to wealth, honour, and ease, we should find in all our gains a burning curse. Who prizes gold with the curse upon it? It is cankered, and will eat into the soul. God knows what is cursed, and what is blessed; and we may well believe his declaration that evil is meaner than the brutes, and more sensual than the wild beasts of the field. All this is a call to escape from the ways of sin. Tremble lest ye be found under the curse; and hasten to flee to him who can turn the curse into a blessing, even Jesus, who bore our sins in his own body on the tree, and so bore away the curse from all believers.

The memorable fact that Satan and the power of evil are under the curse should hearten us in our conflict with spiritual wickednesses. We can overcome them, for the curse of the Lord has gone forth against them.

III. For a third lesson, note THE REMARKABLE PROSTRATION which fell upon the serpent: "Upon thy belly shalt thou go." So does the serpent move, and so doth evil labour to make progress. Satan moves always as a fallen one: not with the dignity of holiness, but grovelling low. God has put upon his every movement the indication that he is no longer great and wise. The movements of the Prince of darkness are base and sensual:—"Upon thy belly shalt thou go." His seed also take to the same posture in going. I have seen the foes of the truth contending against the faith of God, and I have marked their policies, their plots, and their plans; and I have said to myself, "Verily, it is written, Upon thy belly shalt thou go." Beings engaged in evil designs have no other way of going, but with tricks, devices, concealments, double meanings. When men deny the Scriptures and the truth of God, they always go to work in an underhand, mean, and serpentine style: "Upon thy belly shalt thou go." If guilty man begins to plot for his own advantage, scheme for his own glory, and aim at perverting the truth, you will notice that he never takes a bold, open, manly stand, but he dodges, he conceals, he twists and shifts: "Upon thy belly shalt thou go." Sin is a mean and despicable thing. The greatest potentate of evil was here doomed to cringe and crawl, and his seed have never forgotten their father's posture.

All the objects of the powers of evil are grovelling. What do they seek after? When men forsake the way of holiness, they rush after polluted and idle amusements. What is there in the world's pleasure which is ennobling? Still is carnal mirth a grovelling thing: "Upon thy belly shalt thou go." A professing man gives up the separated way, and enters upon modern society, and he no longer walks with God. What is his general course? Within a short time we find him careless of all religion, and tolerant of licentiousness. It is ever so: "Upon thy belly shalt thou go." If you give way to evil, you shall go down, down, down, till your god is your belly, and you glory in your shame. If a man would be great, let him serve God. If a man would rise to the angels, ay, rise to God, let him obey the command of his Maker. But if he wishes to degrade himself below the adder, which "glides obscure through bush and brake," his easy method is to follow Satan, and rebel against the Most High.

IV. Observe, in the fourth place, THE PERPETUAL DEGRADATION put upon the serpent: "And dust shalt thou eat all the days of thy life." Satan is now to live a defeated life, for such is the force of the expression, "His enemies shall lick the dust." It signifies that they are utterly defeated. So Satan all his life long exists as a conquered and chained enemy: his power is broken, and he knows it well. He is defeated as to the whole of his great scheme, and he is to be defeated in the details of it all the days of his life. When he met our Lord in the wilderness, he crept upon his belly with serpentine temptations; but our Lord by his holiness made him eat dust! How often was he in our Lord's lifetime made to feel that his conqueror had come! He cringed before him, and implored that he might not be tormented before his time. When he saw the Lord Jesus upon the cross, having planned, as he thought, to crush him by death, he began to dread defeat. When he heard him cry, "It is finished," and felt his iron heel upon his head, he knew, to his eternal horror, that he had only fashioned for the Christ an opportunity of redeeming mankind. What a mouthful of dust he had to eat in that day! None more wretched in the universe than Satan, whose works the bleeding Saviour had destroyed. It was a day of bitter defeat for the enemy when our Lord rose from the dead. The old serpent had watched the pale corpse; but when he saw it live, and when the angel rolled away the stone, and Jesus, the Christ, came forth to die no more, I warrant you the serpent ate the dust that day. And when the apostles stood forth—men whom Satan despised, humble fishermen—and the Holy

Ghost came down upon them; again it was fulfilled, "Dust shalt thou eat." When the nations were converted, and the idols were broken, and the truth mightily prevailed; then did Satan remember the words, "Dust shalt thou eat all the days of thy life." He has more humiliation yet to come. Arise, and preach Christ and win souls, and the great enemy of souls shall find his power diminished, and his name abhorred, and again he shall lick the dust.

For ever dust shall be the serpent's meat, for what he does gain always disappoints him. He thought he had obtained a great advantage when he won the woman to disobedience; but he had made a rod for his own back, since her seed would become his eternal antagonist. The fall of man led up to the incarnation and the atonement; and by these Satan is thrown down. By man has come the resurrection, and so the defeat of death, who was first-born of hell. The victory of the devil in Eden is blotted out by the victory of Jesus at Calvary.

If Satan ever knows pleasure at all, it is of the foulest and most unsatisfactory kind: dust is his meat. There is nothing satisfying in the pleasures of rebellion. He remains a disappointed, restless being. The most cunning error which he invents, and sustains by philosophy, is no more than dust. His whole cause, for which he has laboured these thousands of years with a horrible perseverance—his whole cause, I say—will dissolve into dust, and will be blown away as smoke. Still doth he feed himself upon dust. Let those who are servants of Satan know assuredly that, as they are living in sin, they will have to eat at their father's table, and learn the emptiness of all the pleasures of sin, and the worthlessness of all the treasures of evil. Everything that sin can bring you is just so much dust—foul eating, insufficient, clogging, killing. Though you hoard up wealth, gold is nothing but dust to a dying man. Though you gain all earthly honour, it, too, dissolves in dust. This is the misery of that great spirit who is called the Prince of darkness, that he must eat dust all his days. But what misery it must be to be only some poor subject in that unhallowed kingdom, and still to be doomed to the same loathsome fare! "Dust shalt thou eat all the days of thy life." Note that right well: and may God deliver you from such feeding!

V. Let us, in the next place, think upon THE CEASELESS WAR with which God threatens the serpent: "I will put enmity between thee and the woman, and between thy seed and her seed." He reckoned upon an easy conquest, and had apparently gained it; but he would find his victim become his antagonist, and at length his conqueror. Satan can never know peace: he seeketh rest and findeth none. When he talked to that woman with his guileful words of flattery, he thought he had made a friend of her. The charming creature in whom God had embodied the perfection of beauty, had he not seduced her from obedience to the great King? Had he not used her as the instrument to make her husband a traitor to his God? They were great friends—those two. She felt, in the moment that she took the fruit, that she owed much to the serpent for giving her the gentle hint whereby she was led to find the opening of her eyes, and the uplifting of her nature to be as God. How grievously was she deceived! Nor was the serpent to find himself advantaged. The league was broken, and the deceiver and his victim were at enmity. God declares most solemnly, "I will put enmity between thee and the woman:" God will see that there be no peace. There is a war to be waged between Satan and the woman's seed, so long as the world stands. Sometimes it looks as if there was going to be peace; for the world flatters the church, and the church seeks to conform herself to the world. As before Noah's flood the sons of God and the daughters of men were joined in unhallowed alliance, so again and again there have been attempts at truce. But peace there cannot be. To-day Satan tempts the ministers of Christ to soften down the gospel, adapt it to the age, and make it popular; and he also labours to throw down the division between the church and the world. "Fill up the gulf!" says he; "Cover it over like an old sewer, and forget that it ever existed!" Thus he speaks like the sinner in the Proverbs: "Cast in thy lot among us, let us all have one purse." But mark this, all ye that hear me—though all the pulpits should be captured, and though it should seem that the very elect were deceived, yet God will not leave himself without witness, but will find, somewhere or other, some chosen ones of the seed of the woman to carry on the holy war even to the end. Jehovah hath laid his hand upon his throne, and he has sworn to have war with evil from generation to generation. See how it was in Israel when the high-priest of God, even Eli, winked at sin, when his own sons, as priests, committed iniquity at the tabernacle door; and all Israel was thus made to do evil. Would not the lamp of truth go out? Would not the worship of the Lord be utterly abhorred? Ah, no! a little child was brought by his mother into the tabernacle to be the servant of the Lord, and in him the Lord found a champion. In the night did God call Samuel; and he answered, "Here am I." This Samuel stood before the Lord, and gave forth prophecies which made both the ears of him that heard thereof to tingle, and the Lord was again great in Israel. Do not tremble for the ark of the Lord. God will not suffer the old serpent to spread his slime over all things. Satan's throne shall always be opposed.

This enmity is to be kept up by God himself. He said, "*I will put enmity between thee and the woman, and between thy seed and her seed.*" See here the church of God announced in this verse! You have not only the gospel here, but the church also. Christ, the seed of the woman, is the head; and all who are in Christ are his body; he and they are the one seed. In these words the Lord set up the church which continues to this day; a seed which is opposed to Satan, and to evil; a seed which will remain, by the power of the Spirit of God, waging constant war with the powers of evil. Do we belong to that seed? In this seed there is a deep-seated hatred to everything that is false and evil. God will see that this seed shall never yield to the power of evil; for still it shall stand true, "I will put enmity between thee and the woman." As long as there is false doctrine, there shall be a protesting reformer; as long as there is any form of wickedness extant, there shall be a witness born from on high to contend with it. This seed is born, not of blood, nor of the will of the flesh, but of the Spirit of God, who dwells in the true seed of the woman; and this seed shall be valiant for the Lord of hosts till the last enemy shall be destroyed.

Which side are you on, my friend, this morning? I put the question very pointedly to everyone here: Are you born from above? That which is born of the flesh is flesh, and that which is born of the Spirit is spirit; and only this last is the true seed of the woman.

VI. Sixthly, observe that we see in the text THE LIMITED ACHIEVEMENT of the old serpent. What will he accomplish by all his schemes? "Thou shalt bruise his heel." That is all. This is after the serpent's manner. Satan is "an adder in the path, that biteth the horse heels, so that his rider shall fall backward." If he dares not attack you openly, he will assail you from behind. He is as a snake in the grass, biting at the heel of the traveller. The result of Satan's six thousand years of cunning and enmity is, that he has bruised the heel of his victim.

That bruised heel is painful enough. Behold our Lord in his human nature sore bruised: he was betrayed, bound, accused, buffeted, scourged, spit upon. He was nailed to the cross; he hung there in thirst and fever, and darkness and desertion. They pierced his hands and his feet; and last, they set his heart abroach, and forthwith there flowed from it both blood and water. Satan by death bruised the heel of the woman's seed. It is a sad business; but when our Lord thought of the resurrection, the salvation of his chosen, and the conquest of the world, it seemed to him to be a light thing; for "he endured the cross, despising the shame."

Behold the seed of the woman as further comprehending all the Lord's believing people! Satan has bruised their heel to the utmost of his power. Through the long persecutions he has been assailing the heel of the church. Many of the saints the devil cast into prison, and others he caused to be tortured for Christ's sake; but their souls were not conquered. He could only bruise their heel, their spirit soared out of his reach. And you, to-day, when tempted and tried, and cast down, may be comforted because your Head is not hurt, for Jesus reigns in heaven. The waters are black, and they cover the body, but our Head is above the billows, and the body is safe. The serpent's bruises stay in the heel, and spread no further. The suffering of the church, however great, is but a light affliction, not worthy to be compared with the far more exceeding and eternal weight of glory. Thank God, the enemy can only bruise your heel.

The cause of God and truth in the world may, by Satan's subtle power, be for a while sadly bruised as to the heel of its progress, but it cannot be wounded in the heart of its truth. The kingdom advances painfully, because of the bruised heel; but it fails not, but even when lame it takes the prey. Some doctrine which, possibly, may have been stated in a questionable manner is more fully studied, more carefully made known; and so even the heel-bruise works for good. Though the church of God may be under a cloud for a time, yet she will break out with all the greater splendour before long.

"Thou shalt bruise his heel." Make the best thou canst of it, Satan, it does not come to much! All that thou art at thy greatest is but a heel-nibbler, and nothing more. Thou art not allowed to poison the heel, but only to bruise it. Though the man of God walks limpingly a while, and suffers where the fangs have been, yet, leaning on his Beloved, he comes up from the wilderness without fail, and forgetting the bruises of his heel, he rejoices in the triumphs of his glorious Head.

VII. Now we come to the seventh lesson. We have marked the limited triumph of Satan, and we now observe HIS FINAL DOOM. "I will put enmity between thee and the woman, between thy seed and her seed; it shall bruise thy head." Here is the end of the great conflict. Satan, who heads the powers of evil in the world, is to fight it out with all his cunning and strength, and he is so far to succeed as to bruise the heel of the champion with whom he fights; but in the end the seed of the woman is to bruise his head. This was accomplished when the Lord Jesus died, and by dying honoured the law, put away sin, slew death, and defeated hell. When the great Substitute drank the cup of wrath to its utmost dregs for every believing soul, when he unhinged the gate of the sepulchre and carried it away, as Samson carried the gates of Gaza—post, and bar, and all; when he opened the doorways of heaven and led captivity captive; then, indeed the head of the dragon was broken. What can Satan now do? Is not the accuser of the brethren cast down? He is still doing his little best in bitterness and malice; but the Christ hath crushed him. Yes, the very Christ who "was despised and rejected of men," the man of the thorn crown and the marred visage, the man of bleeding shoulders and pierced hands and feet, the man who was born of a virgin, the seed of the woman, hath broken the power of the enemy. Hallelujah! Hallelujah! He hath cast down the Prince of darkness from his high places! Did he not himself say, "I beheld Satan as lightning fall from heaven"? He hath bruised the serpent's head.

This is done in all believers also, and shall be done yet more effectually. Brethren, in that day when the Holy Spirit led us to trust in the Lord Jesus, we bruised the serpent's head. He had been accustomed to command, and we to obey, and thus sin had dominion over us; but as soon as ever we believed in Christ, that dominion was ended, and Dagon fell before the ark of the Lord. I see the serpent rise above me. This great python, with opened jaws, gapes upon me as though he would swallow me up quick. But I am not afraid. O serpent, I have bruised thy head in Christ Jesus my Lord; for I, too, am of the seed of the woman! The serpent cannot lift himself against the chosen seed. What can he do with a broken head? He knows that God has decreed that every believer shall triumph over him. It is written, "God shall bruise Satan under your feet shortly." Hallelujah! once again.

This bruise upon the head of the evil is a mortal stroke. If he had been bruised upon the tail, or upon the neck, he might have survived; but the Lord shall utterly slay the kingdom of evil, and crush out its power. Reigning evil shall cease; and grace shall reign through righteousness unto eternal life. There shall be a new heaven and a new earth, wherein dwelleth righteousness. Christ himself, the seed of the woman, shall come a second time, and he shall reign on earth amongst his ancients gloriously. Then shall he ride forth prosperously, because of truth and righteousness : and his right hand shall exalt his people. His foot shall tread down their enemy. May you and I be among the happy throng that shall salute the Seed of the woman in his second advent! May we reign with him in that day! By the Seed of the woman is Paradise restored to us, and all the mischief of the fall is undone : for he restoreth that which he took not away.

And now, my hearer, which side are you on? Do any of you think that ye shall not surely die? You talk like your father, and his children you are. Do any of you say, God is a hard governor? Has he said, "Ye shall not eat of the fruit of the trees of the garden"? You are like your own father in this also. And do you move in snaky, cunning ways? Are you given to craft and policy? Dare you tell a lie, and then forge another to prop up the first? You are of your father the devil, for his works you do. Are you opposed to God and truth and righteousness? and do you cry out for what is called "liberty," that is, licentiousness and permission to indulge your own passions? Then you are on the evil side. Do you aspire to know good and evil? Young man, would you go into evil haunts to see vice, and learn its ways? Do you long to see "life," as they call it? Are you familiar with the sensual and the profane? Ah! then you are listening to that old deceiver, who allures you into his deadly nets: I pray you, escape from his seductions.

Is it well with you? Do you look to Jesus, the seed of the woman? Are you trusting in him to break the power of the enemy? Do you wish the power of sin to be broken in yourself? Do you desire to have the very head of it crushed to powder? Do you pine to be free from sin, and holy as God is holy? Are you trusting in Jesus to have this same thing wrought in you? Ah! then you are on the conquering side. Victory shall be yours through the blood of the Lamb.

Thus have we found much gospel in the wonderful sentence pronounced upon that old serpent, the devil; but yet we have only skimmed the surface. To the eternal God be glory, world without end. Amen.

Portion of Scripture read before Sermon—Genesis iii.

Hymns from "Our Own Hymn Book"—917, 470, 477.

Metropolitan Tabernacle Pulpit.

CHRIST THE CONQUEROR OF SATAN.

A Sermon

DELIVERED ON LORD'S-DAY MORNING, NOVEMBER 26TH, 1876, BY

C. H. SPURGEON,

AT THE METROPOLITAN TABERNACLE, NEWINGTON.

"And I will put enmity between thee and the woman, and between thy seed and her seed; it shall bruise thy head, and thou shalt bruise his heel."—Genesis iii. 15.

THIS is the first gospel sermon that was ever delivered upon the surface of this earth. It was a memorable discourse indeed, with Jehovah himself for the preacher, and the whole human race and the prince of darkness for the audience. It must be worthy of our heartiest attention.

Is it not remarkable that this great gospel promise should have been delivered so soon after the transgression? As yet no sentence had been pronounced upon either of the two human offenders, but the promise was given under the form of a sentence pronounced upon the serpent. Not yet had the woman been condemned to painful travail, or the man to exhausting labour, or even the soil to the curse of thorn and thistle. Truly "mercy rejoiceth against judgment." Before the Lord had said "Dust thou art and unto dust thou shalt return," he was pleased to say that the seed of the woman should bruise the serpent's head. Let us rejoice, then, in the swift mercy of God, which in the early watches of the night of sin came with comfortable words unto us.

These words were not directly spoken to Adam and Eve, but they were directed distinctly to the serpent himself, and that by way of punishment to him for what he had done. It was a day of cruel triumph to him : such joy as his dark mind is capable of had filled him, for he had indulged his malice, and gratified his spite. He had in the worst sense destroyed a part of God's works, he had introduced sin into the new world, he had stamped the human race with his own image, and gained new forces to promote rebellion and to multiply transgression, and therefore he felt that sort of gladness which a fiend can know who bears a hell within him. But now God comes in, takes up the quarrel personally, and causes him to be disgraced on the very battle-field upon which he had gained a temporary success. He tells the dragon that he

No. 1,326.

will undertake to deal with him; this quarrel shall not be between the serpent and man, but between God and the serpent. God saith, in solemn words, "I will put enmity between thee and the woman, between thy seed and her seed," and he promises that there shall rise in fulness of time a champion, who, though he suffer, shall smite in a vital part the power of evil, and bruise the serpent's head. This was the more, it seems to me, a comfortable message of mercy to Adam and Eve, because they would feel sure that the tempter would be punished, and as that punishment would involve blessing for them, the vengeance due to the serpent would be the guarantee of mercy to themselves. Perhaps, however, by thus obliquely giving the promise, the Lord meant to say, "Not for your sakes do I this, O fallen man and woman, nor for the sake of your descendants; but for my own name and honour's sake, that it be not profaned and blasphemed amongst the fallen spirits. I undertake to repair the mischief which has been caused by the tempter, that my name and my glory may not be diminished among the immortal spirits who look down upon the scene." All this would be very humbling but yet consolatory to our parents if they thought of it, seeing that mercy given for God's sake is always to our troubled apprehension more sure than any favour which could be promised to us for our own sake. The divine sovereignty and glory afford us a stronger foundation of hope than merit, even if merit can be supposed to exist.

Now we must note concerning this first gospel sermon that on it the earliest believers stayed themselves. This was all that Adam had by way of revelation, and all that Abel had received. This one lone star shone in Abel's sky; he looked up to it and he believed. By its light he spelt out "sacrifice," and therefore he brought of the firstlings of his flock and laid them upon the altar, and proved in his own person how the seed of the serpent hated the seed of the woman, for his brother slew him for his testimony. Although Enoch the seventh from Adam prophesied concerning the second advent, yet he does not appear to have uttered anything new concerning the first coming, so that still this one promise remained as man's sole word of hope. The torch which flamed within the gates of Eden just before man was driven forth lit up the world to all believers until the Lord was pleased to give more light, and to renew and enlarge the revelation of his covenant, when he spake to his servant Noah. Those hoary fathers who lived before the flood rejoiced in the mysterious language of our text, and resting on it, they died in faith. Nor, brethren, must you think it a slender revelation, for, if you attentively consider, it is wonderfully full of meaning. If it had been on my heart to handle it doctrinally this morning, I think I could have shown you that it contains all the gospel. There lie within it, as an oak lies within an acorn, all the great truths which make up the gospel of Christ. Observe that here is the grand mystery of the incarnation. Christ is that seed of the woman who is here spoken of; and there is a hint not darkly given as to how that Incarnation would be effected. Jesus was not born after the ordinary manner of the sons of men. Mary was overshadowed of the Holy Ghost, and "the holy thing" which was born of her was as to his humanity the seed of the woman only; as it is written, "Behold a virgin shall conceive and bear a son, and they shall call his name Immanuel." The promise plainly teaches that the deliverer would be born of a woman, and, carefully viewed, it also foreshadows the divine method of the Redeemer's conception and birth. So also is the doctrine of the two seeds plainly taught here—" I will put 'enmity between thee and the woman, between thy seed and her seed." There was evidently to be in the world a seed of the woman on God's side against the serpent, and a seed of the serpent that should always be upon the evil side even as it is unto this day. The church of God and the synagogue of Satan both exist. We see an Abel and a Cain, an Isaac and an Ishmael, a Jacob and an Esau; those that are born after the flesh, being the children of their father the devil, for his works they do, but those that are born again—being born after the Spirit, after the power of the life of Christ, are thus in Christ Jesus the seed of the woman, and contend earnestly against the dragon and his seed. Here, too, the great fact of the sufferings of Christ is clearly foretold—" Thou shalt bruise his heel." Within the compass of those words we find the whole story of our Lord's sorrows from Bethlehem to Calvary. " It shall bruise thy head ": there is the breaking of Satan's regal power, there is the clearing away of sin, there is the destruction of death by resurrection, there is the leading of captivity captive in the ascension, there is the victory of truth in the world through the descent of the Spirit, and there is the latter-day glory in which Satan shall be bound, and there is, lastly, the casting of the evil one and all his followers into the lake of fire. The conflict and the conquest are both in the compass of these few fruitful words. They may not have been fully understood by those who first heard them, but to us they are now full of light. The text at first looks like a flint, hard and cold; but sparks fly from it plentifully, for hidden fires of infinite love and grace lie concealed within. Over this promise of a gracious God we ought to rejoice exceedingly.

We do not know what our first parents understood by it, but we may be certain that they gathered a great amount of comfort from it. They must have understood that they were not then and there to be destroyed, because the Lord had spoken of a " seed." They would argue that it must be needful that Eve should live if there should be a seed from her. They understood, too, that if that seed was to overcome the serpent and bruise his head, it must augur good to themselves: they could not fail to see that there was some great, some mysterious benefit to be conferred upon them by the victory which their seed would achieve over the instigator of their ruin. They went on in faith upon this, and were comforted in travail and in toil, and I doubt not both Adam and his wife in the faith thereof entered into everlasting rest.

This morning I intend to handle this text in three ways. First, we shall notice *its facts;* secondly, we shall consider *the experience within the heart of each believer which tallies to those facts;* and then, thirdly, *the encouragement* which the text and its connection as a whole afford to us.

I. THE FACTS. The facts are four, and I call your earnest attention to them. The first is *Enmity was excited.* The text begins, " I will put enmity between thee and the woman." They had been very friendly; the woman and the serpent had conversed together. She thought at the time that the serpent was her friend; and she was so much his friend that she took his advice in the teeth of God's precept, and was willing to believe bad things of the great Creator, because this wicked, crafty serpent insinuated the same. Now, at the moment when God spake, that friendship between the woman and the serpent had already in a measure come to an end, for she had accused the serpent to God, and said, "The serpent beguiled me, and I did eat." So far, so good. The friendship of sinners does not last long; they have already begun to quarrel, and now the Lord comes in and graciously takes advantage of the quarrel which had commenced, and says, "I will carry this disagreement a great deal further, I will put enmity between thee and the woman." Satan counted on man's descendants being his confederates, but God would break up this covenant with hell, and raise up a seed which should war against the Satanic power. Thus we have here God's first declaration that he will set up a rival kingdom to oppose the tyranny of sin and Satan, that he will create in the hearts of a chosen seed an enmity against evil, so that they shall fight against it, and with many a struggle and pain shall overcome the prince of darkness. The divine Spirit has abundantly achieved this plan and purpose of the Lord, combating the fallen angel by a glorious man: making man to be Satan's foe and conqueror. Henceforth the woman was to hate the evil one, and I do not doubt but what she did so. She had abundant cause for so doing, and as often as she thought of him it would be with infinite regret that she could have listened to his malicious and deceitful talk. The woman's seed has also evermore had enmity against the evil one. I mean not the carnal seed, for Paul tells us, "They which are the children of the flesh, these are not the children of God: but the children of the promise are counted for the seed." The carnal seed of the man and the woman are not meant, but the spiritual seed, even Christ Jesus and those who are in him. Wherever you meet these, they hate the serpent with a perfect hatred. We would if we could destroy from our souls every work of Satan, and out of this poor afflicted world of ours we would root up every evil which he has planted. That seed of the woman, that glorious *One*,—for he speaks not of seeds as of many but of seed that is one,—you know how he abhorred the devil and all his devices. There was enmity between Christ and Satan, for he came to destroy the works of the devil and to deliver those who are under bondage to him. For that purpose was he born; for that purpose did he live; for that purpose did he die; for that purpose he has gone into the glory, and for that purpose he will come again, that everywhere he may find out his adversary and utterly destroy him and his works from amongst the sons of men. This putting of the enmity between the two seeds was the commencement of the plan of mercy, the first act in the programme of grace. Of the woman's seed it was henceforth said, "Thou lovest righteousness, and hatest wickedness: therefore God, thy God, hath anointed thee with the oil of gladness above thy fellows."

Then comes the second prophecy, which has also turned into a fact, namely *the coming of the champion*. The seed of the woman by promise is to champion the cause, and oppose the dragon. That seed is the Lord Jesus Christ. The prophet Micah saith, "But thou, Bethlehem Ephratah, though thou be little among the thousands of Judah, yet out of thee shall he come forth unto me that is to be ruler in Israel;

whose goings forth have been from of old, from everlasting. Therefore will he give them up, until the time that she which travaileth hath brought forth." To none other than the babe which was born in Bethlehem of the blessed Virgin can the words of prophecy refer. She it was who did conceive and bear a son, and it is concerning her son that we sing, "Unto us a child is born, unto us a Son is given: and his name shall be called Wonderful, Counsellor, the Mighty God, the Everlasting Father, the Prince of Peace." On the memorable night at Bethlehem, when angels sang in heaven, the seed of the woman appeared, and as soon as ever he saw the light the old serpent, the devil, entered into the heart of Herod if possible to slay him, but the Father preserved him, and suffered none to lay hands on him. As soon as he publicly came forward upon the stage of action, thirty years after, Satan met him foot to foot. You know the story of the temptation in the wilderness, and how there the woman's seed fought with him who was a liar from the beginning. The devil assailed him thrice with all the artillery of flattery, malice, craft and falsehood, but the peerless champion stood unwounded, and chased his foeman from the field. Then our Lord set up his kingdom, and called one and another unto him, and carried the war into the enemy's country. In divers places he cast out devils. He spake to the wicked and unclean spirit and said, "I charge thee come out of him," and the demon was expelled. Legions of devils flew before him : they sought to hide themselves in swine to escape from the terror of his presence. "Art thou come to torment us before our time?" was their cry when the wonder-working Christ dislodged them from the bodies which they tormented. Yea, and he made his own disciples mighty against the evil one, for in his name they cast out devils, till Jesus said, "I beheld Satan as lightning fall from heaven." Then there came a second personal conflict, for I take it that Gethsemane's sorrows were to a great degree caused by a personal assault of Satan, for our Master said, "This is your hour, and the power of darkness." He said also, "The Prince of this world cometh." What a struggle it was. Though Satan had nothing in Christ, yet did he seek if possible to lead him away from completing his great sacrifice, and there did our Master sweat as it were great drops of blood, falling to the ground, in the agony which it cost him to contend with the fiend. Then it was that our Champion began the last fight of all and won it to the bruising of the serpent's head. Nor did he end till he had spoiled principalities and powers and made a show of them openly.

"Now is the hour of darkness past,
Christ has assumed his reigning power;
Behold the great accuser cast
Down from his seat to reign no more."

The conflict our glorious Lord continues in his seed. We preach Christ crucified, and every sermon shakes the gates of hell. We bring sinners to Jesus by the Spirit's power, and every convert is a stone torn down from the wall of Satan's mighty castle. Yea, and the day shall come when everywhere the evil one shall be overcome, and the words of John in the Revelation shall be fulfilled. "And the great dragon was cast out, that old serpent, called the Devil, and Satan, which deceiveth the whole world: he was cast out into the earth, and his angels were cast out with him. And I heard a loud voice saying in heaven, Now is come salvation, and strength, and the kingdom of our God, and the power of his Christ: for the accuser of our brethren is cast down, which accused them before our God day and night." Thus did the Lord God in the words of our text promise a champion who should be the seed of the woman, between whom and Satan there should be war for ever and ever: that champion has come, the man-child has been born, and though the dragon is wroth with the woman, and makes war with the remnant of her seed which keep the testimony of Jesus Christ, yet the battle is the Lord's, and the victory falleth unto him whose name is Faithful and True, who in righteousness doth judge and make war.

The third fact which comes out in the text, though not quite in that order, is that *our Champion's heel should be bruised.* Do you need that I explain this? You know how all his life long his heel, that is, his lower part, his human nature, was perpetually being made to suffer. He carried our sicknesses and sorrows. But the bruising came mainly when both in body and in mind his whole human nature was made to agonize; when his soul was exceeding sorrowful even unto death, and his enemies pierced his hands and his feet, and he endured the shame and pain of death by crucifixion. Look at your Master and your King upon the cross, all distained with blood and dust! There was his heel most cruelly bruised. When they take down that precious body and wrap it in fair white linen and in spices, and lay it in Joseph's tomb, they weep as they handle that casket in which the Deity had dwelt, for there again Satan had bruised his heel. It was not merely that God had bruised him, "though it pleased the Father to bruise him," but the devil had let loose Herod, and Pilate, and Caiaphas, and the Jews, and the Romans, all of them his tools, upon him whom he knew to be the Christ, so that he was bruised of the old serpent. That is all, however! It is only his heel, not his head, which is bruised! For lo, the Champion rises again; the bruise was not mortal nor continual. Though he dies, yet still so brief is the interval in which he slumbers in the tomb that his holy body hath not seen corruption, and he comes forth perfect and lovely in his manhood, rising from his grave as from a refreshing sleep after so long a day of unresting toil! Oh the triumph of that hour! As Jacob only halted on his thigh when he overcame the angel, so did Jesus only retain a scar in his heel, and that he bears to the skies as his glory and beauty. Before the throne he looks like a lamb that has been slain, but in the power of an endless life he liveth unto God.

Then comes the fourth fact, namely, that while his heel was being bruised, *he was to bruise the serpent's head.* The figure represents the dragon as inflicting an injury upon the champion's heel, but at the same moment the champion himself with that heel crushes in the head of the serpent with fatal effect. By his sufferings Christ has overthrown Satan, by the heel that was bruised he has trodden upon the head which devised the bruising.

> "Lo, by the sons of hell he dies;
> But as he hangs 'twixt earth and skies,
> He gives their prince a fatal blow,
> And triumphs o'er the powers below."

Though Satan is not dead, my brethren, I was about to say, would God he were, and though he is not converted, and never will be, nor will the malice of his heart ever be driven from him, yet Christ has so far broken his head that he has missed his mark altogether. He intended to make the human race the captives of his power, but they are redeemed from his iron yoke. God has delivered many of them, and the day shall come when he will cleanse the whole earth from the serpent's slimy trail, so that the entire world shall be full of the praises of God. He thought that this world would be the arena of his victory over God and good, instead of which it is already the grandest theatre of divine wisdom, love, grace, and power. Even heaven itself is not so resplendent with mercy as the earth is, for here it is the Saviour poured out his blood, which cannot be said even of the courts of paradise above. Moreover he thought, no doubt, that when he had led our race astray and brought death upon them, he had effectually marred the Lord's work. He rejoiced that they would all pass under the cold seal of death, and that their bodies would rot in the sepulchre. Had he not spoiled the handiwork of his great Lord? God may make man as a curious creature with intertwisted veins and blood nerves, and sinews and muscles, and he may put into his nostrils the breath of life; but, "Ah," saith Satan, "I have infused a poison into him which will make him return to the dust from which he was taken." But now, behold, our Champion whose heel was bruised has risen from the dead, and given us a pledge that all his followers shall rise from the dead also. Thus is Satan foiled, for death shall not retain a bone, nor a piece of a bone, of one of those who belonged to the woman's seed. At the trump of the archangel from the earth and from the sea they shall arise, and this shall be their shout, "O death, where is thy sting? O grave, where is thy victory?" Satan, knowing this, feels already that by the resurrection his head is broken. Glory be to the Christ of God for this!

In multitudes of other ways the devil has been vanquished by our Lord Jesus, and so shall he ever be till he shall be cast into the lake of fire.

II. Let us now view OUR EXPERIENCE AS IT TALLIES WITH THESE FACTS. Now, brothers and sisters, we were by nature, as many of us as have been saved, the heirs of wrath even as others. It does not matter how godly our parents were, the first birth brought us no spiritual life, for the promise is not to them which are born of blood, or of the will of the flesh, or of the will of man, but only to those who are born of God. "That which is born of the flesh is flesh"; you cannot make it anything else and there it abides, and the flesh, or carnal mind, abideth in death; "it is not reconciled to God, neither indeed can be." He who is born into this world but once, and knows nothing of the new birth, must place himself among the seed of the serpent, for only by regeneration can we know ourselves to be the true seed. How does God deal with us who are his called and chosen ones? He means to save us, and how does he work to that end?

The first thing he does is, he comes to us in mercy, and *puts enmity between us and the serpent.* That is the very first work of grace. There was peace between us and Satan once; when he tempted we yielded; whatever he taught us we believed; we were his willing slaves. But perhaps you, my brethren, can recollect when first of all you began to feel uneasy and dissatisfied; the world's pleasures no longer pleased you; all the juice seemed to have been taken out of the apple, and you had nothing left but the hard core, which you could not feed upon at all. Then you suddenly perceived that you were living in sin, and you were miserable about it, and though you could not get rid of sin yet you hated it, and sighed over it, and cried, and groaned. In your heart of hearts you remained no longer on the side of evil, for you began to cry, "O wretched man that I am, who shall deliver me from the body of this death?" You were already from of old in the covenant of grace ordained to be the woman's seed, and now the decree began to discover itself in life bestowed upon you and working in you. The Lord in infinite mercy dropped the divine life into your soul. You did not know it, but there it was, a spark of the celestial fire, the living and incorruptible seed which abideth for ever. You began to hate sin, and you groaned under it as under a galling yoke; more and more it burdened you, you could not bear it, you hated the very thought of it. So it was with you: is it so now? Is there still enmity between you and the serpent? Indeed you are more and more the sworn enemies of evil, and you willingly acknowledge it.

Then came the champion: that is to say, "Christ was formed in you the hope of glory." You heard of him and you understood the truth about him, and it seemed a wonderful thing that he should be your substitute and stand in your room and place and stead, and bear your sin and all its curse and punishment, and that he should give his righteousness, yea, and his very self, to you that you might be saved. Ah, then you saw how sin could be overthrown, did you not? As soon as your heart understood Christ then you saw that what the law could not do, in that it was weak through the flesh, Christ was able to accomplish, and that the power of sin and Satan under which you had been in bondage, and which you now loathed, could and would be broken and destroyed because Christ had come into the world to overcome it.

Next, do you recollect how you were led to see *the bruising of Christ's heel* and to stand in wonder and observe what the enmity of the serpent had wrought in him? Did you not begin to feel the bruised heel yourself? Did not sin torment you? Did not the very thought of it vex you? Did not your own heart become a plague to you? Did not Satan begin to tempt you? Did he not inject blasphemous thoughts, and urge you on to desperate measures; did he not teach you to doubt the existence of God, and the mercy of God, and the possibility of your salvation, and so on? This was his nibbling at your heel. He is at his old tricks still. He worries whom he can't devour with a malicious joy. Did not your worldly friends begin to annoy you? Did they not give you the cold shoulder because they saw something about you so strange and foreign to their tastes? Did they not impute your conduct to fanaticism, pride, obstinacy, bigotry, and the like? Ah, this persecution is the serpent's seed beginning to discover the woman's seed, and to carry on the old war. What does Paul say? "But as then he that was born after the flesh persecuted him that was born after the Spirit, even so it is now." True godliness is an unnatural and strange thing to them, and they cannot away with it. Though there are no stakes in Smithfield, nor racks in the Tower, yet the enmity of the human heart towards Christ and his seed is just the same, and very often shows itself in "trials of cruel mockings" which to tender hearts are very hard to bear. Well, this is your heel being bruised in sympathy with the bruising of the heel of the glorious seed of the woman.

But, brethren, do you know something of the other fact, namely, that *we conquer, for the serpent's head is broken in us?* How say you? Is not the power and dominion of sin broken in you? Do you not feel that you cannot sin because you are born of God? Some sins which were masters of you once, do not trouble you now. I have known a man guilty of profane swearing, and from the moment of his conversion he has never had any difficulty in the matter. We have known a man snatched from drunkenness, and the cure by divine grace has been very wonderful and complete. We have known persons delivered from unclean living, and they have at once become chaste and pure, because Christ has smitten the old dragon such blows that he could not have power over them in that respect. The chosen seed sin and mourn it, but they are not slaves to sin; their heart goeth not after it: they have to say sometimes "the thing I would not that I do," but they are wretched when it is so. They consent with their heart to the law of God that it is good, and they sigh and cry that they may be helped to obey it, for they are no longer under the slavery of sin; the serpent's reigning power and dominion is broken in them.

It is broken next in this way, that the guilt of sin is gone. The great power of the serpent lies in unpardoned sin. He cries "I have made you guilty: I brought you under the curse." "No," say we, "we are delivered from the curse and are now blessed, for it is written, 'Blessed is the man whose transgression is forgiven, and whose sin is covered.' We are no longer guilty, for who shall lay anything to the charge of God's elect? Since Christ hath justified, who is he that condemneth?" Here is a swinging blow for the old dragon's head, such as he never will recover.

Oftentimes the Lord also grants us to know what it is to overcome temptation, and so to break the head of the fiend. Satan allures us with many baits; he has studied our points well, he knows the weakness of the flesh: but many and many a time, blessed be God, we have foiled him completely to his eternal shame! The devil must have felt himself mean that day when he tried to overthrow Job, dragged him down to a dunghill, robbed him of everything, covered him with sores, and yet could not make him yield. Job conquered when he cried, "Though he slay me yet will I trust in him." A feeble man had vanquished a devil who could raise the wind and blow down a house, and destroy the family who were feasting in it. Devil as he is, and crowned prince of the power of the air, yet the poor bereaved patriarch sitting on the dunghill covered with sores, being one of the woman's seed, through the strength of the inner life won the victory over him.

> "Ye sons of God oppose his rage,
> Resist, and he'll be gone:
> Thus did our dearest Lord engage
> And vanquish him alone."

Moreover, dear brethren, we have this hope that the very being of sin in us will be destroyed. The day will come when we shall be without spot or wrinkle, or any such thing; and we shall stand before the throne of God, having suffered no injury whatever from the fall and from all the machinations of Satan, for "they are without fault before the throne of God." What triumph that will be! "The Lord will tread Satan under your feet shortly." When he has made you perfect and free from all sin, as he will do, you will have bruised the serpent's head indeed.

And your resurrection, too, when Satan shall see you come up from the grave like one that has been perfumed in a bath of spices, when he shall see you arise in the image of Christ, with the same body which was sown in corruption and weakness raised in incorruption and power, then will he feel an infinite chagrin, and know that his head is bruised by the woman's seed.

I ought to add that every time any one of us is made useful in saving souls we do as it were repeat the bruising of the serpent's head. When you go, dear sister, among those poor children, and pick them up from the gutters, where they are Satan's prey, where he finds the raw material for thieves and criminals, and when through your means, by the grace of God, the little wanderers become children of the living God, then you in your measure bruise the old serpent's head. I pray you do not spare him. When we by preaching the gospel turn sinners from the error of their ways, so that they escape from the power of darkness, again we bruise the serpent's head. Whenever in any shape or way you are blessed to the aiding of the cause of truth and righteousness in the world, you, too, who were once beneath his power, and even now have sometimes to suffer from his nibbling at your heel, you tread upon his head. In all deliverances and victories you overcome, and prove the promise true,—"Thou shalt tread upon the lion and adder: the young lion and the dragon shalt thou trample under feet. Because he hath set his love upon me, therefore will I deliver him: I will set him on high, because he hath known my name."

III. Let us speak awhile upon THE ENCOURAGEMENT which our text and the context yields to us; for it seems to me to abound.

I want you, brethren, to exercise faith in the promise and be comforted. The text evidently encouraged Adam very much. I do not think we have attached enough importance to the conduct of Adam after the Lord had spoken to him. Notice the simple but conclusive proof which he gave of his faith. Sometimes an action may be very small and unimportant, and yet, as a straw shows which way the wind blows, it may display at once, if it be thought over, the whole state of the man's mind. Adam acted in faith upon what God said, for we read, "And Adam called his wife's name Eve (or Life); because she was the mother of all living" (verse 20). She was not a mother at all, but as the life was to come through her by virtue of the promised seed, Adam marks his full conviction of the truth of the promise though at the time the woman had borne no children. There stood Adam, fresh from the awful presence of God, what more could he say? He might have said with the prophet, "My flesh trembleth for the fear of thee," but even then he turns round to his fellow-culprit as she stands there trembling too, and he calls her Eve, mother of the life that is yet to be. It was grandly spoken by Father Adam : it makes him rise in our esteem. Had he been left to himself he would have murmured or at least despaired, but no, his faith in the new promise gave him hope. He uttered no word of repining against the condemnation to till with toil the unthankful ground, nor on Eve's part was there a word of repining over the appointed sorrows of motherhood ; they each accept the well-deserved sentence with the silence which denotes the perfection of their resignation; their only word is full of simple faith. There was no child on whom to set their hopes, nor would the true seed be born for many an age, still Eve is to be the mother of all living, and he calls her so. Exercise like faith, my brother, on the far wider revelation which God has given to you, and always extract the utmost comfort from it. Make a point, whenever you receive a promise from God, to get all you can out of it : if you carry out that rule, it is wonderful what comfort you will gain. Some go on the principle of getting as little as possible out of God's word. I believe that such a plan is the proper way with a man's word ; always understand it at the minimum, because that is what he means ; but God's word is to be understood at the maximum, for he will do exceeding abundantly above what you ask or even think.

Notice by way of further encouragement that we may regard our reception of Christ's righteousness as an instalment of the final overthrow of the devil. The twenty-first verse says, " Unto Adam also and to his wife did the Lord God make coats of skins, and clothed them." A very condescending, thoughtful, and instructive deed of divine love! God heard what Adam said to his wife, and saw that he was a believer, and so he comes and gives him the type of the perfect righteousness, which is the believer's portion—he covered him with lasting raiment. No more fig leaves, which were a mere mockery, but a close fitting garment which had been procured through the death of a victim ; the Lord brings that and puts it on him, and Adam could no more say, " I am naked." How could he, for God had clothed him. Now, beloved, let us take out of the promise that is given us concerning our Lord's conquest over the devil this one item and rejoice in it, for Christ has delivered us from the power of the serpent who opened our eyes and told us we were naked, by covering us from head to foot with a righteousness which adorns and protects us, so that we are comfortable in heart, and beautiful in the sight of God, and are no more ashamed.

Next, by way of encouragement in pursuing the Christian life, I would say to young people, expect to be assailed. If you have fallen into trouble through being a Christian, be encouraged by it ; do not at all regret or fear it, but rejoice ye in that day, and leap for joy, for this is the constant token of the covenant. There is enmity between the seed of the woman and the seed of the serpent still, and if you did not experience any of it you might begin to fear that you were on the wrong side. Now that you smart under the sneer of sarcasm and oppression rejoice and triumph, for now are ye partakers with the glorious seed of the woman in the bruising of his heel.

Still further encouragement comes from this. Your suffering as a Christian is not brought upon you for your own sake ; ye are partners with the great seed of the woman, ye are confederates with Christ.

You must not think the devil cares much about you: the battle is against Christ in you. Why, if you were not in Christ, the devil would never trouble you. When you were without Christ in the world you might have sinned as you like, your relatives and work-mates would not have been at all grieved with you, they would rather have joined you in it; but now the serpent's seed hates Christ in you. This exalts the sufferings of persecution to a position far above all common afflictions. I have heard of a woman who was condemned to death in the Marian days, and before her time came to be burned a child was born to her, and she cried out in her sorrow. A wicked adversary, who stood by said, "How will you bear to die for your religion if you make such ado?" "Ah," she said, "Now I suffer in my own person as a woman, but then *I* shall not suffer, but Christ in me." Nor were these idle words, for she bore her martyrdom with exemplary patience, and rose in her chariot of fire in holy triumph to heaven. If Christ be in you, nothing will dismay you, but you will overcome the world, the flesh, and the devil by faith.

Last of all, let us resist the devil always with this belief, that he has received a broken head. I am inclined to think that Luther's way of laughing at the devil was a very good one, for he is worthy of shame and everlasting contempt. Luther once threw an inkstand at his head when he was tempting him very sorely, and though the act itself appears absurd enough, yet it was a true type of what that greater Reformer was all his life long, for the books he wrote were truly a flinging of the inkstand at the head of the fiend. That is what we have to do: we are to resist him by all means. Let us do this bravely, and tell him to his teeth that we are not afraid of him. Tell him to recollect his bruised head, which he tries to cover with a crown of pride, or with a popish cowl, or with an infidel doctor's hood. We know him, and see the deadly wound he bears. His power is gone; he is fighting a lost battle; he is contending against omnipotence. He has set himself against the oath of the Father; against the blood of the incarnate Son; against the eternal power and Godhead of the blessed Spirit, all of which are engaged in the defence of the seed of the woman in the day of battle. Therefore, brethren, be ye steadfast in resisting the evil one, being strong in faith, giving glory to God.

> "'Tis by thy blood, immortal Lamb,
> Thine armies tread the tempter down;
> 'Tis by thy word and powerful name
> They gain the battle and renown.
>
> "Rejoice ye heavens; let every star
> Shine with new glories round the sky:
> Saints, while ye sing the heavenly war,
> Raise your Deliverer's name on high."

PORTION OF SCRIPTURE READ BEFORE SERMON—Genesis iii.

HYMNS FROM "OUR OWN HYMN BOOK"—335, 477, 322.

The New Park Street Pulpit.

THE INCARNATION AND BIRTH OF CHRIST.

A Sermon

Delivered on Sabbath Morning, December 23, 1855, by the

REV. C. H. SPURGEON,

AT NEW PARK STREET CHAPEL, SOUTHWARK.

"But thou, Beth-lehem Ephratah, though thou be little among the thousands of Judah, yet out of thee shall he come forth unto me that is to be ruler in Israel; whose goings forth have been from of old, from everlasting."—Micah v. 2.

THIS is the season of the year when, whether we wish it or not, we are compelled to think of the birth of Christ. I hold it to be one of the greatest absurdities under heaven to think that there is any religion in keeping Christmas-day. There are no probabilities whatever that our Saviour Jesus Christ was born on that day, and the observance of it is purely of Popish origin; doubtless those who are Catholics have a right to hallow it, but I do not see how consistent Protestants can account it in the least sacred. However, I wish there were ten or a dozen Christmas-days in the year; for there is work enough in the world, and a little more rest would not hurt labouring people. Christmas-day is really a boon to us; particularly as it enables us to assemble round the family hearth and meet our friends once more. Still, although we do not fall exactly in the track of other people, I see no harm in thinking of the incarnation and birth of the Lord Jesus. We do not wish to be classed with those

"Who with more care keep holiday
The wrong, than others the right way."

The old Puritans made a parade of work on Christmas-day, just to show that they protested against the observance of it. But we believe they entered that protest so completely, that we are willing, as their descendants, to take the good accidentally conferred by the day, and leave its superstitions to the superstitious.

To proceed at once to what we have to say to you: we notice, first, *who it was that sent Christ forth.* God the Father here speaks, and says, "Out of thee shall he come forth unto *me* that is to be the ruler in Israel." Secondly, *where did he come to at the time of his incarnation?* Thirdly, *what did he come for?* "To be ruler in Israel." Fourthly, *had he ever come before?* Yes, he had. "Whose goings forth have been from of old, from everlasting."

I. First, then, WHO SENT JESUS CHRIST? The answer is returned to us by the words of the text. "Out of thee," saith Jehovah, speaking by the mouth of Micah "out of thee shall he come forth unto me." It is a sweet thought that Jesus Christ, did not come forth without his Father's permission, authority, consent, and assistance. He was sent of the Father, that he might be the Saviour of men. We are, alas! too apt to forget, that while there are distinctions as to the persons in the Trinity, there are no distinctions of honor; and we do very frequently ascribe the honor of our salvation, or at least the depths of its mercy and the extremity of its benevolence, more to Jesus Christ than we do to the Father. This is a very great mistake. What if Jesus came? Did not his Father send him? If he was made a child did not the Holy Ghost beget him? If he spake wondrously, did not his Father pour grace into his lips, that he might be an able minister of the new covenant? If his Father did forsake him when he drank the bitter cup of gall, did he not love him still? and did he not, by-and by, after three days, raise him from the

No. 57.

dead, and at last receive him up on high, leading captivity captive? Ah! beloved, he who knoweth the Father, and the Son, and the Holy Ghost as he should know them, never setteth one before another; he is not more thankful to one than the other; he sees them at Bethlehem, at Gethsemane, and on Calvary, all equally engaged in the work of salvation. "He shall come forth unto *me*." O Christian, hast thou put thy confidence in the man Christ Jesus? Hast thou placed thy reliance solely on him? And art thou united with him? Then believe that thou art united unto the God of heaven; since to the man Christ Jesus thou art brother, and holdest closest fellowship, thou art linked thereby with God the Eternal, and "the Ancient of days" is thy Father and thy friend. "He shall come forth unto *me*." Did you never see the depth of love there was in the heart of Jehovah, when God the Father equipped his Son for the great enterprise of mercy? There had been a sad day in Heaven once before, when Satan fell, and dragged with him a third of the stars of heaven, and when the Son of God launching from his great right hand the Omnipotent thunders, dashed the rebellious crew to the pit of perdition; but if we could conceive a grief in heaven, that must have been a sadder day, when the Son of the Most High left his Father's bosom, where he had lain from before all worlds. "Go," saith the Father, "and thy Father's blessing on thy head!" Then comes the unrobing. How do angels crowd around to see the Son of God take off his robes! He laid aside his crown; he said, "My father, I am Lord over all, blessed for ever, but I will lay my crown aside, and be as mortal men are." He strips himself of his bright vest of glory; "Father," he says, "I will wear a robe of clay, just such as men wear." Then he takes off all those jewels wherewith he was glorified; he lays aside his starry mantles and robes of light, to dress himself in the simple garments of the peasant of Galilee. What a solemn disrobing that must have been! And next, can you picture the dismissal! The angels attend the Saviour through the streets, until they approach the doors: when an angel cries, "Lift up your heads, O ye gates, and be ye lifted up ye everlasting doors, and let the king of glory through!" Oh! methinks the angels must have wept when they lost the company of Jesus—when the Sun of Heaven bereaved them of all its light. But they went after him. They descended with him; and when his spirit entered into flesh, and he became a babe, he was attended by that mighty host of angels, who after they had been with him to Bethlehem's manger, and seen him safely laid on his mother's breast, in their journey upwards appeared to the shepherds and told them that he was born king of the Jews. *The Father* sent him! Contemplate that subject. Let your soul get hold of it, and in every period of his life think that he suffered what *the Father* willed; that every step of his life was marked with the approval of the great I AM. Let every thought that you have of Jesus be also connected with the eternal, ever-blessed God; for "he," saith Jehovah, "shall come forth unto *me*." Who sent him, then? The answer is, his Father.

II. Now, secondly, WHERE DID HE COME TO? A word or two concerning Bethlehem. It seemed meet and right that our Saviour should be born in Bethlehem, and that because of Bethlehem's history, Bethlehem's name, and Bethlehem's position—little in Judah.

1. First, it seemed necessary that Christ should be born in Bethlehem, *because of Bethlehem's history*. Dear to every Israelite was the little village of Bethlehem. Jerusalem might outshine it in splendour; for there stood the temple, the glory of the whole earth, and "beautiful for situation, the joy of the whole earth was Mount Zion;" yet around Bethlehem there clustered a number of incidents which always made it a pleasant resting-place to every Jewish mind; and even the Christian cannot help loving Bethlehem. The first mention, I think, that we have of Bethlehem is a sorrowful one. There Rachel died. If you turn to the 35th of Genesis you will find it said in the 16th verse—"And they journeyed from Bethel; and there was but a little way to come to Ephrath; and Rachel travailed, and she had hard labour. And it came to pass, when she was in hard labour, that the midwife said unto her, Fear not; thou shalt have this son also. And it came to pass, as her soul was in departing, (for she died) that she called his name Ben-oni: but his father called him Benjamin. And Rachel died, and was buried in the way to Ephrath, which is Bethlehem. And Jacob set a pillar upon her grave, that is the pillar of Rachel's grave unto this day." A singular incident this—almost prophetic. Might not Mary have called her own son Jesus, her Ben-oni; for he was to be the child of sorrow? Simeon said to her—"Yea, a sword shall pierce through thine own soul also, that

the thoughts of many hearts may be revealed." But while she might have called him Ben-oni, what did God his Father call him? Benjamin, the son of my right hand. Ben-oni was he as a man; Benjamin as to his Godhead. This little incident seems to be almost a prophecy that Ben-oni—Benjamin, the Lord Jesus, should be born in Bethlehem. But another woman makes this place celebrated. That woman's name was Naomi. There lived at Bethlehem in after days, when, perhaps, the stone that Jacob's fondness had raised had been covered with moss and its inscription obliterated, another woman named Naomi. She too was a daughter of joy, and yet a daughter of bitterness. Naomi was a woman whom the Lord had loved and blessed, but she had to go to a strange land; and she said, " Call me not Naomi (pleasant) but let my name be called Mara (bitter) for the Almighty hath dealt very bitterly with me." Yet was she not alone amid all her losses, for there cleaved unto her Ruth the Moabitess, whose Gentile blood should unite with the pure untainted stream of the Jew, and should thus bring forth the Lord our Saviour, the great king both of Jews and Gentiles. That very beautiful book of Ruth had all its scenery laid in Bethlehem. It was at Bethlehem that Ruth went forth to glean in the fields of Boaz; it was there that Boaz looked upon her, and she bowed herself before her lord; it was there her marriage was celebrated; and in the streets of Bethlehem did Boaz and Ruth receive a blessing which made them fruitful, so that Boaz became the father of Obed, and Obed the father of Jesse, and Jesse the father of David. That last fact gilds Bethlehem with glory—the fact that David was born there—the mighty hero who smote the Philistine giant, who led the discontented of his land away from the tyranny of their monarch, and who afterwards, by a full consent of a willing people, was crowned king of Israel and Judah. Bethlehem was a royal city, because the kings were there brought forth. Little as Bethlehem was, it was much to be esteemed; because it was like certain principalities which we have in Europe, which are celebrated for nothing but for bringing forth the consorts of the royal families of England. It was right, then, from history, that Bethlehem should be the birth-place of Christ.

2. But again: *there is something in the name of the place.* "Bethlehem Ephratah." The word *Bethlehem* has a double meaning. It signifies "the house of bread," and "the house of war." Ought not Jesus Christ to be born in "the house of bread?" He is the Bread of his people, on which they feed. As our fathers ate manna in the wilderness, so do we live on Jesus here below. Famished by the world, we cannot feed on its shadows. Its husks may gratify the swinish taste of worldlings, for they are swine; but we need something more substantial, and in that blest bread of heaven, made of the bruised body of our Lord Jesus, and baked in the furnace of his agonies, we find a blessed food. No food like Jesus to the desponding soul or to the strongest saint. The very meanest of the family of God goes to Bethlehem for his bread; and the strongest man, who eats strong meat, goes to Bethlehem for it. House of Bread! whence could come our nourishment but from thee? We have tried Sinai, but on her rugged steeps there grow no fruits, and her thorny heights yield no corn whereon we may feed. We have repaired even to Tabor itself, where Christ was transfigured, and yet there we have not been able to eat his flesh and drink his blood. But Bethlehem, thou house of bread, rightly wast thou called; for there the bread of life was first handed down for man to eat. And it is also called "the house of war;" because Christ is to a man "the house of bread," or else "the house of war." While he is food to the righteous he causeth war to the wicked, according to his own word—" Think not that I am come to send peace on the earth; I am not come to send peace, but a sword. For I am come to set a man at variance against his father, and the daughter against her mother, and the daughter-in-law against her mother-in-law. And a man's foes shall be they of his own household." Sinner! if thou dost not know Bethlehem as "the house of bread," it shall be to thee a "house of war." If from the lips of Jesus thou dost never drink sweet honey—if thou art not like the bee, which sippeth sweet luscious liquor from the Rose of Sharon, then out of the selfsame mouth there shall go forth against thee a two-edged sword; and that mouth from which the righteous draw their bread, shall be to thee the mouth of destruction and the cause of thine ill. Jesus of Bethlehem, house of bread and house of war, we trust we know thee as our bread. Oh! that some who are now at war with thee might hear in their hearts, as well as in their ears the song—

"Peace on earth, and mercy mild,
God and sinners reconciled."

And now for that word *Ephratah*. That was the old name of the place which the Jews retained and loved. The meaning of it is, "fruitfulness," or "abundance." Ah! well was Jesus born in the house of fruitfulness; for whence cometh my fruitfulness and thy fruitfulness, my brother, but from Bethlehem? Our poor barren hearts ne'er produced one fruit, or flower, till they were watered with the Saviour's blood. It is his incarnation which fattens the soil of our hearts. There had been pricking thorns on all the ground, and mortal poisons, before he came; but our fruitfulness comes from him. "I am like a green fir-tree; from thee is my fruit found." "All my springs are in thee." If we be like trees planted by the rivers of water, bringing forth our fruit in our season, it is not because we were naturally fruitful, but because of the rivers of water by which we were planted. It is Jesus that makes us fruitful. "If a man abide in me," he says, "and my words abide in him, he shall bring forth much fruit." Glorious Bethlehem Ephratah! Rightly named! Fruitful house of bread—the house of abundant provision for the people of God!

3. We notice, next, *the position of Bethlehem*. It is said to be "little among the thousands of Judah." Why is this? Because Jesus Christ always goes among little ones. He was born in the little one "among the thousands of Judah." Not Bashan's high hill, not on Hebron's royal mount, not in Jerusalem's palaces, but in the humble, yet illustrious, village of Bethlehem. There is a passage in Zechariah which teaches us a lesson:—It is said that the man on the red horse stood among the myrtle-trees. Now the myrtle-trees grow at the bottom of the hill; and the man on the red horse always rides there. He does not ride on the mountain-top; he rides among the humble in heart. "With this man will I dwell, saith the Lord, with him who is of a humble and contrite spirit, and who trembleth at my word." There are some little ones here this morning—" little among the thousands of Judah." No one ever heard your name, did they? If you were buried, and had your name on your tombstone, it would never be noticed. Those who pass by would say, "It is nothing to me: I never knew him." You do not know much of yourself, or think much of yourself; you can scarcely read, perhaps. Or if you have some talents and ability, you are despised amongst men; or, if you are not despised by them, you despise yourself. You are one of the little ones. Well, Christ is always born in Bethlehem among the little ones. Big hearts never get Christ inside of them; Christ lieth not in great hearts, but in little ones. Mighty and proud spirits never have Jesus Christ, for he cometh in at low doors, but he will not come in at high ones. He who hath a broken heart, and a low spirit, shall have the Saviour, but none else. He healeth not the prince and the king, but "the broken in heart, and he bindeth up their wounds." Sweet thought! He is the Christ of the little ones. "Thou, Bethlehem Ephratah, though thou be little among the thousands of Judah, yet out of thee shall he come forth unto me that is to be ruler in Israel."

We cannot pass away from this without another thought here, which is, *how wonderfully mysterious was that providence which brought Jesus Christ's mother to Bethlehem at the very time when she was to be delivered!* His parents were residing at Nazareth; and what should they want to travel at that time for? Naturally, they would have remained at home; it was not at all likely that his mother would have taken a journey to Bethlehem while in so peculiar a condition; but Cæsar Augustus issues a decree that they are to be taxed. Very well, then, let them be taxed at Nazareth. No; it pleases him that they should all go to their city. But why should Cæsar Augustus think of it just at that particular time? Simply because, while man deviseth his way, the king's heart is in the hand of the Lord. Why, what a thousand chances, as the world has it, met together to bring about this event! First of all, Cæsar quarrels with Herod; one of the Herods was deposed; Cæsar says, "I shall tax Judea, and make it a province, instead of having it for a separate kingdom." Well, it must be done. But when is it to be done? This taxing, it is said, was first commenced when Cyreneus was governor. But why is the census to be taken at that particular period—suppose, December? Why not have had it last October? and why could not the people be taxed where they were living? Was not their money just as good there as anywhere else? It was Cæsar's whim; but it was God's decree. Oh! we love the sublime doctrine of eternal absolute predestination. Some have doubted its being consistent with the free agency of man. We know well it is so, and we never saw any difficulty in the subject; we believe metaphysicians have made difficulties; we see none ourselves. It is for us to believe, that man does as he pleases, yet notwithstanding he always does as God decrees. If Judas betrays

Christ, "thereunto he was appointed;" and if Pharoah hardens his heart, yet, "for this purpose have I raised thee up, for to show forth my power in thee." Man doth as he wills; but God maketh him do as *he* willeth, too. Nay, not only is the will of man under the absolute predestination of Jehovah; but all things, great or little, are of him. Well hath the good poet said, "Doubtless the sailing of a cloud hath Providence to its pilot; doubtless the root of an oak is gnarled for a special purpose, God compasseth all things, mantling the globe like air." There is nothing great or little, that is not from him. The summer dust moves in its orbit, guided by the same hand which rolls the stars along; the dewdrops have their father, and trickle on the rose leaf as God bids them; yea, the sear leaves of the forest, when hurled along by the tempest, have their allotted position where they shall fall, nor can they go beyond it. In the great, and in the little, there is God—God in everything, working all things according to the counsel of his own will; and though man seeks to go against his Maker, yet he cannot. God hath bounded the sea with a barrier of sand; and if the sea mount up wave after wave, yet it shall not exceed its allotted channel. Everything is of God; and unto him who guideth the stars and wingeth sparrows, who ruleth planets and yet moveth atoms, who speaks thunders and yet whispers zephyrs, unto him be glory; for there is God in everything,

III. This brings us to the third point: WHAT DID JESUS COME FOR? He came to be "ruler in Israel." A very singular thing is this, that Jesus Christ was said to have been "born the king of the Jews." Very few have ever been "born king." Men are born princes, but they are seldom born kings. I do not think you can find an instance in history where any infant was born king. He was the prince of Wales, perhaps, and he had to wait a number of years, till his father died, and then they manufactured him into a king, by putting a crown on his head; and a sacred chrism, and other silly things; but he was not born a king. I remember no one who was born a king except Jesus; and there is emphatic meaning in that verse that we sing—

"Born thy people to deliver;
Born a child, and yet a king."

The moment that he came on earth he was a king. He did not wait till his majority that he might take his empire; but as soon as his eye greeted the sunshine he was a king; from the moment that his little hands grasped anything, they grasped a sceptre: as soon as his pulse beat, and his blood began to flow, his heart beat royally, and his pulse beat an imperial measure, and his blood flowed in a kingly current. He was born a king. He came "to be ruler in Israel." "Ah!" says one, "then he came in vain, for little did he exercise his rule; 'he came unto his own, and his own received him not;' he came to Israel and he was not their ruler, but he was 'despised and rejected of men,' cast off by them all, and forsaken by Israel, unto whom he came." Ay, but "they are not all Israel who are of Israel," neither because they are the seed of Abraham shall they all be called. Ah, no! He is not ruler of Israel after the flesh, but he is the ruler of Israel after the spirit. Many such have obeyed him. Did not the apostles bow before him, and own him as their king? And now, doth not Israel salute him as their ruler? Do not all the seed of Abraham after the spirit, even all the faithful, for he is "the father of the faithful," acknowledge that unto Christ belong the shields of the mighty, for he is the king of the whole earth? Doth he not rule over Israel? Ay, verily he doth; and those who are not ruled over by Christ are not of Israel. He came to be a ruler over Israel. My brother, hast thou submitted to the sway of Jesus? Is he ruler in thine heart, or is he not? We may know Israel by this: Christ is come into their hearts, to be ruler over them. "Oh!" saith one, "I do as I please, I was never in bondage to any man." Ah! then thou hatest the rule of Christ. "Oh!" says another, "I submit myself to my minister, to my clergyman, or to my priest, and I think that what he tells me is enough, for he is my ruler." Dost thou? Ah! poor slave, thou knowest not thy dignity; for nobody is thy lawful ruler but the Lord Jesus Christ. "Ay," says another, "I have professed his religion, and I am his follower." But doth he rule in thine heart? Doth he command thy will? Doth he guide thy judgment? Dost thou ever seek counsel at his hand in thy difficulties? Art thou desirous to honor him, and to put crowns upon his head? Is he thy ruler? If so, then thou art one of Israel; for it is written, "He shall come to be ruler in Israel." Blessed Lord Jesus! thou art ruler in thy people's hearts, and thou ever shalt be; we want no other ruler save thyself, and we will submit to none other. We are free, because we are the servants of Christ; we are at liberty, because he is our ruler, and we know no bondage and no slavery, because Jesus Christ alone is monarch of our hearts. He came "to be ruler in Israel;" and mark you, that mission of his is not quite fulfilled yet, and shall not be till the latter-day glories. In a little while you shall see Christ come again, to be ruler over his people Israel, and ruler over them not only as spiritual Israel, but even as natural Israel, for the Jews shall be restored to their land, and the tribes of Jacob shall yet sing in the halls of their temple; unto God there shall yet again be offered Hebrew songs of praise, and the heart of the unbelieving Jew shall be melted at the feet of the true Messias. In a short time, he who at his birth was hailed king of the Jews by Easterns, and at his death was written king of the Jews by a Western, shall be called king of the Jews everywhere—yes, king of the Jews and Gentiles also—in that universal monarchy whose dominion shall be co-extensive with the habitable globe, and whose duration shall be coeval with time itself. He came to be a ruler in Israel, and a ruler most decidedly he shall be, when he shall reign among his people with his ancients gloriously.

IV. And now, the last thing is, DID JESUS CHRIST EVER COME BEFORE? We answer, yes: for our text says, "Whose goings forth have been of old, from everlasting."

First, *Christ has had his goings forth in his Godhead*. "From everlasting." He has not been a secret and a silent person up to this moment. That new-born child there has worked wonders long ere now; that infant slumbering in its mother's arms is the infant of to-day, but it is the ancient of eternity; that child who is there hath not made its appearance on the stage of this world; his name is not yet written in the calendar of the circumcised; but still though you wist it not, " his goings forth have been of old, from everlasting."

1. Of old *he went forth as our covenant head in election,*"according as he hath chosen us in *Him,* before the foundation of the world."

"Christ be my first elect, he said,
Then chose our souls in Christ our Head."

2. He had goings forth for his people, *as their representative before the throne, even before they were begotten in the world.* It was from everlasting that his mighty fingers grasped the pen, the stylus of ages, and wrote his own name, the name of the eternal Son of God; it was from everlasting that he signed the compact with his Father, that he would pay blood for blood, wound for wound, suffering for suffering, agony for agony, and death for death, in the behalf of his people; it was from everlasting that he gave himself up, without a murmuring word, that from the crown of his head to the sole of his foot he might sweat blood, that he might be spit upon, pierced, mocked, rent asunder, suffer the pain of death, and the agonies of the cross. His goings forth as our Surety were from everlasting. Pause, my soul, and wonder! Thou hadst goings forth in the person of Jesus from everlasting. Not only when thou wast born into the world did Christ love thee, but his delights were with the sons of men before there were any sons of men. Often did he think of them; from everlasting to everlasting he had set his affection upon them. What! believer, has he been so long about thy salvation, and will he not accomplish it? Has he from everlasting been going forth to save me, and will he lose me now? What! has he had me in his hand, as his precious jewel, and will he now let me slip between his precious fingers? Did he choose me before the mountains were brought forth, or the channels of the deep scooped out, and will he lose me now? Impossible!

"My name from the palms of his hands
Eternity cannot erase;
Impress'd on his heart it remains,
In marks of indelible grace."

I am sure he would not love me so long, and then leave off loving me. If he intended to be tired of me, he would have been tired of me long before now. If he had not loved me with a love as deep as hell and as unutterable as the grave, if he had not given his whole heart to me, I am sure he would have turned from me long ago. He knew what I would be, and he has had long time enough to consider of it; but I am his choice, and there is an end of it; and unworthy as I am, it is not mine to grumble, if he is but contented with me. But he is contented with me—**he must be contented with me**—for he has known me long enough to know my faults. He knew me before I knew myself; yea, he knew me before I was myself. Long before my members were fashioned they were written in his book, " when as yet there were none of them," his eyes of affection were set on them. He knew how badly I would act towards him, and yet he has continued to love me;

" His love in times past forbids me to think,
He'll leave me at last in trouble to sink."

No; since " his goings forth were of old from everlasting," they will be " to everlasting."

Secondly, we believe that Christ *has come forth of old, even to men, so that men have beheld him.* I will not stop to tell you that it was Jesus who walked in the garden of Eden in the cool of the day, for his delights were with the sons of men; nor will I detain you by pointing out all the various ways in which Christ came forth to his people in the form of the angel of the covenant, the Paschal Lamb, the brazen serpent, the burning bush, and ten thousand types with which the sacred history is so replete; but I will rather point you to four occasions when Jesus Christ our Lord has appeared on earth as a man, before his great incarnation for our salvation. And, first, I beg to refer you to the 18th chapter of Genesis, where Jesus Christ appeared to *Abraham,* of whom we read, " The Lord appeared unto him in the plains of Mamre: and he sat in the tent door in the heat of the day; and he lift up his eyes and looked, and lo, three men stood by him; and when he saw them, he ran to meet them from the tent door, and bowed himself toward the ground." But whom did he bow to? He said " My Lord," only to one of them. There was one man between the other two, the most conspicuous for his glory, for he was the God-man Christ; the other two were created angels. who for a time had assumed the appearance of men. But this was the man Christ Jesus. " And he said, My Lord, if now I have found favour in thy sight, pass not away, I pray thee, from thy servant: Let a little water, I pray you, be fetched, and wash your feet, and rest yourselves under the tree." You will notice that this majestic man, this glorious person, stayed behind to talk with Abraham. In the 22nd verse it is said,—" And the men turned their faces from thence and went towards Sodom;" that is, two of them, as you will see in the next chapter· " but Abraham stood yet before the Lord." You will notice that this man, the Lord, held sweet fellowship with Abraham, and allowed Abraham to plead for the city he was about to destroy. He was in the positive form of man; so that when he walked the streets of Judea it was not the first time that he was a man; he was so before, in " the plain of Mamre, in the heat of the day." There is another instance—his appearing to *Jacob,* which you have recorded in the 32nd chapter of Genesis and the 24th verse. All his family were gone, " And Jacob was left alone, and there wrestled a man with him until the breaking of the day. And when he saw that he prevailed not against him, he touched the hollow of his thigh; and the hollow of Jacob's thigh was out of joint, as he wrestled with him. And he said, Let me go, for the day breaketh. And he said, I will not let thee go, unless thou bless me. And he said unto him, What is thy name? And he said, Jacob. And he said, Thy name shall be called no more Jacob, but Israel; for as a prince hast thou power with God." This was a man, and yet God. " For as a prince hast thou power with God and with men, and hast prevailed." And Jacob knew that this man was God, for he says in the 30th verse: "for I have seen God face to face, and my life is preserved." Another instance you will find in the book of *Joshua.* When Joshua had crossed the narrow stream of Jordan, and had entered the promised land, and was about to drive out the Canaanites, lo! this mighty man-God appeared to Joshua. In the 5th chapter, at the 13th verse, we **read**—" And it came to pass, when Joshua was by Jericho, that he lifted up his eyes and looked, and, behold, there stood a man over against him with his sword drawn in his hand, and Joshua went unto him, and (like a brave warrior, as he was,) said unto him, Art thou for us, or for our adversaries? And he said, Nay; but as Captain of the host of the Lord am I now come." And **Joshua** saw at once that there was divinity in him; for Joshua fell on his face to the earth, and did worship, and said to him, " What saith *my lord* unto his servant?" Now, if this had been a created angel he would **have** reproved Joshua, and said, " I am one of your fellow servants." But no; " **the** captain of the Lord's host said unto Joshua, Loose thy shoe from thy foot; for the place whereon thou standest is holy. And Joshua did so." Another remarkable instance is that recorded in the third chapter of the book of Daniel, where we read the account of Shadrach, Meshach, and Abednego being cast into the fiery furnace, which was so fierce that it destroyed the men who threw them in. Suddenly the king said to his counsellors—" Did not we cast three men bound into the midst of the fire? They answered and said unto the king, True, O king. He answered and said, Lo, I see four men loose, walking in the midst of the fire, and they have no hurt; and the form of the fourth is like the Son of God." How should Nebuchadnezzar know that? Only that there was something so noble and majestic in the way in which that wondrous Man bore himself, and some awful influence about *him*, who so marvellously broke the consuming teeth of that biting and devouring flame, so that it could not so much as singe the children of God. Nebuchadnezzar recognized his humanity. He did not say, "I see three men and an angel," but he said, "I see four positive men, and the form of the fourth is like the Son of God." You see, then, what is meant by his goings forth being "from everlasting."

Observe for a moment here, that each of these four great occurrences happened to the saints *when they were engaged in very eminent duty, or when they were about to be engaged in it.* Jesus Christ does not appear to his saints every day. He did not come to see Jacob till he was in affliction; he did not visit Joshua before he was about to be engaged in a righteous war. It is only in extraordinary seasons that Christ thus manifests himself to his people. When Abraham *interceded* for Sodom, Jesus was with him, for one of the highest and noblest employments of a Christian is that of intercession, and it is when he is so engaged that he will be likely to obtain a sight of Christ. Jacob was engaged in *wrestling*, and that is a part of a Christain's duty to which some of you never did attain; consequently, you do not have many visits from Jesus. It was when Joshua was *exercising bravery* that the Lord met him. So with Shadrach, Meshach, and Abednego: they were in the high places of *persecution*, on account of their adherence to duty, when he came to them, and said, " I will be with you, passing through the fire." There are certain peculiar places we must enter, to meet with the Lord. We must be in great trouble, like Jacob; we must be in great labour, like Joshua; we must have great intercessory faith, like Abraham; we must be firm in the performance of duty, like Shadrach Meshach, and Abednego; or else we shall not know him "whose goings forth have been of old, from everlasting;" or, if we know him, we shall not be able to "comprehend with all the saints what is the height, and depth, and length, and breadth of the love of Christ, which passeth knowledge."

Sweet Lord Jesus! thou whose goings forth were of old, even from everlasting, thou hast not left thy goings forth yet. Oh! that thou wouldst go forth this day, to cheer the faint, to help the weary, to bind up our wounds, to comfort our distresses! Go forth, we beseech thee, to conquer sinners, to subdue hard hearts—to break the iron gates of sinners' lusts, and cut the iron bars of their sins in pieces! O Jesus! go forth; and when thou goest forth, come thou to me! Am I a hardened sinner? Come thou to me; I want thee:

> "Oh! let thy grace my heart subdue;
> I would be led in triumph too;
> A willing captive to my Lord,
> To sing the honours of thy word."

Poor sinner! Christ has not left going forth yet. And when he goes forth, recollect, he goes to Bethlehem. Have you a Bethlehem in your heart? Are you little? He will go forth to you yet. Go home and seek him by earnest prayer. If you have been made to weep on account of sin, and think yourself too little to be noticed, go home, little one! Jesus comes to little ones; his goings forth were of old, and he is going forth now. He will come to your poor old house; he will come to your poor wretched heart; he will come, though you are in poverty, and clothed in rags, though you are destitute, tormented, and afflicted; he will come, for his goings forth have been of old from everlasting. Trust him, trust him, trust him; and he will go forth to abide in your heart for ever.

Metropolitan Tabernacle Pulpit.

"GOD WITH US."

A Sermon

Delivered on Lord's-Day Morning, December 26th, 1875, by

C. H. SPURGEON,

AT THE METROPOLITAN TABERNACLE, NEWINGTON.

"They shall call his name Emmanuel, which being interpreted is, God with us."—Matthew i. 23.

THOSE words, "being interpreted," salute my ear with much sweetness. Why should the word "Emmanuel" in the Hebrew, be interpreted at all? Was it not to show that it has reference to us Gentiles, and therefore it must needs be interpreted into one of the chief languages of the then existing Gentile world, namely, the Greek. This "being interpreted" at Christ's birth, and the three languages employed in the inscription upon the cross at his death, show that he is not the Saviour of the Jews only, but also of the Gentiles. As I walked along the quay at Marseilles, and marked the ships of all nations gathered in the port, I was very much interested by the inscriptions upon the shops and stores. The announcements of refreshments or of goods to be had within were not only printed in the French language, but in English, in Italian, in German, in Greek, sometimes in Russian and Swedish. Upon the shops of the sail-makers, the boat-builders, the ironmongers, or the dealers in ship stores, you read a polyglot announcement, setting forth the information to men of many lands. This was a clear indication that persons of all nations were invited to come and purchase, that they were expected to come, and that provision was made for their peculiar wants. "Being interpreted" must mean that different nations are addressed. We have the text put first in the Hebrew "Emmanuel," and afterwards it is translated into the Gentile tongue, "God with us;" "being interpreted," that we may know that we are invited, that we are welcome, that God has seen our necessities and has provided for us, and that now we may freely come, even we who were sinners of the Gentiles, and far off from God. Let us preserve with reverent love both forms of the precious name and wait the happy day when our Hebrew brethren shall unite their "Emmanuel" with our "God with us."

No. 1,270.

Our text speaks of a *name* of our Lord Jesus. It is said, "They shall call his name Emmanuel." In these days we call children by names which have no particular meaning. They are the names, perhaps, of father or mother or some respected relative, but there is no special meaning as a general rule in our children's names. It was not so in the olden times. Then names meant something. Scriptural names, as a general rule, contain teaching, and especially is this the case in every name ascribed to the Lord Jesus. With him names indicate things. "His name shall be called Wonderful, Counsellor, the Mighty God, the everlasting Father, the Prince of Peace," because he really is all these. His name is called Jesus, but not without a reason. By any other name Jesus would not be so sweet, because no other name could fairly describe his great work of saving his people from their sins. When he is said to be called this or that, it means that he really is so. I am not aware that anywhere in the New Testament our Lord is afterwards called Emmanuel. I do not find his apostles, or any of his disciples, calling him by that name literally; but we find them all doing so in effect, for they speak of him as "God manifest in the flesh", and they say, "The word was made flesh and dwelt among us, and we beheld his glory, the glory as of the only-begotten of the Father, full of grace and truth." They do not use the actual word, but they again interpret and give us free and instructive renderings, while they proclaim the sense of the august title and inform us in divers ways what is meant by God being with us in the person of the Lord Jesus Christ. It is a glorious fact, of the highest importance, that since Christ was born into the world God is with us.

You may divide the text, if you please, into two portions :—"GOD," and then "God WITH US." We must dwell with equal emphasis upon each word. Never let us for a moment hesitate as to the Godhead of our Lord Jesus Christ, for his Deity is a fundamental doctrine of the Christian faith. It may be we shall never understand fully how God and man could unite in one person, for who can by searching find out God. These great mysteries of godliness, these "deep things of God," are beyond our measurement : our little skiff might be lost if we ventured so far out upon this vast, this infinite ocean, as to lose sight of the shore of plainly revealed truth. But let it remain as a matter of faith that Jesus Christ, even he who lay in Bethlehem's manger, and was carried in a woman's arms, and lived a suffering life and died on a malefactor's cross, was, nevertheless, "God over all, blessed for ever," "upholding all things by the word of his power." He was not an angel—that the apostle has abundantly disproved in the first and second chapters of the epistle to the Hebrews: he could not have been an angel, for honours are ascribed to him which were never bestowed on angels. He was no subordinate deity or being elevated to the Godhead, as some have absurdly said—all these things are dreams and falsehoods; he was as surely God as God can be, one with the Father and the ever-blessed Spirit. If it were not so, not only would the great strength of our hope be gone, but as to this text the sweetness had evaporated altogether. The very essence and glory of the incarnation is that he was God who was veiled in human flesh: if it was any other being who thus came to us in human flesh, I see nothing very remarkable in it,. nothing comforting, certainly. That an angel should become a man is a matter of no great consequence to me: that some other superior being should assume the nature of man brings no joy to my heart, and opens no well of consolation to me. But "God with us" is exquisite delight. "GOD with us": all that "God" means, the Deity, the infinite Jehovah with us; this, this is worthy of the burst of midnight song, when angels startled the shepherds with their carols, singing "Glory to God in the highest, and on earth peace, good will to men." This was worthy of the foresight of seers and prophets, worthy of a new star in the heavens, worthy of the care which inspiration has manifested to preserve the record. This, too, was worthy of the martyr deaths of apostles and confessors who counted not their lives dear unto them for the sake of the incarnate God; and this, my brethren, is worthy at this day of your most earnest endeavours to spread the glad tidings, worthy of a holy life to illustrate its blessed influences, and worthy of a joyful death to prove its consoling power. Here is the first truth of our holy faith—"Without controversy great is the mystery of godliness, God was manifest in the flesh." He who was born at Bethlehem is God, and "God with us." God—there lies the majesty; "God with us," there lies the mercy. *God*—therein is glory; "God *with us*," therein is grace. God alone might well strike us with terror; but "God with us" inspires us with hope and confidence. Take my text as a whole, and carry it in your bosoms as a bundle of sweet spices to perfume your hearts with peace and joy. May the Holy Spirit open to you the truth, and the truth to you. I would joyfully say to you in the words of one of our poets—

"Veil'd in flesh the Godhead see;
Hail the incarnate Deity!
Pleased as man with men to appear,
Jesus our Immanuel here."

First, *let us admire this truth;* then *let us consider it more at length,* and after that *let us endeavour personally to appropriate it.*

I. LET US ADMIRE THIS TRUTH. "God with us." Let us stand at a reverent distance from it as Moses when he saw God in the bush stood a little back, and put his shoes from off his feet, feeling that the place whereon he stood was holy ground. This is a wonderful fact, God the Infinite once dwelt in the frail body of a child, and tabernacled in the suffering form of a lowly man. "God was in Christ." "He made himself of no reputation, and took upon him the form of a servant, and was made in the likeness of men."

Observe first, the wonder *of condescension* contained in this fact, that God who made all things should assume the nature of one of his own creatures, that the self-existent should be united with the dependent and derived, and the Almighty linked with the feeble and mortal. In the case before us the Lord descended to the very depth of humiliation, and entered into alliance with a nature which did not occupy the chief place in the scale of existence. It would have been great condescension for the infinite and incomprehensible Jehovah to have taken upon himself the nature of some noble spiritual being, such as a seraph or a cherub; the union of the divine with a created spirit would have been an unmeasurable stoop, but for God to be one with man is far more. Remember that in the person of Christ manhood was not merely quickening spirit, but also suffering, hungering, dying, flesh and blood. There was taken to himself by our Lord all that materialism which makes up a body, and a body is after all but the dust of the earth, a structure fashioned from the materials around us. There is nothing in our bodily frame but what is to be found in the substance of the earth on which we live. We feed upon that which groweth out of the earth, and when we die we go back to the dust from whence we were taken. Is not this a strange thing that this grosser part of creation, this meaner part, this dust of it, should nevertheless be taken into union, with that pure, marvellous, incomprehensible, divine being of whom we know so little, and can comprehend nothing at all? Oh, the condescension of it! I leave it to the meditations of your quiet moments. Dwell on it with awe. I am persuaded that no man has any idea how wonderful a stoop it was for God thus to dwell in human flesh, and to be "God with us."

Yet, to make it appear still more remarkable, remember that the creature whose nature Christ took was a being that had sinned. I can more readily conceive the Lord's taking upon himself the nature of a race which had never fallen; but, lo, the race of man stood in rebellion against God, and yet a man did Christ become, that he might deliver us from the consequences of our rebellion, and lift us up to something higher than our pristine purity. "God sending his own Son in the likeness of sinful flesh, has condemned sin in the flesh." "Oh, the depths," is all that we can say, as we look on and marvel at this stoop of divine love.

Note, next, as you view this marvel at a distance, what *a miracle of power* is before us. Have you ever thought of the power displayed in the Lord's fashioning a body capable of union with Godhead? Our Lord was incarnate in a body, which was truly a human body, but yet in some wondrous way was prepared to sustain the indwelling of Deity. Contact with God is terrible; "He looketh on the earth and it trembleth; he toucheth the hills and they smoke." He puts his feet on Paran, and it melts, and Sinai dissolves in flames of fire. So strongly was this truth inwrought into the minds of the early saints, that they said, "No man can see God's face and live;" and yet here was a manhood which did not merely see the face of God, but which was inhabited by Deity. What a human frame was this which could abide the presence of Jehovah! "A body hast thou prepared me." This was indeed a body curiously wrought, a holy thing, a special product of the Holy Spirit's power. It was a body like our own, with nerves as sensitive, and muscles as readily strained, with every organization as delicately fashioned as our own, and yet God was in it. It was a frail barque to bear such a freight. Oh, man Christ, how couldst thou bear the Deity within thee! We know not how it was, but God knoweth. Let us adore this hiding of the Almighty in human weakness, this comprehending of the Incomprehensible, this revealing of the Invisible, this localization of the Omnipresent. Alas, I do but babble! What are words when we deal with such an unutterable truth? Suffice it to say, that the divine power was wonderfully seen in the continued existence of the materialism of Christ's body, which else had been consumed by such a wondrous contact with divinity. Admire the power which dwelt in "God with us."

Again, as you gaze upon the mystery, consider what *an ensign of good will* this must be to the sons of men. When the Lord takes manhood into union with himself in this matchless way it must mean good to man. God cannot mean to destroy that race which he thus weds unto himself. Such a marriage as this, between man and God, must mean peace; war and destruction are never thus predicted. God incarnate in Bethlehem, to be adored by shepherds, augurs nothing but "peace on earth and mercy mild." O ye sinners who tremble at the thought of the divine wrath, as well you may, lift up your heads with joyful hope of mercy and favour, for God must be full of grace and mercy to that race which he so distinguishes above all others by taking it into union with himself. Be of good cheer, O men of women born, and expect untold blessings for "unto us a child is born, unto us a Son is given." If you look at rivers you can often tell whence they come, and the soil over which they have flowed by their colour: those which flow from melting glaciers are known at once. There is a text concerning a heavenly river which you will understand if you look at it in this light: "He showed me a pure river of the water of life, clear as crystal, proceeding out of the throne of God, and *of the Lamb.*" Where the throne is occupied by Godhead, and the appointed Mediator, the incarnate God, the once bleeding Lamb, then the river must be pure as crystal, and be a river, not of molten lava of devouring wrath, but a river of the water of life. Look you to "God with us" and you will see that the consequences of incarnation must be pleasant, profitable, saving, and ennobling to the sons of men.

I pray you to continue your admiring glance, and look upon God with us once more *as a pledge of our deliverance.* We are a fallen race, we are sunken in the mire, we are sold under sin, in bondage and in slavery to Satan; but if God comes to our race, and espouses its nature, why then we must retrieve our fall, it cannot be possible for the gates of hell to keep those down who have God with them. Slaves under sin and bondsmen beneath the law, hearken to the trump of jubilee, for one has come among you, born of a woman, made under the law, who is also mighty God, pledged to set you free. He is a Saviour, and a great one: able to save, for he is Almighty, and pledged to do it, for he has entered the lists and put on the harness for the battle. The champion of his people is one who will not fail nor be discouraged till the battle is fully fought and won. Jesus coming down from heaven is the pledge that he will take his people up to heaven, his taking our nature is the seal of our being lifted up to his throne. Were it an angel that had interposed, we might have some fears; were it a mere man, we might go beyond fear, and sit down in despair; but if it be "God with us," and God has actually taken manhood into union with himself, then let us "ring the bells of heaven" and be glad; there must be brighter and happier days, there must be salvation to man, there must be glory to God. Let us bask in the beams of the Sun of Righteousness, who now has risen upon us, a light to lighten the Gentiles, and to be the glory of his people Israel.

Thus we have admired at a distance.

II. And, now, in the second place, let us come nearer and CONSIDER THE SUBJECT MORE CLOSELY. What is this? What means this, "God with us"? I do not expect this morning to be able to set forth all the meaning of this short text, "God with us," for indeed, it seems to me to contain the whole history of redemption. It hints at man's being without God, and God's having removed from man on account of sin. It seems to tell me of man's spiritual life, by Christ's coming to him, and being formed in him the hope of glory. God communes with man, and man returns to God, and receives again the divine image as at the first. Yea, heaven itself is "God with us." This text might serve for a hundred sermons without any wire drawing; yea, one might continue to expatiate upon its manifold meanings for ever. I can only at this time give mere hints of lines of thought which you can pursue at your leisure, the Holy Spirit enabling you.

This glorious word Emmanuel means, first, that God in Christ is *with us in very near association.* The Greek particle here used is very forcible, and expresses the strongest form of "*with.*" It is not merely "in company with us" as another Greek word would signify, but "with," "together with," and "sharing with." This preposition is a close rivet, a firm bond, implying, if not declaring, close fellowship. God is peculiarly and closely "with us." Now, think for a while, and you will see that God has in very deed come near to us in very close association. He must have done so, for *he has taken upon himself our nature,* literally our nature,—flesh, blood, bone, everything that made a body; mind, heart, soul, memory, imagination, judgment, everything that makes a rational man. Christ Jesus was the man of men, the second Adam, the model representative man. Think not of him as a deified man any more than you would dare to regard him as a humanized God, or demigod. Do not confound the natures nor divide the person: he is but one person, yet very man as he is also very God. Think of this truth then, and say, "He who sits on the throne is such as I am, sin alone excepted." No, 'tis too much for speech, I will not speak of it; it is a theme which masters me, and I fear to utter rash expressions. Turn the truth over and over, and see if it be not sweeter than honey and the honey-comb.

"Oh joy! there sitteth in our flesh,
  Upon a throne of light,
  One of a human mother born,
  In perfect Godhead bright!"

Being with us in our nature, God was with us in *all our life's pilgrimage.* Scarcely can you find a halting-place in the march of life at which Jesus has not paused, or a weary league which he has not traversed. From the gate of entrance even to the door which closes life's way the footprints of Jesus may be traced. Were you in the cradle? He was there. Were you a child under parental authority? Christ was also a boy in the home at Nazareth. Have you entered upon life's battle? Your Lord and Master did the same; and though he lived not to old age, yet through incessant toil and suffering he bore the marred visage which attends a battered old age. Are you alone? So was he, in the wilderness, and on the mountain's side, and in the garden's gloom. Do you mix in public society? So did he labour in the thickest press. Where can you find yourself, on the hill top, or in the valley, on the land or on the sea, in the daylight or in darkness,—where, I say, can you be without discovering that Jesus has been there before you? What the world has said of her great poet we might with far more truth say of our Redeemer—

> "A man so various that he seemed to be
> Not one, but all mankind's epitome."

One harmonious man he was, and yet all saintly lives seem to be condensed in his. Two believers may be very unlike each other, and yet both will find that Christ's life has in it points of likeness to their own. One shall be rich and another shall be poor, one actively laborious and another patiently suffering, and yet each man in studying the history of the Saviour shall be able to say—his pathway ran hard by my own. He was made in all points like unto his brethren. How charming is the fact that our Lord is "God with us," not here and there, and now and then, but evermore.

Especially does this come out with sweetness in his being "God with us" *in our sorrows*. There is no pang that rends the heart, I might almost say not one which disturbs the body, but what Jesus Christ has been with us in it all. Feel you the sorrows of poverty? He "had not where to lay his head." Do you endure the griefs of bereavement? Jesus "wept" at the tomb of Lazarus. Have you been slandered for righteousness' sake, and has it vexed your spirit? He said "Reproach hath broken mine heart." Have you been betrayed? Do not forget that he too had his familiar friend, who sold him for the price of a slave. On what stormy seas have you been tossed which have not also roared around his boat? Never glen of adversity so dark, so deep, apparently so pathless, but what in stooping down you may discover the footprints of the Crucified One. In the fires and in the rivers, in the cold night and under the burning sun, he cries, "I am with thee. Be not dismayed, for I am both thy companion and thy God."

Mysteriously true is it that when you and I shall come to *the last, the closing scene*, we shall find that Emmanuel has been there. He felt the pangs and throes of death, he endured the bloody sweat of agony and the parching thirst of fever. He knew the separation of the tortured spirit from the poor fainting flesh, and cried, as we shall, "Father, into thy hands I commend my spirit." Ay, and the grave he knew, for there he slept, and left the sepulchre perfumed and furnished to be a couch of rest, and not a charnel-house of corruption. That new tomb in the garden makes him God with us till the resurrection shall call us from our beds of clay to find him God with us in newness of life. We shall be raised up in his likeness, and the first sight our opening eyes shall see shall be the incarnate God. "I know that my Redeemer liveth, and though after my skin worms devour this body, yet in my flesh shall I see God." "God with us." I in my flesh shall see him as the man, the God. And so *to all eternity* he will maintain the most intimate association with us. As long as ages roll he shall be "God with us." Has he not said, "Because I live ye shall live also"? Both his human and divine life will last on for ever, and so shall our life endure. He shall dwell among us and lead us to living fountains of waters, and so shall we be for ever with the Lord.

Now, my brethren, if you will review these thoughts, you shall find good store of food; in fact, a feast even under that one head. God in Christ is with us in the nearest possible association.

But, secondly, *God in Christ is with us in the fullest reconciliation.* This, of course, is true, if the former be true. There was a time when we were parted from God; we were without God, being alienated from him by wicked works, and God also was removed from us by reason of the natural rectitude of character which thrusts iniquity far from him. He is of purer eyes than to behold iniquity, neither can evil dwell with him. That strict justice with which he rules the world requires that he should hide his face from a sinful generation. A God who looks with complacency upon guilty men is not the God of the Bible, who is in multitudes of places set forth as burning with indignation against the wicked. "The wicked and him that loveth violence his soul hateth." But, now the sin which separated us from God has been put away by the blessed sacrifice of Christ upon the tree, and the righteousness, the absence of which must have caused a gulf between unrighteous man and righteous God, that righteousness, I say, has been found, for Jesus has brought in everlasting righteousness. So that now in Jesus God is with us, reconciled to us, the sin which caused his wrath being for ever put away from his people. There are some who object to this view of the case, and I, for one, will not yield one jot to their objections. I do not wonder that they cavil at certain unwise statements, which I like no better than they do; but, nevertheless, if they oppose the atonement as making a recompense to injured justice, their objections shall have no force with me. It is most true that God is always love, but his stern justice is not opposed thereto. It is also most certainly true that towards his people he always was, in the highest sense, love, and the atonement is the result and not the cause of divine love; yet, still viewed in his rectoral character, as a judge and lawgiver, God is "angry with the wicked every day," and apart from the reconciling sacrifice of Christ, his own people were "heirs of wrath even as others." There was anger in the heart of God, as a righteous judge, against those who have broken his holy law, and the reconciliation has a bearing upon the position of the judge of all the earth as well as upon man. I for one shall never cease to say, "O Lord, I will praise thee, for though thou wast angry with me, thine anger is turned away, and thou comfortest me." God can now be with man, and embrace sinners as his children, as he could not have righteously done had not Jesus died. In this sense, and in this sense only, did Dr. Watts write some of his hymns which have been so fiercely condemned. I take leave to quote two verses, and to commend them as setting forth a great truth if the Lord be viewed as a judge, and represented as the awakened conscience of man rightly perceives him. Our poet says of the throne of God:

> "Once 'twas the seat of dreadful wrath,
> And shot devouring flame;
> Our God appeared, consuming fire,
> And vengeance was his name.

"Rich were the drops of Jesus' blood,
Which calmed his frowning face,
Which sprinkled o'er the burning throne,
And turn'd the wrath to grace."

So that now Jehovah is not God against us, but "God with us," he has "reconciled us to himself by the death of his Son."

A third meaning of the text "God with us" is this, *God in Christ is with us in blessed communication*. That is to say, now he has come so near to us as to enter into commerce with us, and this he does in part by hallowed conversation. Now he speaks to us and in us. He has in these last days spoken to us by his Son and by the Divine Spirit with the still small voice of warning, consolation, instruction, and direction. Are you not conscious of this? Since your souls have come to know Christ, have you not also enjoyed intercourse with the Most High? Now, like Enoch, you "walk with God," and, like Abraham, you talk with him as a man talketh with his friend. What are those prayers and praises of yours but the speech which you are permitted to have with the Most High; and he replies to you when his Spirit seals home the promise or applies the precept, when with fresh light he leads you into the doctrine or bestows brighter confidence as to good things to come. Oh yes, God is with us now, so that when he cries, "Seek ye my face" our heart says to him, "Thy face, Lord, will I seek." These Sabbath gatherings, what mean they to many of us but "God with us." That communion table, what means it but "God with us"? Oh, how often in the breaking of bread and the pouring forth of the wine in the memory of his atoning death have we enjoyed his real presence, not in a superstitious, but in a spiritual sense, and found the Lord Jesus to be "God with us." Yes, in every holy ordinance, in every sacred act of worship, we now find that there is a door opened in heaven and a new and living way by which we may come to the throne of grace. Is not this a joy better than all the riches of earth could buy?

And it is not merely in speech that the Lord is with us, but God is with us now by powerful *acts* as well as words. "God with us," why it is the inscription upon our royal standard which strikes terror to the heart of the foe, and cheers the sacramental host of God's elect. Is not this our war cry, "The Lord of hosts is with us, the God of Jacob is our refuge." As to our foes within, God is with us to overcome our corruptions and frailties; and as to the adversaries of truth without, God is with his church, and Christ has promised that he ever will be with her "even to the end of the world." We have not merely God's word and promises, but we have seen his acts of grace on our behalf, both in providence and in the working of his blessed Spirit. "The Lord hath made bare his holy arm in the eyes of all the people." "In Judah is God known: his name is great in Israel. In Salem also is his tabernacle, and his dwelling place in Zion. There brake he the arrows of the bow, the shield, and the sword, and the battle." "God with us"—oh, my brethren, it makes our hearts leap for joy, it fills us with dauntless courage. How can we be dismayed when the Lord of hosts is on our side?

Nor is it merely that God is with us in acts of power on our behalf, but in emanations of his own life into our nature by which we are at first new born, and afterwards sustained in spiritual life. This is more wonderful still. By the Holy Spirit the divine seed which "liveth and abideth for ever" is sown in our souls, and from day to day we are strengthened with might by his Spirit in the inner man.

Nor is this all, for as the masterpiece of grace, the Lord, by his Spirit, even dwells in his people. God is not incarnate in us as in Christ Jesus, but only second in wonder to the incarnation is the indwelling of the Holy Spirit in believers. Now is it "God with us" indeed, for God dwelleth in us. "Know ye not," says the apostle, "that your bodies are the temples of the Holy Ghost." "As it is written, I will dwell in them, and I will walk in them." Oh, the heights and depths then comprehended in those few words, "God with us."

I had many more things to say unto you, but time compels me to sum them up in brief. The Lord becomes "God with us" *by the restoration of his image in us.* "God with us" was seen in Adam when he was perfectly pure, but Adam died when he sinned, and God is not the God of the dead but of the living. Now we, in receiving back the new life and being reconciled to God in Christ Jesus, receive also the restored image of God, and are renewed in knowledge and true holiness. "God with us" means sanctification, the image of Jesus Christ imprinted upon all his brethren.

God is with us, too, let us remember, and leave the point, *in deepest sympathy*. Brethren, are you in sorrow? God is in Christ sympathetic to your grief. Brethren, have you a grand object? I know what it is, it is God's glory; therein also you are sympathetic with God, and God with you. What, let me inquire, is your greatest joy? Have you not learned to rejoice in the Lord? Do you not joy in God by Jesus Christ? Then God also joyeth in you. He rests in his love, and rejoices over you with singing, so that there is God with us in a very wonderful respect, inasmuch as through Christ our aims and desires are like those of God. We desire the same thing, press forward with the same aim, and rejoice in the same objects of delight. When the Lord says, "This is my beloved Son, in whom I am well pleased," our heart answers, "Ay, and in him we are well pleased too." The pleasure of the Father is the pleasure of his own chosen children, for we also joy in Christ; our very soul exults at the sound of his name.

III. I must leave this delightful theme when I have said two or three things about OUR PERSONAL APPROPRIATION of the truth before us.

"God with us." Then, if Jesus Christ be "God with us," let us come to God without any question or hesitancy. Whoever you may be you need no priest or intercessor to introduce you to God, for God has introduced himself to you. Are you children? Then come to God in the child Jesus, who slept in Bethlehem's manger. Oh, ye greyheads, ye need not keep back, but like Simeon come and take him in your arms, and say, "Lord, now lettest thou thy servant depart in peace according to thy word, for mine eyes have seen thy salvation." God sends an ambassador who inspires no fear: not with helmet and coat of mail, bearing lance, does heaven's herald approach us, but the white flag is held in the hand of a child, in the hand of one chosen out of the people, in the hand of one who died, in the hand of one who though he sits in glory wears the nail-print still. O man, God comes to you as one like yourself. Do not be afraid to come to the gentle Jesus. Do not imagine that you need to be prepared for an audience with him, or that you want the intercession of a saint, or the intervention of priest or minister. Anyone could have come to the babe in Bethlehem. The horned oxen, methinks, ate of the hay on which he slept and feared not. Jesus is the friend of each one of us, sinful and unworthy though we be. You, poor ones, you need not fear to come, for, see, in a stable he is born, and in a manger he is cradled. You have not worse accommodation than his, you are not poorer than he. Come and welcome to the poor man's Prince, to the peasants' Saviour. Stay not back through fear of your unfitness; the shepherds came to him in all their deshabille. I read not that they tarried to put on their best garments, but in the clothes in which they wrapped themselves that cold midnight they hastened just as they were to the young child's presence. God looks not at garments, but at hearts, and accepts men when they come to him with willing spirits, whether they be rich or poor. Come, then; come, and welcome, for God indeed is "God with us."

But, oh, let there be no delay about it. It did seem to me, as I turned this subject over, yesterday, that for any man to say, "I will not come to God," after God has come to man in such a form as this, were an unpardonable act of treason. Peradventure, you knew not God's love when you sinned, as you did; peradventure, though you persecuted his saints, you did it ignorantly in unbelief; but, behold your God extends the olive branch of peace to you, extends it in a wondrous way, for he himself comes here to be born of a woman, that he may meet with you who were born of women too, and save you from your sin. Will you not hearken now that he speaks by his Son? I can understand that you ask to hear no more of his words when he speaks with the sound of a trumpet, waxing exceeding loud and long, from amidst the flaming crags of Sinai; I do not wonder that you are afraid to draw near when the earth rocks and reels before his awful presence; but now he restrains himself and veils the splendour of his face, and comes to you as a child of humble mien, a carpenter's son. Oh, if he comes so, will you turn your backs upon him? Can ye spurn him? What better ambassador could you desire? This embassage of peace is so tenderly, so gently, so kindly, so touchingly put, that surely you cannot have the heart to resist it. Nay, do not turn away, let not your ears refuse the language of his grace, but say, "If God is with us, we will be with him." Say it, sinner, say, "I will arise and go to my Father and will say unto him, Father, I have sinned."

And as for you who have given up all hope, you that think yourselves so degraded and fallen that there can be no future for you,— there is hope for you yet, for you are a man, and the next being to God is a man. He that is God is also man, and there is something about that fact which ought to make you say, "Yes, I may yet discover, mayhap, brotherhood to the Son of man who is the Son of God, I, even I, may yet be lifted up to be set among princes, even the princes of his people, by virtue of my regenerated manhood which brings me into relation with the manhood of Christ, and so into relation with the Godhead." Fling not yourself away, oh man, you are something too hopeful after all to be meat for the worm that never dies, and fuel for the fire that never can be quenched. Turn you to your God with full purpose of heart, and you shall find a grand destiny in store for you.

And now, my brethren, to you the last word is, let us be with God since God is with us. I give you for a watchword through the year to come, " Emmanuel, God with us." You, the saints redeemed by blood, have a right to all this in its fullest sense, drink into it and be filled with courage. Do not say, "We can do nothing." Who are ye that can do nothing? God is with you. Do not say "The church is feeble and fallen upon evil times,"—nay, "God is with us." We need the courage of those ancient soldiers who were wont to regard difficulties only as whetstones upon which to sharpen their swords. I like Alexander's talk—when they said there were so many thousands, so many millions perhaps of Persians. "Very well," says he, "it is good reaping where the corn is thick. One butcher is not afraid of a thousand sheep." I like even the talk of the old Gascon, who said when they asked him, "Can you and your troops get into that fortress? it is impregnable." "Can the sun enter it?" said he. "Yes." "Well, where the sun can go we can enter." Whatever is possible or whatever is impossible, Christians can do at God's command, for God is with us. Do you not see that the word, "God with us," puts impossibility out of all existence? Hearts that never could else be broken will be broken if God be with us. Errors which never else could be confuted can be overthrown by "God with us." Things impossible with men are possible with God. John Wesley died with that upon his tongue, and let us live with it upon our hearts.—" The best of all is God with us." Blessed Son of God, we thank thee that thou hast brought us that word. Amen.

PORTION OF SCRIPTURE READ BEFORE SERMON—Hebrews i. ii.

HYMNS FROM "OUR OWN HYMN BOOK"—249, 256 (vers. 3, 4), 260.

Metropolitan Tabernacle Pulpit.

THE GREAT MYSTERY OF GODLINESS.

A Sermon

Delivered on Lord's-day Morning, December 22nd, 1867, by

C. H. SPURGEON,

AT THE METROPOLITAN TABERNACLE, NEWINGTON.

"And without controversy great is the mystery of godliness: God was manifest in the flesh, justified in the Spirit, seen of angels, preached unto the Gentiles, believed on in the world, received up into glory."—1 Timothy iii. 16.

The apostle had just reminded Timothy that the church of the living God is the pillar and ground of the truth, and he had pressed it upon him to behave himself aright in the midst of those faithful men to whom the Lord had committed the gospel; and, lest by any means the youthful minister should think that the treasure committed to the church was of little value, he declares that beyond all controversy it was great and precious. Every heathenish religion had its mystery, its secret doctrine revealed only to the initiated, which was held to be the essence of the faith. The mystery of some religions was mere froth, foolish if untrue, and if true of no consequence to any one; but even those who do not believe the facts of our religion can hold no controversy with us about the unspeakable greatness of them, if they be indeed true. Be a man what he may, if he be reasonable he will admit that Christianity does not deal in trifles. Like the eagle, it does not hawk for flies, it aspires to conquer the loftiest themes of thought. Right or wrong, the subjects with which we deal are not secondary, but wear about them an awful interest which none but the frivolous despise. Jesus sits in no second place among teachers. Paul mentions what the mystery of godliness is, and declares that it concerns the manifestation of God in human flesh, that he might save men from their sin. Now, saith he, without controversy this is a great matter, if it be received by us as true, it becomes us to act as those who are put in trust with a priceless deposit with which we dare not be otherwise than faithful. There is no room for indifference where the gospel is concerned—it is either the most astounding of impostures, or the most amazing of revelations; no man can safely remain undecided about it, it is too weighty, too solemn to be snuffed at as a matter of no concern. Foes and friends alike confess that the mystery of godliness is great: it is no rippling rill of dogma, but a broad ocean of thought, no molehill of discovery, but an Alp of revelation, no single beam of light but a sun shining at its strength.

I shall, this morning, first take up *the apostle's summary* of our religion; secondly, I shall give a few *notes upon it*; and, thirdly, draw one or two *inferences from it*.

No. 786.

I. First let us carefully look at THE SUMMARY OF TRUE RELIGION handed by the apostle to his son in the faith.

1. The first article in this most authentic apostle's creed declares that "*God was manifest in the flesh ;*" this is claimed as an especially valuable part of the great mystery of godliness. My brethren, if you will carefully consider it, this is one of the most extraordinary doctrines that was ever declared in human hearing, for were it not well attested, it would be absolutely incredible that the infinite God who filleth all things, who was and is, and is to come, the Almighty, the Omniscient, and the Omnipresent, actually condescended to veil himself in the garments of our inferior clay. He made all things, and yet he deigned to take the flesh of a creature into union with himself: the Infinite was linked with the infant, and the Eternal was blended with mortality. That manger at Bethlehem, tenanted by the express image of the Father's glory, was a great sight indeed to those who understood it. Well might the angels troop forth in crowds from within the gates of pearl, that they might behold him whom heaven could not contain, finding accommodation in a stable with a lowly wedded pair. Wonder of wonders! God over all, blessed for ever, became one with a newborn babe which slept in a manger where the horned oxen fed.

"God was manifest in the flesh." In this Paul testifies not merely to our Lord's birth, but to the whole of the divine manifestation in his life of two or three and thirty years. He was abundantly manifest among the multitudes, and before his disciples during the latter part of his life. He was God in miracles most plenteous, but he was man in sufferings most pitiable. He was the Son of the Highest, and nevertheless, "a man of sorrows and acquainted with grief." He trod the billows of the obedient sea, and yet he owned not a foot of land in all Judea. He fed thousands by his power, and yet all faint and weary he sat upon a well, and cried, "Give me to drink." He cast out devils, but was himself tempted of the devil. He healed all manner of diseases, and was himself exceeding sorrowful even unto death. Winds and waves obeyed him, every element acknowledged the august presence of deity, and yet he was tempted in all points like as we are. Our Lord's manhood was no phantasm, no myth, no mere appearance in human shape: beyond all doubt "the Word was made flesh, and dwelt among us." "Handle me and see, saith he; "a Spirit hath not flesh and bones as ye see me have." "Reach hither thy finger, and behold my hands; and reach hither thy hand, and thrust it into my side: and be not faithless, but believing." Yet with equal certainty, *God* was manifest in him. As the light streams through the lantern, so the glory of Godhead flamed through the flesh of Jesus, and those who were his nearest companions bear witness: "We beheld his glory, the glory as of the only begotten of the Father, full of grace and truth."

That revelation of God in the flesh became yet more extraordinary when, at last, our Lord condescended to be put to death by his own creatures. Arraigned before human tribunals, condemned as guilty of the gravest crimes, he is taken from prison and from judgment, with none to declare his generation; he is fastened to the accursed wood, and put to a death of deepest shame, and bitterest torture. O ye whose loving eyes have looked upon the ensanguined rills which gush from the wounds of your bleeding Lord, and have delighted to behold the lily of the valleys reddened into the rose of Sharon with the crimson of his own blood, you can see God in Christ as you behold rocks rending, the sun darkened, and the dead arising from their tomb sat the moment of his departure from the earth—behold in the writhing form of the Crucified Man at once the vengeance and the love of God, nor less behold divine power sustaining the load of human guilt, and divine compassion enduring such agonies for rebels so ill deserving. Truly this Son of man was also the Son of God.

Beloved, this is a mystery surpassing all comprehension. If any man should attempt to explain, or even to define the union of the divine and human in the Lord Jesus, he would soon prove his folly. The schoolmen of the dark ages were very fond of asking puzzling questions about what they called the hypostatical union of the deity and humanity of Christ. They could not cast so much as a ray of light upon the subject; they amused themselves with enigmas and lost themselves in labyrinths. It is enough for us to know that the incarnation is a glorious fact, and it suffices us to hold it in its simplicity. God was manifest in the flesh of Jesus Christ the incarnate Word.

Beloved, this is a *great* mystery—*great because it treats of God.* Any doctrine which relates to the Infinite and the Eternal is of the utmost weight. We should be all ear and all heart when we have to learn concerning God. Reason teaches us that he who made us, who is our preserver, and at whose word we are so soon to return to the dust, should be the first object of our thoughts. Turn ye hither, ye wayward children of Adam, and behold this great mystery, for your God is here. A bush burning and unconsumed would attract your curious gaze: what think ye of a man who was in union with the God who is a consuming fire? The truth of God manifest in flesh is great if you consider the *great honour which is thereby conferred upon manhood.* How is man honoured in God's taking the nature of man into union with himself, for verily he took not upon him the nature of angels, but he took upon him the seed of Abraham! Whichever of all the creatures shall come nearest to the Creator will evidently have the preeminence in the ranks of creatureship, which then shall bear the palm? Shall not the seraphs be chosen? Shall not the swift-winged sons of fire be chief among heaven's courtiers? Behold, and be astonished, a worm is preferred, a rebellious child of the earth is chosen! Human nature is espoused into oneness with the divine! There is no gulf between God and redeemed man at this hour. God is first, over all, blessed for ever, but next comes man in the person of the man Christ Jesus. Well may we say with David, "When I consider thy heavens, the work of thy fingers, the moon and the stars, which thou hast ordained; what is man, that thou art mindful of him? and the son of man, that thou visitest him? For thou hast made him a little lower than the angels, and hast crowned him with glory and honour. Thou madest him to have dominion over the works of thy hands; thou hast put all things under his feet." Man is royal now that Christ is human. Man is exalted since Christ is humiliated. Man may go up to God now that God has come down to man. This is great, is it not? A mystery, certainly, but great in every way. See that ye despise it not, lest ye miss the abounding benefit which flows to man through this golden channel.

My brethren, the mystery appears greatest of all because *it is so nearly connected with our eternal redemption.* There could have been no putting away of sin by vicarious suffering if God had not become incarnate. Sin is not removed except by an atonement, neither would any person have sufficed to atone but one of like nature to those who had offended. By man came death; by man also must come resurrection. Jesus appears as man to save his people from their sins, by taking the sins of his people upon himself, and offering a propitiation for them. What a wondrous sight was the dying Redeemer! The cross is the focus of all human history—I was almost going to say it is the centre of the life of God, if such a thing can be. All the ages meet in Calvary. Jesus is the central Sun of all events. O, gaze again, and marvel more and more that God should put himself into the place of his offending creature, and in the person of his dear Son, should offer to eternal justice a compensation for the insults which sin had cast upon law and rule! There is no greatness in heaven or earth if it be not here in the bleeding flesh of Jesus, the Son of God. All else is dwarfed into nothing in his presence.

Beloved, the manifestation of God in Jesus crucified will appear to be great to you if you have ever drank deep into its meaning. If, standing at the foot of the cross, you have seen all your sins punished in the person of the incarnate God, and have heard the voice which saith, "There is therefore now no condemnation to them that are in Christ Jesus," you cannot think lightly of the Word made flesh. If you have learned that his blood has brought perfect pardon to all believers, and that through the rent veil of his flesh the saints have access to God and entrance into heaven, you will lay hold upon the great truth of an incarnate Deity with a grasp which neither the trials of life nor the terrors of death shall unclasp; you will hate the very thought of denying the Godhead of the Lord that bought you—you will be jealous for his great name, and burn with sacred zeal for his glory. Your heart will cry out indignantly, "Away from me, ye rejecters of the divine Redeemer; if you rob Christ of his glory. I count ye the worst of thieves. 'Whosoever denieth the Son, the same hath not the Father,' and in denying Jesus ye reject the one God himself!"

2. The apostle mentions, in the next place, the important witness by which the mission of Jesus was confirmed. He was "*Justified in the Spirit.*" By the word "Spirit," we understand the Holy Spirit, although it may be understood of the spiritual nature of Christ, in which he was always justified, though in the flesh he was condemned of men. It appears more natural to confine the expression to the Holy Spirit. Every religion demands our attention in proportion to the certainty of its teachings, and the value of its confirmatory testimony. How matchless is the seal which is set upon the mystery of godliness, since the Holy Spirit has been pleased himself, personally and repeatedly to confirm it! If we demand trustworthy evidence, behold the Holy Spirit bearing witness to our most holy faith, both in heaven and in earth!—"It is the Spirit that beareth witness, because the Spirit is truth." Observe what part the Holy Spirit took in connection with our Lord. The formation of the immaculate body of the holy child Jesus was by the energy of the Holy Ghost—as the angel said to Mary, "The Holy Ghost shall come upon thee, and the

power of the Highest shall overshadow thee: therefore also that holy thing which shall be born of thee shall be called the Son of God." Afterwards, the Holy Spirit owned this same most sacred person, in whom God was manifested, by descending upon him at his baptism in the waters of Jordan. John, who was the forerunner and witness of Jesus, bore record, saying, "I saw the Spirit descending from heaven like a dove, and it abode upon him; and I knew him not: but he that sent me to baptise with water, the same said unto me, Upon whom thou shalt see the Spirit descending, and remaining on him, the same is he which baptiseth with the Holy Ghost. And I saw, and bare record that this is the Son of God." The heavens were opened, and the Spirit, the voice of God, proclaimed, "This is my beloved Son, in whom I am well pleased." On one or two other occasions we have it upon the testimony of witnesses who were present, that an audible voice was heard out of the excellent glory, saying, "This is my beloved Son: hear ye him!" The greatest attestation which the Holy Spirit gave to Christ was the raising of him from the dead. In some respects Christ rose from the dead by his own power, but it is a scriptural doctrine that he was "declared to be the Son of God with power according to the spirit of holiness by the resurrection from the dead." The power by which we are converted is evidently the Holy Spirit, and we read in the Ephesians, "The exceeding greatness of his power to us-ward who believe, according to the working of his mighty power, which he wrought in Christ, when he raised him from the dead." Moreover, let us not forget that forty days after our Master had been taken up from us, while the disciples were gathered together with one accord in one place, suddenly they heard a sound as of a rushing mighty wind, which filled all the place where they were sitting; the Holy Ghost, whom Jesus had promised, had come to make good the word of the Lord. Ye have not forgotten the miraculous flames of fire which sat upon each of the disciples, and how they spake with other tongues as the Spirit gave them utterance! You know how that day three thousand were converted to the faith by the testimony of those first champions of Christ! Thus the Holy Spirit bore witness with signs, and miracles, and wondrous gifts, that he who professed to be incarnate Deity, was most truly God and the Saviour of men.

Beloved, if you complain that this attestation has now ceased, and that the record of miracles is rather a strain upon your faith than an assistance to it, I would remind you that the Spirit of God has not ceased from the midst of the church. The Holy Ghost no longer operates upon material substances, the sick are not healed, and the dead are not raised—this we freely confess; but he still acts with equally wonderful results upon the minds of men. In this very house there have been miracles performed, which, in lasting value, put the raising of the dead to the blush. Many of us who are now present bear witness that by the Spirit of God we have been new created, raised from spiritual corruption, delivered from the dominion of Satan, and translated into the kingdom of God. The swine of drunkenness have been made lovers of holiness, the beasts of sensuality have become partakers of the divine nature; what better sign is needed? When hearts of adamant melt like wax, and streams of penitence flow from souls as hard as flinty rocks, who will refuse to believe? Let the gospel be judged by its fruits.

and we are satisfied with the trial. If it does not turn the moral desert into an Eden, transform the lion into a lamb, and raise up the beggar from the dunghill, then let it be rejected; but since it has done this, and is doing it, let its despisers beware lest they commit the sin against the Holy Ghost while they reject the solemn evidences which he daily thrusts before our eyes. Brethren, in our own souls the blessed Spirit has borne most overwhelming witness when we have been bowed in penitence at Jesus' feet, and anon have been lifted up into loftiest joy as we found pardon in his blood. The Spirit of God is with us still, working with the word of God. See the savage casting away his weapons, the cannibal softened into the man. What philosophy could not do and did not care to attempt—what civilisation never could have accomplished alone, the cross of Christ has effectually performed. The Spirit of God is with us, and both in the holiness of the saints, and in the conversions of unbelievers, he bears witness that God was in Christ.

3. Our apostle writes, as the next part of the great mystery of godliness, that Christ "*was seen of angels.*" Jesus was seen of angels at his birth; they appeared to the shepherds, and bade them hasten to Bethlehem, while they themselves looked on with holy wonder—

> "They saw the heaven-born child, in human flesh array'd,
> Benevolent and mild, while in a manger laid;
> And praise to God, and peace on earth,
> For such a birth, proclaim'd aloud."

Our Lord was watched by holy spirits in the wilderness where, after he had conquered that arch tempter, angels ministered unto him. He was with the wild beasts at one moment, and anon seraphic spirits waited in his train. An angel ministered unto him in Gethsemane, when his sweat was as it were great drops of blood. Upon Calvary they watched him too, and doubtless, as the poet says—

> "Around the bloody tree they press'd with strong desire
> That wondrous sight to see, the Lord of life expire;
> And, could their eyes have known a tear,
> Had dropp'd it there in sad surprise."

Visions of angels were seen by the witnesses of his resurrection. Two clothed in white sat the one at the head and the other at the foot where the body of Jesus had lain. Angels met him at his ascension, when the clouds received him out of the sight of his gazing followers; and they attended him up to glory, crying, "Lift up your heads, O ye gates; and be ye lift up, ye everlasting doors; and the King of glory shall come in."

The apostle mentions this to show the greatness of our religion, since the noblest intellects are interested in it. Did you ever hear of angels hovering around the assemblies of philosophical societies? Very interesting papers are sometimes produced speculating upon geological facts; startling discoveries are every now and then made as to astronomy and the laws of motion; we are frequently surprised at the results of chemical analyses; yet I do not remember ever reading even in poetry that angelic beings have shown any excitement at the news. The fact is, that the story of the world's history in geologic times, and all the facts about this world, are as well known to angels as the letters of the alphabet are to us; all our profound sciences and recondite theories to them must seem utterly contemptible. Those august minds which have been long ago created of God, and preserved from defilement by his decree, are better able to judge than we are of the importance of things; and when we find them deeply interested in a matter, it cannot be of small account. Concerning an incarnate God, it is said, "which things the angels desire to look into." Their views of God's manifesting himself in the flesh are such, that over the mercy-seat they stand with outspread wings gazing in reverent admiration, and before the throne they sing, "Worthy is the Lamb, for he was slain." The doctrine of incarnate Deity, may be folly to the Greeks, and the vainglorious wiseacres of this world may call it commonplace, but to angels it is an ever flowing fount of adoring admiration. They turn from every other sight to view the incarnate Redeemer, regarding his condescending deed of grace as a bottomless ocean of mystery, a topless steep of wonder. Jesus was seen of angels, and they still delight to gaze upon him—this to the apostle's mind was conclusive evidence that the doctrines of our faith are of the greatest importance.

4. Then, he passes on to the next truth, Jesus Christ was *preached unto the Gentiles.* Was this a great thing? Is preaching a wonder? Yes. The preaching of the gospel proves conclusively the grandeur of our religion. The nearest to Christ were the angels—he was seen of them: the furthest from Christ were fallen Gentiles, who had given themselves up to the worship of the works of their own hands, to these also Jesus came. That Jesus Christ was preached to the Gentiles at all, was a wonder which it behoves us not to forget. As Paul says, "Wherefore remember, that ye being in time past Gentiles in the flesh, who are called Uncircumcision by that which is called the Circumcision in the flesh made by hands: that at that time ye were without Christ, being aliens from the commonwealth of Israel, and strangers from the covenants of promise, having no hope, and without God in the world: but now in Christ Jesus ye who sometimes were far off are made nigh by the blood of Christ. For he is our peace, who hath made both one, and hath broken down the middle wall of partition between us; having abolished in his flesh the enmity, even the law of commandments contained in ordinances; for to make in himself of twain one new man, so making peace." The Gentiles were brutalised with grovelling vices, and no form of spiritual faith had ever found footing among them, was then the most spiritual of all religions to be taught to *them,* and carried to them by no other means than that of preaching? This surprised our apostle; and what surprises me still more is this, that Christ was preached to the Gentiles *by Jews*—that those whose bigotry at that time was invincible, so that they could not imagine such a thing as a Gentile being in covenant with God, were the very men who with indefatigable ardour went among the Gentiles to preach Jesus Christ. If you had told an intelligent Jew that some of his fellow countrymen would become apostles to the Gentiles, to declare that the wall which surrounded the favoured nation was broken down, he would have smiled incredulously, and exclaimed, "Impossible! You may cut the Jew in pieces first. The belief that his race is peculiarly favoured of God lies in the very heart and marrow of the Israelite; he will never consent to become one with the Gentile dogs." Yet Jesus the King of the Jews, Israel's hope and consolation, was first published to the heathen by Jews, and chiefly by one who

boasted that he was a "Hebrew of the Hebrews; as touching the law, a Pharisee." Paul, the most ferocious of bigots, who counted that he did God's service when he hunted out the disciples of Christ, became the Gentile's friend and spiritual father. This is a startling fact.

It is a most noteworthy fact in the history of our faith, that Jesus is still preached among the nations, and the church labours to make him everywhere known. What other religion spends so much energy in seeking converts? If any of you were foolish enough to wish to become Jews, you would not be welcomed among the Jewish fraternity. No Israelite ever attempts to proselyte us to his opinions. It would be a novelty indeed to hear of Jewish missionaries sent out to convert the heathen from their superstitions, or to recover Christians from their errors. No; the Jew does not want us, he prefers to keep his heritage for himself and his heirs. How far different is it with the followers of Jesus, whose very watchword is "preach the gospel to every creature!" In the case of all other religions, the preaching to the Gentiles is absent. I am not aware of any Mahometan society for the conversion of the world to the Prophet. I never saw in the streets of London a Brahmin, come from far, to convert the crowds of London to the doctrines of the Shasters; nor have I ever seen a Buddhist thrusting himself into the midst of peril to win the savage to his creed. Let any other faith than the Christian show me a man traversing alone the centre of Africa, like Livingstone, or dwelling alone with Bushmen, as Moffat has done. The fact is, that the spirit of false creeds is rather monopoly than extension; but as for the religion of Christ, it is expansive as the arch of heaven. If I could, I would have all men saved. If it were possible, I would have every one of you partakers of Christ Jesus this very morning; and we would cheerfully lay down our lives if we could extend the kingdom of Jesus Christ to the utmost bounds of the earth. What is it that keeps up this incessant preaching of Christ? Nothing but the real force of our faith. O ye heathen, if your religions be true, why do ye not promulgate them? Gods of the heathen, if ye be gods, why do ye not command your worshippers to convert the nations to your allegiance? But, no, they confess the worthlessness of their system, in that these systems are not preached among the Gentiles, and have no vitality to secure their spread. When these religions do attempt to spread themselves, which is rarely enough, how do they do it? Mahomet put a scimitar into the hand of each one of his followers, and said, "That is the strength of Islamism: use that sharp argument upon the nations." But Christ refused all carnal weapons, and chose the simple preaching of the word. What other faith can dare to depend upon preaching— upon one man's testimony to other men about truth precious to himself? Surely this goes to show that the things which we believe are powerful, and worthy to be considered with attentive respect.

5. Another great part of the mystery is that Christ is *believed on in the world*. I will acknowledge that I have often wondered at this sentence, and have asked why Paul should write it down as a great mystery that Christ should be believed on in the world. And yet it is a marvel of marvels. If you think how sunken the world was in vice, how darkened the understanding of man was with ignorance, it is astounding that such men should receive so holy and so spiritual a religion as that which Jesus Christ preached by his servants. We come to you who

are fond of sin, and we tell you that you must give up your favourite pleasures, that cherished vices must be abandoned, that holiness which is distasteful to you must rule your life; and yet obnoxious as these things are to flesh and blood, when the Holy Spirit comes with the word, you believe them, and accept them joyfully. The apostle, in his first epistle to the Corinthians, uses the following language: "Be not deceived: neither fornicators, nor idolaters, nor adulterers, nor effeminate, nor abusers of themselves with mankind, nor thieves, nor covetous, nor drunkards, nor revilers, nor extortioners, shall inherit the kingdom of God. And such were some of you: but ye are washed, but ye are sanctified, but ye are justified in the name of the Lord Jesus, and by the Spirit of our God." Was not this extraordinary that such horrible characters should become lovers of the pure and holy Jesus? Must not a religion which can change such as these be something more than a cunningly devised fable? In another place, we are told of all mankind, "There is none that understandeth, there is none that seeketh after God. They are all gone out of the way, they are together become unprofitable; there is none that doeth good, no, not one." Is it not a wonder that such depraved minds should perceive beauties in the Lord Jesus, and yield their full confidence to him? Indeed, to every saved man, it is the greatest miracle of all that he is himself a believer. When I come to look at the truths upon which I rest, they are very simple indeed, and yet around them so many doubts are cast by the evil of my own heart, that I stand amazed that my faith retains her hold. I believe that Christ died for my sins with much more assurance than I believe anything else; no fact in history is one-half so certain to me, and yet, at times, it is so hard to believe it, that it is clear to me that true faith is not of man, but is a fruit of the Spirit. Great must be the truth which forces itself upon the conviction of minds so dark and so benighted as ours.

The apostle winds up his summary of the mystery by reminding us that Christ was "*received up into glory.*" This is no small truth surely, that the Apostle and High Priest of our profession has not gone from us into obscurity, but is at this day sitting upon the throne of God! At this hour Jesus is King of kings and Lord of lords, upholding all things by the word of his power. He shall shortly come to be our Judge. He shall descend from heaven with a shout, with the trump of the archangel and the voice of God, and all men shall be gathered before him to receive their final sentence. This is no small truth, but a great one to be proclaimed with zeal. Thus, throughout, the burden of our religion is far from trivial. "Great is the mystery of godliness."

II. I must now detain you with a few NOTES UPON THIS SUMMARY. Paul has here given us an outline of the Christian faith, and we note upon it as follows:—

First, *it is all concerning Christ.* Out of these six articles of Paul's creed, they all speak of Christ; from which I gather that if we are to preach the gospel faithfully, we must preach much concerning Jesus Christ. My dear brethren, this must be the first, the midst, and end of our ministry. That man of whom it cannot be said that he preaches Christ, does not behave himself aright in the house of God; he evidently is not a messenger sent from heaven. It is all our business here to cry with John the Baptist, "Behold the Lamb of God, which taketh away the sin of the world." Brethren, as it is ours to preach Christ, so it is yours to receive him. If you have received a gospel, of which Christ is not the top and bottom, throw it away. If you are resting on anything beside Christ Jesus, you are resting upon a rotten foundation. Get off from it, lest you be deceived at the last. But if Christ is all in all to you, and his work and person are the sum and substance of your hope, then be of good cheer; where Jesus is honoured, souls are safely sheltered.

I notice, in the second place, that there is *not here a single word upon sacramentarianism.* Now, in these days, we are perpetually told by men who are manifestly in earnest, that the great thing is the sacrament. According to their teaching, God has committed to bishops and priests the fulness of his grace, which we meekly and reverently may receive at their venerable hands. We are told that, in connection with a few drops of water, sprinkled by the successors of the apostles, children become regenerate; through the laying on of the same blessed hands, we afterwards become confirmed in the faith, and assured of our salvation. Through priestly power we are made partakers of the very body and blood of Christ, which, according to them, becomes literally present through their operation. When we come to die, they can anoint us with oil, consecrated by their power, and by this unction all our sins are forgiven us. The top and the bottom of the system is the priest, the priest, the priest. A man like ourselves, and not a whit better, but ten thousand times worse for his infamous impudence in pretending to be what he is not, this man, dressed out in as many colours as the peacock, is the divinely appointed medium of grace. If this be the truth, Paul did not know it, for, if he had known it, he would say, "Great is the mystery of godliness; God dwells in the priests, hasten and kiss their feet, for by their ceremonials you get salvation." Paul says nothing of the kind. He has nothing to reveal about candles, and copes, and pompous processions; all he has to say is this, "God was manifest in the flesh, justified in the Spirit, seen of angels, preached unto the Gentiles, believed on in the world, received up into glory," and that is all. How different this simple gospel from the complex machinery of Popery and Anglicanism!

I want you to notice still further, that in this summary there is *no exhibition of mere doctrine.* I believe, most firmly, in the doctrines commonly called Calvinistic, and I hold them to be very fraught with comfort to God's people; but if any man shall say that the preaching of these is the whole of the preaching of the gospel, I am at issue with him. Brethren, you may preach those doctrines as long as you like, and yet fail to preach the gospel; and I will go further, and affirm that some who have even denied those truths, to our great grief, have nevertheless been gospel preachers for all that, and God has saved souls by their ministry. The fact is, that while the doctrines of election, final perseverance, and so on, go to make up a complete ministry, and are invaluable in their place, yet the soul and marrow of the gospel is not there, but is to be found in the great fact that "God was manifest in the flesh, justified in the Spirit," and so on. Preach Christ, young man, if you want to win souls. Preach all the doctrines, too, for the building up of believers, but still the main business is to preach Jesus who came into the world to seek and to save that which was lost. The apostle tells us in the Corinthians that first of all he delivered unto us as soul-saving truth, "how that Christ died for our sins, according to the Scriptures, and that he was buried, and that he rose again on the third day, according to the Scriptures." Facts about Christ Jesus, and the promise of life through him, these are the faith of the gospel.

Let me also say that I do not perceive anything in this summary *tending remarkably to exalt prophecy.* I would not make this remark were it not that there is a certain troublesome sect abroad nowadays to whom the one thing needful is a perpetual speculation upon prophecy. All the bells in their steeple ring out "prophecy! prophecy! prophecy!" They plume themselves upon an expected secret rapture, and I know not what vain imaginings beside. Where prophecy is preached in connection with their shibboleth, there the gospel is preached, and all ministers beside their own, however honoured by God, are railed at by them as part of Babylon, against whom men are to be warned. They, forsooth, are wise men, and can afford superciliously to look down upon their fellow Christians as the slaves of sect and system, being, I venture to say, far more sectarian than the worst of us, and more bigoted to their system than Romanists themselves. My dear friends, if you have any time to spare, and cannot find any practical work for Jesus, study the dark places of prophecy, but do not read modern prophetical works, for that is a sheer waste of time and nothing better. Hold off as you would from a serpent from the idea that the study or preaching of prophecy is the gospel, for the belief that it is so, is mischievous beyond conception. The gospel which is to be vehemently declared is this:—"God was manifest in the flesh, justified in the Spirit, seen of angels, preached unto the Gentiles, believed on in the world, received up into glory." So long as London is reeking with sin, and millions are going down to hell, let us leave others to prophesy, let us go with anxious hearts to seek after souls, and see if we cannot by the Spirit's power win sinners from going down into the pit.

You will, doubtless, have observed that this summary of the gospel is *very simple.* Whenever you meet with teaching which is cloudy and complicated, you may generally conclude that it is not the gospel of your salvation, for the truth of Christ is so plain that he who runs may read, and the wayfaring man though a fool need not err therein. Perhaps some of you have been thinking that conversion and salvation are dark and mysterious things, and that you have to pass through many singular operations and feelings in order to be saved. Now, beloved, the whole of our faith lies in a nutshell. He that believeth in Jesus Christ the incarnate God, is saved. These few truths if grasped by the mind, received and trusted in by the heart, will save you. It is at the cross that salvation must be found. We have not written over our religion, "Mystery, mystery, mother of harlots," this is the sign of Babylon, but we have this to tell you, "He that believeth and is baptised shall be saved; he that believeth not shall be damned," and the things which you have to believe are just these simplicities: Jesus the Son of God has come into this world as man to save men; he has bled and died; he is proclaimed and preached; he is to be received and believed in; he has gone up to glory to prepare a place for them that trust him, and that is all.

III. THE INFERENCES I draw from this are just these. If this be a great gospel, then *how important it is for us to receive it.* If the gospel were a laborious system of ethics, there are many in this house who never could be saved, for they could not understand it; but since it is so simple, why do men refuse it? "Jesus Christ came into the world to save sinners, of whom I am chief." O will you not lay hold upon that truth? I do pray the Spirit of God to take off your minds from all philosophies and mysteries, that you may come to Jesus only. Trust in Christ and you are saved. Receive this simple truth. God calls it great; angels think it great; the Holy Spirit attests it to be great; we who preach it feel it to be great; they who receive it acknowledge it to be great; Christ in glory bears witness that it is great; O accept this great salvation! May the Spirit lead you to believe in the great Saviour of great sinners.

Again, if it be so great, *how important it is for us to spread it!* It does not require us to go to college in order to tell of Jesus: we can each in our sphere publish his fame abroad. If this simple truth be the message of God to perishing sinners, then in the name of common humanity, and above all, in the name of the love of Christ, let us deliver it.

How this text ought to encourage us to spread the gospel. When I am preaching the gospel, many may say, "Oh, he is only telling us commonplace truth." Just so, I know that; and yet I feel within myself as if I was wheeling up God's great cannon, which will blow the gates of hell to pieces yet. "What! none of the venerable mysteries of Rome? What, none of the new philosophical discoveries? None of the imposing ceremonies? No, brethren, not one of them, they are all wooden guns, shams and counterfeits, and if ever they are fired off they will go to shivers. This plain truth, that "God was made flesh and dwelt among us," is God's great battering-ram against which nothing can stand. Never lose heart in the gospel, my brethren, but think you hear the apostle calling across the ages, "Great is the mystery of godliness." Look for nothing greater, the gospel is great enough. Keep to it, never think you have told men times enough about it. As Napoleon told his warriors at the pyramids, "A thousand ages look down upon you!" bleeding martyrs who from their graves, call to you to be faithful; confessors who ascended to heaven in fiery chariots, implore you to be steadfast. Hold fast that ye have received! Attempt not to mend the truth, venture not to shape it according to the fancy of the times, but proclaim it in all its native purity. By this hammer the gods of Rome and Greece were dashed to shivers, by this lever the world was turned upside down; it is this gospel which has brought glory to God, filled heaven with redeemed souls, and made hell to tremble in all its palaces of flame. Bind it about your heart, and defy the hosts of Rome or hell to unloose its folds. Wrap it about your loins in death, and hold it as a standard in both your hands in life. This simple truth, that "Jesus Christ has come to seek and to save that which is lost," and that "whosoever believeth in him shall not perish, but have everlasting life," must be your jewel, your treasure, your life.

PORTION OF SCRIPTURE READ BEFORE SERMON—1 Tim. iii. 14—16; iv.

Metropolitan Tabernacle Pulpit.

THE HEXAPLA OF MYSTERY.

A Sermon

DELIVERED ON LORD'S DAY MORNING, DECEMBER 22ND, 1872, BY

C. H. SPURGEON,

AT THE METROPOLITAN TABERNACLE, NEWINGTON.

"And without controversy great is the mystery of godliness: God was manifest in the flesh, justified in the Spirit, seen of angels, preached unto the Gentiles, believed on in the world, received up into glory."—1 Timothy iii. 16.

THE apostle tells us in the preceeding verse that the Lord has a double design in maintaining his church in the world. The first is that it may be the place of his abode, for the church of the living God is "the house of God," the home wherein he reveals himself unto his own children, the resting-place of his love which he has of old appointed. Jehovah still inhabits the praises of Israel, and still he fulfills his promise to his chosen, "I will dwell in them and walk in them" (2 Cor. vi. 16). Blessed is the church which has realised this first design of God, and so has continued to enjoy the Lord's presence and power. May we in this place be a building fitly framed together, and grow unto a holy temple in the Lord, for a habitation of God through the Spirit. God's next purpose in sustaining a church in the world is that it may preserve and uphold his truth among men, for the church of the living God is "the pillar and ground of the truth." The gospel must be believed, practised, and proclaimed by men of God, or it will not have power. God does not trust the conservation of his truth to books, or to the most accurately written creeds, or to some one person supposed to be infallible, but he puts the incorruptible seed into the hearts of his chosen, and in such good soil its vitality and its growth secure its preservation. Even the inspired word, as a letter, has small power till it gains a lodging-place for the truth in a warm heart, and then it grows and yields fruit, till its boughs spread far and wide, and its seeds are wafted on the wings of every wind, to spring up on the hills and among the vallies where none had looked for them. As long as one copy of the Holy Scriptures remains in the world we shall have the pure truth among us, but it will be like an unplanted seed. For the propagation of the gospel, human voices are required; for the establishment and confirmation of it among men, human lives are needed; and God intends that his gospel shall be set forth and held up, published, defended, maintained, and supported in the world by his church; not alone by his ministers, nor by a hierarchical establishment, but by the entire company of faithful men. To the sacramental host of his elect has he committed the banner of the truth, which they are always to unfold, and carry on by the power of his Spirit, from victory to victory. In this sense, the church of the living God is, and ever must be, "the pillar and ground of the truth;" let us take care, in our measure to make her so.

While dealing with this question, it was most fitting for the apostle to tell us what the truth is, and now is the most proper time for each one of us to learn what are the vital and essential truths which the church of God is for ever to maintain. Our text is for this reason deeply interesting; it deals not with questionable and debatable topics, but with things verily, and, indeed, received among us. Its testimony is short, but weighty. We cannot spare a single word from it, and it would be a crime to add anything to it. The apostle calls it a "mystery," and so, indeed, it is, for exceeding greatness of meaning, but not for obscurity of language, for it is as plain as it is full. Neither is it a mystery because it speaks of recondite opinions, or philosophical theories, for it deals only with facts, and is an historical summary of actual occurrences.

Observe that the comprehensive summary of the gospel here given is contained in six little sentences, which run with such regularity of measure in the original Greek, that some have supposed them to be an ancient hymn; and it is possible that they may have been used as such in the early church. There is a poetic form about the six sentences. You are aware, of course, that the Orientals do not consider it essential to sacred psalms and hymns that they should resound with jingling rhymes; we are the slaves of mere sound in that respect, but they are free. Their fashion of verse-making has more respect to the sense than ours, and lies, as a rule, very much in introducing pleasant parallels and contrasts. These you have here, whether the six paragraphs are verses of a hymn or no. Note that "manifest in *the flesh*" is contrasted with "justified in *the spirit;*" "seen of angels," who are nearest to the throne of God, is fitly set by the side of "preached unto the Gentiles," who stand at the opposite pole, and are far off. And then the third duplicate is made up of the evident opposites, "believed on *in the world*," "received up *into glory.*" Thus, all through, the lights and shades are set over against each other by evident design. Moreover, you will perceive an equally plain parallelism, if you will read attentively. The first two stanzas deal with the revealing of the Lord Jesus;—he is manifest in the flesh, and he is yet more fully made manifest by being justified in the spirit. Then follows a making known of the Lord by sight to angels, and by hearing to the Gentiles; and, in the third pair of lines, there is a twofold reception,—the one by grace among men who believe, and the other into his actual glory in heaven. To all this add that pairs are also discernable in the first and last, the second and fourth, and the two middle lines. Just for an instant notice that the first clause of the series deals with Christ's descent, and the last with his ascent; the second and the fifth are both intensely spiritual; and the third and fourth have to do with the senses only. Thus you find another set of parallels, whose existence can hardly be a mere accident.

Note this, for it teaches us that our memories need to be helped and strengthened in every way, and so it is well to have condensed truth to carry about with us, and exceedingly advantageous to us to have it arranged for us in such a shape that we are likely to recollect it. The apostle has been led by the Spirit to give us goodly words, helping our infirmities; of this help we should gratefully avail ourselves to the utmost. If we be somewhat instructed in the word we have here an example of practical usefulness; we may for ourselves and for others, especially for the young, try to put truth into forms which will help it to retain its hold upon the memory.

I shall call my text a hexapla of essential truth, a sixfold mystery of godliness. You have six great points clearly set forth before you, and these constitute the main, the essential elements of our holy faith, which the church of God is for ever to set forth, and uphold to the end of time.

The apostle has said, " without controversy great is the mystery of godliness." When he says "without controversy," I suppose he means that there ought to be no controversy about these facts, though controversies have arisen concerning them, and always will, since the most self-evident truth will always find self-evident fools to contradict it. He means that, in the church of God, at any rate, there is no question about these fundamentals. Outside of the church these statements are denied, but inside the house of God no one ever questions them for a moment; and he who does so is by that very act proven to have no part nor lot in the matter. Without controversy all Christians agree that these are truths, and also that they are no trifles, but involve a mystery, and a great mystery; that is to say, that they were things hidden in themseves, and so concealed that reason could not have found them out; and even now, though they be revealed, they concern matters so vast and so profound that none of us comprehend them to the full, and the best instructed scribe in the kingdom recognises in them infinite deeps which he cannot hope fully to explore. The facts are unquestioned by the church of God, and are without dispute, among the faithful, regarded as containing in their inner depths a world of weighty meaning, even the great mystery of godliness.

Have you ever noticed that there are six New Testament mysteries? There may be more, but these six are the chief. The first is the mystery of the incarnation, which is now before us; " Great is the mystery of godliness, God was manifest in the flesh." The next is the mystery of the union of Christ with his church, of which we read, in Ephesians v. 31, 32, " For this cause shall a man leave his father and mother, and shall be joined unto his wife, and they two shall be one flesh. This is a great mystery: but I speak concerning Christ and the church." Thrice blessed union with Jesus, may our souls find their heaven in thy holy mystery.

> "Oh teach us, Lord, to know and own
> This wondrous mystery,
> That thou with us art truly ONE,
> And we are ONE with thee!"

The third mystery is the mystery of the calling of the Gentiles, to which Paul refers in Ephesians iii. 4—6, where he says, " Whereby, when ye read, ye may understand my knowledge in the mystery of Christ;

which in other ages was not made known unto the sons of men, as it is now revealed unto his holy apostles and prophets by the Spirit; that the Gentiles should be fellow-heirs, and of the same body, and partakers of his promise in Christ by the gospel." Herein we have a joyful portion, for which we can never be too grateful. The fourth mystery concerns the Jews, and deals with the restoration of Israel, whom we ought to remember with abounding sympathy and brotherly love. Of this you will read in Romans xi. 25, 26: "For I would not, brethren, that ye should be ignorant of this mystery, lest ye should be wise in your own conceits; that blindness in part is happened to Israel, until the fulness of the Gentiles be come in. And so all Israel shall be saved: as it is written, There shall come out of Sion the Deliverer, and shall turn away ungodliness from Jacob." For a fifth mystery I would bid you remember the doctrine of the removal of corruption from the body, and of its resurrection as spoken of in the famous passage, "Behold, I shew you a mystery; we shall not all sleep, but we shall all be changed, in a moment, in the twinkling of an eye, at the last trump: for the trumpet shall sound, and the dead shall be raised incorruptible, and we shall be changed." And then, alas! to close the list, there is that mystery of iniquity which began to work so soon, and worketh yet more and more of evil.

Our text, then, is one of six mysteries, but it has this pre-eminence, that it is a *great* mystery, and is besides peculiarly *the* mystery. It is called "the mystery of godliness," because it most intimately concerns a godly life, because those who receive it in their hearts become thereby godly men; and because, moreover, it builds up its believers in godliness, and is to them a grand motive for the reverent love and holy fear of the Lord their God.

Let so much as we have already spoken stand for our preface, and let us now, by the Holy Spirit's aid, consider one by one the six branches of the mystery which is now before us

I. The first sentence is "GOD WAS MANIFEST IN THE FLESH." I believe that our version is the correct one, but the fiercest battlings have been held over this sentence. It is asserted that the word *Theos* is a corruption for " *Os* ;" so that, instead of reading " *God* was manifest in the flesh," we should read, " *who* was manifest in the flesh." There is very little occasion for fighting about this matter, for if the text does not say "God was manifest in the flesh," who does it say was manifest in the flesh? Either a man, or an angel, or a devil. Does it tell us that a man was manifest in the flesh? Assuredly that cannot be its teaching, for every man is manifest in the flesh, and there is no sense whatever in making such a statement concerning any mere man, and then calling it a mystery. Was it an angel, then? But what angel was ever manifest in the flesh? And if he were, would it be at all a mystery that he should be " seen of angels "? Is it a wonder for an angel to see an angel? Can it be that the devil was manifest in the flesh? If so, he has been "received up into glory," which, let us hope, is not the case. Well, if it was neither a man, nor an angel, nor a devil, who was manifest in the flesh, surely he must have been God; and so, if the word be not there, the sense must be there, or else nonsense. We believe that, if criticism should grind the text in a mill, it would get out of it no more and no less than the sense expressed by our grand old version. God himself was manifest in the flesh. What a mystery is this! A mystery of mysteries! God the invisible was manifest; God the spiritual dwelt in flesh; God the infinite, uncontained, boundless, was manifest in the flesh. What infinite leagues our thought must traverse between Godhead self-existent, and, therefore, full of power and self-sufficiency, before we have descended to the far-down level of poor flesh, which is as grass at its best, and dust in its essence! Where find we a greater contrast than between God and flesh, and yet the two are blended in the incarnation of the Saviour. God was manifest in the flesh; truly God, not God humanised, but God as God. He was manifest in real flesh; not in manhood deified and made superhuman, but in actual flesh.

> Oh joy! there sitteth in our flesh,
> Upon a throne of light,
> One of a human mother born,
> In perfect Godhead bright!
>
> For ever God, for ever man,
> My Jesus shall endure;
> And fix'd on Him, my hope remains
> Eternally secure.

Matchless truth, let the church never fail to set it forth, for it is essential to the world's salvation that this doctrine of the incarnation be made fully known.

O my brethren, since it is "without controversy," let us not controvert but sit down and feed upon it. What a miracle of condescension is here, that God should manifest himself in flesh. It needs not so much to be preached upon as to be pondered in the heart. It needs that ye sit down in quiet, and consider how he who made you became like you, he who is your God became your brother man. He who is adored of angels once lay in a manger; he who feeds all living things hungered and was athirst; he who oversees all worlds as God, was, as a man, made to sleep, to suffer, and to die like yourselves. This is a statement not easily to be believed. If he had not been beheld by many witnesses, so that men handled him, looked upon him, and heard him speak, it were a thing not readily to be accepted that so divine a person should be manifest in flesh. It is a wonder of condescension!

And it is a marvel, too, of benediction, for God's manifestation in human flesh conveys a thousand blessings to us. Bethlehem's star is the morning star of hope to believers. Now man is nearest to God. Never was God manifest in angel nature, but he is manifest in flesh. Now, between poor puny man that is born of a woman, and the infinite God, there is a bond of union of the most wonderful kind. God and man in one person is the Lord Jesus Christ! This brings our manhood near to God, and by so doing it ennobles our nature, it lifts us up from the dunghill and sets us among princes; while at the same time it enriches us by endowing our manhood with all the glory of Christ Jesus in whom dwelleth all the fulness of the Godhead bodily. Lift up your eyes, ye down-trodden sons of man! If ye be men ye have a brotherhood with Christ, and Christ is God. O ye who have begun to despise yourselves and think that ye are merely sent to be drudges upon earth, and slaves of sin, lift up your heads and look for redemption in the Son of Man, who has broken the captives' bonds. If ye be believers in the Christ of God, then are ye also the children of God, and if children then heirs,—heirs of God, joint heirs with Jesus Christ.

What a fulness of consolation there is in this truth, as well as of benediction; for if the Son of God be man, then he understands me and will have a fellow feeling for me. He knows my unfitness to worship sometimes—he knows my tendencies to grow weary and dull—he knows my pains, my trials, and my griefs:

> "He knows what fierce temptations mean,
> For he has felt the same."

Man, truly man, yet sitting at the right hand of the Father, thou, O Saviour, art the delight of my soul. Is there not the richest comfort in this for you, the people of God?

And, withal, there is instruction, too, for God was manifest in the flesh; and if you desire to see God, you must see him in Christ Jesus. It does not say God was veiled in the flesh, though under certain aspects that might be true; but God was "*manifest* in the flesh." The brightness of the sun might put out our eyes if we gazed upon it, and we must needs look through dim glass, and then the sun is manifested to us; so the excessive glory of the infinite Godhead cannot be borne by our mind's eye till it comes into communication and union with the nature of man, and then God is manifest to us. My soul, never try to gaze upon an absolute God: the brightness will blind thine eye: even our God is a consuming fire! Ask not to see God in fire in the bush, nor God in lightning upon Mount Sinai; be satisfied to see God in the man Christ Jesus, for there God is manifested. Not all the glory of the sky, and of the sea, nor the wonders of creation or providence, can set forth the Deity as does the Son of Mary, who from the manger went to the cross, and from the cross to the tomb, and from the tomb to his eternal throne. Behold ye now the Lamb of God, for God is manifest in him! People of God, look ye nowhere else for God.

I shall leave the point when I have put a personal question. Have we each one of us seen God in Christ Jesus? Remember, this is essential to salvation. We speak not now that which is harsh or severe, we only speak that which is honest and true; if you rebel against it we still can say no less. Ye cannot be right anywhere unless ye are right about the person of the Lord Jesus. If you do not accept him as the Son of God he cannot be a Saviour to you, and without him for a Saviour you are as surely lost as you are born, whatever profession you may make. I trust we can say, many of us, "Yes, Jesus Christ is to us Lord, to the glory of God the Father, and we worship him, and obey him, putting all our trust in him, and rendering our adoration to him." If you be not now his worshippers, may the blessed Spirit bring you to Jesus, and not suffer you to attempt to go to the Father first, for the Lord Jesus hath told us "no man cometh unto the Father but by me." May you go to the throne of God by the way of the cross, for that is the only open way, and may you go by that road at once.

II. The second clause concerns our Lord's vindication by the Spirit. He who was "manifest in the flesh" was also "JUSTIFIED IN THE

Spirit." When our Lord came in human flesh and declared himself to be the Son of God there were many reasons why his statement would be doubted, for he came in such poverty, weakness, and disrepute. In any case, the appearance of God in flesh would need great proof, but the circumstances which surrounded our Saviour were such as to cast, especially in carnal minds, great doubt upon his pretensions; but our Lord, however the flesh might seem to cloud his claims, was "justified in the Spirit," which may mean, and perhaps does, that his spiritual nature as man was so elevated by his Godhead that it abundantly justified his claim to be the Son of God. What a spirit was his for purity and dignity! What nobility ever came near to his! What a mind was his, what wisdom dwelt in him! Even as a child he baffled Rabbis, and as a man he confounded all who would entrap him in his speech. Was there ever such teaching as his? Listen to him, and you feel that the spirit which flashes from those eyes and distils from those lips justifies his claim to be the Son of the Highest.

Hearken also to his words of command, when his Godhead glows through his humanity and proves him divine. He speaks, and it is done; he commands and it stands fast. At his bidding waves sleep and winds rest; pain flies, strength returns, health smiles, and death lives! Has not his spiritual nature, by deeds so astounding, fully justified him?

And see, dear friends, how he was justified—not only by his own spirit, which wrought beyond the reach and compass of all other spirits —but he was justified by the Holy Spirit which rested upon him without measure, and made his human spirit strong. It was this anointing which made him the chief of all prophets, teachers, and revealers of the mind of God. All who heard him confessed his unrivalled power, even when they resisted it. The Spirit of God bore witness in him—his words were full of unction; the Spirit of God bore witness with him—his words went to men's hearts. The Spirit of God bore witness to Christ, and justified all his claims at the time of his baptism, when out of the excellent glory there appeared the form of a dove, and a voice cried out of heaven, "This is my beloved Son." That same Spirit justified him audibly again in his transfiguration; but silently, and yet more evidently, the seal of God was always on him, everywhere the Spirit witnessed to him. Only blind eyes, blinded by hate, refused to see the divine light which hung about his every word and act, as radiance enrobes a star. Above all, our Lord's claims were justified by the Spirit in his resurrection, when he was "declared to be the Son of God with power, acccording to the Spirit of holiness by his resurrection from the dead." Nor less so when, after forty days, he was received up into glory, and the Spirit of God justified all that Christ had said, by coming down like a rushing mighty wind and cloven tongues of fire, and resting upon his disciples. If Christ had not risen from the dead he would have been a convicted impostor, and after his rising from the dead, if the Spirit of God had not been given, his claim would still have remained under a cloud! But now it is clear that "he hath ascended on high, and received gifts for men, yea, for the rebellious also, that the Lord God might dwell among them;" for the scattering of the Spirit of God among men was that promised largess which our mighty Conqueror distributed among his people, when he entered upon the possession of his crown.

The Holy Spirit has justified Christ. This is a part of the testimony of the church—that Christ's claims are to be justified by the spirit of his teaching, and also by the Holy Spirit whose supernatural power will accompany the proclamation of the gospel. Now, let the church always stand to this. I am afraid we are on wrong ground when we begin to defend the gospel by mere reason. The true defence of the gospel is the spirit of Christ; Jesus is justified in the Spirit, and needs no other justification. O, brethren, if we exhibit the spirit of Christ we shall answer cavillers, and if the Spirit of God rests on the ministry of the church, cavillers will cease to cavil; they will see her glory and they will be ashamed. The Holy Ghost is our strength, our glory, the abiding witness that our great Leader is Lord and God.

Brethren, has the Holy Spirit ever justified Christ in your soul? He has come to save, has the Holy Spirit revealed him as your Saviour? He has come to blot out sin, has the Holy Ghost ever revealed him in all his power to pardon you? This is the sure vindication of Christ— your own personal experience of his preciousness and his power: if the Holy Ghost has given you that, none can confound you, but if you have it not you lack the one thing needful. God grant you may not lack it long!

III. The third clause of our hexapla is, "SEEN OF ANGELS." This is an important point, for angels had waited to see the Lord, patiently gazing on the mercy-seat. There had been rumours in heaven of this mystery of the manifold wisdom of God, but they had not understood it; and it is now in Christ that the mystery of incarnate God has been revealed to them. If I may so say, the brightness of the Godhead had confounded even the angels; they were not able to see God, but when God came and manifested himself in the flesh, then God was seen of angels. The Godhead was seen in Christ by angels, as they had never seen it before. They had beheld the attribute of justice, they had seen the attribute of power, they had marked the attribute of wisdom, and seen the prerogative of sovereignty; but never had angels seen love, and condescension, and tenderness, and pity, in God as they saw these things resplendent in the person and the life of Christ. They were astounded to think that God was such a one. They knew him to be thrice holy, for they had chanted "Holy, holy, holy," in their perpetual sanctus; but they did not know him to be love—essential love—as they knew it when they saw that "he spared not his own Son, but freely delivered him up for us all." The angels, seeing God thus manifest in flesh, ministered to him; they watched around the manger; they were messengers to his foster-parent to warn him of intended evil to the child; and they waited on the Redeemer in the desert of his temptation. One of their number strengthened him in the garden, another rolled away the stone from his grave, while others sat at the head and foot of the sepulchre where Jesus had lain. I doubt not it is true as we sang just now:—

> "They brought his chariot from above,
>   To bear him to his throne;
> Clapped their triumphant wings, and cried,
>   'The glorious work is done.'"

Jesus was all along seen of angels, and this is one reason why they sing so sweetly of him—why they tune their notes so heartily to the song, "Worthy is the Lamb that was slain;" for they saw him live, and die, saw him labour and suffer; and therefore is their song so vivid and so full of adoration. "Thou wast slain," say they, though they cannot add, "and hast redeemed us unto God by thy blood." Now the joy of this truth lies here: it brings the angel host so near to us, for they saw Jesus and waited on him, and we see him, and therefore our eyes and the angels' eyes meet upon the person of Christ. We have one common love, one common Lord; and now the ministering spirits that waited upon him are ready to wait upon us. They love the members for the sake of the Head. Beloved, we rejoice this day to know that Christ is head of angels and principalities and powers, as well as head of his church; and so in him broken unity is restored, and the household of God is one in him. Angelic eyes beheld and loved; they love on still, and wonder yet. Fair spirits, charmed with the beauty of our Bridegroom, ye rejoice with us, and make it your delight to swell his train!

One question, and we leave the point. Have you ever seen Jesus? He was seen of angels. Has your eye ever seen him—your inner, spiritual eye? If not, the Lord help you this morning to look unto him and be saved! It is nothing that he was seen of angels, unless he be seen of me also, even as of one born out of due time. O! to see him as my Saviour, my all, and rest in him! This is the main business. May God grant us that gladness!

IV. Briefly, the fourth part of the great mystery does not look, at first sight, to be at all mysterious. There is much of mystery in the facts that God was "manifest in the flesh, justified in the Spirit, and seen of angels;" but the next appears very common-place—"PREACHED UNTO THE GENTILES." Yet it is not without a marvel: those who reflect will see a great mystery of grace in it. Until Christ came, nothing was "preached to the Gentiles." They were accounted dogs, and few were the crumbs that fell to them from the master's table; but after our Lord had ascended on high he was proclaimed to the Gentiles. To a Jew especially this would seem a very strange thing. The Jew thought that if the Gentile perished, it was but a matter of course; but for the Gentiles to be visited with the gospel was strange indeed. That God should work effectually in Peter to the apostleship of the circumcision was to them readily a matter of faith, but that the same should be equally mighty in Paul towards the Gentiles was incredible yet true. Well, blessed be God, you and I are partakers in this mystery, for we have heard and believed the love which God hath toward us. We are Gentiles also, but unto us has the gospel been preached as well as unto the ancient people; yea, and we have been more highly favoured than they, for at this day, more are the children of the desolate than the children of the married wife. God hath multiplied the seed of Abraham after the Spirit among the Gentiles, whereas the seed of Abraham after the flesh have, in these times, rejected the Saviour. Rejoice then, in the mystery, that Christ is *preached* among the Gentiles. Mark you, *preached!* For he is to be set forth in that manner. The church is ever to maintain this great, uncontroverted mystery, that the setting forth of Christ to the Gentiles is to be by preaching, and not by any other means of man's devising. Suppose I could take my pencil now, and draw the Saviour with such matchless skill, that a Raffaelle or a Titian could not rival me: God has never ordained that so Christ should be set forth to the Gentiles. Or, suppose I should perform the ceremony of the mass with all the exactness, and with all the gorgeousness which the church of Rome would require; such a setting forth of Christ among the Gentiles would not be according to the divine mystery. Christ is to be *preached* among the Gentiles: the appointed way of manifesting the incarnate God to the sons of men is by preaching—the church must always maintain this. The strongest castle of the walls of Zion for offence and defence must ever be the pulpit. God is pleased by the foolishness of preaching to save them that believe. I hate to see, as I do sometimes, in certain modern buildings, the pulpit stuck in the corner, and the altar in the most conspicuous place. The altar of sacrifice, indeed, the place of defilement and remembrance of sin, how comes that to be in the holy place at all? God has never ordained it to be there. Where in Holy Scripture have we mention of a material altar in the assemblies of believers? Our only altar is the spiritual altar of our Lord's person, whereof they have no right to eat that serve the tabernacle of outward forms of rites and ceremonies. Altars belong to Jews and heathens, and even they never bow before them; none but your Popish idolaters have fallen so low as that. The most prominent agency in the church of God is the preaching of Christ—this is the trumpet of heaven and the battering-ram of hell! By this door salvation comes, for faith cometh by hearing, and hearing by the word of God, and how shall they hear without a preacher? God's way of creating faith in men's hearts is not by pictures, music, or symbols, but by the hearing of the word of God. This may seem a strange thing, and strange let it seem, for it is a mystery, and a great mystery, but a fact beyond all controversy; for ever let the church maintain that Christ is to be preached unto the Gentiles. A part of the greatness of the mystery lies in the persons who preached the gospel. It was a strange thing that Jesus should be preached unto the Gentiles by unlearned and ignorant men. One of the apostles, it is true, was of another class, but he declares that he never preached with excellency of speech, but in all simplicity he laid bare the mystery of God in plain language. It was wonderful that Christ should be preached unto the Gentiles so rapidly. It was but the other day the hundred and twenty were in the upper room, and within a few years there was no part of the civilized globe which had not heard the name of Jesus; they had penetrated Scythia, they had subdued the barbarians, their only weapon being the cross; they had triumphed at Athens, in the stronghold of classic learning; they had passed into Rome, and set up the cross amidst the luxurious vices of the capital. No place was untrodden by the Christian missionary, and no place was unaffected by the power of the gospel which he preached. This is a great mystery: the Lord repeat the mystery again and again! O that preaching might once again be recognised to be God's power unto salvation, and used everywhere—in the church, in the lecture hall, in the street—in foreign lands and at home; for the voice of truth in the **preaching** of Jesus is the great power of God.

One question here, and we leave it—Have you reverently heard the gospel? for there goes with the declaration that God saves through preaching, the warning, "Take heed how ye hear," for if God waits to bless by hearing, woe unto the men who hear inattentively and disrespectfully, woe unto the hearers only who are not doers of the word! A responsibility goes with hearing, and God grant that you may be obedient hearers, so that we who preach may give a good account of you at the last, that our ministry may not have been in vain, but may have been to you the voice of God to your salvation.

V. And now the fifth part of the mystery is a very remarkable one: like that which preceded, it does not appear to be mysterious on the surface, but it is so: "BELIEVED ON IN THE WORLD." This is the most glorious of all the six points, this wonderful fact that Jesus is "believed on in the world." Why, when the humble preachers went out first to tell of Jesus, their story was so strange you could not imagine that any would believe it. And then the doctrines that they taught were so contrary to all the prejudices of flesh and blood, so humbling to human pride, so insulting to all our self-esteem, that it was not probable that men would accept them. And the world, too, what a world it was! It was steeped up to its throat in cruelty, in vice, in luxury, in sins infamous and unmentionable, and was it likely that a pure Saviour, with a perfect doctrine like his, would find followers? But he did; he was "believed on in the world." Why, I think the first preachers must have been ready to leap for joy when they found that men believed them. If I had been Peter, I should scarce have slept for joy for many a night if I had found three thousand willing to believe my testimony, and willing to be baptised into Christ! And Paul—oh, methinks, with all his sorrows, he must have been a very happy man—must have been struck with wonder to see that though he went into idolatrous lands to tell this new, and strange, and incredible story, yet in every place there were found men or women who received it joyfully.

Mark well that the church is bound to maintain this mystery, that it is by believing in Christ that the efficacy of his sacrifice comes to men. The mystery is not that Christ is served in the world, that is not put here; not that Christ is worshipped in the world, that is not the first point—those things will be sure to follow: but the vital mystery is that Christ is "believed on in the world," that is to say, trusted as the Saviour. Men leave all other trusts, and trust in him; they give up their self-righteousness, they leave their vaunted sacraments, they forsake all ways and modes of self-salvation, and come and trust in Christ,—this is the great mystery. "Well," says one, "I do not see that there is a mystery in it." Have you ever believed in Jesus yourself, beloved friend? If you have, you will say "this is the finger of God." Belief in Jesus is as great a work of divine power as the making of this globe. One of the visitors to this place lately said, "I am willing to be a believer, if the preacher can persuade me." Very likely, but no preacher can create true faith—it needs a mightier power than the preacher's, even the power of the Holy Ghost. God gives to his elect the blessing of faith, and others wilfully remain in unbelief. Faith, simple as it is, is supernatural, divine, and not to be attained by human aid, nor human eloquence; they who have it know that it is a blessed mystery, this believing on Jesus Christ in the world.

Have you this faith? Do you believe in Jesus? Everything else in my text leads up to this. If he be manifest in the flesh what is that unless I believe in him? What if he be justified in the Spirit. What is that unless faith in him justifies me? What if he be seen of angels, how does that help me unless I see him too? And even if he be preached among the Gentiles, that does but involve greater guilt upon my soul if, after hearing, I have not believed in him? O dear hearers, I may not long speak to you, and every time that I am kept away from addressing you I feel a deep anxiety that by some means my preaching may be made effectual to your salvation. Many of you have believed in my Lord—this is my comfort; but, on the other hand, how many there are who still hear, and hear, and hear, and that is all. How long halt ye? How long cause ye us to labour for nought? No one is so worth trusting as the Saviour is, and nothing is so true as that he came to save sinners.

VI. The last point of the church's witness is that Jesus was "RECEIVED UP INTO GLORY." Only this word about it: he was so received because his work is finished. He would never have gone into his glory if he had not finished all his toil. He would have accepted no reward had he not fully earned it. My soul, believe thou that Christ is received up into glory; that will let thee know that thou art resting in a finished work, an atonement which has put away all sin, a satisfaction which has made all believers accepted in the Beloved. He has gone into glory, thus he is personally rewarded; and moreover, he has thus representatively taken possession of all that he has purchased. Is Christ in glory? then the believer is in glory, not literally but in his covenant Head. What Christ takes possession of he claims in our name: "I go to prepare a place for you." O ye who sorrow over the present, rejoice also; for even now at this moment heaven is yours,—your Jesus has taken possession in your name.

And oh, it is joyous to know that our great Lord is eternally exalted! If he were not exalted what comfort could we have? He is received up into glory! Men say he is not God—they cannot hurt him, for he is received up into glory! They revile his gospel—they cannot dim the lustre of his crown, he is received up into glory! They would fain slay his people if they could, but *he* is received up into glory! They struggle and they strive against his cause, and would fain overthrow it; but O, what matters it, he is everlastingly exalted, and he will shortly come—that same Jesus who was received into glory shall so come, in like manner as he was seen to go up into heaven. Here are great wells of comfort. He has to his glory gone, and has taken to himself his great power; but every hour is bringing nearer the time when he shall lay bare his sword in the midst of his foes, and shall unveil his face in the midst of his friends. Let us rejoice in him this day, and go our way to bear, with all the church of the living God, the six-fold testimony of our text concerning our precious Saviour. Amen.

PORTION OF SCRIPTURE READ BEFORE SERMON.—Luke ii. 1—32.

Metropolitan Tabernacle Pulpit.

THE MAN CHRIST JESUS.

A Sermon

Delivered on Lord's-day Morning, April 12th, 1885, by

C. H. SPURGEON,

AT THE METROPOLITAN TABERNACLE, NEWINGTON.

"Now consider how great this man *was*."—Hebrews vii. 4.

Consider how great Melchizedek was. There is something majestic about every movement of that dimly-revealed figure. His one and only appearance is thus fitly described in the Book of Genesis,—" And Melchizedek king of Salem brought forth bread and wine: and he was the priest of the most high God. And he blessed him, and said, Blessed be Abram of the most high God, possessor of heaven and earth: and blessed be the most high God, which hath delivered thine enemies into thy hand. And he gave him tithes of all." We see but little of him, yet we see nothing little in him. He is here and gone, as far as the historic page is concerned, yet is he "a priest for ever," and "it is witnessed that he liveth." Everything about him is on a scale majestic and sublime.

"Consider how great this man was" in the combination of his offices. He was duly appointed both priest and king: king of righteousness and peace, and at the same time priest of the Most High God. It may be said of him that he sat as a priest upon his throne. He exercised the double office to the great blessedness of those who were with him; for his one act towards Abraham would seem to be typical of his whole life; he blessed him in the name of the Most High God. "Consider how great this man was," that he not only ruled his people with righteousness and brought them peace, but he was their representative towards God and God's representative to them; and in each character distributed divine blessings.

"Consider how great this man was" in the power of his benedictions. Abraham had already been greatly blessed, so much so that he is described as "he that received the promises." Yet a receiver of promises so great, a man with whom God had entered into solemn covenant, was yet blessed by Melchizedek, "and without all contradiction the less is blessed of the better." This great man yet further blessed the blessed Abraham, and the father of the faithful was glad to receive benediction at his hands. No small man this: no priest of second

No. 1,835.

rank; but one who overtops the sons of men by more than head and shoulders, and acts a superior's part among the greatest of them.

"Consider how great this man was" in his supremacy over all around him. He met Abraham when he was returning as a conqueror from the overthrow of the robber kings; and the victorious patriarch bowed before him and gave him tithes of the best of the spoil. Without a moment's hesitation the man of God recognized the priest of God, and paid to him the tribute of a subject to the officer of a great king. In Abraham's bowing all the line of Aaronic priesthood did homage unto Melchizedek; for as the apostle saith, "Levi also, who receiveth tithes, paid tithes in Abraham, for he was yet in the loins of his father when Melchizedek met him." So that all kings in Abraham, and all priests in Abraham, did homage unto this man, who, as king and priest, was owned to be supreme. "Consider how great this man was." When Paul had once proved that Melchizedek was greater than Abraham, he felt that he had clearly proved him to be greater than all others, at least to the Hebrews; for the seed of Abraham can recognize none greater than Abraham; and since Abraham by paying tithes acknowledges his subordination to Melchizedek, it is clear that the priest of the Most High God was the greatest of men.

"Consider how great this man was" as to the singularity of his person, "without father, without mother, without descent": that is to say, we know nothing as to his birth, his origin, or his history. Even this explanation hardly answers to the words, especially when it is added, "Having neither beginning of days, nor end of life." So mysterious is Melchizedek that many deeply-taught expositors think that he was veritably an appearance of our Lord Jesus Christ. They are inclined to believe that he was not a king of some city in Canaan, as the most of us suppose, but that he was a manifestation of the Son of God, such as were the angels that appeared to Abraham on the plains of Mamre, and that divine being who appeared to Joshua by Jericho, and to the three holy ones in the furnace. At any rate, you may well "consider how great this man was" when you observe how veiled in cloud is everything about his coming and going—veiled because intended to impress us with the depth of the sacred meanings which were shadowed forth in him. How much more shall this be said of him of whom we ask—

"Thy generation who can tell,
Or count the number of thy years?"

"Consider how great this man was" in the speciality of his office. He had no predecessor in his priesthood, and he had no successor. He was not one who took a holy office and then laid it down; but as far as the historic page of Scripture is concerned we have no note of his quitting this mortal scene; he disappears, but we read nothing of his death any more than of his birth. His office was perpetual, and passed not from sire to son; for he was the type of One "who is made not after the law of a carnal commandment, but after the power of an endless life."

"Consider how great this man was" in his being altogether unique. There is another "after the order of Melchizedek," the glorious Antitype in whom Melchizedek himself is absorbed; but apart from him Melchizedek is unique. Who can equal this strange, mysterious priest, prophet, king, sent of the Most High God to bless the father of the faithful? He is altogether alone: he receives no commission from the hands of men, nor from God by men; and he does not transmit to a successor what he had not received from a predecessor. Melchizedek stands alone: one mighty crag, rising out of the plain; a lone Alp, whose brow is swathed in cloud sublime. "Consider how great this man was;" but think not to measure that greatness.

I shall leave you to that consideration; for my business this morning is not with Melchizedek, but with a greater than he. I shall take my text in its connection, but lift it up to a higher application. Beloved friends, if Melchizedek was so great, how much greater is that man whom Melchizedek represents! If the type is so wonderful what must the Antitype be! I invite you to consider "how great" is he of whom it is written, "The Lord sware and will not repent, Thou art a priest for ever after the order of Melchizedek." I will not say "Consider how great this man *was*," for there is no verb: the "was" is inserted in italics by the translators. We are to consider "how great this man." Say "was" if you will, but read also "*is*," and "*shall be*." Consider how great this man was and is, and is to be, even the Man Christ Jesus.

And first, this morning, let me *exhort you to consider* how great this man is: then let me *assist you to consider* how great this man is: and then *let us practically improve our consideration* of how great this man is, trying to turn it to holy account as the Holy Ghost may enable us.

I. First, then, LET ME EXHORT YOU TO CONSIDER HOW GREAT THIS MAN, THE LORD JESUS CHRIST IS.

This subject *claims* your consideration. I do not think it should be a matter of option with you whether you will now consider the greatness of your Lord or not; it is his due and right that you should consider his greatness. For he of whom we speak,—"this man," is one well known among us. If you be true to your profession he is one most dear to you, to whom you owe all things, aye, owe your very selves. He is one between whom and you there is a troth plighted: you are espoused unto him, your hearts are his, even as his heart is yours. If *you* do not consider him, who will? He has loved you, and given himself for you. Strangers may listen to our teaching at this time, and in vain we may cry,

"Is it nothing to you, all ye that pass by?
Is it nothing to you that Jesus should die?"

But you are no stranger, you are not even a guest in his house, but you are a child living at home with him. He is your brother, and much more; for he is bone of your bone, and flesh of your flesh. All your interests are wrapped up in him. You are one with him: by an endless union, one. I claim, therefore, and I am sure you assent at once to the claim, that you should often consider your Lord, and the greatness of his nature, person, office, and work. His greatness should be your perpetual theme. I would urge that all other thoughts should now be banished, for this is your Lord's own day, and therefore to him it should be dedicated with glad consent. If you are "in the Spirit on the Lord's day," you will, like John in Patmos, give all your thoughts to the Son of Man who walketh among the golden candlesticks. I urge it on you that you do now consider with your whole heart and mind, "how great this man is." Do you not consent to the claim?

Certainly the subject *needs* consideration; for, dear friends, we shall never gain an idea of how great he is unless we do consider, and consider much. Here is a great deep, and it cannot be fathomed by the thoughtless. You think you know Christ, and, blessed be his name, you do know him in a sense; but do you know the thousandth part of him? When the apostle Paul had known Christ for many years he wrote to the Philippians, and he then expressed himself as desiring to know Christ; for though he knew him to his own personal salvation, yet he felt that he did not know him to the full. He owned that he knew the love of Christ, but he added, "it passeth knowledge." Well may each of us who has been for years a student at the Master's feet exclaim, "I find myself a learner yet." I suppose the saints who have been in heaven now for thousands of years, and have been evermore adoring him, are still students of him. This is the philosophy which the most cultured mind shall never fully compass,—"God manifest in the flesh." "Consider how great this man is!" This is a matter worthy of continual research, and calling for profound thought. You must weigh this subject, and turn it over, and meditate upon it the livelong day. You must let it lie both day and night upon your hearts as a bundle of camphire, perfuming the bosom in which it lies. You must look, and look, and look, and look again: still looking unto Jesus. The angels standing on the golden mercy-seat have ever their eyes bent downward, desiring to look within; and that must be your posture. Oh, you servants of the Lord, by looking to Jesus you began to live, by looking to him you shall continue to live, and your life shall find strength and growth. This sacred subject shall ever need more and more consideration from you. Oh the depths of the love, and wisdom, and glory of God in the person of Jesus Christ!

I go a little further, and say that not only does my subject claim your consideration and need your consideration, but it solemnly *commands* it. The text is not a mere piece of advice; it is by inspiration that the apostle bids you to-day out of this sacred page, "Consider how great this man was." He charges you to think of Melchizedek, but much more would he have you remember Melchizedek's Antitype. Oh, do not, my brethren, do not need to be pressed to this divine study: love it, never cease from it. Count every minute wasted in which you are not learning more about Jesus. Reckon all other knowledge to be as mere draff and dogs' meat as compared with the knowledge of Christ crucified. In these days of science, falsely so called, determine with the apostle to know nothing among men save Jesus Christ and him crucified. It is imperative upon you that you love the Lord your God with all your heart, and all your soul, and all your mind; and that God in Christ Jesus should call into exercise every faculty of your inner man, while, with blended intellect and emotion, you consider how great he was.

Follow out this meditation, I pray you, because there is an exceeding great *reward* for any man who will "consider how great this man was." I find for myself that the only possibility of my living is living in Christ and unto Christ. Look you about and try to live by the wisdom of man. Unstable as water and fickle as the wind is the product of human wisdom. The history of philosophy, from the beginning until now, is the history of fools; and never was folly so self-evident as in the philosophy which is now dominant. I believe that within a century it will be found impossible to make men believe that educated men were ever so degraded as to accept the philosophy of the present hour; it will seem to be so altogether absurd and contrary to all reason and common sense, that it will be rejected with scorn as a popular delusion of a dark age. Even to-day this generation is kicking about like footballs the philosophies of preceding ages, and we may rest assured that future generations will do the same with the dotings of to-day. I find, therefore, that I must come back to the revelation of God. Here is a rock beneath my feet—"God was in Christ, reconciling the world unto himself, not imputing their trespasses unto them." Certain great facts concerning God and his Christ have been made known to us by the Holy Ghost, and these are infallibly sure. God's revelation is true, whatever man's dreams may be. On the basis of revelation there is foothold. A personal knowledge of Christ revealed by the Spirit is also a sure matter. I get to Jesus, I speak to him, and meditate upon him, and he rises before me greater than ever, till in his presence all the learning of men condenses into folly. He is "God only wise." Ah, then I live when he is all in all! My heart is glad and my glory rejoiceth when I forget all else save Christ Jesus my Lord. Therefore, brethren, I say that you shall find a great reward in full often coming near to your Lord, and considering again and again how great he is.

Consider his greatness, and I again remind you that the blessing comes only by consideration. I may speak to you this morning about the greatness of my Master, but I shall not succeed in fully declaring it. I am never more vexed with myself than when I have done my very best to extol his dear name! What is it but holding a candle to the sun? What are my lispings compared with the loud acclamations which such an one as he is might well expect from those who love him? You must carefully consider, or you will miss the blessing. It will not be enough for you to hear, or read; you must do your own thinking, and consider your Lord for yourselves. You may even read the Bible itself without profit, if you do not *consider* as well as read. The wine is not made by gathering the clusters, but by treading the grapes in the wine-vat: under pressure the red juice leaps forth. Not the truth as you read it, but the truth as you meditate upon it, will be a blessing to you. "Read, mark, learn, and inwardly digest." "Consider how great this man was." Shut yourselves up with Jesus, if you would know him. "Come, my people, enter thou into thy chambers, and shut thy doors about thee: hide thyself as it were for a little moment, until the indignation be overpast." In Christ there is shelter, and the more you consider him the greater your peace will be. Come and lay your finger into the prints of the nails, and thrust your hand into his side. Commune with the personal Christ, who ever liveth; and evermore "consider how great this man was."

Thus have I exhorted you to this duty; now let me try to help you in it. But what help will mine be unless the Divine Spirit be with me, that the word spoken may be with power?

II. LET ME NEXT ASSIST YOU TO CONSIDER HOW GREAT THIS MAN WAS.

And first, lest the very use of the expression, "this man," should leave anybody for a moment in doubt as to our faith in his Godhead, I bid you consider how great this man was *in his relationship to God*. For though he was man, he was not merely man. He was assuredly and truly man in all respects, "man of the substance of his mother," bone of our bone and flesh of our flesh; and yet he was indeed and of a truth very God. Do not think of him as a divine man, or as a human God; he was neither the one nor the other. He was perfectly man, yet he was infinitely God. Think, then, into what a position of honour and dignity his manhood was uplifted by union with the Godhead in one person. Born, growing, gathering strength, coming to manhood, suffering, dying, in all this he was man; yet he was never at any time less divine. Our Lord's humanity is not to be thought of apart from his deity, for he is one and indivisible. I have sometimes heard objections made against certain expressions in Dr. Watts's hymns in which our Lord is spoken of as the God that bled and died, and so forth. I fear that the objection is frequently aimed less at the poet than at the truth of the deity of our Lord: the objector figures as a critic because he dares not avow himself a heretic. Take note that in the Scriptures you shall find frequent confusions of speech upon the person of our Lord, intentionally made, in order to show that although the natures were distinct, yet they were indissolubly united in the one person of Jesus. Of his one person might popularly be predicated that which in strict accuracy could only be true of his humanity, or only of his deity. To the one person of our Lord will be found to be ascribed what he did both as God and as man, and it is not needful for us to be wise or accurate above what is written by the Spirit of God. It is possible to be so true to the letter as to be false to the spirit. Cavillers have no monopoly of wisdom. My Lord Jesus is to me no less a man because he is God. Oh, how my heart loves him! He is to me fairest of the sons of men, chief among ten thousand, and altogether lovely. But he is to me because of his manhood none the less, but all the more, "God over all, blessed for ever." Into the dust my spirit bows before his majesty, and my soul adores him. I ask you, therefore, to consider the greatness of his manhood because it never was apart from his Godhead, and cannot be thought of except in connection therewith. "The word was made flesh, and dwelt among us, and we beheld his glory, the glory as of the only begotten of the Father, full of grace and truth." Inconceivable is the greatness of the man who is thus one with God.

You, my brethren, are not in doubt upon this vital matter; let me, therefore, ask you to consider "how great this man was" as to *his relationship to men*. Christ Jesus is the second man, the Lord from heaven. Adam, our first father, was the head of the race, and all men were in him as their representative: in him they stood in the garden; in him, alas, they fell when he broke the divine command, and the Lord took up the quarrel of his covenant, and cast him out of Paradise. "Oh, what a fall was there, my brethren: then you and I and all of us fell down." We inherit because of Adam's failure a nature whose tendencies are towards evil. Adam was a very great personage in relation to the race : he was the summary of all the generations, the fountain of the stream of humanity. To him we might apply the language of the prophet, "Thou hast been in Eden, the garden of God. . . . . Thou wast perfect in thy ways from the day that thou wast created, till iniquity was found in thee." As Adam came forth from God, he was as a covering cherub, under whose wings the race nestled down. But now comes in the Lord Jesus Christ as the greater man, the representative man, in whom none are made to fall, but multitudes arise. In this man the Lord is again well pleased with men. Time was when God looked on rebellious man, and it repented him that he had made him ; but now that he turns his eye to this perfect man he feels no such repentance ; but, on the contrary, we read that "God was in Christ reconciling the world unto himself." For the sake of the man Christ Jesus he deals with the innumerable race of sinners in a way of long-suffering and pity, and does not destroy them. Long ago had the flood-gates been pulled up again, and man been swept away by a deluge, not of water but of fire, if it had not been that the long-suffering Lord looks on the Well-Beloved Christ, and therefore spares mankind. Yea, more ; for his sake he sends the gospel of peace to men, and in the name of Jesus glad tidings are sent to every creature. It has sometimes happened that the illustrious deed of one man has served to elevate a class, or even a nation into honour. A grand, heroic deed has welded you not only to that one person but to all his kith and kin. Consider, then, how great this man was, that the divine mind which cannot look upon sin without indignation, nevertheless was so charmed to look upon the person and character of this glorious Man, that an amnesty was proclaimed to the race, and a message was sent to the sons of men bidding them repent and turn to him and live. "Consider," then, "how great this man was."

Come a little closer, and reach forward to that which will delight your hearts far more ; consider *the relationship of Christ to his own people.* Now we get on sure ground, and feel a rock beneath our feet. Long before the heavens and the earth were made, God with prescient eye beheld the person of his Son as God in human nature, and he saw all his elect lying in him. The church is his body, "the fulness of him that filleth all in all." God the Father saw in the divine decree the mystical Christ, and he was well pleased with all his redeemed for Christ Jesus' sake. How wondrous was that transaction when in the council-chamber of eternity the covenant was made, and the Lord Jesus Christ became the surety of that covenant. He entered into covenant with the eternal God on the behalf of his chosen that he would make atonement for their sin, and would perfect the righteousness which should cover everyone of them, and make them to be accepted in the Beloved. No actual sacrifice was offered for thousands of years ; but see "how great this man was," since on the strength of his bare promise the Lord continued to save men for thousands of years, admitting them to his infinite glory before the Mediator had appeared, or the Redeemer had put a hand to the work. Consider that you and I, and all of us who are in Christ, are this day beloved for his sake, accepted for his sake, justified for his sake. Still doth God embrace us in the arms of almighty love for his sake ; for his sake heaven is being prepared for us ; for his sake the treasures of the infinite are given to us; because we are the covenanted ones for whom he pledged his troth, and for whom in the fulness of time he poured out his heart's blood, that he might redeem us unto God. "Consider how great this man was." He is so great that all the saints are blessed in him. He is so great that we, as many as have believed, dwell evermore in the clefts of this great Rock, and find in him our castle and high tower. "For ye are dead, and your life is hid with Christ in God. When Christ, who is our life, shall appear, then shall ye also appear with him in glory." "Consider how great this man was."

Let me help you a little further, dear friends, to "consider how great this man was," by reminding you of *the surroundings of his first advent*. Thousands of years before his birth holy men had been speaking of him. Prophets and seers all pointed to him as The Coming One. "How great this man was," since the wisest and best of mankind all looked forward to his day with gladness. Think of that wonderful system of types, and emblems, and symbols which God ordained by his servant Moses; for the whole of this system was meant to set forth the Messiah, who would yet appear in the fulness of time. To him witnessed each bleeding sacrifice, each censer of sweet incense, each golden vessel, each curtain and wall of tabernacle or temple: all spoke concerning him. Ay, and more than that, all the histories of all the empires were all but concentric rings of which he was the centre; for the Lord Jesus is the centre of history, the sum total of all God's doings and manifestations among the sons of men. That was an august Person towards whom all the past had been labouring, and for whom all the present was agonizing. "How great this man was," that when he came the saints were watching for him: Simeon and Anna could not depart till he appeared. Angels stood on tip-toe ready to descend and sing, "Glory to God in the highest, and on earth peace, good will toward men." Humble shepherds, as they watched their flocks, did but wait for the signal to hasten to adore him; and wise men from the east forgot the fatigues of a long journey that they might lay their gold and incense at his feet. "How great this man was," when, being born and laid in a manger, the whole earth was moved by his appearing.

Consider, too, "how great this man was," not only as to the outward circumstances of his coming, but *as to the secret mystery of his birth*. For this man was not "born in sin," as we are; neither was he "shapen in iniquity." This is a thing to be thought of and considered in our privacy, but it cannot be omitted here. Thus said the angel to the blessed Virgin, "The Holy Ghost shall come upon thee, and the power of the Highest shall overshadow thee: therefore also that holy thing which shall be born of thee shall be called the Son of God." "Conceived by the Holy Ghost, born of the Virgin Mary," he was truly a man, but not fallen man. The method by which the pure human nature of the man Christ Jesus was produced is a great mystery, but it serves to make us see "how great this man was." I will say no more than this, that we have here the fulfilment of the promise, "Behold, a virgin shall conceive, and bear a son, and shall call his name Immanuel." Think of that word of old: "When he bringeth in the firstbegotten into the world, he saith, And let all the angels of God worship him." Let us, therefore worship. Reverently forbearing all idle intrusion into the deep things of God, let us go to Bethlehem, and "consider how great this man was."

Now, let us look at *his life*. After he emerged from the obscurity of his childhood, what a life was that of our Lord! His greatest adversaries, unless they have been mad, have never dared to speak against his character. If the Christian religion were supposed to be an invention, the existence of the narrative of the life of Jesus would be more wonderful than the facts themselves. The conception of a perfect character requires a perfect mind, and a perfect mind would never have prepared a fiction and imposed it upon men as a veritable history. If the life of Jesus be a fable, then a perfect being has deceived us; and this it is not possible for us to imagine. The life of Jesus Christ is great throughout. It is so tender and so gentle that it is never little and mean: it is so unselfish that it never ceases to be majestic; it is so condescending that it is pre-eminently sublime. Above all, it is full of truth, transparent, artless, natural. No one ever thought of Jesus as acting a part yet; he is reality itself. He is so simple, so unaffected, so truly "the holy child Jesus," that in this he is great above all. Never was a man so wholly seen as the Christ; and yet never was man so little understood. You have read memoirs of departed worthies, and you have felt, "The biographer did well to say no more upon this point;" but you never felt that anything need be reserved as to the character of Jesus. If his chroniclers had kept on writing till the world itself had been made a library of the lives of Christ they would never have recorded an unworthy act or a regrettable word. It is not only that his pursuits were majestic, for he came to save men; that his motives were divine, for he revealed the Father; but it is *himself* that is so great—I mean his soul, his spirit, the man himself. Look at Alexander, he is a great conqueror, but what a pitiful creature he appears when the drunkard's bowl has maddened him. What a poor thing is Napoleon as seen in privacy! In his captivity he was as petulant as a spoiled child. Consider the Lord Jesus, and it does not matter where you view him: in the wilderness he is grandly victorious over temptation, in the crowd he is greatly wise in answering those who would entrap him. Behold him in his agony in the Garden; was there ever such an Agoniser? Behold him as the crucified; did ever cross hold such a sufferer? When Jesus is least he is greatest, and when he is in the direst darkness his brightness is best revealed. In death he destroys death; in the grave he bursts the sepulchre. "Consider how great this man was": the field of his life is ample; do not be slow to investigate it.

Beloved, I cannot speak as I would of him. The blaze of this Sun blinds me! Yet consider how great this man was *in his death;* for then he appeared as the great Sin-offering, putting away the sin of his people. The Lord had made to meet in him the iniquity of us all. What a weight was on him, yet he sustained it! The wrath of God on account of sin fell upon him who had never sinned, and he bore it all. A penalty which must have made a hell for us for ever was exacted of our Lord upon the cross, and he discharged it. He drank the whole of our bitter cup. He bore in himself all that was necessary to vindicate the divine justice until he could truly say, "It is finished." "Lama Sabachthani" is the most terrible word that ever came from human lips; and therefore "It is finished" is the greatest utterance that tongue ever gave forth. The work was colossal; what if I say it was infinite; and therefore our Lord Jesus when he cried "It is finished," had reached the summit of greatness. "Consider how great this man was."

Now, beloved, consider for a minute "how great this man was" when *he rose again;* for he could not be holden with the bonds of death, and his body could not see corruption. It was a great thing in itself for Christ to rise, but what I want you to remember is, that we all rose in him. "As in Adam all die, even so in Christ shall all be made alive"; and especially his covenanted people were raised up together with him. There was for his redeemed a death in his death and a rising again in his rising again; for we have been made partakers of his resurrection, and we live in newness of life by his rising from the dead. This is his cry as he rises from the tomb, "Because I live ye shall live also." "Consider how great this man was" whose life imparts life to all who are in him.

But *he has gone up on high,* and has led captivity captive. Think of the gifts which were showered down from heaven in consequence of this man's ascent into the highest. For the Holy Spirit descended never to return till the close of this dispensation, and now all the gifts that rest in the church of God, and all the works of regeneration, illumination, sanctification, and the like, which are wrought by the blessed Paraclete, are the effects of the entrance of this man into the secret place of the tabernacles of the Most High. Every soul regenerated, every heart comforted, every mind quickened, every eye illuminated, every creature spiritually blessed, reflects glory upon this man. How great is he!

Beloved, I would we had time this morning to introduce you to this man as he now sits *at the right hand of God,* even the Father. There is no need for me to depict him; if there were it were impossible to me. What said the man who loved him best, and knew him best? "When I saw him I fell at his feet as dead." "Consider how great this man is" now, when every angel pays him homage, and at the name of Jesus every knee doth bow, of things in heaven; as by-and-by every knee shall bow of things on earth, and things that are under the earth, for Jesus Christ is Lord to the glory of God the Father. "Consider how great this man is," and then remember that he shall shortly come to be our Judge! Possibly, while I am yet speaking to you, he may appear; no man knoweth the day nor the hour; but "how great this man is" will be clearly seen when, in flaming fire, he shall take vengeance upon those that will not obey him. How "great" will he be when in the manifestation of his glory all believers shall be glorified. I think I hear, even now, sounding out of my theme, shouts of "hallelujah, hallelujah," from assembled worlds. Yes, the music peals forth loud and long, "King of kings, and Lord of lords. HALLELUJAH. For he shall reign for ever and ever. HALLELUJAH!" Break forth with your loud hosannas, oh, ye waiting spirits of believing men, for the time is at hand when he shall be admired in all them that believe! Consider how great this man is. I have but reached the fringe of my subject. We see but the skirts of our Lord's garments; his actual glory is unspeakable, unsearchable. Oh, the depths! Oh, the depths!

III. This in a few words is THE PRACTICAL IMPROVEMENT of the whole subject, with which we must wind up. Consider how great this man was, and as you consider, believe in his infinite power to bless men. He is full of blessing as the sun is full of light, that he may shine upon his needy creatures. Christ is full of blessing that he may bless poor, needy, empty sinners. Dost thou say, poor sinner, "I am so great a sinner that he cannot save me"? Consider what this man did when he was here on earth; he went about and laid his hands on the diseased, and they were cured; he looked at devils, and they fled; he spoke to fevers and they disappeared. And he in heaven is, and if I may so say, greater than when he was here below, for here on earth he was veiled in humiliation, but now he is enthroned in infinite majesty, "able to save to the uttermost them that come unto God by him, seeing he ever liveth to make intercession for them." Believe in the infinite blessedness treasured up in Christ for every believing soul, and come and take your share of it this morning. All that you want, and all that you wish—come and receive freely, for he doth graciously dispense it, and it is a part of his glory that he delights to enrich the children of men. Let faith in Jesus be one lesson—may God write it on each heart.

And then let us ascribe to our Lord Jesus Christ all the honour that our thoughts can compass. Let us give to him this day our very selves over again. Consider how great this man was, and go away feeling how greatly you are indebted to him, what great things you ought to do for him, and how little your greatest thing is when you have done it as compared with the greatness of his deservings.

> "Let him be crowned with majesty
> That bowed his head to death;
> And be his honour sounded high
> By all things that have breath."

Do not you feel that question pressing upon your heart?

> "Oh what shall I do
> My Saviour to praise!"

Do something; and having done it do more, and yet more. Give up your whole being to the showing forth of how great this Man is!

Once more, considering how great this Man is, do not be afraid, nor troubled, nor tumbled up and down in your thoughts about anything that is happening, or is yet to happen. "Consider how great this man was." Our wise men are going to do away with the old faith; modern culture means to stamp out old-fashioned orthodoxy. Christianity itself is getting to be effete, and something better is to supersede it. Listen! "Why do the heathen rage, and the people imagine a vain thing? The kings of the earth set themselves, and the rulers take counsel together, against the Lord, and against his anointed. He that sitteth in the heaven shall laugh : the Lord shall have them in derision. Yet have I set my king upon my holy hill of Zion." One said to me the other day, "The current of thought does not seem to run in the direction of evangelical religion." Well, I said I should not believe in evangelical religion an atom the more if the current of thought did run that way. We do not believe according to the counting of heads. The currents of men's thoughts are so uncertain that you can better tell the flight of birds, or the changing of English weather. The gospel is perhaps the surer to be true because there are so few who believe it. It is according to our expectation that God's revealed truth should be abhorred and hated by the wise men of every generation. I shall not believe the gospel any the less if I am left alone, nor shall I believe it any the more if the whole world shall cry it up. Let God be true and every man a liar. He whose faith stands upon the concensus of popular opinion has placed his feet upon the sand, but he who has read his Bible and has been taught of the Spirit of God what truth is, will hold to it come what may. When you consider how great this man is, it seems to me that to be a fool for his sake is the highest wisdom, and that to cling to what he says is the best philosophy, and to believe him, and none beside is not alone a duty but a necessity of every Christian spirit. Be of good cheer, dear friends! Let no man's heart fail him because of modern doubt. Let no man be troubled because of the fierceness of the fight. I can hear already the sounding of the trumpets of the Lord's coming. He is not far away; even if thousands of years intervene before his feet shall touch the Mount of Olivet the victory will never be doubtful. All is done that is required for winning the battle, his blood has been shed, his life has been accepted as a ransom. The eternal decree has settled it, nothing can change it! "He shall see of the travail of his soul, and shall be satisfied." Amen.

PORTIONS OF SCRIPTURE READ BEFORE SERMON—Psalm ii. 110; Hebrews vii. 1—10, 17, 21, 22.

HYMNS FROM "OUR OWN HYMN BOOK"—72, 392, 60.

Metropolitan Tabernacle Pulpit.

FOUND BY JESUS, AND FINDING JESUS.

A Sermon

INTENDED FOR READING ON LORD'S-DAY, AUGUST 26TH, 1894,

DELIVERED BY

C. H. SPURGEON,

AT THE METROPOLITAN TABERNACLE, NEWINGTON,

On Lord's-day Evening, June 24th, 1888.

"The day following Jesus would go forth into Galilee, and findeth Philip, and saith unto him, Follow me. Now Philip was of Bethsaida, the city of Andrew and Peter. Philip findeth Nathanael, and saith unto him, We have found him, of whom Moses in the law, and the prophets, did write, Jesus of Nazareth, the son of Joseph."—John i. 43—45.

For a soul to come to Jesus, is the grandest event in its history. It is spiritually dead till that day; but it then begins to live, and a saved man may reckon his age from the time in which he first knew the Lord. That day of first knowing Christ is important in the highest degree, because it affects all the man's past career; it sheds another light on all the years that have gone by. If he has lived in sin, as no doubt he has, the transaction of that day blots out all the sin. The day in which a man comes to Christ, that very day his transgressions and iniquities are blotted out, even as the thick clouds are driven from the sky when God's strong wind chases them away. Is not that a grand day in which our sins are cast into the depths of the sea so that henceforth it can be said of them, "They may be sought for, but they shall not be found; yea, they shall not be, saith the Lord"? I say that the day in which a soul comes into contact with Christ is the greatest day of its history, because all the past is changed by it; and as for the present, what a different life does a man begin to live on the day in which he finds the Lord! He commences to live in the light instead of being dead in the darkness; he begins to enjoy the privileges of liberty, instead of suffering the horrors of slavery; he is started on the way to heaven, instead of continuing on the road to hell. He is such a new creature that he cannot tell how changed he is. One said to me, "Sir, the change in me is of this kind; either the whole world is altered, or else I am." So is it when we are brought to know Christ; it is a real, total, radical change. With many, it is a most joyous alteration; they feel like the man who had been lame, and who,

No. 2,375.

when Peter spoke to him in the name of Jesus, and lifted him up, so that his feet and ankle bones received strength, was not satisfied with walking, for we read, "He leaping up stood, and walked, and entered with them into the temple, walking, and leaping, and praising God." He was walking, and leaping, and praising God; do you wonder at it? If you had lost the use of your legs for a while, you would feel like leaping and praising God when you had them all right again; and thus is it with a soul when it first finds the Saviour. Oh! happy, happy day, when the miraculous hand of Christ takes away the infirmities of the soul, and makes the lame man to leap as a hart, and causes the tongue of the dumb to sing!

The day in which a man comes to Christ is also a wonderful day in its effect upon all his future. It is as when the helm of a ship is put right about; the man now sails in a totally different direction. His future will never be what his past was. There may be faults; there may be infirmities and shortcomings; but there will never be the old love of sin any more. "Sin shall not have dominion over you." This is God's own promise to us, given through his servant Paul. When Christ comes to our soul, he so breaks the neck of sin, that though it lives a struggling, dying life, and often makes a deal of howling in the heart, yet it is doomed to die. The cross of Christ has broken its back, and broken its neck, too, and die it must. Henceforth the man is bound for holiness, and bound for heaven.

Now, dear friends, have any of you come to Christ? I know that you have, the great mass of you, and I bless God, and so do you, that it is so with you; but if there are any of you who have never come to the Saviour, I wish that this might be the night when you should find him. I am but a poor lame preacher; you are not often troubled with the sight of one sitting down and preaching; yet I think that if I had lost my legs, and had always to lie on my back, I would like even then to preach Christ crucified, and to—

"Tell to sinners round,
What a dear Saviour I have found."

I do pray that some of you to-night, made to think all the more by the infirmity of the preacher, may be led to seek and to find the Saviour, and then it shall be a happy day indeed for you, as it has been for so many more.

I am going to talk to you about Philip's conversion, and first, I ask you to notice, in our text, *the convert's description of it:* "Philip findeth Nathanael, and saith unto him, We have found him, of whom Moses in the law, and the prophets, did write, Jesus of Nazareth, the son of Joseph." That is Philip's description of it: "We have found Jesus." It was a true description, but it was not all the truth; so, in the second place, we will notice *the Holy Spirit's description of it:* "The day following Jesus would go forth into Galilee, and findeth Philip." Philip's account of the incident is that he found Christ; but the Holy Spirt's record of it is that Christ found Philip. They are both true, however; although the latter is the fuller. We will talk a little about both descriptions of Philip's conversion.

I. First then, THE CONVERT'S DESCRIPTION OF HIS COMING TO CHRIST is given in these words, "We have found . . . Jesus," and what he says is perfectly true.

If any one of you is saved, it will be by finding Christ, by your personally making a discovery of him, as that man did who found the treasure that was hid in the field. There must be a search after Christ; but if there be a search after him, we may be certain of this one thing, that there will first be a consciousness of needing him.

Philip had sought Christ, or else he would never have said that he had found him; but, before that, *Philip knew that there was need of a Messiah.* When he looked round about on the world, and on the church, he said to himself, "Oh, that the promised Messiah would come! There is great need of him. The people need him, the church needs him, the world needs him." When Philip looked into his own heart, he said, "Oh, for the coming of the Messiah! I feel that I want him; I have urgent need of him." Dear hearer, do you feel that you need a Saviour? You never will seek him until you do feel your need of him. You must recognize that there is sin in you, sin for which you cannot make atonement, sin that you cannot overcome. You must realize that you need another and a stronger arm than your own, that you need divine help, that you need One who can be your Brother, to sympathize with you, and be patient with you, and yet who can be the Mighty God to conquer all your sin for you. You do need a Saviour; that is the first thing that will prompt you to search for him.

Wanting a Messiah, *Philip read the Scriptures concerning him.* He speaks about Moses and the prophets, and of what they had written concerning the promised Deliverer. O my dear hearers, if you want to find Christ, you must search the Scriptures, for they testify of him! Oh, that you did search the Scriptures more, with the definite object of finding the Saviour! Probably, the great majority of unconverted people never read their Bibles at all; or they read only just enough to satisfy their curiosity, or their conscience. Perhaps they read the Bible as a part of literature which cannot be quite ignored; but they do not take down the Holy Book, and read it carefully and prayerfully, saying, "Oh, that I might find holiness here! Oh, that I might find Christ here!" If they did, it would not be long before they found Jesus. Well does Dr. Watts sing,—

> "Laden with guilt, and full of fears,
> I fly to thee, my Lord,
> And not a glimpse of hope appears
> But in thy written Word.
> The volume of my Father's grace
> Does all my griefs assuage;
> Here I behold my Saviour's face
> Almost in every page."

He who reads the Bible with the view of finding Christ, will not be long before some passage of Scripture will seem to leap up, to attract his attention, as though it were set on fire, and then it will speak to him of Jesus, whispering to him of the great sacrifice on Calvary, and speaking to his heart of divine love and mercy. Philip was a searcher after Christ in the place where Christ loves to be,—in the pages of Scripture,—and you must be the same if you desire to find Jesus.

But then *Philip also gave himself to prayer*. We are not told so, but we feel sure of it. He asked the Lord to reveal Christ to him, to guide him to where the Christ would be, to let him know the Christ. Oh, if you want to be saved, be much in prayer! I do not mean merely saying prayers; what is the good of that? I do not mean simply saying fine words of your own, merely for the sake of uttering them. Prayer is communing with God; it is asking the Lord for what you really feel that you need. What waggon-loads of sham prayers are shot down at God's door, as if they were so much rubbish thrown away! Let it not be so with your prayers; but speak to the Lord out of your very soul when you come to the throne of grace. I cannot give you a better prayer than the one we have been singing,—

> "Gracious Lord, incline Thine ear,
> My requests vouchsafe to hear;
> Hear my never-ceasing cry;
> Give me Christ, or else I die.
>
> "Lord, deny me what Thou wilt,
> Only ease me of my guilt;
> Suppliant at Thy feet I lie,
> Give me Christ, or else I die.
>
> "Thou dost freely save the lost!
> Only in Thy grace I trust:
> With my earnest suit comply;
> Give me Christ, or else I die.
>
> "Thou hast promised to forgive
> All who in Thy Son believe;
> Lord, I know Thou canst not lie;
> Give me Christ, or else I die."

With the open Bible before you to guide your understanding, kneel down, and say, "O God, graciously reveal Christ to me by thy Holy Spirit; bring me to know him, bring me this day to find him as my own Saviour!"

It is certain, also, that *Philip realized that he might claim the Messiah for himself.* One of the things that every man, who would find the Saviour, must do, is to make sure of his right to come and take the Saviour. The question that puzzles many is, "May I have the Saviour?" My dear friends, every sinner in the world is permitted to come and trust the Saviour, if he wills to do so. "Whosoever will, let him take the water of life freely." "But," asks some troubled soul, "will Christ have me?" That is not the question; the question is, "Will you have Christ?" He says, "Him that cometh to me I will in no wise cast out." It is you who cast out the Saviour, not the Saviour who casts you out. The bolt to the door is on the inside; it is you who have bolted it, and it is you who must undo the bolt, and invite the Saviour to enter your heart. He is willing enough to come in; wherever there is a soul that wants him, he comes at once; therefore, do not raise any quibbling questions about whether a sinner may come to Christ, or may not come. Is he not bidden to come?

We are told to preach the gospel to every creature, and he who gave us our great commission also added, "He that believeth and is baptized shall be saved; but he that believeth not shall be damned."

Philip accepted Christ as the Messiah. Do you ask, "What am I to do that I may find the Saviour?" Well, what you have to do is practically this, accept him. If you were sick, and the doctor stood before you, with the medicine ready prepared, you would not say, "What am I to do with this medicine, sir? Am I to rub my hand on the outside of the bottle?" You know very well that there are certain directions as to how much is to be taken, and how often. What you have to do with the medicine is to take it. "But I cannot make that medicine work for my restoration." Who said you could? All you have to do is to take it. It is just this that you have to do with Christ; take him, accept him, receive him. Remember the twelfth verse of this chapter out of which our text is taken: "As many as received him, to them gave he power to become the sons of God, even to them that believe on his name." That is it, you see, receive him, believe on his name. "But surely I am to do some good works." Certainly, you will do good works after you have received Christ; but for your soul's salvation, you are to do no good works, but simply to receive Christ. "Oh, but I must lead a holy life!" Yes, and you will lead a holy life after you have received Christ; but in order to the leading of a holy life you must have a new heart, and to get a new heart, you have to receive Christ. He will change you, he will renew you, he will make you a new creature in himself. What you have to do is to receive him, and to believe on his name. O my dear hearers, I do trust that I am speaking to some this evening who will understand what I am saying. I fear that I am addressing many who will not believe, though I may put the truth as plainly as it can be preached. You know that you may hold a candle right against a blind man's eyes, and yet he will not see even then. The Holy Spirit must open your eyes to see what is meant by this receiving Christ, or else you will not understand what you are to do. You are not to give anything to Christ; you are to take all from him. You are not to bring anything to Christ; you are to come to him just as you are, and he will bring to you everything that you need. Then, when you have accepted him by the simple act of faith, you will say with Philip, "We have found Jesus." That is the convert's description, and a very good one, too: "We have found Jesus."

II. But now, secondly, what is THE HOLY GHOST'S DESCRIPTION? I will read to you the very words again; here they are: "The day following Jesus would go forth into Galilee, and findeth Philip." Jesus finds Philip before Philip finds Jesus; Philip finds Jesus because Jesus has found Philip.

Now, notice, that *this is the previous work;* it came before Philip's own finding. Jesus would go forth into Galilee to find Philip. Dear friends, I recollect very well that, after I had found the Lord, I did not at first fully understand the doctrines of grace. I had heard them preached; but I had not comprehended them. I think at the time I should have been very much puzzled with the doctrine of election, if anybody had spoken to me about it; but I was sitting down, one day, gratefully reflecting on what God had done for me. I knew that my sins were pardoned, I knew that I was accepted in Christ Jesus, and I knew that I was renewed in heart, and in one moment the revelation came to me, "All this is the work of God." The instant I saw that truth, I said to myself, "Yes, that is the fact, and God be glorified for it! But why has this great work been wrought in me?" I knew that there was no merit in me before the Lord had dealt in mercy with my soul, so I said to myself, "This is the effect of sovereign distinguishing grace." Then I understood in a moment how it is that God begins with us, and that it is God's will and God's eternal purpose, which, after all, lie deeper down than our will or our purpose; and God's will and God's eternal purpose must have the glory. What a revelation it was to me! I saw the doctrines of grace immediately; and I think that anybody who has been brought to find the Saviour, and who prayerfully studies the reasons for his salvation, can see the same truth that the Lord revealed to me.

Because, first of all, you began to be thoughtful, did you not? Who made you thoughtful? You would never have found the Saviour if you had not become thoughtful instead of careless and indifferent. Who made you think of divine things? What influence was it which wrought upon you, and caused you to feel that you must think about eternity, and heaven, and hell? Surely it was God the Holy Ghost going forth, in the name of Jesus Christ, and dealing with you in mercy.

Then you had a sense of your need and of your sinfulness. There was a time when you had no such sense; then, who gave it to you? Where do you think that repentance, that sorrow for sin, that desire after Christ, came from? Did all that grow in your own fallen human nature? Ah, believe me, that dunghill never brought forth such fair flowers as these! No, it was Christ who sowed the good seed in your soul; it was he who made you feel your need of him.

Next, when you read the Bible, you understood it. You perceived that Jesus was the only Saviour of sinners, you saw his fitness to meet your case, and you understood the plan of salvation. Who made you understand it? I know that it is plain enough for a child to comprehend; but no one ever does understand spiritual things except by the operation of the Spirit of God. It was the Holy Spirit who gave you the spiritual power by which you were able to grasp the simple truth concerning the way of salvation.

Then you began to pray. I have spoken of that matter already. But who taught you to pray? You had not been accustomed to real prayer; you had often had great mouthfuls of words, that was all; but now you began to cry, "God be merciful to me, a sinner!" Oh, the groaning of your spirit, and the anguish of your heart, as you cried to God! Who gave you that anguish? Who broke you all to pieces, and made every broken bone cry out for mercy? Who, indeed, but Christ who wrought mightily in your soul by the power of the Holy Spirit?

And when you yielded yourself up to Christ, when you believed in

Jesus, and found salvation, where did that faith come from? Is it not always the work of the Spirit of God? Is not faith the gift of God, and do you not confess that it is so in your case? Once, when I was a little child, I thought I saw a needle moving across the table; and I should have been wondering who made the needle march as it did, but I was old enough to understand that somebody was moving a magnet underneath the table, and the needle was following the magnet which I could not see. Thus the Lord, with his mighty magnet of grace, is often at work upon the hearts of men, and we think that their desire after God, and their faith in Christ, are of themselves. In a sense, the desire and the faith are their own; but there is a divine force that is at work upon them, producing these results. It is Jesus finding Philip, though Philip does not know it. Philip thinks that he is finding Jesus, but behind the veil it is Jesus finding Philip. This was the previous work.

And, dear friends, *this was very delightful work for the Lord Jesus Christ.* Notice how it is put: "The day following Jesus would go forth into Galilee, and findeth Philip." O my blessed Lord, how he will go forth to find a soul! A journey is never too long for him, and he never wastes a day. "The day following Jesus would go forth, and findeth Philip." Oh, may my Lord delight to come forth, and find some of you! You are to-night in a place where he has found a good many; I pray that he may find some of you. Perhaps you do not know how it was that you came here. You did not mean to come out to-night; but here you are in this crowd, in the thick of this great throng. My Lord has found many a precious jewel here; to its own self it seemed nothing but a poor pebble, but to him it was a diamond of the first water. O my Master, find some more of thy jewels to-night! Lord Jesus, come and find Philip, and find Mary, and then let Philip and Mary declare that they have found thee!

When our dear Master goes forth to find a soul, *it is very effectual work.* He said to Philip, "Follow me," and Philip at once followed him. Christ did not need to preach a long sermon; his discourse contained only two words, "Follow me." I will gladly end my sermon just here if my Master will preach to some of you his two-worded sermon, "Follow me," "*Follow me*," "Follow me." "Come, poor soul, you do not know the way! 'Follow me.' You want some one to go before you, to be your leader. 'Follow me.' You want some one to be your shelter, your companion, your all. 'Follow me.'" That is what you have to do, good woman. You have been worrying about what you have heard from different preachers; Christ says to you, "Follow me." That is what you have to do, young man. You have been reading those rubbishing modern thought books till you do not know whether you are on your head or on your heels. Burn them. Jesus says, "Follow me." I know that some of you have been distracted with all sorts of silly talk; let that go to the dogs. Jesus says, "Follow me." The crucified Saviour says, "Follow me." Take him for your atonement. The risen Saviour says, "Follow me." Take him for your life. The Saviour on the throne says, "Follow me." Take him for your joy. The Saviour coming in glory hereafter says, "Follow me." Take him to be your hope. "Follow me," "Follow me," that is the text for to-night, and that is the sermon, too. Jesus said to Philip, "Follow me," and Philip followed him directly; and he not only followed Christ himself, but he began immediately to try to get others to follow him.

Please to notice also that *Philip was found by Christ in a very different way from the other disciples.* Two of them had been found through the teaching of John the Baptist; but Philip had apparently had no teaching. Another of the little company had been found through the private call of his brother; Philip may not have had any relative or friend to speak to him, but the Saviour just said to him, "Follow me," and he followed him. Dear friends, do not begin comparing your conversion with somebody else's. If the Lord Jesus Christ calls you, and says to you, "Follow me," and you follow him, if there never was another soul converted in exactly the same way, it does not matter at all. If you have come to him, if you have trusted in him, you are saved.

The pith of all that I have to say is this. Do not get worrying yourselves, as some of you do, about God's eternal purpose, and about the secret working of the Holy Spirit, and about how this can be consistent with your following Christ when he bids you. They are perfectly consistent. Some persons have asked me at times to reconcile these two things; and I have said to them, "Very well, tell me the difficulties, and I will reconcile them." It would be quite as easy to state them as to meet them, for in fact there are none. "Oh, but," says one, "you tell me to believe in Christ, and yet you constantly preach that faith is the work of the Spirit of God." I know that I do. "You say that God has a chosen people?" Yes, I do. "And yet you say that men are to choose Christ?" I do. "Well, how do you reconcile those two things?" Show me that there is any difficulty about the two things, and then I will reconcile them. You imagine the difficulty, for there is none in reality, there does not exist any in practical life. I believe that God has predestinated whether I am going down to the Lord's supper at the close of this service; but I shall go down as well as my legs can carry me. "Oh!" say you, "you make it out to be a matter of your own free will?" Yes, I do. "And yet you believe it to be God's eternal purpose?" Yes, I do. "Well, then, reconcile the two things." Again I say that there is no difficulty in the case, there is nothing to be reconciled, for both statements are true. You might as well ask me to reconcile the land and the water, or to reconcile the dog star, Sirius, and a farthing rushlight. There is no quarrel between them, and I have no time to waste on needless argument. Come you to Christ; and if you do, it will be because the Holy Spirit draws you. If you find the Saviour, it will be because the Saviour first found you. Perhaps, in heaven, you may see some difficulties, and get them explained; down here, you need not see them, and you need not ask to have them explained. Salvation is all of God's grace, from first to last; yet is it true that the grace of God leads men to do what Moses did, according to our subject this morning,*—to make a choice,

---

* See the *Metropolitan Tabernacle Pulpit*, No. 2,030, "Moses: his Faith and Decision."

and to choose rather to suffer affliction with the people of God than to enjoy the pleasures of sin for a season. God grant that you may make an equally wise choice!

I have done when I have said this one thing more. Philip, and Peter, and Andrew, were all of Bethsaida: "Now Philip was of Bethsaida, the city of Andrew and Peter." These three good men, these three apostles, were all of Bethsaida. That ought to be some comfort to many of you, my dear hearers, because there are numbers of you, who are here to-night, who are of Bethsaida. Sitting all round me, I see people who, I believe, are of Bethsaida. "Oh!" say you, "we never were there in all our lives." Listen. Bethsaida was one of the places in which Christ had done many of his mighty works; and you remember that, when the people repented not, Jesus uttered over them that sad lamentation, "Woe unto thee, Chorazin! woe unto thee, Bethsaida! for if the mighty works, which were done in you, had been done in Tyre and Sidon, they would have repented long ago in sackcloth and ashes. But I say unto you, It shall be more tolerable for Tyre and Sidon at the day of judgment than for you. And thou, Capernaum, which art exalted unto heaven, shalt be brought down to hell: for if the mighty works, which have been done in thee, had been done in Sodom, it would have remained until this day. But I say unto you, That it shall be more tolerable for the land of Sodom in the day of judgment, than for thee."

Now, there are some of you here who have heard the gospel for many years, and have seen the power of the grace of God in your families, and it will be more tolerable for Tyre and Sidon, and for Sodom and Gomorrah, in the day of judgment, than it will be for you, inasmuch as you have rejected the Saviour. But, as there were these three men, Philip, and Peter, and Andrew, who were of Bethsaida,—and I should think that the home of James and John was not very far off from the same place,—why should not you come to Christ? Why should not you become members of his Church, and, if it be the Lord's will, preachers of his Word? God grant that it may be so!

Oh, how I long in my soul for the salvation of every one of you! Many of you, who have come here to-night, are strangers to me. I trust that you will not be strangers to my Master. To-night, I pray you, here in the very heat of midsummer, ere yet the harvest shall be past, and the summer shall be ended, "Seek ye the Lord while he may be found, call ye upon him while he is near: let the wicked forsake his way, and the unrighteous man his thoughts: and let him return unto the Lord, and he will have mercy upon him; and to our God, for he will abundantly pardon." Receive Christ, trust in him. God grant that you may do so, for Jesu's sake! Amen.

Exposition by C. H. Spurgeon.

JOHN I. 29—51.

Verse 29. *The next day—*

This chapter is a record of the events that occurred on different days. Sometimes God does great things in a single day; one extraordinary day may have more in it than a hundred ordinary years. It is well for us to try to live by the day, and not to let any day pass without some good action having been done in it. Let us never have to cry, "I have lost a day."

29. *John seeth Jesus coming unto him, and saith, Behold the Lamb of God, which taketh away the sin of the world.*

We ought never to be slow in delivering such a message as that which John the Baptist uttered. I do not wonder that, as soon as ever John knew that Jesus was the Messiah, he told the good news to others. Hast thou found Jesus? Tell thy brother to-night; or, if not to-night, go as soon as thou canst, and bid him, "Behold the Lamb of God, which taketh away the sin of the world."

30—34. *This is he of whom I said, After me cometh a man which is preferred before me: for he was before me. And I knew him not: but that he should be made manifest to Israel, therefore am I come baptizing with water. And John bare record, saying, I saw the Spirit descending from heaven like a dove, and it abode upon him. And I knew him not: but he that sent me to baptize with water, the same said unto me, Upon whom thou shalt see the Spirit descending, and remaining on him, the same is he which baptizeth with the Holy Ghost. And I saw, and bare record that this is the Son of God.*

John was acquainted with Jesus, for they were related to one another, and were brought up together; but he did not officially know him as the Messiah until he saw the Holy Spirit descending and remaining on him; for that was the Lord's token by which he was to recognize him. He refused, therefore, to follow any knowledge or judgment of his own. He would not know Jesus as the Christ until he saw the private mark for which the Lord had told him to look. As soon as he saw that, then John said that he knew him; and as soon as he thus knew him, he began to preach him. Has the Lord given thee in thy soul a token that Christ is thy Saviour? Dost thou know him by the witness of the Holy Ghost? Then go and speak of him to others, and, like John, say, "Behold the Lamb of God." Let this be your one business between here and heaven.

35, 36. *Again the next day after John stood, and two of his disciples; and looking upon Jesus as he walked, he saith, Behold the Lamb of God!*

"Again the next day." See how the Evangelist goes by days in his record. John preached the same sermon two days running; and, if you proclaim Christ and him crucified, you may preach him two hundred days running, but you will never preach him too often. If you preach Christ as the Lamb of God, the great Sin-bearer, you may be always at that blessed work. There are some who very seldom preach Christ as bearing the sin of men; so that others of us must do it all the oftener to make up for their shortcomings. As for me, I can say with Charles Wesley,—

> "His only righteousness I show,
> His saving truth proclaim;
> 'Tis all my business here below,
> To cry, 'Behold the Lamb!'"

37. *And the two disciples heard him speak, and they followed Jesus.*

It is hard preaching when you preach away your congregation; but John did this deliberately. He wished these two no longer to be his disciples, but to become the disciples of Jesus. He had mastered the meaning of his own words, "He must increase, but I must decrease," and he was quite willing that it should be so: "The two disciples heard him speak, and they followed Jesus."

38, 39. *Then Jesus turned, and saw them following, and saith unto them, What seek ye? They said unto him, Rabbi, (which is to say, being interpreted, Master,) where dwellest thou? He saith unto them, Come and see.*

He gave them a full invitation to come to the place where he tarried, and see for themselves. That is what Jesus still says, "Come and see." If any of you want to know him, "Come and see." You are perfectly welcome to "Come and see" all that Jesus has to show you.

39. *They came and saw where he dwelt, and abode with him that day: for it was about the tenth hour.*

The best part of that day was the portion which they spent with Jesus; it was the best day they had ever enjoyed, for they lived with Jesus. It was also the beginning of better days for these two disciples; for, having once lived with Jesus, they learnt never to live without him. Oh, that we also may abide with him!

40, 41. *One of the two which heard John speak, and followed him, was Andrew, Simon Peter's brother. He first findeth his own brother Simon, and saith unto him, We have found the Messias, which is, being interpreted, the Christ.*

Where should missionary work begin? A brother should begin with his brother. It is all very well to have a desire to go to the heathen in Africa; you had better begin work as a missionary in England, and then go to Africa. He who cannot win his brother is not likely to win anybody else. "He first findeth his own brother Simon:" this Andrew, who was afterwards to bring so many to Christ, must begin at home, and succeed there. If we are not faithful with one or two relatives, how can God trust us with a pulpit and a congregation?

42. *And he brought him to Jesus. And when Jesus beheld him, he said, Thou art Simon the son of Jona:*

"Simon, son of a dove, thy name may point thee out as being timid; mind where thou dost wing thy flight."

42. *Thou shalt be called Cephas, which is by interpretation, A stone.*

Something more solid than the son of a pigeon; something more stable than the son of a dove. Christ changes men's names, and changes their natures, too. He can make the most fickle of us to become firm and steadfast. Oh, that he would thus work by his grace upon us!

43, 44. *The day following Jesus would go forth into Galilee, and findeth Philip, and saith unto him, Follow me. Now Philip was of Bethsaida, the city of Andrew and Peter.*

"The day following." See, friends, what a wonderful chapter this is. There is a book called, *The Book of Days;* I call this chapter the chapter of days. Every day seems memorable for some great event.

"Bethsaida, the city of Andrew and Peter," was a poor, miserable village; but God greatly honoured it. Great works often begin in little places. The best of beings came out of the despised town of Nazareth; and three of the best of men, Philip, Andrew, and Peter, came out of Bethsaida.

45. *Philip findeth Nathanael, and saith unto him, We have found him, of whom Moses in the law, and the prophets, did write, Jesus of Nazareth, the son of Joseph.*

True faith may make blunders. Jesus was not the son of Joseph, except by reputation; and he was Jesus of Bethlehem quite as much as he was Jesus of Nazareth; but true faith is accepted of God even though it makes some mistakes. It believes God's Word, and it believes God's Son, and therefore it shall be accepted.

46. *And Nathanael said unto him, Can there any good thing come out of Nazareth? Philip saith unto him, Come and see.*

Christ had said, "Come and see." Now Philip uses the same words, "Come and see." It is always right to follow the example that the Lord Jesus has set us.

47, 48. *Jesus saw Nathanael coming to him, and saith of him, Behold an Israelite indeed, in whom is no guile! Nathanael saith unto him, Whence knowest thou me?*

You may remember that, a short time ago, I preached a sermon upon Nathanael.* He was a kind of Jewish John Blunt, a man who always spoke his mind. He had a mind, and he had a mind to speak it, and he spoke his mind. So, the moment that Christ spoke of him, he asked, "Whence knowest thou me?" He was conscious that Christ did know him, and being a man who was altogether free from cunning and craftiness, he pointedly asked how Christ came to know him.

48. *Jesus answered and said unto him, Before that Philip called thee, when thou wast under the fig tree, I saw thee.*

What was he doing under the fig tree? Jesus knew, and Nathanael knew, but nobody else knew, and perhaps nobody else ever will know. That was a secret between Christ and Nathanael. He was doing something there that he regarded as quite private, and the Saviour's allusion to his being under the fig tree was the plainest proof he could have of Christ's divinity. "Oh!" thought he, "he who can remind me of that secret transaction must be God."

49, 50. *Nathanael answered and saith unto him, Rabbi, thou art the Son of God; thou art the King of Israel. Jesus answered and said unto him, Because I said unto thee, I saw thee under the fig tree, believest thou? thou shalt see greater things than these.*

You who are honest in heart, you who can be convinced by a single argument,—and, mark you, one good argument is as convincing as twenty good arguments, and a great deal better than a hundred bad ones,—you who are willing to be led by a single thread shall be led. If you are willing to believe on what is clear evidence, you shall have more evidence: "thou shalt see greater things than these." God will show much to that man who has eyes with which to see it. He who will not see, and does not wish to see, shall grow more and more blind, and the darkness shall thicken about him.

51. *And he saith unto him, Verily, verily, I say unto you, Hereafter ye shall see heaven open, and the angels of God ascending and descending upon the Son of man.*

He could see actually what Jacob saw only in a dream, when he beheld that wonderful stairway of light which leads from earth to heaven, even the Lord Jesus Christ, who by his manhood and his Godhead bridges the distance between us and God.

HYMNS FROM "OUR OWN HYMN BOOK"—605, 576, 606.

---

* See the *Metropolitan Tabernacle Pulpit*, No. 2,021, "Nathanael; or, the Ready Believer and his Reward."

Metropolitan Tabernacle Pulpit.

THE ESSENCE OF SIMPLICITY.

A Sermon

DELIVERED ON LORD'S DAY MORNING, DECEMBER 29TH, 1872, BY

C. H. SPURGEON,

AT THE METROPOLITAN TABERNACLE, NEWINGTON.

"Jesus heard that they had cast him out; and when he had found him, he said unto him, Dost thou believe on the Son of God? He answered and said, Who is he, Lord, that I might believe on him?"—John ix. 35, 36.

THIS text is from the story of the blind man to whom Jesus had given sight. His narrative of the cure provoked the anger of the Jews and their rulers; and, as the man could not be brought to see with them that one who had opened his eyes could also be a bad man, they cast him out of their assembly, and by that act signified to him that he would be, or already was, cast out of the Jewish Church, set aside from the synagogue, and made the victim of the greater excommunication. This was one of the most fearful calamities that could befall a Jew, and I do not doubt but what the man considered it to be so. Now, it is not at all likely that any person here is feeling the same trouble, but many may be suffering from something similar. It may be that you have excommunicated yourselves. Within the court of your own bosom conscience has held a solemn court, and pronounced upon you a sentence which continually rings in your ears. You scarcely dare mingle with those who assemble in the house of God, for you feel yourselves unworthy to be among them. Up till lately you were upon the best of terms with yourselves, and reckoned that all was right with God. You hoped that you stood on as good a footing, at any rate, as other men, and perhaps were somewhat better than many around you; but now a process of enlightenment has come over your mind—practices have been seen to be seriously evil which before were regarded as trifles, and sin itself has worn another aspect than any which it bore in former times. Does such a person stand here this morning? Then let me assure him that his state of mind is well known to me, for I knew its horrors by the space of many months together. I, too, felt that I was cut off from the congregation of the hopeful, and must not hope for mercy from God. I dared not lift so much as mine eyes towards heaven, but complained to the Lord as Jonah did—"I am shut out of thy sight." Hence with

No. 1,088.

brotherly sympathy I speak to any man who reckons himself a castaway, shut out from the house of the Lord.

The man in the narrative, most happily for him, at the time when the sentence began to cast its gloom over him, was met by the Lord Jesus Christ, who at once proceeded to afford him the necessary cordial. Christ has come as the consolation of Israel, and where he finds that men are burdened in spirit he commences his gracious work : but, observe, he brings but one cordial, and prescribes but one way by which its efficacy can be realised. He spoke to the oppressed man concerning the Son of God and personal faith in him, for this is the master-consolation for broken hearts, this is the surest and best means of bringing joy to souls which sit in the dungeons of despondency. Our Lord began by saying to the cast-out one, "Dost thou believe on the Son of God?" Now, if any here present are in the state which I have thus hurriedly sketched, feeling themselves guilty before God, with spirits ill at ease, with hearts alarmed at coming and deserved judgment, I would come in Christ's name to them this morning with words of comfort, but they will be no other than those which Jesus uttered of old. I have nothing to speak to you by way of comfort but concerning the Son of God, and concerning him only, by demanding that ye believe on him, for only as you receive him by faith will he be to you a relief from sorrow. He that believeth on the Lord Jesus shall not be ashamed, but without faith you are without salvation.

We shall this morning labour to bring you all to the point in hand. There shall be between the doctrine of the gospel and your soul this morning, O thou who art not yet a believer, a direct encounter. Thou shalt come up this morning and face the gospel, whether thou spurn it or accept it. Thou shalt know, if the plainest words can tell it thee, that if thou believest in Christ Jesus thou shalt be saved, and it shall be put to thee whether thou wilt do this or not, and thou shalt either believe on the Son of God or incur anew the sin of putting from thee the only name given under heaven among men whereby thou canst be saved. I say thou shalt be brought to this if words can bring thee to it, and then I must leave the work of deciding you in the hands of God the Holy Ghost. I entreat you who love the Lord, and have prevalence in prayer, to aid me with your supplications, that the result of bringing the sinner face to face with the gospel may be that he may decide to believe in Jesus, that faith may be given him, that the Son of God may become the object of his soul's confidence, and that in no case the hearer may be left to continue in unbelief, and to reject the Son of God. You have seen at the mouth of the coal pits how the full wagons as they run down the incline draw the empty ones up to the pit's mouth that they also may be filled : I would to God that you who have grace may exert the power God has given you with himself; and so by prevalent intercession you may draw others to the Saviour. While we are preaching do you be praying, and God will work by us both. Look upon the unsaved around you with an eye of pity, then look to Christ, your exalted Saviour, with the eye of faith, and say to him, "Jesu, thou who hast redeemed myriads by thy blood, now work by thine eternal Spirit, and redeem also by power. Let the Spirit that rested on thine own ministry, the Spirit that was with thy servants at Pentecost, the Spirit that has converted us also to thy truth, work mightily among the congregation this morning, that all these may be led to obey thee. When thy cross is lifted high, let it bring life to the dead throughout the camp, and be to the awakened a lighthouse of safety, to the despairing a pillar of hope."

I. The run of our discourse this morning being solemnly practical, we shall, in the most distinct manner, lay down and define THE MATTER IN HAND. With thee, my anxious friend, the greatest and weightiest business that can concern thee is that thou find salvation. Thou hast it not at present, thy conscience tells thee that; and though thou art well aware that thou must obtain it, or be for ever lost, yet thou hast as yet but small prospect of ever finding it. Thou hast sinned, and punishment awaits thee; neither canst thou escape! The point above all points with thee is that thou be saved, and if thou be really awakened thou desirest to be saved from sin as well as from its punishment; thou wouldst not only escape from the consequences of doing wrong, but from the propensity to do wrong; from the constant power and defilement of past sin, and from the tendency to sin again. Thou desirest also to be forgiven, and by forgiveness to be set clear from the anger of a justly offended God, and to be rendered acceptable to the Most High; and if thou be in thy right mind thou desirest that all this should be done really and truly, not in pretence or fiction, but in deed and in truth. God forbid that thou shouldst ever be content with the name of being saved, with an external and professional salvation of outward rites and ceremonies, while your heart remains unpurified and your nature uncleansed. In some other departments we may be deceived and not be very great losers, but in soul matters we must make all things sure; for if we are deceived there, it is all over with us indeed. Let me be cheated with base metal instead of gold, if you will, but not with falsehoods in the place of saving truth, or deceptive notions in lieu of gracious operations. Let me be deceived as to the food I eat, and find every morsel of it adulterated, if so it must be; but not in the life-bread eternal, which my soul craves after. Be true to my soul, if all else be a lie!

Do you, my hearer, desire salvation from the power and guilt of sin, and do you desire it to be thorough and real? Do you not also long for it *now*? If God has at all quickened you, you long to be saved at once, and tremble at the idea of delay. Sin is bitter to you *now*, it is a present plague. The matter before us now is present salvation, personal salvation to be realised for your own self. If there be such a thing as looking up to the smiling face of a reconciled Father in heaven, you desire to enjoy it *now*: if it be possible for the load of sin to be rolled from off a mortal's shoulders for ever, you desire to be quit of that burden at this instant: if there be, indeed, a fountain in which, if a man be washed, every stain shall disappear, you long to plunge beneath its cleansing flood at once, and be made whiter than the driven snow. If your soul is so far awakened I bless God indeed, for there is nothing beneath the sun—and, indeed, there is nothing above it—that can rival in importance your soul's salvation.

Now the matter which I must press upon you is this. If you are ever to be saved, God has declared that salvation must come to you as a gift of his grace, as an act of his free favour, and can only be received by you through your believing in his Son. As Christ consoled the man in the temple by saying to him, "Dost thou believe on the Son of God?" so to-day there is no consolation, much less salvation for thee, except through believing in God's own Son. A hundred times have you heard the story of God's only begotten Son, who is the lover of men's souls; but we must tell it you yet again. God will not save men on the ground of their merits; indeed, if they have any merits they do not require saving. If God owes you anything, produce the account and you shall have it. If there be any obligations on God's part towards you, say what they are, and if they can be proved to exist, God will never give you less than you can justly claim. Alas! my friend, if you are lodged where you deserve to be, where will it be but in the pit of hell? It were well for you then to have done with all claims and demands. God will only save you as a guilty person who deserves to be destroyed, but whom he saves becauses he chooses to save him—because he resolves to manifest in him the abundance of his mercy. "By grace are ye saved," is the immutable purpose of heaven; and it is further decreed, that this grace shall be received by men through the channel of faith, and by that channel only. God will save only those who trust in his Son. Jesus Christ the Lord came into this world and took upon himself our nature, as we taught you last Sabbath Day, and being found in fashion as a man, he took the transgressor's place; the transgressions of his people were numbered upon him, imputed to him, charged to his account, and he suffered for them as if they had been his own sins. He was scourged, tormented, crucified, and slain; the stripes he bore were the chastisments due to human sin, and the death he endured was the death threatened to transgressors; and now, whosoever will trust in Jesus shall participate in the result of all the Redeemer's substitutionary agonies, and the case shall stand thus—the sufferings of Christ shall be instead of the believer's suffering, and the merits of Christ shall be instead of the obedience which man ought to have rendered. Faith in Jesus makes us righteous through the righteousness of another; it causes us to be accepted in the Beloved, perfect in Christ Jesus. As by the first Adam we fell, so by the second Adam we rise again. Now the way to partake in the benefits of the death of the Lord Jesus is simply by believing in him. Here let it be understood that believing in Jesus is not a mysterious and complex action. It does not require a week to explain what faith is. Faith believes what God has revealed concerning Christ, and it therefore trusts in Christ as the divinely-appointed Saviour. I believe that Jesus was God's Son, that God sent him into the world to save sinners, that to do so he became a substitute to justice for all those who trust him, and, as I trust him, I know that he was my substitute and that I am clear before God. Since Jesus died for me, God's justice cannot put me to eternal death for whom Jesus my substitute has died; God's truth cannot demand a second time the debt which has already been fully paid on my behalf. The *rationale* of the whole thing is as plain as possible, and whoever in this world, old or young, Jew or Gentile, literate or illiterate, rich or poor, debauched or moral, will trust in Jesus shall be saved—nay he is saved the moment he does so; but whosoever of woman born refuses to trust in Jesus is condemned already, because he hath not believed on the Son of God. Let a man's character be what it may, if in that character there be no faith, he is a lost soul; but on the other hand, let that character have been what it may, if now he cometh to the cross and believeth in Jesus, he beginneth from that moment a new life; God will give to him all the graces and excellencies of character which will adorn his faith, and his faith shall save him. Trusting in Jesus, believing in Jesus, that is the matter. I want to bring my hammer down upon this anvil at every stroke, and if the Lord will be pleased to place before me some heart that he has melted in the furnace of conviction, the strokes will tell, if the Eternal God will lay-to his almighty arm and smite with energy divine. If any soul be but brought to faith in Jesus the work is done; to believe in the Son of God is the point, and nothing else.

II. This being the matter in hand, we will make an advance, in the second place, to notice that there is A QUESTION IN OUR TEXT WHICH INVOLVES THE WHOLE BASIS OF FAITH. The man said to Jesus, "Who is he, Lord, that I might believe on him?" This man all through the narrative proves himself to be a very shrewd fellow. I do not know that holy Scripture gives us an instance of a more common-sense man than this man whose eyes were opened; and so, when he is told that he must believe in the Son of God, he comes to the point at once, and says, "Who is he, Lord, that I might believe on him?" as if that was all he wanted to know—"Who is he?" and then the faith would surely come. When a soul is seeking faith, this question is the main point; the hinge of the whole matter lies there. This man did not say, "Lord, who am I that I should believe?"—not at all; that would have been wide of the point. If I read a story in the newspapers, about the truthfulness of which there is a question, I do not begin asking what my own character is, as though that had anything to do with it, but I ask who the authority for the story may be. I do not look within, but I look to the person claiming belief. The story is true or not, whatever I may be. My character does not concern the truth or falsehood of the statement, I must enquire into the statement itself. So this man did not make any remarks about what he might have been or might still be, but he hung the issue on this nail—"Who is he, Lord, that I might believe on him?" So now, dear hearer, all the arguments for thy faith lie within the compass of that question, "Who is he, Lord, that I should believe in him?" Thou needest not say, "Who am I that I should believe? I have lived a life that has been defiled with sin; I have gone from one transgression to another; I have resisted conscience; I have stood out against the gospel; I have defiled myself by sins against light and knowledge." It mattereth not. There thou standest, with all thy defilement taken for granted, and God says to thee, "Whosoever believeth on the Lord Jesus Christ hath everlasting life." That is the saving matter; that, and nothing more nor less. Wilt thou believe in the Lord Jesus or not? What thou art is nothing to the point. If God's witness be true, it is true whether thou be black or white, whether thou be a big sinner or a little sinner; and if it be false it will not be any the truer, whether you be good or bad, worthy or unworthy. If Jesus be able to save he ought to be trusted; and if he be not able none ought to rely upon him—the whole question turns on that.

Neither raise any quibbles as to your present condition. You say, "But I at this moment feel myself so hard of heart; I cannot weep as some can; repentance is hid from my eyes; prayer is heavy, groaning work with me; even while I am listening to the gospel this morning my attention is not riveted as it ought to be upon the truth which I know to be vital; I am destitute of every good point; I am empty of everything that can recommend me to mercy." I answer, what of that? Suppose I tell a man that the sum of ten thousand pounds has been left him in a will, is it anything to the point if he shows me his rags, his empty cupboard, and his wretched bed? Does his poverty make me a liar? Why does the man introduce such extraneous matter into the good news? Either it is true or it is not; his condition has nothing to do with the truth or falsehood of my declaration. If the man were wrapped in scarlet and fine linen, that would not make my statement any the truer; and if the dogs lick him as they did Lazarus, that does not give him a right to deny my truthfulness when I tell him a fact. So, O sinner, your condition has nothing to do with the question whether Jesus is to be trusted or not. "God so loved the world that he gave his only begotten Son, that whosoever believeth in him should not perish, but have everlasting life." Will you believe in him? Will you trust the Lord Jesus? If you desire to trust him the subject for enquiry is, "Is he worth trusting?" But it is a question far away from the point to say, "I am this," or "I am that." Is not this so? I appeal to your own common sense.

"But still, as to the future," says one; "I might go back to my old sins. I cannot trust myself, I have made some reformations before, and they have been but poor ventures; my ship has gone out to sea, and foundered in the first gale; I cannot expect with such temptations as will await me, that I shall bear up and enter heaven." Now, what has the question of believing in Jesus to do with thy good resolutions, or thy miserable failures? Whosoever trusts Christ shall be saved. If thou be lost trusting him in the future, God's word will not be true. The question is, Canst thou trust Christ? and that turns on that other "is he worthy to be trusted?" No other question can be admitted for a single moment. The case is something like that of a man in yonder sea; his ship is wrecked; she is breaking to pieces; her decks have been swept; he barely retains his hold on a floating spar. See! the life-boat comes up close to his side, and is ready to take him on board. Now, if there be a question in that man's mind about getting into that life-boat in order to be saved, the only rational one that I can conceive is, "Will the boat carry me to shore? Is she sea-worthy? Will she outlive the breakers? Can she reach the land safely?" You cannot conceive the poor fellow's saying, "I quiver too much with ague to be rescued by that boat," or "The sea has washed the last rag from off my back, the boat will not suit me," or "Another time I may be wrecked on the coast of Africa, and there may be a life-boat." No, no. Man alive, there is the boat! Is she sea-worthy? That is the question. If so, get into her. If Christ be not worth trusting, do not trust him;

and if he be worthy of all confidence, then have done with idle questions and cast yourself upon him. "If we receive the witness of men, the witness of God is greater: for this is the witness of God which he hath testified of his Son. He that believeth on the Son of God hath the witness in himself: he that believeth not God hath made him a liar; because he believeth not the record that God gave of his Son. And this is the record, that God hath given to us eternal life, and this life is in his Son. He that hath the Son hath life; and he that hath not the Son of God hath not life" (1 John v. 9—12).

Still, we will keep to this point—Jesus is worth trusting, worthy of the sinner's unwavering faith. He is worth trusting, O sinner, because first of all *he* on whom thou art bidden to rely this day by the command of the gospel, *is God himself.* Thou hast offended God, and it is God who came into the world to save sinners. Against Christ thy sins were launched as arrows from a bow, but he against whom those bolts were shot has come in the fulness of his power and the infinity of his mercy to save them that believe. Canst thou not trust thyself in almighty hands—almighty to save? Is anything impossible with God? An angel could not save thee, but surely God himself can? How canst thou limit the Holy one of Israel? How canst thou set bounds to boundless love, or limits to limitless grace? If Jesus were man and not God, unbelief would have good excuse; but if the Saviour be divine, where can distrust find a cloak for itself?

I feel this morning as if I could not help believing in Christ now that I know him to be divine. Faith has grown to be a necessary act of my mind. Save me! Who shall persuade me that he cannot? Come forth ye devils with your arguments and plead with me, and ye cannot inject a doubt into my soul while I know him to be God; he can shake the heavens when he pleases and make the earth to tremble; he bears up the universe upon his shoulders; cannot he save my poor soul? Ay, that he can. "Who is he that I might believe on him?" He is divine, and therefore I believe.

But next, the Lord Jesus Christ, in whom the sinner is bidden to trust, is *commissioned by God to save.* He came into the world as a Saviour, not alone on his own account, but as Messiah sent of God. He has the full concurrence of the sacred Trinity. It is the will of the Father, it is the will of the Holy Spirit, as well as the will of the Son, that whosoever believeth in Jesus should be saved. He was anointed of the Lord for his peculiar work. Now, I feel as if this was a special ground for trust in him. If Christ were an amateur Saviour who had taken up the trade of saving on his own account, there might be a question; but if God has divinely commissioned him to save, O soul, why canst thou doubt any more? Warranted of God, authorised of the Eternal, O heart, rest thou in him.

Then, mark, the Lord Jesus Christ *has actually done all that is necessary* for him to do for the salvation of all who trust him. Years ago, before Jesus Christ came into the world, if I had been sent to preach the gospel, I must have cried "Jesus will take upon him the sins of believers and lay down his life for his church," but now I have a more encouraging message;—Jesus has carried his people's sins away for ever, he has suffered on their behalf all that was required to make an end of their transgressions. Whatever was demanded by the justice of God as a recompense for the injured honour of the law he has rendered. The equivalent for all the sufferings which all the elect would have suffered in hell, Christ has suffered everything necessary that God might be just, and yet the justifier of him that believeth, Christ has endured. The cup of vengeance is not full, and to be drained; it is empty, and turned bottom upwards, Jesus has drank it dry. The labours needful for our redemption, superlatively greater than the labours of Hercules, have all been accomplished. Christ has gone into the grave, has gone out of the grave, and gone up to his glory. He has entered heaven because his work is done; and now he sits down at the right hand of the Father in the posture of rest and honour, because he has perfected for ever all those who put their trust in him. Now, soul, how canst thou refuse to believe in Jesus? To me the argument seems impossible to be resisted. If it be so, that Christ hath died, the just for the unjust, and that all who trust him shall be saved, I will also trust him, and I shall find peace through his blood.

Moreover, soul, the point we trust God's grace is bringing thee to is this—Jesus deserves to be trusted, and trust him we will—for *he is full of power to save,* for he is now upon the throne, and all power is given him in heaven and in earth. He is full of power to save we know, because he is saving souls every day. Some of us are the living witnesses that he can forgive sin, for we are pardoned, accepted, and renewed in heart; and the only way in which we obtained those boons was this—we trusted him, we did nothing else but trust him. If any soul here that believes in Jesus should perish, I must perish with him. I sail in that boat, and if it sinks I have no other to fly to. I avow before you all that I have no other confidence; I have not so much as the shred of a reliance in any sacrament I have undergone or enjoyed, in any sermon I have ever preached, in any prayer I have ever prayed, in any communion with God I have ever known. My hope lies in the blood and righteousness of Jesus Christ; and I shake off as though it were a viper, into the fire, as a deadly thing only fit to be burned, all pretence of relying on anything I may be, or can be, or ever shall be, or do. "None but Jesus,"—this is the settled pillar upon which we must build; it will bear us up, but nothing else can. Now, since by the authority of infallible Scripture, we know that Jesus has this power, wherefore is it that souls seeking rest do not obey the command, and rest themselves freely upon him. This is the climax of human depravity, that it rejects the witness of God himself, and chooses to perish in unbelief.

Moreover, remember also that Jesus Christ this morning is by no means unwilling to save sinners, but on the contrary, he delights to do it. You have never to drag mercy out of Christ, as money from a miser, but it flows freely from him, like the stream from the fountain, or the sunlight from the sun. If he can be happier, he is made happier by giving of his mercy to the undeserving. When a poor wretch who only deserves hell, comes to him, and he says, "I have blotted out thy sins," it is joy to Christ's heart to do it. When a poor blasphemer bows his knee, and says, "Lord, be merciful to me a sinner," it makes Christ's heart glad to say, "Thy blasphemies are forgiven: I suffered for them on the tree." When a poor little child, by her bedside, cries, "Gentle Jesus, teach a little child to pray, and forgive the sins which I have done;" the Saviour loves to say, " Suffer these little children to come to me, for this also is a part of my recompense for the wounds I endured in my hands, my feet, and my side." When any of you come to him and confess your transgressions and trust yourselves in his hands, it will be a new heaven to him; it will put new stars into his ever bright and lustrous crown; it will make him see of the travail of his soul and give him satisfaction. Have we not here also arguments to prove that Jesus is worthy to be trusted ?

III. This leads us in the third place to say, by all these answers to the question,—" Who is he ? " EVERY SINNER IN THIS TABERNACLE IS SHUT UP THIS MORNING TO THE ALTERNATIVE OF FAITH OR UNBELIEF. You are shut up either to trust in Christ, in whom God commands you to trust, or to refuse to trust him. I am not sent to preach to some of you this morning, but to every one who has ears to hear. I have never learned to preach a restricted gospel to a part of a congregation; the commission received by every true minister of Christ is, " Go ye into all the world and preach the gospel to every creature : he that believeth and is baptised shall be saved ; he that believeth not shall be damned." As you are all creatures, the gospel is hereby preached to all of you ; sensible or insensible, spiritually dead or spiritually alive, so long as you are able to hear the gospel, one message comes to you all out of the excellent glory. " Whosoever will, let him come and take of the water of life freely." " Believe in the Lord Jesus Christ and thou shalt be saved." But I know what will be your course of action unless the Spirit of God prevent it. Many of you will try to decline the alternative between believing and not believing, which I have put so nakedly before you. You will not like to say, " I will not trust Christ," and yet you will not trust in him. What, then, will you do ? Why, you will ring the changes on the old bells , " But I am such a sinner. I am so unworthy ! " I have already shown that the plea is not relevant and ought not to be thrust into the business. The question is one and indivisible, " Wilt thou believe on the Son of God ?" Why then do you raise another question about yourself which has nothing to do with it. Yet I will take you on your own ground and answer you. Granted that you are a special and abominable sinner : then of all men in the world you are the man who should trust Christ, because it is written, " This is a faithful saying and worthy of all acceptation, that Christ Jesus came into the world to save *sinners*." You have been a drunkard, a fornicator, an adulterer, a thief, in fact, a devil of a man ; well then, you have been a sinner ;—that is all it comes to, and Jesus Christ came into the world to save sinners; therefore instead of being shut out by your character, you are shut in by it. You are the sort of man that Christ came to save. You cannot run away and say, " He did not come to save me because I am not a sinner." You dare not do that.

Very likely you will turn round upon me and say, " My reason for unbelief is that I do not feel as I should." I again say the plea ought never to be urged. Because I feel a pain in my foot this morning, is that a reason why I should not trust in an honest man, or believe a statement which comes to me upon good authority. I will, however, take you on your own ground. You are so sinful that you are, in all respects, undeserving; well, then, Jesus came to save his people from their sins. Clearly, you are one of the very sort of persons whom he came to save, for you are full of sins. His salvation is all of grace, and since you have no good thing about you whatsoever, you are a most fit case for mercy, free mercy, great mercy! Salvation, all of grace, exactly suits you. You are an empty vessel, then it is clear you want to be filled; you are a filthy vessel, then you need washing; and Jesus proposes both to cleanse and fill. His overtures are exactly adapted to your circumstances. You are the very man for grace to bless.

"Ah, but," says another, "I feel myself lost, utterly lost." What! are we first to do battle with some of you because you feel too little, and then with others because they feel too much; then we must come back to our one fixed point, and remind you again that both excuses are wide of the mark, and that the one point is—will you, or will you not, believe in the Lord Jesus, whom God has set forth to be the Saviour of men? But still if you are crushed with sorrowful feelings, there are special reasons for your attending to the gospel call, since some invitations are especially directed to you, such as, "Ho everyone that thirsteth come ye to the waters," and "If any man thirst, let him come unto me and drink." If there are special messages of grace for you who are somewhat awakened to a sense of need, then I entreat you, hasten to accept the testimony of God that so your souls may live.

The one question for every unconverted sinner here is, Wilt thou believe on Jesus Christ? But I hear you saying, "Well, I must do better in the future; I think after all I may perhaps, by some exertions of my own, get into a better condition." How can you hope so? Have you not made a pretty mess of it up till now? You had better give up the vain attempt. If you have done so badly in the past, you have little encouragement to try the future. Let despair drive you to faith. The worst of your conduct is you are going clean contrary to God's plan. God says, "I will not save you on the ground of merit, for you have none." That is really a gracious declaration of his, for it only shuts out false hopes, since "by the works of the law shall no flesh living be justified." Now, if you say, "I will seek salvation on the ground of works," you are flying in God's face. Is this wise? I should far rather recommend you to accept at once what he so freely gives. Follow the course of action adopted by a person the other day in dealing with another. He wanted to purchase something of his brother. His brother had asked him a certain amount for it, and he said, "I will give you half." "No," said the brother, "sooner than take so small a price I will give it to you." "Thank you; I will have it," was the immediate reply. That is what I would have you do. Do not offer your petty price to God, when he is ready to give the blessing without money and without price! I never knew such fools as men are about the things of God. If they can get a good thing for nothing, all the world over they will have it without pressing, and yet they rebel against free grace. Years ago we paid twenty millions to set free the slaves in Jamaica, but before the bill was carried there were no end of objections raised in the House of Commons and elsewhere. Many persons pleaded their objections, but I never heard of a negro appearing at the bar of the house to urge objections on behalf of the slaves. No black man came forward to say that the blacks were unworthy and undeserving, neither did the slaves propose that a part of the money should be paid by themselves. O no, it is not in human nature to request others to encumber their free gifts in that fashion; yet here we are so false to all that is reasonable that we want to encumber sovereign grace. When God says, "I will blot out your transgressions now and save you once for all; only trust my dear Son;" 'tis strange, 'tis passing strange, 'tis madness at its consummation, that men should invent objections, and plead for a gospel with conditions and hard terms.

Now, what will men do if driven out of this? I have often seen the sinner in the next place turn to downright falsehood and say, "It is too late," though he knows right well it never can be too late; for the gospel says, "He that believeth and is baptised shall be saved." It does not say, if he believes when he is twenty-five years of age, or thirty-five, or fifty-five, or one hundred and five, but it stands the same for all ages. It is never too late to believe a truth, and that is the point. —"Wilt thou believe on the Son of God? Then the sinner will say that he feels within himself that there is no hope, and so because he happens to believe a lie he will make out that God's truth also is a lie, and refuse to believe that which God solemnly declares, namely, that there is salvation in Jesus Christ! But I cannot stay to mention all these falsehoods, nor indeed to run into all the subterfuges of men who seek to escape from their own mercies. I saw in Pompeii, on a shop door, the motto, "Eme et Habe bis"—"Buy and you shall have," and I could not but think that if I were walking the streets of the New Jerusalem, I should have seen a very different device, "Come, buy wine and milk, without money and without price." Now if there could be a shop opened in London in which all the goods were to be had without money and without price, would you quarrel with the shopkeeper, and petition for an Act of Parliament to shut his shop up, and say it was wicked, because you would rather go on the old terms and pay for all you have? Not a bit of it. Yet why is it you stand out against free grace's golden motto, "Trust in Christ and you shall have." Here is instantaneous pardon, perfect pardon, everlasting pardon, sonship through Christ, safety on earth, glory in heaven, and all for nothing, all for nothing;— the free gift of a gracious God to undeserving sinners, who trust in Jesus! Never angel had a more gracious, more god-like message of mercy than I have, how I wish I could glow with a seraph's zeal, and cry with a cherub's voice while proclaiming it. Would God that men would leave their foolish reasonings, and believe in Jesus Christ.

IV. Lastly, on this alternative, this day, may hang EVERLASTING THINGS TO MANY OF YOU. I remember well, for the anniversary of the season has almost come round, when I was placed in a similar condition to many now present, when I knew myself to be ruined and undone, and heard, for the first time truly to understand it, that word, "Look unto me, and be ye saved, all ye ends of the earth." I know how it stood that morning. I was like Naaman by the Jordan's brink. There flowed the flood. The old nature said, "Are not Abana and Pharpar, rivers of Damascus, better than all the waters of Israel? May I not wash in them and be clean?" Human nature said, "I want to feel something :

I want to have John Bunyan's experience; I want to have my mother's experience; I want to feel a broken heart; I want to groan more bitterly; I want to be kept awake so many more nights; and all that sort of thing." Suppose I had resisted still; if God's grace had not come in and made all that wicked pride of mine give way, I might have been at this hour I know not where, if still living among men. I might have been in hell, gnawing my tongue to think I should ever have heard a plain gospel sermon, and should have put far from me the gospel when it was proclaimed, and all because I would not believe what is indisputably true, and would not trust in him whom no one ever trusted in vain. This morning I know there are some in my condition here, in whom the good Spirit will say, "Wash and be clean;" and the soul will sigh, "It seems too good to be true:" but the good Spirit will reply, "Are not my ways higher than your ways, and my thoughts than your thoughts?" Unbelief will say, "Your sins are many," but the good Spirit will answer, "Though your sins be as scarlet, they shall be as white as snow; though they be red like crimson, they shall be as wool." Then the heart will suggest, "But I have rebelled against thee, O God, so long;" and the sweet Spirit of God will whisper, "I have blotted out thy sins like a cloud, and like a thick cloud thine iniquities: Return unto me, for I am married unto thee, saith the Lord." And I do trust that now, at this very moment, many a heart will say, "I will, then, simply rest my soul's salvation upon Christ the Son of God, who is the only Saviour of the lost: I will never from this day hope to be a self-saved man, nor look to anything but to him who on the bloody tree endured the wrath of God in the behalf of as many as believe on him." Soul, if thou dost so trust Jesus, as surely as thou livest thou art saved! Go in peace. Not I speak these words only this morning from these poor lips of clay, but he who was nailed on the tree, whom all heaven adores, speaks this morning through me—and he saith to one, "Daughter, be of good cheer, thy sins be forgiven thee;" and to another, "Son, thy sins be forgiven thee: take up thy bed and walk." O forgiven one, I charge thee do it, and as thou goest out of this house this morning, saved, and full of joy, tell others about it; never leave off telling about it, and live to love him who has saved thee! I saw the other day a picture by Rubens, in which he has painted Mary Magdalene kissing the feet of Christ while still they are gushing with founts of blood on the cross. It was a strange picture, but I felt if I had been there I would have kissed them too, though they had been crimson with his gore. O blessed feet! O blessed Saviour! O blessed Father who gave his Son to be so blessed a Saviour! O blessed Spirit of the blessed God that led our wicked, proud hearts into obedience and trust in Jesus: yea, blessed be the God and Father of our Lord Jesus Christ, who hath begotten us unto a lively hope by the resurrection of Jesus Christ from the dead. The Lord bless you. Amen.

PORTIONS OF SCRIPTURE READ BEFORE SERMON—Romans iii. 9—31; iv. 1—13.

Metropolitan Tabernacle Pulpit.

SALVATION BY WORKS, A CRIMINAL DOCTRINE.

A Sermon

Delivered on Lord's-day Morning, April 18th, 1880, by

C. H. SPURGEON,

at the Metropolitan Tabernacle, Newington.

"I do not frustrate the grace of God: for if righteousness come by the law, then Christ is dead in vain."—Galatians ii. 21.

THE idea of salvation by the merit of our own works is exceedingly *insinuating*. It matters not how often it is refuted, it asserts itself again and again; and when it gains the least foothold it soon makes great advances. Hence Paul, who was determined to show it no quarter, opposed everything which bore its likeness. He was determined not to permit the thin end of the wedge to be introduced into the church, for well he knew that willing hands would soon be driving it home: hence when Peter sided with the Judaizing party, and seemed to favour those who demanded that the Gentiles should be circumcised, our brave apostle withstood him to the face. He fought always for salvation by grace through faith, and contended strenuously against all thought of righteousness by obedience to the precepts of the ceremonial or the moral law. No one could be more explicit than he upon the doctrine that we are not justified or saved by works in any degree, but solely by the grace of God. His trumpet gave forth no uncertain sound, but gave forth the clear note, "By grace are ye saved through faith; and that not of yourselves: it is the gift of God." Grace meant grace with him, and he could not endure any tampering with the matter, or any frittering away of its meaning.

So fascinating is the doctrine of legal righteousness that the only way to deal with it is Paul's way. Stamp it out. Cry war to the knife against it. Never yield to it; but remember the apostle's firmness, and how stoutly he held his ground: "To whom," saith he, "we gave place by subjection, no, not for an hour."

The error of salvation by works is exceedingly *plausible*. You will constantly hear it stated as a self-evident truth, and vindicated on account of its supposed practical usefulness, while the gospel doctrine of salvation by faith is railed at and accused of evil consequences. It is affirmed that if we preach salvation by good works we shall encourage virtue; and so it might seem in theory, but history proves by many instances that as a matter of fact where such doctrine

No. 1,534.

has been preached virtue has become singularly uncommon, and that in proportion as the merit of works has been cried up, morality has gone down. On the other hand, where justification by faith has been preached, conversions have followed, and purity of life has been produced even in the worst of men. Those who lead godly and gracious lives are ready to confess that the cause of their zeal for holiness lies in their faith in Christ Jesus; but where will you meet with a devout and upright man who glories in his own works?

Self-righteousness is *natural to our fallen humanity*. Hence it is the essence of all false religions. Be they what they may, they all agree in seeking salvation by our own deeds. He who worships his idols will torture his body, will fast, will perform long pilgrimages, and do or endure anything in order to merit salvation. The Romish Church holds up continually before the eyes of its votaries the prize to be earned by self-denial, by penance, by prayers, or by sacraments, or by some other performances of man. Go where you may, the natural religion of fallen man is salvation by his own merits. An old divine has well said, every man is born a heretic upon this point, and he naturally gravitates towards this heresy in one form or another. Self-salvation, either by his personal worthiness, or by his repentance, or by his resolves, is a hope ingrained in human nature, and very hard to remove. This foolishness is bound up in the heart of every child, and who shall get it out of him?

This erroneous idea *arises partly from ignorance*, for men are ignorant of the law of God, and of what holiness really is. If they knew that even an evil thought is a breach of the law, and that the law once broken in any point is altogether violated, they would be at once convinced that there can be no righteousness by the law to those who have already offended against it. They are also in great ignorance concerning themselves, for those very persons who talk about self-righteousness are as a rule openly chargeable with fault; and if not, were they to sit down and really look at their own lives, they would soon perceive even in their best works such impurity of motive beforehand, or such pride and self-congratulation afterwards, that they would see the gloss taken off from all their performances, and they would be utterly ashamed of them. Nor is it ignorance alone which leads men to self-righteousness, they are also deceived by *pride*. Man cannot endure to be saved on the footing of mercy; he loves not to plead guilty and throw himself on the favour of the great King; he cannot brook to be treated as a pauper, and blessed as a matter of charity; he desires to have a finger in his own salvation, and claim at least a little credit for it. Proud man will not have heaven itself upon terms of grace; but so long as he can he sets up one plea or another, and holds to his own righteousness as though it were his life. This self-confidence also arises from wicked *unbelief*, for through his self-conceit man will not believe God. Nothing is more plainly revealed in Scripture than this,—that by the works of the law shall no man be justified, yet men in some shape or other stick to the hope of legal righteousness; they will have it that they must prepare for grace, or assist mercy, or in some degree deserve eternal life. They prefer their own flattering prejudices to the declaration of the heart-searching God. The testimony of the Holy Spirit concerning the deceitfulness of the heart is cast aside, and the declaration of God that there is none that doeth good, no, not one, is altogether denied. Is not this a great evil? Self-righteousness is also much promoted by the almost universal *spirit of trifling* which is now abroad. Only while men trifle with themselves can they entertain the idea of personal merit before God. He who comes to serious thought, and begins to understand the character of God, before whom the heavens are not pure, and the angels are charged with folly,—he, I say, that comes to serious thought and beholds a true vision of God, abhors himself in dust and ashes, and is for ever silenced as to any thought of self-justification. It is because we do not seriously examine our condition that we think ourselves rich and increased in goods. A man may fancy that he is prospering in business, and yet he may be going back in the world. If he does not face his books or take stock, he may be living in a fool's paradise, spending largely when on the verge of bankruptcy. Many think well of themselves because they never think seriously. They do not look below the surface, and hence they are deceived by appearances. The most troublesome business to many men is thought; and the last thing they will do is to weigh their actions, or test their motives, or ponder their ways, to see whether things be right with them. Self-righteousness being supported by ignorance, by pride, by unbelief, and by the natural superficiality of the human mind, is strongly entrenched and cannot readily be driven out of men.

Yet self-righteousness is *evidently evil*, for it makes light of sin. It talks of merit in the case of one who has already transgressed, and boasts of excellence in reference to a fallen and depraved creature. It prattles of little faults, small failures, and slight omissions, and so makes sin to be a venial error which may be readily overlooked. Not so faith in God, for though it recognises pardon, yet that pardon is seen to come in a way which proves sin to be exceeding sinful. On the other hand, the doctrine of salvation by works has not a word of comfort in it for the fallen. It gives to the elder son all that his proud heart can claim, but for the prodigal it has no welcome. The law has no invitation for the sinner, for it knows nothing of mercy. If salvation be by the works of the law, what must become of the guilty, and the fallen, and the abandoned? By what hopes can these be recalled? This unmerciful doctrine bars the door of hope, and hands over the lost ones to the executioner, in order that the proud Pharisee may air his boastful righteousness, and thank God that he is not as other men are.

It is the intense selfishness of this doctrine which condemns it as an evil thing. It naturally exalts self. If a man conceives that he will be saved by his own works he thinks himself somewhat, and glories in the dignity of human nature: when he has been attentive to religious exercises he rubs his hands and feels that he deserves well of his Maker; he goes home to repeat his prayers, and ere he falls asleep he wonders how he can have grown to be so good and so much superior to those around him. When he walks abroad he feels as if he dwelt apart in native excellence, a person much distinguished from "the vulgar herd," a being whom to know is to admire. All the while he considers himself to be very humble, and is often amazed at his own condescension. What is this but a most hateful spirit? God, who sees the heart, loathes it.

He will accept the humble and the contrite, but he puts far from him those who glory in themselves. Indeed, my brethren, what have we to glory in? Is not every boast a lie? What is this self-hood but a peacock feather, fit only for the cap of a fool? May God deliver us from exalting self; and yet we cannot be delivered from so doing if we hold in any degree the doctrine of salvation by our own good works.

At this time I desire to shoot at the very heart of that soul-destroying doctrine, while I show you, in the first place, that *two great crimes are contained in the idea of self-justification*. When I have brought forth that indictment, I shall further endeavour to show that *these two great crimes are committed by many*, and then, thirdly, it will be a delight to assert that *the true believer does not fall into these crimes*. May God, the Holy Spirit, help us while meditating upon this important theme.

I. First, then, TWO GREAT CRIMES ARE CONTAINED IN SELF-RIGHTEOUSNESS. These high crimes and misdemeanours are frustrating the grace of God, and making Christ to have died in vain.

The first is *the frustration of the grace of God*. The word here translated "frustrate" means to make void, to reject, to refuse, to regard as needless. Now, *he that hopes to be saved by his own righteousness rejects the grace or free favour of God, regards it as useless, and in that sense frustrates it*. It is clear, first, that if righteousness come by the law, the grace of God is no longer required. If we can be saved by our own merits we need justice, but we certainly do not want mercy. If we can keep the law, and claim to be accepted as a matter of debt, it is plain that we need not turn suppliants, and crave for mercy. Grace is a superfluity where merit can be proved. A man who can go into court with a clear case and a bold countenance asks not for mercy of the judge, and the offer of it would insult him. "Give me justice," he says; "give me my rights"; and he stands up for them as a brave Englishman should do. It is only when a man feels that the law condemns him that he puts in a plea for mercy. Nobody ever dreamed of recommending an innocent man to mercy. I say, then, that the man who believes that by keeping the law, or by practising ceremonies, or by undergoing religious performances, he can make himself acceptable before God, most decidedly puts the grace of God on one side as a superfluous thing as far as he is concerned. Is it not clearly so? And is not this a crimson crime—this frustration of the grace of God?

Next, *he makes the grace of God to be at least a secondary thing*, which is only a lower degree of the same error. Many think that they are to merit as much as they can by their own exertions, and then the grace of God will make up for the rest. The theory seems to be that we are to keep the law as far as we can, and this imperfect obedience is to stand good, as a sort of composition, say a shilling in the pound, or fifteen shillings in the pound, according as man judges of his own excellence; and then what is required over and above our own hard-earned money the grace of God will supply: in short, the plan is every man his own Saviour, and Jesus Christ and his grace make-weights for our deficiencies. Whether men see it or not, this admixture of law and grace is most dishonouring to the salvation of Jesus Christ. It makes the Saviour's work to be incomplete, though on the cross he cried, "It is finished." Yea, it even treats it as being utterly ineffectual, since it appears to be of no avail till man's works are added to it. According to this notion, we are redeemed as much by our own doings as by the ransom price of Jesus' blood, and man and Christ go shares, both in the work and in the glory. This is an intense form of arrogant treason against the majesty of divine mercy: a capital crime, which will condemn all who continue in it. May God deliver us from thus insulting the throne of grace by bringing a purchase-price in our hand, as if we could deserve such peerless gifts of love.

More than that, he who trusts in himself, his feelings, his works, his prayers, or in anything except the **grace of God,** *virtually gives up trusting in the grace of God altogether:* for be it known unto you, that God's grace will never share the work with man's merit. As oil will not combine with water, so neither will human merit and heavenly mercy mix together. The apostle saith in Romans xi. 6, "If by grace, then it is no more of works: otherwise grace is no more grace. But if it be of works, then is it no more grace: otherwise work is no more work." You must either have salvation wholly because you deserve it, or wholly because God graciously bestows it though you do not deserve it. You must receive salvation at the Lord's hand either as a debt or as a charity, there can be no mingling of the ideas. That which is a pure donation of favour cannot also be a reward of personal deserving. A combination of the two principles of law and grace is utterly impossible. Trust in our own works in any degree effectually shuts us out from all hope of salvation by grace; and so it frustrates the grace of God.

This is another form of this crime, that when men preach up human doings, sufferings, feelings, or emotions as the ground of salvation, *they take off the sinner from confidence in Christ,* for as long as a man can maintain any hope in himself he will never look to the Redeemer. We may preach for ever and ever, but as long as there remains latent in any one bosom a hope that he can effectually clear himself from sin and win the favour of God by his own works, that man will never accept the proclamation of free pardon through the blood of Christ. We know that we cannot frustrate the grace of God: it will have its way, and the eternal purpose shall be fulfilled; but as the tendency of all teaching which mixes up works with grace is to take men off from believing in the Lord Jesus Christ, its tendency is to frustrate the grace of God, and every act is to be judged by its tendency even if the Lord's divine power prevents its working out its natural result. No man can lay another foundation than that which is laid, but inasmuch as they try to do so they are guilty of despising the foundation of God as much as those builders of the olden time who rejected the stone which God had chosen to be the head of the corner. May the grace of God keep us from such a crime as this, lest the blood of other men's souls should crimson our garments.

This hoping to be saved by our own righteousness *robs God of his glory.* It as good as says, "We want no grace; we need no free favour." It reads of the new covenant which infinite love has made, but by clinging to the old covenant it puts dishonour upon it. In its heart it murmurs, "What need of this covenant of grace? The covenant of works answers every purpose for us." It reads of the great gift of grace in the person of Jesus Christ, and it does despite thereto by the secret thought that human doings are as good as the life and death of the Son of God. It cries, "We will not have this man to save us." A self-righteous hope casts a slur upon the glory of God, since it is clear that if a man could be saved by his own works, he would naturally have the honour of it; but if a man be saved by the free grace of God, then God is glorified. Woe unto those who teach a doctrine which would pluck the crown royal from the head of our sovereign Lord and disgrace the throne of his glory. God help us to be clear of this rank offence against high heaven.

I grow warm upon such a subject as this, for my indignation rises against that which does dishonour to my Lord, and frustrates his grace. This is a sin so gross that even the heathen cannot commit it. They have never heard of the grace of God, and therefore they cannot put a slight upon it: when they perish it will be with a far lighter doom than those who have been told that God is gracious and ready to pardon, and yet turn on their heel and wickedly boast of innocence, and pretend to be clean in the sight of God. This is a sin which devils cannot commit. With all the obstinacy of their rebellion, they can never reach to this. They have never had the sweet notes of free grace and dying love ringing in their ears, and therefore they have never refused the heavenly invitation. What has never been presented to their acceptance cannot be the object of their rejection. Thus, then, my hearer, if you should fall into this deep ditch you will sink lower than the heathen, lower than Sodom and Gomorrah, and lower than the devil himself. Wake up, I pray, and do not dare to frustrate the grace of God.

The second great crime which self-justification commits is *making Christ to be dead in vain*. This is plain enough. If salvation can be by the works of the law, why did our Lord Jesus die to save us? O, thou bleeding Lamb of God, thine incarnation is a marvel, but thy death upon the accursed tree is such a miracle of mercy as fills all heaven with astonishment. Will any dare to say that thy death, O incarnate God, was a superfluity, a wanton waste of suffering? Do they dare think thee a generous but unwise enthusiast whose death was needless? Can there be any who think thy cross a vain thing? Yes, thousands virtually do this, and, in fact, all do so who make it out that men might have been saved in some other way, or may now be saved by their own willings and doings.

They who say that the death of Christ goes only part of the way, but that man must do something in order to merit eternal life,—these, I say, make this death of Christ to be only partially effective, and, in yet clearer terms, ineffectual in and of itself. If it be even hinted that the blood of Jesus is not price enough till man adds his silver or his gold, then his blood is not our redemption at all, and Christ is no Redeemer! If it be taught that our Lord's bearing of sin for us did not make a perfect atonement, and that it is ineffectual till we either do or suffer something to complete it, then in the supplemental work lies the real virtue, and Christ's work is in itself insufficient. His death cry of "It is finished," must have been all a mistake, if still it is not finished; and if a believer in Christ is not completely saved by what Christ has done, but must do something himself to complete it, then salvation was not finished, and the Saviour's work remains imperfect till we, poor sinners, lend a hand to make up for his deficiencies. What blasphemy lies in such a supposition! Christ on Calvary made a needless, and a useless offering of himself if any man among you can be saved by the works of the law.

This spirit also rejects the covenant which was sealed with Christ's death. For if we can be saved by the old covenant of works, then the new covenant was not required. In God's wisdom the new covenant was brought in because the first had grown old, and was void by transgression, but if it be not void, then the new covenant is an idle innovation, and the sacrifice of Jesus ratified a foolish transaction. I loathe the words while I pronounce them. No one ever was saved under the covenant of works, nor ever will be, and the new covenant is introduced for that reason; but if there be salvation by the first, then what need was there of the second? Self-righteousness, as far as it can, disannuls the covenant, breaks its seal, and does despite to the blood of Jesus Christ which is the substance, the certificate, and the seal of that covenant. If you hold that a man can be saved by his own good works, you pour contempt upon the testament of love which the death of Jesus has put in force, for there is no need to receive as a legacy of love that which can be earned as the wage of work.

O sirs, this is a sin against each person of the sacred Trinity. It is a sin against the Father. How could he be wise and good, and yet give his only Son to die on yonder tree in anguish, if man's salvation could be wrought by some other means? It is a sin against the Son of God: you dare to say that our redemption price could have been paid somehow else, and that therefore his death was not absolutely needful for the redemption of the world; or if needful, yet not effectual, for it requires something to be added to it before it can effect its purpose. It is a sin against the Holy Ghost, and beware how you sin against him, for such sins are fatal. The Holy Ghost bears witness to the glorious perfection and unconquerable power of the Redeemer's work, and woe to those who reject that witness. He has come into the world on purpose that he may convince men of the sin of not believing in Jesus Christ: and therefore if we think that we can be saved apart from Christ we do despite to the Spirit of his grace.

The doctrine of salvation by works is a sin against all the fallen sons of Adam, for if men cannot be saved except by their own works what hope is left for any transgressor? You shut the gates of mercy on mankind; you condemn the guilty to die without the possibility of remission. You deny all hope of welcome to the returning prodigal, all prospect of Paradise to the dying thief. If heaven be by works, thousands of us will never see its gates. I know that I never shall. You fine fellows may rejoice in your prospects, but what is to become of us? You ruin us all by your boastful scheme.

Nor is this all. It is a sin against the saints, for none of them have any other hope except in the blood and righteousness of Jesus Christ. Remove the doctrine of the atoning blood, and you have taken all away; our foundation is gone. If you speak thus you offend the whole generation of godly men. I go further: work-mongering is a sin against the perfect ones above. The doctrine of salvation by works would silence the hallelujahs of heaven. Hush, ye choristers, what meaning is there in your song? You are chanting, "Unto him that loved us, and washed us from our sins in his own blood." But why sing ye so? If salvation be by works, your ascriptions of praise are empty flatteries. You ought to sing, "Unto ourselves who kept our garments clean, to us be glory for ever and ever"; or at least "unto ourselves whose acts made the Redeemer's work effectual be a full share of praise." But a self-lauding note was never heard in heaven, and therefore we feel sure that the doctrine of self-justification is not of God. I charge you, renounce it as the foe of God and man. This proud system is a sin of deepest dye against the Well-beloved. I cannot endure to think of the insult which it puts upon our dying Lord. If you have made Christ to live in vain, that is bad enough; but to represent him as having *died* in vain! What shall be said of this? That Christ came to earth for nothing is a statement most horrible; but that he became obedient to the death of the cross without result is profanity at its worst.

II. I will say no more concerning the nature of these sins, but in the second place proceed to the solemn fact that THESE TWO GREAT CRIMES ARE COMMITTED BY MANY PEOPLE. I am afraid they are committed by some who hear me this day. Let everyone search himself and see if these accursed things be not hidden in his heart, and if they be, let him cry unto God for deliverance from them.

Assuredly these crimes are chargeable on *those who trifle with the gospel.* Here is the greatest discovery that was ever made, the most wonderful piece of knowledge that ever was revealed, and yet you do not think it worth a thought. You come now and then to hear a sermon, but you hear without heart; you read the Scriptures occasionally, but you do not search them as for hid treasure. It is not your first object in life thoroughly to understand and heartily to receive the gospel which God has proclaimed: yet such ought to be the case. What, my friend, does your indifference say that the grace of God is of no great value in your esteem? You do not think it worth the trouble of prayer, of Bible-reading, and attention. The death of Christ is nothing to you—a very beautiful fact, no doubt; you know the story well, but you do not care enough about it to wish to be a partaker in its benefits. His blood may have power to cleanse from sin, but you do not want remission; his death may be the life of men, but you do not long to live by him. To be saved by the atoning blood does not strike you as being half so important as to carry on your business at a profit and acquire a fortune for your family. By thus trifling with these precious things you do, as far as you can, frustrate the grace of God and make Christ to die in vain.

Another set of people who do this are *those who have no sense of guilt.* Perhaps they are naturally amiable, civil, honest, and generous people, and they think that these natural virtues are all that is needed. We have many such, in whom there is much that is lovely, but the one thing needful is lacking. They are not conscious that they ever did anything very wrong, they think themselves certainly as good as others, and in some respects rather better. It is highly probable that you are as good as others, and even better than others, but still do you not see, my dear friend, if I am addressing one such person, that, if you are so good that you are to be saved by your goodness, you put the grace of God out of court, and make it vain? The whole have no need of the physician, only they that are sick require his skill, and therefore it was needless that Christ should die for such as you, because you, in your own opinion, had done nothing worthy of death. You claim that you have done nothing very bad; and yet there is one thing in which you have grievously transgressed, and I beg you not to be angry when I charge you with it. You are very bad, because you are so proud as to think yourself righteous, though God hath said that there is none righteous, no, not one. You tell your God that he is a liar. His Word accuses you, and his law condemns you; but you will not believe him, and actually boast of having a righteousness of your own. This is high presumption and arrogant pride, and may the Lord purge you from it. Will you lay this to heart, and remember that if you have never been guilty of anything else this is sin enough to make you mourn before the Lord day and night? You have as far as you could by your proud opinion of yourself made void the grace of God, and declared that Christ died in vain. Hide your face for shame, and entreat for mercy for this glaring offence.

Another sort of people may fancy that they shall escape, but we must now come home to them. *Those who despair* will often cry, " I know I cannot be saved except by grace, for I am such a great sinner; but, alas, I am too great a sinner to be saved at all. I am too black for Christ to wash out my sins." Ah, my dear friend, though you know it not, you are making void the grace of God, by denying its power and limiting its might. You doubt the efficacy of the Redeemer's blood, and the power of the Father's grace. What! The grace of God, is not that able to save? Is not the Father of our Lord Jesus able to forgive sin? We joyfully sing,—

"Who is a pardoning God like thee?
Or who hath grace so rich and free?"

And you say he cannot forgive you, and this in the teeth of his many promises of mercy. He says, "All manner of sin and of blasphemy shall be forgiven unto men." "Come now, and let us reason together, saith the Lord: though your sins be as scarlet, they shall be as white as snow; though they be red like crimson, they shall be as wool." You say that this is not true. Thus you frustrate the grace of God, and you make out that Christ died in vain, at least for you, for you say that he cannot cleanse you. Oh say not so: let not thine unbelief give the lie to God. Oh, believe that he is able to save even thee, and freely, at this very moment, to put all thy sin away, and to accept thee in Christ Jesus. Take heed of despondency, for if thou dost not trust him thou wilt make void his grace.

And those, I think, commit this sin in a large measure, *who make a mingle-mangle of the gospel.* I mean this: when we preach the gospel we have only to say, "Sinners, you are guilty; you never can be anything else but guilty in and of yourselves: if that sin of yours be pardoned it must be through an act of sovereign grace, and not because of anything in you, or that can be done by you. Grace must be given to you because Jesus died, and for no other reason; and the way by which you can have that grace is simply by trusting Christ. By faith in Jesus Christ you shall obtain full forgiveness." This is pure gospel. If the man turns round and enquires, "How am I warranted to believe in Christ?" If I tell him that he is warranted to believe in Christ because he feels a law-work within, or because he has holy desires, I have made a mess of it: I have put something of the man into the question and marred the glory of grace. My answer is, "Man, your right to believe in Christ lies not in what you are or feel, but in God's command to you to believe, and in God's promise which is made to every creature under heaven, that whosoever believeth in Jesus Christ shall be saved." This is our commission, "Go ye into all the world, and preach the gospel to every creature. He that believeth and is baptized shall be saved." If you are a creature, we preach that gospel to you. Trust Christ and you are saved. Not because you are a sensible sinner, or a penitent sinner, or anything else, but simply because God, of his free grace, with no consideration rendered to him on your part, but gratis and for nothing, freely forgives all your debts for the sake of Jesus Christ. Now I have not mangled the gospel; there it is, with nothing of the creature about it but the man's faith, and even that is the Holy Spirit's gift. Those who mingle their "ifs," and "buts," and insist upon it "you must do this, and feel that, before you may accept Christ," frustrate the grace of God in a measure, and do damage to the glorious gospel of the blessed God.

And so, once more, do *those also who apostatise.* Do I speak to any here who were once professors of religion, who once used to offer prayer in the assembly, who once walked as saints, but now have gone back, breaking the Sabbath, forsaking the house of God, and living in sin? You, my friend, say by your course of life,—"I had the grace of God, but I do not care about it: it is worth nothing. I have rejected it, I have given it up: I have made it void: I have gone back to the world." You do as good as say, "I did once trust in Jesus Christ, but he is not worth trusting." You have denied him, you have sold your Lord and Master. I will not now go into the question as to whether you ever were sincere, though I believe you never were, but on your own showing such is your case. Take heed lest these two terrible crimes should rest upon you, that you do frustrate the grace of God, and make Christ to be dead in vain.

III. On my third point I shall carry with me the deep convictions, and the joyful confidences, of all true believers. It is this, that NO TRUE BELIEVER WILL BE GUILTY OF THESE CRIMES. In his very soul he loathes these infamous sins.

First of all, *no believer in Christ can bear to think of the frustrating of the grace of God or the making of it void.* Come, now, honest hearts, I speak to you. Do you trust in grace alone, or do you in some measure rest in yourselves? Do you even in a small degree depend upon your own feelings, your own faithfulness, your own repentance? I know you abhor the very thought. You have not even the shadow of a hope nor the semblance of a confidence in anything you ever were, or ever can be, or ever hope to be. You fling this away as a foul rag full of contagion, which you would hurl out of the universe if you could. I do avow that though I have preached the gospel with all my heart, and glory in it, yet I cast my preachings away as dross and dung if I think of them as a ground of reliance. and though I have brought many souls to Christ, blessed be his name, I never dare for one moment put the slightest confidence in that fact as to my own salvation, for I know that I, after having preached to others, may yet be a castaway. I cannot rest in a successful ministry, or an edified church, but I repose alone in my Redeemer. What I say of myself I know that each one of you will say for himself. Your almsgivings, your prayers, your tears, your suffering persecution, your gifts to the church, your earnest work in the Sunday-school or elsewhere—did you ever think of putting these side by side with the blood of Christ as your hope? No, you never dreamed of it; I am sure you never did, and the mention of it is utterly loathsome to you: is it not? Grace, grace, grace is your sole hope.

Moreover, you have not only renounced all confidence in works, but you renounce it this day more heartily than ever you did. The older you are, and the more holy you become, the less do you think of trusting in yourself. The more we grow in grace the more we grow in love with grace; the more we search into our hearts, and the more we know of the holy law of God, the deeper is our sense of unworthiness, and consequently the higher is our delight in rich, free, unmerited mercy, the free gift of the royal heart of God. Tell me, does not your heart leap within you when you hear the doctrines of grace? I know there are some who never felt themselves to be sinners, who shift about as if they were sitting on thorns when I am preaching grace and nothing else but grace; but it is not so with you who are resting in Christ. "Oh, no," you say, "ring that bell again, sir! Ring that bell again; there is no music like it. Touch that string again, it is our favourite note." When you get down in spirits and depressed what sort of book do you like to read? Is it not a book about the grace of God? What do you turn to in the Scriptures? Do you not turn to the promises made to the guilty, the ungodly, the sinner, and do you not find that only in the grace of God, and only at the cross foot is there any rest for you? I know it is so. Then you can rise up and say with Paul, "I do not frustrate the grace of God. Some may, if they like, but God forbid that I should ever make it void, for it is all my salvation and all my desire."

The true believer is also free from the second crime: *he does not make Christ to be dead in vain.* No, no, no, he trusts in the death of Christ; he puts his sole and entire reliance upon the great Substitute who loved and lived and died for him. He does not dare to associate with the bleeding sacrifice, his poor bleeding heart, or his prayers, or his sanctification, or anything else. "None but Christ, none but Christ," is his soul's cry. He detests every proposal to mix anything of ceremony or of legal action with the finished work of Jesus Christ. The longer we live, I trust, dear brethren, the more we see the glory of God in the face of Jesus Christ. We are struck with admiration at the wisdom of the way by which a substitute was introduced,—that God might smite sin and yet spare the sinner; we are lost in admiration at the matchless love of God, that he spared not his own Son; we are filled with reverent adoration at the love of Christ, that when he knew the price of pardon was his blood his pity ne'er withdrew. What is more, we not only joy in Christ, but we feel an increasing oneness with him. We did not know it at first, but we know it now, that we were crucified with him, that we were buried with him, that we rose again with him. We are not going to have Moses for a ruler, or Aaron for a priest, for Jesus is both king and priest to us. Christ is in us, and we are in Christ, and we are complete in him, and nothing can be tolerated as an aid to the blood and righteousness of Jesus Christ our Lord. We are one with him, and being one with him we realize more every day that he did not die in vain. His death *has* bought us real life: his death *has* already set us free from the bondage of sin, and *has* even now brought us deliverance from the fear of eternal wrath. His death has bought us life eternal, has bought us sonship and all the blessings that go with it, which the Fatherhood of God takes care to bestow; the death of Christ has shut the gates of hell for us, and opened the gates of heaven; the death of Christ has wrought for us mercies, not visionary or imaginary, but real and true, which this very day we do enjoy, and so we are in no danger of thinking that Christ died in vain.

It is our joy to hold two great principles which I will leave with you, hoping that you will suck marrow and fatness out of them. These are the two principles. The grace of God cannot be frustrated, and Jesus Christ died not in vain. These two principles I think lie at the bottom of all sound doctrine. *The grace of God cannot be frustrated after all.* Its eternal purpose will be fulfilled, its sacrifice and seal shall be effectual: the chosen ones of grace shall be brought to glory. There shall be no failures as to God's plan in any point whatever: at the last when all shall be summed up it shall be seen that grace reigned through righteousness unto eternal life, and the topstone shall be brought out with shoutings of " Grace, grace unto it." And as grace cannot be frustrated, so *Christ did not die in vain.* Some seem to think that there were purposes in Christ's heart which will never be accomplished. We have not so learned Christ. What he died to do shall be done; those he bought he will have; those he redeemed shall be free; there shall be no failure of reward for Christ's wondrous work: he shall see of the travail of his soul and shall be satisfied. On these two principles I throw back my soul to rest. Believing in his grace that grace shall never fail me. " My grace is sufficient for thee," saith the Lord, and so shall it be. Believing in Jesus Christ, his death must save me. It cannot be, O Calvary, that thou shouldst fail; O Gethsemane, that thy bloody sweat should be in vain. Through divine grace, resting in our Saviour's precious blood, we must be saved. Joy and rejoice with me, and go your way to tell it out to others. God bless you in so doing, for Jesus' sake. Amen.

Portion of Scripture read before Sermon—Gal. i. 11 ; ii.

Hymns from "Our Own Hymn Book"—178, 647, 554.

Metropolitan Tabernacle Pulpit.

THE GOSPEL OF THE GLORY OF CHRIST.

A Sermon

Delivered on Lord's-day Morning, March 31st, 1889, by

C. H. SPURGEON,

AT THE METROPOLITAN TABERNACLE, NEWINGTON.

"*The light of the glorious gospel of Christ.*"—2 Corinthians iv. 4.

Shining in the centre of the verse, like a pearl in its setting, you find these words. Literally and accurately translated, they run thus: "The light of the gospel of the glory of Christ." This is the form given to my text in the Revised Version, and I shall follow it, because it, word for word, follows the original.

Paul was a man of one idea. The gospel of Christ had saturated his soul as the dew saturated Gideon's fleece. He could think of nothing else, and speak of nothing else, but the glory of Christ crucified. Important events in politics transpired in the apostle's day, but I cannot remember an allusion to them. Great social problems were to be solved, but his one and only solution was the preaching of that great Saviour who is to cleanse the Augean stables of the world. For Paul there was but one thing worth living for, and that one thing was worth dying for. He did not count even his life dear unto him that he might win Christ, and be found in him. Hence his spirits rose or sank according to the prosperity or decline of the kingdom of Christ. When he writes an epistle, his mood varies according to the spiritual condition of the people to whom he writes. If their faith groweth exceedingly, and if from them sounds forth the word of God, then is he jubilant in his tone; but if they are declining in grace, if there are divisions among them, if false doctrine is ravaging them like a wolf in the sheep-fold, then he is solemn in spirit, and he writes with a heavy hand. In this case Paul laments the condition of those who could not see what was so plain to himself—namely, the gospel of the glory of Christ. He saw most clearly the glory of his Lord, and that precious gospel which is built up thereon, and he marvelled that others could not see it also. Considering their case with care, he sorrowfully perceived that they must first have shut their eyes by wilful unbelief, and that, therefore, Satan had exercised his evil power, and had utterly blinded them. The blaze of the gospel is so bright that, even with their eyes averted, some measure of light must have entered their minds, unless some special evil power had operated to

No. 2,077.

hold them in darkness. The devil himself must have blinded them, and even he found it a great task to shut out the glorious light, and to accomplish it he had to assume all his power as "the god of this world." It needed that the cunning with which he apes the Godhead should be put forth to the full to close the perceptive faculties of men against the clear and forcible light of the truth of the gospel. The light of the glorious gospel, like that of the morning dawn, would have been seen even by dim eyes, had not the infernal prince blindfolded the thoughts of men, and made their minds as dark as his own. The light of the gospel is intense, and by a faithful ministry it is flashed in the very faces of men; and therefore, in fear of losing his subjects, the prince of darkness hastens to blind their eyes. Jesus comes to give sight, and Satan comes to destroy it. They each know the value of those eyes by which men look and live. The battle rages at the mental Eye-gate. The conflict between the two champions is raised upon the question—shall men behold the light, or shall they abide in darkness?

I wonder whether there are any here at this time who have long been willing unbelievers, and have at last come to be quite unable to perceive any glory in the gospel of our Lord Jesus. When they hear it faithfully preached, they flippantly criticize the style of the speaker; but the matter of which he speaks appears to them to be of small consequence. They pass by the cross itself, and the sorrow of the Lord is nothing to them. These may be very intelligent men and women in other matters, and yet have no perception of spiritual truth. They can perceive a thousand beauties in nature, but none in grace; they have drunk of the Castalian fountain, but have not even sipped of "the waters of Shiloah that go softly." They can descant at large upon the sublime and beautiful; but they see neither beauty nor sublimity in him who is all that is lovely, and all that is heavenly. I pray that while I am speaking of the light of the gospel of the glory of Christ, that light may penetrate their minds. May God, who commanded the light to shine out of darkness, speak again the almighty fiat, saying, "Let there be light"; and there shall be light. May the miracle of the old creation be repeated in the new creation, to the praise of the glory of divine grace.

First, this morning, I shall ask you to think upon Paul's words, and *consider his name for the gospel*—it is "the gospel of the glory of Christ." Secondly, let us *consider the light which streams from that gospel of the glory of Christ*. When we have thought of these two things, let us *consider what to do with this light*, this marvellous light of the gospel of the glory of Christ.

I. At the outset, LET US CONSIDER PAUL'S NAME FOR THE GOSPEL: "the gospel of the glory of Christ."

It is very evident that the apostle felt that the gospel was solely and altogether of Christ. The Anointed was, in his view, the one subject of the glad tidings, from beginning to end. When he was born, the angels proclaimed good tidings of great joy to the sons of men; and after his death, his human messengers went forth to all nations with messages of love. His death is the birth of our hope; his resurrection is the rising of our buried joy; his session at the right hand of

God is the prophecy of our eternal bliss. Christ is the author of the gospel, the subject of the gospel, and the end of the gospel. His hand is seen in every letter of that wonderful epistle of divine love called the New Testament, or New Covenant. He, himself, is glad tidings to us in every point, and the gospel is from him in every sense. That is not gospel which does not relate to Jesus. If there is no blood-mark upon it, the roll of tidings may be rejected as a forgery. As Christ is the subject, so is he the object of the gospel: his glory is promoted by the gospel. It is the gospel of his glory among the sons of men in all ages, and it will be so throughout eternity. The gospel and the sinners saved by it will glorify the Son of God for ever.

To Paul the gospel was always a glorious gospel. He never had dim views of its excellence. He never spoke of it as though it stood in doubtful competition with Judaism, or heathenism, or the philosophies of the Stoics and the Epicureans. These things were but dross to him in comparison with the "much fine gold" of the gospel. He spoke of it in glowing terms: he felt it to be a great privilege and responsibility to be put in trust with it, and to be allowed to preach it. It was the joy of his heart to live upon it himself, and it was his one aim to proclaim it to others. "The glorious gospel of the blessed God" was his one absorbing science, and he determined to know nothing else. O you that are beginning to think lightly of the old gospel, and dream that it is becoming powerless, may the Spirit that rested upon the apostle rest on you, till you also shall perceive the glory of the divine method of grace, and shall speak of it fervently as "the glorious gospel of Christ"!

Returning to the literal translation, we remark that the apostle saw that the excellence of the gospel lay in the glory of Christ. I shall try to show you this. The glorious Saviour is the substance of the glorious gospel. In speaking of this theme, I can only repeat what you know already, and in that repetition I shall not strive after elaborate expressions, but tell the story simply, after the manner of the apostle, who says, "Seeing then that we have such hope, we use great plainness of speech." The glory of Christ would be insulted by attempts to set it forth with finery of words. Let it be seen in its own light.

The glory of the gospel, then, lies very much in *the glory of our Lord's person*. He who is the Saviour of men is God—"God over all, blessed for ever." Is it not written, "When he bringeth in the first begotten into the world, he saith, And let all the angels of God worship him"? With the angels of God we worship Jesus Christ as God. Our Redeemer is also man—man like ourselves, with this exception, that in him there is no taint of natural depravity, and no act of sin has ever stained his character. Behold the glory of him who is God and man mysteriously united in one Person! He is unique: he is the brightness of the Father's glory, and the brother born for adversity. This is the gospel—that the Son of God himself gloriously undertook the salvation of men, and therefore was made flesh, and dwelt among us, and we beheld his glory. If we had here a vast hospital full of sick folk, it would be the best of news for those languishing therein, if I could tell them that a great physician had devoted himself to their healing; and the more I could extol the physician who had come to visit them, the more would there be of good news for them. If I could say to them, "The physician who is coming to succour you is possessed of infallible wisdom and unerring skill, and in him are united loving tenderness and infinite power," how they would smile upon their beds! Why, the very news would half restore them! Should it not be much more so with desponding and despairing souls when they hear that he who has come to save is none other than the glorious Christ of God? The mysteriously majestic person of Christ is the mainstay of the gospel. He who is able to save is no angel, and no mere man; but he is " Emmanuel, God with us." Infinite are his resources, boundless is his grace. O ye guilty ones, who lie upon beds of remorse, ready to die of grief, here is a Saviour such as you need. When you think of what you are, and despair; think also of what he is, and take heart. If I made you doubt the Deity of the Saviour, I should cut away the foundation of your only hope; but while you see him to be God, you remember that nothing is too hard for him. If I caused you to doubt his proper manhood, I should also rob you of comfort, since you would not recognize in him the tender sympathy which grows out of kinship. Beloved, the Lord Jesus stands before you, commissioned by the eternal God, with the Spirit of the Lord resting upon him without measure; and thus, being in nature and person the first and the best, his message of salvation is to you most full and sure, and his glory is gospel to you.

The glory of Christ lies not only in his person, but *in his love*. Remember this, and see the gospel which lies in it. From all eternity the Son of God has loved his people: even from of old "his delights were with the sons of men." Long before he came on earth he so loved the men whom his Father gave him that he determined to be one with them, and for their redemption to pay the dreadful price of life for life. He saw the whole company of his chosen in the glass of his fore-knowledge, and loved them with an everlasting love. Oh the love which glowed in the heart of our Redeemer "in the beginning"! That same love will never know an end. Herein to us is his glory. He loved us so, that heaven could not hold him; he loved us so, that he descended to redeem us; and having come among us amid our sin and shame, he loves us still. "Having loved his own which were in the world, he loved them unto the end." Love, thou hast reached thine utmost glory in the heart of the divine Saviour! And the glory of this love, which is without beginning, boundary, change, or close, is the very life-blood of the gospel. The love of Jesus is the glad tidings of great joy. Our great Physician loves the sick, and delights to heal them. He comes into the wards among the palsied and the plague-stricken with an intense longing to bless them. Jesus is the sinner's Friend. How rapturously does my soul sing of him as "Jesu, lover of my soul"! A gracious gospel lies in the glory of the love of Christ!

This being so, beloved, we next see the glory of *his incarnation*. To us it was the glory of Christ that he was born at Bethlehem, and dwelt at Nazareth. It looks like dishonour that he should be the carpenter's son; but throughout all ages this shall be the glory of the Mediator, that he deigned to be partaker of our flesh and blood. There is glory in his poverty and shame; glory in his having nowhere to lay his head; glory in his weariness and hunger. Surpassing glory springs from Gethsemane and the bloody sweat, from Calvary and the death of the cross. All heaven could not yield him such renown as that which comes from the spitting and the scourging, the nailing and the piercing. A glory of grace and tenderness surrounds the incarnate God; and this, to those convinced of sin, is the gospel. When we see God in human flesh we expect reconciliation. When we see that he took our infirmities and bare our sicknesses, we hope for pardon and healing. Born of a virgin, our Lord has come among us, and has lived on earth a life of service and of suffering: there must be hope for us. He came not into the world to condemn the world, but that the world through him might be saved. See, I pray you, the glory of his life of doing good, of working miracles of mercy, of tender care for the fallen; and ask yourselves whether there is not in his life among men good news for all sad hearts. Did God himself cover his glory with a veil of our inferior clay? Then he means well to men. Humanity, thus honoured by union with the Godhead, is not utterly abhorred. In the Word made flesh we see the glory of God, and noting how love predominates, how condescending pity reigns, we see in this a gospel of grace for all believing men.

The glory of Christ is further seen in *his atoning sacrifice*. But you stop me and say, "That was his humiliation and his shame." Yes, it is true, and therefore it is his glory. Is not the Christ to every loving heart most of all glorious in the death of the cross? What garment doth so well become our Beloved as the vesture dipped in his own blood? He is altogether lovely, let him be arrayed as he may; but when our believing hearts behold him covered with the bloody sweat, we gaze upon him with adoring amazement and rapturous love. His flowing crimson bedecks him with a robe more glorious than the imperial purple. We fall at his feet with sevenfold reverence when we behold the marks of his passion. Is he not most of all illustrious as our dying substitute? Beloved, here lies the marrow of the gospel. Jesus Christ suffered in our stead. "He his own self bare our sins in his own body on the tree." That glory of his cross, which we again aver to be greater glory than any other, is gospel to us. On his cross he bore the whole weight of divine justice in our place; the iron rod of Jehovah, which must have broken us in pieces like potters' vessels, fell on him. He "became obedient to death, even the death of the cross," and in that act he slew death, and overcame him that had the power of death, that is, the devil.

> " His cross a sure foundation laid
> For glory and renown,
> When through the regions of the dead
> He passed to reach the crown."

But the glory of his sacrificial death, by which he blotted out our sin and magnified the law, is the gospel of our salvation.

We will now travel a little further, to *his resurrection*, wherein his glory is more palpable to us. He could not be holden by the bonds of death. He was dead: his holy body could die, but it could not see corruption; so, having slept a little while within the chamber of the tomb, he arose and came forth to light and liberty—the living Christ glorified by his resurrection. Who shall tell the glory of the risen Lord?

> "Rising, he brought our heaven to light,
> And took possession of the joy."

Rising, he sealed our justification. Rising, he rifled the sepulchre and released the captives of death. He was "declared to be the Son of God with power by the resurrection from the dead." Let us rejoice that he is not dead, but ever liveth to make intercession for us. This is the gospel to us; for because he lives we shall live also. "He is able to save them to the uttermost that come unto God by him, seeing he ever liveth to make intercession for them." Oh the glory of our risen Lord! Consider it deeply, meditate upon it earnestly; and, as you do so, hear the clear sound of glad tidings of great joy. For our greatest consolation we do not look to this precept or to that promise, so much as to Jesus himself, who has by his rising from the dead given us the surest pledge and guarantee of our deliverance from the prison of guilt, the dungeon of despair, and the sepulchre of death.

Once more, lift up your eyes a little higher, and note *the glory of our Lord's enthronement and of his second coming*. He sits at the right hand of God. He that once was hung up upon the tree of shame now sitteth on the throne of universal dominion. Instead of the nail, behold the sceptre of all worlds in his most blessed hand. All things are put under his feet. Jesus, who was made a little lower than the angels for the suffering of death, is now crowned with glory and honour, and this is the gospel to us. For thus it is plain that he has conquered all our enemies, and has all power in heaven and in earth on our behalf. His acceptance with God is the acceptance of all whom he loves; and he loves all who trust him. His sitting in glory is a pledge that the whole of the redeemed by blood shall sit there in due time. His second coming, for which we daily look, is our divinest hope. Mayhap, before we fall asleep the Lord shall descend from heaven with a shout, with the trump of the archangel and the voice of God; and then shall the righteous shine forth as the sun in the kingdom of their Father. Then will our weary days be ended: the strife of tongues, the struggle against sin, the stratagems of error, all will be finished, and truth and holiness shall reign supreme. O my brethren, if I could but break loose from the impediments of mouth and tongue, and speak my heart without these cumbrous organs, then would I make you rejoice in the glory of my divine Master upon his throne to-day, and in his glorious appearing at the appointed hour. If we could see him as John did in Patmos, we might swoon at his feet; but it would be with the rapture of hope, and not with the chill of despair.

Mark this: the less you make of Christ, the less gospel you have to trust in. If you get rid of Christ from your creed, you have at the same time destroyed all its good news. The more gospel we would preach, the more of Christ we must proclaim. If you lift up Christ, you lift up the gospel. If you dream of preaching the gospel without exalting Christ in it, you will give the people husks instead of true bread. In proportion as the Lord Jesus is set up on a glorious high throne, he becomes salvation to the sons of men. A little Christ means a little gospel; but the true gospel is the gospel of the glory of Christ.

II. Secondly, LET US CONSIDER THE LIGHT OF THIS GOSPEL. Our apostle speaks of "the light of the gospel of the glory of Christ."

That light is, first of all, *unveiled*. Whatever light there was in the law—and there was much—it was latent light. The veil on the face of Moses was typical of the way in which the ceremonials of the law were hidden from the sight of men. We forget that a great majority of those things whereof we read in the law were never seen by the Israelites as a people. Do not suppose that any Israelite ever looked within the veil: none but the high priest ever entered there. Even the holy place outside the veil was reserved for the priests. The most of the sacrificial types were as much matters of faith to the Israelites as the meaning is a matter of faith to us. They did not see even the patterns of the heavenly things: they had to be told of them; and in the hearing, they had to exercise faith, as we also do. But, my brethren, our gospel is one, not of the veil which hides, but of the lamp which shines. We use no reserve among you. I solemnly declare before God that I believe nothing which I do not preach among you openly, and I give no sense to the words which I use but that which is natural to them. "For we are not as many, which corrupt the word of God: but as of sincerity, but as of God, in the sight of God speak we in Christ." We have heard of preachers who, under the rose, believe very differently from what they openly say. The trust-deed requires some little consonance with evangelical doctrine, but they loathe it in their souls, and tell their brethren so in private. But as for us, "we have renounced the hidden things of dishonesty, not walking in craftiness, nor handling the word of God deceitfully." We dare preach everything that we believe, and preach it as plainly as possible. The more you know us through and through, the more glad we shall be. Our gospel is one which may be advertised on every hoarding: we have nothing to conceal. I have heard of William Gadsby, of Manchester, that, travelling on a coach one day, he asked two heretical divines to tell him how a sinner is justified in the sight of God. "No," said they, "you don't catch us in that fashion. Whatever answer we gave you, would be repeated all over Manchester within a week." "Oh," says he, "then I will tell *you*. A sinner is justified in the sight of God by faith in the blood and righteousness of Jesus Christ. Go and tell that all over Manchester, and all over England, as quickly as you like; for I believe nothing that I am ashamed of." Light rejoices to proclaim itself. The gospel is a light, and lights are not meant to be hidden under bushels or beds. If they are buried in that way they will burn their way to resurrection, and the bushels and the beds will be consumed, and make all the greater light. The gospel of the blessed God is intended to be conspicuous as the lighthouse on the rock, which is seen afar. It is so illuminating that everyone in the house may see by it. The gospel which is not known is of no value: it is as much intended to be understood as light is meant to be seen.

This light, in the next place, *is all its own*. You cannot illuminate the gospel: it is itself an illumination. Should I not be an idiot if I were to say to my deacon behind me, "Dear friend, kindly get me a candle, I want to show these people the sun. I do not see the sun just now, but I will lead them into the street, and by the help of this candle we will search the sky till we find him out"? I think I hear you say, "Our pastor is out of his mind." Such conduct might well justify the suspicion. It is not by human light that we can show the gospel of God. Not by rhetoric and reasoning do men perceive the light of the gospel. There is a self-manifesting and a self-evidencing power in the gospel. It runs on its own feet, and needs no crutches. If men would read their Bibles they would, as a rule, believe their Bibles; but they will not read them. If men would hear the gospel attentively, they would, as a general rule, believe the gospel; but they will not give it the attention it deserves. It needs no effort to see a bright light. If men would only open their eyes to the light of the gospel, they would see it. If they would only think upon the glory of the gospel of Christ, its light would find its way into their souls. Where the gospel shines in all its brilliance, men have to put up their shutters to keep out its light; and they do even worse, for they call in the devil to gouge out their eyes, that they may not be forced to see. In itself the gospel has such a wonderful power of making itself felt, that, if men did not resist its influence, it would reveal divine things to them. I wish I could induce unbelievers here to read the story of the crucifixion every morning, and to keep on reading it and studying it; for I am persuaded that the light which streams from the cross would, by the blessing of God, open their eyes, and enter their souls savingly.

For, mark you, the light of the gospel of the glory of Christ is *divine light*. Paul tells us this when he says, "For God, who commanded the light to shine out of darkness, hath shined in our hearts, to give the light of the knowledge of the glory of God in the face of Jesus Christ." The gospel is either divine, or it is a lie: it has a supernatural power about it, or else it is an imposture. The true power of the gospel of Christ lies not in its natural reasonableness, nor in its adaptation to human need, nor in its moral beauty, but in the attendant power of the Spirit of God. God is in the gospel, and therefore it is mighty. We may preach to you for a thousand years together, and never a soul of you will receive Christ, unless the same Spirit that spake light into the primeval dark shall say, "Let there be light." Salvation is a supernatural process. God himself must come upon the scene before the eyes of a man born blind will see. How this truth exalts God and lowers man! Yes; and the lower we are brought, the better. When we get to feel our utter helplessness, then will our extremity prove to be the opportunity of the grace of God. O heavenly light, shine now into the soul of all who hear or read this sermon!

This light is *a revealing light*. Whenever the light of the glory of Christ comes streaming into the heart, it reveals the hidden things of darkness. When the glory of Christ is seen, then we see our own shame and sinfulness. Did it need God himself to redeem us? then we must have been in dire bondage. Did it need that the incarnate God should die? then sin must be exceeding sinful. That is a deep pit which needs that God should come from heaven to lift us out of it. We never see the impotence and depravity of human nature so well as in the light of the glory of Christ; but when he is seen as undertaking this tremendous work, and as putting his almighty shoulder to it, then we clearly perceive what help man needed, and how great was his fall. What a revelation it is when the light shines into the secret chambers of imagery, and the idol gods are made manifest in all their hideousness! May God send this light to many, that their ruin, their doom, their remedy, and their way of obtaining it, may be plainly perceived.

The light of the gospel also *enlivens*. No other light will give life to the dead. You may make the strongest light in the world flash frequently upon a corpse, but there will be neither breath nor pulse. But the light of the gospel of the glory of Christ brings life with it. "The life was the light of men." "Awake thou that sleepest, and arise from the dead, and Christ shall give thee light." Darkness is death, but the light of God is life. Let but this Sun of Righteousness arise, and he not only brings healing, but life. Shine, glorious Lord: let thy glory shine forth, and as it pours its brilliance into the minds of men, their dead hearts shall beat with the life of hope and holiness, and they will see the Lord!

This light is *photographic*—you get that in the neighbourhood of the text, in the last verse of the third chapter. See the Revised Version: "But we all, with unveiled face, reflecting as a mirror the glory of the Lord, are transformed into the same image from glory to glory, even as from the Lord the Spirit." The light of the gospel of the glory of Christ imprints Christ's image upon the character of believers. We see him, and, seeing his love, we learn to love; seeing his life, we learn to live; seeing his full atonement, we hate evil; seeing his resurrection, we rise to newness of life. By the power of the Spirit working from day to day, we are quietly transformed from our old likeness, and conformed to the likeness of Christ, till our deformity is lost in a blessed comeliness of conformity to him. If we saw him more clearly and more constantly, we should grow into his likeness more rapidly. No sanctification is worth having but that which comes of communion with the holy Lord through the power of the Holy Ghost. You may read the biographies of good men, and you may copy them in all simplicity, and yet in the end you may become a caricature of perfection, and not the very image thereof. The perfect character of Jesus is yet the most easy to imitate. It is safe to copy Jesus; for in him is no excess or defect; and, strange to say, that character which is in some aspects inimitable is in others the most imitable of all. I have often been depressed in view of the high character of certain saints whom I honour, because I have felt that I could never be like them, under any circumstances. I know one who is full of faith and of all goodness; but he is always solemn, and constantly absorbed "in meditations high." I never could grow exactly like him; for there are certain mirthful elements in my constitution; and if they were taken away, I should not be the same man. When I look at my Lord, I see much in him that is supernatural, but nothing that is unnatural. We see in him humanity in perfection; but the perfection never conceals the humanity. He is so holy as to be a perfect model; so human as to be a model available for poor creatures such as we are. Beloved, the light of the gospel of the glory of Christ is photographic.

Yet, further, *it creates peace and joy.* This light brings delight. I cannot imagine a man unhappy who clearly perceives the light of the glory of Christ. Is Christ glorious? Then it does not much matter what becomes of me. Have you never heard of dying and wounded soldiers in Napoleon's wars who still clung to their emperor with an idolatrous love in the hour of death? Lifting himself upon his elbow, the soldier of the Old Guard gave one more cheer for the great captain. If the dying warrior saw Napoleon riding over the field, he would with his last gasp cry, "*Vive l'Empereur!*" and then expire. We read of one, that when the surgeons were trying to extract a bullet from his chest, he said, "Go a little deeper, and you will find the Emperor." He had him on his heart. Infinitely more commendable is the loyalty of the believer to the Lord Christ. Though we die in a ditch, what does it matter so long as "God also hath highly exalted him, and given him a name which is above every name: that at the name of Jesus every knee should bow, of things in heaven, and things in earth, and things under the earth; and that every tongue should confess that Jesus Christ is Lord, to the glory of God the Father"? It makes the sick saint well to think of the triumphs of his Lord. Have you never, when you have been sitting here heavy in heart, been borne aloft on wings of delight when we have been singing:

> "Bring forth the royal diadem,
> And crown him Lord of all"?

Surely there is a gospel in the glory of Christ to our sad hearts. That gospel lifts us out of the damps of doubt and fear into the clear blue of heavenly fellowship. God grant that we may feel this uplifting more and more! Thus have I tried to describe the qualities of this light; but you must see it for yourselves.

III. And now I close by saying, LET US CONSIDER WHAT WE SHALL DO WITH THIS LIGHT.

Do with it! *Look towards it.* Let us first indulge ourselves with a long and steady gaze upon it. No man can look long at the sun, for it would blind him; but you may look at Jesus, the Sun of Righteousness, as long as you please, and your eyes will grow stronger the longer you gaze on his perfections. I beseech you, beloved in the Lord, to get alone, and give yourself to meditate upon the glory of the once-despised Jesus. Track him from the cradle to the cross, from the cross to the crown. I cannot suggest to you any subject more instructive, more comforting, more ennobling than this. Look at this light; for it is a pleasant thing to behold this sun. Have you never heard how the Laplanders climb the hills when the sun is at last about to appear after the weary winter months? How they rejoice in the first beams of the rising sun! So let us rise to lofty meditation, and look to our Lord and Master, till we perceive his mediatorial glory, and are blessed thereby. Have you no time? Give up your newspaper for a week that you may sanctify the time to the noble end of considering the glory of your Lord; and I will warrant that you shall get a thousand times more out of such thought than from skimming the daily journal. Look unto Jesus, and the light within will grow like the glory of heaven.

Next, if you say that a man cannot always stand looking at the sun, I admit the statement, and change the advice. *See all things by this light.* How differently things look in sunlight to what they do by gaslight or candle-light! Let us regard all things by their appearance in the light of the glory of Christ. Then, if you hear a sermon which does not glorify Christ, it will be a lost discourse to you. Do not endure to see your Lord set in a low place. Hear no more of that talk which makes little of his blood and of his substitution. You read a book, a very clever book, but instead of honouring Christ, it glorifies human nature, and you have soon had enough of it. Only that is good gospel which glorifies Christ. In this light you see things truly. Many of the wise men of the period ought to be treated as Diogenes treated Alexander. The conqueror of the world said to the man in the tub, "What can I do for you?" He thought he could do everything for the poor philosopher. Diogenes only replied, "Get out of the sunlight." These wise people cannot do us a greater favour than to remove their learned selves from standing between us and the sunlight of the ever-blessed gospel of the glory of Christ. These Alexanders may go on ruling the Christian world and the infidel world, but they have not conquered *us;* for our faith and joy lie outside the world, in yonder Sun of Righteousness, whose light is the rejoicing of our eyes.

Beloved, when asked what we should do with this light, I answer again, *value it.* Esteem the glorious gospel of Christ more than all besides. See at what rate the devil reckons it! He takes the trouble himself to come up from the bottomless pit to blind men's eyes, for fear they should see it. When he perceives the blaze of the gospel of the glory of God, he saith to himself, "Ah! they will be seeing the truth, and so they will escape from me. I must go myself, and blind them." So the "God of this age," as he esteems himself, comes to unbelievers, and blindfolds them in one way or another. He thrusts the hot iron of fatal unbelief upon men's inward eyes, and seals them in blackest night, lest they should see "the light of the gospel of the glory of Christ." Since, then, he thinks so much of this light, let us spread it with all diligence. If Satan hates it, let *us* love it. If this is the great gun which he dreads, let us wheel it to the front, and keep up a constant cannonade from it.

The gospel is our *Mons Meg,* the biggest gun in the castle; but it is not out of date: it will carry a ball far enough to reach the heart of the sinner who is furthest from God. Satan trembles when he hears the roar of the gospel gun. Let it never be silent.

Let us also *hold it out with the greatest confidence.* This light must win in the long run. If you came to this building in the middle of the night, somebody might say to you, "How can we get the darkness out of this building?" It would be a hopeless task. How could it be done? You cannot pump out the darkness; but if you fill the house with light the darkness will vanish of itself. Preach Christ, and away goes the god of this world. Exalt Christ, and down goes the devil. Beloved, let us persuade men to let this light shine around them. They cannot see it because of unbelief; but if it shines around them, it may bring them eyes. God the Holy Spirit blessing it, light will beget sight. Induce your friends to hear the gospel and read the Word of God, and who can tell but they will be saved?

And, lastly, let all who try to preach and teach *keep Christ always in the front.* The gospel must have Christ as its centre and its circumference; in fact, as its all in all. The gospel is not the gospel without Christ. The gospel will have no dominant idea in it but Christ. It is a noble steed, but it will bear no rider but him whose vesture is dipped in blood. I have read of the famous horse Bucephalus, that when he was brought out with his royal trappings upon him, he would not allow one even of the highest nobles of the court to mount him; he would carry no one but Alexander, the king. The gospel is glorious in its going when it bears Jesus in the saddle; but if you preach yourself, or human philosophy, the gospel will fling you over its head. Let us sing with the blessed Virgin, "My soul doth magnify the Lord, and my spirit doth rejoice in God my Saviour." This is a gospel sonnet: this is a song which our Well-Beloved deserves of us. O ye preachers and teachers, lift up Christ! He is as the serpent on the pole, and all who look to him shall live for ever. Look to him, all ye that are dying of serpent-bites; for looking ye shall live. God bless these words in which I have desired to glorify my Lord! Amen.

PORTIONS OF SCRIPTURE READ BEFORE SERMON—2 Cor. iii.; iv. 1—7.

HYMNS FROM "OUR OWN HYMN BOOK"—416, 425, 414.

Metropolitan Tabernacle Pulpit.

THE COMMON SALVATION.

A Sermon

DELIVERED ON LORD'S-DAY MORNING, APRIL 10TH, 1881, BY

C. H. SPURGEON,

AT THE METROPOLITAN TABERNACLE, NEWINGTON.

"The common salvation."—Jude 3.

JUDE says, "Beloved, when I gave all diligence to write unto you of the common salvation, it was needful for me to write unto you." The apostle did not write for writing's sake, and in this he sets us an example: we are not to speak for speaking's sake, nor even to preach for preaching's sake. When we take upon us to write concerning divine things it ought to be because it is needful for us to write, and when we speak in the name of God it should be because we have something to say which it is needful should be said. Unless a man feels an imperative necessity to speak he will not speak as an ambassador of God. I wot that Jude would not have given all diligence to write if he had not first felt that necessity was laid upon him so to do. Before you instruct others endeavour to feel the obligation which rests upon you to impart the light which you have received, for if you have been called of God unto this ministry woe is unto you if you preach not the gospel. The souls of others require the truth which you have been commissioned to teach; but you also require to teach it to them; for, if you do not warn them, their blood may stain your skirts. "That the soul be without knowledge is not good:" neither is it good to any that he should withhold what he knows. That men should live and die in ignorance of Christ is terrible to conceive of, therefore when you speak or write do it because it is needful to be done, and needful that you should do it. You know how it behoved Christ to suffer, and even so it behoves us to hold forth the word of life.

The necessity in the present case was that he should write of the common salvation. If it was common—commonly understood and commonly received—why should he need to write about it? Surely a common subject has enough written upon it already, and it affords no room for freshness and novelty, which are so much desired by readers. Yet experience and observation prove that it is more needful to preach the common doctrines of the gospel than any other truths, and that just those things which appear to be the most elementary and the most generally received are those upon which it is most important to lay stress

No. 1,592.

again and again. If there be certain high doctrines, speculative theories, and dogmas which are rather outgrowths of the gospel than the gospel itself, let them be preached in due proportion; but if they be not preached, the risk and danger will not be extreme. As for the root facts, the fundamental doctrines, the primary truths of Scripture, we must from day to day insist upon them. We must never say of them, "Everybody knows them"; for, alas! everybody forgets them. We must not cease from proclaiming them from fear of being charged with uttering mere platitudes; that which is revealed of the Holy Ghost must not be spoken of so reproachfully. Let men call the doctrines of the gospel platitudes if they will; we will only answer, that on such platitudes our salvation rests. After all, on certain grand, wide, well-known truths of universal acceptance the church of God is builded; her basis is not a difficult philosophy, but a plain revelation. Let us not strain after matters of ultra refinement, theories of cultured intellects; but let us obey the necessity which calls upon us to write and to speak of the common salvation. The gospel message is full of world-wide truisms and well-known facts. What said Paul,—"This is a faithful saying, and worthy of all acceptation, that Christ Jesus came into the world to save sinners." If worthy of all acceptation it is surely worthy of all proclamation. It is worth while for the whole church continually to rehearse that Jesus came to save sinners, for common truth as it is there is a necessity that we should perpetually and diligently make it known. The common salvation should be commonly spoken of; but I fear it is uncommonly neglected in these days.

The immediate necessity to write of the common salvation arose out of certain men who had crept into the church unawares. Some of these attacked the gospel on its practical side with Antinomian subtlety. They cried up the grace of God, but said little of the holy living which it produces. They made light of sin under pretence of magnifying the grace of God; they called careful watchfulness a legal spirit, derided humble self-examination, and claimed as children of God to be in no sense bound by the precepts of the moral law. The apostle calls it "turning the grace of our God into lasciviousness." Side by side with these there crept in another gang of evil ones, "who denied the only Lord God, and our Lord Jesus Christ." They robbed Christ of his divine glory, and so denied his atonement and sovereignty as to dethrone him from being either the Saviour or the King of his church. This was the essence of Arianism. They said that Jesus Christ was an admirable example, that he was one of a number of persons who have discovered important truths, and that he is therefore to be greatly admired; but they asserted that still higher truth would yet be discovered as the race proceeded in its progress, and so forth. These "men of thought" crept into the church, and stabbed at the heart of the common salvation. We used to have in our churches a sad amount of the Antinomian leaven; we had among us men who preached the doctrine of grace without the grace of the doctrine, and professors who for evermore spoke about "the truth," but seemed little careful about following "the way" or exhibiting "the life." I hope that this evil principle has pretty well departed from us, though I fear that in its removal it has dragged away precious truth with it; and now we are assailed by quite another school of thought. I see no choice in the two kinds of foes, they are equally bad: these last are denying this truth and paring down the other, moving landmarks and overthrowing monuments, shaking every wall and kicking at every foundation. Having crept in among us unawares, defiant of common honesty, they preach against the gospel from our own pulpits and wage war against our Zion from within her own gates. It is essential at this day that such as fear God, and are his servants, should again and again both write and preach concerning "the common salvation," and over and over again rehearse the first lessons of Christ, the very alphabet of grace. We must make the joyful sound of the common salvation to be more common than ever. I wish to ring it out this morning with all the power that I have and with all that God will grant me by his Holy Spirit. If these men assailed certain speculations of theology it would little matter. What is the chaff to the wheat, saith the Lord? Let the chaff be removed, by all means. If they assailed certain peculiarities of method, either in work, or life, or teaching, it might be well for us to be taught something by their censures. If they attacked the specialities of a single person or sect, and the particular view of truth held by a mere party, it would not signify, for what are the fashions of men's minds? Who is Paul, and who is Apollos? But it is at the very root of the tree that they lay their axe, and, therefore, we must end all hesitation, take up our weapons, and for the sake of the common salvation earnestly contend for the faith which was once delivered unto the saints. Our subject, then, is "the common salvation." Oh to speak in the power of the Spirit.

I. Our first observation at this time shall be that PRESENT SALVATION IS ENJOYED BY THE FOLLOWERS OF CHRIST, otherwise there could be among them no "common salvation." Those who are sanctified by God the Father, and preserved in Jesus Christ, and called, are saved. In the church of God salvation is this day the privilege of all believers. *It is not a matter of the future alone,* a blessing to be sought for on a dying bed and reached in heaven; but it is a blessing for this world and this present time. Those greatly mistake the meaning of salvation who suppose it signifies nothing more than escaping from hell when you die and entering into heaven when the time has come. Salvation means being at once delivered from the power of sin, and being once for all washed from the guilt of sin. The very word used here—"the common salvation"—shows that Jude did not regard it as a hidden treasure put away from human reach throughout this mortal life. How could it have been common in such a case? He did not regard it as a distant attainment to be reached after twenty, thirty, or forty years of holy living, but as a thing to be tasted, and handled, and received as soon as faith enters the soul; for how else could it be common? "Unto us who are saved," says the apostle, "who hath saved us, and called us with an holy calling," saith the Scripture in another place. Salvation has come to our house, we have it, it is a common blessing in the household of faith.

As salvation is not a future benefit only, so *it is not a benefit reserved for a few of the more saintly people among believers.* It is supposed by some that you cannot know whether you are saved till you are in the article of death; or that, if any do know it, it must be a few eminent teachers or specially holy persons, who have lived a very religious life, and consequently know that they are saved. It is to be confessed that the more holy and godly our life the brighter our evidence of salvation becomes; but still, the blessing itself is common to all the children of God, and those whose faith is feeble, and whose spiritual life is weak, are still saved in the Lord. Beloved hearer, you ought not to rest without knowing that you are saved. You may know it: if it be true you ought to know it. I do not think that you have any right to sit quietly on that seat for ten minutes without knowing that you are saved; for it is an awful thing to be in doubt as to whether you are under the bondage of sin, in doubt as to your being at peace with God. This is not a subject upon which uncertainty can be endured. You say, "'Tis a point I long to know." It is well that you long to know it: I beg you to long to know it so intensely that you must either know it or become unutterably wretched. Let every doubt on that point be like a sword in your bones. May God cause your heart either to rejoice with full assurance, or else to be in agony as with death pangs till you are confident that you are built on the sure foundation. The salvation which is in Christ Jesus is the common salvation of all who know the gospel and live upon it. Among simple-minded believers salvation is the inheritance of every one of them, and the knowledge that they are saved is an everyday possession. We who have joined in church-fellowship in this place can truly say, "We rejoice in Christ Jesus, and have no confidence in the flesh": "Being justified by faith, we have peace with God through our Lord Jesus Christ." We count it no presumption to say that we are saved, for the word of God has told us so in those places where salvation is promised to faith in Christ Jesus. The presumption would lie in doubting the word of God; but in simply believing what he says there is far greater humility than in questioning it. Being, then, partakers of like precious faith we share in salvation bought with precious blood, which though it be costly beyond all price is, nevertheless, to all believers the common salvation.

This common salvation consists in many works of grace for us and in us. In part it consists of deliverance from spiritual death. We were dead in trespasses and sins, but the Spirit of God has quickened us into a new and heavenly life, and thus we have salvation from spiritual death. This belongs to-day to all believers; for how can a man be a believer and not have the inner life? Having that life he is conscious that it is there. True, he may fall into a fainting fit, and lie swooning, scarcely conscious of being alive; but such is not his usual condition. Healthy life is conscious life, and rejoices in being, acting, and growing. You who are strangers to the people of God may think me fanatical, but, indeed, I am only speaking words of truth and soberness when I say that the conscious possession of a heavenly life is common among believers, and is, in fact, a large part of the common salvation.

This common salvation consists in deliverance from that awful distance at which we once stood from God. We were far off from him by wicked works, and when the quickening began in us we felt that distance, and we mourned it, fearing also that it never could be removed. But now in Christ Jesus we are brought nigh, and have become dwellers in the house of the Lord. Abba, Father, is the cry which the blessed God hears and accepts, as it rises from our hearts. Once God was not in all our thoughts, but now our thoughts are sanctified, and sweetened by a sense of his presence ; and we find our greatest joy in feeling that he is all around us and within us, that in him we live and move and have our being. Blessed is the common salvation which has brought us nigh to God by the blood of Jesus, and made us children and heirs of the Most High.

We have also been saved from the gloom of heart which once hung over us, because we were conscious of being under God's displeasure. We thought that we could never be forgiven, but we are forgiven; we concluded that our heavenly Father would never accept us, but we are accepted in the Beloved ; we wrote ourselves down among the condemned, but now are we justified by faith which is in Christ Jesus our Lord. The darkness hath passed, and the true light shines into the spirits of the faithful. Peace with God is a sweet part of the common salvation.

Now are we delivered also from the love of sin. We cannot find pleasure in it as once we did. We sin, but it costs us dear. When we do so we lament it with our whole soul. It was our natural way to run the downward road, but now when our feet tread that path it is as wanderers who are out of their way. Once sin was our element, as the water is the living element of fish ; but it is far otherwise now, for sin is death to us. Transgression now breeds sorrow in our conscience, and creates misery in the heart, for it is alien to the life of God which is in us. If we could have our desire we would never offend again : we would have our souls clear as the firmament above us, and never should an evil thought or a loose desire flit over the pure heavens of our sanctified minds. We would do God's will on earth as it is done in heaven ; I say "we," for I speak for all believers in the Lord Jesus. We are all rescued from the iron yoke of the love of evil, and this is a most precious part of the common salvation.

The Lord has also delivered us from that cowardly fear of man which bringeth a snare, and holdeth men as slaves to evil customs. He has also brought us out of the dark dungeon of spiritual ignorance, and renewed us in knowledge ; thus has he broken the dominion of the former lusts of our ignorance, and given us liberty to serve him with godly fear. Pride, too, is laid in the dust, and we are saved from that dreadful tyrant. The dominant power of selfishness is destroyed, and we have learned to love. The woes of others afflict us, the joys of others rejoice us, our soul flows out beyond the narrow confines of our own ribs. Our heart is enlarged with love towards God and to all his creatures. Blessed salvation this! And it is common to all believers.

We have again and again heard it said that evangelical ministers preach salvation to sinful men and talk to them of a future life, whereas if we were practical we should denounce the sinner, and speak only of present reformation in this life. The charge is, I fear, oftener made in malice than in ignorance. But if in ignorance I would reply,—O fools and slow of heart, neither to hearken nor to understand. Our constant theme is immediate salvation from sin, and we are perpetually insisting upon it that this salvation is a present business, to be attended to at once for the purposes of to-day. It is false, utterly false, that we have so preached about the world to come as to have pushed out of sight the duties and temptations of this present life. No, we have regarded the life to come as commenced here below, and have viewed heaven itself as to a great extent the fruit of a heavenly disposition which must be implanted in us while yet on earth. Ah, if men did not hate the gospel they would not so often repeat stale objections and groundless accusations. It is surely time that infidelity should invent something fresh in the way of objection, for this has long passed the stage of toleration, and has become a worn-out impertinence.

Salvation from sin, leading upward to perfection and heaven, is called in the text "the common salvation." It is, then, the salvation of all God's people—the salvation about which all true Christians are agreed; for, notwithstanding all you hear about our divisions into sects, the church is really one. The denominations of the Christian church are very like the divisions of a ploughed field by means of furrows which mark the surface, but the land remains to all intents and purposes one field. I speak not of mere professors, but truly spiritual people; such are all one in Christ Jesus, and their salvation is in all respects the same. If they have not all things common, at least they have one and the same salvation. All converted men and women believe in the same essential truths, feel the working of the same Spirit within them, and press forward to the same end, namely, perfecting holiness in the fear of the Lord. You shall take a high churchman, who is a truly spiritual man, and there are such people, and you shall set him down side by side with the most rigid member of the Society of Friends, and when they begin to talk of Jesus, of the work of the Holy Spirit in the soul, and the desire of their hearts after God, you will hardly know which is which. The nearer we come to him who is the salvation of God, the more plainly we see that among the children of God the basis of agreement is far wider than the ground of division. Andrew Fuller well and pithily said, "There are, I conceive, four things which essentially belong to the common salvation; its necessity, its vicarious medium, its freeness to the chief of sinners, and its holy efficacy." We may differ on the "five points," but we are agreed upon these four points. Ask any true Christian if it be not so. You shall get together, if you like, a collection of the odds and ends of Christianity—and certainly there are some queer Christian people about, whose light comes from above, so they say,—I think through a crack in the roof; but if they are really genuine, and their hearts are right, you shall find that even in these wrong-headed folk there is an agreement upon their need of a Saviour, their faith in his death, the freeness of his grace, and the change of heart which it produces. All believers in Christ have a common delight in a common salvation.

II. We go a step further, and note, secondly, that THIS SALVATION IS IN SOME RESPECTS COMMON IN THE WIDEST POSSIBLE SENSE. It is common because *it is to be preached to all nations,* to all classes, to all characters, to all ages, and to all conditions of men—in fact, it is to be preached to every creature under heaven. It is the common salvation so far as this, that a proclamation of mercy through Jesus Christ is to be made to all mankind; for it is declared that if they believe in Christ Jesus they shall be saved. You need not be afraid of being too free and unreserved in your delivering of the gospel. Let the great trumpet be blown, and let every mortal ear attend. I am as firm an adherent to the doctrines of sovereign grace as any man living; but never shall this tongue hesitate to declare the common salvation. Whenever I am called upon to address a congregation, I will always cry, "Ho, every one that thirsteth, come ye to the waters!" "Whosoever will, let him take of the water of life freely." The invitation of the gospel is so far-reaching that it may well be called "the common salvation."

It is common in the widest sense, because *every man that believeth in Christ Jesus will be saved*; not the Jew only, but the Gentile also; not the poor man only, but the rich man also; not the black man only, or the white man only, but men of every colour; not the ignorant or the learned, the rude or the refined, exclusively, but every soul of Adam born that believeth in Christ Jesus shall be saved. "For God so loved the world that he gave his only begotten Son, that whosoever believeth in him should not perish, but have everlasting life." And so to thee, dear hearer, whoever thou mayest be, comes this common salvation. It is a command addressed to thee, and a promise made sure to thee: "Believe in the Lord Jesus Christ, and thou shalt be saved."

It is common in this wide sense, that *if any man be saved he will be saved by this common salvation*. Men talk as if there were half-a-dozen different roads to heaven, and yet there is but one: they prattle as if there were seven or eight Saviours at the least, or as if every man must be his own Saviour, as we heard the other day of every man being his own lawyer; and yet there is but one name given among men whereby we must be saved. He who tries to be his own Saviour has a fool for his client. He will utterly fail to his eternal confusion: why did Jesus die to save us if we can save ourselves? All of Adam born who enter eternal life come in by the one door. Infants are saved through Christ, and if any attain to heaven from among the heathen it must be by virtue of the salvation of Christ. He is the common life for all that live, the common bread for all who are fed by God, the common joy of all who have been blessed of the Lord. Thus in its publication, in its promise, and in its efficacy the salvation of Christ is the one and only gospel of life to men. As there is but one common air, one common sea, one common earth, so there is but one common salvation. O that we may be among those who prove its power in their own person by being saved in the Lord with an everlasting salvation.

III. But I am persuaded that this is not what Jude meant, so I come, in the third place, to say that IT IS COMMON TO ALL BELIEVERS. Do you recollect what this same Jude once said to the Saviour? He asked him, "Lord, how is it that thou wilt manifest thyself unto us and not unto the world?" He understands that matter now; but he is not looking so much at the "not unto the world" as at the first fact in his question, "Thou wilt manifest thyself unto us." He is evidently full of joy that the manifestation of the salvation of Jesus is common to all believers. Upon that blessed fact let us dwell.

Certain offices, gifts, attainments and enjoyments are given to some and not to others. "Are all apostles? are all prophets? are all teachers? are all workers of miracles? Have all the gifts of healing? do all speak with tongues? do all interpret?" It is not every believer that possesses full assurance, or enjoys ecstasy, or is made largely useful to others. But all believers have the common salvation. There they share and share alike, and every one of them is saved in Christ Jesus and called. An apostle may say to the newest of his converts, "I long to see you, that I may impart unto you some spiritual gift, to the end ye may be established; that is, that I may be comforted together with you by the mutual faith both of you and me."

For, first, it is a common salvation which all believers possess, since it springs from *the same grace.* There are not some saved by grace and others by works, many by pure grace and more partly by works; but salvation is altogether of grace in every case, and that grace is the same in all who possess it. All believers are chosen by the same electing love, for the same reason, namely, to the glory of the Father's grace; and being so chosen, they are all ordained unto the same life, secured by the same covenant, and given into the hands of the same Surety. Eternal love encompasses, enriches, comforts, and preserves each individual believer, and guarantees to each the same inheritance in Christ Jesus. Brother, are you saved by grace? so am I. Am I saved by grace? Then my sister, if thou believest in Christ, thou art saved as I am.

It is a common salvation—common because we are all saved by *the same Saviour.* We are not some of us looking to Jesus, and others to Moses, or to ourselves ; neither are we some of us looking to the atoning death, and others to the perfect life of Christ ; but we are all saved by the same one work, life, death, resurrection and intercession of Christ Jesus. When he made atonement by blood it was for all his redeemed ; when he rose it was to justify all who are in him ; when he stands at the right hand of God to plead, he intercedes for all the saints ; and when he cometh it will be that all his saints may be with him where he is, and may behold his glory. Do not fall into the modern notion, which divides up Christ, and allots something to one class of believers, and another portion to others of the chosen. They tell us there are such and such promises for Israel, and other promises for the church ; I have not so read the word, for I am persuaded that all believers are the Israel of God. God loveth all his saints, and the same blessedness shall be to them all, and you may rejoice and be glad that God will not give special raptures and upsoarings into the skies to a portion of his family, and leave the rest in the cold. In all that is "salvation" we have a common heritage, for Christ belongs to us all, and we are all members of his body, partakers of his life, and sharers of his glory.

It is a common salvation because we are all saved through the *same faith,* we believe the same precious truth, and receive Christ in the same way. All the saved possess faith, though not all to the same degree. Would God we were all strong in faith ! Still, faith is a child-like confidence in God in the greatest as much as in the least of God's people, and this is the essential requisite to salvation in every case. He that believeth in Christ is not condemned, but he that believeth not is condemned already. To all participation in Christian privilege we have only one right : " If thou believest with all thy heart thou mayest." Faith makes a man a fellow-commoner with the saints of God.

It is a common salvation because faith and spiritual life are wrought in us by the *same Spirit.* Faith does not come to one by the operation of free will and to another by free grace, but to every one by the same Spirit. You, then, my brother, are plucked like a brand from the burning by the power of the Spirit of God, so also is thy friend who rejoices with thee. All are quickened by the same Spirit, and kept alive by the same Quickener. The love of the Spirit should be joyfully acknowledged by us all without exception, for the Spirit has wrought all our works in us.

It is a common salvation as to *its results;* for all believers are equally born again, and they are all renewed by him, who saith, "Behold I make all things new." Brought into the one family of God, they are all made children of God and joint heirs with Christ Jesus. They are all justified, accepted, preserved, guided, upheld, and comforted. Their feet are set upon the selfsame rock, they are led in the same King's highway, and a new song is prepared for every one of their mouths. The common salvation, like the common table of a household, satisfies all their mouths with good things, and renews their youth like the eagle's.

By-and-by they shall meet in *the same heaven.* There will be no division before the throne between the different tribes and denominations of believers. One family, we dwell in him even now, with all our petty strifes; but the great family relationship shall be more fully developed by-and-by when imperfections and errors shall be cast aside. The saints before the throne will sing a common hymn unto the common Saviour as they gather in the common home, saved with a common salvation.

Brethren, I am right glad of all this. I feel inclined to stop the sermon and ask you to join in singing Charles Wesley's verse—

> " Partners of a glorious hope,
> Lift your hearts and voices up ;
> Jointly let us rise and sing
> Christ our Prophet, Priest, and King."

To me it is a joyous thing that God's best gifts should be the commonest. It is so in nature: the sunshine, the dew, the air, the heavens, these cannot become the particular estate of a few; they are common blessings. When Richard the Second banished Bolingbroke that nobleman is represented as saying—

> " This must my comfort be,
> That sun that warms you here, shall shine on me ;
> And those his golden beams, to you here lent,
> Shall point on me, and gild my banishment."

There is no monopolizing the best gifts, for heaven ordains them to be the right of all mankind; and so the chief things of the covenant of grace are common to all believers. One may have greater powers of speech than another; but God hath spoken to the silent brother the same promises. Gifts are to this man and to that; but the gift of salvation is to all who believe. The choicest saint may have far less of this world's riches than his brother; but the riches of God's grace are all his own by equal title. We live on common ground here, fed by our Father with the same bread from heaven. Thank God that in so many points the saints have fellowship, for all these should make them of one mind and of one heart towards each other. Some of God's children are not learned, but they shall all be taught of the Lord; all are not experienced in the deep things of God, but they are all entitled to the best things of God. There are some few points in which we are unlike, even as children of the same family differ in age, and height, or in the colour of their eyes or hair ; but we are one in so many vital and conspicuous features, that we should with one voice and heart praise our common Father. We may not all wear the same form of garment, but we all breathe the same life. We may not eat from the same ware, but we all eat the same bread. We may not all drink from a silver chalice, but the wine is from the one cluster. "Now there are diversities of gifts, but the same Spirit. And there are differences of administrations, but the same Lord. And there are diversities of operations, but it is the same God which worketh all in all." It is a great comfort to my heart that, among you who are bound to me by such loving ties, I can speak without hesitation of the common salvation ; for you know it, feel it, love it, rejoice in it, even as I do this day.

IV. That brings me to close, by noticing that this fact of the common salvation was mentioned by Jude that he might use it as an argument. So then THIS FACT HAS MANY LESSONS IN IT.

First, this common salvation *forbids a monopolizing spirit.* The old divines used to say that enclosures were contrary to law. I am afraid that I may not say so now; for almost everywhere the commons have been taken from the poor man and his goose. May there yet be an end to such enclosings. But enclosures in spiritual things are contrary to the law of Christ. Who are we that we should cut off from fellowship with us those whose fellowship is with the Father and his Son Jesus Christ? Yet we have those around us who make it a point of Christianity to be *exclusive.* Their exclusions are perpetual. Shut that door! Shut that door! Shut that door! seems to be the one great command of their house, and the second is like unto it—make more doors, one within the other, and take care to bolt them all. Their sheep must keep within their fold without fail, for if they once get a bite of pasture outside the enclosure their doom is sealed. In many forms this spirit has has been among our denominations, but I do not believe in it. If the spirit of Christianity begets in us love to all mankind, much more, my brethren, are we to love those in whom there is the life of God. Is it really so, that this man is to be un-Christianized because of a mistake and the other because of a misapprehension? Doth God make thy brother a Christian and dost thou try to unmake him? Doth God think so much of him as to forgive him, to give him power in prayer, and enjoyment of his presence, and dost thou think so lightly of him that thou wilt hardly own him to be a partaker in Christ at all? Does the Father smile on all his children, and do we frown on half of them? If I could do it, the last thing I should attempt would be to wall in my own special company and say, "The temple of the Lord are we." I would not wish to set a fence round about the baptized and say, "These be the church of Christ, even as many as have been immersed in water that they may be buried into his death." Beloved brethren, our Lord hath a people that are on other points as right as right can be who on the point of baptism are as wrong as wrong can be; but, for all that, they are his people, and in other respects are sound in the faith and valiant for the Lord our God. Unto such our love goeth forth, and must go forth, despite their grievous error. Upon other matters there are distinctions among believers, but yet there is a common salvation enjoyed by the Arminian as well as by the Calvinist, possessed by the Presbyterian as well as by the Episcopalian, prized by the Quaker as well as by the Baptist. Those who are in Christ are more near of kin than they know of, and their intense unity in deep essential truth is a greater force than most of them imagine: only give it scope and it will work wonders. As for us, let us not be among the men of whom Jude says, "These be they that separate themselves, sensual, having not the Spirit."

Next, this doctrine *fosters the spirit of benediction.* Jude begins his epistle with "Mercy unto you, and peace, and love be multiplied." Brothers and sisters, fill your lungs with this healthy air. You are saved with a common salvation; desire the profit, the growth, the happiness of all who partake of this one salvation. You are in one ship; seek the good of all who sail with you. You are enlisted in one army; pray the Captain of salvation to make every soldier strong in the Lord and in the power of his might. The common salvation should excite us to seek the prosperity of every part of Zion; we would seek the good, not of our Tabernacle alone, but of every tabernacle or temple where Christians meet to worship the Most High.

Next, this fact *arouses in us a common spirit of contention for the one faith.* For what saith the apostle? "It is needful that I write unto you of the common salvation, and exhort you that you should earnestly contend for the faith once delivered to the saints." When the gospel is assailed we must all rise in its defence, for it is the common salvation which is involved in it. When they frightened this nation years ago with the rumour of an invasion by the French, the Russians, or somebody or other, what was the result? Everybody became warlike. Our young men joined rifle clubs, and our elderly men furbished up their old blunderbusses. Everybody hastened to arm himself to protect the common country from the coming foe; and had the enemy really arrived even the women would have shouldered their brooms to sweep the intruder over our white cliffs. Every man, woman, and child would have found some fork, or scythe, or spade, or axe wherewith to protect the common fatherland. Community of interest begets community of feeling. We are all Englishmen, and we all sing, "Britons never will be slaves"; so, in this case, when the gospel of Jesus Christ is assailed, it does not matter by whom, I feel I may call upon all Christians to take action for the common salvation. Brothers, rouse you to the fight, for more than our hearths and homes is now attacked. Do they deny the deity of Christ? It is not only *my* religion that is assailed, it is yours as well. Do they turn the grace of God into lasciviousness? It is not this branch of the church that is now endangered. The entire church is placed in jeopardy. This gospel is not my heritage or yours, it is the common domain of all the faithful, and I beseech you feel it to be so. In your own spheres and in your own ways hold the truth, and hold it firmly. You who can neither preach nor write in defence of sound doctrine can at least give negative help by refusing to countenance error. Do not go to hear those who preach false doctrine, do not encourage them in any way, do not bid them God speed. Love all them that love the Lord Jesus Christ in sincerity, but if a word be spoken against the Lord or against the gospel which he has revealed, turn your back upon the speaker. Be like the loving John, who, when he went to take a bath, found Cerinthus, the heretic, there, and departed at once with all speed. I want to see more backbone in all professors, more determination never to stultify their faith by pretending to believe that black is white and that white is a shade of black. Love: do I not preach it with all my heart, and do I not bid you manifest it in your deeds? But with that love mingle a firm adherence to the truth as it is in Jesus, and a zealous resolve that it shall not lose its honour while you are capable of upholding it. Let the common salvation be protected by the earnest zeal of the entire body of the church and by us also.

This fact, I think, *puts everyone of us to the question,* It is a common salvation, but have I a part in it? It belongs to all the people of God, but am I one of them? I should like you this morning, when you get home, to write on a piece of paper, if you will, whether you are saved or not. It would be a timely searching. Here you are, on this tenth of April—write down "Saved, bless the Lord for it," and if you are obliged to feel you could not write that down, go up into your chamber and cry mightily unto God till you can. Well, if you are able to write "saved," then inasmuch as it is a common salvation go and try to spread that salvation among others. "Others save," says Jude. I know, he says, "others save with fear," but still he says "others save;" try as far as ever you can to bring others to the Saviour. A man's salvation that he never wishes to spread among others is a salvation that is not worth having. You are not saved from selfishness if you do not wish to see your children, and relatives, and neighbours, yea, and all the world brought to Jesus' feet. If it be a common salvation go and make it common.

And, lastly, this text *calls for a common song of praise* from all those who have the common salvation, and I cannot suggest to you a better doxology than that with which Jude closes his epistle: "Now unto him that is able to keep you from falling, and to present you faultless before the presence of his glory with exceeding joy, to the only wise God our Saviour, be glory and majesty, dominion and power, both now and ever. Amen."

PORTION OF SCRIPTURE READ BEFORE SERMON—Epistle of Jude.

HYMNS FROM "OUR OWN HYMN BOOK"—84 (Song II.), 674, 486.

Metropolitan Tabernacle Pulpit.

NUMBER 1,500, OR LIFTING UP THE BRAZEN SERPENT.

A Sermon

Delivered on Lord's-day Morning, October 19th, 1879, by

C. H. SPURGEON,

AT THE METROPOLITAN TABERNACLE, NEWINGTON.

"And Moses made a serpent of brass, and put it upon a pole, and it came to pass, that if a serpent had bitten any man, when he beheld the serpent of brass, he lived."—Numbers xxi. 9.

This discourse when it shall be printed will make fifteen hundred of my sermons which have been published regularly week by week. This is certainly a remarkable fact. I do not know of any instance in modern times in which fifteen hundred sermons have thus followed each other from the press from one person, and have continued to command a large circle of readers. I desire to utter most hearty thanksgivings to God for divine help in thinking out and uttering these sermons,—sermons which have not merely been printed, but have been *read* with eagerness, and have also been translated into foreign tongues; sermons which are publicly read on this very Sabbath day in hundreds of places where a minister cannot be found; sermons which God has blessed to the conversion of multitudes of souls. I may and I must joy and rejoice in this great blessing which I most heartily ascribe to the undeserved favour of the Lord.

I thought the best way in which I could express my thankfulness would be to preach Jesus Christ again, and set him forth in a sermon in which the simple gospel should be made as clear as a child's alphabet. I hope that in closing the list of fifteen hundred discourses the Lord will give me a word which will be blessed more than any which have preceded it, to the conversion of those who hear it or read it. May those who sit in darkness because they do not understand the freeness of salvation and the easy method by which it may be obtained, be brought into the light by discovering the way of peace through believing in Christ Jesus. Forgive this prelude; my thankfulness would not permit me to withhold it.

Concerning our text and the serpent of brass. If you turn to John's gospel you will notice that its commencement contains a sort of orderly list of types taken from Holy Scripture It begins with the creation.

God said, " Let there be light," and John begins by declaring that Jesus, the eternal Word, is "the true light, which lighteth every man that cometh into the world." Before he closes his first chapter John has introduced a type supplied by Abel, for when the Baptist saw Jesus coming to him he said, "Behold the Lamb of God which taketh away the sin of the world." Nor is the first chapter finished before we are reminded of Jacob's ladder, for we find our Lord declaring to Nathanael, "Hereafter ye shall see heaven open, and the angels of God ascending and descending upon the Son of man." By the time we have reached the third chapter we have come as far as Israel in the wilderness, and we read the joyful words, "As Moses lifted up the serpent in the wilderness, even so must the Son of man be lifted up, that whosoever believeth in him should not perish, but have everlasting life." We are going to speak of this act of Moses this morning, that we may all of us behold the brazen serpent and find the promise true, "every one that is bitten, when he looketh upon the brazen serpent, shall live." It may be that you who have looked before will derive fresh benefit from looking again, while some who have never turned their eyes in that direction may gaze upon the uplifted Saviour, and this morning be saved from the burning venom of the serpent, that deadly poison of sin which now lurks in their nature, and breeds death to their souls. May the Holy Spirit make the word effectual to that gracious end.

I. I shall invite you to consider the subject first by noticing THE PERSON IN MORTAL PERIL for whom the brazen serpent was made and lifted up. Our text saith, "It came to pass that if a serpent had bitten any man, when he beheld the serpent of brass, he lived."

Let us notice that the fiery serpents first of all came among the people because *they had despised God's way and God's bread.* "The soul of the people was much discouraged because of the way." It was God's way, he had chosen it for them, and he had chosen it in wisdom and mercy, but they murmured at it. As an old divine says, "It was lonesome and longsome," but still it was God's way, and therefore it ought not to have been loathsome: his pillar of fire and cloud went before them, and his servants Moses and Aaron led them like a flock, and they ought to have followed cheerfully. Every step of their previous journey had been rightly ordered, and they ought to have been quite sure that this compassing of the land of Edom was rightly ordered, too. But, no; they quarrelled with God's way, and wanted to have their own way. This is one of the great standing follies of men; they cannot be content to wait on the Lord and keep his way, but they prefer a will and way of their own.

The people, also, quarrelled with God's food. He gave them the best of the best, for "men did eat angels' food;" but they called the manna by an opprobrious title, which in the Hebrew has a sound of ridicule about it, and even in our translation conveys the idea of contempt. They said "Our soul loatheth this light bread," as if they thought it unsubstantial, and only fitted to puff them out, because it was easy of digestion, and did not breed in them that heat of blood and tendency to disease which a heavier diet would have brought with it. Being discontented with their God they quarrelled with the bread which he set upon their table, though it surpassed any that mortal man has ever eaten before or since. This is another of man's follies; his heart refuses to feed upon God's word or believe God's truth. He craves for the flesh-meat of carnal reason, the leeks and the garlic of superstitious tradition, and the cucumbers of speculation; he cannot bring his mind down to believe the Word of God, or to accept truth so simple, so fitted to the capacity of a child. Many demand something deeper than the divine, more profound than the infinite, more liberal than free grace. They quarrel with God's way, and with God's bread, and hence there comes among them the fiery serpents of evil lusting, pride, and sin. I may be speaking to some who have up to this moment quarrelled with the precepts and the doctrines of the Lord, and I would affectionately warn them that their disobedience and presumption will lead to sin and misery. Rebels against God are apt to wax worse and worse. The world's fashions and modes of thought lead on to the world's vices and crimes. If we long for the fruits of Egypt we shall soon feel the serpents of Egypt. The natural consequence of turning against God like serpents is to find serpents waylaying our path. If we forsake the Lord in spirit, or in doctrine, temptation will lurk in our path and sin will sting our feet.

I beg you carefully to observe concerning those persons for whom the brazen serpent was specially lifted up that *they had been actually bitten by the serpents*. The Lord sent fiery serpents among them, but it was not the serpents being *among* them that involved the lifting up of a brazen serpent, it was the serpents having actually poisoned them which led to the provision of a remedy. "It shall come to pass that *everyone that is bitten*, when he looketh upon it, shall live." The only people who did look and derive benefit from the wonderful cure uplifted in the midst of the camp, were those who had been stung by the vipers. The common notion is that salvation is for good people, salvation is for those who fight against temptation, salvation is for the spiritually healthy: but how different is God's word. God's medicine is for the sick, and his healing is for the diseased. The grace of God through the atonement of our Lord Jesus Christ is for men who are actually and really guilty. We do not preach a sentimental salvation from fancied guilt, but real and true pardon for actual offences. I care nothing for sham sinners: you who never did anything wrong, you who are so good in yourselves that you are all right—I leave you, for I am sent to preach Christ to those who are full of sin, and worthy of eternal wrath. The serpent of brass was a remedy for those who had been bitten.

What an awful thing it is to be bitten by a serpent! I dare say some of you recollect the case of Gurling, one of the keepers of the reptiles in the Zoological Gardens. It happened in October, 1852, and therefore some of you will remember it. This unhappy man was about to part with a friend who was going to Australia, and according to the wont of many he must needs drink with him. He drank considerable quantities of gin, and though he would probably have been in a great passion if any one had called him drunk, yet reason and common-sense had evidently become overpowered. He went back to his post at the gardens in an excited state. He had some months before seen an exhibition of snake-charming, and this was on his poor muddled brain. He must emulate the Egyptians, and play with serpents. First he took out of its cage a Morocco venom-snake, put it round his neck, twisted it about, and whirled it round about him. Happily for him it did not arouse itself so as to bite. The assistant-keeper cried out, "For God's sake put back the snake," but the foolish man replied, "I am inspired." Putting back the venom-snake, he exclaimed, "Now for the cobra." This deadly serpent was somewhat torpid with the cold of the previous night, and therefore the rash man placed it in his bosom till it revived, and glided downward till its head appeared below the back of his waistcoat. He took it by the body, about a foot from the head, and then seized it lower down by the other hand, intending to hold it by the tail and swing it round his head. He held it for an instant opposite to his face, and like a flash of lightning the serpent struck him between the eyes. The blood streamed down his face, and he called for help, but his companion fled in horror; and, as he told the jury, he did not know how long he was gone, for he was "in a maze." When assistance arrived Gurling was sitting on a chair, having restored the cobra to its place. He said, "I am a dead man." They put him in a cab, and took him to the hospital. First his speech went, he could only point to his poor throat and moan; then his vision failed him, and lastly his hearing. His pulse gradually sank, and in one hour from the time at which he had been struck he was a corpse. There was only a little mark upon the bridge of his nose, but the poison spread over the body, and he was a dead man. I tell you that story that you may use it as a parable and learn never to play with sin, and also in order to bring vividly before you what it is to be bitten by a serpent. Suppose that Gurling could have been cured by looking at a piece of brass, would it not have been good news for him? There was no remedy for that poor infatuated creature, but there is a remedy for you. For men who have been bitten by the fiery serpents of sin Jesus Christ is lifted up: not for you only who are as yet playing with the serpent, not for you only who have warmed it in your bosom, and felt it creeping over your flesh, but for you who are actually bitten, and are mortally wounded. If any man be bitten so that he has become diseased with sin, and feels the deadly venom in his blood, it is for him that Jesus is set forth to-day. Though he may think himself to be an extreme case, it is for such that sovereign grace provides a remedy.

The bite of the serpent was painful. We are told in the text that these serpents were "fiery" serpents, which may perhaps refer to their colour, but more probably has reference to the burning effects of their venom. It heated and inflamed the blood so that every vein became a boiling river, swollen with anguish. In some men that poison of asps which we call sin has inflamed their minds. They are restless, discontented, and full of fear and anguish. They write their own damnation, they are sure that they are lost, they refuse all tidings of hope. You cannot get them to give a cool and sober hearing to the message of grace. Sin works in them such terror that they give themselves over as dead men. They are in their own apprehension, as David says, "free among the dead, like the slain that lie in the grave, whom God remembers no more." It was for men bitten by the fiery serpents that the brazen serpent was lifted up, and it is for men actually envenomed by sin that Jesus is preached. Jesus died for such as are at their wits' end: for such as cannot think straight, for those who are tumbled up and down in their minds, for those who are condemned already—for such was the Son of man lifted up upon the cross. What a comfortable thing that we are able to tell you this.

The bite of these serpents was, as I have told you, mortal. The Israelites could have no question about that, because in their own presence "much people of Israel died." They saw their own friends die of the snake-bite, and they helped to bury them. They knew why they died, and were sure that it was because the venom of the fiery serpents was in their veins. They were left without an excuse for imagining that they could be bitten and yet live. Now, we know that many have perished as the result of sin. We are not in doubt as to what sin will do, for we are told by the infallible word, that "the wages of sin is death," and, yet again, "Sin, when it is finished, bringeth forth death." We know, also, that this death is endless misery, for the Scripture describes the lost as being cast into outer darkness, "where their worm dieth not, and their fire is not quenched." Our Lord Jesus speaks of the condemned going away into everlasting punishment, where there shall be weeping, and wailing, and gnashing of teeth. We ought to have no doubt about this, and the most of those who profess to doubt it are those who fear that it will be their own portion, who know that they are going down to eternal woe themselves, and therefore try to shut their eyes to their inevitable doom. Alas, that they should find flatterers in the pulpit who pander to their love of sin by piping to the same tune. We are not of their order. We believe in what the Lord has said in all its solemnity of dread, and, knowing the terrors of the Lord, we persuade men to escape therefrom. But it was for men who had endured the mortal bite, for men upon whose pallid faces death began to set his seal, for men whose veins were burning with the awful poison of the serpent within them—for them it was that God said to Moses, "Make thee a fiery serpent, and set it upon a pole: and it shall come to pass, that every one that is bitten, when he looketh upon it, shall live."

There is no limit set to the stage of poisoning: however far gone, the remedy still had power. If a person had been bitten a moment before, though he only saw a few drops of blood oozing forth, and only felt a little smart, he might look and live, and if he had waited, unhappily waited, even for half an hour, and speech failed him, and the pulse grew feeble, yet if he could but look he would live at once. No bound was set to the virtue of this divinely ordained remedy, or to the freedom of its application to those who needed it. The promise had no qualifying clause,—"It shall come to pass that everyone that is bitten, when he looketh upon it, shall live," and our text tells us that God's promise came to pass in every case, without exception, for we read—"It came to pass, that if a serpent had bitten *any man*, when he beheld the serpent of brass, he lived." Thus, then, I have described the person who was in mortal peril.

II. Secondly, let us consider THE REMEDY PROVIDED FOR HIM. This was as singular as it was effectual. *It was purely of divine origin*, and it is clear that the invention of it, and the putting of power into it, was entirely of God. Men have prescribed several fomentations, decoctions, and operations for serpent bites: I do not know how far any of them may be depended upon, but this I know—I would rather not be bitten in order to try any of them, even those that are most in vogue. For the bites of the fiery serpents in the wilderness there was no remedy whatever, except this which God had provided, and at first sight that remedy must have seemed to be a very unlikely one. A simple look to the figure of a serpent on a pole—how unlikely to avail! How and by what means could a cure be wrought through merely looking at twisted brass? It seemed, indeed, to be almost a mockery to bid men look at the very thing which had caused their misery. Shall the bite of a serpent be cured by looking at a serpent? Shall that which brings death also bring life? But herein lay the excellency of the remedy, that it was of divine origin; for when God ordains a cure he is by that very fact bound to put potency into it. He will not devise a failure, nor prescribe a mockery. It should always be enough for us to know that God ordains a way of blessing us, for if he ordains, it must accomplish the promised result. We need not know *how* it will work, it is quite sufficient for us that God's mighty grace is pledged to make it bring forth good to our souls.

This particular remedy of a serpent lifted on a pole was *exceedingly instructive*, though I do not suppose that Israel understood it. We have been taught by our Lord and know the meaning. It was a serpent impaled upon a pole. As you would take a sharp pole and drive it through a serpent's head to kill it, so this brazen serpent was exhibited as killed, and hung up as dead before all eyes. It was the image of a dead snake. Wonder of wonders that our Lord Jesus should condescend to be symbolised by a dead serpent. The instruction to us after reading John's gospel is this: our Lord Jesus Christ, in infinite humiliation, deigned to come into the world, and to be made a curse for us. The brazen serpent had no venom of itself, but it took the form of a fiery serpent. Christ is no sinner, and in him is no sin. But the brazen serpent was in the form of a serpent; and so was Jesus sent forth by God "in the likeness of sinful flesh." He came under the law, and sin was imputed to him, and therefore he came under the wrath and curse of God for our sakes. In Christ Jesus, if you will look at him upon the cross, you will see that sin is slain and hung up as a dead serpent: there too is death put to death, for "he hath abolished death and brought life and immortality to light:" and there also is the curse for ever ended because he has endured it, being "made a curse for us, as it is written, cursed is every one that hangeth on a tree." Thus are these serpents hung up upon the cross as a spectacle to all beholders, all slain by our dying Lord. Sin, death, and the curse are as dead serpents now. Oh, what a sight! If you can see it what joy it will give you. Had the Hebrews understood it, that dead serpent, dangling from a pole, would have prophesied to them the glorious sight which this day our faith gazes upon—Jesus slain, and sin, death, and hell slain in him. The remedy, then, to be looked to was exceedingly instructive, and we know the instruction it was intended to convey to us.

Please to recollect that in all the camp of Israel *there was but one remedy* for serpent-bite, and that was the brazen serpent; and there was but one brazen serpent, not two. Israel might not make another. If they had made a second it would have had no effect: there was one, and only one, and that was lifted high in the centre of the camp, that if any man was bitten by a serpent he might look to it and live. There is one Saviour, and only one. There is none other name given under heaven among men whereby we must be saved. All grace is concentrated in Jesus, of whom we read, "It pleased the Father that in him should all fulness dwell." Christ's bearing the curse and ending the curse, Christ's being slain by sin and destroying sin, Christ bruised as to his heel by the old serpent, but breaking the serpent's head,—it is Christ alone that we must look to if we would live. O sinner, look to Jesus on the cross, for he is the one remedy for all forms of sin's poisoned wounds.

There was but one healing serpent, and that one was *bright and lustrous*. It was a serpent of brass, and brass is a shining metal. This was newly-made brass, and therefore not dimmed, and whenever the sun shone, there flashed forth a brightness from this brazen serpent. It might have been a serpent of wood or of any other metal, if God had so ordained; but he commanded that it must be of brass, that it might have a brightness about it. What a brightness there is about our Lord Jesus Christ! If we do but exhibit him in his own true metal he is lustrous in the eyes of men. If we will but preach the gospel simply, and never think to adorn it with our philosophical thought, there is enough brightness in Christ to catch a sinner's eye, aye, and it does catch the eyes of thousands. From afar the everlasting gospel gleams in the person of Christ. As the brazen standard reflected the beams of the sun, so Jesus reflects the love of God to sinners, and seeing it they look by faith and live.

Once more, this remedy was *an enduring one*. It was a serpent of brass, and I suppose it remained in the midst of the camp from that day forward. There was no use for it after Israel entered Canaan, but, as long as they were in the wilderness, it was probably exhibited in the centre of the camp, hard by the tabernacle door, upon a lofty standard. Aloft and open to the gaze of all hung this image of a dead snake— the perpetual cure for serpent venom. Had it been made of other materials it might have been broken, or have decayed, but a serpent of brass would last as long as fiery serpents pestered the desert camp. As long as there was a man bitten there was the serpent of brass to heal him. What a comfort is this, that Jesus is still able to save to the uttermost all that come to God by him, seeing he ever liveth to make intercession for them. The dying thief beheld the brightness of that serpent of brass as he saw Jesus hanging at his side, and it saved him; and so may you and I look and live, for he is "Jesus Christ, the same yesterday, to-day, and for ever."

> "Faint my head, and sick my heart,
> Wounded, bruis'd, in every part,
> Satan's fiery sting I feel
> Poison'd with the pride of hell:
> But if at the point to die,
> Upward I direct mine eye,
> Jesus lifted up I see,
> Live by him who died for me."

I hope I do not overlay my subject by these figures. I wish not to do so, but to make it very plain to you. All you that are really guilty, all you who are bitten by the serpent, the sure remedy for you is to look to

Jesus Christ, who took our sin upon himself, and died in the sinner's stead, "being made sin for us that we might be made the righteousness of God in him." Your only remedy lies in Christ, and nowhere else. Look unto him and be ye saved.

III. This brings us, in the third place, to consider THE APPLICATION OF THE REMEDY, or the link between the serpent-bitten man and the brass serpent which was to heal him. What was the link? It was of the most simple kind imaginable. The brazen serpent might have been, if God had so ordered it, carried into the house where the sick man was, but it was not so. It might have been applied to him by rubbing: he might have been expected to repeat a certain form of prayer, or to have a priest present to perform a ceremony, but there was nothing of the kind; he had only to look. It was well that the cure was so simple for the danger was so frequent. Bites of the serpent came in many ways; a man might be gathering sticks, or merely walking along, and be bitten. Even now in the desert serpents are a danger. Mr. Sibree says that on one occasion he saw what he thought to be a round stone, beautifully marked. He put forth his hand to take it up, when to his horror he discovered that it was a coiled-up living serpent. All the day long when fiery serpents were sent among them the Israelites must have been in danger. In their beds and at their meals, in their houses and when they went abroad, they were in danger. These serpents are called by Isaiah "flying serpents," not because they do fly, but because they contract themselves and then suddenly spring up, so as to reach to a considerable height, and a man might be well buskined and yet not be beyond the reach of one of these malignant reptiles. What was a man to do? He had nothing to do but to stand outside his tent door, and look to the place where gleamed afar the brightness of the serpent of brass, and the moment he looked he was healed. He had nothing to do but to look,—no priest was wanted, no holy water, no hocus-pocus, no mass-book, nothing but a look. A Romish bishop said to one of the early Reformers, when he preached salvation by simple faith, "O Mr. Doctor, open that gap to the people and we are undone." And so indeed they are, for the business and trade of priestcraft are ended for ever if men may simply trust Jesus and live. Yet it is even so. Believe in him, ye sinners, for this is the spiritual meaning of looking, and at once your sin is forgiven, and what perhaps is more, its deadly power ceases to operate within your spirit. There is life in a look at Jesus; is not this simple enough?

But please to notice how *very personal* it was. A man could not be cured by anything anybody else could do for him. If he had been bitten by the serpent and had refused to look to the serpent of brass, and had gone to his bed, no physician could help him. A pious mother might kneel down and pray for him, but it would be of no use. Sisters might come in and plead, ministers might be called in to pray that the man might live; but he must die despite their prayers if he did not look. There was only one hope for his life—*he must look to that serpent of brass.* It is just so with you. Some of you have written to me begging me to pray for you: so I have, but it avails nothing unless you yourselves believe in Jesus Christ. There is not beneath the copes of heaven, nor in heaven, any hope for any one of you unless you will believe in Jesus Christ. Whoever you may be, however much bitten of the serpent, and however near to die, if you will look to the Saviour you shall live; but if you will not do this you must be damned, as surely as you live. At the last great day I must bear witness against you that I have told you this straight out and plainly. "He that believeth and is baptized shall be saved: he that believeth not shall be damned." There is no help for it; you may do what you will, join what church you please, take the Lord's Supper, be baptized, go through severe penances, or give all your goods to feed the poor, but you are a lost man unless you look to Jesus, for this is the one remedy; and even Jesus Christ himself cannot, will not, save you unless you look to him. There is nothing in his death to save you, there is nothing in his life to save you, unless you will trust him. It has come to this, *you must look*, and look for yourself.

And then, again, it is *very instructive*. This looking, what did it mean? It meant this—self-help must be abandoned, and God must be trusted. The wounded man would say, "I must not sit here and look at my wound, for that will not save me. See there where the serpent struck me, the blood is oozing forth, black with the venom! How it burns and swells! My very heart is failing. But all these reflections will not ease me. I must look away from this to the uplifted serpent of brass." It is idle to look anywhere except to God's one ordained remedy. The Israelites must have understood as much as this, that God requires us to trust him, and to use his means of salvation. We must do as he bids us, and trust in him to work our cure; and if we will not do this we shall die eternally.

This way of curing was intended that they might magnify the love of God, and attribute their healing entirely to divine grace. The brazen serpent was not merely a picture, as I have shown you, of God's putting away sin by spending his wrath upon his Son, but it was a display of divine love. And this I know because Jesus himself said, "As Moses lifted up the serpent in the wilderness, even so must the Son of man be lifted up. For God so loved the world that he gave his only-begotten Son": plainly saying that the death of Christ upon the cross was an exhibition of God's love to men; and whosoever looks to that grandest display of God's love to man, namely, his giving his only-begotten Son to become a curse for us, shall surely live. Now, when a man was healed by looking at the serpent he could not say that he healed himself; for he only looked, and there is no virtue in a look. A believer never claims merit or honour on account of his faith. Faith is a self-denying grace, and never dares to boast. Where is the great credit of simply believing the truth, and humbly trusting Christ to save you? Faith glorifies God, and so our Lord has chosen it as the means of our salvation. If a priest had come and touched the bitten man he might have ascribed some honour to the priest; but when there was no priest in the case, when there was nothing except looking to that brazen serpent, the man was driven to the conclusion that God's love and power had healed him. I am not saved by anything that I have done, but by what the Lord has done. To that conclusion God will have us all come; we must all confess that if saved it is by his free, rich, sovereign, undeserved grace displayed in the person of his dear Son.

IV. Allow me one moment upon the fourth head, which is THE CURE EFFECTED. We are told in the text that "if a serpent had bitten any man, *when* he beheld the serpent of brass, he lived;" that is to say, *he was healed at once.* He had not to wait five minutes, nor five seconds. Dear hearer, did you ever hear this before? If you have not, it may startle you, but it is true. If you have lived in the blackest sin that is possible up to this very moment, yet if you will now believe in Jesus Christ you shall be saved before the clock ticks another time. It is done like a flash of lightning; pardon is not a work of time. Sanctification needs a lifetime, but justification needs no more than a moment. Thou believest, thou livest. Thou dost trust to Christ, thy sins are gone, thou art a saved man the instant thou believest. "Oh," saith one, "that is a wonder." It is a wonder, and will remain a wonder to all eternity. Our Lord's miracles when he was on earth were mostly instantaneous. He touched them and the fevered ones were able to sit up and minister to him. No doctor can cure a fever in that fashion, for there is a resultant weakness left after the heat of the fever is abated. Jesus works perfect cures, and whosoever believeth in him, though he hath only believed one minute, is justified from all his sins. Oh the matchless grace of God!

This remedy healed again and again. Very possibly after a man had been healed he might go back to his work, and be attacked by a second serpent, for there were broods of them about. What had he to do? Why, to look again, and if he was wounded a thousand times he must look a thousand times. You, dear child of God, if you have sin on your conscience, look to Jesus. The healthiest way of living where serpents swarm is never to take your eye off the brazen serpent at all. Ah, ye vipers, ye may bite if ye will; as long as my eye is upon the brazen serpent I defy your fangs and poison-bags, for I have a continual remedy at work within me. Temptation is overcome by the blood of Jesus. "This is the victory which overcometh the world, even our faith."

This cure was of universal efficacy to all who used it. There was not one case in all the camp of a man that looked to the serpent of brass and yet died, and there never will be a case of a man that looks to Jesus who remains under condemnation. The believer *must* be saved. Some of the people had to look from a long distance. The pole could not be equally near to everybody, but so long as they could see the serpent it healed those that were afar off as well as those who were nigh. Nor did it matter if their eyes were feeble. All eyes were not alike keen; and some may have had a squint, or a dimness of vision, or only one eye, but if they did but look they lived. Perhaps the man could hardly make out the shape of the serpent as he looked. "Ah," he said to himself, "I cannot discern the coils of the brazen snake, but I can see the shining of the brass;" and he lived. Oh, poor soul, if thou canst not see the whole of Christ nor all his beauties, nor all the riches of his grace, yet if thou canst but see him who was made sin for us thou shalt live. If thou sayest, "Lord, I believe; help thou mine unbelief," thy faith will save thee; a little faith will give thee a great Christ, and thou shalt find eternal life in him.

Thus I have tried to describe the cure. Oh that the Lord would work that cure in every sinner here at this moment. I do pray he may.

It is a pleasant thought that if they looked to that brazen serpent by any kind of light they lived. Many beheld it in the glare of noon, and saw its shining coils, and lived; but I should not wonder that some were bitten at night, and by the moonlight they drew near and looked up and lived. Perhaps it was a dark and stormy night, and not a star was visible. The tempest crashed overhead, and from the murky cloud out flashed the lightning, cleaving the rocks asunder. By the glare of that sudden flame the dying man made out the brazen serpent, and though he saw but for a moment yet he lived. So, sinner, if your soul is wrapped in tempest, and if from out the cloud there comes but one single flash of light, look to Jesus Christ by it and you shall live.

V. I close with this last matter of consideration: here is A LESSON FOR THOSE WHO LOVE THEIR LORD. What ought we to do? We should imitate Moses, whose business it was to set the brazen serpent upon a pole. It is your business and mine to lift up the gospel of Christ Jesus, so that all may see it. All Moses had to do was to hang up the brazen serpent in the sight of all. He did not say, "Aaron, bring your censer, and bring with you a score of priests, and make a perfumed cloud." Nor did he say, "I myself will go forth in my robes as lawgiver, and stand there." No, he had nothing to do that was pompous or ceremonial. he had but to exhibit the brass serpent and leave it naked and open to the gaze of all. He did not say, "Aaron, bring hither a cloth of gold, wrap up the serpent in blue and scarlet and fine linen." Such an act would have been clean contrary to his orders. He was to keep the serpent unveiled. Its power lay in itself, and not in its surroundings. The Lord did not tell him to paint the pole, or to deck it with the colours of the rainbow. Oh, no. Any pole would do. The dying ones did not want to see the pole, they only needed to behold the serpent. I dare say he would make a neat pole, for God's work should be done decently, but still the serpent was the sole thing to look at. This is what we have to do with our Lord. We must preach *him*, teach *him*, and make *him* visible to all. We must not conceal him by our attempts at eloquence and learning. We must have done with the polished lancewood pole of fine speech, and those bits of scarlet and blue, in the form of grand sentences and poetic periods. Everything must be done that Christ may be seen, and nothing must be allowed which hides him. Moses may go home and go to bed when the serpent is once uplifted. All that is wanted is that the brazen serpent should be within view both by day and night. The preacher may hide himself, so that nobody may know who he is, for if he has set forth Christ he is best out of the way.

Now, you teachers, teach your children Jesus. Show them Christ crucified. Keep Christ before them. You young men that try to preach, do not attempt to do it grandly. The true grandeur of preaching is for Christ to be grandly displayed in it. No other grandeur is wanted. Keep self in the background, but set forth Jesus Christ among the people, evidently crucified among them. None but Jesus, none but Jesus. Let him be the sum and substance of all your teaching.

Some of you have looked to the brazen serpent, I know, and you have been healed, but what have you done with the brazen serpent since? You have not come forward to confess your faith and join the church. You have not spoken to any one about his soul. You put the brazen serpent into a chest and hide it away. Is this right? Bring it out, and set it on a pole. Publish Christ and his salvation. He was never meant to be treated as a curiosity in a museum; he is intended to be exhibited in the highways that those who are sin-bitten may look at him. "But, I have no proper pole," says one. The best sort of pole to exhibit Christ upon is a high one, so that he may be seen the further. Exalt Jesus. Speak well of his name. I do not know any other virtue that there can be in the pole but its height. The more you can speak in your Lord's praise, the higher you can lift him up the better, but for all other styles of speech there is nothing to be said. Do lift Christ up. "Oh," says one, "but I have not a long standard." Then lift him up on such as you have, for there are short people about who will be able to see by your means. I think I told you once of a picture which I saw of the brazen serpent. I want the Sunday-school teachers to listen to this. The artist represented all sorts of people clustering round the pole, and as they looked the horrible snakes dropped off their arms, and they lived. There was such a crowd around the pole that a mother could not get near it. She carried a little babe, which a serpent had bitten. You could see the blue marks of the venom. As she could get no nearer, the mother held her child aloft, and turned its little head that it might gaze with its infant eye upon the brazen serpent and live. Do this with your little children, you Sunday-school teachers. Even while they are yet little, pray that they may look to Jesus Christ and live; for there is no bound set to their age. Old men snake-bitten came hobbling on their crutches. "Eighty years old am I," saith one, "but I have looked to the brazen serpent, and I am healed." Little boys were brought out by their mothers, though as yet they could hardly speak plainly, and they cried in child language, "I look at the great snake and it bless me." All ranks, and sexes, and characters, and dispositions looked and lived. Who will look to Jesus at this good hour? O dear souls, will you have life or no? Will you despise Christ and perish? If so, your blood be on your own skirts. I have told you God's way of salvation, lay hold on it. Look to Jesus at once. May his Spirit gently lead you so to do. Amen.

PORTIONS OF SCRIPTURE READ BEFORE SERMON—Numbers xxi. 4—9; John iii. 1—18.

HYMNS FROM "OUR OWN HYMN BOOK"—240, 539, 331.

Metropolitan Tabernacle Pulpit.

THE BLOOD OF SPRINKLING.

A Sermon

Delivered on Lord's-day Morning, February 28th, 1886, by

C. H. SPURGEON,

AT THE METROPOLITAN TABERNACLE, NEWINGTON.

> And to Jesus the mediator of the new covenant, and to the blood of sprinkling, that speaketh better things than that of Abel. See that ye refuse not him that speaketh. For if they escaped not who refused him that spake on earth, much more shall not we escape, if we turn away from him that speaketh from heaven."—Hebrews xii. 24, 25.

We are joyfully reminded by the apostle that we are *not* come to Mount Sinai and its overwhelming manifestations. After Israel had kept the feast of the Passover, God was pleased to give his people a sort of Pentecost, and more fully to manifest himself and his law to them at Sinai. They were in the wilderness, with the solemn peaks of a desolate mountain as their centre; and from the top thereof, in the midst of fire, and blackness, and darkness, and tempest, and with the sound of a trumpet, God spake with them. "The earth shook, the heavens also dropped at the presence of God: even Sinai itself was moved at the presence of God, the God of Israel." We are not come to the dread and terror of the old covenant, of which our apostle saith in another place, "The covenant from the Mount Sinai gendereth unto bondage" (Gal. iv. 24.) Upon the believer's spirit there rests not the slavish fear, the abject terror, the fainting alarm, which swayed the tribes of Israel; for the manifestation of God which he beholds, though not less majestic, is far more full of hope and joy. Over us there rests not the impenetrable cloud of apprehension; we are not buried in a present darkness of despair; we are not tossed about with a tempest of horror; and, therefore, we do not exceedingly fear and quake. How thankful we should be for this! Israel was privileged even in receiving a fiery law from the right hand of Jehovah; but we are far more favoured, since we receive "the glorious gospel of the blessed God."

Our apostle next tells us what we *are* come to. I suppose he speaks of all the saints after the death and resurrection of our Lord and the descent of the Holy Ghost. He refers to the whole church, in the midst of which the Holy Spirit now dwells. We are come to a more joyous sight than Sinai, and the mountain burning with fire. The Hebrew worshipper, apart from his sacrifices, lived continually beneath the shadow of the

No. 1,888.

darkness of a broken law ; he was startled often by the tremendous note of the trumpet, which threatened judgment for that broken law ; and thus he lived ever in a condition of bondage. To what else could the law bring him ? To convince of sin and to condemn the sinner is its utmost power. The believer in the Lord Jesus Christ lives in quite another atmosphere. He has not come to a barren crag, but to an inhabited city, Jerusalem above, the metropolis of God. He has quitted the wilderness for the land which floweth with milk and honey, and the material mount which might be touched for the spiritual and heavenly Jerusalem. He has entered into fellowship with an innumerable company of angels, who are to him, not cherubim with flaming swords to keep men back from the tree of life, but ministering spirits sent forth to minister to the heirs of salvation. He is come to the joyous assembly of all pure intelligences who have met, not in trembling, but in joyous liberty, to keep the feast with their great Lord and King. He thinks of all who love God throughout all worlds, and he feels that he is one of them; for he has come to "the general assembly and church of the first-born, which are written in heaven." Moreover, he has come "to God the Judge of all," the umpire and rewarder of all the chosen citizens who are enrolled by his command, the ruler and judge of all their enemies. God is not to them a dreadful person who speaks from a distance; but he is their Father and their Friend, in whom they delight themselves, in whose presence there is fulness of joy for them. Brethren, our fellowship is with the Father, our God. To him we have come through our Lord Jesus Christ. Moreover, in the power of the Spirit of God we realize the oneness of the church both in heaven and earth, and the spirits of just men made perfect are in union with us. No gulf divides the militant from the triumphant; we are one army of the living God. We sometimes speak of the holy *dead;* but there are none such: they live unto God ; they are perfected as to their spirits even now, and they are waiting for the moment when their bodies also shall be raised from the tomb to be again inhabited by their immortal souls. We no longer shudder at the sepulchre, but sing of resurrection. Our condition of heart, from day to day, is that of men who are in fellowship with God, fellowship with angels, fellowship with perfect spirits.

We have also come to Jesus, our Saviour, who is all and in all. In him we live ; we are joined unto him in one spirit; he is the Bridegroom of our souls, the delight of our hearts. We are come to him as the Mediator of the new covenant. What a blessed thing it is to know that covenant of which he is the Mediator! Some in these days despise the covenant ; but saints delight in it. To them the everlasting covenant, "ordered in all things, and sure," is all their salvation and all their desire. We are covenanted ones through our Lord Jesus. God has pledged himself to bless us. By two immutable things wherein it is impossible for him to lie, he has given us strong consolation, and good hope through grace, even to all of us who have fled for refuge to the Lord Jesus. We are happy to live under the covenant of grace, the covenant of promise, the covenant symbolized by Jerusalem above, which is free, and the mother of us all.

Then comes the last thing of all, mentioned last, as I shall have to show you, for a purpose. We have come "*to the blood of sprinkling.*"

On that first day at Sinai no blood of sprinkling was presented; but afterwards it was used by divine order to ratify the national covenant which the tribes made with Jehovah at the foot of the hill. Of that covenant the Lord says, "which my covenant they brake, although I was an husband unto them." *He* never brake his covenant, but *they* brake it; for they failed to keep that condition of obedience without which a covenant founded upon works falls to the ground. We have come to the blood of sprinkling which has fallen upon a covenant which never shall be broken; for the Lord hath made it to endure though rocks and hills remove. This is called by the Holy Ghost "a better covenant, which was established upon better promises." We are, come to the covenant of grace, to Jesus the Mediator of it, and to his blood, which is the seal of it. Of this last we are going to speak at this time—"The blood of sprinkling which speaketh better things than that of Abel."

I shall need this morning to occupy all the time with what I regard as only the first head of my discourse. *What is it?* "The blood of sprinkling." It will be our duty afterwards to consider *where we are*— "we are come unto this blood"; and, thirdly, to remember *what then?* "See that ye refuse not him that speaketh."

I. First, What is it? What is this "blood of sprinkling"? In a few words, "the blood of sprinkling" represents the pains, the sufferings, the humiliation, and the death of the Lord Jesus Christ, which he endured on the behalf of guilty man. When we speak of the blood, we wish not to be understood as referring solely or mainly to the literal material blood which flowed from the wounds of Jesus. We believe in the literal fact of his shedding his blood; but when we speak of his cross and blood we mean those sufferings and that death of our Lord Jesus Christ by which he magnified the law of God; we mean what Isaiah intended when he said, "He shall make his soul an offering for sin"; we mean all the griefs which Jesus vicariously endured on our behalf at Gethsemane, and Gabbatha, and Golgotha, and specially his yielding up his life upon the tree of scorn and doom. "The chastisement of our peace was upon him, and with his stripes we are healed." "Without shedding of blood there is no remission"; and the shedding of blood intended is the death of Jesus, the Son of God.

Remember that his sufferings and death were not apparent only, but true and real; and that they involved an incalculable degree of pain and anguish. To redeem our souls cost our Lord an exceeding sorrowfulness "even unto death"; it cost him the bloody sweat, the heart broken with reproach, and specially the agony of being forsaken of his Father, till he cried, "My God, my God, why hast thou forsaken me?" Our Mediator endured death under the worst possible aspects, bereft of those supports which are in all other cases of godly men afforded by the goodness and faithfulness of God. His was not merely a natural death, but a death aggravated by supernatural circumstance, which infinitely intensified its woe. This is what we mean by the blood of Christ, his sufferings, and his death.

These were voluntarily undertaken by himself out of pure love to us, and in order that we might thereby be justly saved from deserved punishment. There was no natural reason on his own account why he should suffer, bleed, and die. Far from it,—"He only hath immortality." But out of supreme love to us, that man might be forgiven without the violation of divine rectitude, the Son of God assumed human flesh, and became in very deed a man, in order that he might be able to offer in man's place a full vindication to the righteous and unchangeable law of God. Being God, he thus showed forth the wondrous love of God to man by being willing to suffer personally rather than the redeemed should die as the just result of their sin. The matchless majesty of his divine person lent supreme efficacy to his sufferings. It was a man that died, but he was also God, and the death of incarnate God reflects more glory upon law than the deaths of myriads of condemned creatures could have done. See the yearning of the great God for perfect righteousness: he had sooner die than stain his justice even to indulge his mercy. Jesus the Lord, out of love to the Father and to men, undertook willingly and cheerfully for our sakes to magnify the law, and bring in perfect righteousness. This work was so carried out to the utmost, that not a jot of the suffering was mitigated, nor a particle of the obedience foregone: "he became obedient unto death, even the death of the cross." Now he hath finished transgression, made an end of sin, and brought in everlasting righteousness: for he has offered such an expiation that God is just, and the justifier of him that believeth. God is at once the righteous Judge, and the infinitely loving Father, through what Jesus hath suffered.

Brethren, though I have said that there was no reason why the Son of God should bleed and die on his own account, yet towards us there was a reason. Our Lord from of old in the eternal covenant was constituted the head and representative of all who were in him; and so, when the time came, he took the place, bore the sin, and suffered the penalty of those whom the Father gave him from before the foundations of the world. He is as much the representative man as the first Adam was the representative man; and as in Adam the sin was committed which ruined us, so in the second Adam the atonement was made which saves us. "As in Adam all die, even so in Christ shall all be made alive." There was no other person so fit to undertake the enterprise of our redemption as this second man, who is the Lord from heaven. He properly, but yet most generously and spontaneously, came and shed his precious blood, in the room and place and stead of sinners, to bring the guilty near to God.

But the text does not merely speak of the blood *shed*, which I have explained to you, but of "the blood *of sprinkling*." This is the atonement applied for divine purposes, and specially applied to our own hearts and consciences by faith. For the explanation of this sprinkling we must look to the types of the Old Testament. In the Old Testament the blood of sprinkling meant a great many things; in fact, I cannot just now tell you all that it signified. We meet with it in the Book of Exodus, at the time when the Lord smote all the first-born of Egypt. Then the blood of sprinkling meant *preservation*. The basin filled with blood was taken, and a bunch of hyssop was dipped into it, and the lintel and the two side-posts of every house tenanted by Israelites were smeared with the blood; and when God saw the blood upon the house of the Israelite, he bade the destroyer pass that family by, and leave their first-born unharmed. The sprinkled blood meant preservation : it was Israel's passover and safeguard.

The sprinkled blood very frequently signified the *confirmation* of a covenant. So it is used in Exodus xxiv., which I read to you just now. The blood was sprinkled upon the book of the covenant, and also upon the people, to show that the covenant was, as far as it could be, confirmed by the people who promised, "All that the Lord hath said will we do." The blood of bulls and of goats in that case was but a type of the sacrificial blood of the Lord Jesus Christ. The lesson which we learn from Exodus xxiv. is that the blood of sprinkling means the blood of ratification or confirmation of the covenant, which God has been pleased to make with men in the person of our Lord Jesus Christ. Since Jesus died, the promises are Yea and Amen to all believers, and must assuredly be fulfilled. The covenant of grace had but one condition, and that condition Jesus has fulfilled by his death, so that it has now become a covenant of pure and unconditional promise to all the seed.

In many cases the sprinkling of the blood meant *purification*. If a person had been defiled, he could not come into the sanctuary of God without being sprinkled with blood. There were the ashes of a red heifer laid up, and these were mixed with blood and water; and by their being sprinkled on the unclean, his ceremonial defilement was removed. There were matters incident to domestic life, and accidents of outdoor life, which engendered impurity, and this impurity was put away by the sprinkling of blood. This sprinkling was used in the case of recovery from infectious disease, such as leprosy; before such persons could mingle in the solemn assemblies, they were sprinkled with the blood, and thus were made ceremonially pure. In a higher sense this is the work of the blood of Christ. It preserves us, it ratifies the covenant, and wherever it is applied it makes us pure; for "the blood of Jesus Christ his Son cleanseth us from all sin." We have our hearts sprinkled from an evil conscience; for we have come unto the obedience and sprinkling of the blood of Jesus Christ.

The sprinkling of the blood meant, also, *sanctification*. Before a man entered upon the priesthood the blood was put upon his right ear, and on the great toe of his right foot, and on the thumb of his right hand, signifying that all his powers were thus consecrated to God. The ordination ceremony included the sprinkling of blood upon the altar round about. Even thus hath the Lord Jesus redeemed us unto God by his death, and the sprinkling of his blood hath made us kings and priests unto God for ever. He is made of God unto us sanctification, and all else that is needed for the divine service.

One other signification of the blood of the sacrifice was *acceptation and access*. When the high priest went into the most holy place once a year, it was not without blood, which he sprinkled upon the ark of the covenant, and upon the mercy-seat, which was on the top thereof. All approaches to God were made by blood. There was no hope of a man drawing near to God, even in symbol, apart from the sprinkling of the blood. And now to-day our only way to God is by the precious sacrifice of Christ; the only hope for the success of our prayers, the acceptance of our praises, or the reception of our holy works, is through the ever-abiding merit of the atoning sacrifice of our Lord Jesus Christ. The

Holy Ghost bids us enter into the holiest by the blood of Jesus; there is no other way.

There were other uses besides these, but it may suffice to put down the sprinkling of the blood as having these effects, namely, that of preservation, satisfaction, purification, sanctification, and access to God. This was all typified in the blood of bulls and of goats, but actually fulfilled in the great sacrifice of Christ.

With this as an explanation, I desire to come still closer to the text, and view it with great care; for to my mind it is singularly full of teaching. May the Holy Spirit lead us into the truth which lies herein like treasure hid in a field!

First. *The blood of sprinkling is the centre of the divine manifestation under the gospel.* Observe its innermost place in the passage before us.* You are privileged by almighty grace to come first to Mount Zion, to climb its steeps, to stand upon its holy summit, and to enter the city of the living God, the heavenly Jerusalem. In those golden streets, surrounding the hallowed shrine, you behold an innumerable company of angels. What a vision of glory! But you must not rest here; for the great general assembly, the festal gathering, the solemn convocation of the enrolled in heaven, is being held, and all are there in glad attire, surrounding their God and Lord. Press onward to the throne itself, where sits the Judge of all, surrounded by those holy spirits who have washed their robes, and, therefore, stand before the throne of God in perfection.

Have you not come a long way? Are you not admitted into the very centre of the whole revelation? Not yet. A step further lands you where stands your Saviour, the Mediator, with the new covenant. Now is your joy complete; but you have a further object to behold. What is in that innermost shrine? What is that which is hidden away in the holy of holies? What is that which is the most precious and costly thing of all, the last, the ultimatum, God's grandest revelation? The precious blood of Christ, as of a lamb without blemish and without spot—the blood of sprinkling. This comes last; it is the innermost truth of the dispensation of grace under which we live. Brethren, when we climb to heaven itself, and pass the gate of pearl, and wend our way through the innumerable hosts of angels, and come even to the throne of God, and see the spirits of the just made perfect, and hear their holy hymn, we shall not have gone beyond the influence of the blood of sprinkling; nay, we shall see it there more truly present than in any other place beside. "What!" say you, "the blood of Jesus in heaven?" Yes. The earthly sanctuary, we are told, was purified with the blood of bulls and of goats, "but the heavenly things themselves with better sacrifices than these" (Heb. ix. 23). When Jesus entered once for all into the holy place, he entered by his own blood, having obtained eternal redemption for us: so saith the apostle in the ninth chapter of this epistle. Let those who talk lightly of the precious blood correct their view ere they be guilty of blasphemy; for the revelation of God knows no lower deep, this is the heart and centre of all. The manifestation of Jesus under the gospel is not only the revelation of the Mediator,

---

* For this line of thought I am much indebted to a chapter in an admirable book, entitled "Every-day Life," by C. H. Waller, M.A. Shaw and Co.

but especially of his sacrifice. The appearance of God the Judge of all, the vision of hosts of angels and perfect spirits, do but lead up to that sacrifice which is the source and focus of all true fellowship between God and his creatures. This is the character which Jesus wears in the innermost shrine where he reveals himself most clearly to those who are nearest to him. He looks like a lamb that has been slain. There is no sight of him which is more full, more glorious, more complete, than the vision of him as the great sacrifice for sin. The atonement of Jesus is the concentration of the divine glory; all other revelations of God are completed and intensified here. You have not come to the central sun of the great spiritual system of grace till you have come to the blood of sprinkling—to those sufferings of Messiah which are not for himself, but are intended to bear upon others, even as drops when they are sprinkled exert their influence where they fall. Unless you have learned to rejoice in that blood which taketh away sin, you have not yet caught the key-note of the gospel dispensation. The blood of Christ is the life of the gospel. Apart from atonement you may know the skin, the rind, the husk of the gospel; but its inner kernel you have not discovered.

I next ask you to look at the text and observe that *this sprinkling of the blood*, as mentioned by the Holy Ghost in this passage, *is absolutely identical with Jesus himself*. Read it. "To Jesus the mediator of the new covenant, and to the blood of sprinkling, that speaketh better things than that of Abel. See that ye refuse not *him* that speaketh." He saith it is the blood that speaketh; and then he proceeds to say, "See that ye refuse not *him* that speaketh." This is a very unexpected turn, which can only be explained upon the supposition that Jesus and the blood are identical in the writer's view. By what we may call a singularity in grammar, in putting *him* for *it*, the Spirit of God intentionally sets forth the striking truth, that the sacrifice is identical with the Saviour. "We are come to the Saviour, the mediator of the new covenant, and to the blood of sprinkling that speaketh; see that ye refuse not *him*." Beloved friends, there is no Jesus if there is no blood of sprinkling; there is no Saviour if there is no sacrifice. I put this strongly, because the attempt is being made nowadays to set forth Jesus apart from his cross and atonement. He is held up as a great ethical teacher, a self-sacrificing spirit, who is to lead the way in a grand moral reformation, and by his influence to set up a kingdom of moral influence in the world. It is even hinted that this kingdom has never had prominence enough given to it because it has been overshadowed by his cross. But where is Jesus apart from his sacrifice? He is not there if you have left out the blood of sprinkling, which is the blood of sacrifice. Without the atonement, no man is a Christian, and Christ is not Jesus. If you have torn away the sacrificial blood, you have drawn the heart out of the gospel of Jesus Christ, and robbed it of its life. If you have trampled on the blood of sprinkling, and counted it a common thing, instead of putting it above you upon the lintel of the door, and all around you upon the two side-posts, you have fearfully transgressed. As for me, God forbid that I should glory save in the cross of our Lord Jesus Christ, since to me that cross is identical with Jesus himself. I know no Jesus but he who died the just for the unjust. You can separate Jesus and the blood materially; for by the spear-thrust, and all his other wounds, the blood was drawn away from the body of our Lord; but spiritually this "blood of sprinkling" and the Jesus by whom we live, are inseparable. In fact, they are one and indivisible, the selfsame thing, and you cannot truly know Jesus, or preach Jesus, unless you preach him as slain for sin; you cannot trust Jesus except you trust him as making peace by the blood of his cross. If you have done with the blood of sprinkling, you have done with Jesus altogether; he will never part with his mediatorial glory as our sacrifice, neither can we come to him if we ignore that character. Is it not clear in the text that Jesus and the blood of sprinkling are one? What God hath joined together, let no man put asunder. Note this right carefully.

Thirdly, observe that *this "blood of sprinkling" is put in close contact with "the new covenant."* I do not wonder that those who are lax in their views of the atonement have nothing honourable to say concerning the covenants, old or new. The doctrine of the covenants is the marrow of divinity; but these vain-glorious spirits affect to despise it. This is natural, since they speak slightingly of the atonement. What covenant is there without blood? If it be not ratified, if there be no sacrifice to make it sure, then is it no covenant in the sight of God or of enlightened men. But, O beloved, ye who know your Lord, and follow on to know him yet better, to you the covenant of promise is a heritage of joy, and his atonement is most precious as the confirmation of it. To us the sacrificial death of our Lord is not *a* doctrine, but *the* doctrine, not an outgrowth of Christian teaching, but the essence and marrow of it. To us Jesus in his atonement is Alpha and Omega, in him the covenant begins and ends. You see how it was confirmed by blood. If it be a man's covenant, if it be confirmed, it standeth; but this is God's covenant, confirmed with promises, oaths and blood, and it stands fast for ever and ever. Every believer is as much interested in that covenant as was Abraham the father of believers; for the covenant was made with Abraham and his spiritual seed; and in Christ it is confirmed to all that seed for ever by his most precious blood. That, also, is evident enough in the text: fail not to consider it well.

But, fourthly, I want you to notice that according to the text *the blood is the voice of the new dispensation.* Observe that on Sinai there was "the sound of a trumpet, and the voice of words; which voice they that heard entreated that the word should not be spoken to them any more." You look, therefore, under the new dispensation, for a voice, and you do not come to any till you reach the last object in the list, and there see "the blood of sprinkling that speaketh." Here, then, is the voice of the gospel; it is not the sound of a trumpet, nor the voice of words spoken in terrible majesty; but the blood speaks, and assuredly there is no sound more piercing, more potent, more prevailing. God heard the voice of Abel's blood and visited Cain with condign punishment for killing his brother; and the precious blood of Jesus Christ, the Son of God, cries in the ears of God with a voice which is ever heard. How can it be imagined that the Lord God should be deaf to the cry of his Son's sacrifice? Lo, these many ages the blood has cried —"Forgive them! Forgive them! Accept them! Deliver them from going down into the pit, for I have found a ransom!"

The blood of sprinkling has a voice of instruction to us even as it has a voice of intercession with God. It cries to us, "See the evil of sin! See how God loveth righteousness! See how he loveth men! See how impossible it is for you to escape from the punishment of sin except by this great sacrifice in which the love and the justice of God equally appear! See how Jehovah spared not his own Son, but freely delivered him up for us all."

What a voice there is in the atonement!—a voice which pleads for holiness and love, for justice and grace, for truth and mercy. "See that ye refuse not him that speaketh."

Do you not hear it? If you take away the blood of sprinkling from the gospel, you have silenced it. It has no voice if this be gone. "Oh," they say, "the gospel has lost its power"! What wonder when they have made it a dumb gospel! How can it have power when they take away that which is its life and speech? Unless the preacher is evermore preaching this blood, and sprinkling it by the doctrine of faith, his teaching has no voice either to rouse the careless or to cheer the anxious. If ever there should come a wretched day when all our pulpits shall be full of modern thought, and the old doctrine of a substitutionary sacrifice shall be exploded, then will there remain no word of comfort for the guilty or hope for the despairing. Hushed will be for ever those silver notes which now console the living, and cheer the dying; a dumb spirit will possess this sullen world, and no voice of joy will break the blank silence of despair. The gospel speaks through the propitiation for sin, and if that be denied, it speaketh no more. Those who preach not the atonement exhibit a dumb and dummy gospel; a mouth it hath, but speaketh not; they that make it are like unto their idol.

Let me draw you nearer still to the text. Observe, that *this voice is identical with the voice of the Lord Jesus;* for it is put so. "The blood of sprinkling that speaketh. See that ye refuse not *him* that speaketh." Whatever the doctrine of the sacrifice of Jesus may be, it is the main teaching of Jesus himself. It is well to notice that the voice which spoke from Sinai was also the voice of Christ. It was Jesus who delivered that law the penalty of which he was himself to endure. He that read it out amidst the tempest was Jesus. Notice the declaration—"Whose voice then shook the earth." Whenever you hear the gospel, the voice of the precious blood is the voice of Jesus himself, the voice of him that shook the earth at Sinai. This same voice shall by-and-by shake, not the earth only, but also heaven. What a voice there is in the blood of sprinkling, since indeed it is the voice of the eternal Son of God, who both makes and destroys! Would you have me silence the doctrine of the blood of sprinkling? Would any one of you attempt so horrible a deed? Shall we be censured if we continually proclaim the heaven-sent message of the blood of Jesus? Shall we speak with bated breath because some affected person shudders at the sound of the word "*blood*"? or some "cultured" individual rebels at the old-fashioned thought of sacrifice? Nay, verily, we will sooner have our tongue cut out than cease to speak of the precious blood of Jesus Christ. For me there is nothing worth thinking of or preaching about but this grand truth, which is the beginning and the end of the whole Christian system, namely, that God gave his Son to die that sinners might live.

This is not the voice of the blood only, but the voice of our Lord Jesus Christ himself. So saith the text, and who can contradict it?

Further, my brethren, from the text I learn another truth, namely, that *this blood is always speaking*. The text saith not "the blood of sprinkling that spoke," but "that speaketh." It is always speaking, it always remaineth a plea with God and a testimony to men. It never will be silenced, either one way or the other. In the intercession of our risen and ascended Lord his sacrifice ever speaketh to the Most High. By the teaching of the Holy Ghost the atonement will always speak in edification to believers yet upon the earth. It is the blood that speaketh. According to our text, this is the only speech which this dispensation yields us. Shall that speech ever be still? Shall we decline to hear it? Shall we refuse to echo it? God forbid. By day, by night, the great sacrifice continues to cry to the sons of men, "Turn ye from your sins, for they cost your Saviour dear. The times of your ignorance God winked at, but now commandeth all men everywhere to repent, since he is able to forgive and yet be just. Your offended God has himself provided a sacrifice; come and be sprinkled with its blood, and be reconciled once for all." The voice of this blood speaks wherever there is a guilty conscience, wherever there is an anxious heart, wherever there is a seeking sinner, wherever there is a believing mind. It speaketh with sweet, familiar, tender, inviting voice. There is no music like it to the sinner's ear: it charms away his fears. It shall never cease its speaking so long as there is a sinner yet out of Christ; nay, so long as there is one on earth who still needs its cleansing power because of fresh backslidings. Oh, hear ye its voice! Incline your ear and receive its blessed accents: it says, "Come now, and let us reason together, saith the Lord; though your sins be as scarlet, they shall be as white as snow; though they be red like crimson, they shall be as wool."

This part of my discourse will not be complete unless I bid you notice that we are expressly told that *this precious blood speaks "better things than that of Abel."* I do not think that the whole meaning of the passage is exhausted if we say that Abel's blood cries for vengeance, and that Christ's blood speaks for pardon. Dr. Watts puts it:—

> "Blood has a voice to pierce the skies:
> 'Revenge!' the blood of Abel cries;
> But the dear stream when Christ was slain
> Speaks peace as loud from ev'ry vein."

That is quite true; but I conceive that it is not all the sense, and perhaps not even *the* sense here intended. Revenge is scarcely a good thing; yet Abel's blood spake good things, or we should hardly read that Christ's blood speaks "better things." What does the blood of Abel speak? The blood of Abel speaks to a complete and believing obedience to God. It shows us a man who believes God, and, notwithstanding the enmity of his brother, brings to God the appointed sacrifice of faith, strictly following up, even to the bitter end, his holy obedience to the Most High. That is what the blood of Abel says to me; and the blood of Jesus says the same thing most emphatically. The death of Jesus Christ was the crown and close of a perfect life; it was a fit completion of a course of holiness. In obedience to the Great Father, Jesus even laid down his life. But if this be all the blood of Jesus speaks, as some say that it is, then it does not speak better things than the blood of Abel; for it only says the same things in a louder voice. The martyrdom of any saint has a voice for obedience to God as truly as the martyrdom of Jesus; but the death of our Lord says far more, infinitely more, than this: it not only witnesses to complete obedience, but it provides the way by which the disobedient may be forgiven and helped to obedience and holiness. The cross has a greater, deeper, gladder gospel for fallen men than that of a perfect example which they are unable to follow.

The blood of Abel said this, too—that he was not ashamed of his faith, but witnessed a good confession concerning his God, even to the death; he put his life in his hand, and was not ashamed to stand at the altar of God, and avow his faith by obediently offering the ordained sacrifice. Now, I grant you that the blood of Jesus also declares that he was a faithful and true witness, who willingly sealed his witness with his blood. He proved by shedding his blood that he could not be turned aside from truth and righteousness, even though death stood in his way; but if that is all that the blood of sprinkling speaketh, it saith no better things than the blood of Abel. "Be faithful unto death," is the voice of Abel as well as of Jesus. Jesus must have said more than this by his blood-shedding.

The blood of Abel said good things; that is implied in the fact that the blood of Jesus Christ says better things; and no doubt the blood of Abel rises to the dignity of teaching self-sacrifice. Here was a man, a keeper of sheep, who by his mode of life laid out his life for the good of those committed to his charge; and at the last, in obedience to God, he yielded himself up to die by a brother's hand. It was the first draught of a picture of self-sacrifice. Our Lord Jesus Christ also made a complete self-sacrifice. All his life long he gave himself to men. He lived never for himself. The glory of God and the good of men were united in one passion which filled his whole soul. He could say, "The zeal of thine house hath eaten me up." His death was the completion of his perfect self-sacrifice. But if that were all, the blood of Jesus saith no better thing than Abel's death saith, though it may say it more emphatically.

Our Lord's blood saith "better things than that of Abel"; and what doth it say? It saith, "There is redemption through his blood, the forgiveness of sins according to the riches of his grace." "He his own self bare our sins in his own body on the tree, that we being dead to sins should live unto righteousness: by whose stripes we were healed." "He hath made him to be sin for us, who knew no sin; that we might be made the righteousness of God in him." The voice of the blood is this, "For I will be merciful to their unrighteousness, and their sins and their iniquities will I remember no more." "The blood of Jesus Christ his Son cleanseth us from all sin." Now, my brethren, these are better things than Abel's blood could say, and they are what the blood of Jesus speaks to every one upon whom it is sprinkled by faith. It must be applied to each one of us by faith, or it says nothing to us. But when it falls on each believing individual, it saith to him words of blessing which pacify his conscience and delight his soul.

The apostle says that "Ye are come to the blood of sprinkling." Is it so? Has that blood of sprinkling ever been applied to you? Do you feel it? Are you preserved? Are you cleansed? Are you brought nigh to God? Are you sanctified unto God's service by the atoning sacrifice? If so, then go you out, and in firm confidence that never can be shaken, make your glory in the blood of sprinkling. Tell every sinner whom you meet that if the Lord Jesus wash him he shall be whiter than snow. Preach the atoning sacrifice of the Lamb of God, and then sing of it. Recollect that wondrous threefold song in the fifth chapter of the Revelation, where, first of all, the elders and living creatures round about the throne, sing a new song, saying, "Thou wast slain, and hast redeemed us to God by thy blood out of every kindred, and tongue, and people, and nation." Then ten thousand times ten thousand, and thousands of thousands of angels take up the strain and cry, "Worthy is the Lamb that was slain." Nor is this all; for the apostle tells us, "Every creature which is in heaven, and on the earth, and under the earth, and such as are in the sea, and all that are in them, heard I saying, Blessing, and honour, and glory, and power, be unto him that sitteth upon the throne, and unto the Lamb for ever and ever." See you not that they all extol the Lord Jesus in his sacrificial character as the Lamb slain? I have scant patience with those who dare to put this great truth into the background, and even sneer at it or misrepresent it of set purpose. Sirs, if you would be saved you must have the blood of Jesus sprinkled upon you. He that believeth not in Christ Jesus, in Jesus the atoning sacrifice, must perish. The eternal God must repulse with infinite disgust the man who refuses the loving sacrifice of Jesus. Inasmuch as he counted himself unworthy of this wondrous sacrifice, this marvellous expiation, there remaineth no other sacrifice for sin, and nothing for him but that eternal blackness and darkness and thunder which were foreshadowed at Sinai. Those who refuse the atonement which wisdom devised, which love provided, and which justice has accepted, have signed their own death-warrant, and none can wonder that they perish. The Lord lead us to glory in Christ crucified. Amen.

PORTIONS OF SCRIPTURE READ BEFORE SERMON—Exodus xx. 1—21; xxiv. 1—8.

HYMNS FROM "OUR OWN HYMN BOOK"—236, 279, 291.

Metropolitan Tabernacle Pulpit.

THE BLOOD OF SPRINKLING
(Second Sermon).

A Sermon

Delivered on Lord's-day Evening, February 28th, 1886, by

C. H. SPURGEON,

At the Metropolitan Tabernacle, Newington.

> "Ye are come . . . . to Jesus the mediator of the new covenant, and to the blood of sprinkling, that speaketh better things than that of Abel. See that ye refuse not him that speaketh."—Heb. xii. 24, 25.

In the former part of this sermon the text grew upon me so largely that it was quite impossible to express all its meaning. In as condensed a manner as possible I explained what was meant by "the blood of sprinkling," and I also enlarged upon the high position which this precious blood occupies in the gospel dispensation; but I was obliged to leave for this second occasion two practical questions which the text is sure to raise if it be carefully thought upon.

The doctrinal portion of our meditation was greatly blest to our hearts, for God the Holy Ghost refreshed us thereby: may he now fulfil his sacred office with equal power, by revealing the things of Christ to us in a way which shall cause self-examination, and arouse us to give more earnest heed than ever to the voice of him that speaketh from heaven. No theme can excel in value and excellence that of the precious blood of Jesus. Unless the Holy Spirit shall prepare our hearts, even with such a topic as this before us, we shall be nothing profited; but if he will show these choice truths unto us, we shall be comforted, quickened, edified, and sanctified by them.

It is a considerable disadvantage to some of you that you have not heard the former part of the sermon; but I hope you will read it at your leisure, and then, if you read this in connection with it, the whole subject will be before you.* Not that I can set it all out in words: I only mean that it will be before you as the ocean is before us when we sit on the beach, or as the heavens are before us when we gaze upon Arcturus with his sons. Finite language fails to convey the infinite; and if ever there was a text which deserved to be called infinite, it is that which is now before us.

Having touched, as with a swallow's wing, the surface of our great

---

* See "The Blood of Sprinkling," No. 1,888.

theme under the first division of the sermon, I have now to speak with you upon the second, which is this : *Where are we with reference to this blood of sprinkling?* The text says, "Ye are come." We are not come to Mount Sinai, but we are come to Mount Zion ; to angels and their God ; to saints and their Mediator, and to the blood of sprinkling. This having had its share of our thoughts, we are to conclude with the question, *What then?* If we have come to this blood of sprinkling, what then ? The answer is, "See that ye refuse not him that speaketh." Let us give to the wondrous truths revealed to us by the sacrifice of Jesus the most earnest heed, that our souls may hear and live. May the Holy Spirit enable us to hear the heavenly voice at this hour! "Faith cometh by hearing"; may it come at this time by our reverently hearing the voice of the blood of sprinkling !

II. My business under the second head of my discourse is to answer the question, WHERE ARE WE? I have to explain what is meant by the expression which is found in the twenty-second verse of the chapter, "Ye are come." Link the twenty-second verse with this twenty-fourth, and read, "Ye are come to the blood of sprinkling."

Well, first, ye are *come to the hearing of the gospel of the atoning sacrifice.* The Israelites left Egypt, and, having passed the Red Sea, they entered the desert, and at length came to the mount of God, even to Sinai, that terrible mountain. In the valley around that throne of God they were gathered together in their thousands. What a sight that vast multitude must have been! Probably two millions or more were encamped before the mount. Then, "The Lord came from Sinai, and rose up from Seir unto them ; he shined forth from Mount Paran ; and he came with ten thousands of his saints ; from his right hand went a fiery law for them." Israel crouched in the valley below, subdued by the terrible majesty of the scene, and overawed by the trumpet voice which pealed forth from the midst of the thick darkness. The Lord spake with them, but their uncircumcised ears could not bear his glorious voice, and they entreated that Moses might act as mediator, and speak in God's stead.

You and I have not come to such a terrible sight at this hour. No quivering mountain smokes before you, no terrible lightnings appal you, no thunders distress you.

"Not to the terrors of the Lord,
The tempest, fire, and smoke ;
Not to the thunder of that word
Which God on Sinai spoke:

"But we are come to Sion's hill
The city of our God,
Where milder words declare his will,
And spread his love abroad."

Among the great things which you are called upon to consider under the gospel is "the blood of sprinkling." Count yourselves happy that you are privileged to hear of the divinely appointed way of reconciliation with God. You are come to hear, not of your sin and its doom, not of the last judgment and the swift destruction of the enemies of God, but of love to the guilty, pity for the miserable, mercy for the wicked.

compassion for those who are out of the way. You are come to hear of God's great expedient of wisdom, by which he, by the same act and deed, condemns sin, and lets the sinner live ; honours his law, and yet passes by transgression, iniquity, and sin. You are come to hear, not of the shedding of your own blood, but of the shedding of his blood who, in his infinite compassion, deigned to take the place of guilty men—to suffer, that they might not suffer, and die, that they might not die. Blessed are your ears, that they hear of the perfect sacrifice! Happy are your spirits, since they are found where free grace and boundless love have set forth a great propitiation for sin! Divinely favoured are you to live where you are told of pardon freely given to all who will believe on the name of the Lord Jesus, as the Lamb of God which taketh away the sin of the world. You hear at this hour not law, but gospel; not the sentence of judgment, but the proclamation of grace. "See that ye refuse not him that speaketh." It is no small thing for the kingdom of God to have come so nigh unto you. Awake to a sense of your privilege: you do not sit in heathen midnight, nor in Popish gloom, nor in Jewish mist; but day has dawned on you: do not refuse the light.

In a better sense, going a little further, we have not only come to the blood of sprinkling by hearing about it, but we have come to it because *the great God now deals with us upon methods which are founded and grounded upon the atoning sacrifice of Christ.* If God were to deal with us upon the terms laid down at Sinai, he need not be long in finding the "two or three witnesses" to prove that we have broken his law. We should be ourselves compelled to plead guilty ; no witnesses would be required. Truly, he hath not dealt with us after our sins. We are so faulty that we can draw no comfort from the prospect of judgment by law ; we appeal to mercy alone ; for on any other ground our case is hopeless. "This do, and thou shalt live" is a covenant which brings us no ray of comfort; for its only word to us is that thunderbolt— "The soul that sinneth, it shall die."

By the works of the law none can be justified, for by that law we are all condemned. Read the Ten Commandments, and pause at each one, and confess that you have broken it either in thought, or word, or deed. Remember that by a glance we may commit adultery, by a thought we may be guilty of murder, by a desire we may steal. Sin is any want of conformity to perfect holiness, and that want of conformity is justly chargeable upon every one of us. Yet the Lord does not, under the gospel dispensation, deal with us according to law. He does not now sit on the throne of judgment, but he looks down upon us from the throne of grace. Not the iron rod, but the silver sceptre, is held over us. The long-suffering of God rules the age, and Jesus the Mediator is the gracious Lord-lieutenant of the dispensation. Instead of destroying offending man from off the face of the earth, the Lord comes near to us in loving condescension, and pleads with us by his Spirit, saying, "You have sinned, but my Son has died. In him I am prepared to deal with you in a way of pure mercy and unmingled grace."

O sinner, the fact that you are alive proves that God is not dealing with you according to strict justice, but in patient forbearance ; every moment you live is another instance of omnipotent long-suffering. It is the sacrifice of Christ which arrests the axe of justice, which else must execute you. The barren tree is spared because the great Dresser of the vineyard, who bled on Calvary, intercedes and cries, "Let it alone this year also." O my hearer, it is through the shedding of the blood and the mediatorial reign of the Lord Jesus that you are at this moment on praying ground and pleading terms with God! Apart from the blood of atonement you would now be past hope, shut up for ever in the place of doom. But see how the great Father bears with you! He stands prepared to hear your prayer, to accept your confession of sin, to honour your faith, and to save you from your sin through the sacrifice of his dear Son.

Through our Lord Jesus sovereign grace and infinite love find a free way to the most undeserving of the race. Through the divine sacrifice the Lord saith, "Come now and let us reason together: though your sins be as scarlet, they shall be as white as snow;" "Believe on the Lord Jesus Christ, and thou shalt be saved." Thus the rebel is treated as a child, and the criminal as a beloved one. Because of yonder death on Calvary's cruel tree, God can invite guilty men to come to him, and he can receive them to the bosom of his love. O my dear hearers, do remember this! I am not sent to scold you, but to woo you, not sent to thunder at you, but to let the soft cleansing drops from the heart of Jesus fall upon you. I beg you not to turn away, as men may well do when the tidings are heavy; but hearken diligently, for the message is full of joy. You are now in the house of prayer, addressed by one of the Lord's ambassadors, and the tidings are of peace through a propitiation which God himself has provided and accepted. We cry not to you, "Prepare for vengeance;" but we proclaim, "a God ready to pardon." We do not threaten that he will no more have mercy upon you; but we tell you that he waiteth to be gracious. If I had to say, "You have provoked him past bearing, and he now means to destroy you," what a miserable man should I be! How could I bring such evil tidings to my fellow-creatures? Then would it have been woe to me that my mother bare me for so hard a fate. Thank God, it is not so. By virtue of the blood of sprinkling the language of boundless love is heard among our apostate race, and we are entreated to acquaint ourselves with God, and be at peace.

No, my hearer, the day of grace is not over: you are not come to Sinai. No, you are not yet condemned past all hope; for you are still within reach of Jesus the Mediator. There is forgiveness. The fountain which was opened of old for sin and for uncleanness is open still. If you have sinned like David, if you will but accept the sprinkling of the blood of Jesus, I am able to speak to you as Nathan did to the guilty king, and say, "The Lord hath put away thy sin; thou shalt not die." At any rate, God is dealing with you now on gospel terms; he sits on Zion, not on Sinai; he pronounces invitations of grace, and does not utter the stern sentence of justice.

Further, there is a far more effectual way of coming to the blood of sprinkling than this—*when by faith that blood is sprinkled upon our souls.* This is absolutely needed: the blood *shed* must become to each one of us the blood *sprinkled*. "How can I know," says one, "that the blood of Christ is upon me?" Dost thou trust thyself with Christ? Dost thou believe that he made an atonement on the cross; and wilt thou venture thy eternal destiny upon that fact, *trusting* in what Jesus did, and in that alone? If thou dost thus trust, thou shalt not trust in vain. Dost thou apply thy heart to the precious blood of Jesus? Then that precious blood is applied to thy heart. If thine heart bleeds for sin, bring it to the bleeding heart of Jesus, and it shall be healed. I showed, in the early part of this discourse, that the blood sprinkled on the lintel and the two side-posts of the door preserved the Israelites on the night of the Passover: it shall also preserve you. The blood sprinkled upon the defiled made them ceremonially clean: it shall cleanse you. Have I not often quoted those blessed words: "The blood of Jesus Christ his Son cleanseth us from all sin"? That blood put upon the sons of Aaron dedicated them to God; and if it be applied to you, it shall consecrate you to God, and you shall become the accepted servant of the Most High. Oh, what a blessed thing to know assuredly that we have come to the blood of sprinkling by a true and humble faith! Canst thou say that thou dost alone rely on Jesus for salvation? Canst thou call heaven and earth to witness that thou hast no other confidence? Then remember the word of the Lord: "He that believeth in him hath everlasting life. He that believeth in him is not condemned." "Therefore being justified by faith, we have peace with God." Are not these words full of strong assurance? Indeed, we have not come to Mount Sinai, the place of trembling; but to Zion, the place which is beautiful for situation, the joy of the earth; the vision of peace, the home of infinite blessedness. Conscience no longer thunders at you for your sins; for your sins are gone. The expiation has covered them: the sprinkling of the blood has put them all away. Your iniquities are cast into the depths of the sea; God has cast them behind his back. The handwriting of ordinances that was against you Christ has taken away, nailing it to his cross, as a record in which there is no more condemning force. The debt is paid, the bill is receipted. Who can lay anything to the charge of God's elect? O beloved! it is a most blessed thing to come to the blood of sprinkling.

> "The terrors of law and of God
> With me can have nothing to do;
> My Saviour's obedience and blood
> Hide all my transgressions from view."

The act of faith, whereby we accept and trust in the Lord Jesus as our Mediator and Sacrifice, is the true and effectual coming to the blood of sprinkling. May none of us forget thus to come! He is the Lamb of God, which taketh away the sin of the world, and those who come to him shall be led into full salvation. Have you thus come? If you have not, why do you delay? He saith, "Him that cometh to me I will in no wise cast out." Come to him, for he is calling you; come to him, even as you now are, and he will receive you without fail.

Further, to come to this blood of sprinkling means *thankfully to enjoy all that comes to us through the blood of sprinkling.* I have intruded upon this somewhat already. Brothers and sisters, if you have come to the blood of sprinkling, believe in the full pardon which God has given you, and in your consequent peace with God. It is a blessed word in the Creed, "I believe in the forgiveness of sins." Do you believe in the forgiveness of sins? I have seen some of the children of God who have believed in Jesus, but it has been with a faith which did not realize the full blessing promised to it; for they were as troubled about their sins as if they had never been forgiven. Now, a man who receives a free pardon from the Queen, and goes his way out of prison, rejoices in that pardon as a reality, and therefore walks abroad without fear. You must believe in the pardon of God as a reality, and act accordingly. If he has absolved you for Jesus' sake, then you are absolved. Why tremble like a guilty wretch waiting for the verdict? Why talk about fearing divine wrath? If you are pardoned, the deed of grace is done, and can never be undone; for the gifts and calling of God are without repentance on his part. His remission of sin is a clear gaol delivery, a sure plea, a full quittance.

> "Oh! how sweet to view the flowing
> Of our Lord's atoning blood,
> With divine assurance knowing
> He has made my peace with God!"

I want every child of God in his inmost soul to come to the blood of sprinkling by full assurance of his justification, and then to go on to enjoy constant access to the mercy-seat, and communion with the Lord God. We may now with holy boldness speak with God in prayer, for the mercy-seat is sprinkled with the blood. O pardoned one, be not backward to enjoy thy liberty of fellowship! Thou art clean through the blood, and therefore thou mayest enter into the closest communion with the divine Father; thou art consecrated by the blood, and therefore thou mayest abound in the service of thy God. Treat thy God as a child should treat a father, and be not so awed by his majesty as to be cast down and distressed because of past sin, seeing it is pardoned. Take the good that God provides thee; enjoy the peace the blood has bought thee; enter into the liberty that thy ransom price has ensured thee. Do not stand in feelings, and fears, and dreams; but come unto this blood of sprinkling, and rest there, and be filled with joy and peace through believing. With such a ransom found for thee, dream not of going down into the pit, but ascend with gladness into the hill of the Lord, and stand in his holy place.

I think, once more, that this coming to the blood of sprinkling means also that *we feel the full effect of it in our lives*. The man who knows that Jesus shed his blood for him, and has had that blood applied to his conscience, becomes a sin-hating man, consecrated to him who has cleansed him. "The love of Christ constraineth us; because we thus judge, that if one died for all, then were all dead: and that he died for all, that they which live should not henceforth live unto themselves, but unto him which died for them, and rose again." I believe that there is no fruitful source of virtue like faith in the precious blood of Jesus. I hope your conduct will always support me in this assertion. Those who are debtors for salvation to their dying Lord should be the most holy of men. You people who think that you will get to heaven by some other way than by "the blood of sprinkling" have no sure bonds to hold you to holiness. You trust partly to your own works, and partly to what Jesus has done. Well, you do not owe him much, and therefore you will not love him much, and therefore you will not feel bound to live strict, holy, gracious lives. But the man who knows that his many sins are all washed away through the blood of Jesus, and that thus he is saved, he is the man who will serve the Lord with all his heart. He who has received a finished righteousness and complete salvation is under boundless obligations of gratitude, and the force of these obligations will urge him to a consecrated life. Over him the supreme power of gratitude will exert its sacred influence, and he will be not only carefully obedient, but ardently zealous in the service of his Redeemer. We know it is so, and we mean to prove it by our daily conduct. Brethren, I would have you exhibit more and more the influence of the precious blood in sanctifying your lives. Are there not Christians who hold the doctrine of the atoning blood, and yet are no better than others? Alas! it is so. But it is one thing to hold a doctrine, and another thing for that doctrine to take hold upon your heart and influence your life. Oh, if we believed practically what we believe professionally, what manner of persons should we be in all holy conversation and godliness! Hear me, my brother, and answer the appeals I make to thee as in the presence of the Lord. Blood-bought; canst thou live for thyself? Blood-washed; canst thou defile thy garments? Marked with the King's own name, in the King's own blood; how canst thou yield thyself to other rulers? God grant that we may come unto the blood of sprinkling till it shall purify our nature, and fill us with an all-consuming enthusiasm for him whose heart was pierced for us!

I ask you, then, to put the question closely home, "Have I come unto this blood of sprinkling? If not, why should I not come at once?" I read the other day an imaginary story, which describes the need of looking well to this great business. Receive it as a parable:—A little daughter of the house of Israel, had heard the commandment concerning the Passover night, and as she lay ill in her bed she cried, "Father, have you sprinkled the blood upon the lintel and the two side-posts?" Her father answered, "Not yet, my child. It shall be done." The daughter was distressed, and filled with fear. After waiting a little while she again cried, "Father, father, have you sprinkled the blood upon the door?" He answered carelessly, "Child, I have told Simeon to sprinkle it, and I have no doubt it is done." "But, father," cried she, "it is near midnight, and the destroying angel will soon be abroad; are you *sure* that the blood is over the door? Jehovah our God hath said that we must sprinkle the blood upon the lintel and the two side-posts, or else the destroyer will not pass over us. Father, are you sure it is done?" The father passed over her enquiry: he had been eating of the lamb with his friends, and thought that this was sufficient; he did not care to give too much prominence to the ghastly idea of blood. He was of a liberal mind, and would not believe that a merciful God would smite his household for so small an omission.

Then his daughter arose from her bed, made strong by the God of Israel. Nothing would content her until she had been outside into the street, and seen for herself whether the saving mark was over the door of her father's house. It was almost midnight, but by the light of the moon she looked, and no blood-mark was there! How great was her distress! "Father," she cried, "make haste and bring the basin." There it stood, filled with blood; for the Paschal Lamb had been slain. The father, at her entreaty, dashed the hyssop into it, struck the lintel and the two side-posts and shut the door, and as he did so, the midnight hour arrived. They were saved so as by fire. The daughter's obedient care and reverence of the Lord had warded off the sword of the destroyer. Oh that the holy anxiety of some one now present would work the like blessing for other households! Ask, dear child, ask the question, "Father, have you come to the blood of sprinkling? Is the blood of the Lamb above your head, between you and God? Is it on both sides of you, when you come in and go out?" O soul, be thus anxious about thyself, and rest not till thou hast by faith been purged with hyssop, and cleansed by the blood of the one sacrifice for sin.

III. The last part of our subject is this: WHAT THEN? According to our text, the blood of Jesus is the voice of the new dispensation. It is the blood which speaks, and it speaks better things than the blood of Abel. What then is our duty? How doth the apostle express our obligation? "See that ye refuse not him that speaketh."

I would have a quarter of an hour's very quiet talk with you, without excitement or quibbling debate. Lend me your ears, for I speak in all love for your souls. I want, dear friends, that this great truth of atonement which I so often preach may have a fair hearing, and not be left to lie among the lumber of forgotten things.

Do not refuse the voice of Jesus by cold indifference. God was made flesh, and dwelt among men, and in due time he took upon himself our sin, and suffered for it in his own body on the tree, that sin might be put away by the sacrifice of himself. By his death upon the cross our Lord made atonement for the sin of man, and those who believe in him are delivered from evil and its consequences. The main point is that Jesus died for us, the just for the unjust. His atoning blood has a voice: "See that ye refuse not him that speaketh." The text says: See to it; look to it; make sure of it; be careful about it. Do not miss the salvation of your Lord through neglect; for he who dies by neglecting the healing medicine will as surely perish as he who stabs himself. Be in earnest to accept the Saviour: I beseech you so to do, for I am afraid that many refuse him that speaketh, because they never think of him, or of his sacrifice. It seems to me that if I were a young man I would give this matter very early notice. However deeply I might be engaged in business, I should feel that my first concern ought to be to set myself right with God. Other matters would be sure to drop into order if I could be right with the Lord of all. If I heard it said that salvation came by the blood of Christ, I think I should pull myself together and resolve to understand this singular statement. I would not let it go by me, but would endeavour to reach the bottom of it, and practically understand it. I would meditate much upon teaching so wonderful as this—that the Son of God in man's stead honoured the justice of God by death, and so put away sin.

When I was a youth I had a great longing to begin life on right principles: I longed to find deliverance from sin. I would wake up with the sun in summer time to read my Bible, and such books as Bunyan's "Grace Abounding," Baxter's "Call to the Unconverted,"

Alleine's "Alarm," and Doddridge's "Rise and Progress of Religion in the Soul." In these books I tried to spell out the way of salvation; but the chief thing I longed to know was, "How can man be just with God? How can God be just with man, and yet put away his sin?" Do you not think that these questions are of high importance? I beg that they may not have the cold shoulder from you. Give this question due space. I know that a great many things demand your attention nowadays; but I claim for this, which is the innermost revelation of God, that it should have an early and earnest hearing. God incarnate in Christ Jesus bleeding and dying for human sin is a marvel of love too great to be passed over without thought. I pray you, therefore, "refuse not him that speaketh." Do not say, "I pray thee, have me excused." I do not suppose that you will become an infidel or act as a blasphemer towards this grand truth. I will not accuse you of denying the fact of the atonement; but my great fear is lest you should be indifferent to it. If it be so, that God himself has come to earth to bleed and die to save guilty man, it is the greatest, gladdest news that ever came to our poor erring race, and every member of that race should receive it with hopeful attention.

When you resolve to study the doctrine, *do not approach it with prejudice through misapprehension.* Those that hate the gospel of Christ are very busy in caricaturing the doctrine of the atonement. They assert that we preach that God was not merciful by nature, but must needs be appeased by the blood of his own Son. They charge us with saying that Jesus by his death made God loving. We distinctly teach the very opposite of that statement. What we do say is this, that God is infinitely loving—that, in fact, God is love; but that love does not cause him to be unjust or unholy; for *that* in the long run would not be love. God is the Judge of all the earth, and he must do right. The Lord, as the great moral governor, if he makes a law, and threatens a penalty, must execute that penalty, or else his law will lose its authority. If the penalty threatened be not executed, there is a tacit acknowledgment that it was threatened in error. Could you believe in a fallible God? The Lord has made a law which is perfect, and just, and good. Would you rather be without law? What reasonable person desires anarchy? He has backed up that law with a threatening. What is the use of a law if to break it involves no evil consequences? A government that never punishes offenders is no government at all. God, therefore, as moral ruler, must be just, and must display his indignation against wrong and evil of every kind. It is written on the conscience of men that sin must be punished. Would you have it go unpunished? If you are a just man, you would not. To meet the case, therefore, the Lord Jesus Christ, by himself bearing the penalty of death, has honoured the divine law. He has shown to all intelligences that God will not wink at sin, that even his infinite mercy must not come in the way of his justice. This is the doctrine: do not listen to those who twist and pervert it. It is the love of God which has provided the great atonement by which, in a judgment better than ours, the law finds a glorious vindication, and the foundation of moral government is strengthened. Do consider this matter, and judge it fairly, with candid minds. We do assure you from God's Word that apart from the atonement of our Lord Jesus you can never be saved either from the guilt or power of evil. You will find no peace for your conscience that is worth having, no thorough and deep peace, except by believing in this atoning sacrifice; neither will you meet with a motive strong enough to rescue you from the bonds of iniquity. Therefore, "See that ye refuse not him that speaketh." Hear, and your soul shall live. Cavil, and you will die in your sins.

Do not refuse the voice of the Lord Jesus by rejecting the principle of expiation. If God is content with this principle, it is not for us to raise objection. The Lord God is infinitely more concerned to fix matters on a right foundation than ever we can be; and if he feels that the sacrifice of Jesus meets the case at all points, why should we be dissatisfied with it? If there were a flaw in the proceedings his holy eyes would see it. He would not have delivered up his own Son to die unless that death would perfectly fulfil the design intended by it. A mistake so expensive he would never have perpetrated. Who are you to raise the question? If God is satisfied, surely you should be? To refuse the atonement because we are too wise to accept so simple a method of mercy is the utmost height of folly. What! will ye refuse him that speaketh because the present phase of human madness dares to dispute the divine way of human redemption? I pray you, do not so.

Once more. *Do not refuse this voice of mercy by preferring your own way of salvation.* You have, no doubt, a way of salvation in your own mind, for few men have given up all hope. Perhaps your chosen hope is that you will be saved by doing your best. Alas! no man does his best; and the best acts of a rebel must be unaccepted of his king. So long as he is a rebel his acts are those of a rebel, and of no esteem with his prince. Perhaps your hope lies in saying so many prayers, and going to church, or attending chapel; or you are so unwise as to trust to a minister or priest. Now, we beseech you, hear the witness of God which he has given us in this book, and learn that other foundation can no man lay than that which is laid, which is Jesus Christ the righteous. There is one salvation, and there can be no other; all other hopes are lying vanities, and arrogant insults to Jesus. God hath set forth Christ to be a propitiation for sin. There is no other propitiation, or atonement, or way of acceptance; and if you reject this way, you must die in your sins.

I cannot help it if you do not like this teaching, although I shall be grieved if you refuse it. I can only tell you the truth, and leave it with your own hearts. Do not wilfully refuse it. When I meet you face to face in that last day, to which we all must come, I shall not be clear of your blood unless I tell you what is assuredly the truth—that in the precious blood of Christ is the only cleansing from sin, and the only acceptance with God. By believing in Jesus, as slain for you, you shall be saved; but do what you may, pray as you may, fast as you may, give alms as you may, you shall not enter heaven by any other road. The way to glory is by the way of the cross. "Without shedding of blood there is no remission." Look to him whom you have pierced, and mourn for your sins. Look not to any other, for no other is needed, no other is provided, no other can be accepted. Jesus is the sole messenger of the covenant of life and peace. "See that ye refuse not him that speaketh."

"See that ye *refuse* not." Then there is a choice about it. If you had never heard the gospel, you could not have refused it; but now that you have heard the message, it lies within your power, and it is an awfully dangerous power, to refuse him that speaketh. Oh, can you, will you, dare you refuse my bleeding Saviour—refuse the Lord of love? I see him now. The thorn-crown is about his brow. He is hanging on his cross expiring in unutterable pangs! Can you refuse him while he presents such a spectacle of sacrifice? His eyes are red with weeping; have you no tears for such sorrow? His cheeks are all distained with the brutal soldiers' spittle: have you no love and homage for him? His hands are fastened to the wood—his feet the same: and there he hangs to suffer in the sinner's stead. Will you not yield yourselves to him? I could joyfully bow before that cross-foot to kiss his dear feet distained with blood. What a charm he has for me! And you—do you refuse him?

He is no mere man. It is God himself who hangs upon the cross. His body is that of a man, but it is in union with the Godhead. He who died at Calvary is God over all, and this makes his death so effectual. He whom you have offended, in order to be justly able to pardon you, hangs there and dies for you: and do you turn your back on him? O sirs, if you be wise you will come, as I said I fain would come, and kiss those bleeding feet, and look up and say, "My Lord, I am reconciled to thee—how could I be otherwise? My enmity is dead. How can I be an enemy to him that died for me? In shame, and scorn, and misery, Jesus dies that I may live. O Lord Jesus, thou hast wrought in me, not reconciliation merely, but full submission and hearty love. I joy to sink myself in thee, and to be thine for ever." See that ye refuse not my Lord. May the sweet Spirit who loves the cross, and, like a dove, hovers round it now, descend upon you all who hear my message! May the Holy Ghost apply the blood of sprinkling to you; and may you feel that, instead of refusing him that speaketh, you rejoice in his name!

When the text says, "See that ye refuse not," it tacitly and pleadingly says, "See that ye accept him." Dear hearers, I trust you will receive my Lord into your hearts. When we read of refusing, or receiving, we perceive an action of the will. Jesus must be willingly received: he will not force himself upon any man. Whosoever accepts Jesus is himself accepted of Jesus. Never was there a heart willing to receive him to whom Jesus denied himself. Never! But you must be willing and obedient. Grace works this in you; but in you this must be. Till the heart entertains Jesus gladly nothing is done. All that is short of a willing hearing of Jesus, and a willing acceptance of his great atonement, is short of eternal life. Say, wilt thou have this Saviour, or dost thou decline his love? Wilt thou give him a cold refusal? Oh, do not so; but, on the contrary, throw open the doors of thy heart, and entreat thy Lord and Saviour to come in.

I do not wonder that the Israelites asked that they might no longer hear the voice of thunder from the top of Sinai; it was too terrible for human ear; but you have no such excuse if you refuse him that speaketh;

for Jesus speaks in notes more sweet than music, more tender than a mother's sonnet to her babe. Let me remind you, that he was wont to say, "Come unto me, all ye that labour and are heavy laden, and I will give you rest. Take my yoke upon you, and learn of me; for I am meek and lowly in heart: and ye shall find rest unto your souls." He declared that all manner of sin and of blasphemy should be forgiven unto men. He stood and cried, on the last day of the feast, "If any man thirst, let him come unto me, and drink." I am telling you no fables; for Christ, who was born at Bethlehem and died on Calvary, by his own blood which he shed for many, assures you that there is forgiveness for every man of you who, confessing his sin, will come and put his trust in him.

"See that ye refuse not him that speaketh;" for though you hear only my poor feeble voice pleading with you, with an honest, loving heart at the back of it, yet God the Holy Ghost is speaking, and Jesus Christ himself is speaking to you. Refuse *me* if you please, but do not refuse my Lord. The blood of Jesus says, " I was poured out for the guilty. I was shed to manifest divine love. I am sprinkled to cleanse from sin." Each drop as it falls creates peace of heart. Stand where that blood is falling. Let it sprinkle you.

Thus the blood speaks. Will you not answer, "Lord, we come to thee, for thou hast drawn us. Thy wounds have wounded our hearts. Thy death has killed our enmity. Sprinkle us unto thyself. Bedew us with thy blood. Let us be accepted in the Beloved"? Amen. So may God hear us!

PORTION OF SCRIPTURE READ BEFORE SERMON—Hebrews x.

HYMNS FROM "OUR OWN HYMN BOOK"—302, 294, 580, 288.

Metropolitan Tabernacle Pulpit.

THE TEACHING OF THE FOOT-WASHING.

A Sermon

Delivered on Lord's-day Morning, October 12th, 1879, by

C. H. SPURGEON,

AT THE METROPOLITAN TABERNACLE, NEWINGTON.

"Jesus knowing that the Father had given all things into his hands, and that he was come from God, and went to God; he riseth from supper, and laid aside his garments; and took a towel, and girded himself. After that he poureth water into a bason, and began to wash the disciples' feet, and to wipe them with the towel wherewith he was girded."—John xiii. 3—5.

It seems to me that the true text of this enacted sermon of the foot-washing is to be found in the first verse of the chapter: "Having loved his own which were in the world, he loved them unto the end." Our Lord washed the feet of his disciples to show that to the last moment of his intercourse with them he was full of the deepest and truest love to them, and was willing to perform the most menial action for their good. Nor was this all, for we may regard that one condescending act as the pledge and type of his daily kindness towards all his own which are in the world. Those deeds of love, which the foot-washing sets forth, are continuous among us, and are the sure tokens of his abiding love to us. Our Lord's affection for his people is not a transient passion. He loved them or ever the earth was, he continues still to love them, and he always will love them when these heavens and this earth shall have passed away. In token of the continuance of his love, he has left on record this washing of his disciples' feet, not because he did it once only, but because it is the type of what he is always doing. Even in his glory he is caring for his saints with that same condescending love which led him to wash their feet, and he is acting towards them spiritually in the selfsame way.

The love of Christ will assuredly endure all the strain that can ever be put upon it, for at the time when he acted as menial servant to his disciples his love was enduring, and enduring right gloriously, three great trials, any one of which might have broken it had it not been altogether omnipotent. For, first, he was about to go away from them. Much of human love needs the presence of its object for its maintenance; it is, alas, seldom true that "absence makes the heart grow fonder." Jesus was about to depart out of this world unto the Father, and, with the exception of one brief interval, he was no more to walk in the midst of his

No. 1,499

chosen, or sit at table with them. Out of sight, however, they would not be out of mind. Though he was just about to take the last terrible journey of death, yet he forgot them not, but graciously made them see that he would remember them still. If you will remember the style of his going, his thoughtfulness of his friends becomes the more remarkable. He was about to leave them by a cruel and ignominious death, and according to the common conduct of men it would not have been wonderful if he had sought pity and comfort from his friends; instead of which, he forgot himself and all the pain, and grief, and death which lay before him, and spent all his time and strength upon the comfort and establishment of his followers. When he knew that the hour was come when he must depart out of the world with pangs unutterable, he still loved his own with an all-absorbing love. There was much in the prospect of his grievous departure which might for a season have diverted his thoughts from them; but they lay so close to the centre of his soul that even under such circumstances he washed their feet.

Next, it is to be remembered, that our Lord was well aware that one of them had already entertained the idea of betraying him. There sat one at the table who had held a secret interview with the Pharisees and chief priests, and had taken money as a bribe for his Master's blood. You cannot so dissociate a leading disciple from the rest as not to feel that the whole band was thereby disgraced, and the Lord might very well have said, "I will discard my apostles, for they have betrayed me"; especially when you recollect that those who did not sell him or betray him nevertheless all forsook him and fled,—forsook him when they ought to have rallied round him, and have spoken up for him at the judgment-seat. None of them appeared in answer to the question, "Who shall declare his generation?" Like timid hares, they fled at the first bark of the dogs. It would not have been wonderful, had his been a human love, if he had said, "They are unworthy of me: their confidence dies out when they see my sorrow: they betray me, they forsake me, therefore I will let them go, and care for them no more." No, but knowing what they were, our Lord took a towel and girded himself and washed their feet, ay, washed the traitor's feet, and gently handled that heel which had been lifted up against him; washing from it the dust gathered in its secret walk upon the traitor's errand.

> "The sight might kings themselves convert,
> God only could so far submit:
> Satan is in the traitor's heart,
> The Lord Most High is at his feet."

This act of tender, considerate affection, performed under such circumstances, to men who acted towards him in such ungenerous style, proves to us that his love will bear the strain of our ill-behaviour, our want of fidelity, and our thousand grievous failures. Having loved his own, which are in the world, he loves them to the end.

There was a third strain, and a powerful one, too. Our Saviour knew that the Father had committed all things into his hands, he knew that there was but a brief interval before he should die, and then he would ascend to the Father's right hand, and sit there eternally as God over all, blessed for evermore, yet he did not disdain to do a slave's work for his beloved ones. Oftentimes circumstances alter affections. A man grows rich and great, and forgets his friends. This we would not suspect of Jesus if his had not been a greater change than we mortals can possibly experience; but his was a surpassing accession of glory: from being plunged in ignominy and shame he was exalted to receive the homage of angels, and the adoration of the whole universe. One would think that in the prospect of such honours, though he loved his own, he would not so love them as to become their servitor, and all in disarray stoop down before them, even to their feet, and do the service of a bondsman. No wonder that Peter raised an objection suggested by reverential awe. Who could without protest receive such humble service from such hands? Yet our Lord did this with heaven's supernal glory descending on him! He disrobed himself, though angels longed to cast the imperial purple about his shoulders. With all things in his hand, he yet took a towel and wiped the disciples' feet.

Beloved, if our Lord's love bore these three strains, we may, like the apostle, be persuaded that neither death nor life, nor angels, nor principalities, nor powers, nor things present, nor things to come, nor height, nor depth, nor any other creature shall be able to separate us from the love of God which is in Christ Jesus our Lord.

I invite you now, therefore, to see your Saviour's enduring and continuing love as set forth to us in this symbolic washing of his disciples' feet, and in like acts of which it is an emblem. I shall ask you to view it, first, as *the type of his continuous love;* and secondly, *as the example of that love as it should be reflected by his people.* May the Holy Spirit be our interpreter, and open to us this choice cabinet of love-tokens.

I. First: We will look upon this washing of the disciples' feet as THE TYPE OF OUR LORD'S CONTINUOUS LOVE TO US. We will view it in four lights. First, *Christ Jesus still acts as the host of his people.* Has it never struck you how much the life of Christ with his people lay in intense familiarity with them? How in common things he displayed his brotherhood with them? He began his ministry at a feast at Cana of Galilee, working his first miracle at a wedding. Again and again we find him eating with his disciples. The last thing he did was to sit at supper with them, and he still saith to his church, "Behold, I stand at the door and knock: if any man open to me I will enter in and sup with him and he with me." His own figure for the opening of the new dispensation is a supper: "Blessed is he that shall eat bread at the marriage supper of the Lamb." We do not always view our intercourse with Christ in this homely light, and I fear we forget that the acquaintance of Christ with his people was one of great intimacy and familiar communion, for they did eat and drink with him and he with them. At this time also Jesus is the host of his church, providing the gospel supper and entertaining us right royally. Instead of meat he gives us his flesh to eat, rarest of dainties, and he cries, "My flesh is meat indeed, and my blood is drink indeed." He prepares a table before us in the presence of our enemies. He satisfies our mouth with good things, so that our youth is renewed like the eagle's. And, mark you, the Lord is a host who goes through with his divine hospitalities, and leaves nothing incomplete. In the East the master of the house would wash his guests' feet if they were persons whom he sought to honour. You remember how Abraham bade the angels turn in to his tent, and also said to them, "Let a little water, I pray you, be fetched, and wash your feet." Even so our Master entertains us at his table, not as paupers, but as guests, ay, and not as guests of an ordinary kind, but as friends of the highest class, dear to his soul, whose feet he will wash. He can truly say of us, "Since thou wast precious in my sight thou hast been honourable, and I have loved thee." He treats us as distinguished persons who shall not sit among mean men, but shall have their portion among princes. This foot-washing once done was a fair representation of that honourable entertainment which the King extends to all believing souls when he bids them come to his banqueting table and drink of the wine which he has mingled. I like to think of the Lord as my host, and of myself as no mere waif and stray, but as a welcome guest, to whom he is daily fulfilling all a host's part, granting me all I want, yea, all that I wish for. He himself gives us honours and comforts more than could be expected even from our most familiar friend. See, he even washes our feet! What better token need we of his abiding love? Since he continues to entertain his whole church, and treats us all as distinguished visitors, it is clear that he loves us still.

My second rendering of the passage is that *he cares for our minor matters with a personal interest.* Jesus washed their feet—this showed a very tender and familiar consideration of their little wants. That he should ease their weary hearts I can understand, that he should enlighten their clouded brains I can understand; but that he should wash their feet is wonderful. A little soil on their ancles, will he attend to that? Ay, that he will, and personally too. He will himself take the basin and the towel and wash their feet. Had they been diseased with leprosy it would seem natural that he should touch them and say, "Be clean"; or had they been blind or halt it would have been probable that he would touch their eyes or heal their limbs; but a mere defilement of their feet is so a small a matter, would he attend to that? He might have left them to wash one another's feet, might he not? Surely he had but to suggest it and they would have cheerfully waited on each other. Peter, at any rate, would have been first to obey, and to his Lord's command he would have replied, "Wash them? That I will, with delight." But no; the Lord laid aside his own garments and took a towel, and himself performed the kindly deed for them. Brothers and sisters, take your little things to Christ, those trials of which your heart says, "They are too small: though they prick me like thorns in the flesh, and give me pain, yet they are really too trifling for me to mention in prayer." Not so; the Lord loves us to trust him thoroughly. This is a token of his love, of his continued affection, that even to the little things he will look, even to your small affairs he will condescend, and you may ask him—oh, it is bold asking, but you may do it—you may ask him to wash your feet, for he will do even that. Do not, I pray you, cause your own love to be put under suspicion through a deficiency in your childlike confidence in your condescending Lord. I confess I have often required more faith to pray about some tiny matter of my own than about a thousand things which concern my Master's kingdom, and yet when faith is broad and large, love knows that all matters which grieve the minds of his servants touch the heart of the Master, and that all which works our good works also his delight. We must believe in him so much that we can trust each day's cares with him, believing that he still washes his disciples' feet, by attending to their minor needs and griefs.

> "He overrules all mortal things,
> And manages our mean affairs;
> On humble souls the King of kings
> Bestows his counsels and his cares."

We will now take a third reading of it. This washing of the disciples' feet means that *he provides refreshment for his people.* I do not suppose that many here present know what an intense pleasure it is in extremely hot countries to have the feet washed upon coming in after a weary walk. The servant from a pitcher pours forth fresh cool water upon the feet when they are aching with a long journey and hot with burning heat and dust, and the result is delightfully refreshing. Our Lord washed his disciples' feet, not only because cleansing was desirable, but also for their pleasure and solace. He takes great pleasure in giving joy to his followers. He desires that his joy should be in us that our joy may be full. He does not want us to be like paupers, who have to be content with bare necessaries, but to be gentlemen-commoners upon his bounty who shall be served right royally, like princes of the blood whom even the king himself doth not disdain to wait upon.

When doth the Lord give us these refreshments? He often does this after a journey,—I mean after a severe trial. When, as pilgrims to heaven, we have been wearied by the greatness of the way, the Master comes, and manifests himself to us, and refreshes us. Sometimes, also, this good cheer comes before the trial, for these disciples were now about to enter upon a very rough road: they were doomed to travel through the rest of their lives without the personal presence of their Master, and he seems to say, "Before you set out I will wash your feet. A little refreshment of this kind will strengthen you at the starting, and when you are further on your way the very remembrance of it will come to you like a cool stream of water fresh from the ewer." So the Master was pleased to refresh them after a journey and before a journey, and the refresnment was intended, as I have already said, for their souls' delight. It was a feast at which they sat, and he wished them to enjoy everything that could make them happy at his table. Brethren, I have told you that this foot-washing is a type of our Lord's continuous love to us, a type which is followed by action like itself; and so it is in this respect, for he is often refreshing us. Have you not tasted of his cordials? We speak far less of our spiritual delights than we might do; but if we would open our mouths we could tell of rapturous times, when, though sore weary and cast down, we have been graciously revived. Sweet promises have been applied to us by our Lord's own hands, like cold water poured upon hot and weary feet, and by this means we have been bathed in rest. A sense of his love has come over us like a dream, and yet we were never more awake in our lives. We have been entranced and yet most sober and calm. Our Lord's love is a dear delight, and, when we realize it, the bells of heaven seem to be ringing close against our ears, and choirs of angels to have come down from glory to make music in our chambers. At such times we often wonder why we were so gladdened, but when next day an extraordinary trouble sets in we discover the reason, and perceive that we have been well nourished that we may go a forty-days' journey in the strength of this meat.

Yes, we have had those refreshments in this house when the word has been preached, or when some joyful hymn has borne us on its wings to heaven; or, best of all, at the communion table. Nor here alone, for in our own quiet chambers, and in the night watches, the Lord has refreshed our hearts, for he giveth songs in the night. These sweet renewals and upliftings are the tokens that having loved his own he loves them to the end. This is the foot-washing over again, for Christ is still busy at his works of love. Though he lays not aside his garment to-day, nor comes among us like a servant, yet even from the highest throne in glory he has ways of executing the same purposes of kindness. Still he gives us inward delight, and this joy becomes our strength, making us swift as a young roe, to run upon his gracious errands. The weariness which makes the feet heavier is removed by joyful fellowship, and so we are washed and refreshed. We who are his ministers need much of this, that we may be as hinds let loose, giving goodly words.

Our fourth view of the text is more full and accurate, namely, that *Christ continues to guard the purity of his church;* for though it was not all his meaning, yet by washing their feet he certainly intended their cleansing; for after he had done it he said, "Ye are clean: he that is washed is clean every whit." Our Lord watches over the purification of all those who are his own, and this is a great joy to us who love his church, and are concerned for her honour. To see professors defile themselves is heart-breaking work to loving pastors, and our only comfort is that Jesus is quite as jealous of the holiness of his people as ever we can be. Beloved, I live while I see your pure and holy conversation; but when I see impurity, worldliness, and evil among you, it cuts me to the heart, and were it not that I know my Lord is watching over the purity of his people I would fain lay me down and die. From the occasion which our Lord selected for the foot-washing it is clear that he would have us seek the special purifying power of his presence during religious ordinances. I really cannot tell at what point of the evening's proceedings our Lord washed his disciples' feet, and if you read the chapter you will be somewhat puzzled. It is "before the passover," yet it is said, "supper being ended," which I suppose would be better rendered, "supper being in progress"; for after the washing our Lord took a sop, dipped it, and gave it to Judas, and therefore the supper was not over. Or if one supper may have come to an end another was just commencing. Was this feast the passover? Was it the Lord's Supper? Was it the first of the *agapè*, or love feasts, in which the early church delighted? Which was it? I do not know, and I am not much concerned to know. The Lord Jesus Christ made the passover melt into the Lord's Supper; so that you cannot tell where one ends and the other begins. No violent jerk occurred in leaving the lines of the Jewish dispensation for the Christian; for our Lord's disciples went up to the temple to pray after the veil was rent in twain, and the legal ceremonies had lost their meaning. There was a gradual sliding of the one economy into the other, and on the memorable night of the washing of the feet I suspect that our Master ate and drank with his disciples at a common meal, just as the early Christians did when they met together at their love-feasts: then probably followed the actual passover celebration, a night before its time; and this gradually dissolved into the Lord's Supper, of which the cup was "the cup after supper." Anyhow, it does not matter much; but it is clear that we need our feet washed before we come to his table,—"Let a man examine himself, and so let him eat of this bread." We also need our feet washed while we are at his table, for there is sin in our holiest things, and even when we come most near to our Lord we need that he wash us, according to that text, "If we walk in the light as he is in the light, we have fellowship one with another, and the blood of Jesus Christ his Son cleanseth us from all sin." Even when we walk in the light, and have clearest fellowship with God, the Lord Jesus continues to cleanse us from all sin. And I am sure we want washing after supper. When we come away from worship we have need to get alone, and cry, "Cleanse thou me from secret faults. Let my want of devotion or my coldness in it be forgiven. Let my lack of zeal, my scantiness of faith, and the wandering of my heart be all washed away by thee, my Lord and Master, for much I need it."

Our Lord is so anxious for the purification of his people that he is frequently giving them a sweet sense that their transgressions in holy things are put away, and thus he seems to say to them, "I have accepted your sacrifice, I have received your prayers and tears, and presented them unto my Father. I have washed you, and you are clean: go in peace." This is one of the acts of his continuous love, this daily washing of our feet.

This frequent washing by our Lord we must all have; it is *absolutely necessary*. There is a "must" in the case: as we must be born again, so we must be made holy. It would be to our Lord's dishonour to be followed by disciples who do not walk in integrity and uprightness. As he is himself perfectly holy he desires to have around him a holy people purged from all defilement. He is so anxious that he should have such a people, that sooner than they shall not be washed he will act the part of a servant and wash their feet himself. "Be ye clean that bear the vessels of the Lord." Ye that follow in his footsteps, walk with clean feet. Come not up with the miry clay still sticking to you, but wash, wash daily, and follow your pure Master with pure and cleansed hearts, with careful and obedient feet, so that all may see that you are the disciples of the Undefiled. His ministers especially need this or the people will never cry, "How beautiful upon the mountains are the feet of him that bringeth good tidings." Brethren, pray for us that we may experience this to the highest degree.

These constant washings which are the testimonial of Christ's continued love we must all receive. Did he not say to Peter, "If I wash thee not, thou hast no part with me"? If Jesus does not make you holy you are not his. Brother, if you live in sin, and love it, you cannot love God. Unless he truly purges your life and makes you to walk in a clean path, you are not his, for he purges his own: such as riot in iniquity prove that they are of their father, the devil, for his works they do. Whom Jesus loves he purifies. He loved his church and gave himself for it that he might sanctify and cleanse it. If, then, you are unholy, ungracious, dishonest, unrighteous, how can you say that you belong to his church? He washes the feet of all who are his disciples, and if your feet are filthy you belong not to the faithful band.

This washing must be *spiritual:* no external form will suffice. Christ washed the feet of Judas with water, but inasmuch as Judas had never been bathed in the laver of regeneration, and had never been purged in the fount of forgiving love, that washing which Christ gave to his feet did him no spiritual good; and you, my friend, may use what external ablutions you will, and perform whatever religious ceremonies you please, but unless your spirit has been renewed by the Holy Ghost, and your heart purged in the sight of God, you still have no part nor lot with Christ's disciples.

The mercy is that this purification, which is so needful, and which must be of a spiritual kind, is *very readily given.* I admire the beauty of the figure in its simple ease. The Scripture does not say that our Master was nailed to the cross and poured forth a stream from his heart, in order to wash his disciples' feet. No, although the act by which he cleansed them was very condescending, yet it was not painful or laborious. He layeth aside his garments, girdeth on the towel, and taketh the ewer, and straightway proceeds therewith to wash the disciples' feet. It was easily done, and whatever there was upon the feet was soon removed: it needed no suffering, no dire grief on Jesus' part. For our first washing from the guilt and condemnation of sin it needed that Jesus should lay down his life, and fill the cleansing fount with atoning blood; but for the after removal of sin the Lord useth an easy process of love. He doth by his Spirit speedily cleanse us from iniquity, even as our feet are soon washed. How, readily, therefore, we ought to go to Christ about the purging of our consciences from dead works. I have heard it said that the sinner finds great difficulty in going to Christ at first: that is sadly true, but I have also noticed that sometimes there is a difficulty in continuing to go to him every day of our lives. To go as a sinner and get washed from sin needs faith, but it also requires a steady confidence to resort to Jesus under a thousand conscious failures and backslidings year after year. I sit down in my chamber, and I feel I am a forgiven man: about that I am quite sure, and therefore I shall never be cast into hell: but this day I spoke unadvisedly with my lips, or I grew angry in temper, or I am conscious that I was proud, or else I have been frivolous and worldly, or I have been selfish; and at the remembrance of those sins I lose my peace and feel I cannot pray. Communion with God seems gone while these faults stare me in the face. The arch-enemy whispers, "You cannot get back into your former happy state." At such times let us say to him, "O thou enemy, I can and will return into fellowship, for my dear Lord and Master has only to take the basin and wash my feet, and this he can do right speedily." O my brother, when a sense of sin revives upon the conscience, do not be persuaded by unbelief that there is an impossibility of again escaping it, but go straight away to your Master and say, "Wash me, and I shall be whiter than snow," and he will cleanse you, and once again you shall joy and rejoice in him. Remember the words of our hymn concerning the fountain of divine grace:—

> "This fountain from guilt not only makes pure,
> And gives, soon as felt, infallible cure;
> But if guilt removèd return, and remain,
> Its power may be provèd again and again."

Mark, however, that this washing *must be given us by our Lord himself.* He must first wash our feet before we can wash one another's feet. I think I see the Well-beloved now as he pours the pure water on their ancles! Mark how he takes their feet into his kind and tender hands, and washes them clean, and then wipes them with the towel! He continues to do this to us even now in a spiritual sense. It is his own dear love that takes away sin from the conscience, so that it does not linger there to foul and mar it. Often methinks he seems to kiss those feet and say, "Dear child, thou art clean now. Watch thy footsteps, and keep thy garments that they be not defiled again: yet even if they be I will wash them again, for I live still to cleanse thee and put away thy transgressions. I mean ere long to make thee as perfect as myself, without spot or wrinkle or any such thing." Nor may I leave this point till I bid you mark the condescension of this personal washing, for Abraham did not himself wash the angels' feet, but said, "Let a little water be fetched, and wash your feet;" and Joseph did not personally wash his brethren's feet, but the steward of his house brought them in and gave them water, and they washed their feet; but Jesus does it all himself. O my soul, bow down before him and adore his love unparalleled.

Thus I have shown you that this foot-washing is a symbol of our Redeemer's continuous acts of love. Jesus is always our host, and therefore he washes our feet; he always cares for our little matters, and in this sense washes even our feet; he is always providing refreshments for his people in their pilgrimage to heaven, and thus he washes their feet; he is always guarding the purity of his church and people, and so in the fullest sense he washes their feet.

II. Secondly, we come to practical matters as to ourselves. AS THE MODEL OF HIS OWN LOVE IN HIS PEOPLE our Lord washed their feet. The love of the saints is their Lord's love in them, which has filled their vessels to the brim and is now running over. Christ's love is the sun and our love is the moonlight which we are able to give forth because the sun hath looked upon us. Love is first freely imparted and then plenteously diffused. Jesus says, "The water that I shall give him shall be in him a well of water;" and then again, "Out of his belly shall flow rivers of living water." What we receive we impart, and the grace which works *in* us at the first ere long works *by* us.

Let us look at this foot-washing in reference to ourselves, and our duty and office in the midst of our brethren. We learn, first, that *there will always be need of service in the church,* and always need of service in the particular direction of promoting purity. The apostles were twelve strong men, surely they did not require a servant! Yes, they did. They must have a servant, they could not do without a servant; and therefore their Lord supplied the vacant place. And now that the Lord is gone his church still needs servants, and servants to wash feet, or else all will go amiss. On earth the church will never be so clean that it will have no need of foot-washing; the church will never be able dispense with purifying service till the Lord shall come. You, my brother Christian, may never expect to join a church where there will be nothing for you to do; do not even desire such a position of idleness. We shall never get among a community so pure that we shall see no faults in our brethren, and never shall we ourselves be so good that they will see no faults in us; therefore, let us render and receive a happy, mutual service in the church by which the sanctification of one and all will be promoted. In those words, "If I then, your Lord and Master, have washed your feet; ye also ought to wash one another's feet," our Lord speaks as though he would have us reckon upon acting as servants for the benefit of each other. Let us cheerfully accept the position.

We see next that *we are not to advocate the abrogation of such service*, or pretend that we have reached a point at which we can dispense with it. The Stoic would say, "Washing feet! What is the good of it? What need of washing a man's feet? If he needs it, let him wash them himself. The first law of nature is self-love: let every man see to himself. What have I to do with my brother's feet? Let him wash his own. What has he to do with my feet? Let him mind his own business." That is anti-Christianity: but Christianity says, "I am willing that others should help me to be holy, and I am also willing to help others to the same end. I am so imperfect that I am willing that anybody should point out my faults, and rebuke me for them, and I am so anxious that my brother should be holy that I will lovingly help him to conquer sin." Sometimes it is more humbling to have your own feet washed than to wash other people's, and hence sometimes our naughty pride says, "Thou shalt never wash my feet." Yet it must be so, and pride must sit still like a child, and be both washed and wiped. Again, I perceive that to many it is easy to stoop to the poor, but hard to yield to their equals in estate or in ability. I know those who will do a thousand things for a poor man, but they would not do the like service to those of their own rank. You say, "As for that poor soul, I do not mind conceding many points to him, but this other man will crow over me if I yield to his weakness, and he will expect me to do it again, and so I may be thought to be a person of no spirit, who can easily be put upon, and made a general hack." That also is the speech of anti-Christianity. True Christianity impels us to render and to accept that service which is mutual among true saints. He who kindly reminds me of my faults helps me to be better; let me not be angry with him, but value him for his faithfulness. On the other hand, I must never hint at a failing in a brother unless I believe that he will be the better for it, and even then I must do it gently, for I am not to scald my brethren's feet, but to use cool, sparkling, living water in the washing of them. Refining by fire is God's work: refreshing with water is ours. We are to rebuke in love, not in wrath; we are to wipe as well as wet, to comfort as well as correct.

In the world they criticise: this is the business of the public press, and it is very much the business of private circles. Hear how gossips say, "Do you see that spot? What a terrible walk that man must have had this morning: look at his feet! He has been very much in the mire you can see, for there are the traces upon him." That is the world's way. Christ's way is very different. He says nothing, but takes the basin and begins to wash away the stain. Do not judge and condemn, but seek the restoration and the improvement of the erring. Say to your faulty brother, "I am very anxious if I may to take away your spots. I would not wish to point them out if I did not feel that I should thereby help you to get rid of them." I fear that many professors follow the world's way, and indulge in what we call gossip, which is usually slander and misrepresentation, or, in other words, lying. The best of men may have to endure this, but it is a great pity it should be so. Why will people find pleasure in throwing dirty water over their neighbours? Do you make yourself any better by blackening others? Do you expect to rise by pulling others down? Scorn such attempts. An ambition which suggests such evil means is only worthy of a fiend. O ye who truly love your Lord cease from cruel witticisms, and spend your strength in humble and loving washings of your brethren's feet, and so shall we all become more happy, because more like our Lord.

This foot-washing among disciples *should be done very cheerfully.* Nobody asked the Master to bring the basin: no one would have thought of such a thing: it was his own heart of love that made him do it, out of spontaneous affection for those whom he had chosen. Let us be also ready to perform any office for our brethren, however lowly. If there is a position in the church where the worker will have to toil hard and get no thanks for it, take it, and be pleased with it. If you can perform a service which few will ever seek to do themselves, or appreciate when performed by others, yet occupy it with holy delight. Covet humble work, and when you get it be content to continue in it. There is no great rush after the lowest places, you will rob no one by seeking them. The first place we must have an election for and poll the whole community, but for the very lowest there is no great ambition, therefore select such a place, and while you will escape envy you will also gain a quiet conscience. If we were Christ's more thoroughly we should cheerfully and voluntarily push ourselves into the places of self-sacrifice, counting it our chief honour to serve God and the church in ways which are obscure and despised, because in so doing we shall be saved from the pharisaic spirit which desires the praise of man.

When we do anything for Christ's people, not only should we do it cheerfully but *thoroughly.* How well our Lord took up the servant's place. He disrobed himself until he stood prepared for his task in much the same undress as an attendant at the Turkish baths, who takes off all his upper garments. Our Lord was ready to do his work; he put off all that would hinder him, for he meant real washing, and not a mere form. When you are going to serve your brethren, do it heartily; give your Lord zealous and earnest service; strip to your shirt sleeves, if need be, to serve Christ and his people. Do not attempt to play the fine gentleman; is it not far nobler to be a real Christian?

Observe how each point of our Lord's procedure is marked by the evangelist. "He riseth from supper, and laid aside his garments; and took a towel, and girded himself. After that he poureth water into a bason, and began to wash the disciples' feet, and to wipe them with the towel wherewith he was girded." He might have left them to wipe themselves, but, no, he must finish his love work—"He wiped them with the towel wherewith he was girded." Whenever you serve a brother for Christ's sake do it thoroughly. Begin it heartily, go on with it steadfastly, and do not leave off till the deed is done. If anything is to be done slovenly let it be something which is done for yourself; but Jesus and his people must have the best which our ability can render. Give the saints of God the pick and choice of your productions: if you wash their feet wash them well. The foot of the meanest servant of Christ is more honourable than the head of the greatest emperor that ever wore a diadem. It will be seen in eternity to be a greater honour to have performed the most menial service for a true child of God than to have been honoured and decorated with stars and garters in the service of the mightiest monarch. Lay yourselves out for thorough service of your Lord in his people, and try to be always doing this.

I feel quite sure of my ground in having said that this foot-washing was meant to be a type of what our Lord is always doing, because he puts it thus : "If I then, your Lord and Master, have washed your feet; ye also ought to wash one another's feet." Evidently the inference would be "If I did this but once, ye ought to wash one another's feet once;" but since the moral is, "You ought always to wash one another's feet," the doctrine is that in effect our Lord is always washing the feet of his people. Let us carry out the lesson, and be always in a servant's attitude among our fellow disciples. Let us be always on bended knee with the basin and the towel near at hand; let us be willing to relieve those who are in need, to restore those who stumble, to reclaim those who wander, and to edify and perfect all the body of Christ as far as our ability will permit. Be it ours to promote the holiness of all our fellow Christians at all times. You say it is the pastor's business to look after the church. I know it is, but the true pastor's wisdom is to set the members of the church looking after one another. "Bear ye one another's burdens, and so fulfil the law of Christ." In my own case the pastorate of one person over five thousand members is ridiculous, unless it be exercised by impressing all the members with the necessity, the duty, the privilege of mutual oversight, each one seeking to do good to the other according as he hath opportunity. Let this mind be in you which is also in Christ Jesus, who washed his disciples' feet. Love one another, I do implore you, and in honour prefer one another. Look not every man on his own things, but every man also on the things of others. Let brotherly love continue, and ever so live that when your Master looks down upon you he may joy and rejoice in you, as I trust he does this day.

May this, our beloved church, be for many a year a pattern of unity and peace within, and of strength and activity without, that so a witness may be borne for pure and undefiled religion, and a model set up in which shall be seen the handiwork of the Spirit, who creates love in the hearts of the saints. Little children, love one another. Amen.

PORTION OF SCRIPTURE READ BEFORE SERMON—John xiii. 1—17.

Metropolitan Tabernacle Pulpit.

JESUS, THE KING OF TRUTH.

A Sermon

Delivered on Thursday Evening, December 19th, 1872, by

C. H. SPURGEON,

AT THE METROPOLITAN TABERNACLE, NEWINGTON.

"Pilate therefore said unto him, Art thou a king then? Jesus answered, Thou sayest that I am a king. To this end was I born, and for this cause came I into the world, that I should bear witness unto the truth. Every one that is of the truth heareth my voice."—John xviii., 37.

The season is almost arrived when by the custom of our fellow-citizens we are led to remember the birth of the holy child Jesus, who was born "king of the Jews." I shall not, however, conduct you to Bethlehem, but to the foot of Calvary; there we shall learn, from the Lord's own lips, something concerning the kingdom over which he rules, and thus we shall be led to prize more highly the joyous event of his nativity.

We are told, by the apostle Paul, that our Lord Jesus Christ before Pontius Pilate witnessed a good confession. It was a good confession as to the manner of it, for our Lord was truthful, gentle, prudent, patient, meek, and yet, withal, uncompromising, and courageous. His spirit was not cowed by Pilate's power, nor exasperated by his sneers. In his patience he possessed his soul, and remained the model witness for the truth—both in his silence and in his speech. He witnessed a good confession also, as to the matter of it; for, though he said but little, that little was all that was needful. He claimed his crown rights, and, at the same time, declared that his kingdom was not of this world, nor to be sustained by force. He vindicated both the spirituality and the essential truthfulness of his sovereignty. If ever we should be placed in like circumstances, may we be able to witness a good confession too! We may never, like Paul, be made to plead before Nero; but, if we should, may the Lord stand by us, and help us to play the man before the lion! In our families, or among our business acquaintances, we may have to meet some little Nero, and answer to some petty Pilate; may we then also be true witnesses. O that we may have grace to be prudently silent or meekly outspoken, as the matter may require, in either case being faithful to our conscience and our God! May the sorrowful visage of Jesus, the faithful and true witness, the Prince of the kings

No. 1,086.

of the earth, be often before our eye, to check the first sign of flinching, and to inspire us with dauntless courage!

We have before us, in the words of the text, a part of our Saviour's good confession touching his kingdom.

I. Note, first of all, that OUR LORD CLAIMED TO BE A KING. Pilate said, "Art thou a king, then?" asking the question with a sneering surprise that so poor a being should put forth a claim to royalty. Do you wonder that he should have marvelled greatly to find kingly claims associated with such a sorrowful condition? The Saviour answered, in effect, "It is even as thou sayest, I am a king." The question was but half earnest; the answer was altogether solemn: "I am a king." Nothing was ever uttered by our Lord with greater certainty and earnestness.

Now, notice, that our Lord's claim to be a king was made without the slightest ostentation or desire to be advantaged thereby. There were other times when, if he had said "I am a king," he might have been carried upon the shoulders of the people, and crowned amid general acclamations. His fanatical fellow countrymen would gladly have made him their leader at one time; and we read that they would have "taken him by force and made him a king." At such times he said but little about his kingdom, and what he did say was uttered in parables, and explained only to his disciples when they were alone. Little enough did he say in his preaching concerning his birthright as the Son of David and a scion of the royal house of Judah; for he shrank from worldly honours, and disdained the vain glories of a temporal diadem. He who came in love to redeem men, had no ambition for the gewgaws of human sovereignty. But now, when he is betrayed by his disciple, accused by his countrymen, and in the hands of an unjust ruler; when no good can come of it to himself; when it will bring him derision rather than honour; he speaks out plainly and replies to his interrogator, "Thou sayest that I am a king."

Note well the clearness of our Lord's avowal; there was no mistaking his words: "I am a king." When the time has come for the truth to be spoken, our Lord is not backward in declaring it. Truth has her times most meet for speech, and her seasons for silence. We are not to cast our pearls before swine, but when the hour has come for speech we must not hesitate, but speak as with the voice of a trumpet, giving forth a certain sound, that no man may mistake us. So, though a prisoner given up to die, the Lord boldly declares his royalty, though Pilate would pour derision upon him in consequence thereof. O, for the Master's prudence to speak the truth at the right time, and for the Master's courage to speak it when the right time has come. Soldiers of the cross, learn of your Captain.

Our Lord's claim to royalty must have sounded very singularly in Pilate's ear. Jesus was, doubtless, very much careworn, sad, and emaciated in appearance. He had spent the first part of the night in the garden in an agony; in the midnight hours he had been dragged from Annas to Caiaphas, and from Caiaphas to Herod; neither at daybreak had he been permitted to rest, so that, from sheer weariness, he must have looked very unlike a king. If you had taken some poor ragged creature in the street, and said to him, "Art thou a king, then?" the question could scarcely have been more sarcastic. Pilate, in his heart, despised the Jews as such, but here was a poor Jew, persecuted by his own people, helpless and friendless; it sounded like mockery to talk of a kingdom in connection with him. Yet never earth saw truer king! None of the line of Pharaoh, the family of Nimrod, or the race of the Cæsars, was so intrinsically imperial in himself as he, or so deservedly reckoned a king among men by virtue of his descent, his achievements, or his superior character. The carnal eye could not see this, but to the spiritual eye it is clear as noon-day. To this day, pure Christianity, in its outward appearance, is an equally unattractive object, and wears upon its surface few royal tokens. It is without form or comeliness, and when men see it, there is no beauty that they should desire it. True, there is a nominal Christtianity which is accepted and approved of men, but the pure gospel is still despised and rejected. The real Christ of to-day, among men, is unknown and unrecognised as much as he was among his own nation eighteen hundred years ago. Evangelical doctrine is at a discount, holy living is censured, and spiritual-mindedness is derided. "What," say they, "This evangelical doctrine, call you it the royal truth? Who believes it now-a-days? Science has exploded it. There is nothing great about it; it may afford comfort to old women, and to those who have not capacity enough for free thought, but its reign is over, never to return." As to living in separation from the world, it is called Puritanism, or worse. Christ in doctrine, Christ in spirit, Christ in life —the world cannot endure as king. Christ chanted in cathedrals, Christ personified in lordly prelates, Christ surrounded by such as are in king's houses, *he* is well enough; but Christ honestly obeyed, followed, and worshipped in simplicity, without pomp or form, they will not allow to reign over them. Few now-a-days will side with the truth their fathers bled for. The day for covenanting to follow Jesus through evil report and shame appears to have gone by. Yet, though men turn round upon us, and say, "Do you call your gospel divine? Are you so preposterous as to believe that your religion comes from God and is to subdue the world?"—we boldly answer; "Yes!" Even as beneath the peasant's garb and the wan visage of the Son of Mary we can discern the Wonderful, the Counsellor, the Mighty God, the Everlasting Father! so beneath the simple form of a despised gospel we perceive the royal lineaments of truth divine. We care nothing about the outward apparel or the external housing of truth; we love it for its own sake. To us, the marble halls and the alabaster columns are nothing, we see more in the manger and the cross. We are satisfied that Christ is the king still where he was wont to be king, and that is not among the great ones of the earth, nor among the mighty and the learned, but amongst the base things of the world and the things which are not, which shall bring to nought the things that are, for these hath God from the beginning chosen to be his own.

Let us add, that our Lord's claim to be a king shall be acknowledged one day by all mankind. When Christ said to Pilate, according to our version, "Thou sayest that I am a king," he virtually prophesied the future confession of all men. Some, taught by his grace, shall in this life rejoice in him as their altogether lovely King. Blessed be God, the Lord Jesus might look into the eyes of many of us, and say, "Thou sayest that I am a king," and we would reply, "We do say it joyfully." But the day shall come when he shall sit upon his great white throne, and then, when the multitudes shall tremble in the presence of his awful majesty, even such as Pontius Pilate, and Herod, and the chief priests, shall own that he is a king! Then to each of his astounded and overwhelmingly convinced enemies he might say, "Now, O despiser, thou sayest that I am a king," for to him every knee shall bow, and every tongue shall confess that he is Lord!

Let us remember, here, that when our Lord said to Pilate, "Thou sayest that I am king," he was not referring to his divine dominion. Pilate was not thinking of that at all, nor did our Lord, I think, refer to it: yet, forget not that, as divine, he is the King of kings and Lord of lords. We must never forget that, though he died in weakness as man, yet he ever lives and rules as God. Nor do I think he referred to his mediatorial sovereignty, which he possesses over the earth for his people's sake; for the Lord has all power committed unto him in heaven and in earth, and the Father has given him power over all flesh, that he may give eternal life to as many as are given him. Pilate was not alluding to that, nor our Lord either, in the first place; but he was speaking of that rule which he personally exercises over the minds of the faithful, by means of the truth. You remember Napoleon's saying, "I have founded an empire by force, and it has melted away; Jesus Christ established his kingdom by love, and it stands to this day, and will stand." That is the kingdom to which our Lord's word refers, the kingdom of spiritual truth in which Jesus reigns as Lord over those who are of the truth. He claimed to be a king, and the truth which he revealed, and of which he was the personification, is, therefore, the sceptre of his empire. He rules by the force of truth over those hearts which feel the power of right and truth, and therefore willingly yield themselves to his guidance, believe his word, and are governed by his will. It is as a spiritual Lord that Christ claims sovereignty among men; he is king over minds that love him, trust him, and obey him, because they see in him the truth which their souls; pine for. Other kings rule our bodies, but Christ our souls, they govern by force, but he by the attractions of righteousness; theirs is, to a great extent, a fictitious royalty, but his is true, and finds its force in truth.

So much, then, upon Christ's claims to be a king.

II. Now, observe, secondly, that OUR LORD DECLARED THIS KINGDOM TO BE HIS MAIN OBJECT IN LIFE. "To this end was I born, and for this cause came I into the world." To set up his kingdom was the reason why he was born of the virgin. To be King of men, it was necessary for him to be born. He was always the Lord of all; he needed not to be born to be a king in that sense, but to be king through the power of truth, it was essential that he should be born in our nature. Why so? I answer, first, because it seems unnatural that a ruler should be alien in nature to the people over whom he rules. An angelic king of men would be unsuitable; there could not exist the sympathy which is the cement of a spiritual empire. Jesus, that he might govern by force of love and truth alone, became of one nature with mankind; he was a man among men, a real man—but a right noble and kingly man, and so a King of men.

But, again, the Lord was born that he might be able to save his people. Subjects are essential to a kingdom; a king cannot be a king if there be none to govern. But all men must have perished through sin, had not Christ come into the world and been born to save. His birth was a necessary step to his redeeming death; his incarnation was necessary to the atonement.

Moreover, truth never exerts such power as when it is embodied. Truth spoken may be defeated, but truth acted out in the life of a man is omnipotent, through the Spirit of God. Now, Christ did not merely speak the truth, but he *was* truth. Had he been truth embodied in an angelic form, he had possessed small power over our hearts and lives; but perfect truth in a human form has royal power over renewed humanity. Truth embodied in flesh and blood has power over flesh and blood. Hence, for this purpose was he born. So when ye hear the bells ringing out at Christmas, think of the reason why Jesus was born; dream not that he came to load your tables and fill your cups; but in your mirth look higher than all earth-born things. When you hear that in certain churches there are pompous celebrations and ecclesiastical displays, think not for this purpose was Jesus born. No; but look within your hearts, and say, for this purpose was he born : that he might be a King, that he might rule through the truth in the souls of a people who are by grace made to love the truth of God.

And then he added, "For this cause came I into the world;" that is, he came out of the bosom of the Father that he might set up his kingdom, by unveiling the mysteries which were hid from the foundation of the world. No man can reveal the counsel of God, but one who has been with God; and the Son who has come forth of the ivory palaces of gladness, announces to us tidings of great joy! For this cause also came he into the world, from the obscure retirement of Joseph's workshop, where, for many years he was hidden like a pearl in its shell. It was needful that he should be made known, and that the truth to which he witnessed should be sounded in the ears of the crowd. Since he was to be a King, he must leave seclusion, and come forth to do battle for his throne; he must address the multitudes on the hill-side; he must speak by the sea-shore; he must gather disciples, and send them forth by two and two to publish on the housetops the secrets of mighty truth! He came not forth because he loved to be seen of men, or courted popularity; but for this purpose—that, the truth being published, he might set up his kingdom. It was needful that he should come out into the world and teach, or truth would not be known, and consequently could not operate. The sun must come forth, like a bridegroom out of his chamber, or the kingdom of light will never be established; the breath must come forth from the hiding-place of the winds, or life will never reign in the valley of dry bones. During three years, our Lord lived conspicuously, and emphatically "came into the world." He was seen of men so closely as to be beheld, looked upon, touched, and handled. He was intended to be a pattern, and therefore, it was needful that he should be seen. The life of a man who lives in absolute retirement may be admirable for himself and acceptable with God, but it cannot be exemplary to men: for this cause the Lord came forth into the world, that all he did might influence mankind. His enemies were permitted to watch his every action, and to endeavour to entrap him in his speech, by way of test; his friends saw him in privacy, and knew what he did in solitude; thus his whole life was reported—he was observed on the cold mountain-side at midnight, as well as in the midst of the great congregation. This was permitted to make the truth known, for every action of his life was truth, and tended to set up the kingdom of truth in the world.

Let us pause here. Christ is a king, a king by force of truth in a spiritual kingdom; for this purpose was he born; for this cause came he into the world. My soul, ask thyself this question:—Has this purpose of Christ's birth and life been answered in thee? If not, what avails Christmas to thee? The choristers will sing, "Unto us a child is born; unto us a Son is given." Is that true to thee? How can it be unless Jesus reigns in thee, and is thy Saviour and thy Lord? Those who can in truth rejoice in his birth are those who know him as their bosom's Lord, ruling their understanding by the truth of his doctrine; their admiration by the truth of his life; their affections by the truth of his person. To such he is not a personage to be pourtrayed with a crown of gold and a robe of purple, like the common theatrical kings of men; but one brighter and more heavenly, whose crown is real, whose dominion is unquestionable, who rules by truth and love! Do we know this King?

This question may well come home to us, for, beloved, there are many who say, "Christ is my King," who know not what they say, for they do not obey him. He is the servant of Christ who trusts in Christ, who walks according to Christ's mind, and loves the truth which Jesus has revealed: all others are mere pretenders.

III. But now I must pass on. Our Lord, in the third place, REVEALED THE NATURE OF HIS ROYAL POWER. I have already spoken on that, but I must do so again. We should have thought the text would have run thus: "Thou sayest that I am a king; to this end was I born, and for this cause came I into the world, that I should establish my kingdom." It is not so in words, but so it must mean, for Jesus was not incoherent in his speech. We conclude that the words employed have the same meaning as that which the context suggests, only it is differently expressed. If our Lord had said, "That I might establish a kingdom," he might have misled Pilate; but when he availed himself of the spiritual explanation, and said that his kingdom was truth, and that the establishment of his kingdom was by bearing witness to the truth, then, though Pilate did not understand him—for it was far above his comprehension—yet, at any rate, he was not misled.

Our Lord, in effect, tells us that truth is the pre-eminent characteristic of his kingdom, and that his royal power over men's hearts is through the truth. Now, the witness of our Lord among men was emphatically upon real and vital matters. He dealt not with fiction, but with facts; not with trifles, but with infinite realities. He speaks not of opinions, views, or speculations, but of infallible verities. How many preachers waste time over what may be or may not be! Our Lord's testimony was pre-eminently practical and matter-of-fact, full of verities and certainties. I have sometimes, when hearing sermons, wished the preacher would come to the point, and would deal with something that really concerned our soul's welfare. What concern have dying men with the thousand trivial questions which are flitting around us? We have heaven or hell before us, and death within a stone's-throw; for God's sake do not trifle with us, but tell us the truth at once! Jesus is king in his people's souls, because his preaching has blessed us in the grandest and most real manner, and set us at rest upon points of boundless importance. He has not given us well-chiselled stones, but real bread. There are a thousand things which you may not know, and you shall be very little the worse for not knowing them; but O, if you do not know that which Jesus has taught, it shall go ill with you. If you are taught of the Lord Jesus, you shall have rest for your cares, balm for your sorrows, and satisfaction for your desires. Jesus gives sinners who believe in him the truth which they need to know; the assurance of sin forgiven through his blood, favour ensured by his righteousness, and heaven secured by his eternal life.

Moreover, Jesus has power over his people because he testifies not to symbols, but to the very substance of truth. The Scribes and Pharisees were very fluent upon sacrifices, offerings, oblations, tithes, fastings, and the like; but what influence could all that exert over aching hearts? Jesus has imperial power over contrite spirits, because he tells them of his one real sacrifice and of the perfection which he has secured to all believers. The priests lost their power over the people because they went no further than the shadow, and sooner or later all will do so who rest in the symbol. The Lord Jesus retains his power over his saints because he reveals the substance, for grace and truth are by Jesus Christ. What a loss of time it is to debate upon the fashion of a cope, or the manner of celebrating communion, or the colour suitable for the clergyman's robes in Advent, or the precise date of Easter. Vanity of vanities, all is vanity! Such trifles will never aid in setting up an everlasting kingdom in men's hearts. Let us take care lest we also set great store by externals, and miss the essential, spiritual life of our holy faith. Christ's kingdom is not meat and drink, but righteousness and peace, and joy in the Holy Ghost!

The power of King Jesus in the hearts of his people lies much in the fact that he brings forth unalloyed truth, without mixture of error. He has delivered to us pure light and no darkness; his teaching is no combination of God's word and man's inventions; no mixture of inspiration and philosophy; silver without dross is the wealth which he gives his servants. Men taught of his Holy Spirit to love the truth, recognise this fact and surrender their souls to the royal sway of the Lord's truth, and it makes them free, and sanctifies them; nor can anything make them disown such a sovereign, for as the truth lives and abides in their hearts, so Jesus, who is the truth, abides also. If you know what truth is, you will as naturally submit yourselves to the teachings of Christ as ever children yield to a father's rule.

The Lord Jesus taught that worship must be true, spiritual, and of the heart, or else it would be nothing worth. He would not take sides with the temple at Gerizim or that on Zion, but he declared that the time was come when those who worshipped God would worship him in spirit and in truth. Now, regenerate hearts feel the power of this, and rejoice that it emancipates them from the beggarly elements of carnal ritualism. They accept gladly the truth that pious words of prayer or praise are vanity, unless the heart has living worship within it. In the great truth of spiritual worship, believers possess a Magna Charta, dear as life itself. We refuse to be again subject to the yoke of bondage, and cleave to our emancipating king.

Our Lord taught, also, that all false living was base and loathsome. He poured contempt on the phylacteries of hypocrites and the broad borders of the garments of oppressors of the poor. With him, ostentatious alms, long prayers, frequent fasts, and the tithe of mint and cummin, were all nothing when practised by those who devoured widows' houses. He cared nothing for white-washed sepulchres and platters with outsides made clean, he judged the thoughts and intents of the heart. What woes were those which he denounced upon the formalists of his day! It must have been a grand sight to have seen the lowly Jesus roused to indignation, thundering forth peal on peal his denunciations of hypocrisy. Elias never called fire from heaven one half so grandly. "Woe unto you Scribes and Pharisees, hypocrites," is the loudest roll of heaven's artillery! See how, like another Samson, Jesus slays the shams of his age, and piles them heaps upon heaps to rot for ever. Shall not he who teaches us true living be king of all the sons of truth? Let us even now salute him as Lord and King.

Besides, beloved, our Lord came not only to teach us the truth, but a mysterious power goes forth from him, through that Spirit which rests on him without measure—which subdues chosen hearts to truthfulness, and then guides truthful hearts into fulness of peace and joy. Have you never felt when you have been with Jesus, that a sense of his purity has made you yearn to be purged of all hypocrisy and every false way? Have you not been ashamed of yourself when you have come forth from hearing his word, from watching his life, and, above all, from enjoying his fellowship—quite ashamed that you have not been more real, more sincere, more true, more upright, and so a more loyal subject of the truthful King? I know you have. Nothing about Jesus is false or even dubious; he is transparent—from head to foot he is truth in public, truth in private, truth in word, and truth in deed. Hence it is that he has a kingdom over the pure in heart, and is vehemently extolled by all those whose hearts are set upon righteousness.

IV. And now, in the fourth place, our Lord DISCLOSED THE METHOD OF HIS CONQUEST. "To this end was I born, and for this cause came I into the world, *that I should bear witness for the truth.*" Christ never yet set up his kingdom by force of arms. Mahomet drew the sword, and converted men by giving them the choice of death or conversion; but Christ said to Peter, "Put up thy sword into its sheath." No compulsion ought to be used with any man to lead him to receive any opinion, much less to induce him to espouse the truth. Falsehood requires the rack of the Inquisition, but truth needs not such unworthy aid; her own beauty, and the Spirit of God, are her strength. Moreover, Jesus used no arts of priestcraft, or tricks of superstition. The foolish are persuaded of a dogma, by the fact that it is promulgated by a learned doctor of high degree, but our Rabboni wears no sounding titles of honour; the vulgar imagine that a statement must be correct if it emanates from a person who wears lawn sleeves, or from a place where the banners are of costly workmanship, and the music of the sweetest kind : these things are arguments with those who are amenable to no other ; but Jesus owes nothing to his apparel, and influences none by artistic arrangements. None can say that he reigns over men by the glitter of pomp, or the fascination of sensuous ceremonies. His battle-axe is the truth; truth is both his arrow and his bow, his sword and his buckler. Believe me, no kingdom is worthy of the Lord Jesus but that which has its foundations laid in indisputable verities; Jesus would scorn to reign by the help of a lie.

True Christianity was never promoted by policy or guile, by doing a wrong thing, or saying a false thing. Even to exaggerate truth is to beget error, and so to pull down the truth we would set up. There are some who say, "Bring out one line of teaching, and nothing else, lest you should seem inconsistent." What have I to do with that ? If it be God's truth, I am bound to deliver it all, and to keep back none of it. Policy, like a sailing vessel, dependant on the wind, tacks about hither and thither; but the true man, like a vessel having its motive power within, goes straight onward in the very teeth of the hurricane. When God puts truth into men's souls, he teaches them never to tack or trim, but to hold to truth at all hazards. This is what Jesus always did. He bore witness to the truth, and there left the matter; being guileless as a lamb.

Here it will be fit to answer the question, " What truth did he witness to ?" Ah, my brethren, what truth did he *not* witness to ? Did he not mirror all truth in his life ? See how clearly he set forth the truth that God is love. How melodious, how like a peal of Christmas bells, was his witness to the truth that " God so loved the world, that he gave his only begotten Son, that whosoever believeth in him might not perish but have everlasting life." He also bore witness that God is just. How solemnly he proclaimed that fact ! His flowing wounds, his dying agonies rang out that solemn truth, as with a knell which even the dead might hear. He bore witness to God's demand for truth in the inward parts ; for he often dissected men and laid them bare, and opened up their secret thoughts and discovered them to themselves, and made them see that only sincerity could bear the eye of God. Did he not bear witness to the truth that God had resolved to make for himself a new people and a true people ? Was he not always telling of his sheep who heard his voice, of the wheat which would be gathered into the garner, and of the precious things which would be treasured up when the bad would be thrown away ? Therein he was bearing witness that the false must die, that the unreal must be consumed, that the lie must rust and rot; but that the true, the sincere, the gracious, the vital, shall stand every test, and outlast the sun. In an age of shams, he was always sweeping away pretences and establishing truth and right by his witness. And now, beloved, this is the way in which Christ's kingdom is to be set up in the world. For this cause was the church born, and for this end came she into the world, that she might set up Christ's kingdom by bearing witness to the truth. I long, my beloved, to see you all witness-bearers. If you love the Lord, bear witness to the truth. You must do it personally; you must also do it collectively. Never join any church whose creed you do not entirely and unfeignedly believe, for if you do you act a lie, and are, moreover, a partaker in the error of other men's testimonies. I would not for a moment say anything to retard Christian unity, but there is something before unity, and that is, "truth in the inward parts" and honesty before God. I dare not be a member of a church whose teaching I knew to be false in vital points. I would sooner go to heaven alone than belie my conscience for the sake of company. You may say, "But I protest against the error of my church." Dear friends, how can you consistently protest against it when you profess to agree with it, by being a member of the church which avows it? If you are a minister of a church, you do in effect say before the world, "I believe and teach the doctrines of this church;" and if you go into the pulpit and say you do not believe them, what will people conclude? I leave you to judge that. I saw a church tower the other day, with a clock upon it, which startled me by pointing to half-past ten when I thought it was only nine; I was, however, quite relieved when I saw that another face of the clock indicated a quarter past eight. "Well," thought I, "whatever time it may be, that clock is wrong, for it contradicts itself." So if I hear a man say one thing by his church-membership and another by his private protest, why, whatever may be right, he certainly is not consistent with himself.

Let us bear witness to the truth, since there is great need of doing so just now, for witnessing is in ill repute. The age extols no virtue so much as "liberality," and condemns no vice so fiercely as bigotry, *alias* honesty. If you believe anything and hold it firmly, all the dogs will bark at you. Let them bark: they will have done when they are tired! You are responsible to God, and not to mortal men. Christ came into the world to bear witness to the truth, and he has sent you to do the same; take care that you do it, offend or please; for it is only by this process that the kingdom of Christ is to be set up in the world.

Now, the last thing is this. Our Saviour, having spoken of his kingdom and the way of establishing it, DESCRIBED HIS SUBJECTS: "Everyone that is of the truth heareth my voice." That is to say, wherever the Holy Spirit has made a man a lover of truth, he always recognises Christ's voice and yields himself to it. Where are the people who love the truth? Well, we need not enquire long. We need not Diogenes' lantern to find them, they will come to the light; and where is light but in Jesus? Where are those that would not seem to be what they are not? Where are the men who desire to be true in secret and before the Lord? They may be discovered where Christ's people are discovered ; they will be found listening to those who bear witness to the truth. Those who love pure truth, and know what Christ is, will be sure to fall in love with him and hear his voice. Judge ye, then, this day, brethren and sisters, whether ye are of the truth or not ; for if you love the truth, you know and obey the voice which calls you away from your old sins, from false refuges, from evil habits, from everthing which is not after the Lord's mind. You have heard him in your conscience rebuking you for that of the false which remains in you ; encouraging in you that of the true which is struggling there. I have done, when I have urged on you one or two reflections.

The first is, beloved, Dare we avow ourselves on the side of truth at this hour of its humiliation ? Do we own the royalty of Christ's truth when we see it every day dishonoured. If gospel truth were honoured everywhere, it would be an easy thing to say " I believe it ;" but now, in these days, when it has no honour among men, dare we cleave to it at all costs ? Are you willing to walk with the truth through the mire and through the slough ? Have you the courage to profess unfashionable truth ? Are you willing to believe the truth against which science, falsely so-called, has vented her spleen ? Are you willing to accept the truth although it is said that only the poor and uneducated will receive it ? Are you willing to be the disciple of the Galilean, whose apostles were fishermen ? Verily, verily, I say unto you, in that day in which the truth in the person of Christ shall come forth in all its glory, it shall go ill with those who were ashamed to own it and its Master.

In the next place, if we have heard Christ's voice, do we recognise our life-object ? Do we feel, " For this end were we born, and for this cause came we into the world, that we might bear witness to the truth ? " I do not believe that you, my dear brother, came into the world to be a linendraper, or an auctioneer, and nothing else. I do not believe that God created you, my sister, to be merely and only a sempstress, a nurse, or a housekeeper. Immortal souls were not created for merely mortal ends. For this purpose was I born, that, with my voice in this place, and everywhere else, I might bear witness to the truth. You acknowledge that : then I beg you, each one, to acknowledge that you have a similar mission. "I could not occupy the pulpit," says one. Never mind that : bear witness for the truth where you are, and in your own sphere. O waste no time or energy, but at once testify for Jesus.

And now, last of all, do you own Christ's superlative dignity, beloved ? Do you see what a King, Christ is ? Is he such a King to you as none other could be ? It was but yesterday a prince entered one of our great towns, and they crowded all their streets to welcome him—yet he was but a mortal man. And then at night they illuminated their city, and made the heavens glow as though the sun had risen before his appointed hour. Yet what had this prince done for them? Loyal subjects were they, and that was the reason of their joy. But O, beloved, we need not ask, "What has Christ done for us?"—we will ask, "What has he not done for us?" Emmanuel, we owe all to thee! Thou art our new creator, our Redeemer from the lowest pit of hell! In thyself resplendent and altogether lovely, thy beauties command our adoration! Thou hast lived for us, thou hast bled for us, thou hast died for us; and thou art preparing a kingdom for us, and thou art coming again to take us to be with thee where thou art! All this commands our love. All hail! all hail! Thou art our King, and we worship thee with all our soul!

Beloved, I beseech you love Christ, and live for him while you can. Work while opportunity serves. While I have been laid aside, and able to do nothing, the great sorrow of my heart has been my inability to do him service. I heard my brethren shouting in the battle-field, and I saw my comrades marching to the fight, and I lay like a wounded soldier in the ditch, and could not stir, save that I breathed a prayer that you might all be strong in the Lord and in the power of his might. This was my thought: "Oh, that I had preached better while I could preach, and lived more for the Master while I could serve him!" Don't incur such regrets in the future by present sluggishness, but live now for him who died for you!

If any present in this assembly have never obeyed our King, may they come to trust in him to-night; for he is a tender Saviour, and is willing to receive the biggest and blackest sinner who will come to him. Whosoever trusts in him, will never find him fail; for he will save to the uttermost them that come unto God by him. May he bring you to his feet, and reign over you in love. Amen.

PORTION OF SCRIPTURE READ BEFORE SERMON—Psalm lxxxv.

Metropolitan Tabernacle Pulpit.

THE INDWELLING AND OUTFLOWING OF THE HOLY SPIRIT.

A Sermon

DELIVERED ON LORD'S-DAY MORNING, MAY 28TH, 1882, BY

C. H. SPURGEON,

AT THE METROPOLITAN TABERNACLE, NEWINGTON.

"He that believeth on me, as the scripture hath said, out of his belly shall flow rivers of living water. (But this spake he of the Spirit, which they that believe on him should receive: for the Holy Ghost was not yet given; because that Jesus was not yet glorified.)"—John vii. 38, 39.

"Nevertheless I tell you the truth; It is expedient for you that I go away: for if I go not away, the Comforter will not come unto you; but if I depart, I will send him unto you."—John xvi. 7.

IT is essential, dear friends, that we should worship the living and true God. It will be ill for us if it can be said, "Ye worship ye know not what." "Thou shalt worship the Lord thy God, and him only shalt thou serve." The heathen err from this command by multiplying gods, and making this and that image to be the object of their adoration. Their excess runs to gross superstition and idolatry. I fear that sometimes we who "profess and call ourselves Christians" err in exactly the opposite direction. Instead of worshipping more than God I fear we worship less than God. This appears when we forget to pay due adoration to the Holy Spirit of God. The true God is triune, Father, Son, and Holy Spirit; and though there be but one God yet that one God has manifested himself to us in the trinity of his sacred persons. If, then, I worship the Father and the Son, but forget or neglect to adore the Holy Spirit, I worship less than God. While the poor heathen in his ignorance goes far beyond and transgresses, I must take care lest I fall short and fail too. What a grievous thing it will be if we do not pay that loving homage and reverence to the Holy Spirit which is so justly his due. May it not be the fact that we enjoy less of his power and see less of his working in the world because the church of God has not been sufficiently mindful of him? It is a blessed thing to preach the work of Jesus Christ, but it is an evil thing to omit the work of the Holy Ghost; for the work of the Lord Jesus itself is no blessing to that man who does not know the work of the Holy Spirit. There is the ransom price, but it is only through the Spirit that we know the redemption: there is the precious blood, but it is as though the fountain had never been filled unless the Spirit of God lead us with repenting

No. 1,662.

faith to wash therein. The bandage is soft and the ointment is effectual, but the wound will never be healed till the Holy Spirit shall apply that which the great Physician has provided. Let us not therefore be found neglectful of the work of the divine Spirit, lest we incur guilt, and inflict upon ourselves serious damage.

You that are believers have the most forcible reasons to hold the Holy Ghost in the highest esteem; for what are you now without him? What were you, and what would you still have been, if it had not been for his gracious work upon you? He quickened you, else you had not been in the living family of God to-day. He gave you understanding that you might know the truth, else would you have been as ignorant as the carnal world is at this hour. It was he that awakened your conscience, convincing you of sin: it was he that gave you abhorrence of sin, and led you to repent: it was he that taught you to believe, and made you see that glorious Person who is to be believed, even Jesus, the Son of God. The Spirit has wrought in you your faith and love and hope, and every grace. There is not a jewel upon the neck of your soul which he did not place there.

> "For every virtue we possess,
> And every victory won,
> And every thought of holiness,
> Are his alone."

What have we learned, if we have learned aright, except by the teaching of the Holy Ghost? What can we say either in prayer to God or in teaching to men that shall be acceptable unless we receive the unction of the Holy One of Israel? Brethren, who is it that has comforted us in our distresses, directed us in our perplexities, strengthened us in our weaknesses, and helped our infirmities in ten thousand ways? Is it not the Comforter whom the Father hath sent in Jesus' name? Can I speak too highly of the riches of his grace toward us? Can I too much extol the love of the Spirit? I know I cannot, and you that know what he has wrought in you delight to hear him highly spoken of and his work and offices set forth. We are bound by a thousand ties to seek his honour who has wrought in us our salvation. Let us never grieve him by our ingratitude, but let us endeavour to extol him. For my part, it shall be the labour of this morning to impress upon you the necessity for his work, and the superlative value of it.

Beloved brethren, notwithstanding all that the Spirit of God has already done in us, it is very possible that we have missed a large part of the blessing which he is willing to give, for he is able to "do exceeding abundantly above all that we ask or think." We have already come to Jesus, and we have drunk of the life-giving stream: our thirst is quenched, and we are made to live in him. Is this all? Now that we are living in him, and rejoicing to do so, have we come to the end of the matter? Assuredly not. We have reached as far as that first exhortation of the Master, "If any man thirst, let him come unto me and drink": but do you think that the generality of the church of God have ever advanced to the next, "He that believeth on me, as the Scripture hath said, out of his belly shall flow rivers of living water"? I think I am not going beyond the grievous truth if I say that only here and there will you find men and women who have believed up to that point. Their thirst is quenched, as I have said, and they live, and because Jesus lives they shall live also, but health and vigour they have not: they have life, but they have not life more abundantly. They have little life with which to act upon others: they have no energy welling up and overflowing to go streaming out of them like rivers. They have not thought it possible perhaps, or thinking it possible they have not imagined it possible to themselves; or believing it possible to themselves they have not aspired to it, but they have stopped short of the fullest blessing. Their wading into the sacred river has contented them and they know nothing of "waters to swim in." Like the Israelites of old, they are slow to possess all the land of promise, but sit down when the war has hardly begun. Brothers, let us go in to get of God all that God will give us: let us set our heart upon this, that we mean to have by God's help all that the infinite goodness of God is ready to bestow. Let us not be satisfied with the sip that saves, but let us go on to the baptism which buries the flesh and raises us in the likeness of the risen Lord: even that baptism into the Holy Ghost and into fire which makes us spiritual and sets us all on flame with zeal for the glory of God and eagerness for usefulness by which that glory may be increased among the sons of men.

Thus I introduce you to my texts, and by their guidance we will enter upon the further consideration of the operations of the Holy Spirit, especially of those to which we would aspire.

I. We will commence with the remark that THE WORK OF THE SPIRIT IS INTIMATELY CONNECTED WITH THE WORK OF CHRIST. It is a great pity when persons preach the Holy Spirit's work so as to obscure the work of Christ; and I have known some do that, for they have held up before the sinner's eye the inward experience of believers, instead of lifting up first and foremost the crucified Saviour to whom we must look and live. The gospel is not "Behold the Spirit of God" but "Behold the Lamb of God." It is an equal pity when Christ is so preached that the Holy Spirit is ignored; as if faith in Jesus prevented the necessity of the new birth, and imputed righteousness rendered imparted righteousness needless. Have I not often reminded you that in the third chapter of John, where Jesus taught Nicodemus the doctrine, "Except a man be born again of water and of the spirit he cannot enter the kingdom of heaven," we also read those blessed words, "And as Moses lifted up the serpent in the wilderness, even so must the Son of man be lifted up: that whosoever believeth in him should not perish, but have eternal life. For God so loved the world, that he gave his only begotten Son, that whosoever believeth in him should not perish, but have everlasting life." The necessity for regeneration by the Spirit is there put very clearly, and so is the free promise that those who trust in Jesus shall be saved. This is what we ought to do: we must take care to let both these truths stand out most distinctly with equal prominence. They are intertwined with each other and are necessary each to each: what God hath joined together let no man put asunder.

They are so joined together that, first of all, *the Holy Spirit was not given until Jesus had been glorified.* Carefully note our first text; it is a very striking one: "This spake he out of the Spirit which they that believe on him should receive, for the Holy Ghost was not yet." The word "given" is not in the original: it is inserted by the translators to help out the sense, and they were perhaps wise in making such an addition, but the words are more forcible by themselves. How strong the statement, "For the Holy Ghost was not yet." Of course, we none of us dream that the Holy Spirit was not yet existing, for he is eternal and self-existent, being most truly God, but he was not yet in fellowship with man to the full extent in which he now is since Jesus Christ is glorified. The near and dear intercourse of God with man which is expressed by the indwelling of the Spirit could not take place till redeeming work was done and the Redeemer was exalted. As far as men were concerned, and the fulness of the blessing was concerned, indicated by the outflowing rivers of living water, the Spirit of God was not yet. "Oh," say you, "but was not the Spirit of God in the church in the wilderness, and with the saints of God in all former ages?" I answer, Certainly, but not in the manner in which the Spirit of God now resides in the church of Jesus Christ. You read of the prophets, and of one and another gracious man, that the Spirit of God came upon them, seized them, moved them, spake by them; but he did not dwell in them. His operations upon men were a coming and a going: they were carried away by the Spirit of God, and came under his power, but the Spirit of God did not rest upon them or abide in them. Occasionally the sacred endowment of the Spirit of God came upon them, but they knew not "the communion of the Holy Ghost." As a French pastor very sweetly puts it, "He appeared unto men; he did not incarnate himself in man. His action was intermittent: he went and came, like the dove which Noah sent forth from the ark, and which went to and fro, finding no rest; while in the new dispensation he dwells, he abides in the heart, as the dove, his emblem, which John the Baptist saw descending and alighting upon the head of Jesus. Affianced of the soul, the Spirit went off to see his betrothed, but was not yet one with her; the marriage was not consummated until the Pentecost, after the glorification of Jesus Christ." You know how our Lord puts it, "He dwelleth with you and shall be in you." That indwelling is another thing from being *with* us. The Holy Spirit was with the Apostles in the days when Jesus was with them; but he was not in them in the sense in which he filled them at and after the Day of Pentecost. The operations of the Spirit of God before our Lord's ascension were not according to the full measure of the gospel, but now the Spirit of God has been poured upon us from on high; now he has descended, and now he abides in the midst of the church, and now we enter into him and are baptized into the Holy Ghost, while he enters into us and makes our bodies to be his temples. Jesus said, "I will send you another Comforter, which shall abide with you for ever;" not coming and going, but remaining in the midst of the church. This shows how intimately the gift of the Holy Ghost is connected with our Lord Jesus Christ, inasmuch as in the fullest sense of his indwelling the Holy Ghost could not be with us until Christ had been glorified. It has been well observed that our Lord sent out seventy evangelists to preach the gospel, even as he had aforetime sent out the twelve; and no doubt they preached with great zeal and produced much stir; but the

Holy Ghost never took the trouble to preserve one of their sermons, or even the notes of one. I have not the slightest doubt that they were very crude and incomplete, showing more of human zeal than of divine unction, and hence they are forgotten; but no sooner had the Holy Spirit fallen than Peter's first sermon is recorded, and henceforth we have frequent notes of the utterances of apostles, deacons, and evangelists. There was an abiding fulness, and an overflowing of blessing, out of the souls of the saints after the Lord was glorified, which was not existing among men before that time.

Observe, too, that the Holy Spirit was given after the ascent of our divine Lord into his glory, partly *to make that ascent the more renowned.* When he ascended up on high he led captivity captive and gave gifts to men. These gifts were men in whom the Holy Spirit dwelt, who preached the gospel unto the nations. The shedding of the Holy Spirit upon the assembled disciples on that memorable day was the glorification of the risen Christ upon the earth. I know not in what way the Father could have made the glory of heaven so effectually to flow from the heights of the New Jerusalem and to come streaming down among the sons of men as by giving that chief of all gifts, the gift of the Holy Spirit when the Lord had risen and gone into his glory. With emphasis may I say of the Spirit at Pentecost that he glorified Christ by descending at such a time. What grander celebration could there have been? Heaven rang with hosannahs, and earth echoed the joy. The descending Spirit is the noblest testimony among men to the glory of the ascended Redeemer.

Was not the Spirit of God also sent at that time *as an evidence of our divine Master's acceptance?* Did not the Father thus say to the church, "My Son has finished the work, and has fully entered into his glory; therefore give I you of the Holy Spirit"? If you would know what a harvest is to come of the sowing of the bloody sweat and of the death wounds, see the first fruits. Behold how the Holy Spirit is given, himself to be the first fruits, the earnest of the glory which shall yet be revealed in us. I want no better attestation from God of the finished work of Jesus than this blazing, flaming seal of tongues of fire upon the heads of the disciples. He must have done his work, or such a boon as this would not have come from it.

Moreover, if you desire to see how the work of the Spirit comes to us in connection with the work of Christ, recollect that *it is the Spirit's work to bear witness of Jesus Christ.* He does not take of a thousand different matters and show them to us, but he shall take "of mine," saith Christ, "and he shall show them unto you." The Spirit of God is engaged in a service in which the Lord Jesus Christ is the beginning and the end. He comes to men that they may come to Jesus. Hence he comes to convince us of sin that he may reveal the great sacrifice of sin: he comes to convince us of righteousness that we may see the righteousness of Christ; and of judgment that we may be prepared to meet him when he shall come to judge the quick and dead. Do not think that the Spirit of God has come or ever will come among us to teach us a new gospel, or something other than is written in the Scriptures. Men come to me with their fudges and fancies, and tell me that they were revealed to them by the Holy Spirit. I abhor their blasphemous impertinence, and refuse to listen to them for a minute. They tell me this and that absurdity, and then father it upon the Spirit of wisdom. It is enough to try our patience to hear their foolish ravings; but to find the Holy Spirit charged with them is more than we can bear. We have tests and judgments by which to know whether they who claim to speak by the Holy Spirit do so or not : for the testimony of the Spirit is ever most honourable to our Lord Jesus Christ, and does not concern itself with the trifles of time and the follies of the flesh.

It is by the gospel of Jesus Christ that the Spirit of God works in the hearts of men. " Faith cometh by hearing, and hearing by the word of God": the Holy Spirit uses the hearing of the word of God for the conviction, conversion, consolation, and sanctification of men. His usual and ordinary method of operation is to fasten upon the mind the things of God, and to put life and force into the consideration of them. He revives in men's memories things that have long been forgotten, and he frequently makes these the means of affecting the heart and conscience. The men can hardly recollect hearing these truths, but still they were heard by them at some time or other. Saving truths are such matters as are contained in their substance in the word of God, and lie within the range of the teaching, or the person, or work, or offices of our Lord Jesus Christ. It is the Spirit's one business here below to reveal Christ to us and in us, and to that work he steadily adheres.

Moreover, *the Holy Spirit's work is to conform us to the likeness of Jesus Christ.* He is not working us to this or that human ideal, but he is working us into the likeness of Christ that he may be the first-born among many brethren. Jesus Christ is that standard and model to which the Spirit of God by his sanctifying processes is bringing us till Christ be formed in us the hope of glory.

Evermore it is for the glory of Jesus that the Spirit of God works. He works not for the glory of a church or of a community: he works not for the honour of a man or for the distinction of a sect: his one great object is to glorify Christ. "He shall glorify me" is our Saviour's declaration, and when he takes of the things of Christ and shows them unto us, we are led more and more to reverence and love and adore our blessed Lord Jesus Christ.

I will not detain you longer with this. You will see how the works of Jesus and of the Spirit are joined together indissolubly, so that we may neither set the work of Jesus before the work of the Spirit nor the work of the Spirit before the work of Jesus, but we are glad to joy in both and to make much of them. As we delight in the Father's love and the grace of our Lord Jesus, so do we equally rejoice in the communion of the Holy Ghost, and these three agree in one.

II. We will now advance another step, and here we shall need our second text. THE OPERATIONS OF THE HOLY SPIRIT ARE OF INCOMPARABLE VALUE. They are of such incomparable value that the very best thing we can think of was not thought to be so precious as these are. Our Lord himself says, "It is expedient for you that I go away: for if I go not away, the Comforter will not come unto you." Beloved friends, the presence of Jesus Christ was of inestimable value to his disciples, and yet it was not such an advantage to his servants as the indwelling of the Holy Spirit. Is not this a wonderful statement? Well might our Lord preface it by saying, "Now I tell you the truth," as if he felt that they would find it a hard saying, for a hard saying it is. Consider for a moment what Christ was to his disciples while he was here, and then see what must be the value of the Spirit's operations when it is expedient that they should lose all that blessing in order to receive the Spirit of God. Our Lord Jesus Christ was to them their teacher, they had learned everything from his lips: he was their leader, they had never to ask what to do, they had only to follow in his steps: he was their defender, whenever the Pharisees or Sadducees assailed them he was like a brazen wall to them: he was their comforter, in all times of grief they resorted to him, and his dear sympathetic heart poured out floods of comfort at once. What if I were to say that the Lord Jesus Christ was everything to them, their all in all. What a father is to his children, ay, what a mother is to her suckling, that was Jesus Christ to his disciples; and yet the Spirit of God's abiding in the church is better even than all this.

Now take another thought. What would you think if Jesus Christ were to come among us now as in the days of his flesh: I mean not as he will come, but as he appeared at his first advent. What joy it would give you! Oh, the delights, the heavenly joys, to hear that Jesus Christ of Nazareth was on earth again, a man among men! Should we not clap our hands for joy? Our one question would be, "Master, where dwellest thou? for we should all long to live just where he lived. We could then sympathize with the negroes when they flocked into Washington in large numbers to take up their residence there. Why, think you, did they come to live in that city? Because Massa Abraham Lincoln lived there who had set them free, and they thought it would be glorious to live as near as possible to their great friend. If Jesus lived anywhere, it would not matter where, if it were in the desert or on the bleakest of mountains, there would be a rush to the place. How would the spot be crowded; what rents they would pay for the worst of tenements if Jesus was but in the neighbourhood. But do you not see the difficulty? We could not all get near him in any literal or corporeal fashion. Now that the church is multiplied into millions of believers, some of the Lord's followers would never be able to see him, and the most could only hope to speak with him now and then. In the days of his flesh the twelve might see him every day, and so might the little company of disciples, but the case is altered now that multitudes are trusting in his name.

If our Lord were at this time living in the United States we should be much grieved to have an ocean between us and our leader: all the companies that could be formed would not be able to run enough boats to carry us over. If the Master personally came here to this little island, it would not hold all the vast company of the faithful who would flock to it. It is much better to have the Holy Spirit, because he is dwelling with us and in us. The difficulties of the bodily presence are too great, and so, though we would be thankful, like the apostles, if we had known Christ after the flesh, yet we do not marvel that they expressed little sorrow when they said that after the flesh they knew even him no more. The Comforter had filled the void caused by his absence, and made them rejoice because the Lord had gone unto his Father.

Are we not apt to think that if our Lord Jesus were here it would give unspeakable strength to the church? Would not the enemy be convinced if they saw him? No, they would not. If they hear not Moses and the prophets neither would they be converted though one rose from the dead. Jesus rose, but they did not therefore believe. If our Lord had lingered here all this while his personal presence would not have converted unbelievers, for nothing can do that but the power of the Holy Ghost.

"But," you say, "surely it would thrill the church with enthusiasm." Fancy the Lord himself standing on this platform this morning in the same garb as when he was upon earth. Oh, what rapturous worship! What burning zeal! What enthusiasm! We should go home in such a state of excitement as we never were in before. Yes, it is even so, but then the Lord is not going to carry on his kingdom by the force of mere mental excitement, not even by such enthusiasm as would follow the sight of his person. The work of the Holy Spirit is a truer work, a deeper work, a surer work, and will more effectually achieve the purposes of God than even would the enthusiasm to which we should be stirred by the bodily presence of our well-beloved Saviour. The work is to be spiritual, and therefore the visible presence has departed. It is better that it should be so. We must walk by faith, and by faith alone; how could we do this if we could see the Lord with these mortal eyes? This is the dispensation of the unseen Spirit, in which we render glory to God by trusting in his word, and relying upon the unseen energy. Now, faith works and faith triumphs though the world seeth not the foundation upon which faith is built, for the Spirit who works in us cannot be discerned by carnal minds: the world seeth him not, neither knoweth him.

Thus you see that the operations of the Holy Spirit must be inestimably precious. There is no calculating their value, since it is expedient that we lose the bodily presence of Christ rather than remain without the indwelling of the Spirit of God.

III. Now go back to my first text again and follow me in the third head. Those operations of the Spirit of God, of which I am afraid some Christians are almost ignorant, are of wondrous power. The text says, "He that believeth on me, out of the midst of him shall flow rivers of living water." THESE OPERATIONS ARE OF MARVELLOUS POWER. Brethren, do you understand my text? Do rivers of living water flow out of you?

Notice, first, that this is to be *an inward work* : the rivers of living water are to flow out of the midst of the man. The words are according to our version, "Out of his belly"—that is, from his heart and soul. The rivers do not flow out of his mouth: the promised power is not oratory. We have had plenty of words, floods of words; but this is heart work. The source of the rivers is found in the inner life. It is an inward work at its fountain head. It is not a work of talent and ability, and show, and glitter, and glare : it is altogether an inward work. The life-flood is to come out of the man's inmost self, out of the bowels and essential being of the man. Homage is shown too generally to outward form and external observance, though these soon lose their interest and power; but when the Spirit of God rests within a man it exercises a home rule within him and he gives great attention to what an old divine was wont to call "the home department." Alas, many neglect the realm within which is the chief province under our care. O my brother in Christ, if you would be useful, begin with yourself. It is out of your very soul that a blessing must come. It cannot come out of you if it is not in you: and it cannot be in you unless God the Holy Ghost places it there.

Next, it is *life-giving* work. Out of the heart of the man, out of the centre of his life, are to flow rivers of living water; that is to say, he is instrumentally to communicate to others the divine life. When he speaks, when he prays, when he acts, he shall so speak and pray and act that there shall be going out of him an emanation which is full of the life of grace and godliness. He shall be a light by which others shall see. His life shall be the means of kindling life in other men's bosoms. "Out of his belly shall flow rivers of living water."

Note *the plenitude* of it. The figure would have been a surprising one. if it had said, "Out of him shall flow a river of living water"; but it is not so: it says rivers. Have you ever stood by the side of a very abundant spring? we have some such not far from London. You see the water bubbling up from many little mouths. Observe the sand dancing as the water forces its way from the bottom; and there, just across the road, a mill is turned by the stream which has just been created by the spring, and when the water-wheel is turned you see a veritable river flowing forward to supply Father Thames. Yet this is only one river; what would you think if you saw a spring yielding such supplies that a river flowed from it to the north, and a river to the south, a river to the east, and a river to the west; this is the figure before us: rivers of living water flowing out of the living man in all directions. "Ah," say you, "I have not reached to that." A point is gained when you know, confess, and deplore your failure. If you say, "I have all things and abound," I am afraid you will never reach the fulness of the blessing; but if you know something of your failure, the Lord will lead you further. It may be that the spirit of life which comes forth of you is but a trickling brooklet, or even a few tiny drops; then be sure to confess it, and you will be on the way to a fuller blessing. What a word is this! Rivers of living water!! Oh that all professing Christians were such fountains.

See how *spontaneous* it is: "Out of the midst of him shall flow." No pumping is required; nothing is said about machinery and hydraulics; the man does not want exciting and stirring up, but, just as he is, influence of the best kind quietly flows away from him. Did you ever hear a great hubbub in the morning, a great outcry, a sounding of trumpets and drums, and did you ever ask, "What is it?" Did a voice reply, "The sun is about to rise, and he is making this noise that all may be aware of it"? No, he shines, but he has nothing to say about it; even so the genuine Christian just goes about flooding the world with blessing, and so far from claiming attention for himself, it may be that he himself is unconscious of what he is effecting. God so blesses him that his leaf does not wither, and whatsoever he doeth is prospering, for he is like a tree planted by the rivers of water that bringeth forth its fruit in its season: his verdure and fruit are the natural outcome of his vigorous life. Oh, the blessed spontaneity of the work of grace when a man gets into the fulness of it, for then he seems to eat and drink and sleep eternal life, and he spreads a savour of salvation all round.

And this is to be *perpetual*,—not like intermittent springs which burst forth and flow in torrents, and then cease,—but it is to be an everyday outgushing. In summer and winter, by day and by night, wherever the man is, he shall be a blessing. As he breathes, he shall breathe benedictions; as he thinks, his mind shall be devising generous things; and when he acts, his acts shall be as though the hand of God were working by the hand of man.

I hope I hear many sighs rising up in the place! I hope I hear friends saying, "Oh that I could get to that." I want you to attain the fulness of the favour. I pray that we may all get it; for because Jesus Christ is glorified therefore the Holy Spirit is given in this fashion, given more largely to those in the kingdom of heaven than to all those holy men before the Lord's ascent to his glory. God gives no stinted blessing to celebrate the triumph of his Son: God giveth not the Spirit by measure unto him. On such an occasion heaven's grandest liberality was displayed. Christ is glorified in heaven above, and God would have him glorified in the church below by vouchsafing a baptism of the Holy Ghost to each of us.

So I close by this, which I hope will be a very comforting and inspiriting reflection:—

IV. THESE OPERATIONS OF THE SPIRIT OF GOD ARE EASILY TO BE OBTAINED BY THE LORD'S CHILDREN. Did you say you had not received them? They are to be had, they are to be had at once. First, they are to be had by *believing in Jesus.* "This spake he of the Spirit, which they that believe on him should receive." Do you not see that it is faith which gives us the first drink and causes us to live, and this second more abundant blessing of being ourselves made fountains from which rivers flow comes in the same way? Believe in Christ, for the blessing is to be obtained, not by the works of the law, nor by so much of fasting, and striving, and effort, but by belief in the Lord Jesus for it. With him is the residue of the Spirit. He is prepared to give this to you, ay, to every one of you who believe on his name. He will not of course make all of you preachers; for who then would be hearers? If all were preachers the other works of the church would be neglected; but he will give you this favour, that out of you there shall stream a divine influence all round you to bless your children, to bless your servants, to bless the workmen in the house where you are employed, and to bless the street you live in. In proportion as God gives you opportunity these rivers of living water will flow in this channel and in that, and they will be pouring forth from you at all times, if you believe in Jesus for the full blessing, and can by faith receive it.

But there is another thing to be done as well, and that is *to pray;* and here I want to remind you of those blessed words of the Master, "Everyone that asketh receiveth; and he that seeketh findeth; and to him that knocketh it shall be opened. If a son shall ask bread of any of you that is a father, will he give him a stone? Or if he ask a fish, will he for a fish give him a serpent? Or if he shall ask an egg, will he offer him a scorpion? If ye then, being evil, know how to give good gifts unto your children: how much more shall your heavenly Father give the Holy Spirit to them that ask him?" You see, there is a distinct promise to the children of God, that their heavenly Father will give them the Holy Spirit if they ask for his power; and that promise is made to be exceedingly strong by the instances joined to it. If there be a promise that God can break (which there is not), this is not the promise, for God has put it in the most forcible and binding way. I know not how to show you its wonderful force. Did you ever hear of a man who when his child asked for bread gave him a stone? Go to the worst part of London, and will you find a man of that kind? You shall, if you like, get among pirates and murderers, and when a little child cries, "Father, give me a bit of bread and meat," does the most wicked father fill his own little one's mouth with stones? Yet the Lord seems to say that this is what he would be doing if he were to deny us the Holy Spirit when we ask him for his necessary working: he would be like one that gave his children stones instead of bread. Do you think the Lord will ever bring himself down to that? But he says, "*How much more shall your heavenly Father give the Holy Spirit to them that ask him?*" He makes it a stronger case than that of an ordinary parent. The Lord must give us the Spirit when we ask him, for he has herein bound himself by no ordinary pledge. He has used a simile which would bring dishonour on his own name, and that of the very grossest kind, if he did not give the Holy Spirit to them that ask him. Oh, then, let us ask him at once, with all our hearts. Am I not so happy as to have in this audience some who will immediately ask? I pray that some who have never received the Holy Spirit at all may now be led, while I am speaking, to pray, "Blessed Spirit, visit me; lead me to Jesus." But especially those of you that are the children of God,—to you is this promise especially made. Ask God to make you all that the Spirit of God can make you, not only a satisfied believer who has drunk for himself, but a useful believer, who overflows the neighbourhood with blessing. I see here a number of friends from the country who have come to spend their holiday in London. What a blessing it would be if they went back to their respective churches overflowing; for there are numbers of churches that need flooding; they are dry as a barn-floor, and little dew ever falls on them. Oh that they might be flooded! What a wonderful thing a flood is! Go down to the river, look over the bridge, and see the barges and other craft lying in the mud. All the king's horses and all the king's men cannot tug them out to sea. There they lie, dead and motionless as the mud itself. What shall we do with them? What machinery can move them? Have we a great engineer among us who will devise a scheme for lifting these vessels and bearing them down to the river's mouth? No, it cannot be done. Wait till the tide comes in! What a change! Each vessel walks the water like a thing of life. What a difference between the low tide and the high tide. You cannot stir the boats when the water is gone; but when the tide is at the full see how readily they move; a little child may push them with his hand. Oh, for a flood of grace. The Lord send to all our churches a great springtide! Then the indolent will be active enough, and those who were half dead will be full of energy. I know that in this particular dock several vessels are lying that I should like to float, but I cannot stir them. They neither work for God nor come out to the prayer-meetings, nor give of their substance to spread the gospel. If the flood would come you would see what they are capable of: they would be active, fervent, generous, abounding in every good word and work. So may it be! So may it be! May springs begin to flow in all our churches, and may all of you who hear me this day get your share of the streams. Oh that the Lord may now fill you and then send you home bearing a flood of grace with you. It sounds oddly to speak of a man's carrying home a flood within him, and yet I hope it will be so, and that out of you shall flow rivers of living water. So may God grant for Jesus' sake. Amen.

PORTIONS OF SCRIPTURE READ BEFORE SERMON—John vii. 31—39; xvi. 1—18.

HYMNS FROM "OUR OWN HYMN BOOK"—445, 449, 450.

Metropolitan Tabernacle Pulpit.

THE HOLY SPIRIT'S CHIEF OFFICE.

A Sermon

Intended for Reading on Lord's-day, October 14th, 1894,

DELIVERED BY

C. H. SPURGEON,

AT THE METROPOLITAN TABERNACLE, NEWINGTON,

On Thursday Evening, July 26th, 1888.

"He shall glorify me: for he shall receive of mine, and shall shew it unto you. All things that the Father hath are mine: therefore said I, that he shall take of mine, and shall shew it unto you."—John xvi. 14, 15.

It is the chief office of the Holy Spirit to glorify Christ. He does many things, but this is what he aims at in all of them, to glorify Christ. Brethren, what the Holy Ghost does must be right for us to imitate; therefore, let us endeavour to glorify Christ. To what higher ends can we devote ourselves, than to something to which God the Holy Ghost devotes himself? Be this, then, your continual prayer, "Blessed Spirit, help me ever to glorify the Lord Jesus Christ!"

Observe, that the Holy Ghost glorifies Christ by showing to us the things of Christ. It is a great marvel that there should be any glory given to Christ by showing him to such poor creatures as we are. What! To make us see Christ, does that glorify him? For our weak eyes to behold him, for our trembling hearts to know him, and to love him, does this glorify him? It is even so, for the Holy Ghost chooses this as his principal way of glorifying the Lord Jesus. He takes of the things of Christ, not to show them to angels, not to write them in letters of fire across the brow of night, but to show them unto us. Within the little temple of a sanctified heart, Christ is praised, not so much by what we do, or think, as by what we see. This puts great value upon meditation, upon the study of God's Word, and upon silent thought under the teaching of the Holy Spirit, for Jesus says, "He shall glorify me: for he shall receive of mine, and shall shew it unto you."

Here is a gospel word at the very outset of our sermon. Poor sinner,

No. 2,382.

conscious of your sin, it is possible for Christ to be glorified by his being shown unto you. If you look to him, if you see him to be a suitable Saviour, an all-sufficient Saviour, if your mind's eye takes him in, if he is effectually shown to you by the Holy Spirit, he is thereby glorified. Sinner as you are, unworthy apparently to become the arena of Christ's glory, yet shall you be a temple in which the King's glory shall be revealed, and your poor heart, like a mirror, shall reflect his grace.

> " Come, Holy Spirit, heavenly Dove,
> With all thy quickening powers; "

and show Christ to the sinner, that Christ may be glorified in the sinner's salvation!

If that great work of grace is really done at the beginning of the sermon, I shall not mind even if I never finish it. God the Holy Ghost will have wrought more without me than I could possibly have wrought myself, and to the Triune Jehovah shall be all the praise. Oh, that the name of Christ may be glorified in every one of you! Has the Holy Spirit shown you Christ, the Sin-bearer, the one sacrifice for sin, exalted on high, to give repentance and remission? If so, then the Holy Spirit has glorified Christ, even in you.

Now proceeding to examine the text a little in detail, my first observation upon it is this, *the Holy Spirit is our Lord's Glorifier:* " He shall glorify me." Secondly, *Christ's own things are his best glory:* " He shall glorify me : for he shall receive of mine, and shall shew it unto you;" and, thirdly, *Christ's glory is his Father's glory:* " All things that the Father hath are mine : therefore said I, that he shall take of mine, and shall shew it unto you."

I. To begin, then, THE HOLY SPIRIT IS OUR LORD'S GLORIFIER. I want you to keep this truth in your mind, and never to forget it; that which does not glorify Christ is not of the Holy Spirit, and that which is of the Holy Spirit invariably glorifies our Lord Jesus Christ.

First, then, *have an eye to this truth in all comforts.* If a comfort which you think you need, and which appears to you to be very sweet, does not glorify Christ, look very suspiciously upon it. If, in conversing with an apparently religious man, he prates about truth which he says is comforting, but which does not honour Christ, do not you have anything to do with it. It is a poisonous sweet; it may charm you for a moment, but it will ruin your soul for ever if you partake of it. But blessed are those comforts which smell of Christ, those consolations in which there is a fragrance of myrrh, and aloes, and cassia, out of the King's palace, the comfort drawn from his person, from his work, from his blood, from his resurrection, from his glory, the comfort directly fetched from that sacred spot where he trod the winepress alone. This is wine of which you may drink, and forget your misery, and be unhappy no more ; but always look with great suspicion upon any comfort offered to you, either as a sinner or a saint, which does not come distinctly from Christ. Say, " I will not be comforted till Jesus comforts me. I will refuse to lay aside my despondency until he removes my sin. I will not go to Mr. Civility, or Mr. Legality, for the unlading of my burden; no hands shall ever lift the load of conscious sin from off my heart but those that were nailed to the cross, when Jesus himself bore my sins in his own body on the tree." Please carry this truth with you wherever you go, as a kind of spiritual litmus paper, by which you may test everything that is presented to you as a cordial or comfort. If it does not glorify Christ, let it not console or please you.

In the next place, *have an eye to this truth in all ministries.* There are many ministries in the world, and they are very diverse from one another; but this truth will enable you to judge which is right out of them all. That ministry which makes much of Christ, is of the Holy Spirit; and that ministry which decries him, ignores him, or puts him in the background in any degree, is not of the Spirit of God. Any doctrine which magnifies man, but not man's Redeemer, any doctrine which denies the depth of the Fall, and consequently derogates from the greatness of salvation, any doctrine which makes sin less, and therefore makes Christ's work less,—away with it, away with it. This shall be your infallible test as to whether it is of the Holy Ghost or not, for Jesus says, "He shall glorify me." It were better to speak five words to the glory of Christ, than to be the greatest orator who ever lived, and to neglect or dishonour the Lord Jesus Christ. We, my brethren, who are preachers of the Word, have but a short time to live; let us dedicate all that time to the glorious work of magnifying Christ. Longfellow says, in his *Psalm of Life,* that "Art is long," but longer still is the great art of lifting up the Crucified before the eyes of the sin-bitten sons of men. Let us keep to that one employment. If we have but this one string upon which we can play, we may discourse such music on it as would ravish angels, and will save men; therefore, again I say, let us keep to that alone. Cornet, flute, harp, sackbut, psaltery, dulcimer, and all kinds of music are for Nebuchadnezzar's golden image; but as for our God, our one harp is Christ Jesus. We will touch every string of that wondrous instrument, even though it be with trembling fingers, and marvellous shall be the music we shall evoke from it.

All ministries, therefore, must be subjected to this test; if they do not glorify Christ, they are not of the Holy Ghost.

We should also *have an eye to this truth in all religious movements,* and judge them by this standard. If they are of the Holy Spirit, they glorify Christ. There are great movements in the world every now and then; we are inclined to look upon them hopefully, for any stir is better than stagnation; but, by-and-by we begin to fear, with a holy jealousy, what their effects will be. How shall we judge them? To what test shall we put them? Always to this test. Does this movement glorify Christ? Is Christ preached? Then therein I do rejoice, yea, and will rejoice. Are men pointed to Christ? Then this is the ministry of salvation. Is he preached as first and last? Are men bidden to be justified by faith in him, and then to follow him, and copy his divine example? It is well. I do not believe that any man ever lifted up the cross of Christ in a hurtful way. If it be but the cross that is seen, it is the sight of the cross, not of the hands that lift it, that will bring salvation. Some modern movements are heralded with great noise, and some come quietly; but if they glorify Christ, it is well. But, dear friends, if it is some new theory that is propounded, if it is some old error revived, if it is something very glittering and fascinating, and for a while it bears the multitudes away, think nothing of it; unless it glorifies Christ it is not for you and me. "*Aliquid Christi,*" as one of the old fathers said, "Anything of Christ," and I love it; but nothing of Christ, or something against Christ, then it may be very fine and flowery, and it may be very fascinating and charming, highly poetical, and in consonance with the spirit of the age; but we say of it, "Vanity of vanities, all is vanity where there is no Christ." Where he is uplifted, there is all that is wanted for the salvation of a guilty race. Judge every movement, then, not by those who adhere to it, nor by those who admire and praise it, but by this word of our Lord, "He shall glorify me." The Spirit of God is not in it if it does not glorify Christ.

Once again, brethren, I pray you, *eye this truth when you are under a sense of great weakness*, physical, mental, or spiritual. You have finished preaching a sermon, you have completed a round with your tracts, or you have ended your Sunday-school work for another Sabbath. You say to yourself, "I fear that I have done very poorly." You groan as you go to your bed because you think that you have not glorified Christ. It is as well that you should groan if that is the case. I will not forbid it, but I will relieve the bitterness of your distress by reminding you that it is the Holy Ghost who is to glorify Christ: "He shall glorify me." If I preach, and the Holy Spirit is with me, Christ will be glorified; but if I were able to speak with the tongues of men, and of angels, but without the power of the Holy Ghost, Christ would not be glorified. Sometimes, our weakness may even help to make way for the greater display of the might of God. If so, we may glory in infirmity, that the power of Christ may rest upon us. It is not merely we who speak, but the Spirit of the Lord, who speaketh by us. There is a sound of abundance of rain outside the Tabernacle; would God that there were also the sound of abundance of rain within our hearts! May the Holy Spirit come at this moment, and come at all times whenever his servants are trying to glorify Christ, and himself do what must always be his own work! How can you and I glorify anybody, much less glorify him who is infinitely glorious? But the Holy Ghost, being himself the glorious God, can glorify the glorious Christ. It is a work worthy of God; and it shows us, when we think of it, the absolute need of our crying to the Holy Spirit that he would take us in his hand, and use us as a workman uses his hammer. What can a hammer do without the hand that grasps it, and what can we do without the Spirit of God?

I will make only one more observation upon this first point. If the Holy Spirit is to glorify Christ, I beg you to *have an eye to this truth amid all oppositions, controversies, and contentions*. If we alone had the task of glorifying Christ, we might be beaten; but as the Holy Spirit is the Glorifier of Christ, his glory is in very safe hands. "Why do the heathen rage, and the people imagine a vain thing?" The Holy Spirit is still to the front; the eternal purpose of God to set his King upon the throne, and to make Jesus Christ reign for ever and ever, must be fulfilled, for the Holy Ghost has undertaken to see it accomplished. Amidst the surging tumults of the battle, the result of the conflict is never in doubt for a moment. It may seem as though the fate of Christ's cause hung in a balance, and that the scales were in equilibrium; but it is not so. The glory of Christ never wanes; it must increase from day to day, as it is made known in the hearts of men by the Holy Spirit; and the day shall come when Christ's praise shall go up from all human tongues. To him every knee shall bow, and every tongue shall confess that Jesus Christ is Lord, to the glory of God the Father. Therefore, lift up the hands that hang down, and confirm the feeble knees. If *you* have failed to glorify Christ by your speech as you would, there is Another who has done it, and who will still do it, according to Christ's words, " He shall glorify me." My text seems to be a silver bell, ringing sweet comfort into the dispirited worker's ear, " He shall glorify me."

That is the first point, the Holy Spirit is our Lord's Glorifier. Keep that truth before your mind's eye under all circumstances.

II. Now, secondly, CHRIST'S OWN THINGS ARE HIS BEST GLORY. When the Holy Spirit wants to glorify Christ, what does he do? He does not go abroad for anything, he comes to Christ himself for that which will be for Christ's own glory: " He shall glorify me: for he shall receive of mine, and shall shew it unto you." There can be no glory added to Christ; it must be his own glory, which he has already, which is made more apparent to the hearts of God's chosen by the Holy Spirit.

First of all, *Christ needs no new inventions to glorify him.* " We have struck out a new line of things," says one. Have you? " We have found out something very wonderful." I dare say you have; but Christ, the same yesterday, to-day, and for ever, wants none of your inventions, or discoveries, or additions to his truth. A plain Christ is ever the loveliest Christ. Dress him up, and you have deformed him and defamed him. Bring him out just as he is, the Christ of God, nothing else but Christ, unless you bring in his cross, for we preach Christ crucified; indeed, you cannot have the Christ without the cross; but preach Christ crucified, and you have given him all the glory that he wants. The Holy Ghost does not reveal in these last times any fresh ordinances, or any novel doctrines, or any new evolutions; but he simply brings to mind the things which Christ himself spoke, he brings Christ's own things to us, and in that way glorifies him.

Think for a minute of *Christ's person* as revealed to us by the Holy Spirit. What can more glorify him than for us to see his person, very God of very God, and yet as truly man? What a wondrous being, as human as ourselves, but as divine as God! Was there ever another like to him? Never.

Think of his *incarnation*, his birth at Bethlehem. There was greater glory among the oxen in the stall than ever was seen where those born in marble halls were swathed in purple and fine linen. Was there ever another babe like Christ? Never. I wonder not that the wise men fell down to worship him.

Look at his *life*, the standing wonder of all ages. Men, who have not worshipped him, have admired him. His life is incomparable, unique; there is nothing like it in all the history of mankind.

Imagination has never been able to invent anything approximating to the perfect beauty of the life of Jesus Christ.

Think of his *death*. There have been many heroic and martyr deaths; but there is not one that can be set side by side with Christ's death. He did not pay the debt of nature as others do; and yet he paid our nature's debt. He did not die because he must; he died because he would. The only "must" that came upon him was a necessity of all-conquering love. The cross of Christ is the greatest wonder of fact or of fiction; fiction invents many marvellous things, but nothing than can be looked at for a moment in comparison with the cross of Christ.

Think of our Lord's *resurrection*. If this be one of the things that are taken, and shown to you by the Holy Spirit, it will fill you with holy delight. I am sure that I could go into that sepulchre, where John and Peter went, and spend a lifetime in reverencing him who broke down the barriers of the tomb, and made it a passage-way to heaven. Instead of being a dungeon and a *cul-de-sac*, into which all men seemed to go, but none could ever come out, Christ has, by his resurrection, made a tunnel right through the grave. Jesus, by dying, has killed death for all believers.

Then think of his *ascension*. But why need I take you over all these scenes with which you are blessedly familiar? What a wondrous fact that, when the cloud received him out of the disciples' sight, the angels came to convoy him to his heavenly home!

> "They brought his chariot from above,
>   To bear him to his throne;
> Clapp'd their triumphant wings, and cried,
>   'The glorious work is done.'"

Think of him now, *at his Father's right hand*, adored of all the heavenly host; and then let your mind fly forward to the glory of his Second Advent, the final judgment with its terrible terrors, the millennium with its indescribable bliss, and the heaven of heavens, with its endless and unparalleled splendour. If these things are shown to you by the Holy Spirit, the beatific visions will indeed glorify Christ, and you will sit down, and sing with the blessed Virgin, "My soul doth magnify the Lord, and my spirit hath rejoiced in God my Saviour."

Thus, you see that the things which glorify Christ are all in Christ; the Holy Spirit fetches nothing from abroad, but he takes of the things of Christ, and shows them unto us. The glory of kings lies in their silver and their gold, their silk and their gems; but the glory of Christ lies in himself. If we want to glorify a man, we bring him presents; if we wish to glorify Christ, we must accept presents from him. Thus we take the cup of salvation, calling upon the name of the Lord, and in so doing we glorify Christ.

Notice, next, that *these things of Christ's are too bright for us to see till the Spirit shows them to us*. We cannot see them because of their excessive glory, until the Holy Spirit tenderly reveals them to us, until he takes of the things of Christ, and shows them to us.

What does this mean? Does it not mean, first, that he enlightens our understandings? It is wonderful how the Holy Spirit can take a fool, and make him know the wonders of Christ's dying love; and he does make him know it very quickly when he begins to teach him. Some of us have been very slow learners, yet the Holy Spirit has been able to teach something even to us. He opens the Scriptures, and he also opens our minds; and when there are these two openings together, what a wonderful opening it is! It becomes like a new revelation; the first is the revelation of the letter, which we have in the Book; the second is the revelation of the Spirit, which we get in our own spirit. O my dear friend, if the Holy Ghost has ever enlightened your understanding, you know what it is for him to show the things of Christ to you!

But next, he does this by a work upon the whole soul. I mean this. When the Holy Ghost convinces us of sin, we become fitted to see Christ, and so the blessed Spirit shows Christ to us. When we are conscious of our feebleness, then we see Christ's strength; and thus the Holy Ghost shows him to us. Often, the operations of the Spirit of God may seem not to be directly the showing of Christ to us, but as they prepare us for seeing him, they are a part of the work.

The Holy Ghost sometimes shows Christ to us by his power of vivifying the truth. I do not know whether I can quite tell you what I mean; but I have sometimes seen a truth differently from what I have ever seen it before. I knew it long ago, I owned it as part of the divine revelation; but now I realize it, grip it, grasp it, or what is better, it seems to get a grip of me, and hold me in its mighty hands. Have you not sometimes been overjoyed with a promise which never seemed anything to you before? Or a doctrine, which you believed, but never fully appreciated, has suddenly become to you a gem of the first water, a very Koh-i-Noor, or, "Mountain of Light." The Holy Spirit has a way of focussing light, and when it falls in this special way upon a certain point, then the truth is revealed to us. He shall take of the things of Christ, and show them unto you. Have you never felt ready to jump for joy, ready to start from your seat, ready to sit up in your bed at night, and sing praises to God through the overpowering influence of some grand old truth which has seemed to be all at once quite new to you?

The Holy Spirit also shows to us the things of Christ in our experience. As we journey on in life, we pass up hill and down dale, through bright sunlight and through dark shadows, and in each of these conditions we learn a little more of Christ, a little more of his grace, a little more of his glory, a little more of his sin-bearing, a little more of his glorious righteousness. Blessed is the life which is just one long lesson upon the glory of Christ; and I think that is what every Christian life should be. "Every dark and bending line" in our experience should meet in the centre of Christ's glory, and should lead us nearer and nearer to the power of enjoying the bliss at his right hand for ever and ever. Thus the Holy Spirit takes of the things of Christ, and shows them to us, and so glorifies Christ.

Beloved, the practical lesson for us to learn is this, *let us try to abide under the influence of the Holy Spirit.* To that end, let us think very reverently of him. Some never think of him at all. How many sermons there are without even an allusion to him! Shame on the preachers of such discourses! If any hearers come without praying for the Holy Spirit, shame on such hearers! We know and we confess that he is everything to our spiritual life; then why do we not remember him with greater love, and worship him with greater honour, and think of him continually with greater reverence? Beware of committing the sin against the Holy Ghost. If any of you feel any gentle touches of his power when you are hearing a sermon, beware lest you harden your heart against it. Whenever the sacred fire comes as but a spark, quench not the Holy Spirit, but pray that the spark may become a flame. And you, Christian people, do cry to him that you may not read your Bibles without his light. Do not pray without being helped by the Spirit; above all, may you never preach without the Holy Spirit! It seems a pity when a man asks to be guided of the Spirit in his preaching, and then pulls out a manuscript, and reads it. The Holy Spirit may bless what he reads; but he cannot very well guide him when he has tied himself down to what he has written. And it will be the same with the speaker if he only repeats what he has learnt, and leaves no room for the Spirit to give him a new thought, a fresh revelation of Christ; how can he hope for the divine blessing under such circumstances? Oh, it were better for us to sit still until some of us were moved by the Spirit to get up and speak, than for us to prescribe the methods by which he should speak to us, and even to write down the very words we mean to utter! What room is there for the Spirit's operations then?

"Come, Holy Spirit, heavenly Dove,"

I cannot help breaking out into that prayer, "Blessed Spirit, abide with us, take of the things of Christ, and show them to us, that so Christ may be glorified."

III. I am only going to speak a minute or two on the last point. It is a very deep one, much too deep for me. I am unable to take you into the depths of my text, I will not pretend to do so; I believe that there are meanings here which probably we shall never understand till we get to heaven. "What thou knowest not now, thou shalt know hereafter." But this is the point, CHRIST'S GLORY IS HIS FATHER'S GLORY: "All things that the Father hath are mine: therefore said I, that he shall take of mine, and shall shew it unto you."

First, *Christ has all that the Father has.* Do think of that. No mere man dares to say, "All things that the Father hath are mine." All the Godhead is in Christ; not only all the attributes of it, but the essence of it. The Nicene Creed well puts it, and it is not too strong in the expression: "Light of Light, very God of very God," for Christ has all that the Father has. When we come to Christ, we come to omnipotent omnipresent omniscience; we come to almighty immutability; we come, in fact, to the eternal Godhead. The Father has all things, and all power is given unto Christ in heaven and on earth, so that he has all that the Father has.

And, further, *the Father is glorified in Christ's glory.* Never let us fall into the false notion that, if we magnify Christ, we are depreciating the Father. If any lips have ever spoken concerning the Christ of God so as to depreciate the God of Christ, let those lips be covered with shame. We never did preach Christ up as merciful, and the Father as only just, or Christ as moving the Father to be gracious. That is a slander which has been cast upon us, but there is not an atom of truth in it. We have known and believed what Christ himself said, "I and my Father are one." The more glorious Christ is, the more glorious the Father is; and when men, professedly Christians, begin to cast off Christ, they cast off God the Father to a large extent. Irreverence to the Son of God soon becomes irreverence to God the Father himself. But, dear friends, we delight to honour Christ, and we will continue to do so. Even when we stand in the heaven of heavens, before the burning throne of the infinite Jehovah, we will sing praises unto him and unto the Lamb, putting the two evermore in that divine conjunction in which they are always to be found.

Thus, you see, Christ has all that the Father has, and when he is glorified, the Father also is glorified.

Next, *the Holy Spirit must lead us to see this*, and I am sure that he will. If we give ourselves up to his teaching, we shall fall into no errors. It will be a great mystery, but we shall know enough, so that it will never trouble us. If you sit down and try to study the mystery of the Eternal, well, I believe that the longer you look, the more you will be like persons who look into the sea from a great height, until they grow dizzy, and are ready to fall and to be drowned. Believe what the Spirit teaches you, and adore your Divine Teacher; then shall his instruction become easy to you. I believe that, as we grow older, we come to worship God as Abraham did, as Jehovah, the great I AM. Jesus does not fade into the background; but the glorious Godhead seems to become more and more apparent to us. Our Lord's word to his disciples, "Ye believe in God, believe also in me," as we grow older, seems to turn into this, "Ye believe in me, believe also in God." And as we come to a full confidence in the glorious Lord, the God of nature, and of providence, and of redemption, and of heaven, the Holy Spirit gives us to know more of the glories of Christ.

I have talked with you as well as I could upon this sublime theme, and if I did not know that the Holy Spirit glorifies Christ, I should go home miserable, for I have not been able to glorify my Lord as I would; but I know that the Holy Spirit can take what I have said out of my very heart, and can put it into your hearts, and he can add to it whatever I have omitted. Go ye who love the Lord, and glorify him. Try to do it by your lips and by your lives. Go ye, and preach him, preach more of him, and preach him up higher, and higher, and higher. The old lady, of whom I have heard, made a mistake in what she said, yet there was a truth behind her blunder. She had been to a little Baptist chapel, where a high Calvinist preached, and on coming away she said that she liked "High Calvary" preachers best. So do I. Give me a "High Calvary" preacher, one who will make Calvary the highest of all the mountains. I suppose it was not a hill at all, but only a mound; still, let us lift it higher and higher, and say to all other hills, "Why leap ye, ye high hills? This is the hill which God desires to dwell in; yea, the Lord will dwell in it for ever." The crucified Christ is wiser than all the wisdom of the world. The cross of Christ has more novelty in it than all the fresh things of the earth. O believers and preachers of the gospel, glorify Christ! May the Holy Ghost help you to do so!

And you, poor sinners, who think that you cannot glorify Christ at all, come and trust him,—

"Come naked, come filthy, come just as you are,"

and believe that he will receive you; for that will glorify him. Believe, even now, O sinner at death's door, that Christ can make thee live; for thy faith will glorify him! Look up out of the awful depths of hell into which conscience has cast thee, and believe that he can pluck thee out of the horrible pit, and out of the miry clay, and set thy feet upon a rock; for thy trust will glorify him! It is in the power of the sinner to give Christ the greatest glory, if the Holy Spirit enables him to believe in the Lord Jesus Christ. Thou mayest come, thou who art more leprous, more diseased, more corrupt, than any other; and if thou lookest to him, and he saves thee, oh, then thou wilt praise him! You will be of the mind of the one I have spoken of many times, who said to me, "Sir, you say that Christ can save me. Well, if he does, he shall never hear the last of it." No, and he never will hear the last of it. Blessed Jesus,—

> "I will love thee in life, I will love thee in death,
> And praise thee as long as thou lendest me breath;
> And say when the death-dew lies cold on my brow,
> If ever I loved thee, my Jesus, 'tis now.
>
> "In mansions of glory and endless delight,
> I'll ever adore thee in heaven so bright;
> I'll sing with the glittering crown on my brow,
> If ever I loved thee, my Jesus, 'tis now."

We will do nothing else but praise Christ, and glorify him, if he will but save us from sin. God grant that it may be so with every one of us, for the Lord Jesus Christ's sake! Amen.

Exposition by C. H. Spurgeon.

JOHN XVI. 1—16.

Verse 1. *These things have I spoken unto you, that ye should not be offended.*

Or, "made to stumble." Christ would not have you who are his people caused to stumble by anything that happens to you. He wants you to walk without tripping; his angels bear you up in their hands lest at any time you should dash your foot against a stone. He himself, as your Guardian, comes and speaks beforehand to let you know what is to occur to you, that you may not be caused to stumble by any fresh trial that may assail you.

2. *They shall put you out of the synagogues: yea, the time cometh, that whosoever killeth you will think that he doeth God service.*

Christ's disciples were to expect opposition of the most cruel kind. They were to be put away from those with whom they had long worshipped; they were even to run the risk of losing their lives; but Jesus foretold what would happen to them, that they might not be stumbled at it. Such was their Lord's love to them that he would not have them attacked unawares;

by his grace, they would hold on, and hold out, they would persevere to the end; but there would have to be a struggle, and to help them in the fight, Jesus tells them all about it before it begins. We say, "Forewarned, forearmed." So the disciples were; and so are you. Your Lord tells you that you will not get to heaven without trials: "In the world ye shall have tribulation." And he tells you this that it may not surprise you when it comes, that it may not act upon you like a sudden gust of wind that would upset a little ship; but that you may just keep everything in trim looking for the storm to come: "These things have I spoken unto you, that ye should not be caused to stumble."

3. *And these things will they do unto you, because they have not known the Father, nor me.*

The persecuting Jews professed to be worshippers of Jehovah; but they did not know the Christ, whom he sent, and, therefore, in very truth they did not know the Father either. How can you expect that those who do not know the Father will know the Son, or any of the other children of the divine family? As they rejected the Elder Brother, will they not also reject the younger ones? Is the disciple to be above his Master, or the servant to be treated better than his Lord? Think not so; and therefore expect that you will not be known, even as the Father and the Son were not known.

" 'Tis no surprising thing,
That we should be unknown:
The Jewish world knew not their King,
God's everlasting Son."

4. *But these things have I told you, that when the time shall come, ye may remember that I told you of them. And these things I said not unto you at the beginning, because I was with you.*

Our Lord did tell his disciples something about "these things." He did warn them to expect opposition, but he did not dwell upon that theme, he did not expatiate upon it. He did not at first give that prominence to it which he was about to do, and he explains to his disciples why he had not talked much upon that topic: "because I was with you." It did not matter how they were opposed so long as he was with them; his society more than made up for anything they might have to suffer; and, dear child of God, if you now enjoy the presence of Christ, and the power of his Spirit, you need not mind what happens to you.

5, 6. *But now I go my way to him that sent me; and none of you asketh me, Whither goest thou? But because I have said these things unto you, sorrow hath filled your heart.*

They were cast down because he was going away from them. Love awoke fear. It was a hard thing for them to have to miss him; they could not tell what might happen to them when their Leader was gone from their midst. Do you wonder that they were filled with sorrow? Yet there was no real cause for grief; there was rather reason for rejoicing when they understood the true lesson of Christ's departure. There is no real cause for your sorrow, dear friends. If you knew all things, you would rejoice exceedingly in that very thing that now most troubles you.

7. *Nevertheless I tell you the truth; It is expedient for you that I go away: for if I go not away, the Comforter will not come unto you; but if I depart, I will send him unto you.*

And the Comforter is better for us than the personal presence of Christ. We do not always think so; but it is true. It is better for the Church to have the Holy Spirit in the midst of her, than for Christ to be here in the bodily presence on the earth.

8. *And when he is come, he will reprove the world of sin, and of righteousness, and of judgment:*

The world is not as yet convinced, but it is convicted; though it does not own its guilt, there is more than sufficient evidence to prove it guilty in the sight of God.

9. *Of sin, because they believe not on me;*

What must be the depth of human wickedness that sinners will not accept a Divine Saviour! This is the crowning, crushing proof of human guilt: "They believe not on me."

10. *Of righteousness, because I go to my Father, and ye see me no more;*

Christ was righteous, the righteous One, whom men rejected, for he has gone up to the Father's side, where he could not have been if he had not perfected righteousness. The very going back of Christ to the Father's throne proves that righteousness does exist, and convicts men of sinning against it.

11. *Of judgment, because the prince of this world is judged.*

The gospel judges him, and dethrones him; and as there has been a judgment of the world's king, so there will be a judgment of the world itself.

12. *I have yet many things to say unto you, but ye cannot bear them now.*

Some teachers overload their hearers with truth till I might truly say that they pile on the agony. Truth which cannot be received is often most irksome and burdensome to the hearer; when the mind is not in a fit condition to bear any more instruction, it is cruel work to impose it. Our Lord Jesus did not so overburden his disciples: "I have yet many things to say unto you, but ye cannot bear them now."

13. *Howbeit when he, the Spirit of truth, is come, he will guide you into all truth: for he shall not speak of himself;*

This is a very wonderful expression: "He shall not speak of himself." We have plenty of men, nowadays, who boast that they do speak of or from themselves; that is to say, they profess to borrow from no one, not even from God. They are original thinkers, inventors; they bring forth fresh things out of the depth of their wonderful minds; but even the Holy Ghost is here said not to "speak of himself."

13. *But whatsoever he shall hear, that shall he speak;*

That is just our business, to hear God's message, and then to speak it; and if the Holy Ghost does this, and if Jesus did it, we also may be glad to do the same. We are no inventors of great novelties; we are simply the message-bearers of the Most High, the declarers of the old truths which God has revealed to us.

13—16. *And he will shew you things to come. He shall glorify me: for he shall receive of mine, and shall shew it unto you. All things that the Father hath are mine: therefore said I, that he shall take of mine, and shall shew it unto you. A little while, and ye shall not see me: and again, a little while, and ye shall see me, because I go to the Father.*

How wonderful this is! We are to see Jesus because he has gone to the Father. It looks as if that were a reason why we should not see him; but we see him better, by faith, now that he has gone to the Father, than we could have seen him while he was here below covered with the veil of his humiliation. Yet it is hardly surprising that the disciples were puzzled by their Lord's words: "A little while, and ye shall not see me: and again, a little while, and ye shall see me:" and, "Because I go to the Father."

Hymns from "Our Own Hymn Book"—426, 437, 416.

Metropolitan Tabernacle Pulpit.

THE LEADING OF THE SPIRIT, THE SECRET TOKEN
OF THE SONS OF GOD.

DELIVERED BY

C. H. SPURGEON,

AT THE METROPOLITAN TABERNACLE, NEWINGTON.

"As many as are led by the Spirit of God, they are the sons of God."—Romans viii. 14.

CHILDREN are expected to bear some likeness to their parent. Children of God, born of the grandest of all parents, regenerated by the almighty energy of the divine Spirit, are sure to bear a high degree of likeness to their heavenly Father. We cannot be like God in many of his divine attributes, for they are unique and incommunicable: it is not possible for us to wield his power, or to possess his infinite knowledge, neither can we be independent and self-existent, or possessors of sovereignty or worshipfulness. Man can never be so expressly the image of the Father as Jesus is, for he is in a mysterious sense the only begotten Son of God. We can imitate God, however, in many of his attributes; mainly those of a moral and spiritual kind. We must in these qualities be "imitators of God as dear children," or our heavenly pedigree cannot be made out. The point mentioned in the text must never be matter of question, for if that be doubtful our filial relationship to God is unproved. We must be "led by the Spirit of God." That divine Spirit who is ever with the Father and the Son must be evermore with us so that we are guided, instructed, impelled, quickened, actuated, influenced by him, or else we must not dare to think ourselves the sons of God.

The idea of a divine fatherhood extending over all mankind does not appear to have been recognised by the apostle Paul, in this text at any rate. Here the fatherhood is for some, not for all, and the text discriminates between the "as many as are led by the Spirit of God" and the rest of mankind who are under no such influence. In men who are devoid of the Holy Ghost there is another spirit, and that other spirit marks them out as sons of another father: "they are of their father the devil, for his works they do." There have been two seeds from the beginning, the seed of the woman and the

No. 1,220.

seed of the serpent, and it is both untrue and immoral to believe that God stands in the same relation to the two opposing families. No, my brethren, *our* Father who is in heaven is not to be claimed as father by the unbeliever, for to them Jesus expressly says, "If God were your Father, ye would love me."

The text furnishes us with a very simple but sharp and decisive test, which we shall do well to use upon ourselves. It should be employed to try every one of us. If it had said, "As many as have been baptised are the sons of God," we might have been content to sit very easily in our places. If it had said, "As many as eat and drink at the holy feast of Christian fellowship are the children of God," we might have remembered how short a time ago we were sitting with the saints around the communion table. If the doing of certain external acts, or the utterance of certain prayers, or the avowal of orthodox principles, or abstinence from the grosser vices, had been made the royal mark and heavenly seal of the children of God we might have taken our ease after ascertaining that we are correct as to these things. If being united with an earnest church, and being members of a faithful community, had been divinely ordained to be an unquestionable certificate of sonship with the Lord Most High, we might have rested perfectly satisfied without putting ourselves into the crucible: but, since these things are not so arranged, I trust that none of us will be so unwise as to neglect the examination which the text suggests to every prudent mind. Come, my brethren, take nothing for granted on so weighty a business as your soul's eternal interests, but search for evidence and see to the matter as wise householders would do if their whole substance were at stake. Those who are "led by the Spirit of God" are the sons of God; those who are not led by the Spirit of God are not his sons: therefore search and see what spirit is in you, that ye may know whose children ye are.

To help you in this matter I purpose that we should consider, first, where it is that the Spirit of God leads men, that we may see whether he has ever led us there.

I. WHITHER DOES THE SPIRIT OF GOD LEAD THE SONS OF GOD?

First of all, he leads them to *repentance*. One of the first acts of the Holy Spirit is to guide the sons of God to the mercy-seat with tears in their eyes. He leads us into the abominable chambers of imagery concealed within our fallen nature, unfastens door after door and sets open before our enlightened eyes the secret places polluted with idols and loathsome images portrayed upon the wall. He points out with his hand of light the idol gods, the images of jealousy, the unclean and abominable things within our nature, and thus he astonishes us into humility. We could not have believed that such evil things haunted our souls, but his discoveries undeceive us and correct our boastful estimates of ourselves. Then, with that same finger, he points to our past life and shows us the blots, the errors, the wilful sins, the sins of ignorance, the aggravated transgressions, the offences against light and knowledge, which have marred our career from our youth up: and whereas, previously, we looked upon the page of our life, and thought it fair, when the Spirit has led us into light we see how black our history has been, and, being filled with shame and sorrow, we cry out for the ear of God, that we may there confess our sin, and acknowledge that if he should smite us into hell it would be no more than we deserve. Dear friend, did the Holy Spirit ever lead you to the stool of repentance? Did he ever cause you to see how basely you have treated your God, and how shamefully you have neglected your Saviour? Did he ever make you bemoan yourself for your iniquities? There is no way to heaven but by Weeping-cross. He who never felt the burden of his sin will yet be crushed beneath its enormous weight when, like some tottering cliff, in judgment's dreadful hour, it will fall upon him and grind him to powder. No man ever goes to the chamber of true repentance till the Holy Spirit leads him there, but every child of God knows what it is to look on him whom he has pierced, and mourn for his sin. Holy sorrow for sin is as indispensable as faith in the atoning blood, and the same Spirit who gives us peace through the great sacrifice also works in us a hearty grief for having grieved the Lord. If you have from your youth up never felt any special mourning for sin, then may God begin the gracious work in your heart, for salvation is certainly not wrought in you. You must have repentance, for repentance is absolutely necessary to the divine life. "Except ye repent ye shall all likewise perish." The prodigal must cry, "Father, I have sinned;" the publican must smite on his breast and pray, "God be merciful to me a sinner." As well destroy one of the valves of the heart and yet hope to live as take away repentance, which is the inseparable life-companion of faith. A dry-eyed faith is no faith at all. When a man has his face towards Jesus his back is necessarily turned on his sins. As well look for spring in the garden without the snowdrop as look for grace in the heart without penitence. That faith which is not accompanied by repentance is a spurious faith, and not the faith of God's elect; for no man ever trusts Christ till he feels he needs a Saviour, and he cannot have felt that he needs a Saviour unless he has been wearied with the burden of his sin. The Holy Ghost leads men first to repentance.

He leads them at the same time, while they think little of themselves, to *think much of Jesus.* Were you ever led to the cross, beloved? Did you ever stand there, and feel the burden fall from off your shoulders, and roll away into the Redeemer's sepulchre? When Dr. Neale, the eminent Ritualist, took John Bunyan's " Pilgrim's Progress," and Romanized it, he represented the pilgrim as coming to a certain bath, into which he was plunged and washed, and then his burden was washed away. He explains this to be the bath of baptism, though I have never yet seen in any Ritualistic church a baptistry large enough to wash a pilgrim in. However, according to this doctored edition of the allegory, Christian was washed in the laver of baptism, and all his sins were thus removed. That is the High Church mode of getting rid of sin: John Bunyan's way, and the true way, is to lose it at the cross. Now, mark what happened. According to Dr. Neale's "Pilgrim's Progress," that burden grew again on the pilgrim's back, and I do not wonder that it did, for a burden which baptism can remove is sure to come again: but the burden which is lost at the cross never appears again for ever. There is no effectual cleansing for sin except by faith in that matchless atonement offered once for all on Calvary's bloody tree, and as many as are led there by the Spirit of God are the sons of God. The Spirit of God never led a man to think little of Christ, and much of priests. The Spirit of God never led a man to think little of the atoning blood and of simple faith in it, and much of outward forms and ceremonies. The Spirit of God sinks the man and lifts up the Saviour, lowers flesh and blood into the grave, and gives to man new life in the risen Lord, who also hath ascended up on high. "He shall glorify me," said Christ of the Comforter; and that indeed is the Comforter's office.

Now, my dear friends, has the Spirit ever made the Lord Jesus glorious in your eyes? Brethren and sisters, this is the one point above all others. If the Holy Ghost has never made Christ precious to you, you know nothing about him. If he has not lifted Jesus up and sunk your own confidences, if he has not made you feel that Christ is all you want, and that more than all in him you find, then he has never wrought a divine change in your heart. Repentance and faith must stand gazing upon the bleeding Saviour, or else hope will never join them and bring peace as his companion.

When the Spirit has glorified Jesus he leads us to know *other truths*. The Holy Ghost leads the sons of God into all truth. Others go astray after this falsehood or that, but the sheep of God will not hear the voice of strange leaders, their ears are closed to their flatteries: "a stranger will they not follow, for they know not the voice of strangers." Beloved, no lie is of the truth, and no man who receives a lie has been led by the Spirit of God into it, let him say what he may. On the other hand, truth is like a closed chamber to the unregenerate man; he may read the table of contents of the precious storehouse, but into that secret room he cannot enter: there is one that hath the key of David, who openeth and no man shutteth; and the key with which he openeth is the power of the Holy Ghost. When he opens up a doctrine to a man, the man learns it aright, but he never can know it else. You may go to college, and sit at the feet of the most learned Gamaliel of the day, but you can never know the truth in the heart unless the Holy Ghost shall teach you. We never know a truth in the power of it till it is burned into our soul, as with a hot iron, by an experience of its power, or engraven as upon brass by the mystic revelation of the Spirit. Only the Spirit of God can interweave the truth with the heart, and make it part and parcel of ourselves, so that it is in us and we are in it. Have you thus been led into the truth? If so, give God the glory, for thus the Spirit of God certifies your adoption.

The children of God are led not only into knowledge, but into *love*. They are brought to feel the warmth of love as well as to see the light of truth. The Spirit of God causes every true-born son of God to burn with love to the rest of the family. He who is a stranger to Christian love is a stranger to divine grace. Brethren, we have our disputes, for we dwell where it must needs be that offences come; but we would be slow to take offence and slower still to give it, for we are one in Christ Jesus, and our hearts are knit together by his Spirit. I take it that no honest man ought to hold his tongue concerning any of the errors of the day, it is a mean way of cultivating ease for yourself, and gaining a popularity not worth the having; we must speak the truth whether we offend or please, but this is to be done *in* love and *because* of love. God save us from that suggestion of Satan which advises us to speak only those soft things which please men's ears, for he who gives way to this persuasion is a traitor to truth and to the souls of men. The true man of God must speak against every evil and false way; but there beats in his heart a strong affection to every child of God, whatever his errors and his faults may be. The knife of the surgeon is mercifully cruel to the cancer, not out of ill-will to his patient, but out of an honest desire to benefit him; such affectionate faithfulness we have need to cultivate. Love to the saints is the token of the saints. There is an inner church of God's own elect, within everyone of the Christian denominations, and this church is made up of men spiritually enlightened, who know the marrow and mystery of the gospel, and whenever they meet, however diversified may be their views, they recognise one another by a sort of sacred freemasonry, the one Spirit which quickens them all alike leaps within them as it recognises the one life in the bosoms of others. Despite their mental divergences, ecclesiastical associations, and doctrinal differences, spiritual men no sooner hear the password, and catch the mystic sign, than they cry, "Give me thy hand, my brother, for my heart is even as thy heart. The Spirit of God has led me and he has led thee, and in our way we tread step by step together; therefore let us have fellowship with each other." The outsiders of the camp, the mixed multitude that come up out of Egypt with our Israel, fall both into fighting and lusting; but the children of the living God, who make the central body-guard of the ark of the Lord, are one in heart with each other, and must be so. "We know that we have passed from death unto life, because we love the brethren."

The Holy Spirit leads us into *intense love for the souls of sinners.* If any man shall say, "It is no business of mine whether men are lost or saved," the Spirit of God never led him into such inhumanity. Bowels of iron have never felt the touch of the Spirit of Love. If ever a preacher's spirit and teaching legitimately lead you to the conclusion that you may view the damnation of your fellow men with complacency or indifference, you may be sure that the Spirit of God never led him or you in that direction. The devil has more to do with some men's pitiless theology than they imagine. Christ's eyes wept over the sinner's doom, may the Lord save us from thinking of it in any other spirit. He who does not love his fellow man whom he has seen, how can he love God whom he has not seen? Does God look with complacency upon the ruin of our race? Did he not love men so well that he gave his only begotten Son for them? And will he have his own children cold, stoical, and indifferent to the loss of human souls? Beloved, if we dwell with Cain and cry, "Am I my brother's keeper?" the Spirit of God never led us there; he leads us into tenderness, sympathy, compassion, and tearful effort, if by any means we may save some.

Further, the Spirit of God leads the sons of God into *holiness.* I shall not attempt to define what holiness is. That is best seen in the lives of holy men. Can it be seen in your lives? Beloved, if you are of a fierce, unforgiving spirit, the Holy Ghost never led you there;

if you are proud and hectoring, the Holy Ghost never led you there; if you are covetous, and lustful after worldly gain, the Holy Ghost never led you there; if you are false in your statements, and unjust in your actions, the Holy Ghost never led you there. If I hear of a professor of religion in the ball-room or the theatre, I know that the Holy Ghost never led him there; if I find a child of God mixing with the ungodly, using their speech, and doing their actions, I am persuaded the Holy Ghost never led him there. But if I see a man living as Christ would have lived, loving and tender, fearless, brave, honest, in all things minding to keep a good conscience before God and men, I hope that the Spirit of God has led him; if I see that man devout before his God, and full of integrity before his fellow men, then I hope and believe that the Spirit of God is his leader and influences his character. "The fruit of the Spirit is love, joy, peace, longsuffering, gentleness, goodness, faith, meekness, temperance: against such there is no law. And they that are Christ's have crucified the flesh with the affections and lusts." I do not wish to speak sharply, but I feel that I must speak plainly, and I feel bound to say that there is far too much hypocrisy among professing Christian people. Many wear the name of Christian, and have nothing else that is Christian about them. It is sorrowful that it should be so, but so it is: false professors have lowered the standard of Christian character, and made the church so like the world that it is hard to say where one begins and the other ends. We exercise church discipline as best we can, but for all that there is a seed of mischief which does not develope into open and overt sin which we cannot remove by discipline, for we are forbidden to root up the tares lest we root up the wheat with them. Men and brethren, we must be holy! It is of no use our talking about being orthodox in belief: we must be orthodox in life, and, if we are not, the soundest creed will only increase our damnation. I hear men boast that they are Nonconformists to the backbone, as if that were the essential matter: better far be Christians to the heart. What is the use of ecclesiastical Nonconformity if the heart is still conformed to the world? Another man will glory that he is a Conformist, but what is the good of that unless he is conformed to the image of Christ? Holiness is the main consideration, and if we are not led into it by the Spirit of holiness neither are we the sons of God.

Furthermore, the Holy Ghost leads those who are the children of God into *vital godliness*—the mystic essence of spiritual life. For instance, the Holy Ghost leads the saints to prayer, which is the vital breath of their souls. Whenever they get true access to the mercy-seat it is by his power. The Holy Spirit leads them to search the word, and opens their understandings to receive it; he leads them into meditation, and the chewing of the cud of truth; he leads them into fellowship with himself and with the Son of God. He lifts them right away from worldly cares into heavenly contemplations; he leads them away to the heavenly places, where Christ sitteth at the right hand of God, and where his saints reign with him. Beloved, have you ever felt these leadings? I am talking of them, but do *you* understand them? Are these things matters of constant experience with you? It is easy to say, "Yes, I know what you mean." Have you felt them?

Are these every-day things with you, for, as the Lord liveth, if you have not been led into prayer, and into communion with God, the Spirit of God is not in you, and you are none of his?

The Spirit of God, moreover, leads the sons of God into *usefulness*, some in one path, and some in another, while a few are conducted into very eminent service, and into self-consecration of the highest order. We bless God for missionaries who have been led of the Spirit of God among the wildest tribes to preach Jesus Christ. We thank God for holy women who, at home, have been led into the darkest parts of this city to labour amongst the most fallen and depraved, to lift up Christ before them that he might lift them up to himself. Blessed are those men and women who are led by the Spirit of God into labours more abundant, for the more abundant shall be their joy. Methinks I ought to remind you all that if you are doing nothing for Jesus the Spirit of God has never led you into this idleness. If you eat the fat and drink the sweet in the house of God, but never do a hand's turn for the household, the Spirit of God cannot have taught you this abominable sloth. There is a something for everyone of us to do, a talent committed to the charge of every believer, and if we have the Spirit of God dwelling in us he will tell us what the Lord has appointed us to perform, he will strengthen us for the doing of it, and set his seal and blessing upon it when it is done. Those dead branches of the vine which yield no clusters for the Lord, either by patience in suffering or activity in working, have no evidence that they are of the household of faith. Those who take no part in labours for Jesus can hardly hope that they will ultimately be partakers in his glory with him.

Thus have I, in a plain manner, without diving too deep into the matter, given you an answer to the question, "Whither does the Spirit of God lead the sons of God?"

II. I shall now answer another question with still greater brevity—How does the Spirit lead the sons of God?

The reply would be this: *the Spirit of God operates upon our spirits mysteriously.* We cannot explain his mode of operation, except that we shall probably be right if we conclude that he operates upon our spirits somewhat in the same way in which our spirits operate upon other men's spirits, only after a nobler sort. Now, how do I influence the spirit of my friend? I do it usually by imparting to him something which I know, which I hope will have power over his mind by suggesting motives to him, and so influencing his acts. I cannot operate upon my neighbour's mind mechanically; no tool can touch the heart, no hand can shape the mind. We act upon matter by machinery, but upon mind by argument, by reason, by instruction, and so we endeavour to fashion men as we desire. *One great instrument which the Holy Ghost uses upon the mind is the word of God.* The word, as we have it printed in the Bible, is the great instrument in the hand of the Spirit for leading the children of God in the right way. If you want to know what you ought to do, say as the old Scotchman used to say to his wife, "Reach down yon Bible." That is the map of the way, the heavenly pilgrim's knapsack guide; and if you are led by the word of God the Spirit of God is with the word, and works through it, and you are led by the Spirit of God. Quote chapter and verse for an action, and, unless you have wrested the passage, you may rest assured you have acted rightly. Be sure that such and such a thing is a command of God written in the book, inspired by the Holy Ghost, and you do not need a voice of thunder from heaven or an angelic whisper, you have a more sure word of prophecy, unto which you will do well if you take heed as unto a light that shineth in a dark place.

The Spirit of God also speaks through his ministers. The word preached is often blest, as well as the word written, but this can only be the case when the word preached is in conformity with the word written. At times God's ministers seem to give the written word its own voice, so that it sounds forth as if just spoken by the seer who originally received it. As they speak it drops into the ear like honey from the comb, it leaps forth like water from the well-head; and at such times goes into the heart fresh and warm, with even a greater energy than when we read it alone in our chamber. How often do we feel when we read a truth in a book (even though that book is God's word) our sluggish condition prevents its having such power over us as it has when a man of God who has experienced it, and tasted it, and handled it, speaks of it as the outpouring of his own soul. May God grant that the ministry which you usually attend may be to you the voice of God. May it be guidance to your feet, comfort to your heart, invigoration to your faith, and refreshment to your soul, and while you are sitting in the house of prayer may you feel, "That word is for me: I came here not knowing what to do, but I have received direction; I was faint and weary, but I have obtained consolation and strength. The voice of the pastor has been as the oracle of God to my soul, and now I go my way comforted as Hannah did when the Lord's servant had spoken peace to her soul."

Upon another point I would speak with great caution, and would have you think of it with more caution still, for it is a matter which has been sadly abused and turned to fanatical purposes. The Spirit of God does, I believe, *directly, even apart from the word, speak in the hearts of the saints.* There are inward monitions which are to be devoutly obeyed, guidances mysterious and secret, which must be implicitly followed. It is not a subject for common talk, but is meant for the ear of the intelligent believer who will not misunderstand us. There will come to you sometimes, you know not why, certain inward checks, such as Paul received when he essayed to go into Mysia, but the Spirit suffered him not. There is a certain act which you might do or might not do, but an impulse comes upon you which seems to say, "Not that, or not now." Do not violate that inward restraint. "Quench not the Spirit." At another time a proper thing, a fit thing, will have been forgotten by you for a time, but it comes upon you strongly that it is to be done at once, and for some reason you cannot shake off the impression. Do no violence to that impulse. It is not to every man that the Holy Ghost speaks in such a way; but he has his favoured ones, and these must jealously guard the privilege, for perhaps if they are deaf when he speaks he may never speak to them any more in that way. If we render reverent obedience to divine monitions they will become far more common with us. "Why," says one, "you run into Quakerism." I cannot help that. If this is Quakerism I am so far a Quaker: names do not concern me one way or another. You each one know whether your personal experience gives confirmation to what I have advanced or otherwise, and there let the question end; for, mark you, I advance this with caution, and do not set up such monitions as indispensable signs of a son of God. There is a story told (and many such some of us could tell almost as striking) of a certain friend who one night was influenced to take his horse from the stable, and ride some six or seven miles to a certain house where lived a person whom he had never seen. He arrived at dead of night, knocked at the door, and was answered by the master of the house, who seemed to be in great confusion of mind. The midnight visitor said, " Friend, I have been sent to thee, I know not why, but surely the Lord has some reason for having sent me to thee. Is there anything peculiar about thy circumstances ?" The man, struck with amazement, asked him to come up stairs, and there showed him a halter tied to a beam. He was putting the rope about his neck to commit suicide when a knock sounded at the door, he resolved that he would go down and answer the call, and then return and destroy himself; but the friend whom God had sent talked to him, brought him to a cooler mind, and helped him in the pecuniary difficulty which embarrassed him, and the man lived to be an honourable Christian man. I solemnly declare that monitions equally powerful have guided me, and their results have been remarkable to me at any rate. For the most part these are secrets between God and my own soul, neither am I eager to break the seal and tell them to others. There are too many swine about for us to be very lavish with our pearls. If we were obedient to such impulses if we did not save suicides we might save souls, and might often be in the hands of God as angels sent from heaven : but we are like the horse and the mule, which have no understanding, whose mouth must be held in with bit and bridle ; we are not tender enough to be sensitive to the divine influence when it comes, and so the Lord does not please to speak to many of us in this way so frequently as we could desire. Still, it is true that "as many as are led by the Spirit of God," however he may lead them, "they are the sons of God."

Let me here remark that being " *led* by the Spirit of God" is a remarkable expression. It does not say, "As many as are driven by the Spirit of God." No, the devil is a driver, and when he enters either into men or into hogs he drives them furiously. Remember how the whole herd ran violently down a steep place into the sea. Whenever you see a man fanatical and wild, whatever spirit is in him it is not the Spirit of Christ. The Spirit of Christ is forcible, it worketh mightily, but it is a quiet Spirit ; it is not an eagle, but a dove. He comes as a rushing wind, and fills the house where the disciples are sitting, but at the same time he comes not as a whirlwind from the wilderness to smite the four corners of the habitation, or it would become a ruin. He comes as a flame of fire sitting upon each of the favoured ones, but it is not a flame of fire that burns the house and destroys Jerusalem. No, the Spirit of God is gentle; he does not drive, but lead. " As many as are led by the Spirit of God, they are the sons of God."

The Spirit treats us honourably in thus working; he does not deal with us as with dumb, driven cattle, or soulless waves of the sea; he treats us as intelligent beings, made for thought and reflection. He leads us as a man guideth his child, or as one leadeth his fellow, and we are honoured by subjecting our minds and wills to so divine a Spirit. Never is the will truly free until the Holy Ghost sweetly subdues it to willing obedience.

Thus the Spirit of God works, though we cannot explain the method, for that is a thing too wonderful for us, and sooner may we know the path of an eagle in the air, or the way of a serpent upon a rock. As we cannot walk in search of the springs of the sea, so is this also hidden from all living. We have said somewhat upon the subject, and, as far as we can, have answered the question, "How does the Spirit of God lead the children of God?" but we are of yesterday, and know nothing, and, therefore, confessing our ignorance, we pass on.

III. The last question is, WHEN DOES THE SPIRIT LEAD THE SONS OF GOD? Ah, brethren, that question needs anxious answering.

The Spirit of God *would* always lead the sons of God, but, alas, there are times when even children of God will not be led. They are wilful and headstrong, and start aside. The healthy condition of a child of God is to be always led by the Spirit of God. Mark this— led by the Spirit every day; not on Sundays only, nor alone at periods set apart for prayer, but during every minute of every hour of every day. We ought to be led by the Spirit in little things as well as in great matters, for, observe, if we were led by the Spirit all our lives in all other matters, yet, if only one action apart from the Spirit were suffered to run to its full results, it would ruin us. The mercy is that the Lord restoreth our souls; but there is never a single hour when a Christian can afford to wander from the way of the Spirit. If you have a guide along an intricate pathway, and you allow him to conduct you for half an hour, and then say, "Now, I shall direct myself for the next five minutes," in that short space you will lose the benefit of having a guide at all. It is clear that a pilot who only occasionally directs the ship is very little better than none. If you were traversing an unknown and difficult pathway it would render all directions useless if you were to say, "They told me to turn to the right at this corner, but I mean to try the left." That one turning will affect the whole of your after journey. If we err, and are really sons of God, our divine leader will make us retrace our steps with bitter tears, and feel what an evil and bitter thing it is to have chosen our own delusions. If we use our divine leader wisely we shall always follow him. Child of God, the Spirit must lead you in everything. "Well, but," say you, "*will* he?" Ah, "Will he?" Yes, to your astonishment. When you are in difficulties, consult the Holy Spirit in the Word. Hear what God speaks in the inspired volume, and if no light comes from thence kneel down and pray. When you see a sign-post in a country road, and it tells you which way to go, you are glad to follow its directions; but if in your perplexities you see no sign-post, what are you to do? *Pray.* Cast yourself upon the divine guidance, and you shall make no mistake; for even if you happen to pick the roughest road it will be the right one if you have selected it with holy caution, and in the fear of God. Beloved, the Lord will never let a vessel be dashed upon the rocks whose tiller has been given into his hands. Give up the helm to God, and your barque will thread the narrow winding channel of life, avoid every sandbank and sunken rock, and arrive safely at the fair havens of eternal bliss.

The question—when are the sons of God led by the Spirit? is to be answered thus,—when they are as they should be they are always distinctly led by him; and though, owing to sin in them, they are not always obedient to the same degree, yet the power which usually influences their lives is the Spirit of God.

Now I close, using the text thus. First as a *test*. Am I a child of God? If so, I am led by the Spirit. Am I led by the Spirit? I am afraid some of you never think of that matter. By whom are you led? Hundreds of religious people are led by their minister or by a Christian friend, and so far so good for them; but their religion will be a failure unless they are led by the Spirit. Let me put the question again that you may not shirk it,—Are you led by the Spirit? If you are you are a child of God, and if not you are none of his.

That gives me a second use of the text, namely, the use of *consolation*. If you are a child of God you will be led by the Spirit. Now, are you in doubt to-night? Are you embarrassed? Are you in difficulties? Then the sons of God are led by the Spirit, and you will be led. Perhaps you are looking a long way ahead, and you are afraid of difficulties in your old age, or at the death of a relative. Now, God has not given us eyes to pry into the future, and what is the use of our peering where we cannot see? Leave it all to your heavenly Father; and you will be unerringly led by the Holy Ghost. When you come to the place where you thought there would be a difficulty, very likely there will be none. "Who shall roll away the stone from the door of the sepulchre?" said the holy women, but when they came to the sepulchre, lo, the stone was rolled away already. Go on as a child of God, walking by faith, with the full assurance that the path of faith, if not an easy one, will always be a safe one; and all will be well, and you will be led in a right way to a city of habitations.

The last word of all is, the text is an *assurance*. If you are led by the Spirit of God then you are most certainly a son of God. Can you say to-night, "I do yield myself up to the Lord's will. I am not perfect, I wish I were; I am burdened with a thousand infirmities, but yet if the Lord will teach me I am willing to learn, if he will have patience with me I will strive to follow him. Oh, what would I give to be perfectly holy! I long to be pure within. I wish above all things else in this world that I may never grieve my God, but walk with him in the light as he is in the light, and have fellowship with him, while the blood of Jesus Christ his Son cleanses me from all sin"? My brother, be well assured that none ever longed like that but a child of God. Flesh and blood hath not revealed this unto thee. No soul, except an heir of heaven, ever had such wishings, and aspirings, and groanings after holiness, and such sorrows over failures and mistakes. The text does not say, "He who runs in the Spirit is a son of God," but he that is *led* by the Spirit of God. Now, we may stumble whilst we are being led; a man may go very slowly while he is being led; he may go on crutches while he is being led; he may crawl on his hands and knees while he is being led : but none of these absolutely prevent his being truly led. With all your weaknesses and infirmities, the point is—Are you led by the Spirit of God? If you are, all your infirmities and failures are forgiven you for Christ's name's sake, and your being led is the mark of your being born from above. Go home and rejoice in your sonship, and pray God if you have been weak to make you strong, if you have been lame to heal you, and, if you have crept along on your hands and knees, to help you to walk uprightly; but, after all, bless him that his Spirit does lead you. If you can only walk, ask him to make you run; and if you can run, ask him to make you mount on wings as eagles. Do not be satisfied with anything short of the highest attainments; and, at the same time, if you have not reached them, do not despair. Remember that in most families there are babes as well as men and women: the little child in long clothes carried in the arms, and laid on the breast, is just as dear to the parent as the son who in the fulness of his manhood marches by his father's side, and takes his share in the battle of life. You are sons of God if you are led by the Spirit, however small your stature and feeble your grace. The age, strength, or education of the man are not essential to his sonship, but the trueness of his birth is the all-important matter. See ye to it that ye are led by the Spirit, or your parentage is not from above.

If you have been condemned by this sermon, then fly away to Jesus, and penitently and trustfully rest in him. May the Spirit of God lead you to do that, and you are then a child of God. May he bless you now. Amen.

PORTION OF SCRIPTURE READ BEFORE SE. MON—Romans viii. 1—17.

HYMNS FROM "OUR OWN HYMN BOOK"—722, 448, 456.

Metropolitan Tabernacle Pulpit.

THE GREATEST EXHIBITION OF THE AGE.

A Sermon

INTENDED FOR READING ON LORD'S-DAY, MAY 7TH, 1893,

DELIVERED BY

C. H. SPURGEON,

AT THE METROPOLITAN TABERNACLE, NEWINGTON,

On Lord's-day Evening, May 5th, 1889.

"For as often as ye eat this bread, and drink this cup, ye do shew the Lord's death till he come."—1 Corinthians xi. 26.

FIRST, let me say that the Lord's supper is nothing to us unless we partake of it as spiritual persons in a spiritual way. We must understand what we are doing in coming to the communion table; the mere mechanical celebration will be vanity; it may even be a sin. To observe this ordinance aright, you must bring your mind in an awakened state, you must come with holy faith, and love, and concentrated thought. I do pray that we may so come to-night. I know how mechanical we all get. We even stand up and sing, and oftentimes we forget what we are singing while the sounds issue from our lips. We cover our eyes in prayer, but we do not always pray. There is such a thing as preaching from the mouth outward, instead of speaking from the heart; and I believe there is a kind of hearing which is dreadfully superficial, and can do the hearer no good. Now, if you come to the supper to-night, bring your hearts with you; and if your hearts are warm with love to Christ, desire to have them yet fuller of love to your Lord. I remember reading of a Mr. Welch, a very devout minister of the gospel in Suffolk, who was found weeping one day; and when he was asked by a brother minister why he wept, he said it was because he could love Christ more than he did. That was a very good reason for weeping. Now, let us love our Lord much to-night; and if we cannot feel the glow of love as we wish to feel it, let us weep to think that it is so. May the Spirit of God come and put life into our communion, that every child of God here may have real fellowship with Christ in the breaking of bread!

But now, let us get to our work. The Lord's supper, dear friends, is first of all a memorial. "This do in remembrance of me." It is intended to keep alive in our own hearts, and in the minds of others, the wondrous fact that the Son of God was here among men, and laid

No. 2,307.

down his life a sacrifice for sin. It is well known that a custom, a rite, a festival, has a very great historical power to keep up in the minds of men the recollection of a fact; and our Lord has selected this common meal, this supper, as a method by which men should be made to know to the very end of time that he died. There can be no doubt about the death of Christ, because through long ages all history bears record that Christian men and women have met together, and have eaten bread, and have drunk wine, to keep up the memory of his sufferings and death. This is better than if there had been a statue erected, or than if a document had been written, or than if a brass tablet had been inscribed. We are not without memorials of other sorts; especially we are not without books; but this perpetually celebrated feast, kept up without cessation, kept up in every country on the face of the earth, is one of the very best memorials that the death of Christ can have. All of you who come to the table to-night will be helping to keep alive in the memory of men the great fact that Jesus died.

But the Lord's supper is more than a memorial, it is a fellowship, a communion. Those who eat of this bread, spiritually understanding what they do, those who drink of this cup, entering into the real meaning of that reception of the wine, do therein receive Christ spiritually into their hearts. Their heart, soul, mind feeds upon Christ himself, and upon what Christ has done. We do not merely record the fact, but we enjoy the result of it. We do not merely say that Christ died; but we desire to die with him, and to live only as the result of his having died. We take scot and lot with Christ as we come to the table. We say deliberately, "Thine are we, thou Son of God, and all that we have; and thou art ours, and in testimony thereof we eat this bread, and we drink of this cup, to show that we are one with thyself, partners with thee in this great fellowship of love."

Well, now, if you want a permanent memorial, and a perpetual means of fellowship, it will be wise to have a rite or ceremony in which there shall also be a likeness to the fact that has to be remembered. This supper is therefore an exhibition, a showing, a setting forth, a proclamation of the death of Christ. That you may remember that Jesus died, there is something here that bears a resemblance to his death. That you may the better have fellowship with him in his death, here is something which is a vivid picture of that death, and which will help to bring it more clearly before your mind's eye. That is the subject for to-night's meditation,—this supper as a showing forth, an exhibition of Christ's death "till he come."

In speaking of this exhibition, this showing forth, we will consider, first, *what it shows;* secondly, *how it shows it;* and thirdly, *how long it is to show it.*

I. Thinking of this supper, that we are about to celebrate, we will consider, first, WHAT IT SHOWS. "As often as ye eat this bread, and drink this cup, *ye do shew the Lord's death.*"

Brethren, to-night, we are to show, to exhibit, to demonstrate, to set forth, to symbolize, to represent, to picture the death of Christ. He lived, or he could not have died; that fact is, therefore, included in our confession of faith. But the point we specially set forth is this, that he died, he who was born at Bethlehem, the Son of Mary, and who lived here on earth, being also the Son of God, in due time died, he gave his life a ransom for many. Why do we record that fact? To my intense grief, I have heard it said, even among a certain class of preachers, that we dwell too much upon the death of Christ. They ask why we do not talk more about his life. The death of a man, they say, is not so important, by a great many degrees, as his life. The Lord have mercy upon the miserable and ignorant men who talk in that fashion! But we have a reason for making so much of Christ's death. The Lord has instituted no memorial of his life, the memorial that he has instituted is to keep before his people the perpetual remembrance of his death. And why is that the case?

I take it, because *this is the very heart of the gospel of Jesus Christ*. The doctrine that he died, "the Just for the unjust, that he might bring us to God," is essential to the gospel. Leave out the vicarious sacrifice unto death, and you have left out the life of the gospel of Jesus Christ. There are some truths which ought to be preached in due proportion with other truths; but if they are not preached, souls may be saved; but this is a truth which must be preached, and if it be left out, souls will not be saved. I should have more hope of the salvation of a man hearing a Romish priest, with all his superstition, if he preached the death of Christ, than I should of one hearing a Unitarian, with all his intelligence, if he left out the doctrine of the atoning blood of the Lord Jesus Christ. "The blood is the life thereof." "Without shedding of blood is no remission." Because the death of Christ is the life of the gospel, therefore it is that there is an ordinance to set forth that death "till he come."

And this is the more so, in the next place, because *this is the point where the gospel is always being assailed*. You shall find, in almost every controversy, that the fight thickens about the cross. It is around the standard that the foemen cluster. There the sword rings upon the armour, there the loudest shout is heard, there you see the garment rolled in blood. So the cross, the cross is the standard of our Christianity. Round the atoning sacrifice the controversialists gather. They think they are aiming at other things; but the real password is, "Fight neither with small nor great, save only with the Divine Substitute for men." If they could once get rid of the doctrine of the atoning sacrifice, they would destroy that which is the greatest tower of strength to the gospel of Christ; but, thank God, they cannot get rid of the cross! We can still sing,—

> " The cross it standeth fast,
>   Hallelujah!
> Defying every blast,
>   Hallelujah!
> The winds of hell have blown,
> The world its hate hath shown,
> Yet it is not o'erthrown.
>   Hallelujah for the cross!
>   It shall never suffer loss! "

Therefore, set forth the atoning sacrifice of Christ, brethren, in this ordinance, "till he come."

So well does this supper set forth the death of Christ in that respect, that it has been argued by some brethren that, if a man comes to the communion table, unless he is a great liar, he has already made a confession of faith in Christ. I will not go that length; but there is a good deal of truth in the argument. If you truly eat and drink of this supper, you must believe in the atoning sacrifice; you come here under false pretences if you are not a believer in that; for, at the institution of this supper, the Saviour said, "This is my blood of the new testament (or covenant) which is shed for many for the remission of sins." The pardon of sin must be by the shedding of the blood of Christ; and if you reject the blood of Christ, you have rejected the true meaning of this supper, and certainly you cannot come here with a clear conscience. This supper, then, sets forth the great fact that Jesus died; and it is ordained to set that death forth because it is essential to the gospel, and because it is the point which is most fiercely attacked.

And you will notice, brethren, according to our text, that *this showing of the death of Christ is to be kept up through every age "till he come."* It will not be wanted after the coming of Christ, for reasons which we will speak of by-and-by; but until then it will always be wanted. Shall I always have to preach the doctrine of atonement? Yes, always. Shall we always have to set Christ forth evidently crucified among men? Yes, always. First, because we always need to have this truth set forth. You and I, who are firm believers in this glorious truth, yet cannot too often think upon it. I love to come every Lord's-day to the communion table; I should be very sorry to come only once a month, or, as some do, only once a year. I could not afford to come as seldom as that. I need to be reminded, forcibly reminded, of my dear Lord and Master very often. We do so soon forget, and our unloving hearts so soon grow cold. How is it with you, my brethren? I know that it is thus with me. I sing sometimes,—

> "Gethsemane, can I forget?
> Or there thy conflict see,
> Thine agony and bloody sweat,
> And not remember Thee!"

But that is the point of my argument. We need to go often to Gethsemane and there see our Lord's agony and bloody sweat, that we may remember him. I suppose that, until we see his face, we shall never have one communion too many, and we shall never have a thought of Christ that is superfluous. Nay, banish all poetic thought rather than that I should lose a thought of him. Begone the most delightful classical expression, and the most charming thoughts of philosophers, if they would push out one thought of Jesus; for thoughts of Christ are golden thoughts, and thoughts of other things, however burnished by the wit and genius of men, are but poor metal compared with thoughts of Jesus. We need this supper for ourselves, brethren, and we should partake of it often, for that is what is meant by our Lord's words, "As oft as ye drink it." We need that often we should eat this bread, and drink this cup, and show his death for our own sins.

But this supper is as much needed for the sake of others. We are to show Christ's death that others may know about it, that others may be impressed by it, that others may be saved by it. I sometimes wonder, when I am talking to you upon this theme, that I do not preach much better; and yet, when I have done, I say to myself, "Well, how can there be anything better if one only tells the tale truly?" That God came here in human flesh, and for our sins did serve, did die, that he bore the vengeance due to our guilt, the punishment which our transgressions had incurred, brethren, that is poetry. It is essential poetry, even though I only put it into a child's speech. It wants no garnishing. The face of perfect beauty must not be touched with Jezebel's paints; and all the garnishing of eloquence that can be brought to such a fact as this is unnecessary, meretricious, and degrading. Oh, hear you the tale, and then, as you come to the table, remember what it is that you set forth, and say to yourself, "I am, by this action, telling a story more wonderful than all the histories of men put together. I am showing to those who look on something which angels desire to look into, which the most wonderful intelligences will, throughout all the ages, study with ever-growing wonder and delight—God Incarnate, suffering in the sinner's stead." Show that forth, brethren, for it is worth the showing.

II. But now, secondly, having mentioned what it is that this supper shows, let me prove to you HOW IT SHOWS IT.

It does so, first, *very instructively in the emblems themselves.* We want to tell men and to tell our own hearts that Jesus died. Well, see, here is bread; mark you, not a wafer, but a piece of household bread. And here is wine in a cup; not wine and water, but the true juice of the grape, which our Lord called "the fruit of the vine." What then? Here are bread and the fruit of the vine, separately. Bread, representing the flesh of Christ, has a million sermons in it. Shall I tell you its story? It was a grain of wheat, they threw it into the ground, they buried it beneath the clods, it lay there exposed to winter's cold. It sprang up, and many a frost nipped it in the green blade; but there came spring weather, and summertide, and the wheat grew and grew on till it turned into the yellow golden grain. See, they come along with a sharp sickle, and cut it down; it must feel the keen edge. After cutting it down, they take it away in sheaves. They spread it out upon the barn floor. Here are flails, which come hammering down upon it,—in those olden times they did use flails. Now they beat out the grain from the ear; and now, when they have all the grain separated from the straw, it must be winnowed, and the chaff must be blown away. Then they take this corn, and put it between two stones, and grind it. Woe unto thee, O grain, thou art ground into the finest flour! But it has not finished its history of suffering yet. When well ground, and separated from the bran, it is taken, and a woman kneads it with all her might, and makes it into dough. Nor is its suffering ended yet, for she thrusts it into the oven. Now does it feel the heat of the fire; and when the loaf is taken out of the oven, it is cut, or broken, and devoured. It is a story of suffering from the beginning to the end. Now take that cup, and look into its ruddy depths. Do you see that vine yonder? You expected to find it festooned on trelliswork, a lovely object; but looking at it in the winter and spring, you say to yourself, "Is that a vine? It looks like an old, dead stick left in the ground." Yes, it has been cut down. Did you not see the pruner's knife? How sharply he cut! "Surely," you said, "he is killing that vine." No, vines are made to bear much fruit by being closely cut and pruned. But now it is summer, and in the early months of autumn the vine is loaded with red grapes; and those grapes must be taken off the vine, and severed from the branch. See, they are throwing them into the wine-press, heaps upon heaps; look how they are piled up! And what happens now? Men leap in upon them, and with their feet they tread the grapes. The blood of the grape runs out of the wine-press, red like ruddy gore. This is the history of the wine of which you drink, and so it comes to you. And, oh, I need not tell you of your Lord, how he was thrown into the wine-press, and how he suffered even unto death! These elements of bread and wine are stories to you, and emblems of suffering. You notice, too, that these emblems are separate. If I were to take the bread, and crumble it into the cup, and then pass it to you that you might drink of that curious mixture, you would not celebrate the Lord's death at all. It would not be possible, for it is the body with the blood separated from it that sets forth death. While the blood is in the veins, you have life; but when the blood is drawn away from the body, which is set forth to you in the pure white bread and in the red juice of the grape, then you have the picture of death; and in that way you show Christ's sufferings and death in the celebration of this supper. So much I have, I hope, made plain enough for all to understand.

Now notice *the manner of the use of these two elements,* for the manner of their use vividly shows Christ's death. I think it is in the Church Catechism that we are taught that the word "sacrament" means "an outward and visible sign of an inward and spiritual grace." That definition will do for this ordinance, which is the outward and visible sign of an inward and spiritual grace.

It is very remarkable how the emblems before us appeal to our various senses. Notice, first, the Saviour took the bread and the cup. You see them; they are before you, you can see them. After he had blessed them, he said, "Take." Did you ever see, in a very Ritualistic church, that little game played by the priest with his napkin held out under the chin of the communicant, and telling him to open his mouth, and popping the wafer in? This is not eating the Lord's supper, for the command at the institution of the Lord's supper was, "Take, eat." It is essential that you take it in your hand. "Take, eat." So there is another sense that is affected in this sacred exercise, that is, the sense of touch. Jesus took the bread, and brake it, and gave it to the disciples, that they might employ the second sense. They had seen, now they touched. "Take, eat," said the Lord; and they held it in their hands. But never do you have the Lord's supper without an appeal to the ear, for he said, "This is my body." Whenever we break this bread, we say the same, "This bread is Christ's body," so there is an appeal to the ear. You put the bread and the wine into your mouth; there comes in your fourth sense, your taste, so that four senses are made to assist you in realizing that Christ did really die, that his death is no dream, no fiction. It is not merely a man in a book, but a living man who died, a real man who poured out his life unto death for you. I have said that four senses are appealed to; but I might add the sense of smell also. There is an old proverb, "Nothing smells so sweet as bread;" and to a hungry man there is nothing so refreshing as the presence of bread which regales the nostril. The Lord has given us an ordinance here in which he brings our body to support our soul, and to render vivid to our mind by at least four, if not all of our five senses, this most blessed fact, that Jesus Christ, the Son of Mary and the Son of God, did really lay down his life a sacrifice for us.

But now I remind you of another thing. We show the death of Christ, in the next place, by *the mode of the disposal of this bread and this wine,* for these elements go into our bodies. They are received into the inner man, and are digested and assimilated there, and taken up into our system, to build us up; and herein we teach that Christ, dying for us, is to be received by faith into the heart. We are to believe in that death as being for us. We are to appropriate it as our own; we are to trust in it; we are to live upon it. It is to become part and parcel of our spiritual nature, and we are to be built up thereby, for Christ's death on the cross saves nobody to whom Christ does not come into the heart. If thou dost not believe, even Christ lifted up between earth and heaven will not save thee. "As many as received him, to them gave he power to become the sons of God." But without receiving him, Christ is dead in vain so far as thou art concerned. Thou hast no part nor lot in this matter. This fact, I say, we set forth by the method of the disposal of the emblems.

And now, carefully note that *the spirit of this ordinance also is very instructive.* How does it begin? Jesus takes bread, and blesses it. In other words, he gives thanks. It is very usual to call this ordinance the Eucharist, or, the giving of thanks. That is the spirit of it; it is all through a giving of thanks. Now, mark you, there is no reason to give thanks for the death of Christ unless it was an atoning death, and an expiation for sin. I should regret, infinitely regret, that a good man should die as Jesus died unless there was an end to be accomplished by it worthy of that death. The end of Christ's death was that, dying for us, by the shedding of his blood, there might be remission of sins; and for that we may well give thanks. The communion begins with thanksgiving, but how does it continue? It continues by our sitting at ease. There are some who think that, to kneel at the communion is the most reverent posture. So it is, and I doubt not that God accepts their reverence; but it is a most unscriptural posture. There is more presumption than reverence in it, for to alter the ordinance of Christ even on the pretence of reverence is not justifiable. When our Lord first of all instituted the supper, they did not sit down as we do, but they reclined as the Orientals still do, at their ease, so much at their ease that the head of John was on the breast of Jesus. I cannot conceive anything more exactly the opposite of coming up to an altar rail, and kneeling down, than this reclining upon couches with your head upon your next neighbour's bosom. The fact is, that it meant ease, it meant rest; and that is what the posture which we take up should mean. Our nearest approach to that which can be tolerated in our western clime is to sit as much as you can at ease, as a person in this country does at a banquet, as near an approach as possible to the method of the Oriental at his banquet. That is how the feast goes on; it began with a blessing, it proceeds with a restful posture. How does it end? After supper they sang a hymn. It was not a dirge, it was not funereal; they celebrated the death of Christ, but not with funereal rites. They sang a hymn, it was joyous, probably part of the great Hallel of the Jewish Passover. This indicates to us, and we set it forth, that the death of Christ is now a joyous event; that to the whole of his people it is not a thing to sigh over; but that, believing in Christ, it is a thing to thank God for, to be at ease about, and to sing over; and we set that forth by the manner in which we partake of this supper.

One thing more we set forth. *The persons who come to the table must be, according to Christ's rule, believers in him.* They, and they only, have a right to eat of this feast. Others eat and drink unworthily, and drink and eat condemnation to themselves. We do, therefore, say, albeit that there is no limit to the value of the sacrifice of Christ (that were inconceivable), yet he had a special object in it, and he died for a special people, which people are known by their being led to believe in him, to unite with him in a distinct affiance by trusting in him. Not for you all will this avail; but for all of you that believe, for so it is written, "For God so loved the world," so much and no more, "that he gave his only begotten Son, that whosoever believeth in him should not perish, but have everlasting life,"—a universality which, nevertheless, has a speciality hidden in its inner self. Believe this, or else this death is not for thee. Trust Christ, or else thou shalt have no share in the blessings which his death has purchased. And we set that forth when, gathering at the table, we come as believers; but we are obliged to tell others that, if they are not believers, they must not come: they have no right to come.

III. My time has nearly gone, and therefore I must finish with the third point. We have seen what this supper shows, and how it shows it; now we are to consider HOW LONG IT IS TO SHOW IT.

I have tried, as best I could, in a very simple way, to show how this supper does symbolize and set forth the death of Christ. How long are we to do it? "*Till he come.*" Well, now, what does that teach us? When Jesus comes, we are to leave off observing the Lord's supper, but not till he comes.

It teaches us, then, that *there will always be a value in Christ's wondrous death.* God would not have us set forth a thing that is done with, a sucked orange, a mere shell out of which the seed is gone. If the death of Christ were not abundantly efficacious still, he would not have us set it forth. But to-night we can sing, with as much meaning and force as ever we could,—

> " Dear dying Lamb, thy precious blood
> Shall never lose its power,
> Till all the ransom'd Church of God
> Be saved to sin no more."

It is nearly nineteen hundred years since Jesus was here, and yet his blood is still powerful, his death can still take away sin. Come and try it to-night, some of you who have never believed in him; to-night, I say, at the close of this—

"Sweet day, so cool, so calm, so bright,
The bridal of the earth and sky."

Come now, to-night, and yield thyself to the Lamb of God, and wash thee in his precious blood, and thou shalt be whiter than snow. That communion table is just now covered with a white cloth; but when it is uncovered, and you see the bread and the wine, they will say to you, "The atonement is still existing, it is still efficacious, it is still full of power." We celebrate the ordinance because Christ's death is still available for all who trust to it.

The next thing is, dear friends, that by saying that we will partake of this supper till Christ comes, we set forth our belief in *the perpetuity of this ordinance until the influence of Christ's death shall have been infallibly secured*. We are now in a world where men forget; and as long as we are in such a world, we must keep this sign-post, this direction to those who want to journey to heaven. We must never take this sign-post down till there will be no need of it because Christ will have come; and when he shall have come, beloved, we shall not then forget his death. When he shall come, do not think that we shall give up the Lord's supper because we give up thinking of him. Nay, we shall give it up because we shall then never give up thinking of him. He will be present with us; and he being present with us, we shall not need the help which now our weakness requires.

So then, in closing, I say to you that this supper is a window, a window of agate, and *the outlook of this supper is the Second Coming of the Lord from heaven*. This supper is also a gate of carbuncle, and through this gate we are to watch for the return of the Lord Jesus Christ from the throne of his glory to this earth. The Lord shall come. As surely as we are sitting here in this house, so surely will he, before long, appear a second time on earth, "without sin, unto salvation"; and we mean to keep up this feast "till he come."

"See, the feast of love is spread;
Drink the wine, and break the bread:
Sweet memorials, till the Lord
Call us round his heavenly board.
Some from earth, from glory some,
Severed only ' *Till he come!* ' "

Could *you* keep on feasting "till he come", my unsaved hearer? I think that you had better weep and mourn, repent and believe, and so get ready for his appearance. But those who are ready may just keep on feasting upon him, and rejoicing in him, till he puts in his last and glorious appearance. God help us to continue so, for Jesus' sake! Amen.

Exposition by C. H. Spurgeon.
JOHN XVI. 1—20.

This chapter contains some of the most precious words that the Lord Jesus uttered before he died upon the cross.

Verse 1. *These things have I spoken unto you, that ye should not be offended.*

Or, as the Revised Version translates it, "be made to stumble." Christ would not have his children stumble. There is an offence of the cross, but he would not have us needlessly offended. How careful is our dear Saviour not to give us offence! We ought to be very careful not to offend him; but what condescension it is on his part that he should be careful of offending us, or of permitting us to be offended, or made to stumble.

2. *They shall put you out of the synagogues: yea, the time cometh, that whosoever killeth you will think that he doeth God service.*

Can you remain faithful to your Master then, when you lose your position, or your character, or men put you out of the synagogue? When you nearly lose life itself, and when they shall think they are doing God's service by seeking to kill you, can you stand true to Christ then? The Master knew that days of bitter persecution would soon come upon his followers, so he strengthened them against those evil times that were approaching.

3. *And these things will they do unto you, because they have not known the Father, nor me.*

It is ignorance that makes men hate God's people and his Son: "They have not known the Father, nor me." Truly did Paul say, "I did it ignorantly in unbelief;" and for such persecutors there is full and free forgiveness. When they turn unto the Lord, even this sin shall be forgiven them; but they will not forgive themselves for having committed it; and, like Paul, they will count themselves the chief of sinners because they persecuted the Church of God.

4. *But these things have I told you, that when the time shall come, ye may remember that I told you of them.*

"You will then see my foresight, my care for you, my prophetic power. To be forewarned is to be forearmed. You will not be taken by surprise." If any of you who have lately been converted should meet with great opposition, do not be surprised; Jesus has told you to expect it; and if the fire should get seven times hotter, count it no strange thing that the fiery trial has happened unto you. It has happened unto others before you, and will happen to others after you; therefore be prepared for it.

4. *And these things I said not unto you at the beginning, because I was with you.*

"While I was with you, you could run to me, and tell me all about your trials and difficulties. If anybody was hard with you, I could come to your help, and comfort you. You did not need to know these things before, so I did not tell you of them. You do need to know them now, and now I tell you of them."

5. *But now I go my way to him that sent me;*

Christ was going to the cross, and to the grave, and afterwards to heaven.

5. *And none of you asketh me, Whither goest thou?*

For want of asking that question, Christ's disciples were full of grief. Sometimes we do not ask enough questions. We ask too many questions of doubt; it would be well if we were to ask a few more questions of believing curiosity. There are some things that we ought to wish to know; and Christ encourages his people to come to him for information.

6. *But because I have said these things unto you, sorrow hath filled your heart.*

When a poor Christian friend is dying, you are full of sorrow because he is going away from you. Why do you not ask whither he is going? If he is going home to heaven and to glory, why, then be comforted about him, you have no cause for distress on his account.

7. *Nevertheless I tell you the truth; It is expedient for you that I go away:*

"It is better for you that I should be absent than that I should be present." Their Lord was their joy, their Leader, their Teacher, their Comforter. He is going away, and he tells them that his absence will be a gain to them. "It is expedient for *you* that I go away."

7. *For if I go not away, the Comforter will not come unto you; but if I depart, I will send him unto you.*

Now, it is better for us to have the Comforter than to have Christ here in bodily presence; for if Christ were here to-night, in this Tabernacle, where could we put him so as to be equally near each one of us? I should certainly want him up here on the platform; and you, up there in the top gallery, would say, "Well, we are a long way off; why should he not come up here?" You see, if it is bodily presence that is enjoyed, some must be near, and some must be far off; but now that Christ has gone up to heaven, his Spirit is here. Where is that Spirit? On the platform, I hope, and everywhere else. Any of you who desire it may have the Holy Spirit's presence. The Lord says, "I will put my Spirit within you." Better than the bodily presence of Christ is the real, though spiritual, presence of the Holy Ghost.

8. *And when he is come, he will reprove the world of sin, and of righteousness, and of judgment:*

What, a Comforter reprove? Yes. The Holy Spirit never comforts till he has reproved. There must be a reproof of sin before there can be comfort in Christ. And while the Spirit comforts saints, he reproves the world.

9. *Of sin, because they believe not on me;*

The greatest sin in all the world is, not believing on Jesus. Our Lord did not say, "Of sin, because of the evil of drunkenness." That is a great sin, a cursed sin, and there are other great sins; but Christ said, "Of sin, because they believe not on me." That is the root sin, the foundation sin, the sin that keeps a man in his sin.

10. *Of righteousness, because I go to my Father, and ye see me no more;*

It is God's righteousness that takes Christ up to heaven. He has been here; he has lived a perfect life; he has died a sacrificial death; and God has shown his acceptance of him, for he has gone to his reward.

11. *Of judgment, because the prince of this world is judged.*

When Christ came here, there was a crisis, a judgment; and sin was judged and condemned; and the prince of the world, the chief sinner in the world, received his death-blow: "the prince of this world is judged."

12. *I have yet many things to say unto you, but ye cannot bear them now.*

See how Christ teaches us slowly, wisely, prudently. There are some things which some of you young Christians do not know; you could not bear them if you did know them. You shall know them when you can bear them. A man with a doctrine that he cannot handle is often like a child with a tough piece of meat which he cannot bite. Give the child milk, or the crumb of the loaf. Do not put crusts into his mouth till he has teeth to bite them; do not give him meat till he can digest it. See the gentle Saviour's way of imparting instruction. He teaches us much, but not too much at a time.

13. *Howbeit when he, the Spirit of truth is come, he will guide you into all truth: for he shall not speak of himself; but whatsoever he shall hear, that shall he speak: and he will shew you things to come.*

See, my dear brethren in the ministry, how little store the Holy Ghost sets by originality. We have men nowadays straining to be original. Strain the other way, for listen, "He shall not speak of himself,"—not even the Holy Ghost,—"He shall not speak of himself; but whatsoever he shall hear, that shall he speak." He is the Repeater of the Father's message, not the inventor of his own. So let it be with us ministers. We are not to make up a gospel as we go along, as I have heard some say. We are not to shape it to the times in which we live, and suit it to the congregations to which we speak. God forbid! Let this be true of every one of us, "He shall not speak of himself; but whatsoever he shall hear, that shall he speak."

14. *He shall glorify me:*

The Holy Ghost does that; therefore, surely we, who are the preachers of the gospel, should aim at the same object: "He shall glorify me." It should be our one desire to magnify and glorify our Lord Jesus Christ.

14—16. *For he shall receive of mine, and shall shew it unto you. All things that the Father hath are mine: therefore said I, that he shall take of mine, and shall shew it unto you. A little while, and ye shall not see me; and again, a little while, and ye shall see me, because I go to the Father.*

That was a very simple statement, every Sunday-scholar understands it now; but the twelve apostles did not understand it when they heard it.

17, 18. *Then said some of his disciples among themselves, What is this that he saith unto us, A little while, and ye shall not see me: and again, a little while, and ye shall see me: and, Because I go to the Father? They said therefore, What is this that he saith, A little while? we cannot tell what he saith.*

They said this "among themselves." This was not a wise course, for what can ignorance learn of ignorance? Here were disciples questioning one another; none of them knew anything, and yet they were trying to teach one another. If they had all gone to their Master, how much more quickly would they have understood his words! Take everything to Jesus. Try everything by the Word of God. Do not believe what you hear because I say it, or because somebody else says it. Go to the Word of God to learn what you need to know, and to the Spirit of God to teach you the meaning of what you read.

19, 20. *Now Jesus knew that they were desirous to ask him, and said unto them, Do ye enquire among yourselves of that I said, A little while, and ye shall not see me: and again, a little while, and ye shall see me? Verily, verily, I say unto you, That ye shall weep and lament,*

Christ would die; he would go away and be unseen. On the cross he would depart out of this life; in the tomb he would be hidden from his disciples: "Ye shall weep and lament."

20. *But the world shall rejoice:*

But not for long; the world's joy at Christ's death was soon over.

20. *And ye shall be sorrowful, but your sorrow shall be turned into joy.*

I think we may leave off our reading at this verse, with these words to flavour our mouth all this week: "Your sorrow shall be turned into joy." God grant that it may be so with many here present, for Christ's sake! Amen.

Hymns from "Our Own Hymn Book"—282, 820, 802.

Metropolitan Tabernacle Pulpit.

THE WINNOWING FAN.

A Sermon

DELIVERED ON LORD'S-DAY MORNING, JULY 10TH, 1870, BY

C. H. SPURGEON,

AT THE METROPOLITAN TABERNACLE, NEWINGTON.

"Follow peace with all men, and holiness, without which no man shall see the Lord: looking diligently lest any man fail of the grace of God; lest any root of bitterness springing up trouble you, and thereby many be defiled."—
Hebrews xii. 14, 15.

WELL did the apostle declare that the righteous scarcely are saved. It is no child's-play to be a Christian. The Christian life is beyond the poet's meaning, real and earnest. The hills of difficulty which lie before us are no molehills, and the giants and dragons with which we must contend are no phantoms of a disordered brain. When we reach heaven, what monuments of grace we shall be, and how shall we throughout eternity emulate one another's praises, each one feeling himself to be the deepest debtor to sovereign grace! It will be well for us to remember that the religion of Jesus Christ is not a matter of trifling, that the gaining of heaven is not to be achieved by a few half-hearted efforts; and if we will at the same time recollect that all-sufficient succour is prepared for us in the covenant of grace, we shall be in a right state of mind, resolute yet humble, leaning upon the merits of Christ and yet aiming after personal holiness. I trust that in my ministry I shall never keep back the doctrines of the grace of God, but I am anxious at the same time with equal clearness to declare the doctrine that good works are necessary evidences of grace. I am persuaded that if self-righteousness be deadly, self-indulgence is ruinous. Rowland Hill said he had spent a large part of his life in battling with the white devil of Arminianism, but he would now fight the black devil of Antinomianism. I desire to maintain always a balance in my ministry, and while combating self-righteousness to war perpetually with loose living. Antinomianism is a black devil indeed, a devil whose smutty fingers have defiled full many of the pure truths of our holy faith, and made even good men shy of receiving them. We must remember that though we are saved by grace, yet grace does not stupify us, but rather quickens us into action; and though salvation depends upon the merits of Christ, yet those who receive those merits receive with them a faith which produces holiness.

The text before us is so full of weighty matter, and my own heart is so full of solemn searchings, that I despair of speaking to you all that the text has spoken to me. May the Holy Spirit, the author of sanctification,

No. 940.

help me, and bless the word to you. I beg you to notice that there are before us *two things to be followed and two things to be avoided.*

I. There are in the text TWO THINGS TO BE FOLLOWED. The fourteenth verse tells us what they are. "Follow *peace* with all men, and *holiness*, without which no man shall see the Lord." We are to follow peace and holiness, the two are consistent with each other and may be followed together. Peace is to be studied, but not such a peace as would lead us to violate holiness by conforming to the ways of unregenerate and impure men. We are only so far to yield for peace sake as never to yield a principle; we are to be so far peaceful as never to be at peace with sin: peaceful with men, but contending earnestly against evil principles. "Follow peace," but let the following of it be guarded by the other precept, "holiness." With equal ardour we are to follow holiness. Some who have aimed at holiness have made the great mistake of supposing it needful to be morose, contentious, faultfinding, and censorious with everybody else. Their holiness has consisted of negatives, protests, and oppositions for opposition sake. Their religion mainly lies in contrarieties and singularities; to them the text offers this wise counsel, follow holiness, but also follow peace. Courtesy is not inconsistent with faithfulness. It is not needful to be savage in order to be sanctified. A bitter spirit is a poor companion for a renewed heart. Let your determination for principle be sweetened by tenderness towards your fellow men. Be resolute for the right, but be also gentle, pitiful, courteous. Consider the meekness as well as the boldness of Jesus. Follow peace, but not at the expense of holiness. Follow holiness, but do not needlessly endanger peace.

Having thus hinted at the connection between the two, and how the two together make up a complete character, let us now take them one by one.

Follow *peace*, "peace with all" says the text—an amplification of the expression. Follow peace with all the church. There should be no quarrels within the sacred enclosure which the electing love of God has made. Ye are one in the divine choice, ye are one by the Saviour's purchase, ye are one by the Spirit's calling, ye have one Lord, one faith, one baptism, ye are on the way to one heaven; see that ye fall not out by the way. "Let brotherly love continue." Let each esteem others better than himself; let each seek his brother's good to edification. Let us by no means be divided in heart, for schisms grieve the Holy Spirit, destroy our comfort, weaken our graces, afford occasion for gainsayers, and bring a thousand ills upon us. Whereas in these evil days the church is so much divided into denominations and sections, follow peace with all those who love the Lord Jesus Christ in sincerity. Hold what you believe with firmness, for you are not to trifle with God's truth; but wherever you see anything of Christ, there confess relationship, and act as a brother towards your brother in Christ.

Follow peace with all, especially with your own relatives and friends at home. Call we that man a Christian who will not speak with his own brother? We may call him such, but such he cannot be. "If he love not his brother whom he hath seen, how can he love God whom he hath not seen?" When we hear of strifes between husband and wife, between brother and sister, between father and child, we are ashamed that the name of Christ should be connected with such unhallowed contentions. Instead of bidding such persons follow after holiness, I would speak to them as unto carnal, and bid them first bring forth fruits meet for repentance. Do not even publicans and sinners love their own relatives? Are they not often forgiving and gentle? How is it, then, that you, calling yourself a follower of Christ, allow enmity to reign in your spirit? What are your gifts and worshipping while wrath rules within your bosom? What hast thou to do with worshipping God? Leave thy gift before the altar, and go thy way; first be reconciled to thy brother, and then come and offer thy gift.

Follow peace with all your neighbours. A Christian man should not make himself hated by all around him, yet there are some who seem to fancy that they are true to their religion in proportion as they make themselves disagreeable. Win your neighbours by your willingness to oblige; disarm their opposition, if possible, by courtesy, by charitableness, by kindness. "Blessed are the peacemakers, for they shall be called the children of God." "The servant of the Lord must not strive, but be gentle unto all." Do not sow nettles, nor scatter thistle-seeds, but let the peaceful honeysuckle and loving jasmine adorn your porch. Salute each neighbour's dwelling with "peace be to this house." Let the peacefulness of your deportment shame those who delight in ill will and strife; and may the Lord of Peace himself give you peace, always by all means.

"Follow peace with all," that is, even with persecutors. Believers in Paul's day were commanded not to resent the evil done to them; they were to render to no man evil for evil, but to follow that which is good both among themselves and to all. They were put in prison, they were robbed, calumniated, and even cruelly tormented; and yet it is wonderful to observe in history how meekly they endured their afflictions. Scarcely in any case was a word uttered by them inconsistent with the gentleness of their Saviour. Now and then a hot spirit would pronounce a fiery denunciation of the cruelties practised against the followers of Jesus. but as a rule the saints were led like sheep to the slaughter, and suffered in all the glory of patient innocence. Here is the patience of the saints! Even thus it should be at this day. We are to follow peace with the most infidel, the most superstitious, the most wicked, the most cruel. If they will fight, let the fighting be all on one side; or if we take up any weapons, let the weapons be those of longsuffering and of love; let us kill fire with fire, and by the flame of love overcome the flame of hatred. The anvil after all breaks the hammer, because it bears every stroke and returns none; so be it with the Christian. "Love your enemies, bless them that curse you, do good to them that hate you, and pray for them which despitefully use you, and persecute you."

The text says, "*Follow* peace," and the word "follow" indicates a hunter in pursuit of his game. He tracks the footsteps of his prey, he follows it over hill and dale, by the edge of the precipice, over the dangerous ridge, across the brook and along the river, through the wood and down the glen. Follow peace in this way; that is, do not merely be peaceful if nobody irritates you, but go out of your way to be peaceful; give up many things that you have a right to enjoy; the respect that is due to you be willing to forego ; in fine, yield all. but truth for peace sake. "Charity suffereth long, and is kind." "Charity beareth all things, hopeth all things, endureth all things." Often the Alpine hunter, when pursuing the chamois, will leap from crag to crag, will wear out the live-long day, will spend the night upon the mountain's cold brow, and then descend to the valleys, and up again to the hills, as though he could never tire, and could never rest until he has found his prey. So perseveringly, with strong resolve to imitate your Lord and Master, follow peace with all.

Stand thee still awhile, my brother, and let me warn thee that thou canst not follow peace with yonder burden on thy back. What is it ? It is a mass of pride. Thou canst not follow peace if thou be proud. Proud men must raise strife by their pride. Even if they try to exhibit good nature, yet pride neutralises all, and inevitably excites envy and opposition. Even God himself never sees a proud man but he resolves to pull him down : it is a part of the very nature of all intelligent beings to be offended at pride, and to desire its fall. What hast thou to be proud of ? Has God given thee riches? Thou art so much the deeper in his debt. Is that a thing to boast about ? Has God given thee talent? Thou art so much the more in danger of being led astray by thine own presumption. Is thy greater danger a cause for pride? If thy position be higher, thou hast the more responsibility; think less of thy height, and more of the responsibility which it involves. Walk humbly, or thou canst not follow peace.

Nor canst thou follow peace whose heart is full of envy. It is true thou hast not the wealth of another—what would it profit thee if he were as poor as thyself ? It is true thou hast not the talent of another—in what respects wouldst thou be better if that man's gifts were taken from him? Why, man, I will be bound to say, thou hast after all as much as thou wilt make good use of, and if not, thy brother's loss would not make thee the richer. It is wrong to be proud, but it is equally wrong to be envious. An envious man is sure to see faults where they do not exist, and so he makes trouble. Envy paints upon the diseased eyeballs of her victims the faults of others; the faults they see are rather in themselves than in others, yet they think they see them there. Lay aside thy envy. Rejoice that another is happier and better than thou art; rejoice in his happiness, it is the way to increase thine own; rejoice in his goodness, it will make thee better. If thou wouldst double thy joy, enjoy another's joy, and thank God that he hath it.

Nor can you follow peace, my dear friend, you with the swift-moving tongue. It were not amiss that it moved so rapidly if it carried better burdens; but thou art a tale-bearer amongst thy brethren, thy tongue speaketh more than is true, and much more than is kind. If thou perceivest even a little offence in a brother, how quick thou art to spread it with exaggerations of thine own ! How canst thou follow peace till thou hast asked God to bridle thy tongue? What has an untamed, unruly tongue to do with peace ? It is the great creator and fomenter of discord. More mischief is made by idle tittle-tattle than by downright malice. The mischief that men resolve to do is very small compared with what men *and women* incidentally do by mere thoughtless love of saying something. Thou shalt not gossip, is a commandment which lies in "thou shalt not bear false witness," and is akin to "thou shalt not kill." Follow peace with all, and restrain that busy and wicked member, which James calls a world of iniquity, that "setteth on fire the wheel of nature, and is set on fire of hell."

If we would follow peace we must gird our loins with the girdle of forbearance; we must resolve that as we will not give offence, so neither will we take offence, or if offence be felt we must resolve to forgive. After sundown let us never harbour remembrance of an injury. As even the wasp's sting dies when the sun sets, so let our resentments pass away. Boundless is the forgiveness of Christ, so let our forgiveness be. Until seventy times seven, said Christ to Peter; we have not yet reached that, and if we have, let us begin another seventy times seven, for God has forgiven us countless numbers of offences. If any tell us that this is to be mean spirited, let us tell them it is to be Christ-like; and if they call the Master mean spirited, we of his household will be content to be called the same. After all, what is grander than patience? What a holy vengeance it is to heap coals of fire upon an adversary's head by returning kindness for malice? O ye who are the people of God, remember that your name is men of peace, that your God is the God of peace, that your Saviour is the Prince of peace, that the gospel is the gospel of peace, that the ministers are ambassadors of peace, that your heritage on earth is your Saviour's legacy of peace, and that your heaven is peace. "If it be possible, as much as lieth in you live peaceably with all men." This is the winning post towards which you are to run; the crown of olive and not the wreath of laurel is to be your coveted prize.

The second object of pursuit is a still higher attainment—would God we had reached it. "Follow peace with all men, and *holiness*." The amplification of the term "holiness" is the solemn declaration, "without which no man shall see the Lord." Certain theologians are so averse to the preaching of practical holiness, that they have tried to import into these words the idea of imputed righteousness. In imputed righteousness I glory, but it is not mentioned here. No, my hearer, it is utterly impossible that the text should mean anything of the kind, because you will observe that we are to "*follow*" it, whatever it may be. Now, we do not follow imputed righteousness, for as soon as we put our trust in Christ we are justified through his righteousness; it is not a grace to be followed, it is a boon possessed already by every Christian. This text deals with inward, personal holiness, and nothing else. Imputed holiness is a gross misuse of terms; it is not scriptural, and it is a thorough perversion of this passage to force such a sense upon it. This is a holiness produced in us by the Holy Ghost, which we progressively manifest in our hearts and lives.

"Follow holiness, without which no man can see the Lord." I understand by this sentence, in the first place, that no person who is unholy can see or understand Christ the Lord, or God his Father; that is to say, he does not know who Christ is so as to have any real fellowship with him. He may know his name, and know his history, and have some theoretical ideas of what the Redeemer did and is, but he cannot see with spiritual eyesight as holy men do; he cannot, in fact, discern the spiritual character and teaching of the Lord.

But perhaps the great meaning lies in this—without holiness no man can see the Lord in heaven at last. He will see him on the throne of judgment, but he cannot see him as his friend, he cannot see him in that beatific vision which is appointed for the sanctified, he cannot see him so as to find joy and delight in the sight of him; he will not be able to enjoy eternal fellowship with God, he will not be permitted to enter heaven—

> "Those holy gates for ever bar
> Pollution, sin, and shame;
> None can obtain admittance there
> But followers of the Lamb."

God is so holy that he never can have fellowship with unholy creatures. Heaven, the court of God, is so holy that never can unholy beings tread its hallowed pavement. An angel once became unholy, and from the battlements of heaven he was hurled into the deeps of hell. God willed to save his elect, but he would not bring them to heaven until he had sanctified them; he, therefore, sent his Son to die, that from his wounded side might flow the purifying stream. Surely he who would not spare Satan, the bright archangel, will not admit polluted man to heaven; and he who put his Son to death to bring his own elect to heaven, by purifying them from sin, will not bring any of us there if we remain unholy and submit not ourselves to the gospel of Jesus Christ. This is the object of election—" God hath chosen us from the beginning that we should be holy." This is the very end of our calling. "He hath called to virtue and holiness." "As he that hath called you is holy, be ye holy in all manner of conversation." This is the work of the Holy Spirit, he sanctifies the soul, and purifies us day by day. This is the test of likeness to Christ, for it is in true holiness that we are conformed unto the image of God's dear Son. Unholy men cannot enter heaven, it is impossible. Sooner might God die than unholiness live in his presence.

Now, see, my dear friends, the text says, "*Follow* holiness;" *follow* it, that is to say, you will not gain it by standing still. Nobody ever grew holy without consenting, desiring, and agonising to be holy. Sin will grow without sowing, but holiness needs cultivation. Follow it, it will not run after you. You must pursue it with determination, with eagerness, with long-continued perseverance, as a hunter pursues his prey. You have not yet gained all the holiness which you may have and ought to have. You are in some respects holy, all of you who have believed, for you are sanctified and set apart by God the Father; you are also rendered holy, in some respects, by being dedicated to Christ and being consecrated as his servants, but you have need to follow the holiness which the Spirit of God works in you; and I do beseech you, beseeching most of all myself, listen to this word—"Follow holiness."

Ah, dear friends, this is a very high and lofty text, and almost too high to be addressed to some professors; for some who bear the name of Christ have not even followed after morality yet, much less after holiness. Now, holiness is far beyond morality, and you cannot be holy while you are not even moral. I blush to confess that some professors are unchaste; professors, alas! even in this church have vexed us with uncleanness. I may not know who, in each particular case, may now be guilty of this sin, but such have been, such are, such will be, I fear, among the faithful; men who can talk well about Christ, and yet who are living in secret indulgence of lewdness. Persons will dare to profess the religion of Christ who can enjoy a lascivious song and broad talk, who are given to what is softly styled imprudence, which is really impurity. Impure familiarities, glances, and sports, are the commencement of actual crimes. Men and women who in any way injure their delicacy and modesty, by insensible degrees, proceed to overt sin. All men wonder when a professor falls into foul sin, but they would not wonder if they knew how long the transgressor had gone to the verge of the precipice; the wonder would be rather that the moth had not burnt its wings in the candle long before. Oh, hate the very thoughts of uncleanness! Your members are members of Christ, your bodies are to be raised in the image of Christ; defile them not, but walk with the utmost purity as in the sight of the thrice holy God.

Alas! I must further confess that some professors are not yet even honest. Shall I talk with them about being holy, when in their trade they cheat, and misrepresent, and lie! Should we see so many religious bankrupts, so many names before the civil courts, of religious knaves and scoundrels, if there were not good need to preach plain morality even in the visible church of God? I do preach it, I dare not do otherwise, even at the risk of having it thrown in my teeth by the enemies of religion. How can I talk of holiness to those who are dishonest in trading? Shame upon you to couple God's name with your knaveries. Get ye hence. What have ye to do with Christ? Ye are his crucifiers; ye put him to an open shame. I tell such even weeping, that they above all others are the enemies of the cross of Christ.

Mournfully, I must go on and accuse some professors of being drunken. There are still mingled with our churches, even with our Nonconforming churches, those who put but small restraints upon their animal appetites; who are overcharged with drunkenness in their parties and in secret. They talk like the disciples of Christ, and eat and drink like the followers of Epicurus. Men given to wine cannot be filled with the Spirit. What though they are not seen staggering in the streets, is their excess one whit the less sinful than that of the public drunkard? "Ye have lived in pleasure on the earth, and have been wanton; ye have nourished your hearts, as in a day of slaughter." Is not this living unto the flesh? And shall ye not die?

There be some, again, who have not yet attained to be industrious. We have those in the church who are shamefully idle, who if they could but live on the alms of the church, would never do a handsturn for themselves, and how the grace of God can live in a lazy man I know not. If laziness is detestable to good men, much more must it be to God. "My Father worketh hitherto, and I work," says Christ. You find no idleness among angels or saints, yet these men would eat other men's bread, and deserve to be put upon the rations appointed for such by the apostle Paul, "If any will not work, neither let him eat."

Now if I have to speak of such sins as these that are common among ungodly men, well may my heart ache when I see them in the church of

God. I am wearied with the sins of professors, and sore vexed with their inconsistences. I long to present you as a chaste virgin unto Christ, and lo! I see sin and folly in Israel. Achan troubleth the camp. How can we talk of holiness to men who fall short even in morality? Holiness is better than morality, it includes it, it goes beyond it. Holiness affects the heart, holiness respects the motive, holiness regards the whole nature of man. A moral man does not do wrong in act, a holy man hates the thought of doing wrong; a moral man does not swear, but a holy man adores; a moral man would not commit outward sin, a holy man would not commit inward sin, and over that inward sin, if committed, he would pour forth floods of tears. I can hardly explain to you the word "holy," except by calling you to notice that it comes from the same Saxon root as the words "heal," "whole," and "all." A man who is made spiritually whole is a complete man, all the virtues are there; his heart is right as well as his outward acts. Heal, all, whole, wholly, holy, by these steps you reach the word. A holy man aims to be like God, complete in his character, motives, and thoughts, renewed after the image of him that created him in righteousness and true holiness. Did not that word stagger you as I read the chapter this morning? Was not that a wonderful expression? "Partakers of *his* holiness"! That you and I should share in the holiness of God, is not this a lofty thing: and yet we must have no less than this, for without it we shall not see God.

"This is a hard saying," says one, "you judge us too severely." Brethren, I judge you not, it is God's word that judgeth, and I pray you regard its infallible utterance: "Without holiness no man shall see the Lord." In the Greek there are no less than three negatives in this passage, as though it said, "No never, no man shall see the Lord." Is he a great preacher? Without holiness he may preach, and he may win souls, but he shall never see the Lord. Is he a great giver to the cause of God? Yes, very liberal, but without holiness he shall not see the Lord. "He said he believed in Jesus Christ, and he talked a great deal about inward experience." That may be, but without holiness, whoever he may be, he shall never see God face to face. There will be no exception made for any one of us, we must all go into that scale and be weighed there, and if we be devoid of holiness, much more if we be destitute of common morality, we shall never see the Lord. Heaven and earth shall pass away, but this word shall never pass away. If we follow not after holiness, at the gates of heaven we shall find ourselves repulsed; hope as we may, and boast as we may, neither you nor I, without holiness, shall ever get one joyful glimpse of God.

II. Thus have I spoken on the two things to be followed, and now, with the Holy Spirit's help, I will speak on the TWO THINGS TO BE AVOIDED. These are in the next verse: "Looking diligently, lest any man fail of the grace of God." The first thing to be avoided is *failure*. Even those who believe in the doctrine of falling from grace, have honestly conceded that this text does not mean that men may fall from the grace of God, though the marginal reading might imply that. The Greek would not bear such a rendering. There are some persons who for a time appear to possess the grace of God, and for awhile exhibit many outward evidences of being Christians, but at last *the* temptation come, most suitable to their depraved tastes, and they are carried away with it. They fail of the grace of God. They appear to have gained it, but they fail at last ; like a man in business who makes money for a time, but fails in the end. They fail of the grace of God—like an arrow shot from the bow, which goes straight towards the target for a time, but having too little impetus, fails to reach the mark. There are some who did run well, what doth hinder them that they should not obey the truth ?

> "Th' apostate soul doth tire and faint,
> And walk the ways of God no more;
> He is esteemed almost a saint,
> Yet makes his own damnation sure."

Perhaps a more dangerous way of failing of the grace of God may be this. Some have maintained an admirable character to all appearance all their lives, and yet have failed of the grace of God because of some secret sin. They persuaded even themselves that they were believers, and yet they were not truly so; they had no inward holiness, they allowed one sin to get the mastery, they indulged in an unsanctified passion, and so though they were laid in the grave like sheep, they died with a false hope, and missed eternal life. This is a most dreadful state to be in, and perhaps some of us are in it. Let the prayer be breathed, "Search me, O God, and know my heart : try me, and know my thoughts: and see if there be any wicked way in me, and lead me in the way everlasting." Are ye earnest in secret prayer? Do ye love the reading of the Bible? Have ye the fear of God before your eyes? Do you really commune with God? Do you truly love Christ? Ask yourselves these questions often, for though we preach the free gospel of Jesus Christ, I hope as plainly as any, we feel it to be just as needful to set you on self-examination and to excite in you a holy anxiety. It ought to be often a question with you, "Have I the grace of God, or do I fall short of it? Am I a piece of rock crystal which is very like the diamond, but yet is not diamond ? Am I like that famous wheel we have all heard so much of lately which had been revolving on its axis so long, but which had an unseen flaw in it, and therefore at last on its journey it snapped and destroyed many lives? Am I just that? Have I been revolving for years in my profession, and shall I break down at last with the whole weight of my eternal interests to be thereby eternally ruined ?

My dear friends, hear ye earnestly the text, it says, " *Looking diligently* lest any man fail of the grace of God." The word is " *episcopountes,*" a word which signifies overseeing, being true bishops, looking diligently as a man on the watchtower watches for the coming foe. See the sentry pace the rampart, he looks in one direction and he sees the brushwood stirred, he half thinks it is the foe, and suspects an ambush there ; he looks to the front, across the sea, does he not discern a sail in the distance? The attack may be from the seaboard; he looks to the right, across the plain, and if even a little dust should move he watches lest the foe should be on foot. So in the church of God each one should be on his watchtower for himself and for others, watching diligently lest any man fail of the grace of God. The first person who is likely to fail in this church is myself. Each one ought to feel that; the beginning of the watch should therefore be at home.

Depend upon it, dear friends, if there be anyone likely to fall into sin it is yourself. Though I say you, I mean myself as well. Each man is himself most in danger. If you say, "I do not think so," then there is the more reason that you should think so. If upon hearing of anyone falling into sin you have said, "I do not understand it, I know I never should have done so," it is very likely you will, ere long, fall into the same or equally vile sin. You are just the man. Those who think they stand are the men who fall. "If any man thinketh he standeth, let him take heed lest he fall." You who lie low on your faces before God in self-distrust, feeling your liability to err, and asking to be kept every day, you are the least likely to fall of any ; but those who say in Pharasaic confidence, "What fools others are to be led astray in that way, I am not one of them," they are fools themselves. God help you, when you are self-reliant, for your feet have almost gone, if not to any other sin, at all events in the direction of pride; and remember a man may as easily be damned by pride as by dishonesty.

Then, next, exercise watchfulness over others. How many persons might be saved from backsliding by a little oversight! If we would speak to the brother kindly and considerately, when we think he is growing a little cold, we might restore him. We need not always speak directly to him by way of rebuke, but we may place a suggestive book in his way, or speak generally upon the subject. Love can invent many ways of warning a friend without making him angry, and a holy example will also prove a great rebuke to sin. The very presence of some men is a check and guide to others. In the church we ought to bear one another's burden, and so fulfil the law of Christ, exercising the office of bishops over one another, and watching diligently lest any man fail of the grace of God.

The second thing to be avoided is *uprising evil:* "Lest any root of bitterness springing up trouble you, and thereby many be defiled." In the centre of my lawn horse-radish will sprout up; after the smallest shower of rain it rises above the grass and proclaims its vitality. There was a garden there once, and this root maintains its old position. When the gardener cuts it down, it resolves to rise again. Now, if the gardener cannot get it quite out of the ground, it is his business constantly to cut it down. We are but men, and even when associated in church-fellowship, each one brings his own particular poisonous root, and there are sure to be bad roots in the ground. We are to watch diligently lest any of these bitter poisonous roots spring up, for if they do they will trouble us. Sin and error always bring sorrow and division, and thereby many are defiled. Sometimes the root is doctrinal error, and in these days there is a world of it. We must watch diligently lest doctrinal error springs up in our midst. I must confess I have very little charity for many of the errors of modern times, and can never degrade this church by tolerating all sorts of views in it. If men choose errors let them form their own churches; they have no right to thrust their views upon our community. There is a certain form of doctrine which we believe to be scriptural, and if any members deviate from it, their first duty is to leave the church when they can no longer agree with its belief. As long as I am pastor I shall have no controversy about doctrines which are our settled basis of association, but shall bid those who differ go where they can hold their own views in peace; if this should not prove successful, our duty will be to follow peace by extirpating the root of bitterness, and putting the Jonah overboard. Such a case never has occurred, and by God's grace I trust never will, but if it should the church must not hesitate. I am persuaded that doctrinal differences in a church, by breeding the spirit of contention, altogether prevent that church from serving God aright. If we do not agree in the same truth we had better separate; we must be one or we cannot be strong. While we hold one Lord, one faith, one baptism, and are moved by the same spirit, we shall advance to the battle as one man, knit together in the bonds of holy unity; but when roots of bitterness spring up they must be cut down and kept down, or else ultimately they will bring defilement. Doctrinal error leads to practical error, and a church which treats God's doctrine as nothing, will soon allow his precept to be treated in the same way; and this would altogether defile the church of God.

Another root of bitterness, is when *sin* prevails in the church. When they who preached the gospel, or held office in the church, or are members of it, fall into gross and open sin, hell laughs in derision. We should watch diligently against this. Again, I say, each man must watch himself most diligently, and his fellow next. Do, dear friends, guard against the beginning of sin. Rest assured, Christian professors never go into great sins on a sudden; there is first a neglect of private prayer, an indulgence in something which looks innocent but is not, and by degrees it comes to open sin. We cannot, as professors, from the very force of our training and association, plunge into foul sin all of a sudden. It is by degrees that Satan entices us away from our stedfastness, and then at last we fall a prey to the foe. On your knees pray God to crush the eggs of the old dragon before they are hatched; for if you be children of God and go into sin, it will cost you I know not what; it may cost you sorrow to your grave. Poor David, poor David, up to the time of his great sin, what a grand singer he was; but if you read me one of the Psalms, I can tell you whether he wrote it before or after his fall, for before that sad event his songs are jubilant and dance to the music of the timbrel, but afterwards his voice is hoarse, and bass notes preponderate, and you see traces of doubt and unbelief which never appeared before. Beware of his sin lest you fall into his sorrow. And remember, sins which happened to some of God's people of old, and yet they were God's people, if they happened to you would prove that you were not among the people of God at all, for they were placed, many of them, in circumstances which, though they did not excuse the sin, yet somewhat accounted for it. You are not placed in such circumstances, you have more light given you and a clearer revelation of Christ, and therefore more is expected of you, and I tell you in God's sight, if you do not all strive after holiness, it is in vain for you to talk about faith in Christ, for there it stands and always must stand, "Be ye holy, for I am holy;" "Be ye clean, that bear the vessels of the Lord." The Son of Man not only came to seek the lost, but to save them, and what that saving is is explained by his very name. "They shall call his name Jesus, for he shall save his people *from their sins,*" not in their sins, but *from* their sins. Except we, as believers, keep our Lord's commandments and walk according to his will, we shall not be able to comfort ourselves even with the blood of Jesus; for Jesus never died to give us peace while we love sin and live in it. What says the Scripture, "If we walk in the light, as he is in the light, we have fellowship one with another, and the blood of Jesus Christ his Son cleanseth us from all sin," see ye then that only as we are walking in the light as he is in the light, can we have evidence that the blood has cleansed us from sin. God grant us grace to feel the force of this.

If rightly moved by the truths taught in this sermon we shall be very humble. When Isaiah had heard the seraphim cry, "Holy, holy, holy," while the posts of the doors moved, he said, "Woe is me! for I am undone; because I am a man of unclean lips, and I dwell in the midst of a people of unclean lips: for mine eyes have seen the King, the Lord of Hosts." Do you not feel the same? Let humility prevail in your spirit, let it rule in your heart more and more. Do not be afraid of being brought very low; you are never so safe as when you are low. Do not be afraid of having a very humble esteem of yourself. I do not suppose any of us have in our most desponding moments ever grasped the desperate character of our own ruin by nature, and the terrible character of our personal sinfulness apart from Christ. You are undone, in your flesh there dwelleth no clean thing, and even your righteousnesses are as filthy rags. O child of God, get thee to the foot of the cross and lie there. But what then? By all-conquering faith *look up* and say, "Jesus Christ came into the world to save sinners, my faith is fixed on him. O thou precious Lamb of God, like the publican I cry, 'Be merciful to me, a sinner,' renew me, cleanse me, purge me; I hate my sins, deliver me from their power, keep me that I sin not against thee; hold me up and I shall be safe. On the blood which cleanses I depend. O let it come to me in all its purifying, sanctifying, force, and make and keep me pure within!'"

If there be in this house to-day any who have backslidden, I beg them to mourn indeed, and put their trust in Jesus, and begin again. And if there be any professor, young or old, who ought not to be a professor, I ask him either to lay down his profession or make it real. Do not add to your sins this sin of pretending to be a Christian if you are not. Be honest. O do not wound Christ with unnecessary wounds. If you make no profession you will at least be free from the sin of hypocrisy. But I pray you do not sell your birthright for a little pottage. Do not let your God and Saviour go for a little of this world's vanities. May you choose Christ, may you lay hold on him and be laid hold of by him, and may you be kept by him even to the end, that in the last great day Jesus may say of you, "Here am I, and the children whom thou hast given me." If you have never been converted, and have made no profession, still the text has a bearing upon you. Remember, without holiness you cannot see the Lord. "The fear of the Lord is the beginning of wisdom." Faith in Jesus is the basis of holiness. God help you to begin at the cross, and grant you his blessing from this time forth even for ever. Amen.

PORTION OF SCRIPTURE READ BEFORE SERMON—Hebrews xii.

The New Park Street Pulpit.

THE FAINTING WARRIOR.

A Sermon

DELIVERED ON SABBATH MORNING, JANUARY 23RD, 1859, BY THE

REV. C. H. SPURGEON,

AT THE MUSIC HALL, ROYAL SURREY GARDENS.

"O wretched man that I am! who shall deliver me from the body of this death? I thank God, through Jesus Christ our Lord."—Romans vii. 24, 25.

IF I chose to occupy your time with controversial matter, I might prove to a demonstration that the apostle Paul is here describing his own experience as a Christian. Some have affirmed that he is merely declaring what he was before conversion, and not what he was when he became the recipient of the grace of God. But such persons are evidently mistaken, and I believe wilfully mistaken; for any simple-hearted, candid mind, reading through this chapter, could not fall into such an error. It is Paul the apostle, who was not less than the very greatest of the apostles—it is Paul, the mighty servant of God, a very prince in Israel, one of the King's mighty men—it is Paul, the saint and the apostle, who here exclaims, "O wretched man that I am!"

Now, humble Christians are often the dupes of a very foolish error. They look up to certain advanced saints and able ministers, and they say, "Surely, such men as these do not suffer as I do; they do not contend with the same evil passions as those which vex and trouble me." Ah! if they knew the hearts of those men, if they could read their inward conflicts, they would soon discover that the nearer a man lives to God, the more intensely has he to mourn over his own evil heart, and the more his Master honours him in his service, the more also doth the evil of the flesh vex and tease him day by day. Perhaps, this error is more natural, as it is certainly more common, with regard to apostolic saints. We have been in the habit of saying, *Saint* Paul, and *Saint* John, as if they were more saints than any other of the children of God. They are all saints whom God has called by his grace, and sanctified by his Spirit; but somehow we very foolishly put the apostles and the early saints into another list, and do not venture to look on them as common mortals. We look upon them as some extraordinary beings, who could not be men of like passions with ourselves. We are told in Scripture that our Saviour was "tempted in all points like as we are;" and yet we fall into the egregious error of imagining that the apostles, who were far inferior to the Lord Jesus, escaped these temptations, and were ignorant of these conflicts. The fact is, if you had seen the apostle Paul, you would have thought he was remarkably like the rest of the chosen family: and if you had talked with him, you would have said, "Why, Paul, I find that your experience and mine exactly agree. You are more faithful, more holy, and more deeply taught than I, but you have the self-

No. 235.

same trials to endure. Nay, in some respects you are more sorely tried than I." Do not look upon the ancient saints as being exempt either from infirmities or sins; and do not regard them with that mystic reverence which almost makes you an idolater. Their holiness is attainable even by you, and their faults are to be censured as much as your own. I believe it is a Christian's duty to force his way into the inner circle of saintship; and if these saints were superior to us in their attainments, as they certainly were, let us follow them; let us press forward up to, yea, and beyond them, for I do not see that this is impossible. We have the same light that they had, the same grace is accessible to us, and why should we rest satisfied until we have distanced them in the heavenly race? Let us bring them down to the sphere of common mortals. If Jesus was the Son of man, and very man, "bone of our bone, and flesh of our flesh;" so were the apostles; and it is an egregious error to suppose that they were not the subjects of the same emotions, and the same inward trials, as the very meanest of the people of God. So far, this may tend to our comfort and to our encouragement, when we find that we are engaged in a battle in which apostles themselves have had to fight.

And now we shall notice this morning, first, *the two natures*; secondly, *their constant battle*; thirdly, we shall step aside and look at *the weary warrior*, and hear him cry, "O wretched man that I am;" and then we shall turn our eye in another direction, and see that fainting warrior girding up his loins to the conflict, and becoming *an expectant victor*, while he shouts, "I thank God through Jesus Christ our Lord."

I. First, then, THE TWO NATURES. Carnal men, unrenewed men, have one nature—a nature which they inherited from their parents, and which, through the ancient transgression of Adam, is evil, only evil, and that continually. Mere human nature, such as is common to every man, has in it many excellent traits, judging of it between man and man. A merely natural man may be honest, upright, kind, and generous, he may have noble and generous thoughts, and may attain unto a true and manly speech; but when we come to matters of true religion, spiritual matters that concern God and eternity, the natural man can do nothing. The carnal mind, whose ever mind it may be, is fallen, and is at enmity to God, does not know the things of God, nor can it ever know them. Now, when a man becomes a Christian, he becomes so through the infusion of a new nature. He is naturally "dead in trespasses and sins," "without God and without hope." The Holy Spirit enters into him, and implants in him a new principle, a new nature, a new life. That life is a high, holy, and supernatural principle; it is, in fact, the divine nature, a ray from the great "Father of Lights;" it is the Spirit of God dwelling in man. Thus, you see, the Christian becomes a double man—two men in one. Some have imagined that the old nature is turned out of the Christian: not so, for the Word of God and experience teach the contrary; the old nature is in the Christian unchanged, unaltered, just the same, as bad as ever it was; while the new nature in him is holy, pure and heavenly; and hence, as we shall have to notice in the next place—hence there arises a conflict between the two.

Now, I want you to notice what the apostle says about these two natures that are in the Christian, for I am about to contrast them. First, in our text the apostle calls the old nature "the *body* of this death." Why does he call it "the *body* of this death?" Some suppose he means these dying bodies; but I do not think so. If it were not for sin, we should have no fault to find with our poor bodies. They are noble works of God, and are not in themselves the cause of sin. Adam in the garden of perfection, felt the body to be no incumbrance, nor if sin were absent should we have any fault to find with our flesh and blood. What, then, is it? I think the apostle calls the evil nature within him a body, *first*, in opposition to those who talk of the relics of corruption in a Christian. I have heard people say that there are relics, remainders and remnants of sin in a believer. Such men do not know much about themselves yet. Oh! it is not a bone, or a rag which is left; it is the whole body of sin that is there—the whole of it, "from the crown of the head to the sole of the foot." Grace does not maim this body and cut away its members; it leaves it entire, although blessed be God, it crucifies it, nailing it to the cross of Christ. *And again*, I think he calls it a body because it is something tangible. We all know that we have a body; it is a thing we can feel; we know it is there. The new nature is a spirit, subtle, and not easy to detect, I sometimes have to question myself as to whether it is there at all. But as for my old nature, that is a body, I can never find it difficult to recognize its existence, it is as apparent as my flesh and bones. As I never doubt that I am in flesh and blood, so I never doubt but what I have sin within me. It is a body—a thing which I can see and feel, and which, to my pain, is ever present with me.

Understand, then, that the old nature of the Christian is a body; it has in it a substance, or, as Calvin puts it, it is *a mass* of corruption. It is not simply a shred, a remnant—the clout of the old garment; but the whole of it is there still. True, it is crushed beneath the foot of grace; it is cast out of its throne; but it is there, there in all its entireness, and in all its sad tangibility, a body of death. But why does he call it a body of *death?* Simply to express what an awful thing this sin is that remains in the heart. It is a body of *death.* I must use a figure, which is always appended to this text, and very properly so. It was the custom of ancient tyrants, when they wished to put men to the most fearful punishments, to tie a dead body to them, placing the two back to back; and there was the living man, with a dead body closely strapped to him, rotting, putrid, corrupting, and this he must drag with him wherever he went. Now, this is just what the Christian has to do. He has within him the new life; he has a living and undying principle, which the Holy Spirit has put within him, but he feels that every day he has to drag about with him this dead body, this body of death, a thing as loathsome, as hideous, as abominable to his new life, as a dead stinking carcase would be to a living man. Francis Quarles gives a picture at the beginning of one of his emblems, of a great skeleton in which a living man is encased. However quaint the fancy, it is not more singular than true. There is the old skeleton man, filthy, corrupt and abominable. He is a cage for the new principle which God has put in the heart. Consider a moment the striking language of our text, "*The body of this death,*" *it is death incarnate, death concentrated,* death dwelling in the very temple of life. Did you ever think what an awful thing death is? The thought is the most abhorrent to human nature. You say you do not fear death, and very properly; but the reason why you do not fear death is because you look to a glorious immortality. Death in itself is a most frightful thing. Now, inbred sin has about it all the unknown terror, all the destructive force, and all the stupendous gloom of death. A poet would be needed to depict the conflict of life with death—to describe a living soul condemned to walk through the black shades of confusion, and to bear incarnate death in its very bowels. But such is the condition of the Christian. As a regenerate man he is a living, bright, immortal spirit; but he has to tread the shades of death. He has to do daily battle with all the tremendous powers of sin, which are as awful, as sublimely terrific, as even the powers of death and hell.

Upon referring to the preceding chapter, we find the evil principle styled "the old man." There is much meaning in that word "old." But let it suffice us to remark, that in age the new nature is not upon an equal footing with the corrupt nature. There are some here who are sixty years old in their humanity, who can scarce number two years in the life of grace. Now pause and meditate upon the warfare in the heart. It is the contest of an infant with a full-grown man, the wrestling of a babe with a giant. Old Adam, like some ancient oak, has thrust his roots into the depths of manhood; can the divine infant uproot him and cast him from his place? This is the work, this is the labour. From its birth the new nature begins the struggle, and it cannot cease from it until the victory be perfectly achieved. Nevertheless, it is the moving of a mountain, the drying up of an ocean the threshing of the hills, and who is sufficient for these things? The heaven-born nature needs, and will receive, the abundant help of its Author, or it would yield in the struggle, subdued beneath the superior strength of its adversary and crushed beneath his enormous weight.

Again, observe, that the old nature of man, which remains in the Christian, is *evil,* and it cannot ever be anything else but evil; for we are told in this chapter, that "in me,"—that is, in my flesh—"there dwelleth no good thing." The old Adam-nature cannot be improved; it cannot be made better; it is hopeless to attempt it. You may do what you please with it; you may educate it, you may instruct it, and thus you may give it more instruments for rebellion, but you cannot make the rebel into the friend, you cannot turn the darkness into light; it is an enemy to God, and an enemy to God it ever must be. On the contrary, the new life which God has given us cannot sin. That is the meaning of a passage in John, where it is said, "The child of God sinneth not; he cannot sin, because he is born of God." The old nature is evil, only evil, and that continually; the new nature is good, wholly good; it knows nothing of sin, except to hate it. Its contact with sin brings it pain and misery, and it cries out, " Woe is me that I dwell in Meshech, that I tabernacle in the tents of Kedar."

I have thus given you some little picture of the two natures. Let me again remind you that these two natures are essentially unchangeable. You cannot make the new nature which God has given you less divine; the old nature you cannot make less impure and earthly. Old Adam is a condemned thing. You may sweep the house, and the evil spirit may seem to go out of it, but he will come back again and bring with him seven other devils more wicked than himself. It is a leper's house, and the leprosy is in every stone from the foundation to the roof; there is no part sound. It is a garment spotted by the flesh; you may wash, and wash, and wash, but you shall never wash it clean; it were foolish to attempt it. Whilst on the other hand the new nature can never be tainted—spotless, holy, and pure, it dwells in our hearts; it rules and reigns there, expecting the day when it shall cast out its enemy, and without a rival it shall be monarch in the heart of man for ever.

II. I have thus described the two combatants; we shall now come in the next place to THEIR BATTLE. There was never deadlier feud in all the world between nations than there is between the two principles, right and wrong. But right and wrong are often divided from one another by distance, and therefore they have a less intense hatred. Suppose an instance: right holds for liberty, therefore right hates the evil of slavery. But we do not so intensely hate slavery as we should do if we saw it before our eyes: then would the blood boil, when we saw our black brother, smitten by the cow-hide whip. Imagine a slaveholder standing here and smiting his poor slave until the red blood gushed forth in a river; can you conceive your indignation? Now it is distance which makes you feel this less acutely. The right forgets the wrong, because it is far away. But suppose now that right and wrong lived in the same house; suppose two such desperate enemies, cribbed, cabined, and confined within this narrow house, *man*; suppose the two compelled to dwell together, can you imagine to what a desperate pitch of fury these two would get with one another. The evil thing says, "I will turn thee out, thou intruder; I cannot be peaceful as I would, I cannot riot as I would, I cannot indulge lust as I would; out with thee, I will never be content until I slay thee." "Nay," says the new-born nature, "I will kill thee, and drive thee out. I will not suffer stick or stone of thee to remain; I have sworn war to the knife with thee; I have taken out the sword and cast away the scabbard, and will never rest till I can sing complete victory over thee, and totally eject thee from this house of mine." They are always at enmity wherever they are; they were never friends, and never can be. The evil must hate the good, and the good must hate the evil.

And mark although we might compare the enmity to the wolf and lamb, yet the new-born nature is not the lamb in all respects. It may be in its innocence and meekness, but it is not in its strength; for the new-born nature has all the omnipotence of God about it, whilst the old nature has all the strength of the evil one in it, which is a strength not easily to be exaggerated, but which we very frequently under-estimate. These two things are ever desperately at enmity with one another. And even when they are both quiet, they hate each other none the less. When my evil nature does not rise, still it hates the new-born nature; and when the new-born nature is inactive, it has nevertheless a thorough abhorrence of all iniquity. The one cannot endure the other; it must endeavour to thrust it forth. Nor do these at any time allow an opportunity to pass from being revenged upon one another. There are times when the old nature is very active, and then how will it ply all the weapons of its deadly armoury against the Christian. You will find yourselves at one time suddenly attacked with anger, and when you guard yourself against the hot temptation, on a sudden you will find pride rising, and you will begin to say in yourself, "Am I not a good man to have kept my temper down?" And the moment you thrust down your pride there will come another temptation, and lust will look out of the window of your eyes, and you desire a thing upon which you ought not to look, and ere you can shut your eyes upon the vanity, sloth in its deadly torpor surrounds you, and you give yourself up to its influence and cease to labour for God. And then when you bestir yourselves once more, you find that in the very attempt to rouse yourself you have awakened your pride. Evil haunts you go where you may, or stand in what posture you choose. On the other hand the new nature will never lose an opportunity of putting down the old. As for the means of grace, the new-born nature will never rest satisfied unless it enjoys them. As for prayer, it will seek by prayer to wrestle with the enemy. It will employ faith, and hope, and love, the threatenings, the promises, providence, grace, and everything else to cast out the evil. "Well," says one, "I dont find it so." Then I am afraid of you. If you do not hate sin so much that you do everything to drive it out, I am afraid you are not a living child of God. Antinomians like to hear you preach about the evil of the heart, but here is the fault with them, they do not like to be told that unless they hate that evil, unless they seek to drive it out, and unless it is the constant disposition of their new-born nature to root it up, they are yet in their sins. Men who only believe their depravity, but do not hate it, are no further than the devil on the road to heaven. It is not my being corrupt that proves me a Christian, nor knowing I am corrupt, but that I hate my corruption. It is my agonizing death struggle with my corruptions that proves me to be a living child of God. These two natures will never cease to struggle so long as we are in this world. The old nature will never give up; it will never cry truce, it will never ask for a treaty to be made between the two. It will always strike as often as it can. When it lies still it will only be preparing for some future battle. The battle of Christian with Apollyon lasted three hours; but the battle of Christian with himself lasted all the way from the Wicket-gate to the River Jordan. The enemy within can never be driven out while we are here. Satan may sometimes be absent from us, and get such a defeat that he is glad to go howling back to his den, but old Adam abideth with us from the first even to the last. He was with us when we first believed in Jesus, and long ere that, and he will be with us till that moment when we shall leave our bones in the grave, our fears in the Jordan, and our sins in oblivion.

Once more observe, that neither of these two natures will be content in the fight without bringing in allies to assist. The evil nature has old relations, and in its endeavour to drive out the grace that is within, it sends off messengers to all its helpers. Like Cherdorlaomer, the King of Elam, it bringeth other kings with it, when it goeth out to battle. "Ah!" says old Adam, "I have friends in the pit." He sends a missive down to the depths, and willing allies come therefrom—spirits from the vasty deep of hell; devils without number come up to the help of their brother. And then, not content with that, the flesh says:—"Ah! I have friends in this *world*;" and then the world sends its fierce cohorts of temptation, such as the lust of the eyes, and the pride of life. What a battle, when sin, Satan, and the world, make a dead-set upon the Christian at once. "Oh," says one, "it is a terrible thing to be a Christian." I assure you it is. It is one of the hardest things in the world to be a child of God; in fact, it is impossible, unless the Lord makes us his children, and keeps us so.

Well, what does the new nature do? When it sees all these enemies, it cries unto the Lord, and then the Lord sends it friends. First comes in to its help, Jehovah, in the everlasting counsel, and reveals to the heart its own interest in the secrets of eternity. Then comes Jesus with his blood. "Thou shalt conquer," says he; "I will make thee more than a conqueror through my death." And then appears the Holy Spirit, the Comforter. With such assistance, this new-born nature is more than a match for its enemies. God will sometimes leave that new nature alone, to let it know its own weakness; but it shall not be for long, lest it should sink in despair. Are you fighting with the enemy to-day, my dear Christian brethren? Are Satan, the flesh, and the world—that hellish trinity—all against you? Remember, there is a divine trinity for you. Fight on, though like Valiant-for-Truth, your blood runs from your hand and glues your sword to your arm. Fight on! for with you are the legions of heaven; God himself is with you; Jehovah Nissi is your banner, and Jehovah Rophi is the healer of your wounds. You shall overcome; for who can defeat Omnipotence, or trample divinity beneath his foot?

I have thus endeavoured to describe the conflict; but understand me, it cannot be described. We must say, as Hart does in his hymn, when after singing the emotions of his soul, he says—

"But, brethren, you can surely guess,
For you perhaps have felt the same."

If you could see a plain upon which a battle is fought, you would see how the ground is torn up by the wheels of the cannon, by the horse hoofs, and by the trampling of men. What desolation is to be seen, where once the golden crops of harvest grew. How is the ground sodden with the blood of the slain. How frightful the result of this terrible struggle. But if you could see the believers' heart after a spiritual battle, you would find it just a counterpart of the battle-field—as much cut up as the ground of the battle-field after the direst conflict that men or fiends have ever waged. For, think: we are combating man with himself; nay, more, man with the whole world; nay, more, man with hell; God with man, against man, the world and hell. What a fight is that! It were worth an angel's while to come from the remotest fields of ether to behold such a conflict.

III. We come now to notice THE WEARY COMBATANT. He lifts up his voice, and weeping he cries, "O wretched man that I am! who shall deliver me from the body of this death?" It is the cry of a panting warrior. He has fought so long that he has lost his breath, and he draws it in again; he takes breath by prayer. "O wretched man that I am! who shall deliver me from the body of this death?" He will not give up the conflict; he knows he cannot, and he dare not. That thought does not enter into his mind; but the conflict is so sore, the battle so furious, that he is almost defeated; he sits down to refresh himself, and thus he sighs out his soul; like the panting hart, longing for the water brook, he says, "O wretched man that I am." Nay, it is more than that. It is the cry of one who is fainting. He has fought till all his strength is spent, and he falls back into the arms of his Redeemer with this fainting gasp, "O wretched man that I am!" His strength has failed him; he is sorely beaten in the battle; he feels that without the help of God he is so totally defeated that he commences his own wail of defeat, "O wretched man that I am." And then he asks this question, "Who shall deliver me?" And there comes a voice from the Law, "I cannot and I will not." There comes a voice from Conscience, "I can make thee see the battle, but I cannot help thee in it." And then there comes a cry from old Human Nature, and that says, "Ah! none can deliver thee, I shall yet destroy thee; thou shalt fall by the hand of thine enemy; the house of David shall be destroyed, and Saul shall live and reign for ever." And the poor fainting soldier cries again, "Who shall deliver me?" It seems a hopeless case, and I believe that sometimes the true Christian may think himself hopelessly given over to the power of sin.

The wretchedness of Paul, I think, lay in two things, which are enough to make any man wretched. Paul believed the doctrine of human responsibility, and yet he felt the doctrine of human inability. I have heard people say sometimes—"You tell the sinner that he cannot believe and repent without the help of the Holy Spirit, and yet you tell him that it is his duty to believe and repent. How are these two to be reconciled? We reply that they do not want any reconciliation; they are two truths of Holy Scripture, and we leave them to reconcile themselves, they are friends, and friends do not need any reconciliation. But what seems a difficulty as a matter of doctrine is clear as daylight as a matter of experience. I know it is my duty to be perfect, but I am conscious I cannot be. I know that every time I commit sin I am guilty, and yet I am quite certain that I must sin—that my nature is such that I cannot help it. I feel that I am unable to get rid of this body of sin and death, and yet I know I ought to get rid of it. These two things are enough to make any man miserable—to know that he is responsible for his sinful nature, and yet to know that he cannot get rid of it—to know that he ought to keep it down, and yet to feel he cannot—to know that it is his business to keep God's law perfectly, and walk in the commandments of the law blameless, and yet to know by sad experience that he is as unable to do so as he is to reverse the motion of the globe, or dash the sun from the centre of the spheres. Now will not these two things drive any man to desperation? The way in which some men avoid the dilemma, is by a denial of one of these truths. They say, "Well, it is true I am unable to cease from sin;" and then they deny their obligation to do so; they do not cry, "O wretched man that I am;" they live as they like, and say they cannot help it. On the other hand, there are some men who know they are responsible; but then they say, "Ay, but I can cast off my sin," and these are tolerably happy. The Arminian and the hyper-Calvinist both of them get on very comfortably; but the man who believes these two doctrines, as taught in God's Word, that he is responsible for sin and yet that he is unable to get rid of it, I do not wonder that when he looks into himself he finds enough to make him sigh and cry, even to faintness and despair, "O wretched man that I am! who shall deliver me from the body of this death."

And now says one, "Ah, I would not be a Christian, if that is the way in which he faints—if he is always to be fighting with himself, and even until he despairs of victory." Stop a moment. Let us complete the picture. This man is fainting; but he will be restored by-and-bye. Think not that he is hopelessly defeated, he falls to rise, he faints but to be revived afresh. I know a magic, which can awaken his sleeping hopes, and shoot a thrill along the freezing current of his blood. Let us sound the promise in his ear, see how soon he revives. Let us put the cordial to his lips; see how he starts up and plays the man again. "I have been almost defeated" says he, "almost driven to despair. Rejoice not over me, O mine enemy; though I fall, yet shall I rise again." And he lets fly against him once more, shouting, "I thank God through Jesus Christ our Lord." So on he goes again, more than a conqueror, through him that has loved him.

IV. This brings me to this last point, that THE CHRISTIAN IS TO BE A CONQUEROR AT LAST. Do you think that we are for ever to be the drudges and the slaves of sin? Am I for ever to be the galley-slave of my own nature, to tug for freedom and never to escape? Am I always to have this dead man chained to my back, and sniff the pestiferous exhalations of his putrid body? No, no, no, that which is within my heart, is like a caged eagle; and I know that soon the bars which confine me shall be broken; the door of my cage shall be opened, and I shall mount with my eye upon the sun of glory, soaring upward, true to the line, moving neither to the right hand nor to the left, flying till I reach my eyrie in the everlasting rocks of God's eternal love. No, we that love the Lord are not for ever to dwell in Meshech. The dust may besmear our robes, and filth may be upon our brow, and beggared may be our garment, but we shall not be so for ever. The day is coming when we shall rise and shake ourselves from the dust, and put on our beautiful garments. It is true we are now like Israel in Canaan. Canaan is full of enemies; but the Canaanites shall and must be driven out. Amalek shall be slain; Agag shall be hewn in pieces; our enemies shall, every one of them, be dispersed, and the whole land from Dan to Beersheba shall be the Lord's. Christians, rejoice! You are soon to be perfect, you are soon to be free from sin, totally free from it, without one wrong inclination, one evil desire. You are soon to be as pure as the angels in light; nay, more, with your Master's garments on you are to be "holy as the holy one." Can you think of that? Is not that the very sum of heaven, the rapture of bliss, the sonnet of the hill-tops of glory—that you are to be perfect? No temptation can reach you from eye, or ear, or hand; nor if the temptation could reach you would you be hurt by it; for there will be nothing in you that could in any way foster sin. It would be as when a spark falls upon an ocean; your holiness would quench it in a moment. Yes, washed in the blood of Jesus, afresh baptized with the Holy Spirit, you are soon to walk the golden streets, white-robed and white-hearted too, and perfect as your Maker, you are to stand before his throne, and sing his praises to eternity.

Now, soldiers of Christ, to arms again! Once more rush into the fight, you cannot be defeated; you must overcome. Though you faint a little, yet take courage; you shall conquer through the blood of the Lamb.

And now, turning aside for a minute, I shall conclude by making an observation or two to many now present. There are some here who say, "I am never disturbed in that fashion." Then I am sorry for you. I will tell you the reason of your false peace. You have not the grace of God in your hearts. If you had you would surely find this conflict within you. Do not despise the Christian because he is in the conflict; despise yourself because you are out of it. The reason why the devil lets you alone is, that he knows you are his. He does not need to trouble you much now; he will have time enough to give you your wages at the last. He troubles the Christian because he is afraid of losing him; he thinks that if he does not tease him here, he shall never have the chance to do it in eternity; so he will bite him, and bark at him while he may. That is why the Christian is vexed more than you are. As for you, you may well be without any pain, for dead men feel no blows. You may well be without prickings of conscience; for men that are corrupt are not likely to feel wounds, though you stab them from head to foot. I pity your condition, for the worm that dieth not is preparing to feed upon you; the eternal vulture of remorse shall soon wet his horrid beak with the blood of your soul. Tremble; for the fires of hell are hot and unquenchable, and the place of perdition is hideous beyond a madman's dream. Oh that you would think of your last end. The Christian may have an evil present but he has a glorious future; but your future is the blackness of darkness for ever. I adjure you by the living God, you that fear not Christ, consider your ways. You and I must give an account for this morning's service. You are warned, men; you are warned! Take heed to yourselves, that ye think not this life to be everything. *There* is a world to come; there is "after death the judgment." If you fear not the Lord, there is after judgment eternal wrath and everlasting misery.

And now a word to those who are seeking Christ. "Ah!" says one, "sir, I have sought Christ, but I feel worse than I ever was in my life. Before I had any thoughts about Christ I felt myself to be good, but now I feel myself to be evil." It is all right, my friend; I am glad to hear you say so. When surgeons heal a patient's wound, they always take care to cut away the proud flesh, because the cure can never be radical while the proud flesh remains. The Lord is getting rid of your self-confidence and self-righteousness. He is just now revealing to your soul the deadly cancer which is festering within you. You are on the sure road to healing, if you are on the way to wounding. God wounds before he heals; he strikes a man dead in his own esteem before he makes him alive. "Ah," cries one, "but can I hope that I ever shall be delivered?" Yes, my brother, if you now look to Christ. I care not what your sin nor what your despair of heart; if you will only turn your eye to him who bled upon the tree, there is not only hope for you, but there is a certainty of salvation. I myself, while thinking over this subject, felt a horror of great darkness rush over my spirit, as I thought what danger I was in lest I should be defeated, and I could not get a glimpse of light into my burdened spirit, until I turned my eye, and saw my Master hanging on the tree. I saw the blood still flowing; faith laid hold upon the sacrifice, and I said, "This cross is the instrument of Jesus's victory, and shall be the means of mine." I looked to his blood; I remembered that I was triumphant in that blood, and I rose from my meditations, humbled, but yet rejoicing; cast down, but not in despair; looking for the victory. Do likewise. "Jesus Christ came into the world to save sinners: believe that. You are an awakened, conscious and penitent sinner; therefore, he came to save you. Believe his word; trust him. Do nothing for your own salvation of yourself, but trust him to do it. Cast yourself simply and only on him; and, as this Bible is true, you shall not find the promise fail you—"He that seeketh findeth; to him that knocketh it shall be opened."

May God help you, by giving you this new life within! May he help you to look to Jesus, and though long and hard be the conflict, sweet shall be the victory.

Metropolitan Tabernacle Pulpit.

ONWARD!

A Sermon

Delivered on Lord's-Day Morning, May 25th, 1873, by

C. H. SPURGEON,

At the Metropolitan Tabernacle, Newington.

"Brethren, I count not myself to have apprehended: but this one thing I do, forgetting those things which are behind, and reaching forth unto those things which are before, I press toward the mark for the prize of the high calling of God in Christ Jesus."—Philippians iii. 13, 14.

So far as his acceptance with God is concerned a Christian is complete in Christ as soon as he believes. Those who have trusted themselves in the hands of the Lord Jesus are saved: and they may enjoy holy confidence upon the matter, for they have a divine warrant for so doing. "There is therefore now no condemnation to them that are in Christ Jesus." To this salvation the apostle had attained. But while the work of Christ for us is perfect, and it were presumption to think of adding to it, the work of the Holy Spirit in us is not perfect, it is continually carried on from day to day, and will need to be continued throughout the whole of our lives. We are being "conformed to the image of Christ," and that process is in operation, as we advance towards glory. The condition in which a believer should always be found is that of progress: his motto must be, "Onward and upward!" Nearly every figure by which Christians are described in the Bible implies this. We are plants of the Lord's field, but we are sown that we may grow—"First the blade, then the ear, then the full corn in the ear." We are born into the family of God; but there are babes, little children, young men, and fathers in Christ Jesus; yea, and there are a few who are perfect or fully developed men in Christ Jesus. It is a growth evermore. Is the Christian described as a pilgrim? He is no pilgrim who sits down as if rooted to the place. "They go from strength to strength." The Christian is compared to a warrior, a wrestler, a competitor in the games: these figures are the very opposite of a condition in which nothing more is to be done. They imply energy, the gathering up of strength, and the concentration of forces, in order to the overthrowing

No. 1,114.

of adversaries. The Christian is also likened to a runner in a race, and that is the figure now before us in the text. It is clear that a man cannot be a runner who merely holds his ground, contented with his position: he only runs aright who each moment nears the mark. Progress is the healthy condition of every Christian man; and he only realises his best estate while he is growing in grace, "adding to his faith virtue," "following on to know the Lord," and daily receiving grace for grace out of the fulness which is treasured up in Christ Jesus.

Now, to this progress the apostle exhorts us—nay, he does more than exhort, he allures us. He stands among us; he does not lecture us *ex cathedra*, standing like a learned master far above his disciples, but he puts himself on our level, and though not a whit behind the very chief of the apostles, he says, "Brethren, I count not myself to have apprehended." He does not give us the details of his own imperfections and deficiencies, but in one word he confesses them in the gross, and then declares that he burned with eager desire for perfection, so that it was the one passion of his soul to press onward towards the great goal of his hopes, the prize of his high calling in Christ Jesus. We cannot desire to have a better instructor than a man who sympathises with us because he humbly considers himself to be of the same rank as ourselves. Teaching us to run, the apostle himself runs; wishing to fire our holy ambition, he bears testimony to that same ambition flaming within his own spirit. I desire so to speak from this text that every believer may pant for progress in the divine life.

Paul's statements in the text call us to look at him under four aspects: first, as *forming a just estimate of his present condition*—"Brethren, I count not myself to have apprehended;" secondly, as *placing his past in its proper position*—"forgetting the things which are behind;" thirdly, as *aspiring eagerly to a more glorious future*—"reaching forth unto those things which are before;" and fourthly, as *practically putting forth every exertion to obtain that which he desired*—"I press toward the mark for the prize of the high calling of God in Christ Jesus."

First, admire our apostle as PUTTING A JUST ESTIMATE UPON HIS PRESENT CONDITION.

He was not one of those who consider the state of the believer's heart to be a trifling matter. He was not indifferent as to his spiritual condition. He says, "I count,"—as if he had taken stock, had made a careful estimate, and had come to a conclusion. He is not a wise man who says, "I am a believer in Christ, and therefore it little matters what are my inward feelings and experience." He who so speaks should remember that keeping the heart with all diligence is a precept of inspiration, and that a careless walk usually comes to a very sorrowful ending. The apostle did take account; but when he had done so he was dissatisfied: "I count not myself to have apprehended." Nor was that dissatisfaction to be regretted: it was a sign of true grace, a conclusion which is always arrived at when saints judge themselves rightly. Most weighty is that word of Chrysostom, "He who thinks he has obtained everything, hath nothing." Had Paul been satisfied with his attainments he would never have sought for more. Most men cry "hold," when they think they have done enough. The man who could honestly write, " I press forward," you may be quite sure was one who felt that he had not yet apprehended all that might be gained. Self-satisfaction rings the death-knell of progress. There must be a deep-seated discontent with present attainments, or there will never be a striving after the things which are yet beyond.

Now, beloved, remark, that the man who in our text tells us that he had not apprehended was a man vastly superior to any of us. Among them that were born of women there has never lived a greater than Paul the apostle; in sufferings for Christ a martyr of the first class; in ministry for Christ an apostle of foremost degree. Where shall I find such a man for revelations? for he had been caught up into the third heaven, and heard words which it was not lawful for him to utter. Where shall I find his match for character? a character splendidly balanced, as nearly approximating to that of his divine Master as we may well expect to see in mortal men. Yet, after having duly considered the matter, this notable saint said, " I count not myself to have apprehended." Shame, then, on any of us poor dwarfs if we are so vain as to count that we have apprehended! Shame upon the indecent self-conceit of any man who congratulates himself upon his own spiritual condition, when Paul himself said, "Not as though I had already attained, either were already perfect." The injury which self-content will do a man it would be hard to measure, it is the readiest way to stunt him, and the surest method to keep him weak. I should be sorry indeed if I should be addressing one who imagines that he has apprehended, for his progress in grace is barred from this time forth. The moment a man says, " I have it," he will no longer try to obtain it; the moment he cries, " It is enough," he will not labour after more.

Yet, brethren, far too often of late have I come across the path of those who speak as if they have apprehended,—brethren whose own lips praise them, who descant upon their own fulness of grace, with an unction rather too unctuous for my taste. I am not about to condemn them; I cannot say I am not about to censure them, for I intend to do so, from a deep sense of the necessity that they should be censured. These friends assure us that they have reached great heights of grace, and are now in splendid spiritual condition. I should be very glad to know that it is so, if it were true; but I am grieved to hear them act as witnesses for themselves, for then I know that their witness is not true: if it were so, they would be the last men to publish it abroad. There are brethren abroad, whose eminent graciousness is not very clear to others, but it is very evident to themselves; and equally vivid is their apprehension of the great inferiority of most of their brethren. They talk to us, not as men of like passions with ourselves and brethren of the same stock, but as demigods, thundering out of the clouds, giants discoursing to the little men around them. If it be true that they are so superior, I rejoice, yea, and will rejoice; but my suspicion is, that their glorying is not good, and that the spirit which they manifest will prove a snare to them. I meet, I say, sometimes with brethren who feel contented with their spiritual condition. They do not ascribe their satisfactory character to themselves, but to the grace of God; but for all that, they do feel that they are what they ought to be, and what others ought to be but are not. They see in themselves a great deal that is good, very much that is commendable, and a large amount of excellence, which they can hold up for the admiration of others. They have reached the "higher life," and are wonderfully fond of telling us so, and explaining the phenomena of their self-satisfied condition. Though Paul was compelled to say, "In me, that is, in my flesh, there dwelleth no good thing," their flesh appears to be of a better quality: whereas he had spiritual conflicts, and found that without were fightings, and within were fears, these very superior persons have already trodden Satan under their feet, and reached a state in which they have little else to do but to divide the spoil. Now, brethren, whenever we meet with persons who can congratulate themselves upon their personal character, or whenever we get into the state of self-content ourselves, there is an ill savour about the whole concern. I do not know what impression it makes upon you, but whenever I hear a brother talk about himself, and how full he is of the Spirit of God, and all that, I am distressed for him. I think I hear the voice of that stately professor, who said, "God, I thank thee that I am not as other men are." I feel that I would prefer to listen to that other man, who said, "God be merciful to me a sinner," and went down to his house justified rather than the other. When I hear a man crow about himself, I think of Peter's declaration—"Though all men should deny thee, yet will not I," and I hear another cock crow. Self-complacency is the mother of spiritual declension. David said, "My mountain standeth firm: I shall never be moved;" but ere long the face of God was hidden and he was troubled. In the presence of a professor who is pleased with his own attainments, one remembers that warning text: "Let him that thinketh he standeth, take heed lest he fall." Great I! great I! wherever thou art, thou must come down. Great I is always opposed to great Christ. John the Baptist knew the truth when he said, "He must increase, but I must decrease." There is no room in this world for God's glory and man's glory. He who is less than nothing, magnifies God; but he "who is rich, and increased in goods, and hath need of nothing," dishonours God, and he himself "is naked and poor and miserable."

Furthermore, we have observed that the best of men do not talk of their attainments; their tone is self-depreciation, not self-content. We have known some eminently holy men, who are now in heaven, and in looking back upon their lives we note that they were never conscious of being what we all thought them to be. Everybody could see their beauty of character except themselves. *They* lamented their imperfections while *we* admired the grace of God in them. I remember a minister of Christ, now with God—I will not mention his name—if I did, it would be familiar to your ears as household words: it was proposed by some of us, when he left the ministry in his old age, that we should hold a meeting to bid him farewell, and testify our esteem for him. It was my duty to propose the fraternal act, but I hesitated as I saw the blush mantle his cheek, and I paused when he rose and besought us never to think of such a thing, for he felt himself to be one of the most unworthy of all the servants of the Lord. Every man of the associated ministers that day assembled, felt that our venerable friend was by far the superior of us all; and yet his own estimate of himself was lowliest of the lowly. He had sacrificed much, but I never heard him speak of his sacrifices; he lived in habitual fellowship with God, but I never heard him declare it, much less glory in it. Shallow streams brawl and babble, but deep waters flow on in silence. Of all the departed saints whom it has been my lot to esteem highly in love for their works' sake, I do not remember one who dared to praise himself, though I can recollect several poor little spiritual babes who did so to their own injury. If ever true saints speak of what God has done by them, they do it in such a modest way that you might think they were talking of some one five hundred miles away, rather than of themselves. They have scrupulously laid all their crowns at the Saviour's feet, not in word only, but in spirit. When I remember these sacred names of the great departed, I feel it hard to have patience with the unspiritual, unholy boastings of personal holiness and high spirituality, which are getting common in these days. Drums make much noise, but we know by observation that it is not their fulness which makes the sound.

Again, we have noticed that we ourselves, in our own holiest moments, do not feel self-complacent. Whenever we get near to God, and really enter into fellowship with him, the sensations we feel are the very reverse of self-congratulation. Job, in this, was the type of every believing man. Till he saw God he spoke up for his own innocence, and defended himself against the charges of his friends; but when the Lord revealed himself to him, he said, "Mine eye seeth *thee*, therefore I abhor myself and repent in dust and ashes." We never see the beauty of Christ without at the same time perceiving our own deformity. When we neglect prayer and self-examination we grow mighty vain fellows, but when we live near to God in private devotion and heart-searching, we put off our ornaments from us. In the light of God's countenance we perceive our many flaws and imperfections, and instead of saying, "I am clean," we cry out, "Woe is me, for I am a man of unclean lips." Now if this be our own experience, we infer from it that those who think well of themselves must know little of that revealing light which humbles all who dwell in it.

My observation of personal character has been somewhat wide, and I cannot help bearing my testimony that I am greatly afraid of men who make loud professions of superior sanctity. I have had the misfortune to have known, on one or two occasions, superfine brethren, who were, in their own ideas, far above the rest of us, and almost free from human frailties. I confess to have felt very much humbled by their eminent goodness until I found them out: they talked of complete sanctification, of a faith which never staggered, of an old nature entirely dead, until I wondered at them; but I wondered more when I found that all the while they were rotten at the core, were negligent of common duties while boasting of the loftiest spirituality, and were even immoral while they condemned others for comparative trifles. I have now become very suspicious of all who cry up their own wares. I had rather have a humble, timid, fearful, watchful, self-depreciating Christian to be my companion, than any of the religious exquisites who crave our admiration. These great-winged eagles who fly so loftily will, I fear, turn out to be unclean birds. The excessive verdure of a superfinely flourishing religiousness often covers a horrible bog of hypocrisy.

Let me add, once more, that whatever shape self-satisfaction may assume—and it bears a great many—it is at bottom nothing but a shirking of the hardship of Christian soldierhood. The Christian soldier has to fight with sins every day, and if he be a man of God, and God's Spirit is in him, he will find he wants all the strength he has, and a great deal more, to maintain his ground and make progress in the divine life. Now, self-contentment is a shirking of the battle, I do not care how it is come by. Some people shirk watchfulness, repentance, and holy care, by believing that the only sanctification they need is already theirs by imputation. They use the work of the Lord Jesus *for* them as though it could thrust away the necessity of the Spirit's work *in* them. Personal holiness they will not hear of: it is legal. If they come across such a text as "Without holiness no man shall see the Lord;" or, "Be not deceived, God is not mocked, whatsoever a man soweth that shall he also reap," they straightway force another meaning upon it, or else forget it altogether. Another class believe that they have perfection in the flesh, while a third attain to the same complacent condition by the notion that they have overcome all their sins by believing that they have done so; as if believing your battles to be won was the same thing as winning them. This, which they call faith, I take the liberty to call a lazy, self-conceited presumption; and though they persuade themselves that their sins are dead, it is certain that their carnal security is vigorous enough, and highly probable that the rest of their sins are only keeping out of the way to let their pride have room to develop itself to ruinous proportions.

You can reach self-complacency by a great many roads. I have known enthusiasts reach it by sheer intoxication of excitement, while Antinomians come at it by imagining that the law is abolished, and that what is sin in others is not sin in saints. There are theories which afford an evil peace to the mind by throwing all blame of sin upon fate, and others which lower the standard of God's demands so as to make them reachable by fallen humanity. Some dream that a mere dead faith in Jesus will save them, let them live as they list; and others that they are already as good as need be.

Many have fallen into the same condition by another error, for they have said, "Well, we cannot conquer all sin, and therefore we need not aim at it. Some of our sins are constitutional, and will never be got rid of." Under these evil impressions they sit down and say, "It is well, O soul, thou art in an excellent condition; sit still and take thine ease, there is little more to be done, there is no need to attempt more." All this is evil to the last degree.

I have used few theological terms, because it does not matter how we get to be self-satisfied, whether by an orthodox or a heterodox mode of reasoning; it is a mischievous thing in any case. The fact is, my brother, the Lord calls us to this high calling of contending with sin within and without until we die; and it is of no use our mincing the matter, we must fight if we would reign; our sins will have to be contended with till our dying day, and probably we shall have to fight upon our death-bed. Therefore, every day we are bound to be upon our watch-tower against sin around and within us. It is of no use our deluding ourselves with pretty theories, which act only as spiritual opium to cause unhealthy dreams. Sin is a real thing with each one of us, and must be daily wrestled with; there is an evil heart of unbelief within us, and the devil without us, and we must watch, and pray, and cry mightily, and strive, and struggle, and own that we have not yet apprehended. If we dream that we are at the goal already, we shall stop short of the prize. The full soul loatheth the honeycomb; a man full of self, cares for nothing more. Shake off these slothful bands, my brethren; quit you like men—be strong. You are as weak as others, and as likely to sin; watch, therefore, and pray, lest ye enter into temptation.

What is it, at bottom, that makes men contented with themselves? It may be, first of all, a forgetfulness of the awful holiness of the law of God. If the law of the ten commandments is to be read only as its letter runs, I could imagine a man's judging himself and saying, "I have apprehended;" but when we know that the law is spiritual, how can we be self-complacent? My dear brother, if thou thinkest thou hast reached its perfect height, I ask thee to hear these words: "Thou shalt love the Lord thy God with all thy heart, with all thy soul, with all thy mind, and with all thy strength, and thy neighbour as thyself." Canst thou say, in the sight of a heart-searching God, "I have fulfilled all that"? If you can, I am staggered at you, and think you the victim of a strong delusion, which leads you to believe a lie.

Brethren who can take delight in themselves must have lost sight of the heinousness of sin. The least sin is a desperate evil, an assault upon the throne of God, an insult to the majesty of heaven. The simple act of plucking the forbidden fruit cost us Paradise. There is a bottomless pit of sin in every transgression, a hell in every iniquity. If we keep clear of sins of action, and if our tongue be so bridled that we avoid every hasty and unadvised speech, yet do we not know that our thoughts and imaginations, our looks and longings of heart, have in them an infinity of evil? If, after having learned that sin can only be washed out by the death of the Son of God, and that even the flames of hell cannot make atonement for a single sin, a man can then say, "I am content with myself," it is to be feared that he has made a fatal mistake as to his own character.

Is there not a failure, in such cases, to understand the highest standard of Christian living? If we measure ourselves among ourselves, there are many believers here who might be pretty well satisfied. You are as generous as other Christians are, considering your income. You are as prayerful as most other professors, and as earnest in doing good as any of your neighbours; if you are worldly, yet not more worldly than most professors, nowadays, and so you judge yourself not to be far below the standard. But what a standard! Let us seek a better. Brethren, it is a very healthy thing for us who are ministers to read a biography like that of M'Cheyne. Read that through, if you are a minister, and it will burst many of your wind-bags. You will find yourselves collapse most terribly. Take the life of Brainerd amongst the Indians, or of Baxter in our own land. Think of the holiness of George Herbert, the devoutness of Fletcher, or the zeal of Whitfield. Where do you find yourself after reading their lives? Might you not peep about to find a hiding-place for your insignificance?

When we mix with dwarfs we think ourselves giants, but in the presence of giants we become dwarfs. When we think of the saints departed, and remember their patience in suffering, their diligence in labour, their ardour, their self-denial, their humility, their tears, their prayers, their midnight cries, their intercession for the souls of others, their pouring out their hearts before God for the glory of Christ, why, we shrink into less than nothing, and find no word of boasting on our tongue. If we survey the life of the only perfect One, our dear Lord and Master, the sight of his beauty covers our whole countenance with a blush. He is the lily, and we are the thorns. He is the sun, and we are as the night. He is all good, and we are all ill. In his presence we bow in the dust, we confess our sin, and count ourselves unworthy to unloose his shoelatchets.

It is to be feared that there is springing up in some parts of the Christian church a deceitful form of self-righteousness, which leads even good people to think too highly of themselves. It is a fashionable form of fanaticism, very pleasing to the flesh, very fascinating, and very deadly. Many, I fear, are not really living so near to God as they think they are, neither are they as holy as they dream. It is very easy to frequent Bible readings, and conferences, and excited public meetings, and to fill one's self with the gas of self-esteem. A little pious talk with a sort of Christians who always walk on high stilts will soon tempt you to use the stilts yourself; but indeed, dear brother, you are a poor, unworthy worm and a nobody, and if you get one inch above the ground, you get just that inch too high. Remember, you may think yourself to be very strong in a certain direction, because you do not happen to be tried on that point. Many of us are exceedingly good tempered when nobody provokes us. Some are wonderfully patient, because they have a sound constitution, and have no racking pains to endure; and others are exceedingly generous, because they have more money than they want. A ship's seaworthiness is never quite certain till she has been out at sea. The grand thing will be to be sound before the living God in the day of trial. I pray every believer here to get off the high horse, and to remember that he is "naked and poor and miserable" apart from Christ, and only in Jesus Christ is he anything, and that if he thinketh himself to be something when he is nothing, he deceiveth himself, but does not deceive God.

II. In the second place, look at Paul as PLACING THE PAST IN ITS TRUE LIGHT. He says, "Forgetting those things which are behind." What does he mean? Paul does not mean that he forgot the mercy of God which he had enjoyed; far from it. Paul does not mean that he forgot the sins which he had committed; far from it, he would always remember them to humble him. We must follow out the figure which he is using, and so read him. When a man ran in the Grecian games, if he had run half way, and passed most of his fellows, and had then turned to look round and to rejoice over the distance which he had already covered, he would have lost the race. Suppose he had commenced singing his own praises, and said, "I have come down the hill, along the valley, and up the rising ground on this side. See, there are one, two, three, four, five, six runners far behind me." While thus praising himself he would lose the race. The only hope for the racer was to forget all that was behind, and occupy his entire thoughts with the piece of ground which lay in front. Never mind though you have run so far, you must let the space which lies between you and the goal engross all your thoughts and command all your powers. It must be so with regard to all the sins which we have overcome. Perhaps at this moment you might honestly say, "I have overcome a very fierce temper," or, "I have bestirred my naturally indolent spirit." Thank God for that. Stop long enough to say, "Thank God for that," but do not pause to congratulate yourselves as though some great thing had been done, for then it may soon be undone. Perhaps the very moment you are rejoicing over your conquered temper it will leap back upon you, like a lion from the covert, and you will say, "I thought you were dead and buried, and here you are roaring at me again." The very easiest way to give resurrection to old corruptions is to erect a trophy over their graves; they will at once lift up their heads and howl out, "We are alive still." It is a great thing to overcome any sinful habit, but it is needful to guard against it still, for you have not conquered it so long as you congratulate yourself upon the conquest. In the same light we must regard all the grace we have obtained. I know some dear friends who are mighty in prayer, and my soul rejoices to join in their supplications; but I should be sorry indeed to hear them praise their own prayers. We love yonder brother for his generosity, but we hope he will never tell others that he is liberal; yonder dear friend is very humble, but if he were to boast of it, there would be an end of it. Self-esteem is a moth which frets the garments of virtue. Those flies, those pretty flies of self-praise, must be killed, for if they get into your pot of ointment they will spoil it all. Forget the past; thank God who has made you pray so well; thank God who has made you kind, gentle, or humble; thank God who has made you give liberally; but forget it all and go forward, since there is yet very much land to be possessed!

And so with all the work for Jesus which we have done. Some people seem to have very good memories as to what they have performed. They used to serve God wonderfully when they were young! They began early and were full of zeal! They can tell you all about it with much pleasure. In middle life they wrought marvels, and achieved great wonders; but now they rest on their oars, they are giving other people an opportunity to distinguish themselves—their own heroic age is over. Dear brother, as long as ever you are in this world forget what you have already done, and go forward to other service! Living on the past is one of the faults of old churches. We, for instance, as a church, may begin to congratulate ourselves upon the great things God has done by us, for we shall be sure to put it in that pretty shape, although we shall probably mean the great things we have done ourselves. After praising ourselves thus we shall gain no further blessing, but shall decline by little and little. The same is true of denominations. What acclamations are heard when allusion is made to what our fathers did! Oh, the name of Carey, and Knibb, and Fuller! We Baptists think we have nothing to do now but to go upstairs and go to bed, for we have achieved eternal glory through the names of these good men; and as for our Wesleyan friends, how apt they are to harp upon Wesley, Fletcher, Nelson, and other great men! Thank God for them: they were grand men; but the right thing is to forget the past, and pray for another set of men to carry on the work. We should never be content, but "On, on, on," should be our cry! When they asked Napoleon why he continually made wars, he said, "I am the child of war; conquest has made me what I am, and conquest must maintain me." The Christian church is the child of spiritual war; she only lives as she fights, and rides forth conquering and to conquer. God deliver us from the self-congratulatory spirit, however it may come, and make us long and pine after something better!

III. And now the third point. Paul, having put the present and past into their right places, goes on to the future, ASPIRING EAGERLY TO MAKE IT GLORIOUS; for he says, "reaching forth unto those things which are before." Does he not here give us the picture of a runner? He reaches forth. The man, as he speeds, throws himself forward, almost out of the perpendicular. His eye is at the goal already. His hand is far in advance of his feet, the whole body is leaning forward; he runs as though he would project himself to the end of the journey before his legs can carry him there. That is how the Christian should be; always throwing himself forward after something more than he has yet reached, not satisfied with the rate at which he advances, his soul always going at twenty times the pace of the flesh. John Bunyan gives us a little parable of the man on horseback. He is bidden by his master to ride in a hurry to fetch the physician. But the horse is a sorry jade. "Well," saith Bunyan, "but if his master sees that the man on the horse's back is whipping and spurring, and pulling the bridle, and struggling with all his might, he judges that the man would go if he could." That is how the Christian should always be, not only as devout, earnest, and useful as he can be, but panting to be a great deal more so, spurring this old flesh and striving against this laggard spirit if perchance he can do more. Brethren, we ought to be reaching forward to be like Jesus. Never may we say, "I am like so-and-so, and that is enough." Am I like Jesus, perfectly like Jesus? If not, away, away, away from everything I am or have been; I cannot rest until I am like my Lord. The aim of the Christian is to be perfect: if he seeks to be anything less than perfect, he aims at an object lower than that which God has placed before him. To master every sin, and to have and possess and exhibit every virtue,—this is the Christian's ambition. He who would be a great artist must not follow low models. The artist must have a perfect model to copy; if he does not reach to it, he will reach far further than if he had an inferior model to work by. When a man once realises his own ideal, it is all over with him. A great painter once had finished a picture, and he said to his wife with tears in his eyes, "It is all over with me, I shall never paint again, I am a ruined man."

She enquired, "Why"? "Because," he says, "that painting contents and satisfies me; it realises my idea of what painting ought to be, and therefore I am sure my power is gone, for that power lies in having ideals which I cannot reach, something yet beyond me which I am striving after." May none of us ever say, "I have reached my ideal, now I am what I ought to be, there is nothing beyond me." Perfection, brethren, absolute perfection, may God help us to strive after it! That is the model, "Be ye perfect, even as your Father which is in heaven is perfect." "Shall we ever reach it?" says one. Thousands and millions have reached it; there they are before the throne of God, their robes are washed and made white in the blood of the Lamb; and we shall possess the same, only let us be struggling after it by God's good help. Let every believer be striving, that in the details of common life, in every thought, in every word, in every action, he may glorify God. This ought to be our object; if we do not reach it, it is that which we must press for,—that from morning light to evening shade we shall live unto God. Whether we eat or drink, or whatsoever we do, we should do all in the name of the Lord Jesus. This is what we are to seek after, praying always in the Holy Ghost to be sanctified wholly, spirit, soul, and body. "It is a wonderfully high standard," says one. Would you like me to lower it, brother? I should be very sorry to have it lowered for myself. If the highest degree of holiness were denied to any one of us, it would be a heavy calamity. Is it not the joy of a Christian to be perfectly like his Lord? Who would wish to stop short of it? To be obliged to live under the power of even the least sin for ever, would be a horrible thing! No, we never can be content short of perfection; we will reach forward towards that which is before.

IV. And now the apostle is our model, in the fourth place, because he PUTS FORTH ALL HIS EXERTIONS TO REACH THAT WHICH HE DESIRES. He says, "This one thing I do," as if he had given up all else, and addicted himself to one sole object—to aim to be like Jesus Christ. There were many other things Paul might have attempted, but he says, "this one thing I do." Probably Paul was a poor speaker: why did not he try to make himself a rhetorician? No; he came not with excellency of speech. But you tell me Paul was busy with his tent-making. I know he was; what with tent-making, preaching, and visiting, and watching night and day, he had more than enough to do, but all these were a part of his pursuit of the one thing, he was labouring perfectly to serve his Master, and to render himself up as a whole burnt-offering unto God. I invite every soul that has been saved by the precious blood of Christ, to gather up all its strength for this one thing, to cultivate a passion for grace, and an intense longing after holiness. Ah, if we could but serve God as God should be served, and be such manner of people as we ought to be in all holy conversation and godliness, we should see a new era in the church. The greatest want of the church at this day is holiness.

Why did Paul pursue holiness with such concentrated purpose? Because he felt God had called him to it. He aimed at the prize of his high calling. God had elected Paul to be a champion against sin. Selected to be Jehovah's champion, he felt that he must play the man.

Moreover, it was "God in Christ Jesus" who made the choice, and as the apostle looked up and saw the mild face of the Redeemer, and marked the thorn-crown of the King of Sorrows, he felt he must overcome sin, he could not let a single evil live within him; and, though he had not yet apprehended, yet he felt he must press forward till he had apprehended that to which God in Christ had called him.

Moreover, the apostle saw his crown, the crown of life that fadeth not away, hanging bright before his eyes. What, said he, shall tempt me from that path of which yon crown is the end? Let the golden apples be thrown in my way; I cannot even look at them, nor stay to spurn them with my feet. Let the sirens sing on either side, and seek to charm me with their evil beauty, to leave the holy road; but I must not, and I will not. Heaven! Heaven! Heaven! is not this enough to make a man dash forward in the road thither? The end is glorious, what if the running be laborious? When there is such a prize to be had, who will grudge a struggle? Paul pressed forward towards the mark for the prize of his high calling in Christ Jesus. He felt he was a saved man, and he meant through the same grace to be a holy man. He longed to grasp the crown, and hear the "Well done, good and faithful servant," which his Master would award him at the end of his course. Brethren and sisters, I wish I could stir myself and stir you to a passionate longing after a gracious, consistent, godly life, yea, for an eminently, solidly, thoroughly devoted and consecrated life. You will grieve the Spirit if you walk inconsistently; you will dishonour the Lord that bought you; you will weaken the church; you will bring shame upon yourself. Even though you be "saved so as by fire," it will be an evil and a bitter thing to have in any measure departed from God. But to be always going onward, to be never self-satisfied, to be always labouring to be better Christians, to be aiming at the rarest sanctity, this shall be your honour, the church's comfort, and the glory of God. May the Lord help you to perfect holiness in the fear of God. Amen.

PORTION OF SCRIPTURE READ BEFORE SERMON—Philippians iii.

Metropolitan Tabernacle Pulpit.

THE CHILD OF LIGHT WALKING IN LIGHT.

A Sermon

DELIVERED ON LORD'S-DAY MORNING, OCTOBER 2ND, 1887, BY

C. H. SPURGEON,

AT THE METROPOLITAN TABERNACLE, NEWINGTON.

"If we say that we have fellowship with him, and walk in darkness, we lie, and do not the truth: but if we walk in the light, as he is in the light, we have fellowship one with another, and the blood of Jesus Christ his Son cleanseth us from all sin."— 1 John i. 6, 7.

THE apostle warns us against *saying* more than we have made our own by experience. He hints at the solemn difference between empty profession and gracious reality. To have fellowship with God is a great matter; but merely to *say* that we have fellowship with him is a totally different thing. John warns us that if we *say* that which our characters do not support, we lie. He leaves it just so, without a word of softening or excuse. Between saying and being, between saying and doing, there may be all the difference in the world. There is a tendency among men, if there be a good experience, to say that they possess it; if there be a high privilege of grace, to say that they are enjoying it. What a folly is this! It is akin to madness. To unsound minds a precious original suggests a desire to fashion an imitation. To the untruthful mind the genuine is an invitation to be the counterfeit. Let us be upon our guard that we do not flatter ourselves into saying more than is true. Let us not stretch our arm beyond our sleeve, nor boast beyond our line. Every profession will be tried with fire; let us, therefore, see to it that we put in no claim which will not endure the severest test.

There were certain in John's day who said, "We have fellowship with God." How they had come by it they did not explain; perhaps they claimed to have reached it by philosophical speculation, by exact reasoning, or by long-continued meditation. Whatever the road, they said that they had reached the city of God, and were in communion with the Great Being. John saw that they walked in darkness, rejecting the light of divine revelation from above and the pure light of the Holy Spirit within; he saw also that they themselves were not true, and that their lives were not pure, and therefore he warned them that they were speaking and acting a lie. Their life was a lie, for they were not

No. 1,986.

walking in the truth; and their profession that they had fellowship with God was another lie, for God can have no fellowship with falsehood. "God is light, and in him is no darkness at all"; and, therefore, he cannot hold any communion with darkness. John draws the lines very tightly, and judges with unflinching fidelity: he is not inclined to the boasted charity of latitudinarianism, but he curtly dismisses false claims with that plain word "lie." The disciple whom Jesus loved spoke like the Son of Thunder that he was, when he had to deal with shams. It is the part of true love to be honest, and to expose that which would be injurious to those it loves. He who will gloss over a falsehood loves but in word only. Learn, then, that if men boast of fellowship with God, and do not receive the revelation of his word, they lie, and know not the truth.

Let us now speak of the real thing, the fellowship with God which comes of walking in the light. The Christian life is described as walking, which implies *activity*. Christian life feeds upon contemplation, but it displays itself in action. Fellowship with God necessitates action: since to be with God we must "walk with God." The living God is not inactive, motionless, aimless. "My Father," saith Jesus, "worketh hitherto, and I work." Chiefly in the character of active workers or in that of willing sufferers we must maintain fellowship with God. Walking implies activity; but it must be *of a continuous kind*. Neither this step, nor that, nor the next, can make a walk. We must be moving onward and onward, and remain in that exercise, or we cease from walking. Holy walking includes perseverance in obedience, and continuance in service. Not he that begins, but he that continues is the true Christian; final perseverance enters into the very essence of the believer's life: the true pilgrims of Zion go from strength to strength. From strength to strength, did I say? This suggests that walking implies *progress*. He that takes one step and another step, and still stands where he was, has not walked. There is such a thing as the goose-step, and I am afraid many Christians are wonderfully familiar with it: they are where they used to be, and are half inclined to congratulate themselves upon that fact, since they might have backslidden. They have not advanced in the heavenly pilgrimage, and how can they be said to walk? My hearer, is your life a walk *with* God and *towards* God? If so, our subject has to do with you. May the Spirit of all grace lead us into the heart of it!

The things we shall consider this morning will arise out of the text in the following order: First, *the light of our walk:* "if we walk in the light, as he is in the light." Secondly, *the communion of our walk:* "we have fellowship one with another." Thirdly, *the glory of that communion:* "the blood of Jesus Christ his Son cleanseth us from all sin."

I. Consider, first, THE LIGHT OF OUR WALK. True believers do not walk in darkness; they have found the road, and they see it before them. They know whom they have believed, and why they have believed, and so they go forward intelligently. How unhappy are those who are sure of nothing but a groping for the way, and wandering in endless circles of hope and fear! True believers walk onward, because a light shows them their path, and makes them sure of safety and progress. What is meant by walking in the light? It is somewhat singular that last Sunday morning our subject was "The Child of Light walking in Darkness." That darkness is very different from the darkness with which we deal this morning. Children of light may for a time walk in the darkness of sorrow; but from the darkness of untruthfulness, ignorance, sin, and unbelief they have been delivered. In these respects the darkness is past, and the true light now shineth. Moral darkness is contrary to their new-born nature: they cannot endure it. We must distinguish between things that differ, between the darkness of sorrow and the darkness of sin. A metaphor may be used for many purposes, and that of darkness has a wide range of meaning.

What is this light, then, in which the Christian walks? I answer, first, *it is the light of grace.* In our natural state we are in darkness, and under the dominion of the Prince of Darkness. The apostle says of us Gentiles, "Having the understanding darkened, being alienated from the life of God through the ignorance that is in them, because of the blindness of their heart." When the grace of God comes, the dayspring from on high visits us. The Holy Spirit brings us out from under the dominion of the old nature by creating within us a new life, and he brings us out from under the tyranny of the Prince of Darkness by opening our eyes to see and our minds to understand celestial truth. The opening of our blind eyes and the pouring in of the light of truth are from the Lord. This is a work in which he is as fully seen in the glory of his Godhead as when in the natural creation he said, "Let there be light," and there was light. The entrance of God's word into the mind by the power of the Holy Spirit gives us light as to ourselves, our sin, and our danger. With this comes light as to the way of salvation through Jesus Christ, and light as to the mind of God concerning our sanctification. True knowledge takes the place of ignorance, and a desire for purity becomes supreme over the love of sin. Paul says, "Ye were sometime darkness, but now are ye light in the Lord." We accept the revelation of God in the inspired Book; by the attending witness of the Holy Ghost it becomes a revelation of God to our own hearts; and thus all our position—our past, present, and future—is set in a new light. With the driving out of our natural darkness old things pass away, and with the coming in of the divine light all things become new. Blessed is that man to whom the eternal light has come by the effectual working of the Spirit of God, who bringeth to us the light wherein we see God, and Christ, and life everlasting! This is the secret beginning of all our light: "God, who commanded the light to shine out of darkness, hath shined in our hearts, to give the light of the knowledge of the glory of God in the face of Jesus Christ."

The result of this light is seen in various ways. It causes deep sorrow in the beginning, for its first discoveries are grievous to the conscience. Light is painful to eyes long accustomed to darkness. Anon the light brings great joy, for the soul perceives deliverance from the evils which it mourned. Thus light and gladness in the end go together, as it is written, "Light is sown for the righteous, and gladness for the upright in heart." Ever, in each condition, you observe conspicuously that the light of grace is seen as *the light of sincerity*. Until grace comes into our souls we have no heart for the things of God. We may be fussily religious so far as to be attentive to every outward form of worship; but there is no heart-work, no light of truth in all our devotion. But when once the divine light comes in, then we become intensely real in our dealings with God. Hypocrisy and pretence fly before sincere belief and feeling. "Lord, have mercy upon us, miserable sinners," no longer passes our lips flippantly and thoughtlessly; but we are indeed miserable on account of sin. When we seek for mercy we mean it, and do not play at confession and repentance. Our eye is single, and our whole body is full of light: we see what we are at, and arouse ourselves to do it in earnest. We know what we are praying about, and there is no question as to the deep sincerity of our cries and tears. We desire with the whole force of our nature to find pardon and acceptance through the precious blood of Christ. We do not merely say that we desire salvation and eternal life; but we feel that we must have them, and cannot be denied. We cease from playing fast and loose with God. We no longer halt between two opinions, but one thing we seek after, desiring it of the Lord: we would be right with God in all respects. The man that is walking in the light is thoroughly sincere. The shadows of pretence have been chased away: he is in downright earnest in all that he does. O my hearers, many of you have never come so far as this; though this alone is not far. By being in a place of worship you show an outward respect to divine things; but are you worshipping God? Did you worship him just now in the prayer and in the praise? You are listening to me while I talk of the highest things that ever occupied the human mind, but do you long to be a partaker of these things? Do you hunger and thirst after righteousness? Those who are walking in the light are free from pretence, and are living in real earnest: is it so with you? Contentment with unreality is a sign of dwelling in darkness. Careful keeping up of shams, diligent puffing out of wind-bags, and constant creation of make-believes—all this is of the night and its dreams; but to be what you seem to be, to be true in all the phases of your life, this is surely seen in those who walk in the light of God? What can God have to do with shams? What cares he for empty professions? Everything must be true which is to come under his eye.

Next to sincerity I regard *a willingness to know and to be known* as an early result of walking in the light of God. The ungodly come not to the light, lest their deeds should be reproved. There are matters about which they desire no light, but rather say, "Depart from us, we desire not the knowledge of thy ways." Where ignorance affords them a present peace they count it folly to be wise. Alas! it is too commonly the case that men have no inclination to obtain a knowledge which might involve humiliation, repentance, and a retracing of steps. "Let well alone," cry they. How many will say, "Well, we have been Christians after our own way for a good many years, why need we question ourselves?" They look upon a faithful preacher with suspicion: he comes a deal too close home. When he begins to deal with the heart and conscience, they look at him as if he were a dog hunting about for a rat. Truly the emblem is not so very unlike; for wherever there is a self-satisfaction which is afraid of light, we suspect that the rat of hypocrisy is not far off. Beloved, we must not rest content with anything which will not bear the light of day. A religion which we will not submit to the test of self-examination cannot be worth much. No one is afraid to have a genuine sovereign submitted to any test: it is the coiner who is afraid. "Look!" says a man, "I hold a certain creed; my grandmother held it; it has come down to me as an heir-loom. You invite me to examine that creed by the Word of God, but I would rather not. I am not disposed to learn anything which might cause me to change. If you speak too strongly I shall go and hear somebody else, for I cannot bear to be disturbed." This is a foolish prejudice, is it not? Yes, and it may prove the man's ruin. This is the kind of thing that makes a man go out angrily from a sermon, and say, "I will not listen to that man again; he is too personal, and too severe." Nay, friend, can anyone who loves your soul be too severe? Do you wish to be flattered? Do you not know that plain-dealing is more precious than rubies? Would you not say to your physician, "Put me under the severest examination, and let me know the truth"? Would you pay him a fee that he might deceive you. As to your soul, do you not desire to know the very worst of your case? If you would rather be comfortable than be safe, then you and I are not of one mind; for I want to walk in the light, free from deception, knowing truly and thoroughly my own place before the heart-searching God. I would rather not cry, "Peace, peace," where there is no peace. The comfort which grows out of delusion I do not desire. Brethren, we must build on truth, and nothing else but truth.

When men walk in the light they cease to take things for granted, and look below the surface. Certain things have been labelled with the mark of truth, and have passed current; but men who are in the light disregard the labels, and look at the goods themselves. We cannot afford to risk our souls on hearsays: we need personal knowledge. For one, I desire a salvation which will bear the test of the closest examination. I would be saved in such a way that I am neither afraid of conscience, nor of death, nor of the judgment-seat of God. I would be saved in the light. I would be known and read of all men, and I would know even as I am known. We wish to conceal nothing: we can conceal nothing, "for all things are naked and open to the eyes of him with whom we have to do." We would lay bare our bosoms and sincerely cry, "Search me, O God, and know my heart: try me, and know my thoughts: and see if there be any wicked way in me, and lead me in the way everlasting."

A still surer evidence of grace is the *mind's perception of revealed truth and its obedience to it.* Then has true light shone on a man's walk when he perceives the truth revealed by the Holy Spirit in sacred Scripture, and receives it into his heart with a child-like spirit. He that receives Christ also receives Christ's words, and the doctrine which we believe is by no means a matter of indifference. Whatever may be said, brethren, we have received a revelation from God; which we know to be "the faith once for all delivered to the saints." The Lord God has broken through the veil of silence, and has manifested himself to the sons of men. Through the darkness of their minds the carnal cannot see what God has revealed, neither will they believe his truth. The truth of God is spiritual, and the natural man is carnal, and therefore the natural man will not receive the teaching which comes from God. By this test shalt thou know whether the true light is shining upon thee: Dost thou believe what God has revealed in his word? or art thou thine own teacher—maker of thine own faith? He cannot be a disciple who does not learn, but invents. Dost thou hear the teaching of the Lord Jesus, and believe it? I repeat it, thou must not only *say* that thou believest it, but thou must indeed and of a truth believe the things which God has revealed. By this shalt thou know whether thou be a child of light, or a child of darkness. Are the doctrines of grace essential verities with thee? Whatever God has said about sin, righteousness, judgment to come, art thou ready to accept it at once. Whatever he has revealed concerning himself, his Son, his Holy Spirit, the cross, life, death, hell, and the eternal future, dost thou believe it unfeignedly? This is to walk in the light. All other teaching is darkness.

How many correct and amend, and so betray the gospel! They take the garment of truth, and dip it in the blood of their own thought, till it is so distained that they might almost say unto God himself, "Know thou whether this be thy son's coat or not?" If thou be one of those who would twist the Scriptures, and force thine own meaning on them, thou art not in the light. If thou wouldst make them mean other than what God intended them to mean, thou art in the darkness, however learned a philosopher thou mayest be. He only is in the light who distrusts his own wisdom, and bows before the wisdom which cometh from above. If thou wilt sit at Jesus' feet like a child, and hear his words and learn of him, then hath the true light shone upon thee; for he is the light that lighteth every man that cometh into the world. The Holy Spirit comes not to help us to think out a system of belief of our own, but to lead us into all truth, by taking of the things of Christ and showing them unto us.

Brethren, there is a truth and there is a lie, and no lie is of the truth. Can light commune with darkness, or truth with falsehood? I make no claim of implicit faith for what *I* say. God forbid that I should ever become so presumptuous; for that were a sort of blasphemy. But I claim implicit faith for what *God* says. Believing the gospel to be the revelation of God, I claim for it implicit faith. Believing the Lord Jesus to be an infallible teacher, I claim immediate faith in all that he has said. If this implicit faith be refused, it is because there is no light in you. To walk in the light is to know, to love, and to live the truth. To walk in the light of God is to receive our instruction from God. To me the end of all controversy is "Thus saith the Lord." Only let me know that the Lord hath said this or that, and though the revelation should seem impossible to believe, and though it should come into conflict with all my previous notions, I will bow before it without a question. "The Lord hath said it," stands to us instead of all reason, and argument, and evidence; yea, we believe God in the teeth of supposed evidence and reason, saying, "Let God be true, but every man a liar." God will not have fellowship with us if we reject his light; but on the ground of absolute truth he can and will meet us.

If we come unto the light, and believe his witness to the truth, then are we where God can walk with us, and where the precious blood of Jesus Christ cleanses us from all sin.

This, beloved brethren, leads to *a transparency and simplicity of character*. Walking in the light produces Israelites indeed, in whom is no guile. Those who are full of deceit and craftiness upon any subject are not walking in the light of God. God will not have fellowship with any whose minds are crooked and deceitful. Some persons are so warped that nothing is straight to them; their minds seem to see things crookedly; long practice in untruthfulness has given them an evil bias. This is not the case with the man in whom the light of grace is shining. The man who does in reality what he seems to do; the man who says what he means, and means what he says; the man who is truthful, artless and sincere in all his general dealings both before God and man, he it is whose conduct leads us to hope that the light of grace shines within.

This is very evident in *the man's cessation from all guile towards himself*. Remember how David pronounces him blessed "in whose spirit there is no guile." He knew painfully what it was to be full of guile. See him! He has gone astray most grievously. His mind is in the dark. What does David do? There is a foul sin committed: he tries to make himself believe that it is not so very horrible; he labours to hoodwink his conscience. His sin is likely to be seen, and he tries to cover it. He brings back Bathsheba's husband. When he declines to go to his house he must be made drunken. The design has failed. David is afraid, but he is not penitent; on the contrary, he hastens to still greater crime. Uriah is in the wars, and there he is wantonly exposed to death, and is slain in battle. His death is ascribed to the fortune of war. David did not see that it was murder, for he was not walking in the light. He was still in darkness, and therefore he kept all this while acting a deceitful part with his God and his own conscience. His conduct would not bear the light, and so his one idea was to keep out of the light. How changed was all this after Nathan had said to him, "Thou art the man"! When the light of heavenly conviction had penetrated the night of his soul, he made no more excuses, he practised no more subterfuges. He stood in the light, ashamed and confounded. Amazed at the sight of his sin, he abandoned all idea of covering it, and fled at once to the mercy of God crying, "Have mercy upon me, O God, according to thy lovingkindness." In the sobbing and sighing of the fifty-first Psalm he lays bare his heart, and in plainest terms he cries, "Deliver me from bloodguiltiness, O God, thou God of my salvation." He is in the light now, for deceit has gone, and now God can speak comfortably to him, and wash him and make him whiter than snow.

The man who is walking in the light, as God is in the light, is full of *abhorrence of sin*. Sin is practical falsehood; it is moral darkness. The man that abhors evil and injustice; the man that would do good if it cost him his earthly all; the man that would not do wrong though the world should be his reward for doing it—this is the man that walks in the light, and he is the man that shall have fellowship with God, and a sense of cleansing from sin. We cannot attach too great importance to the condition of our minds in reference to sin; for if we wink at it, or take pleasure in it, or persistently practise it, we are abiding in the darkness, and we are under the wrath of God. John says, "Little children, let no man deceive you: he that doeth righteousness is righteous, even as he is righteous." Forget not this practical truth.

I fear I have scarcely brought out the fulness of the meaning. They that are in the light will know what I mean: those who are in darkness cannot imagine what life in the light must be.

II. I come, secondly, to THE COMMUNION OF OUR WALK. Those who are in the light shall not be alone. God himself will be with them, and be their God. The words, "we have fellowship one with another," constitute a wonderfully condescending expression. John would not have dared to coin such an expression; it must have been minted for him by the Spirit from above. Think of God and his people having mutual intercourse! What honour! What joy is this! Thus is the mischief of the Fall removed, and Paradise is restored.

God in the light and man in the light have much in common. Now are they abiding in one element, for they are dwelling in one light. Now are they both concerned about the same thing, and their aims are undivided: God loves truth, and so do those who are renewed in heart. It has come to pass that the great Lord and his enlightened ones see things in the same light. God with his great vision beholds more than we can, yet he does not see more than the truth; and we with our narrow perceptions see the truth, and falsehood we cannot tolerate. Now we can speak with God, seeing we speak truth; and he can converse with us, seeing we are ready to hear the truth. In prayer and praise we are no longer false, and therefore the Lord can hear us. His word falls also upon an honest mind, and so its meaning is perceived. Now also we can act together: the great God and his poor feeble children are striving together for truth and righteousness. Our poor little work he might overlook if he were not so good; but being infinitely condescending, he works through us whenever he sees that our work is done in truth. If our works were works of darkness, he could not co-operate with us; but now that we walk and work in the light, he is able to make us labourers together with himself.

Now we partake with God in sympathy, having a fellow-feeling with him. Does the great Father mourn his prodigal child? So do we mourn over sinners. Do we see Jesus weeping over Jerusalem? So do we mourn for the perishing who will not be saved. Again, as God rejoices over sinners that repent, so do we rejoice in sympathy with him. By coming into the light of love as well as into the light of knowledge we have received power to enter into sympathy with God. Is not this a very wonderful thing? But it is as clear and true as it is wonderful. We would fain bring the whole world into the light. We daily pray, "Thy kingdom come, thy will be done." Our will has grown to be like God's will according to its measure, seeing we have come into the same light as that in which God dwells.

Do you know, dear brothers and sisters, by experience what it is to be honestly dealing with eternal things, to be no longer playing, and toying, and counterfeiting, but to be in real and blessed earnest with God and spiritual facts? Then you have come into fellowship with the great God, for he is in earnest, and in him there is no trifling nor make-believe; but he is acting with intense reality, acting with his whole heart in his contention against sin, his desire for the glory of his Son, his purpose for the salvation of his people.

III. But now I come, in the third place, to that which strikes me most in the text, and it is this—THE GLORY OF THIS COMMUNION: "We have fellowship one with another, and the blood of Jesus Christ his Son cleanseth us from all sin." Here am I a poor creature reading this text. I find that it is possible for men to walk in fellowship with God, the great and ever blessed. I rejoice to learn this, and my heart responds, "If there is any fellowship with God to be known, I will know it. If I can be reconciled to God, and be at friendship with him, I desire it beyond everything. But how can these things be? I see that a great stone lieth at the door. I cannot get out of my prison to begin this walk, because this great stone of sin shuts me in." Then the Lord comes in, and he says, "I saw that this hindrance was in thy road, and so in this very verse I have shown thee how I have taken it away. Precious words! The blood of Jesus Christ his Son cleanseth us from all sin." I gather from the way in which this sentence grows out of the text that this very thing, which looks as if it were the death of all communion with God, is made by infinite grace to be a wide and open channel of communion with him. This stone is rolled away from the door of the sepulchre, and the angel of communion sits down upon it as on a throne. God justifies his people in broad daylight, in a way which defies inspection, and then, by the very method of clearing away their sin, he enters into the nearest and dearest fellowship with them.

To begin with, *here is sin!* What an evil thing it is! How our soul hates it! It is uncleanness to us: a loathsome and abominable evil. You that are in the light know how every beam of light makes you see more of the heinousness, blackness, and accursed nature of sin. Even to feel a tendency towards it in your members makes you groan out, "O wretched man that I am! who shall deliver me." Listen! You are having fellowship with God in this. In him is no sin, but in him is great abhorrence of sin. If you hate sin, God hates it also; and herein you are agreed. The very thought of iniquity, uncleanness, or false-hood, is abhorred of God. His holy nature detests it; and in proportion as you feel the same loathing and detestation, you have fellowship with God. This comes to you by walking in the light, as God is in the light. "Horror hath taken hold upon me," saith David, "because of the wicked that forsake thy law." David was as much in fellowship with God in that horror of sin as he was another day when he could speak of God as his exceeding joy, and rejoice in the mercy which endureth for ever. Yes, beloved, our horror for sin drives us into fellowship with the great Father in that loathing of sin which made him hide his face from his Only-begotten because the sin of man had been made to meet upon him.

Let us go a step further. Sin being once perceived, the next step is that it should *be got rid of.* "Ah!" say you, "I wish I could be cleansed from it; cleansed from all of it; but how can this be? It is not possible for me to purge away my sin." I thought I heard you singing just now :—

> "Could my tears for ever flow,
> Could my zeal no respite show;
> All for sin could not atone,
> Thou must save, and thou alone."

This also is God's thought about sin: he knows how hard it is to remove its pollution. He saw that nothing of ours could remove the horrible blot. Brethren, I know of a surety that all the waters of all the seas might be encarnadined by my scarlet sin, and yet they could not wash out the fatal stain. Not even the fires of hell could burn out the defilement of sin. In this persuasion we have fellowship with the pure and holy God, who saw that there was no means of removing sin but one; he must deliver up his own Son to death, or the sin of man could never be purged away. The sacrifice of the Only-begotten is the unique hope of sinners. The laying of our iniquity upon him who deigned to be the great scape-goat of his people is the sole means for the taking away of the sins of the world. That inward persuasion of the impossibility of the purgation of sin by any doings or feelings of our own, and the consequent perception that in Christ only lies the help of men, has brought us through the light of truth to walk in fellowship with the thrice holy God.

Now go a step further. *The glorious Son of God condescends to become the atonement for sin.* He is taken to the tree; our sins are made to meet upon his blessed head, and there he dies the just for the unjust. He was made sin for us, that we might be made the righteousness of God in him. Standing by the tree of doom, we look up to that blessed Saviour with all-absorbing admiration and love. We admire him as the masterpiece of divine wisdom, grace, power, and truth; and, admiring, we love him; we pledge ourselves to him. Herein we have entered into fellowship with the great Father indeed and of a truth; for the Father loves his Son infinitely: he greatly delights in him. No thought of Christ that the most rapturous enthusiast ever had can reach half way to God's thoughts of Christ. See how holy Bernard seems to go into a delirium of love when he talks about his divine Master! O Bernard, thou canst not tell how the Father loves Jesus, how he delights in his sacrifice, how he takes pleasure in his exaltation! In the putting away of sin by the blood of Jesus the Father has an infinite content, and so have we. Beloved, we rejoice in the divine satisfaction for sin; it is a well of divine delight to us. This satisfaction is not accomplished by anything being hushed up and concealed, but, walking in the light, as God is in the light, we have fellowship with God in the one glorious sacrifice. Suppose I could persuade myself that sin is a trifle, I should not be walking in the light, and I should have no fellowship with God. Suppose I said, "Pooh, pooh! sin can easily be forgiven, I am sure it requires no atonement," I should not be walking in the light, and I should have no fellowship with God. Suppose I said, "Though Jesus died, his death was only the close of his life, and no special reference need be made to it as a sacrifice for sin," I should not be walking in the light, and I should have no fellowship with God.

A step further. Beloved, many of us have come to Jesus Christ by faith; we have looked to him, and have accepted him as our Saviour *cleansing us from all sin.* Joy, joy, joy for ever: the brightest day that ever dawned on us was that day when we saw all our sins numbered on our blessed Scapegoat and carried away into the wilderness of forgetfulness! When God saw the blood of old he passed over Israel, for his justice was satisfied; and it is so with Jesus. How glad and content we are to see how Jesus finished transgression, made an end of sin, and brought in everlasting righteousness! Brethren, the death of Jesus is a cleansing from sin which will bear the light: it is no hole and corner business, no winking at evil, no suspension of law, no making out that sin is no sin. No, the debt is acknowledged, and what is better far, it is paid. The guilty are punished in their substitute, and in him are thus justly set free. We shall all appear before the judgment-seat; and I am glad it is so, for the stain of our sin is so effectually removed by the blood of Jesus that we are clean every whit, and even the eye of divine justice will see no spot in us. We rejoice in perfect whiteness, for the Lord has made us whiter than snow. Yes, we have fellowship with God in this cleansing, for God accepts us in the Beloved. God that made him to be the Lord our Righteousness, God himself justifies us in his Son. He will in the last great day make the whole universe a witness to the righteousness of the salvation of believers. All intelligences shall see that in Christ all who are in him are truly justified, and most justly saved. How the Lord God and his people will have fellowship in their common joy in the work and person of Jesus, as they see the perfection of it, and the way in which all sin is removed by it! Our salvation in Christ is in the light in the most eminent degree: it will bear the full, fierce light of Sinai to be turned upon it, and yet no flaw will be found in it. This is wonderful! This is glorious! Do you wonder that God is well pleased in him! And are not we well pleased! Blessed be his name. Do you not see how we thus have fellowship one with another. Oh, that I had strength to set forth before you the thoughts which fill my soul!

Brethren, we are now at one with God in his master-purpose. Was it not in his heart to create beings with whom he might have fellowship? He made the heavens and the earth; he made the angels; he made all things; but he could find no companionship in all these things. Our Lord, like Adam, found no help-meet for himself in any of the creatures he had made. He desired to produce and bring to himself an order of beings who could be glorified without danger of pride, who could think and feel as the First-born would do; in fact, would become the friends of the Son of God. How were these creatures to be produced? Not by an immediate fiat of creation. Angels he could speak into being by a word; but in the constitution of these beings there would need to be an experience and a discipline to fit them for their lofty position. Their model was to be the Son of Jehovah's love. He was to be the First-born among many brethren. It was needful for these creatures to know sin, and yet to hate it more fully than if they had never known it; to know the love of God, and to be bound by it for ever to an unsinning obedience, which would fill them with boundless happiness. Behold the process by which this new creation, this new order of creatures should come forth. Consider the processes which by the Fall, the incarnation, the Cross, and the new birth work out the sacred result! When you have read the past in this light, then gaze into the future. Now we see how throughout eternity we shall walk in the light, as God is in the light, and have fellowship one with another—fellowship culminating in Jesus Christ the Only-begotten, and the cleansing from all sin by his blood. The blood-washed are to be the friends of God, with whom he shall speak face to face, as he speaks with no angel or seraph. With these he will dwell, and he will be their God, and they shall be his people; and in them and through them he will make known the glories of his Son to wondering worlds. This great purpose has been wrought out to a considerable extent by the Lord's having already made us to walk in the light, as he is in the light, and by washing us in the precious blood; but it doth not even yet appear what we shall be. This much we practically seek after: henceforth we live for Christ! Henceforth our chief glory is the cross! Henceforth our beau-ideal of glory for ourselves is to see Jesus glorified! The torrents have swept us away! We are no longer bound to this earth! We are borne along by the irresistible force of eternal love! God has achieved his purpose in our blood-washed souls; walking in the light we are now in harmony with his master purpose, and we cry: "Father, glorify thy Son"!

I have done; but oh, I wish that all your hearts were brought into the light of God at this moment! Oh, that you would quit the dark ways of self-righteousness, carelessness, thoughtlessness, and sin, and come into the light of truth! Oh, that the light may come to you as to Saul of Tarsus, and at once transform you! May the Spirit of God bring you to know God and his Son Jesus Christ, whom to know is life eternal.

Portion of Scripture read before Sermon—1 John i. and ii.

Hymns from "Our Own Hymn Book"—425, 484, 289.

Metropolitan Tabernacle Pulpit.

WALKING IN THE LIGHT AND WASHED IN THE BLOOD.

A Sermon
DELIVERED ON SUNDAY MORNING, DECEMBER 3RD, 1865, BY
C. H. SPURGEON.
AT THE METROPOLITAN TABERNACLE, NEWINGTON.

"But if we walk in the light, as he is in the light, we have fellowship one with another, and the blood of Jesus Christ his Son cleanseth us from all sin."—1 John i. 7.

THERE are two great powers in conflict in this world. One is the power of good, of which God is the King, and the other is the power of evil, which is represented by the Prince of the power of the air, even Satan. The first principle is set forth by John under the figure of *light*. God himself is essential light, and everything which is good in the world is an emanation from himself. "Every good gift and every perfect gift is from above, and cometh down from the Father of lights, with whom is no variableness, neither shadow of turning." The light is the evident emblem of truth; darkness is the symbol of error. Light represents holiness; darkness is the appropriate figure for sin. Light represents knowledge, especially of spiritual things, since light reveals; darkness is the fit token of the ignorance under which the natural mind labours perpetually. By nature we are all born under the dominion of darkness: we grope our way like blind men, and when we knew God by the light of his works, we glorified him not as God, neither were thankful, but became vain in our imaginations, and our foolish heart was darkened. Naturally, spiritual things are not discernible by man, they are spiritual and spiritually discerned, and the carnal mind cannot perceive them, for it walks in darkness. The guilt of sin is a thing too high for the carnal mind to understand; the glory of the eternal sacrifice it cannot perceive. The excellence of God, the faithfulness of his promise and the validity of his covenant, all such things as these are swathed in mist, so that the carnal mind seeth them not. As soon as ever the grace of God comes into the heart, it makes as great a difference as did the eternal fiat of Jehovah, when he said, "Let there be light," and there was light. As soon as ever God the Holy Ghost begins to work upon the soul of man to illuminate him, he perceives at once his own sinfulness, he abhors that sinfulness, he labours to escape from it, he cries out for a remedy, he finds it in Christ; henceforth he no longer loves sin, he is not guided any longer by the darkness of policy, and selfishness and error, but he walks after the light of the truth of God, of righteousness, of holiness, of true

No. 663

knowledge. God has brought him into light: he sees now what he never saw before; knows, feels, believes, recognises what he never had known anything of aforetime—*he is in the light.* Hence you constantly find the Christian called a child of light, and he is warned that he is of the light and of the day. He is told, "Ye are not of the night nor of darkness." "Ye were sometime darkness, but now are ye light in the Lord: walk as children of light."

You perceive in the text, then, that the Christian is spoken of as a man who is in the light; but there is something more said of him than this. He is practically in the light, "if we *walk in* the light." It is of no use to pretend to have light in the brain, so as to comprehend all knowledge, so as to be sound and orthodox in one's doctrinal opinions— this will be of no vital service, so far as the great point of salvation is concerned. A man may think he has much light, but if it be only notional and doctrinal, and is not the light which enlightens his nature and develops itself in his practical walk, he lies when he talks of being in the light, for he is in darkness altogether. Nor is it truthful to pretend or profess that we have light within in the form of experience if we do not walk in it, for where the light is true, it is quite certain to show itself abroad. If there be a candle within the lantern its light will stream forth into the surrounding darkness, and those who have eyes will be able to see it. I have no right to say I have light, unless I walk in it. The apostle is very peremptory with those who so speak. He says, "He that saith I know him and keepeth not his commandments, is a liar, and the truth is not in him." The Christian, then, is in the light, and he is *practically* in it; his walk and conversation are regulated by truth, by holiness, and by that divine knowledge which God has been pleased to bestow upon him. He walks in the light of faith, in another path than that which is trodden by men who have nothing but the light of sense. He sees Him who is invisible, and the sight of the invisible God operates upon his soul; he looks into eternity, he marks the dread reward of sin, and the blessed gift of God to those who trust in Jesus, and eternal realities have an effect upon his whole manner and conversation: hence he is a man in the light, walking in that light.

There is a very strong description given here—"If we walk in the light *as He is in the light.*" Beloved, the thought of that dazzles me. I have tried to look it in the face, but I cannot endure it. If we walk in the light as God is in the light. Can we ever attain to this? Shall poor flesh and blood ever be able to walk as clearly in the light as He is whom we call "Our Father," of whom it is written "God is light, and in him is no darkness at all." Let us say this much, and then commend this wonderful expression to your meditations. Certainly, this is the model which is set before us, for the Saviour himself said, "Be ye perfect, even as your Father who is in heaven is perfect;" and if we take anything short of absolute perfection as our model of life, we shall certainly, even if we should attain to our ideal, fall short of the glory of God. Beloved, when a schoolmaster writes the copy at the head of the page, he does not expect that the boy will come up to the copy; but then if the copy be not a perfect one, it is not fit to be imitated by a child; and so our God gives us himself as the pattern and copy, "Be ye imitators of God as dear children," for nothing short of himself would be a worthy model. Though we as life-sculptors may feel that we can never rival the perfection of God, yet we are to seek after it, and never to be satisfied until we attain to it. The youthful artist, as he grasps his early pencil, can hardly hope to equal Raphael or Michael Angelo, but still, if he did not have a noble beau ideal before his mind, he would only attain to something very mean and ordinary. Heavenly fingers point us to the Lord Jesus as the great exemplar of his people, and the Holy Spirit works in us a likeness to Him.

But what does it mean, that the Christian is to walk in light as God is in the light? We conceive it to import likeness, but not degree. We are as truly in the light, we are as heartily in the light, we are as sincerely in the light, as honestly in the light, though we cannot be there in the same degree. I cannot dwell in the sun, it is too bright a place for my residence, unless I shall be transformed, like Uriel, Milton's angel, who could dwell in the midst of the blaze of its excessive glory, but I can *walk* in the light of the sun though I cannot dwell in it; and so God is the light, he is himself the sun, and I can walk in the light as he is in the light, though I cannot attain to the same degree of perfection, and excellence, and purity, and truth, in which the Lord himself resides. Trapp is always for giving us truth in a way in which we can remember it, so he says we are to be in the light as God is in the light for *quality*, but not for *equality*; we are to have the same light and as truly to have it and walk in it as God does, though as for equality with God in his holiness and perfection—that must be left until we cross the Jordan and enter into the perfection of the Most High.

Having thus briefly sketched the character of the genuine Christian, observe, beloved, that he is the possessor of two privileges; the first is, *fellowship with God.* "We have fellowship one with another;" and the second is, *complete cleansing from sin—*" and the blood of Jesus Christ his Son cleanseth us from all sin."

The first privilege we will have but a word upon; it is *fellowship with God.* As you read this verse in our translation, it looks very much as if all that was meant was fellowship with your brother Christians; but this, according to able critics, would not convey the sense of the original. The Arabic version renders it, "God with us, and we with him," and several copies read, "we have fellowship with him." Our version almost compels you to think of fellowship with other believers, but such is not the intention of the Spirit. "We have mutual fellowship, between God and our souls there is communion;" this is the sense of the passage. God is light: we walk in light—we agree. "Can two walk together unless they be agreed?" It is clear we are agreed as to the principles which we shall advance: God is the champion of truth, so are we; God is the promoter of holiness, so are we. God seeks that love may reign instead of selfishness, so does the Christian. God hates error, and spares no arrows to destroy it. The Christian also contends earnestly for the faith once delivered to the saints. God is pure, and the pure in heart shall see God. God is holiness, and those who are holy are attracted to God from an affinity of nature, even as the needle is attracted to its pole. If the Lord has visited thee and made thee to walk in light, thou shalt surely have fellowship with God thy Father. He that is in darkness cannot have fellowship with God. Veiled in ignorance, guided by passion, controlled by error, led astray by falsehood, how canst thou aspire to talk with thy God? Thy prayer is but a chattering sound; thy song is the clang of a sounding brass, the noise of a tinkling cymbal; thy devotion bears thee no further than the letter which killeth; but oh, poor soul, if God should take thee out of thy darkness and make thee to see thyself, to see him and follow after truth and righteousness and holiness, why then thy prayer would be heard in heaven, thy song would mingle with the sweet notes of celestial harps, and even thy groans and tears would reach thy Father's heart, for thou wouldst enjoy fellowship with him. If we walk with God as God is in the light, the secret of God is with us, and our secret is with God. He opens his heart to us and we open our heart to him: we become friends: we are bound and knit together, so that being made partakers of the divine nature, having escaped the corruption which is in the world through lust, we lived like Enoch, having our conversation above the skies.

Upon the second privilege we intend to dwell. I have been driven to this text, and yet I have been afraid of it. This text has been handled, the latter part of it I mean. very often out of its connexion. Yet it has had such a comforting influence on many souls, that I have been half afraid to discourse upon it in its connexion, and yet I have felt, "Well, if anything I should say should take away any comfort from any seeking soul, I shall be very sorry, but I cannot help it." I do feel that it is essential to the Christian ministry not to pick passages out of God's Word and rend them away from the connexion, but to take them as they stand. As this text stands, it does not seem to me to gleam with the particular ray of comfort which others see in it, but it has another beam of joy even more radiant. God's Word must be taken as God speaks it: we have no right to divide the living child of divine truth, or wrest it to make it mean other than it does. According to the text, special pardon of sin is the peculiar privilege of those who walk in the light as God is in the light, and it is not the privilege of any one else. Only those who have been brought by divine grace from a state of nature into a state of grace, and walk in the light, may claim the possession of perfect cleansing through the blood of Jesus Christ.

In dwelling upon this latter part of the verse, there seemed to me to be seven things in it, which any thoughtful reader would be struck with. Considered as the privilege of every man who, however limpingly, is walking in the light, this word, which tells of pardon bought with blood, is very precious, a crown set with jewels; to seven choice pearls I invite your loving gaze.

1. The first thing that struck me was THE GREATNESS of everything in the text.

In some places everything is little: you talk with some men—their thoughts, their ideas are all little; almost everything is drawn to a scale, and aspiring minds generally draw their matters to as great a scale as they can find, but that is necessarily a little one. See to what a magnificent scale everything is drawn in our text! Think, beloved, *how great the sin of God's people is!* Will you try and get that thought into your minds, how great is your own sin—your sin before conversion,

—think that over—your sin while seeking the Lord, in putting confidence in your own works and looking after refuges of lies. Your sins since conversion—turn them over. Beloved, one sin towers up like an Alp, but we have many sins heaped upon each other, as in the old fable of the giants who piled Pelion upon Ossa, mountain upon mountain. O God! what an aggregate of sin is there in the life of one of thy most pure and most sanctified children! Multiply this; all the sin of one child of God—multiply it by the number of those contained in that word "*us*," " cleanseth *us* from all sin! How many are God's children? God's Word shall answer. "A number that no man can number, out of all kindreds and peoples and tongues stood before the throne." Can you imagine—deep as hell's bottomless pit; high as heaven's own glory, for sin sought to pluck even God out of his throne; wide as the east is from the west; long as eternity is this great mass of the guilt of the people for whom Christ shed his blood. And yet all this is taken away. "The blood of Jesus Christ his Son cleanseth us from all sin."

Then observe *the greatness of the atonement offered*. Will you inwardly digest those words, "the blood of Jesus Christ his Son"? Blood is at all times precious, but this is no blood of a mere man: it is the blood of an innocent man—better still, it is the blood of man in union with Deity—"His Son!" God's Son! Why! angels cast their crowns before him! All the choral symphonies of heaven surround his glorious throne. "God over all, blessed for ever. Amen." And yet he yields his blood; takes upon himself the form of a servant, and then is scourged and pierced, bruised and torn, and at last slain; for nothing but the blood of Deity could make atonement for human sin. It must be no man, merely; it must be the God-man mediator, the fellow of Jehovah, co-equal and co-eternal with him, who must bear the pangs and bitterness of divine wrath which was due to sin. Think of this— a sacrifice truly, which no human mind can ever properly estimate in the infinity of its value. Here indeed we have greatness—great sin, but a great atonement.

Think again: we have here *great love which provided such a sacrifice.* Oh, how he must have loved, to have descended from heaven to earth, and from earth to the grave! How he must have loved to have chosen us, when we were hating him—when we were enemies, he hath reconciled us unto God by his own death. Dead in trespasses and sins, corrupt, wrapped up in the cerements of evil habits, hateful and hating one another, full of sin and every abomination, yet he loved us so as to yield up his soul unto death for us. We are dealing with great things here indeed, and we must not forget *the greatness of the influence which such an atonement, the result of such love, must have upon the Christian's heart.* Oh, the greatness of the peace which passeth all understanding, which flows from this great atonement! Oh, the greatness of the gratitude which must blaze forth from such a sacred fire as this! Oh, the greatness of the hatred of sin, of the revenge against iniquity, which must spring from a sense of such love, when it is shed abroad in the heart! Ye are citizens enjoying no mean privilege, oh ye blood-bought citizens of a blood-bought city. God has loved you. Ye cannot, though I should allot you a whole life-time—ye cannot get to the depth of that love. God has loved you, and to prove his love he has died in the person of man for you. He loves you, and has overcome the dread result of all your fearful sin; and now, by the love which God has manifested, we do pray you let your holiness, your truthfulness, and your zeal, prove that you understand the greatness of those things. If your heart can really conceive the greatness of the things here revealed, the great sin, the great Saviour offering himself out of great love, that he might make you to be greatly privileged, I am sure your hearts will rejoice.

2. The next thing which sparkles in the text, is its SIMPLE SOLITARINESS: "We have fellowship one with another;" and then it is added, as a simple, gloriously simple statement, "the blood of Jesus Christ his Son cleanseth us from all sin." Observe, here is *nothing said about rites and ceremonies*. It does not begin by saying, "and the waters of baptism, together with the blood of Jesus Christ, his Son, cleanseth us,"—not a word, whether it shall be the sprinkling in infancy, or immersion of believers, nothing is said about it—it is the blood, the blood only, without a drop of baptismal water. *Nothing is here said about sacraments*—what some call "the blessed Eucharist" is not dragged in here—nothing about eating bread and drinking wine—it is the blood, nothing but the blood—"the blood of Jesus Christ his Son." And if nothing is said of rites that God has given, rites that man has invented are equally excluded. Not a syllable is uttered concerning celibacy or monasticism, not a breath about vows of perpetual chastity and poverty, not a hint about confession to a priest and human absolution, not an allusion to penance or extreme unction. "The blood of Jesus Christ his Son cleanseth us from all sin." It was well done by a poor woman, who as she lay sick, heard for the first time the precious gospel of her salvation. She was told that the blood alone cleansed from sin; she believed, and then, putting her hand into her bosom, she took out a little crucifix which she had always worn, hanging from a chain about her neck, and said to the preacher, "Then I don't want this, sir." Ah, truly so, and so may we say of everything that man has devised as a consolation to a poor wounded spirit. "I have found Jesus, and I do not want that, sir." You who want it, keep it; but as for us, if we walk in the light as he is in the light, the blood of Jesus Christ his Son so completely purgeth us from all sin, that we dare not look to anything else, lest we come into the bondage of the beggarly elements of this world. You will perceive, too, that *nothing is said about Christian experience as a means of cleansing*. What, says one, do not the first sentences of the verse imply that? Assuredly not, for you perceive that the first sentence of the verse does not interfere, though it is linked, with the other. If I walk in the light as God is in the light, what then? Does my walking in the light take away my sins? Not at all. I am as much a sinner in the light as in the darkness, if it were possible for me to be in the light without being washed in the blood. Well, but we have fellowship with God, and does not having fellowship with God take away sin? Beloved, do not misunderstand me—no man can have fellowship with God unless sin be taken away; but his fellowship with God, and his walking in light, does not take away his sin—not at all. The whole process of the removal of sin is here, "And the blood of Jesus Christ his Son cleanseth us from all sin." I beg to repeat it—the text does not say that our walking in

the light cleanseth us from sin, it does not say that our having fellowship with God cleanses us from sin—these go with cleansing, but they have no connexion as cause and result—it is the blood, and the blood alone which purges us from sin. The dying thief looked to Christ, and sin was taken away by the blood; and there is a brother in Christ here, who has had such an experience of Christ's love for sixty years that his heart is now like a shock of corn, ripe for heaven; he lives in his Master's presence, he spends the most of his time in his Master's service; but, beloved, there is not a single atom of difference between him and the dying thief, so far as the cleansing away of sin is concerned. The blood cleansed the thief, and the same blood washes this advanced and full-grown Christian, or otherwise he is still unclean.

Observe, yet again, that in the verse *there is no hint given of any emotions, feelings, or attainments, as co-operating with the blood to take away sin.* Christ took the sins of his people and was punished for those sins as if he had been himself a sinner, and so sin is taken away from us; but in no sense, degree, shape or form, is sin removed by attainments, emotions, feelings or experiences. The blood is the alone atonement, the blood without any mixture of aught beside, completes and finishes the work, "For ye are complete in him."

Now I could enlarge for a very long time on this point, but I do not think I shall, I will rather throw into a sentence or two a little direction, and observe that whereas there are some who urge you to look to your doctrinal intelligence as a ground of comfort, I beseech you beloved, look only to the blood; whereas there are others who would set up a standard of Christian experience and urge that this is to be the channel of your consolation, I pray you, while you prize both doctrine and experience, rest nowhere your soul's weight but in the precious blood. Some would lead you to high degrees of fellowship; follow them, but not when they would lead you away from the simple position of a sinner resting upon the blood. There be those who could teach you mysticism, and would have you rejoice in the light within; follow them as far as they have the warrant of God's Word, but never take your foot from that Rock of Ages, where the only safe standing can be found. Certain of my brethren are very fond of preaching Christ in his second advent—I rejoice wherein they preach the truth concerning Christ glorified, but my beloved, I do conjure you do not build your hope on Christ glorified, nor on Christ to come, but on "Christ crucified." Remember that in the matter of taking away sin, the first thing is not the throne, but the cross; not the reigning Saviour, but the bleeding Saviour; not the King in his glory, but the Redeemer in his shame. Care not to be studying dates of prophecies if burdened with sin, but seek your chief, your best comfort in the blood of Jesus Christ which cleanseth us from all sin: here is the pole star of your salvation, sail by it and you shall reach the port of peace.

3. A third brilliant flashes in the light, viz., THE COMPLETENESS of the cleansing. "The blood of Jesus Christ his Son cleanseth us from *all sin,*"—not from some sin, but "from all sin." Beloved, I cannot tell you the exceeding sweetness of this word, but I pray God the Holy Ghost to give you a taste of it. There is original sin, by which we fell in Adam before we were born, and inherited sin through which we

were born in sin and shapen in iniquity; there is actual sin—the sin of my youth and my former transgressions, the sins of my riper years, the sins which defile the hoary head and make that which should be a crown of glory to be a crown of grief—but all these sins original and actual are *all gone! all gone!* Sins against the law, though it be exceeding broad, so that it makes me a sinner in thought, in word, in deed, in heart—all gone. Sins against the gospel, when I kicked against the pricks, when I stifled conscience, when I resisted the Holy Ghost as did also my fathers, when I hated the truth and would not have it because my deeds were evil, and I would not come to the light lest my deeds might be reproved; when I would regard none of the sweet invitations of the gospel—all cleansed away! Sins against Christ Jesus since my conversion when I have backslidden and my heart has been cold towards him; sins against the Holy Spirit when I have followed my own impulses instead of the indwelling Deity,—all gone! The Roman Catholic divides sin into sins venial and sins mortal. Be it so—the blood of Jesus Christ cleanseth us from *all sin*, mortal or venial, deadly or pardonable. Sins of commission—here is a long catalogue—think it over; sins of omission—that is a larger list still. The things which we have left undone which we ought to have done, are probably more numerous than the things which we have done which we ought not to have done—but all are gone. Some sins are greater than others; there is no doubt whatever that adultery, fornication, murder, blasphemy, and such like are greater than the sins of daily life, but whether they be great sins or little sins, they are all gone. That same God who took away the plague of flies from Egypt also took away the plague of thunder and of lightning. All are gone—gone at once. Pharaoh's chariot is drowned in the Red Sea, and the meanest Egyptian is drowned in the self-same way. The depths have covered them; there is not one of them left. There are sins against God—how many are these! Sins of breaking his day and despising his word; profaning his name, forgetting him and not loving him—but He blots out all! Sins against my friends and my enemies, against my neighbour, against my father, my child, my husband—sins in all relationships—yet all are gone! Then, too, remember there are sins of presumption, and sins of ignorance; sins done wilfully, and unknown sins; but the blood cleanseth us from all sin. Shall I enlarge? Surely I need not; but you see the purging is complete. Whether the bill be little or the bill be great, the same receipt can discharge one as the other. The blood of Jesus Christ is as blessed and divine a payment for the sin of blaspheming Peter as it is for the sin of loving John, and our iniquity is gone, all gone at once and all gone for ever. Blessed completeness! What a sweet theme to dwell upon!

4. The next gem that studs the text is the thought of PRESENTNESS.

"Cleanseth" says the text—not "*shall* cleanse." There are multitudes who think that as a dying hope they may look forward to pardon, and perhaps within a few hours of their dissolution they may be able to say, "My sins are pardoned." Such can never have read God's Word, or, if they have read it, they have read it with unbelieving eyes. Beloved, I would not give the snap of my finger for the bare possibility of cleansing when I come to die. Oh how infinitely better to have cleansing now! Some imagine that a sense of pardon is an attainment after many years of Christian experience. For a young Christian to say, "My sins are forgiven," seems to them to be an untimely fig, ripe too soon; but, beloved, it is not so. The moment a sinner trusts Jesus, that sinner is as fully forgiven as he will be when the light of the glory of God shall shine upon his resurrection countenance. Beloved, forgiveness of sin is a present thing—a privilege for this day, a joy for this very hour; and whosoever walks in the light as God is in the light has fellowship with God, and has at this moment the perfect pardon of sin.

You perceive that it is written in the present tense as if to indicate continuance: it will always be so with you, Christian. It was so yesterday—it was "*cleanseth*" yesterday, it is "cleanseth" to-day: it will be "cleanseth" to-morrow: it will be "cleanseth" until you cross the river —every day you may come to this fountain for it "cleanseth!" Every hour you may stand by its brim, for it "cleanseth." I think there is sanctification here as well as justification. I am inclined to believe that this text has been too much limited in its interpretation, and that it signifies that the blood of Jesus is constantly operating upon the man who walks in the light so as to cleanse him from the indwelling power of sin; and the Spirit of God applies the doctrine of the atonement to the production of purity, till the soul becomes completely pure from sin at the last. I desire to feel every day the constantly purifying effect of the sacrifice of my Lord and Master. Look at the foot of the cross, and I am sure you will feel that the precious drops cleanse from all sin.

5. Now in the fifth place, the text presents to us very blessedly the thought of CERTAINTY. It is not "*perhaps* the blood of Jesus Christ cleanses from sin," the text speaks of it as a fact not to be disputed, it does do so. To the believer this is matter of certainty, for the Spirit of God beareth witness with our spirits that we are born of God. Our spirit in the joy and peace which it receives through believing, becomes assured of its being cleansed, and then the Spirit of God comes in as a second witness and bears witness with our spirit that we are born of God. My being cleansed from all sin to-day is to me as much a matter of consciousness, as my being better in health. I was conscious of pain when I lay on my sick bed, and so when I was living in sin as soon as God gave me spiritual life, I was conscious that guilt lay heavily upon me; I am conscious now of pain removed, and so I am

equally conscious of sin removed, and I do not hesitate to say it here, that my consciousness of pardoned sin is at this moment as clear and as distinct as my consciousness of removed pain, while I look at Jesus Christ my Lord by faith. So is it often with the Christian. It is frequently with him a matter of consciousness most positive and infallible that he is truly and really cleansed from all sin by the blood of Jesus Christ; and it is not merely a matter of consciousness, but if you think of it, it is a matter of reasoning. If Jesus Christ did indeed take the sins of all who believe, then it follows necessarily that I trusting in Christ have no longer any sin, for if Christ took my sin, sin cannot be in two places at once. If Christ bears it then I do not bear it; and if Christ was punished for it, then the punishment of my sin has been endured, and I cannot be punished for the sin for which Jesus has been punished, unless God should sovereignly punish men, which would be such an insult to the honesty and justice of God, that it must not be tolerated for a moment in our thoughts. If Jesus Christ has paid the debt it is paid, and—

"Justice can demand no more,
Christ has paid the dreadful score."

So the Christian's being cleansed from sin becomes to him a matter of spiritual argument: he can see it clearly and manifestly.

Yet more, he is so certain of it that it begins to operate upon him in blessed effect. He is so sure that there is no sin laid to his door that he draws nearer to God than a sinner may do defiled with sin. He enters into that which is within the veil: he talks with God as his father; he claims familiar intercourse with the Most High God; and though God be so great that the heaven of heavens cannot contain him, yet he believes that that same God lives in his heart as in a temple. Now this he could not feel if he did not know that sin is put away. Beloved, no man is capable of virtue in the highest sense of the term till it is a matter of certainty to him that his sin is cleansed. You say "That is a strong assertion," but I do assert it—all of you who are doing good works with the view to saving yourselves are missing the mark of pure virtue. You say "Why?" The goodness of an action depends upon its motive; your motive is to save yourselves—that is selfish; your action is selfish, and the virtue of it has evaporated. But the Christian, when he performs good works, does not perform them with any view whatever of merit or self salvation. "I am saved," saith he— "perfectly saved. I have not a sin in God's book against me—I am clean. Great God, before thy bar I am clean through Jesus Christ.

'Loved of my God for him again
With love intense I burn.'

What can I do to prove to all mankind how much, how truly I love my God?" You see then that this must be a matter of certainty, or else it will never have its right effect upon you; and I pray God that you may suck the certainty out of this text and taste its sweetness to your own soul's inward contentment, and be able to say, "Yes, without a doubt, the blood of Jesus Christ his Son cleanseth us from all sin."

6. I hope I shall not weary you, but a few words upon the sixth gem which adorns the text, namely, the DIVINITY of it. "Where?" saith one. Does not divinity gleam in this text? Does it not strike you that the verse is written in a God-like style? The God-like style is very peculiar. You can tell the style of Milton from the style of Wordsworth, or the style of Byron. Read a verse and an educated person knows the author by the ring of the sentences. The God-like style is unique in its excellence. You need never put the name at the bottom when the writing is of the Lord. You know it by the very style of it. "Light be! Light was." Who speaks like that but Deity? Now there is a divine ring about this sentence; "The blood of Jesus Christ his Son cleanseth from all sin." Why if man were talking of so great an atonement he would fetch a compass; he would have to go round about. We cannot afford to say such great things as these in a few words; we must adopt some form of speech that would allow us to extol the truth and indicate its beauties. God seems to put away his pearls as if they were but common pebbles. "The blood of Jesus Christ his Son cleanseth us from all sin"—as if it were as much a matter of every-day work as for a man to wash his hands.

Notice the simplicity of the whole process. It does not seem to take weeks or months, it is done at once. Slowly and by degrees is man's action—we must lay the thing to soak, to fetch the colour from it, subject it to many processes, and expose it to the wind, and rain, and frost, and sun, before it can be cleansed. But here God speaks and it is done. The blood comes into contact with the guilty conscience, and it is all over with sin. As if it were but a handful he moves a mountain of sin, he taketh up the isles as a very little thing; he counteth great oceans of our sin as though they were but a drop of a bucket. Believing in Christ in a moment, by the divine and majestic process which God has ordained, we get the perfect cleansing of sin.

7. In the last place, just a hint upon the WISDOM of the text. What a wise way of cleansing from sin the text speaks of! Beloved, suppose God had devised a plan for pardoning sin which did not turn the sinner's face to God; then you would have a very singular spectacle; you would have a sinner pardoned by a process which enabled him to do without his God; and it strikes me he would be worse than he was before. But here, before ever the sinner can receive pardon he must say, "I will arise and go unto my Father;" and he must come closer into contact with God than he ever came before. He must see God in the flesh of Christ, and must look to him if he would be saved. I do bless God

that I have not to turn my face to hell to get pardon, but I have to turn my face towards heaven; that seems to me to be the wise way, for while it takes away the sin, which was like a disease, it takes away the distance from God, which was the true root of that disease; it turns the sinner's face in the direction of holiness and bliss.

Observe the benefit of this plan of salvation in the fact that it makes the sinner feel the evil of sin. If we were pardoned in a way which did not involve pain to some one, we should say, "Oh, it is easy for God to forgive it;" but when I see the streaming veins of Jesus, and mark the sweat of blood fall to the ground, and hear him cry, "They have pierced my hands and my feet," then I understand that sin is a dreadful evil. If a man should be pardoned without being made to feel that sin is bitter, I do not know that he would be really any the better off—perhaps better unpardoned than pardoned, unless he was led to hate sin.

Our gracious God has also chosen this plan of salvation with the wise design of making man glorify God. I cannot see sin pardoned by the substitutionary atonement of the Lord Jesus, without dedicating myself to the praise and glory of the great God of redeeming love. It would be a pity if man could be pardoned, and afterwards could live a selfish, thankless life, would it not? If God had devised a scheme by which sin could be pardoned, and yet the sinner live to himself, I do not know that the world or the man would be advantaged. But here are many birds killed with one stone, as the proverb puts it. Now henceforth at the foot of the cross, the bands which bound our soul to earth are loosened. We are strangers in the land, and henceforth " God forbid that we should glory, save in the cross of our Lord Jesus Christ, by whom the world is crucified unto us, and we are crucified to the world."

I leave this text with the believer, only adding, if any of you would have it, and joy in it, you must walk in the light. I pray God the Holy Ghost to bring you to see the light of the glory of God, in the face of Jesus Christ; then will you trust him, and then shall you have fellowship with him, and by his blood you shall be cleansed from all sin. God bless you for Jesus' sake. Amen.

PORTION OF SCRIPTURE READ BEFORE SERMON.—1 John i. & ii., 1—11.

Metropolitan Tabernacle Pulpit.

THE ASCENSION AND THE SECOND ADVENT
PRACTICALLY CONSIDERED.

A Sermon

Delivered on Lord's-day Morning, December 28th, 1884, by

C. H. SPURGEON,

At the Metropolitan Tabernacle, Newington.

"And while they looked stedfastly toward heaven as he went up, behold, two men stood by them in white apparel; which also said, Ye men of Galilee, why stand ye gazing up into heaven? this same Jesus, which is taken up from you into heaven, shall so come in like manner as ye have seen him go into heaven."—Acts i. 10, 11.

Four great events shine out brightly in our Saviour's story. All Christian minds delight to dwell upon his birth, his death, his resurrection, and his ascension. These make four rounds in that ladder of light, the foot of which is upon the earth, but the top whereof reacheth to heaven. We could not afford to dispense with any one of those four events, nor would it be profitable for us to forget, or to under-estimate the value of any one of them. That the Son of God was born of a woman creates in us the intense delight of a brotherhood springing out of a common humanity. That Jesus once suffered unto the death for our sins, and thereby made a full atonement for us, is the rest and life of our spirits. The manger and the cross together are divine seals of love. That the Lord Jesus rose again from the dead is the warrant of our justification, and also a transcendently delightful assurance of the resurrection of all his people, and of their eternal life in him. Hath he not said, "Because I live ye shall live also"? The resurrection of Christ is the morning star of our future glory. Equally delightful is the remembrance of his ascension. No song is sweeter than this—"Thou hast ascended on high; thou hast led captivity captive, thou hast received gifts for men, yea, for the rebellious also, that the Lord God might dwell among them."

Each one of those four events points to another, and they all lead up to it: the fifth link in the golden chain is our Lord's second and most glorious advent. Nothing is mentioned between his ascent and his descent. True, a rich history comes between; but it lies in a valley between two stupendous mountains: we step from alp to alp as we journey in meditation from the ascension to the second advent. I say that each of the previous four events points to it. Had he not come a first time in humiliation, born under the law, he could not have come

No. 1,817.

a second time in amazing glory "without a sin-offering unto salvation." Because he died once we rejoice that he dieth no more, death hath no more dominion over him, and therefore he cometh to destroy that last enemy whom he hath already conquered. It is our joy, as we think of our Redeemer as risen, to feel that in consequence of his rising the trump of the archangel shall assuredly sound for the awaking of all his slumbering people, when the Lord himself shall descend from heaven with a shout. As for his ascension, he could not a second time descend if he had not first ascended; but having perfumed heaven with his presence, and prepared a place for his people, we may fitly expect that he will come again and receive us unto himself, that where he is there we may be also. I want you, therefore, as in contemplation you pass with joyful footsteps over these four grand events, as your faith leaps from his birth to his death, and from his resurrection to his ascension, to be looking forward, and even hastening unto this crowning fact of our Lord's history; for ere long he shall so come in like manner as he was seen go up into heaven.

This morning, in our meditation, we will start from the ascension; and if I had sufficient imagination I should like to picture our Lord and the eleven walking up the side of Olivet, communing as they went,—a happy company, with a solemn awe upon them, but with an intense joy in having fellowship with each other. Each disciple was glad to think that his dear Lord and Master who had been crucified was now among them, not only alive but surrounded with a mysterious safety and glory which none could disturb. The enemy was as still as a stone: not a dog moved his tongue: his bitterest foes made no sign during the days of our Lord's after-life below. The company moved onward peacefully towards Bethany—Bethany which they all knew and loved. The Saviour seemed drawn there at the time of his ascension, even as men's minds return to old and well-loved scenes when they are about to depart out of this world. His happiest moments on earth had been spent beneath the roof where lived Mary and Martha and their brother Lazarus. Perhaps it was best for the disciples that he should leave them at that place where he had been most hospitably entertained, to show that he departed in peace and not in anger. There they had seen Lazarus raised from the dead by him who was now to be taken up from them: the memory of the triumphant past would help the tried faith of the present. There they had heard the voice saying, "Loose him, and let him go," and there they might fitly see their Lord loosed from all bonds of earthly gravitation that he might go to his Father and their Father. The memories of the place might help to calm their minds and arouse their spirits to that fulness of joy which ought to attend the glorifying of their Lord.

But they have come to a standstill, having reached the brow of the hill. The Saviour stands conspicuously in the centre of the group, and, following upon most instructive discourse, he pronounces a blessing upon them. He lifts his pierced hands, and while he is lifting them and is pronouncing words of love, he begins to rise from the earth. He has risen above them all to their astonishment! In a moment he has passed beyond the olives, which seem with their silvery sheen to be lit up by his milder radiance. While the disciples are looking, the Lord has ascended into mid-air, and speedily he has risen to the regions of the clouds. They stand spell-bound with astonishment, and suddenly a bright cloud, like a chariot of God, bears him away. That cloud conceals him from mortal gaze. Though we have known Christ after the flesh, now after the flesh know we him no more. They are riveted to the spot, very naturally so : they linger long in the place, they stand with streaming eyes, wonder-struck, still looking upward.

It is not the Lord's will that they should long remain inactive; their reverie is interrupted. They might have stood there till wonder saddened into fear. As it was, they remained long enough; for the angel's words may be accurately rendered, "Why have ye stood, gazing up into heaven?"

Their lengthened gaze needed to be interrupted, and, therefore, two shining ones, such as aforetime met the women at the sepulchre, are sent to them. These messengers of God appear in human form that they may not alarm them, and in white raiment as if to remind them that all was bright and joyous; and these white-robed ministers stood with them as if they would willingly join their company. As no one of the eleven would break silence, the men in white raiment commenced the discourse. Addressing them in the usual celestial style, they asked a question which contained its own answer, and then went on to tell their message. As they had once said to the women, "Why seek ye the living among the dead? He is not here, but is risen;" so did they now say, " Ye men of Galilee, why stand ye gazing up into heaven? this same Jesus, which is taken up from you into heaven, shall so come in like manner as ye have seen him go into heaven." The angels showed their knowledge of them by calling them "men of Galilee," and reminded them that they were yet upon earth by recalling their place of birth. Brought back to their senses, their reverie over, the apostles at once gird up their loins for active service; they do not need twice telling, but hasten to Jerusalem. The vision of angels has singularly enough brought them back into the world of actual life again, and they obey the command, "Tarry ye at Jerusalem." They seem to say,—the taking up of our Master is not a thing to weep about: he has gone to his throne and to his glory, and he said it was expedient for us that he should go away. He will now send us the promise of the Father; we scarcely know what it will be like, but let us, in obedience to his will, make the best of our way to the place where he bade us await the gift of power. Do you not see them going down the side of Olivet, taking that Sabbath-day's journey into the cruel and wicked city without a thought of fear; having no dread of the bloodthirsty crew who slew their Lord, but happy in the memory of their Lord's exaltation and in the expectation of a wonderful display of his power. They held fellowship of the most delightful kind with one another, and anon entered into the upper room, where in protracted prayer and communion they waited for the promise of the Father. You see I have no imagination: I have barely mentioned the incidents in the simplest language. Yet try and realise the scene, for it will be helpful so to do, since our Lord Jesus is to come in like manner as the disciples saw him go up into heaven.

My first business this morning will be to consider *the gentle chiding* administered by the shining ones :—" Ye men of Galilee, why stand ye gazing up unto heaven?" Secondly, *the cheering description* of our Lord which the white-robed messengers used,—"This same Jesus"; and then, thirdly, *the practical truth* which they taught—"This same Jesus, which is taken up from you into heaven, shall so come in like manner as ye have seen him go into heaven."

I. First, then, here is A GENTLE CHIDING. It is not sharply uttered by men dressed in black who use harsh speech, and upbraid the servants of God severely for what was rather a mistake than a fault. No; the language is strengthening, yet tender: the fashion of a question allows them rather to reprove themselves than to be reproved; and the tone is that of brotherly love, and affectionate concern.

Notice, that *what these saintly men were doing seems at first sight to be very right.* Methinks, if Jesus were among us now we would fix our eyes upon him, and never withdraw them. He is altogether lovely, and it would seem wicked to yield our eyesight to any inferior object so long as he was to be seen. When he ascended up into heaven it was the duty of his friends to look upon him. It can never be wrong to look up; we are often bidden to do so, and it is even a holy saying of the Psalmist, "I will direct my prayer unto thee, and will look up"; and, again, "I will lift up mine eyes unto the hills, from whence cometh my help." If it be right to look up into heaven, it must be still more right to look up while Jesus rises to the place of his glory. Surely it had been wrong if they had looked anywhere else,—it was due to the Lamb of God that they should behold him as long as eyes could follow him. He is the Sun: where should eyes be turned but to his light? He is the King; and where should courtiers within the palace gate turn their eyes but to their King as he ascends to his throne? The truth is, there was nothing wrong in their looking up into heaven; but they went a little further than looking; they stood "gazing." A little excess in right may be faulty. It may be wise to look, but foolish to gaze. There is a very thin partition sometimes between that which is commendable and that which is censurable. There is a golden mean which it is not easy to keep. The exact path of right is often as narrow as a razor's edge, and he must be wise that doth not err either on the right hand or on the left. "Look" is ever the right word. Why, it is "Look unto me, and be saved." Look, aye, look steadfastly and intently: be your posture that of one "looking unto Jesus," always throughout life. But there is a gazing which is not commendable, when the look becomes not that of reverent worship, but of an overweening curiosity; when there mingles with the desire to know what should be known, a prying into that which it is for God's glory to conceal. Brethren, it is of little use to look up into an empty heaven. If Christ himself be not visible in heaven, then in vain do we gaze, since there is nothing for a saintly eye to see. When the person of Jesus was gone out of the azure vault above them, and the cloud had effectually concealed him, why should they continue to gaze when God himself had drawn the curtain? If infinite wisdom had withdrawn the object upon which they desired to gaze, what would their gazing be but a sort of reflection upon the wisdom which had removed their Lord? Yet it did seem very right. Thus certain things that you and I may do may appear right, and yet we may need to be chidden out of them into something better: they may be right in themselves, but not appropriate for the occasion, not seasonable, nor expedient. They may be right up to a point, and then may touch the boundary of excess. A steadfast gaze into heaven may be to a devout soul a high order of worship, but if this filled up much of our working time it might become the idlest form of folly.

Yet I cannot help adding that *it was very natural.* I do not wonder that the whole eleven stood gazing up, for if I had been there I am sure I should have done the same. How struck they must have been with the ascent of the Master out of their midst! You would be amazed if some one from among our own number now began to ascend into heaven! Would you not? Our Lord did not gradually melt away from sight as a phantom, or dissolve into thin air as a mere apparition: the Saviour did not disappear in that way at all, but he rose, and they saw that it was his very self that was so rising. His own body, the materialism in which he had veiled himself, actually, distinctly, and literally, rose to heaven before their eyes. I repeat, the Lord did not dissolve, and disappear like a vision of the night, but he evidently rose till the cloud intervened so that they could see him no more. I think I should have stood looking to the very place where his cloudy chariot had been. I know it would be idle to continue so to do, but our hearts often urge us on to acts which we could not justify logically. Hearts are not to be argued with. Sometimes you stand by a grave where one is buried whom you dearly loved: you go there often to weep. You cannot help it, the place is precious to you; yet you could not prove that you do any good by your visits, perhaps you even injure yourself thereby, and deserve to be gently chidden with the question, "why?" It may be the most natural thing in the world, and yet it may not be a wise thing. The Lord allows us to do that which is innocently natural, but he will not have us carry it too far; for then it might foster an evil nature. Hence he sends an interrupting messenger: not an angel with a sword, or even a rod; but he sends some man in white raiment,—I mean one who is both cheerful and holy, and he, by his conduct or his words, suggests to us the question, "Why stand ye here gazing?" *Cui bono?* What will be the benefit? What will it avail? Thus our understanding being called into action, and we being men of thought, we answer to ourselves, "This will not do. We must not stand gazing here for ever," and therefore we arouse ourselves to get back to the Jerusalem of practical life, where in the power of God we hope to do service for our Master.

Notice, then, that the disciples were doing that which seemed to be right, and what was evidently very natural, but that it is very easy to carry the apparently right and the absolutely natural too far. Let us take heed to ourselves, and often ask our hearts, "Why?"

For, thirdly, notice that what they *did was not after all justifiable upon strict reason.* While Christ was going up it was proper that they should adoringly look at him. He might almost have said, "If ye see me when I am taken up a double portion of my spirit shall rest upon you." They did well to look where he led the way. But when he was gone, still to remain gazing was an act which they could not exactly explain to themselves, and could not justify to others. Put the question thus:—"What purpose will be fulfilled by your continuing to gaze into the sky? He is gone, it is absolutely certain that he is gone. He is taken up, and God himself has manifestly concealed all trace of him by bidding yonder cloud sail in between him and you. Why gaze ye still? He told you 'I go unto my Father.' Why stand and gaze?" We may under the influence of great love, act unwisely. I remember well seeing the action of a woman whose only son was emigrating to a distant colony. I stood in the station, and I noticed her many tears and her frequent embraces of her boy; but the train came up and he entered the carriage. After the train had passed beyond the station, she was foolish enough to break away from friends who sought to detain her; she ran along the platform, leaped down upon the railroad and pursued the flying train. It was natural, but it had been better left undone. What was the use of it? We had better abstain from acts which serve no practical purpose; for in this life we have neither time nor strength to waste in fruitless action. The disciples would be wise to cease gazing, for nobody would be benefitted by it, and they would not themselves be blessed. What is the use of gazing when there is nothing to see. Well, then, did the angels ask, "Why stand ye gazing up into heaven?"

Again, put another question,—What precept were they obeying when they stood gazing up into heaven? If you have a command from God to do a certain thing, you need not inquire into the reason of the command, it is disobedient to begin to canvas God's will; but when there is no precept whatever, why persevere in an act which evidently does not promise to bring any blessing? Who bade them stand gazing up into heaven? If Christ had done so, then in Christ's name let them stand like statues and never turn their heads: but as he had not bidden them, why did they do what he had not commanded, and leave undone what he had commanded? For he had strictly charged them that they should tarry at Jerusalem till they were "endued with power from on high." So what they did was not justifiable.

Here is the practical point for us:—*What they did we are very apt to imitate.* "Oh," say you, "I shall never stand gazing up into heaven." I am not sure of that. Some Christians are very curious, but not obedient. Plain precepts are neglected, but difficult problems they seek to solve. I remember one who used always to be dwelling upon the vials and seals and trumpets. He was great at apocalyptic symbols; but he had seven children, and he had no family prayer. If he had left the vials and trumpets and minded his boys and girls, it would have been a deal better. I have known men marvellously great upon Daniel, and specially instructed in Ezekiel, but singularly forgetful of the twentieth of Exodus, and not very clear upon Romans the eighth. I do not speak with any blame of such folks for studying Daniel and Ezekiel, but quite the reverse; yet I wish they had been more zealous for the conversion of the sinners in their neighbourhoods, and more careful to assist the poor saints. I admit the value of the study of the feet of the image in Nebuchadnezzar's vision, and the importance of knowing the kingdoms which make up the ten toes, but I do not see the propriety of allowing such studies to overlay the common-places of practical godliness. If the time spent over obscure theological propositions were given to a mission in the dim alley near the good man's house, more benefit would come to man and more glory to God. I would have you understand all mysteries, brethren, if you could ; but do not forget that our chief business here below is to cry, " Behold the Lamb ! " By all manner of means read and search till you know all that the Lord has revealed concerning things to come ; but first of all see to it that your children are brought to the Saviour's feet, and that you are workers together with God in the upbuilding of his church. The dense mass of misery and ignorance and sin which is round about us on every side demands all our powers ; and if you do not respond to the call, though I am not a man in white apparel, I shall venture to say to you, " Ye men of Christendom, why stand ye gazing up into the mysteries when so much is to be done for Jesus, and you are leaving it undone ? " O ye who are curious but not obedient, I fear I speak to you in vain, but I have spoken. May the Holy Spirit also speak.

Others are contemplative but not active,—much given to the study of Scripture and to meditation thereon, but not zealous for good works. Contemplation is so scarce in these days that I could wish there were a thousand times as much of it ; but in the case to which I refer everything runs in the one channel of thought, all time is spent in reading, in enjoyment, in rapture, in pious leisure. Religion never ought to become the subject of selfishness, and yet I fear some treat it as if its chief end was spiritual gratification. When a man's religion all lies in his saving his own self, and in enjoying holy things for his own self, there is a disease upon him. When his judgment of a sermon is based upon the one question, " Did it feed *me?*" it is a swinish judgment. There is such a thing as getting a swinish religion in which you are yourself first, yourself second, yourself third, yourself to the utmost end. Did Jesus ever think or speak in that fashion ? Contemplation of Christ himself may be so carried out as to lead you away from Christ : the recluse meditates on Jesus, but he is as unlike the busy self-denying Jesus as well can be. Meditation unattended with active service in the spreading of the gospel among men, well deserves the rebuke of the angel, " Ye men of Galilee, why stand ye gazing up into heaven ? "

Moreover, some are careful and anxious and deliriously impatient for some marvellous interposition. We get at times into a sad state of mind, because we do not see the kingdom of Christ advancing as we desire. I suppose it is with you as it is with me,—I begin to fret, and I am deeply troubled, and I feel that there is good reason that I should be, for truth is fallen in the streets, and the days of blasphemy and rebuke are upon us. Then we pine ; for the Master is away, and we cry, " When will he be back again ? Oh, why are his chariots so long in coming ? Why tarries he through the ages ? " Our desires sour into impatience, and we commence gazing up into heaven, looking for his coming with a restlessness which does not allow us to discharge our duty as we should. Whenever anybody gets into that state, this is the word, " Ye men of Galilee, why stand ye gazing up into heaven ? "

In certain cases this uneasiness has drawn to itself a wrong expectation of immediate wonders, and an intense desire for sign-seeing. Ah me, what fanaticisms come of this ! In America years ago, one came forward who declared that on such a day the Lord would come, and he led a great company to believe his crazy predictions. Many took their horses and fodder for two or three days, and went out into the woods, expecting to be all the more likely to see all that was to be seen when once away from the crowded city. All over the States there were people who had made ascension-dresses in which to soar into the air in proper costume. They waited, and they waited, and I am sure that no text could have been more appropriate for them than this, "Ye men of America, why stand ye here gazing up into heaven?" Nothing came of it; and yet there are thousands in England and America who only need a fanatical leader, and they would run into the like folly. The desire to know the times and seasons is a craze with many poor bodies whose insanity runs in that particular groove. Every occurrence is a "sign of the times": a sign, I may add, which they do not understand. An earthquake is a special favourite with them. "Now," they cry, "the Lord is coming"; as if there had not been earthquakes of the sort we have heard of lately hundreds of times since our Lord went up into heaven. When the prophetic earthquakes occur in divers places, we shall know of it without the warnings of these brethren. What a number of persons have been infatuated by the number of the beast, and have been ready to leap for joy because they have found the number 666 in some great one's name. Why, everybody's name will yield that number if you treat it judiciously, and use the numerals of Greece, Rome, Egypt, China, or Timbuctoo. I feel weary with the silly way in which some people make toys out of Scripture, and play with texts as with a pack of cards. Whenever you meet with a man who sets up to be a prophet, keep out of his way in the future; and when you hear of signs and wonders, turn you to your Lord, and in patience possess your souls. "The just shall live by his faith." There is no other way of living among wild enthusiasts. Believe in God, and ask not for miracles and marvels, or the knowledge of times and seasons. To know when the Lord will restore the kingdom is not in your power. Remember that verse which I read just now in your hearing,—"It is not for you to know the times or the seasons." If I were introduced into a room where a large number of parcels were stored up, and I was told that there was something good for me, I should begin to look for that which had my name upon it, and when I came upon a parcel and I saw in pretty big letters, "*It is not for you*," I should leave it alone. Here, then, is a casket of knowledge marked, "*It is not for you* to know the times or the seasons, which the Father hath put in his own power." Cease to meddle with matters which are concealed, and be satisfied to know the things which are clearly revealed.

II. Secondly, I want you to notice THE CHEERING DESCRIPTION which these bright spirits give concerning our Lord. They describe him thus,—" This same Jesus."

I appreciate the description the more because *it came from those who knew him*. "He was seen of angels"; they had watched him all his life long, and they knew him, and when they, having just seen him rise to his Father and his God, said of him, "This same Jesus," then I know by an infallible testimony that he was the same, and that he is the same.

Jesus is gone, but he still exists. He has left us, but he is not dead; he has not dissolved into nothing like the mist of the morning. "This same Jesus" is gone up unto his Father's throne, and he is there to-day as certainly as he once stood at Pilate's bar. As surely as he did hang upon the cross, so surely does he, the self-same man, sit upon the throne of God and reign over creation. I like to think of the positive identity of the Christ in the seventh heaven with the Christ in the lowest deeps of agony. The Christ they spat upon is now the Christ whose name the cherubim and seraphim are hymning day without night. The Christ they scourged is he before whom principalities and powers delight to cast their crowns. Think of it and be glad this morning; and do not stand gazing up into heaven after a myth or a dream. Jesus lives; mind that you live also. Do not loiter as if you had nothing at all to do, or as if the kingdom of God had come to an end because Jesus is gone from the earth, as to his bodily presence. It is not all over; he still lives, and he has given you a work to do till he comes. Therefore, go and do it.

"This same Jesus"—I love that word, for "Jesus" means *a Saviour*. Oh, ye anxious sinners here present, the name of him who has gone up into his glory is full of invitation to you! Will you not come to "this same Jesus"? This is he who opened the eyes of the blind and brought forth the prisoners out of the prison-house. He is doing the same thing to-day. Oh that your eyes may see his light! He that touched the lepers, and that raised the dead, is the same Jesus still, able to save to the uttermost. Oh that you may look and live! You have only to come to him by faith, as she did who touched the hem of his garment; you have but to cry to him as the blind man did whose sight he restored; for he is the same Jesus, bearing about with him the same tender love for guilty men, and the same readiness to receive and cleanse all that come to him by faith.

"This same Jesus." Why, that must have meant that he who is in heaven is the same Christ who was on earth, but it must also mean that *he who is to come will be the same Jesus that went up into heaven.* There is no change in our blessed Master's nature, nor will there ever be. There is a great change in his condition:—

> "The Lord shall come, but not the same
> As once in lowliness he came,
> A humble man before his foes,
> A weary man, and full of woes."

He will be "the same Jesus" in nature though not in condition: he will possess the same tenderness when he comes to judge, the same gentleness of heart when all the glories of heaven and earth shall gird his brow. Our eye shall see him in that day, and we shall recognize him not only by the nail-prints, but by the very look of his countenance, by the character that gleams from that marvellous face; and we shall say, "'Tis he! 'tis he! the self-same Christ that went up from the top of Olivet from the midst of his disciples." Go to him with your troubles, as you would have done when he was here. Look forward to his second coming without dread. Look for him with that joyous expectancy with which you would welcome Jesus of Bethany, who loved Mary, and Martha, and Lazarus.

On the back of that sweet title came this question, "Why stand ye here gazing into heaven?" They might have said, "We stay here because we do not know where to go. Our Master is gone." But oh, it is the same Jesus, and he is coming again, so go down to Jerusalem and get to work directly. Do not worry yourselves; no grave accident has occurred; it is not a disaster that Christ has gone, but an advance in his work. Despisers tell us nowadays, "Your cause is done for! Christianity is spun out! Your divine Christ is gone; we have not seen a trace of his miracle-working hand, nor of that voice which no man could rival." Here is our answer: We are not standing gazing up into heaven, we are not paralyzed because Jesus is away. He lives, the great Redeemer lives; and though it is our delight to lift up our eyes because we expect his coming, it is equally our delight to turn our heavenly gazing into an earthward watching, and to go down into the city, and there to tell that Jesus is risen, that men are to be saved by faith in him, and that whosoever believeth in him shall have everlasting life. We are not defeated, far from it: his ascension is not a retreat, but an advance. His tarrying is not for want of power, but because of the abundance of his long-suffering. The victory is not questionable. All things work for it; all the hosts of God are mustering for the final charge. This same Jesus is mounting his white horse to lead forth the armies of heaven, conquering and to conquer.

III. Our third point is this, THE GREAT PRACTICAL TRUTH. This truth is not one that is to keep us gazing into heaven, but one that is to make each of us go to his house to render earnest service. What is it?

Why, first, that *Jesus is gone into heaven.* Jesus is gone! Jesus is gone! It sounds like a knell. Jesus is taken up from you into heaven! —that sounds like a marriage peal. He is gone, but he is gone up to the hills whence he can survey the battle; up to the throne, from which he can send us succour. The reserve forces of the omnipotent stood waiting till their Captain came, and now that he is come into the centre of the universe, he can send legions of angels, or he can raise up hosts of men for the help of his cause. I see every reason for going down into the world and getting to work, for he is gone up into heaven and "all power is given unto him in heaven and in earth." Is not that a good argument—"Go ye *therefore* and teach all nations, baptising them in the name of the Father, and of the Son, and of the Holy Ghost"?

Jesus will come again. That is another reason for girding our loins, because it is clear that he has not quitted the fight, nor deserted the field of battle. Our great Captain is still heading the conflict; he has ridden into another part of the field, but he will be back again, perhaps in the twinkling of an eye. You do not say that a commander has given up the campaign because it is expedient that he should withdraw from your part of the field. Our Lord is doing the best thing for his kingdom in going away. It was in the highest degree expedient that he should go, and that we should each one receive the Spirit. There is a blessed unity between Christ the King and the commonest soldier in the ranks. He has not taken his heart from us, nor his care from us, nor his interest from us: he is bound up heart and soul with his people, and their holy warfare, and this is the evidence of it, "Behold, I come quickly; and my reward is with me, to give every man according as his work shall be."

Then, moreover, we are told in the text—and this is a reason why we should get to our work—that *he is coming in like manner as he departed.* Certain of the commentators do not seem to understand English at all. "He which is taken up from you into heaven shall so come in like manner as you have seen him go into heaven,"—this, they say, relates to his spiritual coming at Pentecost. Give anybody a grain of sense, and do they not see that a spiritual coming is not a coming in the same manner in which he went up into heaven? There is an analogy, but certainly not a likeness between the two things. Our Lord was taken up; they could see him rise: he will come again, and "every eye shall see him." He went up not in spirit, but in person: he will come down in person. "This same Jesus shall so come in like manner." He went up as a matter of fact: not in poetic figure and spiritual symbol, but as a matter of fact,—"This same Jesus" literally went up. "This same Jesus" will literally come again. He will descend in clouds even as he went up in clouds; and "he shall stand at the latter day upon the earth" even as he stood aforetime. He went up to heaven unopposed; no high priests, nor scribes, nor Pharisees, nor even one of the rabble opposed his ascension; it were ridiculous to suppose that they could; and when he comes a second time none will stand against him. His adversaries shall perish; as the fat of rams shall they melt away in his presence. When he cometh he shall break rebellious nations with a rod of iron, for his force shall be irresistible in that day.

Brethren, do not let anybody spiritualize away all this from you. Jesus is coming as a matter of fact, therefore go down to your sphere of service as a matter of fact. Get to work and teach the ignorant, win the wayward, instruct the children, and everywhere tell out the sweet name of Jesus. As a matter of fact, give of your substance and don't talk about it. As a matter of fact, consecrate your daily life to the glory of God. As a matter of fact, live wholly for your Redeemer. Jesus is not coming in a sort of mythical, misty, hazy way, he is literally and actually coming, and he will literally and actually call upon you to give an account of your stewardship. Therefore, now, to-day, literally not symbolically, personally and not by deputy, go out through that portion of the world which you can reach, and preach the gospel to every creature according as you have opportunity.

For this is what the men in white apparel meant—*be ready to meet your coming Lord.* What is the way to be ready to meet Jesus? If it is the same Jesus that went away from us who is coming, then let us be doing what he was doing before he went away. If it is the same Jesus that is coming we cannot possibly put ourselves into a posture of which he will better approve than by going about doing good. If you would meet him with joy, serve him with earnestness. If the Lord Jesus Christ were to come to-day I should like him to find me at my studying, praying, or preaching. Would you not like him to find you in your Sunday-school, in your class, or out there at the corner of the street preaching, or doing whatever you have the privilege of doing in his name? Would you meet your Lord in idleness? Do not think of it. I called one day on one of our members, and she was whitening the front steps. She got up all in confusion; she said, "Oh dear, sir, I did not know you were coming to-day, or I would have been ready." I replied, "Dear friend, you could not be in better trim than you are: you are doing your duty like a good housewife, and may God bless you." She had no money to spare for a servant, and she was doing her duty by keeping the home tidy: I thought she looked more beautiful with her pail beside her than if she had been dressed according to the latest fashion. I said to her, "When the Lord Jesus Christ comes suddenly, I hope he will find me doing as you were doing, namely, fulfilling the duty of the hour." I want you all to get to your pails without being ashamed of them. Serve the Lord in some way or other; serve him always; serve him intensely; serve him more and more. Go to-morrow and serve the Lord at the counter, or in the workshop, or in the field. Go and serve the Lord by helping the poor and the needy, the widow and the fatherless; serve him by teaching the children, especially by endeavouring to train your own children. Go and hold a temperance meeting, and show the drunkard that there is hope for him in Christ, or go to the midnight meeting and let the fallen woman know that Jesus can restore her. Do what Jesus has given you the power to do, and then, ye men of Britain, ye will not stand gazing up into heaven, but you will wait upon the Lord in prayer, and you will receive the Spirit of God, and you will publish to all around the doctrine of "Believe and live." Then when he comes he will say to you, "Well done, good and faithful servant, enter thou into the joy of thy Lord." So may his grace enable us to do. Amen.

PORTION OF SCRIPTURE READ BEFORE SERMON—Luke xxiv. 49—53, Acts i. 1—12.

HYMNS FROM "OUR OWN HYMN BOOK"—47, 319, 346.

Metropolitan Tabernacle Pulpit.

THE LAMB IN GLORY.

A Sermon

DELIVERED ON LORD'S-DAY MORNING, JULY 14TH, 1889, BY

C. H. SPURGEON,

AT THE METROPOLITAN TABERNACLE, NEWINGTON.

"And I beheld, and, lo, in the midst of the throne and of the four living creatures, and in the midst of the elders, stood a Lamb as it had been slain, having seven horns and seven eyes, which are the seven Spirits of God sent forth into all the earth. And he came and took the book out of the right hand of him that sat upon the throne."—Revelation v. 6, 7.

THE apostle John had long known the Lord Jesus as the Lamb. That was his first view of him, when the Baptist, pointing to Jesus, said, "Behold the Lamb of God, which taketh away the sin of the world." He had been very familiar with this blessed personage, having often laid his head upon his bosom, feeling that this tender goodness of the Saviour proved him to be in nature gentle as a lamb. He had beheld him when he was brought "as a lamb to the slaughter," so that the idea was indelibly fixed upon his mind that Jesus, the Christ, was the Lamb of God. He knew that he was the appointed sacrifice, set forth in the morning and evening Lamb, and in the Paschal Lamb, by whose blood Israel was redeemed from death. In his last days the beloved disciple was to see this same Christ, under the same figure of a lamb, as the great revealer of secrets, the expounder of the mind of God, the taker of the sealed book, and the looser of the seals which bound up the mysterious purposes of God towards the children of men. I pray that we may have on this earth a clear and constant sight of the sin-bearing Lamb, and then, in yonder world of glory, we shall behold him in the midst of the throne and the living creatures and the elders.

The appearance of this Lamb at the particular moment described by John was exceedingly suitable. Our Lord usually appears when all other hope disappears. Concerning the winepress of wrath, it is he who saith, "I have trodden the winepress alone, and of the people there was none with me." In the instance before us, the strong angel had proclaimed with a loud voice, "Who is worthy to open the book, and to loose the seals thereof?" And there was no response from heaven, or earth, or hell. No man was able to open the book, neither to look therein. The divine decrees must remain for ever sealed in mystery unless the once slain Mediator shall take them from the hand

No. 2,095.

of God, and open them to the sons of men. When no one could do this, John wept much. At that grave moment the Lamb appeared. Old Master Trapp says, "Christ is good at a dead lift"; and it is so. When there is utter failure everywhere else, then in him is our help found. If there could have been found another bearer of sin, would the Father have given his Only-Begotten to die? Had any other been able to unfold the secret designs of God, would he not have appeared at the angel's challenge? But he that came to take away the sin of the world now appears to take away the seals which bind up the eternal purposes. O Lamb of God, thou art able to do what none beside may venture to attempt! Thou comest forth when no one else is to be found. Remember, next time you are in trouble, that when no man can comfort and no man can save, you may expect the Lord, the ever-sympathetic Lamb of God, to appear on your behalf.

Before the Lamb appeared, while as yet no one was found worthy to look upon that book which was held in the hand of him that sitteth on the throne, John wept much. By weeping eyes the Lamb of God is best seen. Certain ministers of this age, who make so little of the doctrine of substitutionary sacrifice, would have been of another mind if they had known more contrition of heart and exercise of soul. Eyes washed by repentance are best able to see those blessed truths which shine forth from our incarnate God, the bearer of our sins. Free grace and dying love are most appreciated by the mourners in Zion. If tears are good for the eyes, the Lord send us to be weepers, and lead us round by Bochim to Bethel. I have heard the old proverb, "There is no going to heaven but by Weeping Cross"; and there seems no way of even seeing heaven, and the heavenly One, except by eyes that have wept. Weeping makes the eyes quick to see if there be any hope; and while it dims them to all false confidences, it makes them sensitive to the faintest beam of divine light. "They looked unto him, and were lightened: and their faces were not ashamed." Those who have laid eternal matters to heart so much as to weep over their own need, and that of their fellow-men, shall be the first to see in the Lamb of God the answer to their desires.

Yet observe, that even in this case human instrumentality was permitted; for it is written, "One of the elders saith unto me, Weep not." John the apostle was greater than an elder. Among them that are born of women, in the Church of God we put none before John, who leaned his head upon his Master's bosom; and yet a mere elder of the Church reproves and instructs the beloved apostle! He cheers him with the news that the Lion of the tribe of Juda had prevailed to open the book, and to loose the seven seals thereof. The greatest man in the Church may be under obligations to the least: a preacher may be taught by a convert; an elder may be instructed by a child. Oh that we might be always willing to learn!—to learn of anyone, however lowly. Assuredly, we shall be teachable if we have the tenderness of heart which shows itself in weeping. This will make our souls like waxen tablets, whereon the finger of truth may readily inscribe its teaching. God grant us this preparation of heart!

May we come in a teachable spirit to the text, and may the Lord open our eyes to see and learn with John! It is no small favour that we have the record of the vision. Does not the Lord intend us to be partakers in it? The vision is that of a Lamb, a Lamb that is to open the book of God's secret purposes, and loose the seals thereof. The teaching of the passage is that the Lord Jesus, in his sacrificial character, is the most prominent object in the heavenly world. So far from substitution being done with, and laid aside as a temporary expedient, it remains the object of universal wonder and adoration. He that became a Lamb that he might take away the sin of the world, is not ashamed of his humiliation, but still manifests it to adoring myriads, and is, for that very reason, the very object of their enthusiastic worship. They worship the Lamb even as they worship him that sits upon the throne; and they say, "Worthy is the Lamb," because he was slain and redeemed his people by his blood. His atoning sacrifice is the great reason for their deepest reverence and their highest adoration. Some dare to say that the life of Jesus should alone be preached, and that no prominence should be given to his death. We are not of their religion. I am not ashamed of preaching Christ Jesus in his death as the sacrifice for sin; but, on the contrary, I can boldly say, "God forbid that I should glory, save in the cross of our Lord Jesus Christ." We do not so believe the doctrine of Atonement as to leave it in the dark as a second-rate article of faith; but we hold it to be the first and foremost teaching of inspiration, the greatest well of the believer's comfort, the highest hill of God's glory. As our Lord's sacrificial character is in heaven most prominent, so would we make it most conspicuous among men. Jesus is to be declared as the sin-bearer, and then men will believe and live. May God the Holy Spirit help us in our attempt this morning!

I. Jesus in heaven appears in his sacrificial character; and I would have you note that THIS CHARACTER IS ENHANCED BY OTHER CONSPICUOUS POINTS. Its glory is not diminished, but enhanced, by all the rest of our Lord's character: the attributes, achievements, and offices of our Lord all concentrate their glory in his sacrificial character, and all unite in making it a theme for loving wonder.

We read that *he is the Lion of the tribe of Juda;* by which is signified the dignity of his office, as King, and the majesty of his person, as Lord. The lion is at home in fight, and "the Lord is a man of war: the Lord is his name." Like a lion, he is courageous. Though he be like a lamb for tenderness, yet not in timidity. He is terrible as a lion, "who shall rouse him up?" If any come into conflict with him, let them beware; for as he is courageous, so is he full of force, and altogether irresistible in might. He hath the lion's heart, and the lion's strength; and he cometh forth conquering and to conquer. This it is that makes it the more wonderful that he should become a lamb—

"A lowly man before his foes,
A weary man, and full of woes."

It is wonderful that he should yield himself up to the indignities of the cross, to be mocked with a thorn-crown by the soldiers, and to be spit upon by abjects. O wonder, wonder, wonder, that the Lion of Juda, the offshoot of David's royal house, should become as a lamb led forth to the slaughter!

Further, it is clear that *he is a champion*: "The Lion of the tribe of Juda hath prevailed." What was asked for was worthiness, not only in the sense of holiness, but in the sense of valour. One is reminded of a legend of the Crusades. A goodly castle and estate awaited the coming of the lawful heir: he and he only could sound the horn which hung at the castle gate; but he who could make it yield a blast would be one who had slain a heap of Paynim in the fight, and had come home victorious from many a bloody fray. So here, no man in earth or heaven had valour and renown enough to be worthy to take the mystic roll out of the hand of the Eternal. Our champion was worthy. What battles he had fought! What feats of prowess he had performed! He had overthrown sin; he had met face to face the Prince of darkness, and had overcome him in the wilderness; ay, he had conquered death, had bearded that lion in his den; had entered the dungeon of the sepulchre, and had torn its bars away. Thus he was worthy, in the sense of valour, on returning from the far country to be owned as the Father's glorious Son, heaven's hero, and so to take the book and loose the seals thereof. The brilliance of his victories does not diminish our delight in him as the Lamb. Far otherwise, for he won these triumphs as a Lamb, by gentleness, and suffering, and sacrifice. He won his battles by a meekness and patience before unknown. The more of a conqueror he is, the more astounding is it that he should win by humiliation and death. O beloved, never tolerate low thoughts of Christ! Think of him more and more, as did the blessed Virgin, when she sang, "My soul doth magnify the Lord." Make your thoughts of him great. Be-greaten your God and Saviour, and then add to your reverent thoughts the reflection that still he looks like a lamb that has been slain. His prowess and his lion-like qualities do but set forth more vividly the tender, lowly, condescending relationship in which he stands to us as the Lamb of our redemption.

In this wonderful vision we see Jesus as *the familiar of God*. He it was who, without hesitation, advanced to the burning throne and took the book out of the right hand of him that sat upon it. He was at home there: he counted it not robbery to be equal with God. He is "very God of very God"; to be extolled with equal honour with that which is given unto the Lord God Almighty. He advances to the throne, he takes the book, he communes with Jehovah, he accepts the divine challenge of love, and unseals the mysterious purposes of his glorious Father. To him there is no danger in a close approach to the infinite glory, for that glory is his own. Now, it is he who thus stood on familiar terms with God who also stood in our place, and bore for us the penalty of sin. He who is greater than the greatest, and higher than the highest, became lower than the lowest, that he might save to the uttermost them that come to God by him. He who is Lord of all stooped under all the load and burden of sin. Fall down on your faces and worship the Lamb; for though he became obedient unto death, he is God over all, blessed for ever, the Beloved of the Father.

We observe, in addition to all this, that *he is the prophet of God*.

He it was that had the seven eyes to see all things and discern all mysteries; he it is that opened the seven seals, and thus unfolded the parts of the Book one after another, not merely that they might be read, but might be actually fulfilled; and yet he had been our substitute. Jesus explains everything: the Lamb is the *open sesame* of every secret. Nothing was ever a secret to him. He foresaw his own sufferings; they came not upon him as a surprise.

> "This was compassion like a God,
> That when the Saviour knew
> The price of pardon was his blood,
> His pity ne'er withdrew."

Since then he has not been ignorant of our unworthiness, or of the treachery of our hearts. He knows all about us; he knows what we cost him, and he knows how ill we have repaid him. With all that knowledge of God and of man, he is not ashamed to call us brethren; nor does he reject that truth, so simple, yet so full of hope to us, that he is our sacrifice and our substitute. "He who unveils the eternal will of the Highest is the Lamb of God which taketh away the sin of the world."

Our Lord always was, and is now, *acknowledged to be Lord and God.* All the church doth worship him; all the myriads of angels cry aloud in praises unto him; and to him every creature bows, of things in heaven, and things on earth, and things that are under the earth. When you call him King of kings and Lord of lords, lofty as these titles are, they fall far below his glory and majesty. If we all stood up with all the millions of the human race, and with one voice lifted up a shout of praise to him, loud as the noise of many waters and as great thunders, yet would our highest honours scarcely reach the lowest step of his all-glorious throne. Yet, in the glory of his Deity, he disdains not to appear as the Lamb that has been slain. This still is his chosen character. I have heard of a great warrior, that on the anniversary of his most renowned victory he would always put on the coat in which he fought the fight, adorned, as it was, with marks of shot. I understand his choice. Our Lord to-day, and every day, wears still the human flesh in which he overthrew our enemies, and he appears as one that has but newly died, since by death he overcame the devil. Always, and for ever, he is the Lamb. Even as God's prophet and revealer he remains the Lamb. When you shall see him at the last, you shall say, as John did, "I beheld, and, lo, in the midst of the throne and of the four living creatures, and in the midst of the elders, stood a Lamb as it had been slain."

Write, then, the passion of your Lord upon the tablets of your hearts, and let none erase the treasured memory. Think of him mainly and chiefly as the sacrifice for sin. Set the atonement in the midst of your minds, and let it tinge and colour all your thoughts and beliefs. Jesus bleeding and dying in your room, and place, and stead, must be to you as the sun in your sky.

II. In the second place, let us note that, IN THIS CHARACTER, JESUS IS THE CENTRE OF ALL. "In the midst of the throne, and of the four living creatures, and in the midst of the elders, stood a Lamb as it had been slain." The Lamb is the centre of the wonderful circle which makes up the fellowship of heaven.

From him, as a standpoint, all things are seen in their places. Looking up at the planets from this earth, which is one of them, it is difficult to comprehend their motions—progressive, retrograde, or standing still; but the angel in the sun sees all the planets marching in due course, and circling about the centre of their system. Standing where you please upon this earth, and within human range of opinion, you cannot see all things aright, nor understand them till you come to Jesus, and then you see all things from the centre. The man who knows the incarnate God, slain for human sins, stands in the centre of truth. Now he sees God in his place, man in his place, angels in their place, lost souls in their place, and the saved ones in their place. Know him whom to know is life eternal, and you are in the position of vantage from which you may rightly judge of all things. The proper bearings and relationships of this to that, and that to the next, and so on, can only be ascertained by a firm and full belief in Jesus Christ as the atoning sacrifice.

> "Till God in human flesh I see,
> My thoughts no comfort find,
> The Holy, Just, and sacred Three,
> Are terrors to my mind.
>
> "But if Immanuel's face appears,
> My hope, my joy begins:
> His name forbids my slavish fears,
> His grace removes my sins."

In Christ you are in the right position to understand the past, the present, and the future. The deep mysteries of eternity, and even the secret of the Lord, are all with you when once you are with Jesus. Think of this, and make the Lamb your central thought—the soul of your soul, the heart of your heart's best life.

The Lamb's being in the midst, signifies, also, that *in him they all meet in one.* I would speak cautiously, but I venture to say that Christ is the summing up of all existence. Seek you Godhead? There it is. Seek you manhood? There it is. Wish you the spiritual? There it is in his human soul. Desire you the material? There it is in his human body. Our Lord hath, as it were, gathered up the ends of all things, and hath bound them into one. You cannot conceive what God is; but Christ is God. If you dive down with materialism, which by many is regarded as the drag and millstone of the soul, yet in Jesus you find materialism, refined and elevated, and brought into union with the divine nature. In Jesus all lines meet, and from him they radiate to all the points of being. Would you meet God? Go you to Christ. Would you be in fellowship with all believers? Go you to Christ. Would you feel tenderness towards all that God has made? Go you to Christ; for "of him, and through him, and to him are all things." What a Lord is ours! What a glorious being is the Lamb; for it is only as the Lamb that this is true of him! View him only as God, and there is no such meeting with man. View him as being only man, and then he is far from the centre: but behold him as God and man, and the Lamb of God, and then you see in him the place of rest for all things.

Being in the centre, *to him they all look.* Can you think for a moment how the Lord God looks upon his Only-Begotten? When Jehovah looks on Jesus, it is with an altogether indescribable delight. He saith, "This is my beloved Son, in whom I am well pleased." When he thinks of the passion through which he passed, and the death which he accomplished at Jerusalem, all the infinite heart of God flows high and strong towards his Best-beloved. He hath rest in his Son as he hath nowhere else. His delight is in Jesus; indeed, he hath so much delight in him, that for his sake he takes delight in his people. As the Father's eyes are always on Jesus, so are the eyes of the living creatures and the four-and-twenty elders which represent the church in its divine life and the church in its human life. All who have been washed in his blood perpetually contemplate his beauties. What is there in heaven which can compare with the adorable person of him by whom they were redeemed from among men? All angels look that way, also, waiting his august commands. Are they not all ministering spirits, whom he sends forth to minister to his people? All the forces of nature are waiting at the call of Jesus; all the powers of providence look to him for direction. He is the focus of all attention, the centre of all observation throughout the plains of heaven. This, remember, is as "the Lamb." Not as king or prophet chiefly, but pre-eminently as "the Lamb" is Jesus the centre of all reverence, and love, and thought, in the glory-land above.

Once more, let me say of the Lamb in the centre, that *all seem to rally round him as a guard around a king.* It is for the Lamb that the Father acts: he glorifies his Son. The Holy Spirit also glorifies Christ. All the divine purposes run that way. The chief work of God is to make Jesus the first-born among many brethren. This is the model to which the Creator works in fashioning the vessels of grace: he has made Jesus Alpha and Omega, the beginning and the end. All things ordained of the Father work towards Christ, as their centre; and so stand all the redeemed, and all the angels waiting about the Lord, as swelling his glory and manifesting his praise. If anything could enter the minds of heavenly beings that would contribute to lift Jesus higher, it would be their heaven to speed throughout space to carry it out. He dwelleth as a King in his central pavilion, and this is the joy of the host, that the King is in the midst of them.

Beloved, is it so? Is Jesus the centre of the whole heavenly family? Shall he not be the centre of our Church life? Will we not think most of him—much more of him than of Paul, or Apollos, or Cephas, or any party-leaders that would divide us? Christ is the centre; not this form of doctrine nor that mode of ordinance, but the Lamb alone. Shall we not always delight in him, and watch to see how we can magnify his glorious name? Shall he not be also the centre of our ministry? What shall we preach about but Christ! Take that subject away from me, and I have done. These many years I have preached nothing else but that dear name, and if that is to be dishonoured, all my spiritual wealth is gone: I have no bread for the hungry, nor water for the faint. After all these years my speech has become like the harp of Anacreon, which would resound love alone. He wished to sing of Atreus and of Cadmon, but his harp resounded love alone. It is so with my ministry: with Christ, and Christ alone am I at home. Progressive theology! No string of my soul will vibrate to its touch. New divinity! Evolution! Modern thought! My harp is silent to these strange fingers; but to Christ, and Christ alone, it answers with all the music of which it is capable. Beloved, is it so with you? In teaching you, children, in your life at home, in your dealing with the world, is Jesus the centre of your aim and labour? Does his love fill your heart? In the old Napoleon's days, a soldier was wounded by a bullet, and the doctor probed deep to find it. The man cried out, "Doctor, mind what you are at! A little deeper, and you will touch the Emperor." The Emperor was on that soldier's heart. Truly, if they search deep into our life they will find Christ. Queen Mary said that when she died they would find the name of *Calais* cut upon her heart; for she grieved over the loss of the last British possession in France. We have not lost our Calais, but hold still our treasure; for Christ is ours. We have no other name engraven on our heart but that of Jesus. Truly can we say,

> "Happy if with my latest breath,
> I may but gasp his name;
> Preach him to all, and cry in death,
> 'Behold, behold the Lamb!'"

III. Thirdly, our Lord is seen in heaven as the Lamb slain, and IN THIS CHARACTER HE EXHIBITS PECULIAR MARKS. None of those marks derogate from his glory as the sacrifice for sin; but they tend to instruct us therein.

Note well the words: "Stood a Lamb as it had been slain." "Stood," here is the posture of life; "as it had been slain," here is the memorial of *death*. Our view of Jesus should be twofold; we should see his death and his life: we shall never receive a whole Christ in any other way. If you only see him on the cross, you behold the power of his death; but he is not now upon the cross; he is risen, he for ever liveth to make intercession for us, and we need to know the power of his life. We see him as a lamb "as it had been slain"; but we worship him as one that "liveth for ever and ever." Carry these two things with you as one: a slain Christ, a living Christ. I notice that feeling and teaching in the church oscillates between these two, whereas it should comprehend them both. The Romish church continually gives us a babe Christ, carried by his mother; or a dead Christ, on the cross. Go where we may, these images are thrust upon us. Apart from the sin of image-worship, the thing set forth is not the whole of our Lord. On the other hand, we have a school around us who endeavour to put the cross out of sight, and they give us only a living Christ, such as he is. To them Jesus is only an example and teacher. As a true and proper expiatory substitute they will not have him; BUT WE WILL. We adore the Crucified One upon the throne of God. We believe in him as bleeding and pleading: we see him slain, and behold him reign. Both of these are our joy; neither one more than the other, but each in its own place. Thus, as you look at the Lamb, you begin to sing, "Thou art he that liveth, and wast dead, and art alive for evermore." The mark of our Saviour is life through death, and death slain by death.

Note, next, another singular combination in the Lamb. He is called "a little lamb"; for the diminutive is used in the Greek; but yet how great he is! In Jesus, as a Lamb, we see great tenderness and exceeding familiarity with his people. He is not the object of dread; there is about him nothing like "Stand off, for I am too holy to be approached." A lamb is the most approachable of beings. Yet there is about the little Lamb an exceeding majesty. The elders no sooner saw him than they fell down before him. They adored him, and cried with a loud voice, "Worthy is the Lamb." Every creature worshipped him, saying, "Blessing, and honour, and glory, and power, be unto the Lamb." He is so great that the heaven of heavens cannot contain him; yet he becomes so little that he dwells in humble hearts. He is so glorious that the seraphim veiled their faces in his presence: he is so condescending as to become bone of our bone, and flesh of our flesh. What a wonderful combination of *mercy and majesty*, grace and glory! Never divide what God has joined together: do not speak of our Lord Jesus Christ as some do, with an irreverent, unctuous familiarity; but, at the same time, do not think of him as of some great Lord for whom we must feel a slavish dread. Jesus is your next-of-kin, a brother born for adversity, and yet he is your God and Lord. Let love and awe keep the watches of your soul!

Further, let us look at the peculiar marks of him, and we see that he hath *seven horns and seven eyes*. His power is equal to his vigilance; and these are equal to all the emergencies brought about by the opening of the seven seals of the Book of Providence. When plagues break forth, who is to defend us? Behold the seven horns. If the unexpected occurs, who is to forewarn us? Behold the seven eyes.

Every now and then some foolish person or other brings out a pamphlet stuffed with horrors which are going to happen in a year or two. The whole of it is about as valuable as the Norwood Gipsy's Book of Fate, which you can buy for two-pence; but still, if it were all true that these prophecy-mongers tell us, we are not afraid; for the Lamb has seven horns, and will meet every difficulty by his own power, having already foreseen it by his own wisdom. The Lamb is the answer to the enigma of providence. Providence is a riddle, but Jesus explains it all. During the first centuries, the Church of God was given up to martyrdom: every possible torment and torture was exercised upon the followers of Christ: what could be God's meaning in all this? What but the glory of the Lamb? And now to-day the Lord seems to leave his Church to wander into all kinds of errors: false doctrines are, in some quarters, fearfully paramount. What does this mean? I do not know; but the Lamb knows, for he sees with seven eyes. As a Lamb, as our Saviour, God and man, he understands all, and has the clues of all labyrinths in his hands. He has power to meet every difficulty, and wisdom to see through every embarrassment. We should cast out fear, and give ourselves wholly up to worship.

The Lamb also works to perfection in nature and in providence; for with him are "the seven Spirits of God sent forth into all the earth." This refers not merely to the saving power of the Spirit which is sent forth unto the elect; but to those powers and forces which operate upon all the earth. The power of gravitation, the energy of life, the mystic force of electricity, and the like, are all forms of the power of God. A law of nature is nothing but our observation of the usual way in which God operates in the world. A law in itself has no power: law is but the usual course of God's action. All the Godhead's omnipotence dwells in the Lamb: he is the Lord God Almighty. We cannot put the atonement into a secondary place; for our atoning sacrifice hath all the seven Spirits of God. He is able to save to the uttermost them that come unto God by him. Let us come to God by him. He has power to cope with the future, whatever it may be. Let us secure our souls against all threatening dangers, committing ourselves to his keeping.

How I wish I had power to set the Lord before you this morning evidently glorified! But I fail utterly. My talk is like holding a candle to the sun. I am grateful that my Lord does not snuff me out; perhaps my candle may show some prisoner to the door, and when he has once passed it, he will behold the sun in its strength. Glory be to him who is so great, so glorious, and yet still the Lamb slain for sinners, whose wounds in effect continually bleed our life, whose finished work is the perpetual source of all our safety and our joy.

IV. I close with my fourth point, which is this: Jesus appears eternally as a Lamb, and IN THIS CHARACTER HE IS UNIVERSALLY ADORED.

Before he opened one of the seals this worship commenced. When he had taken the book, the four living creatures and the four-and-twenty elders fell down before the Lamb, and sung a new song, saying, "Thou art worthy to take the book." While yet the book is closed, we worship him. We trust him where we cannot trace him. Before he begins his work as the revealing Mediator, the church adores him for his work as a sacrifice. Jesus our Lord is worshipped not so much for what benefits he will confer as for himself. As the Lamb slain he is the object of heavenly reverence. Many will reverence him, I do not doubt, when he comes in his second Advent, in the glory of the Father. Every knee will bow before him, even of apostates and infidels, when they shall see him take to himself his great power and reign; but that is not the worship which he accepts, nor that which proves the offerer to be saved. You must worship him as a sacrifice, and adore him in his lowly character, as the "despised and rejected of men." You must reverence him while others ridicule him, trust his blood while others turn from it with disdain, and so be with him in his humiliation. Accept him as your substitute, trust in him as having made atonement for you; for in heaven they still worship him as the Lamb.

That adoration *begins with the church of God.* The church of God, in all its phases, adores the Lamb. If you view the church of God as a divine creation, the embodiment of the Spirit of God, then the living creatures fall down before the Lamb. No God-begotten life is too high to refuse obeisance to the Lamb of God. Look at the church on its human side, and you see the four-and-twenty elders falling down and worshipping, having every one harps and vials. Well may the whole company of redeemed men worship the Mediator, since in him our manhood is greatly exalted! Was ever our nature so exalted as it is now that Christ is made Head over all things to his church? Now are we nearest to God, for between man and God no creature intervenes: Immanuel—God with us—has joined us in one. Man is next to the Deity, with Jesus only in between, not to divide, but to unite. The Lord in Christ Jesus hath made us to have dominion over all the works of his hands; he hath put all things under our feet: all sheep and oxen, yea, the fowl of the air, and fish of the sea, and whatsoever passeth through the paths of the sea. O Lord our God, how excellent is thy name in all the earth!

The Lord is adored by the church in all forms of worship. They worship him in prayer; for the vials full of sweet odours are the prayers of saints. They worship him in praise with a new song, and with the postures of lowliest reverence.

But, beloved, the Lamb is not only worshipped by the church, *he is worshipped by angels*. What a wonderful gathering together of certain legions of the Lord's hosts we have before us in this chapter! "Ten thousand times ten thousand, and thousands of thousands." Their company cannot be enumerated in human arithmetic. With perfect unanimity they unite in the hallowed worship, shouting together, "Worthy is the Lamb that was slain."

Nay, it is not merely the church and angelhood; but *all creation*, east, west, north, south, highest, lowest, all adore him. All life, all space, all time, immensity, eternity: all these become one mouth for song, and all the song is, "Worthy is the Lamb."

Now, then, dear friends, if this be so, shall we ever allow anybody in our presence to lower the dignity of Christ, our sacrifice? ["No."] A friend says, emphatically, No; and we all say, No. As with a voice of thunder, we say, No, to all attempts to lower the supreme glories of the Lamb. We cannot have it: our loyalty to him will not permit. Besides, no man will willingly lose his all. Take the Lamb away you take all away. "Who steals my purse, steals trash": who steals my Christ, steals myself, and more than myself—my hopes that are to be my future joys. Life is gone, when his death is rejected, his blood despised. Our souls burn with indignation when this vital truth is assailed.

> "Stand up, stand up for Jesus,
> Ye soldiers of the cross!
> Lift high his royal banner,
> It must not suffer loss!"

Wherever you are, to whatever church you belong, do not associate with those who decry the atonement. Enter not into confederacy with those who, even by a breath, would disparage his precious blood. Do not bear that which assails the Lamb; grow indignant at the foul lie! The wrath of the Lamb may with safety be copied by yourself in this case: you will be angry, and sin not.

Once more, if this be so, if the glorious sacrifice of our Lord Jesus be so much thought of in heaven, cannot you trust it here below? O you that are burdened with sin, here is your deliverance: come to the sin-bearing Lamb. You that are perplexed with doubts, here is your guide: the Lamb can open the sealed books for you. You that have lost your comfort, come back to the Lamb, who is slain for you, and put your trust in him anew. You that are hungering for heavenly food, come to the Lamb, for he shall feed you. The Lamb, the Lamb, the bleeding Lamb: be this the sign upon the standard of the Church of God. Set that ensign to the front, and march boldly on to victory, and then, O Lamb of God, that taketh away the sin of the world, grant us thy peace! Amen.

PORTION OF SCRIPTURE READ BEFORE SERMON—Revelation v.

HYMNS FROM "OUR OWN HYMN BOOK"—412, 338, 395.

Metropolitan Tabernacle Pulpit.

THE HEAVENLY SINGERS AND THEIR SONG.

A Sermon

INTENDED FOR READING ON LORD'S-DAY, AUGUST 13TH, 1893,

DELIVERED BY

C. H. SPURGEON,

AT THE METROPOLITAN TABERNACLE, NEWINGTON,

On Lord's-day Evening, July 14th, 1889.

"And when he had taken the book, the four beasts and four and twenty elders fell down before the Lamb, having every one of them harps, and golden vials full of odours, which are the prayers of saints. And they sung a new song, saying, Thou art worthy to take the book, and to open the seals thereof: for thou wast slain, and hast redeemed us to God by thy blood out of every kindred, and tongue, and people, and nation; and hast made us unto our God kings and priests: and we shall reign on the earth."—Revelation v. 8—10.

This morning* we had a picture of our Lord Jesus Christ appearing in heaven in his sacrificial character, being adored in that character, looking like a Lamb that had been slain, and being worshipped under that aspect in the very centre of heaven. I tried, as far as ever I could, to insist upon it that we must never hide the atoning sacrifice that Christ, as the Lamb of God which taketh away the sin of the world, is always to be brought to the front, to be put foremost in our preaching and in our practice, too. In this verse, we go a step further. This blessed Lamb appears in heaven as the Mediator between God and men. At God's right hand was the book of his eternal purposes. None dared even to look upon it; it was hopeless that any creature should be able to loose the seven seals thereof. But there came forward this glorious Lamb, who had the marks of his slaughter upon him, and he took the book out of the right hand of him that sat upon the throne. Thus he acted as Mediator, Interpreter, taking the will of God, and translating it to us, letting us know the meaning of that writing of the right hand of God which we could never have deciphered, but which, when Christ looses the seals, is made clear to us.

Jesus Christ, then, is seen as our sacrifice in the capacity of Mediator, and in that capacity he becomes the object of the adoration, first, of

---

* See *Metropolitan Tabernacle Pulpit*, No. 2,095, "The Lamb in Glory."

No. 2,321.

the Church, then of all the thousands and ten thousands of angels, and then of every creature that God has made. It would be too large a subject to take in all those hallelujahs; and, therefore, in speaking to-night I select only these three verses to set forth the song of the Church, the adoration of the Church of God, rendered to the bleeding Lamb as the Mediator between God and men.

I shall have only two divisions. First, *behold the worshippers;* and, secondly, *hearken to their song.*

I. First, BEHOLD THE WORSHIPPERS; for, remember, that we must be like them if we are to be with them. It is a well-known rule that heaven must be in us before we can be in heaven. We must be heavenly if we hope to sit in the heavenly places. We shall not be taken up to join the glorified choir unless we have learned their song, and can join their sacred harmony. Look, then, at the worshippers. You are not yet perfectly like them; but you will be, by-and-by, if you have already the main points of likeness wrought in you by the grace of God.

The first point about the worshippers is this, *they are all full of life.* I must confess that I should not like to dogmatize upon the meaning of the four living creatures; but still they do seem to me to be an emblem of the Church in its Godward standing, quickened by the life of God. At any rate, they are living creatures; and the elders themselves are living personages. Yet alas, alas, that it should be needful to say so trite a thing; but the dead cannot praise God! "The living, the living, he shall praise thee, as I do this day." Yet how many dead people there are in this great assembly to-night! If one, who had sufficient powers of penetration as to be able to detect the actions of the spiritual life of man, were to go round this crowd, " Ah! me," he would say, " take this one away, take that one away; these are dead souls in the midst of the living in Zion." I will not dwell upon this very solemn thought; but I wish the conscience of some here to dwell upon it when the service is over; you are dead people in the midst of life; you joined in the song just now, but there was no living praise in your singing. Prayer was offered by my dear brother Hurditch very fervently; but there was no living prayer in you. Do you know that it is so? If so, then take your right place; and God grant you enough life to know the absence of life, lest he should say of you, " Bury my dead out of my sight," and you should be taken away to the house appointed to the dead, since you cannot be allowed to pollute the gathering of living saints! Those in heaven are all full of life; there is no dead worshipper there, no dull, cold heart that does not respond to the praise by which it is surrounded; they are all full of life.

And further note, that *they are all of one mind.* Whether they are four-and-twenty elders, or four living creatures, they all move simultaneously. With perfect unanimity they fall on their faces, or touch their harps, or uplift their golden vials full of sweet odours. I like unanimity in worship here. You remember the lines—

"At once they sing, at once they pray;
They hear of heaven, and learn the way."

We used to sing that hymn when we were children; but is there always real unanimity in our assembly? While one is praising, is not another murmuring? While one is earnest, is not another indifferent? While one is believing, is not another an infidel? O God, grant to our assemblies here below the unanimity that comes of the One Spirit working in us the same result, for so we must be in heaven; and if we are not of one mind here below, we are not like the heavenly beings above! When little bickerings come in, when sectarian differences prevent our joining in the common adoration, it is a great pity. God heal his one Church of all her unhappy divisions, and any one church of any latent differences that there may be, that our unity on earth may be an anticipation of the unanimity of heaven!

Note, next, that as the heavenly worshippers are full of life, and full of unity, so *they are all full of holy reverence*. "When he had taken the book, the four living creatures and four and twenty elders fell down before the Lamb," all reverently fell down before the Lamb. And in the fourteenth verse, after their song was over, and after the angels and the whole creation had taken their turn in the celestial music, we read, "And the four living creatures said, Amen." It was all that they could say; they were overawed with the majestic presence of God and the Lamb. "And the four and twenty elders fell down and worshipped him that liveth for ever and ever." They did not say anything then; they simply fell down and worshipped. It is a grand thing when, at last, we have broken the backs of words with the weight of our feelings, when expressive silence must come in to prove the praises which we cannot utter. It is glorious to be in this reverent state of mind. We are not always so; but they are so in heaven; they are all ready to fall down before the Lord. Do you not think that we often come into our places of worship with a great deal of carelessness? And while the service is going on, are we not thinking of a thousand things? Or if we are attentive, is there enough lowly worship about us? In heaven, they fall down before the Lamb; brothers, sisters, should not we serve God better if we did more of this falling down to worship the Lamb?

Note, next, that while they are all full of reverence, *they are all in a praising condition:* "Having every one of them harps." They did not pass one harp round, and take turns in playing it; nor was there one who had to sit still because he had forgotten his harp; but they had, every one of them, his harp. I am afraid those words do not describe all God's people here to-night. My dear sister, where is your harp? It is gone to be repaired, is it not? My dear brother, where is your harp? You have left it on the willow-tree, by the waters of Babylon, so you have not one here. I must confess that sometimes I have not a harp; I could preach a solemn sermon, but I could not so well render the praise. Our dear friend Hurditch seemed to have brought his harp with him to-night; I am glad he praised the Lord so many times for so many mercies. We do not always have our harps with us; but the living creatures and the elders had, all of them, the apparatus for the expression of their holy joy, "having every one of them harps." Try to be like the spirits above.

But this is not all; *they are all ready for prayer*. In heaven there is prayer, we must correct the common mistake about that matter; and there is something to pray for. Although we do not ask the intercession of saints and angels,—that were far from Scriptural,—still, we believe that the saints do pray. Are they not crying, "O Lord, how long?" Why should they not pray, "Thy kingdom come. Thy will be done, in earth, as it is in heaven"? They would understand that prayer better than we do. We know how God's will is not done on earth, but they know how it is done in heaven; and they could pray, "Thy kingdom come, for thine is the kingdom, and the power, and the glory, for ever, Amen." How sweetly could their lips move over such words as those! Well, they, all of them, had "golden vials full of odours." Are we always furnished and prepared for prayer? This ought to be more easy than always to have a harp; but I am afraid that we have not always our golden vials full of odours; I do not know that they are golden vials at all, I am afraid that ours are of the earth, earthy. But in heaven they have golden vials, pure and precious, and they are full of odours. Sometimes, when you look into your prayer-box, my brother, you have to scrape the bottom to find enough perfume to make even a little incense; but to have our vials full of sweet odours, this is the state of mind in which we should be always. God bring us to that! We shall be getting near heaven, when we can always pray, and certainly near heaven when we can always praise.

"Prayer and praise, with sins forgiven,
Bring to earth the bliss of heaven,"

and make us ready to go up and share that bliss.

Now you see something of what these worshippers were. I do but pause a moment to ask whether we are prepared to go there, whether we are like those who are there. Remember that there is but one place for us besides; if we do not enter heaven, to praise with those perfect spirits, we must be driven from the divine presence to suffer with the condemned. You are not willing to go to hell; will you not be in earnest to go to heaven? You recoil at the idea of "Depart, ye cursed!" Oh, why not even now accept "Come, ye blessed," while Jesus repeats his gracious invitation, "Come unto me all ye that labour, and are heavy laden, and I will give you rest"? I wish that I were able to press this invitation upon you; but I do put it before you. In the name of Jesus, the Lamb of God, that taketh away the sin of the world, I invite you to trust in him, and find your sins forgiven; and so doing, you shall be prepared to meet the Lamb who sits upon the throne, and there for ever to adore his sacrifice, while you enjoy the blessings that flow from it. May we all meet in heaven! It would be a dreadful thing if we could know the destiny of everybody here, and find, among other things, that some here will never see the gate of pearl except from an awful distance, with a great gulf fixed, of which gulf it is said, "They which would pass from hence to you, cannot; neither can they pass to us, that would come from thence." May we be on the right side of that gulf! Be on the right side of it to-night, for Jesus' sake!

II. Now, having thus spoken of the worshippers, I want you to HEARKEN TO THEIR SONGS. We must hearken our best in the short time that we have left. "They sang a new song, saying, Thou art worthy to take the book, and to open the seals thereof: for thou wast slain, and hast redeemed us to God by thy blood out of every kindred, and tongue, and people, and nation; and hast made us unto our God kings and priests: and we shall reign on the earth."

It is rather an unusual thing to take a hymn, and treat it *doctrinally;* but, for your instruction, I must take away the poetry for a moment, and just deal with the doctrines of this heavenly hymn.

The first doctrine is, Christ is put in the front, the deity of Christ, as I hold. They sing, "Thou art worthy, thou art worthy." A strong-winged angel sped his way o'er earth and heaven, and down into the deep places of the universe, crying with a loud voice, "Who is worthy to open the book?" but no answer came, for no creature was worthy. Then came One, of whom the Church cries in its song, "Thou art worthy, thou art worthy." Yes, beloved, he is worthy of all the praise and honour that we can bring to him. He is worthy to be called equal with God, nay, he is himself God, very God of very God; and no man can sing this song, or ever will sing it, unless he believes Christ to be divine, and accepts him as his Lord and God.

Next, the doctrine of this hymn is that the whole Church delights in the mediation of Christ. Notice, it was when he had taken the book that they said, "Thou art worthy to take the book." To have Christ standing between God and man, is the joy of every believing heart. We could never reach up to God; but Christ has come to bridge the distance between us. He places one hand on man and the other upon God; he is the Daysman, who can lay his hand upon both; and the Church greatly rejoices in this. Remember that even the working of providence is not apart from the mediation of Christ. I rejoice in this, that if the thunders be let loose, if plagues and deaths around us fly, the child of God is still under the Mediator's protection, and no harm shall happen to the chosen, for Jesus guards us evermore. All power is given unto him in heaven and in earth, and the Church rejoices in his mediatorship.

But now, notice, in the Church's song, what is her reason for believing that Christ is worthy to be a Mediator. She says, "Thou art worthy, for thou wast slain." Ah, beloved, when Christ undertook to be her Mediator, this was the extreme point to which suretyship could carry him, to be slain! And he has gone to the extreme point, and he has paid life for life. "In the day that thou eatest thereof thou shalt surely die," was the sentence pronounced upon Adam. The second Adam has died; he has bowed his head to the sentence, he has vindicated the law of God, he has gone to the extreme length of all that his mediatorship could possibly demand of him, and this makes the redeemed lift up the song higher and higher and higher: "Thou art worthy, for thou wast slain." Jesus is never more glorious than in his death; his propitiation is the culmination of his glory, after all, as it was the very utmost depth of his shame. Beloved, we rejoice in our Mediator because he died.

Well then, notice, that they sing of the redemption which his death effected, and they do not sing of the redemption of the world. No, not at all: "Thou wast slain, and hast redeemed us to God by thy blood *out of* every kindred, and tongue, and people, and nation." I am not going into a doctrinal discussion to-night. I believe in the infinite value of the atoning sacrifice; I believe that, if God had ordained it to be effectual for the salvation of many more, it was quite sufficient for the divine purpose; but those whom Christ redeemed unto God by his blood are not all mankind. All mankind will not sing this song; all mankind will not be made kings and priests unto God; and all mankind are not redeemed in the sense in which this song is lifted up to God. I want to know, not so much about general redemption, of which you may believe what you like, but about particular redemption, personal redemption: "Thou hast redeemed *us*." "Christ loved the Church, and gave himself for *it*." "Thou hast redeemed us to God by thy blood out of every kindred, and tongue, and people, and nation." My dear hearer, can you join in this song? It is all very well to say, "Oh, yes! we are all sinners; we are all redeemed." Stop, stop; are you a sinner? Do you know it? Sinners are very scarce in London. "Why, there are millions of them!" say you? Yes, yes, yes; nominally, they will say so; but the *bond fide* sinner, who knows his guilt, is a scarce article.

"A sinner is a sacred thing,
 The Holy Ghost hath made him so."

If there is a real sinner in this house to-night, she will be weeping at my Master's feet, washing those blessed feet with her tears. But as for your sham sinners—they are sinners enough, God knows; but they do not really believe that they are sinners. They have never done anything very wrong, nothing very particular, nothing very important, nothing to break their hearts about. Oh! you—why, you cannot even claim to come in among the sinners, you are a sham even there! But as for redemption, that redemption that redeemed everybody will not do you any good, for it redeemed Judas, it redeemed the myriads that are now in hell. A poor redemption that! The redemption that you want is the redemption that would fetch you right out from your fellow-sinners, so that you would be separated unto God, according to that word, "Come out from among them, and be ye separate, saith the Lord, and touch not the unclean thing, and I will receive you, and will be a Father unto you, and ye shall be my sons and daughters."

A thing that is redeemed belonged originally to the person who redeems it; and the redeemed of the Lord always were his: "Thine they were," saith Christ, "and thou gavest them me." They always were God's. You cannot go and redeem a thing that does not belong to you. You may buy it, but you cannot redeem it. Now, that which belonged originally to God came under a mortgage through sin. We, having sinned, came under the curse of the Law; and though God still held to it that we were his, yet we were under this embargo, sin had a lien upon us. Christ came, and saw his own, and he knew that they were his own. He asked what there was to pay to redeem them, to take them out of pawn. It was his heart's blood, his life, himself, that was required; he paid the price, and redeemed them:

and we to-night sing, "Thou hast redeemed us to God by thy blood out of every kindred, and tongue, and people, and nation." He has, by redeeming us, separated us to himself, and made us a peculiar people, bought with blood in a special sense out of all the rest of mankind.

I could tell you a great deal about the universal bearings of Christ's redemption, in which I believe, and in the infinite value of that redemption, in which I believe; but I also say that there was, in the design of God, and in the work of Christ, a peculiar form of redemption, which was only for his own people, even as his intercession is, for he says, "I pray for them, I pray not for the world: but for them which thou hast given me, for they are thine." Whatever some may think about it, there is a speciality and peculiarity about the redemption of Christ; and this makes the very highest note of the song of heaven, "Thou hast redeemed us to God by thy blood out of every kindred, and tongue, and people, and nation."

So much about the heavenly hymn doctrinally.

Now about it *experimentally:* "Thou hast redeemed us to God." I have said, dear friends, that you cannot sing this song unless you know something of it now. Have you been redeemed? Has the embargo that was on you through sin been taken off you? Do you believe in Jesus Christ? For, every man who believeth in Jesus Christ has the evidence of his eternal redemption. Thou hast been bought back with a countless price if thou believest that Jesus is the Christ, and thou art trusting alone in him. That was their experience: "Thou hast redeemed us." They felt free; they remembered when they wore their fetters, but they saw them all broken by Christ. Have you been set free? Have you had your fetters broken? Ask the question, and then let us pass on.

This redemption is the ground of their distinction: "Thou hast redeemed us to God by thy blood." I heard one, the other day, say of a certain minister, "Oh! we want another minister, we are tired of this man; he is always talking so much about the blood." In the last great day, God will be tired of the man who made that speech. God never wearies of the precious blood, nor will his people who know where their salvation lies. They do not, even in heaven, say that it is a dreadful word to mention. "Oh, but I do not like the word!" says some delicate gentleman. Your lordship will not be bothered with it, for you will not go to heaven. Do not trouble yourself; you shall not go where they sing about the blood. But, mark you, if you ever do go there, you will hear it over and over and over again: "Thou hast redeemed us to God by thy blood." How they will ring it out! "Thou, thou, thou hast redeemed us to God by thy blood." How they will emphasize that pronoun, "*Thou*," and address the praise wholly to Jesus, and sound out that word with the full music of their harps, "Thou hast redeemed us to God by thy blood." They are not ashamed of the blood of Jesus up there.

It is this redemption that has made them kings. We cannot realize our kingship to the full here below; though we do in a measure. There is a poor man here, who has but one room to live in; he has no money in his pocket to-night, yet he is a king in the sight of God. There is one here, perhaps, who used to be a drunkard. He could not overcome the evil anyhow; he signed the pledge, wore the blue ribbon, and so on; but still he went back to the drink. By the grace of God he has got his foot upon it now, for he has a new heart and a right spirit. That man is a king; he is a king over his drunken habits. There is one here who used to have a very fierce temper. It was hard to live with him; but Christ has made him a changed man, and now he is a king, ruling over his temper. It is a grand thing to be made a king over yourself. There are some, who have dominion over millions of others, who have never ruled themselves. Poor creatures! Poor creatures! Thank God, if he has given you the mastery of your own nature; that is a glorious conquest; yet this is only the beginning of what is in this song of heaven.

And then they say, "Thou hast made us priests." Oh, the poor creatures we have nowadays in the world, who cannot go to Christ except by a priest! They must go to a priest to confess their sins, and go to a priest to get absolution. We have priests not only in the Church of Rome, but elsewhere; we are sorry to see this accursed priestcraft coming in everywhere. Why, some of you people would like your minister to do all your religion for you, would you not? You take a sitting, and leave your religion to your minister. Christ has made every one of his people a priest, and every child of God is as much a priest as I am; and I am a priest certainly, a priest unto God to offer the spiritual sacrifice of prayer, and praise, and the ministry of the Word. But here is the peculiar joy of all Christians, that God has made them priests. If they do not use their priesthood here, I am afraid that they will never be able to use their priesthood before the throne of God with their fellow-priests. This is the melody of the heavenly song, "Washed in the precious blood, redeemed by that matchless price, we are now made unto our God kings and priests." Even on earth each saint can sing,—

> "I would not change my blest estate,
> For all that earth calls good or great;
> And while my faith can keep her hold,
> I envy not the sinner's gold."

Thus have I spoken of the song doctrinally, and experimentally; now let me speak of it *expectantly*.

There is something to be expected: "And we shall reign on the earth." When John heard that song, the resurrection-day had not yet come. These are the spirits before the throne, disembodied; they are expecting the day of the resurrection. When that day will come, who can tell? But when it comes, the dead in Christ shall rise first. Upstarting at the midnight cry, they shall quit their beds of dust and silent clay, and the saints that are alive and remain shall join them. I will not go into the details of that time; but then shall come a period of halcyon bliss. "The rest of the dead lived not again until the thousand years were finished." Then shall be a time of the saints' reigning upon the earth. Their life shall be regal; their delights, their joys, and their honours, shall be equal to those of kings and princes, nay, they shall far exceed them. Do you and I expect to reign upon the earth? It will seem very odd to one who is very poor, obscure, perhaps ignorant, but who knows his Lord, to find that Christ has made him a priest and a king, and that he shall reign even on the earth with him, and then reign for ever with him in glory; but it would be more singular, it would be perfectly monstrous, if we were to assert of some persons, and of some here present, that they would reign on the earth. The man who lives for himself shall never reign on the earth. "Blessed are the meek: for they shall inherit the earth;" not the men who, in their selfishness, trample down everybody else with iron heel. You shall not reign on the earth; you have lived here simply to hoard money, or to make a name for yourself, or to indulge your passions, or to revenge yourselves upon your fellow-men. You reign, sir? You? God's prison-house is the place for you, not a throne. But when he has made us meek, and humble, and lowly, and reverent, and pure, then we shall become fit to be promoted to this high calling of being priests and kings for Christ unto God in glory, and even here on earth in the day that is coming.

I wish that everybody here would take to searching himself as to whether he is likely to be of that blessed number. Do you with joy accept Christ as your Mediator? Do you see clearly how worthy he is to be the Mediator? Have you been redeemed from among men? Have you been taken away from old associations? Have you broken loose from habits that held you a slave amongst the Egyptians? Have you come into a new society? Has God brought you into a new heaven and a new earth? Has he given you any measure of reigning power over yourself? Do you live as a priest, serving God continually? If you are obliged to keep on saying, "No, no, no," to all these questions, then what shall I say but "Come to Christ"? May you come to him to-night! May he to-night begin in you that blessed process that shall make you meet to be partaker of the inheritance of the saints in light, for Jesus' sake! Amen.

Exposition by C. H. Spurgeon.

PSALM CXXXVI.

When the chorus was taken up by the whole of the people, accompanied by a blast of trumpets, this must have been a magnificent hymn of praise.

Verse 1. *O give thanks unto the* LORD; *for he is good: for his mercy endureth for ever.*

The Psalm begins with the august name, the incommunicable title of the one living and true God, Jah, Jehovah. For this name the Jews had a high respect, which degenerated into superstition, for they would not write it in their Bibles, and put another word instead, in which our translators have imitated them, not to the improvement of the version. Surely, if it is "Jehovah" in the original, we should have it "Jehovah" here. The name is a very wonderful one, "Je-ho-vah." No man knows exactly how it should be pronounced; it is said to consist of a succession of breathings, therefore is it written, "Let every thing that hath breath praise the Lord," whose name is a breathing, and in whom dwells the life of all who breathe.

Let us take care that we never trifle with the name of God. I think that the common use of the word "Hallelujah," or, "Praise ye the Lord," is simply profane. Surely, this is not a word to be dragged in the mire; it should be pronounced with solemn awe and sacred joy.

2. *O give thanks unto the God of gods: for his mercy endureth for ever.*

If there be any other god, if there can be imagined to be any, our God is infinitely above them all. The gods of the heathen are idols, but our God made the heavens. If there be any reverence due to magistrates, of whom we read in Psalm lxxxii., "I have said, Ye are gods," yet are they nothing at all compared with Jehovah, "the God of gods."

3. *O give thanks to the Lord of lords: for his mercy endureth for ever.*

Whatever there be of authority, or lordship, or kingship of any kind, in the world, it is all in subjection to him who is "the Lord of lords." I think I hear the trumpets sounding it out, and all the people joining in chorus, "O give thanks to the Lord of lords: for his mercy endureth for ever." It is ever the same strain, the enduring mercy of God, that bore the strain of Israel's sin, and Israel's need, and Israel's wandering.

4. *To him who alone doeth great wonders: for his mercy endureth for ever.*

Nobody does wonders that can be compared with Jehovah's wonders. Nobody helps him in the doing of his wonders; he asks no aid from any of his creatures.

5. *To him that by wisdom made the heavens: for his mercy endureth for ever.*

Every time you lift up your eyes to that one great arch which spans all mankind, praise the name of the great Builder who made that one enormous span, unbuttressed and unpropped. What a work it was! And it was made by mercy as well as by wisdom. If we go into the scientific account of the atmosphere, of the firmament, and of the stellar heavens, we see that the hand of mercy was at the back of wisdom in the making of it all: "for his mercy endureth for ever."

6. *To him that stretched out the earth above the waters: for his mercy endureth for ever.*

We ought to praise him for the making of every country, especially, I think, we who dwell on these favoured islands, because he has placed our lot in an island.

"He bade the waters round thee flow;
Not bars of brass could guard thee so."

We might have been beneath the tyrant's foot, if it had not been for "the silver streak" that gives us liberty. The whole earth, wherever men dwell, will afford some peculiar reason for their praise to Jehovah.

7—9. *To him that made great lights: for his mercy endureth for ever: the sun to rule by day: for his mercy endureth for ever: the moon and stars to rule by night: for his mercy endureth for ever.*

Why three verses about one thing? Because we are not wont to dwell upon God's goodness as we should. We are therefore bidden, first, to remember light in general, and then the sun, the moon, the stars, each one in particular; and each time we do so, we may say, "His mercy endureth for ever." We are not left in the daytime without the sun; and, when the day is over, the darkness of the night is cheered either by the moon or by the stars, which show us that, not only day unto day, but night unto night, he thinks upon us, "for his mercy endureth for ever." Praise him, praise him, whether it be high noon or midnight, when the day is renewed or when the curtains of your rest are drawn, still praise him, "for his mercy endureth for ever."

10. *To him that smote Egypt in their firstborn: for his mercy endureth for ever:*

It is not a common mercy of which we have to sing, but a peculiar theme for thanksgiving, he "smote Egypt in their firstborn."

11. *And brought out Israel from among them: for his mercy endureth for ever:*

Sing of his goodness to his chosen, even though it involved a terrible stroke upon his proud adversary. There are some who cannot praise God's left hand, but we can; not only the right hand that helps his people out, but the left hand that smites the Egyptians. We praise him still with unabated joy in him. What he doeth, must be right; and in his vengeance there is justice, and justice is mercy to mankind.

12. *With a strong hand, and with a stretched out arm: for his mercy endureth for ever.*

In all God's acts there is some peculiarity which commands especial attention. "He" brought out Israel," praise him for that. He did it "with a strong hand, and with a stretched out arm," therefore again praise him. The ring is precious, but the brilliant in the ring is that to which in this verse you are bidden to look, namely, Jehovah's strong hand, and stretched out arm.

13, 14. *To him which divided the Red sea into parts: for his mercy endureth for ever: and made Israel to pass through the midst of it: for his mercy endureth for ever:*

And when you, too, come to the Red Sea on your way to the heavenly Canaan, when your path is blocked, God will divide it for you; and as he gently leads you through the very deeps, he will have you sing, "His mercy endureth for ever." No floods can drown his love, nor divide you from it. "Who shall separate us from the love of Christ?" Jehovah will split seas in two to make a passage for his people, "for his mercy endureth for ever."

15. *But overthrew Pharaoh and his host in the Red sea: for his mercy endureth for ever.*

This is the deep bass of the hymn, he "overthrew Pharaoh." "The horse and his rider hath he thrown into the sea." We cannot give up that verse; we cannot refuse to sing the song of Moses; we must praise and bless God for all that he did at the Red Sea, even though terrible were his deeds of righteousness, when the chivalry of Egypt sank to the bottom of the sea like a stone.

16. *To him which led his people through the wilderness: for his mercy endureth for ever.*

Here is another point where you can join with Israel. This world is a wilderness to you; but the Lord leads you through it. By his fiery-cloudy pillar, he conducts you all your journey through. By his manna, gently dropping from heaven, he feeds you still; and he will guide you till he brings you over "Jordan's stormy banks"—

"To Canaan's fair and happy land."

17—20. *To him which smote great kings: for his mercy endureth for ever: and slew famous kings: for his mercy endureth for ever: Sihon king of the Amorites: for his mercy endureth for ever: and Og the king of Bashan: for his mercy endureth for ever:*

Here you have the repetitions of God. I have sometimes said that I like the tunes which allow us to repeat the line of a hymn; and, certainly, one likes a Psalm which turns over some great mercy of God, and makes us see the various facets of the wonderful jewel. The psalmist does not merely say that Jehovah smote great kings; but these kings were famous in battle, which rendered their greatness or power the more formidable; but whether men be great, or whether they be valorous, or both, they cannot prevent God's mercy to his people. He will push a way for them against the horns of their adversaries, and they shall be victorious. As if to show the depth of his gratitude, the psalmist gives the names of these kings, and of the countries over which they ruled; and he dwells with emphasis upon these points of the mercy of God to his people, in that he slew famous kings, Sihon king of the Amorites, and Og the king of Bashan.

21, 22. *And gave their land for an heritage: for his mercy endureth for ever: even an heritage unto Israel his servant: for his mercy endureth for ever.*

He gave them those countries which were beyond the land of promise, because these foes tried to stop their way. He did not limit Palestine; but, on the contrary, he stretched the ordained bounds of it, and enclosed the land of the Amorites and Bashan within the territory he gave to his people.

Now comes a soft sweet verse; I think I hear the harps leading the singing:—

23. *Who remembered us in our low estate: for his mercy endureth for ever:*

Can you not sing this to-night? Some of you, who were very poor, very sad, despairing, abhorred of men, slandered, persecuted, very low, perhaps some here, who once were in the slums of this city, now can sing, "Who remembered us in our low estate." Spiritually, our estate was low enough; it had ebbed out, till we had no comfort nor hope left; but the Lord remembered us. That is a blessed prayer, "Lord, remember me." That prayer has been answered for many here; ay, even before we prayed it. He remembered us in our low estate, "for his mercy endureth for ever." Dear heart, are you in a very low estate to-night? Do you feel as if you were at death's dark door, and at hell's dread brink, by reason of the greatness and blackness of your sin? "His mercy endureth for ever." Catch at that rope. Drowning men clutch at straws; but this is no straw. Do cling to it; it will bear your weight. It has been a means of salvation to myriads before you. Trust God's mercy in Christ, and you are saved, "for his mercy endureth for ever." "Who remembered us"—what next?

24. *And hath redeemed us—*

This song is climbing up; it begins to ascend the heavenly ladder; it has already reached redemption.

24, 25. *From our enemies: for his mercy endureth for ever. Who giveth food to all flesh: for his mercy endureth for ever.*

God is the great Feeder of the world. What a commissariat is that of the universe! One cannot think of the wants of the five millions in London without shuddering lest, some day, there should not be food enough for them; but there always is. I will not trace it to the mere fact that trade and commerce supply us. No, there is an over-ruling power at the back of it all, depend upon it. All the world seems eager to supply our markets, and to make the loaf for the labourer; but it is God who has planned it all. Let us praise him "who giveth food to all flesh." As for spiritual meat, he will give us that; I trust we shall all have a portion of meat in due season to-night. If any shall be hungry at the end of the service, it shall be surely from want of willingness to be fed rather than lack of suitability in the Word of God to sustain the spirit, and bless the soul.

26. *O give thanks unto the God of heaven: for his mercy endureth for ever.*

HYMNS FROM "OUR OWN HYMN BOOK"—873, 413, 416.

Metropolitan Tabernacle Pulpit.

"THE MARRIAGE OF THE LAMB."

A Sermon

DELIVERED ON LORD'S-DAY MORNING, JULY 21ST, 1889, BY

C. H. SPURGEON,

AT THE METROPOLITAN TABERNACLE, NEWINGTON.

"Let us be glad and rejoice, and give honour to him: for the marriage of the Lamb is come, and his wife hath made herself ready. And to her was granted that she should be arrayed in fine linen, clean and white: for the fine linen is the righteousness of saints."—Revelation xix. 7, 8.

LAST Lord's-day we saw clearly from God's Word that our Lord is worshipped in heaven under the character of a Lamb. Now, by a Lamb was meant sacrifice, sacrifice for the putting away of sin: according to the text, "Behold the Lamb of God, which taketh away the sin of the world." It is against the great doctrine of atonement and substitutionary death that the attacks of the present unbelieving age are constantly being made; and therefore I set before you the truth that substitution and sacrifice were not a temporary expedient, but that they continue all through the whole history of salvation, and remain in the very highest place, even in heaven itself, and will continue evermore. Do not forget that, whenever we read of Christ as a Lamb, it is to remind us of his sufferings and death in our room, and place, and stead, for the putting away of our sin. Under that character we looked to him, some of us, years ago, and found peace at the first. We are still looking to him under that same character; and when we attain to heaven, we shall not have to change our thought of him, but we shall still see him as a Lamb that has been slain. In our lowest place, when we came out of the Egypt of our bondage, he was the Lamb of God's passover; and in our highest place, in the heavenly temple, we shall still regard him as "the Lamb slain from the foundation of the world."

This morning my principal aim shall be to show you that the blessed and glorious union, which is to be celebrated between the church and her Lord, will be the marriage "*of the Lamb*." The ever blessed and eternal union of hearts with Christ will be in reference to his sacrifice, specially and emphatically. The perfected union of the entire church of God with her divine husband is here described by the beloved apostle, who laid his head upon his Master's bosom, and knew most about him, and who was under the immediate inspiration of the Holy Ghost, in these words: "The marriage of the Lamb is come, and his wife hath made herself ready."

No. 2,096.

Whatever else we think of at this time, my discourse will aim at this as the white of the target—namely, that Jesus Christ as the Lamb, the sacrifice, is not only the beginning, but the end; not only the foundation, but the topstone of the whole sacred edifice of the temple of grace. The consummation of the whole work of redemption is the marriage of the church to Christ; and, according to "the true sayings of God," this is "the marriage of the Lamb."

I will set forth this marriage as best I am able. It is divinely veiled as well as revealed in this Revelation. God forbid we should intrude where the Holy Spirit shuts us out; but still, what we do know of it, let us now think upon, and may the sacred Spirit make it profitable to us!

I. First, I invite your attention to THE ANTECEDENTS OF THIS MARRIAGE. What will happen before the public marriage is celebrated?

One great event will be *the destruction of the harlot church*. I have just read, in your hearing, the previous chapter, which declares the overwhelming destruction which will fall upon that evil system. Any church which puts in the place of justification by faith in Christ another method of salvation, is a harlot church. The doctrine of justification by faith in Christ is the article of a standing or a falling church. Where the blood is precious, there is life; where atonement by the sacrifice is preached and loved, there will the Spirit of God bear effectual testimony; but where human priests are put in the place of Jesus, where pardons can be purchased, where there is an unbloody sacrifice instead of the great propitiation, and sacraments are exalted as the means of regeneration; there the church is no longer a chaste virgin unto Christ, but she hath turned aside from her purity.

The Antichristian system is to be utterly extirpated and burnt with fire; for you will perceive, in the fourteenth verse of the seventeenth chapter, that those who were associated with this false church, " shall make war with the Lamb, and the Lamb shall overcome them: for he is Lord of lords, and King of kings"; and there has been no more wicked nor more determined war with the Lamb, than that which has been waged by superstition supported by unbelief. The harlot church and the beast of infidelity are in real league against the simple faith of Christ. If you point men, no matter where—if you point them away from Christ, you point them to Antichrist. If you teach them what you may, no matter how philosophical it may seem—if in any way it takes them off from building upon the one foundation of Christ's glorious and finished work, you have laid an Antichristian foundation, and all that is built thereon will be destroyed. Everything which sets up itself in opposition to the sacrifice of Christ, is to be hurled down, and made to sink like a millstone in the flood. I would God the hour were come! Oh, that the Lord's own right arm were bare, and that we heard the cry, "Babylon the great is fallen, is fallen." It is ours to expect the speedy coming of our Lord; yet, if he tarry, it may be many a day before "her plagues come in one day." But, wait as we may, so it shall be; the day must come when the true church shall be honoured, and the harlot church shall be abhorred. The **Bride** of Christ is a sort of Cinderella now, sitting among the ashes. She is like her Lord, "despised and rejected of men"; the watchmen smite her, and take away her veil from her; for they know her not, even as they knew not her Lord. But when he shall appear, then shall she appear also, and in his glorious manifestation she also shall shine forth as the sun in the kingdom of the Father.

Furthermore, in the immediate connection, we note that before the marriage of the Lamb, *there was a peculiar voice.* Read the fifth verse: "And a voice came." Where from? "A voice came out of the throne." Whose voice was that? It was not the voice of the Eternal God; for it said, "Praise our God, all ye his servants." Whose voice, then, could it be? No one but God could be upon the throne save the Lamb, who is God. Surely, it was he who said, "Praise our God." The Mediator, God-and-man in one person, was on the throne as a Lamb, and he announced the day of his own marriage. Who should do it but he? "A voice came out of the throne, saying, Praise our God, all ye his servants, and ye that fear him, both small and great." He speaks the word which calls on all the servants of God to praise him, because his complete victory had come. Longing to see of the travail of his soul, earnest to gather in all his elect, he speaks; for the fulness of time has come, when his joy shall be full, and he shall rejoice over the whole company of his redeemed as for ever one with himself.

The voice from the throne is a very remarkable one; for it shows how near akin the exalted Christ is to his people. He saith to all the redeemed, "Praise *our* God, all ye his servants." It reminds me of his memorable words, "I ascend unto my Father, and your Father; and to my God, and your God." He was not then ashamed to associate his people with him in the high possession of his Father and his God; and up there upon the throne, he saith, "Praise *our* God." I do not know how this language strikes you; but to me it forcibly sets forth his love, his condescension, his fraternization, his union with his people. Since I know not how to set it out to you, I must leave you to think over it. He who has gone triumphantly up to the throne, the Saviour whose conflicts are all over, who has gained the everlasting reward of sitting with the Father upon his throne, still joins with us in praise, and saith, "Praise *our* God, all ye his servants." He is not even ashamed to have fellowship with the least of his people; for he adds, "And ye that fear him, both small and great." Truly "the man is near of kin to us, he is our next kinsman."

> " In ties of blood, with sinners one,
> Our Jesus hath to glory gone."

In that glory he still owns his dear relationship, and in the midst of the church he singeth praise unto God. (Heb. ii. 11, 12.)

Next, notice *the response to this voice;* for this also precedes the marriage. No sooner did that one august voice summon them to praise, than immediately "I heard as it were the voice of a great multitude." He heard the mingled sound as of an innumerable host all joining in the song; for the redeemed of the Lord are not a few. No man can count them. "Out of every kindred, and tongue, and people, and nation," they respond in that day to the voice of the Lamb, saying, "Alleluia: for the Lord God omnipotent reigneth." So loud was the sound of all those commingled voices, that it sounded like "many waters"; like cataracts in their roar, or like oceans in their fulness. It was as though all the billows of the Atlantic, and the Pacific, and the Northern, and Southern oceans lifted up their voices, and deep answered unto deep. Nor was the figure too strong; for John heaps upon it another comparison, and says, "As the voice of mighty thunderings." We have lately heard the thunder above the deafening din of our streets, and we have trembled at the dread artillery of heaven. Such was the sound of the mingled voices of the redeemed when they all united to give honour to God, because the marriage of the Lamb had come. Who can imagine the acclamations of that glorious day? We now preach the gospel, as it were, in a corner, and few there are that will applaud the King of kings. Still, the Christ wendeth his way through the world as an unknown or forgotten man; and his church, following behind him, seemeth as a forlorn and forsaken woman—few there be that care for her. But in that day when her Lord is seen as the King of kings, and she is openly acknowledged as his spouse, what welcomes will be heard, what bursts of adoring praise unto the Lord God omnipotent!

Observe that *this tremendous volume of sound will be full of rejoicing and of devout homage.* "Let us be glad and rejoice, and give honour to him." Double joy will be there, and its expression will be homage to the Lord God. The joy of joys will be the delight of Christ in his perfectly gathered church. There is joy in heaven in the presence of the angels of God over one sinner that repenteth; but when all these repenting sinners are gathered into one perfected body, and married to the Lamb, what will be the infinite gladness? Heaven is always heaven, and unspeakably full of blessedness; but even heaven has its holidays, even bliss has its overflowings; and on that day when the springtide of the infinite ocean of joy shall have come, what a measureless flood of delight shall overflow the souls of all glorified spirits as they perceive that the consummation of love's great design is come—"The marriage of the Lamb is come, and his wife hath made herself ready"! We do not know yet, beloved, of what happiness we are capable. We have sometimes wished that we could

> "Sit and sing ourselves away
> To everlasting bliss."

But then we were only feeling the spray of the ocean of blessedness. What must it be to bathe in it? Here we drink from cups of consolation; but what draughts we shall have when we lie down at the well-head, and drink in our joy immediately from God! If you and I enter glory soon without our bodies, we shall not even then know to the utmost degree what will be the bliss of our perfected manhood, when the body shall be raised incorruptible from among the dead, and joined to the sinless soul. Nor would this give us more than a bare idea of the infinite blessedness of myriads of such perfected manhoods united in a perfected church; from which no one single member shall be missing, nor one member maimed, or sick, or stained. Praise the Lord Jesus as you sing—

> "Thou the whole body shalt present
> Before thy Father's face;
> Nor shall a wrinkle, or a spot,
> The beauteous form deface."

Oh, what joy! I feel as if I could not preach to you: I want to get away to think it over, and chew the cud of meditation for myself. You must just sit where you are and muse. Here we have the essence of heavenly music in a few plain words. "The marriage of the Lamb is come." Oh, may I be there! May I be a part of the perfected body of the church of God! Oh, that I might be but part of the soles of her feet, or the least hair of her head! If I may but see the King in his beauty, in the fulness of his joy, when he shall take by the right hand her for whom he shed his precious blood, and shall know the joy which was set before him, for which he endured the cross, despising the shame, I shall be blest indeed!

Thus, I have given you a hint of what will precede the marriage of the Lamb, in all of which you may observe that Jesus wears his character of the Lamb. The harlot church hath fought against the Lamb, and the Lamb hath overcome her forces. He it is that, on the throne, speaks to his people as his brethren; it is to him that the response is given; for the joy and the delight all spring from the fact that the marriage is that of the Lamb whom the Father glorifies, and who glorifies the Father. The voice said, "Let us rejoice, and give honour to him." Was not that his prayer of old, "Father, glorify thy Son, that thy Son also may glorify thee"? To glorify the Father, Jesus died as a sacrifice; and to glorify Jesus, the Father gives him his church, which is redeemed by the blood of the Lamb.

II. Now may I be helped by the Spirit of God, while I lead you on to THE MARRIAGE ITSELF. "The marriage of the Lamb is come." Often as you hear about this marriage of the Lamb, I greatly question whether any here have any precise idea what it means. Dean Alford says, "This figure of a marriage between the Lord and his people, is too frequent and familiar to need explanation." With all deference to the excellent divine, that was a very sufficient reason why he should have carefully explained it, since that which is often noted in Holy Scripture must be of first importance, and should be well understood. I do not wonder that many are shy of such a theme, for it is a difficult one. Alas, how little do I, personally, know of such a matter!

The marriage of the Lamb is *the result of the eternal gift of the Father.* Our Lord says, "Thine they were, and thou gavest them me." His prayer was, "Father, I will that they also, whom thou hast given me, be with me where I am; that they may behold my glory, which thou hast given me: for thou lovedst me before the foundation of the world." The Father made a choice, and the chosen he gave to his Son to be his portion. For them he entered into a covenant of redemption, whereby he was pledged in due time to take upon himself their nature, pay the penalty of their offences, and set them free to be his own. Beloved, that which was arranged in the councils of eternity and settled there between the high contracting parties, is brought to its ultimate end in that day when the Lamb takes unto himself in everlasting union the whole of those whom his Father gave him from of old.

Next: this is *the completion of the betrothal*, which took place with each of them in time. I shall not attempt elaborate distinctions; but as far as you and I were concerned, the Lord Jesus betrothed each one of us unto himself in righteousness, when first we believed on him. Then he took us to be his, and gave himself to be ours, so that we could sing—"My beloved is mine, and I am his." This was the essence of the marriage. Paul, in the Epistle to the Ephesians, represents our Lord as already married to the church. This may be illustrated by the Oriental custom, by which, when the bride is betrothed, all the sanctities of marriage are involved in those espousals; but yet there may be a considerable interval before the bride is taken to her husband's house. She dwells with her former household, and has not yet forgotten her kindred and her father's house, though still she is espoused in truth and righteousness. Afterwards, she is brought home on an appointed day, the day which we should call the actual marriage; but yet the betrothal is, to Orientals, of the very essence of the marriage. Well, then, you and I are betrothed to our Lord to-day, and he is joined to us by inseparable bonds. He does not wish to part with us, nor could we part from him. He is the delight of our souls, and he rejoices over us with singing. Rejoice that he has chosen you and called you, and through the betrothal look forward to the marriage. Feel even now, that though in the world, you are not of it: your destiny does not lie here among these frivolous sons of men. Our home is henceforth on high.

> " My heart is with him on his throne,
>   And ill can brook delay;
> Each moment listening for the voice,
>   ' Rise up, and come away.' "

The marriage day indicates the perfecting of the body of the church. I have already told you that the church will then be completed, and it is not so now. Adam lay asleep, and the Lord took out of his side a rib, and fashioned thereof a help-meet for him: Adam saw her not when she was in the forming, but he opened his eyes, and before him was the perfect form of his help-meet. Beloved, the true church is now in the forming, and is therefore not visible. There are many churches; but as to the one church of Christ, we see it neither here nor there. We speak of the visible church; but the term is not correct. The thing which we see is a mixture of believers and mere pretenders to faith. The church which is affianced unto the heavenly Bridegroom is not visible as yet; for she is in the process of formation. The Lord will not allow such simpletons as we are to see his half-finished work. But the day will come when he shall have completed his new creation, and then will he bring her forth whom he has made for the second Adam, to be his delight to all eternity. The church is not perfected as yet. We read of that part of it which is in heaven, that "They without us should not be made perfect." Unless you and I get there, if we are true believers, there cannot be a perfect church in glory. The music of the heavenly harmonies as yet lacks certain voices. Some of its needful notes are too bass for those already, and others are too high for them, till the singers come who are ordained to give the choir its fullest range. At the Crystal Palace you have seen the singers come trooping in. The conductor is all anxiety if they seem to linger. Still, some are away. The time is nearly up, and you see seats up there on the right, and a vacant block down there on the left. Even so with the heavenly choir: they are streaming in: the orchestra is filling up, but yet there is room, and yet there is demand for other voices to complete the heavenly harmony. Beloved, in the day of the marriage of the Lamb, the chosen shall all be there—the great and the small—even all the believers who are wrestling hard this day with sins and doubts and fears Every living member of the living church shall be there to be married to the Lamb.

By this marriage is meant more than I have told you. There is *the home-bringing.* You are not to live here for ever in these tents of Kedar, among a people of a strange tongue; but the blessed Bridegroom cometh to take you to the happy country, where you shall no longer say, "My soul is among lions." All the faithful shall soon be away to thy land, O Emmanuel! We shall dwell in the land that floweth with milk and honey, the land of the unclouded and unsetting sun, the home of the blessed of the Lord. Happy indeed will be the home-bringing of the perfect church!

The marriage is the *coronal-avowal.* The church is the bride of the great King, and he will set the crown upon her head, and make her to be known as his true spouse for ever. Oh, what a day that will be when every member of Christ shall be crowned in him, and with him, and every member of the mystical body shall be glorified in the glory of the Bridegroom! Oh, may I be there in that day! Brethren, we must be with our Lord in the fight if we would be with him in the victory. We must be with him in wearing the crown of thorns, if we are to be with him in wearing the crown of glory. We must be faithful by his grace, even unto death, if we are to share the glory of his endless life.

I cannot tell you all it means, but certainly this marriage signifies that all who have believed in him shall then *enter into a bliss which shall never end;* a bliss which no fear approacheth, or doubt becloudeth. They shall be for ever with the Lord, for ever glorified with him. Expect not lips of clay fitly to speak on such a theme. Tongues of fire are needed, and words that fall like fire-flakes on the soul.

A day will come, the day of days, time's crown and glory, when, all conflict, risk, and judgment ended for ever, the saints, arrayed in the righteousness of Christ, shall be eternally one with him in living, loving, lasting union, partaking together of the same glory, the glory of the Most High. What must it be to be there! My dear hearers, will you be there? Make your calling and election sure. If you are not trusting in the Lamb on earth, you will not reign with the Lamb in his glory. He that doth not love the Lamb, as the atoning sacrifice, shall never be the bride of the Lamb. How can you hope to be glorified with him if you neglect him in the day of his scorning? O Lamb of God, my sacrifice, I must be one with thee, for this is my very life! I could not live apart from thee. If, my hearer, thou canst thus speak, there is good hope that thou shalt be a participator in the marriage of the Lamb.

III. But we pass on now to dwell emphatically upon the fact that THE CHARACTER UNDER WHICH THE BRIDEGROOM APPEARS IS THAT OF THE LAMB. "The marriage of *the Lamb* is come."

It must be so, because first of all *our Saviour was the Lamb in the eternal covenant;* when this whole matter was planned, arranged and settled by the foresight and decree of eternity. He is "the Lamb slain from the foundation of the world," and the covenant was with him, as one who was to be the surety, the substitute, the sacrifice for guilty men. So, and not otherwise, was it of old.

It was next *as the Lamb that he loved us and proved his love.* Beloved, he did not give us words of love merely when he came from heaven to earth, and dwelt among us "a lowly man before his foes"; but he proceeded to deeds of truest affection. The supreme proof of his love was that he was led as a lamb to the slaughter. When he poured out his blood as a sacrifice, it might have been said, "Behold, how he loved them!" If you would prove the love of Jesus, you would not mention the transfiguration, but the crucifixion. Gethsemane and Golgotha would rise to your lips. Here to demonstration, beyond all possibility of doubt by any true heart, the Well-beloved proved his love to us. See how it runs: "He loved me, and gave himself for me," as if that giving of himself for me was the clear proof that he loved me. Read again: "Christ loved the church, and gave himself for it." The proof of his love to the church was the giving up of himself for it. "Being found in fashion as a man he humbled himself, and became obedient to death, even the death of the cross." "Herein is love, not that we loved God, but that he loved us." So, you see, as a Lamb he proved his love, and as a Lamb he celebrated his marriage with us.

Go a step further. Love in marriage must be on both sides, and *it is as the Lamb that we first came to love him.* I had no love to Christ; how could I have, till I saw his wounds and blood? "We love him, because he first loved us." His perfect life was a condemnation to me, much as I was compelled to admire it; but the love that drew me to him was shown in his substitutionary character, when he bore my sins in his own body on the tree. Is it not so with you, beloved? I have heard a great deal about conversions through admiration of the character of Christ, but I have never met with one: all I have ever met with have been conversions through a sense of need of salvation, and a consciousness of guilt, which could never be satisfied save by his agony and death, through which sin is justly pardoned, and evil is subdued. This is the great heart-winning doctrine. Christ loves us as the Lamb, and we love him as the Lamb.

Further, *marriage is the most perfect union.* Surely, it is as the Lamb that Jesus is most closely joined to his people. Our Lord came very close to us when he took our nature, for thus he became bone of our bone, and flesh of our flesh. He came very near to us when, for this cause, he left his Father and became one flesh with his church. He could not be sinful as she was; but he did take her sins upon himself, and bear them all away, as it is written, "The Lord hath laid on him the iniquity of us all." When "he was numbered with the transgressors," and when the sword of vengeance smote him in our stead, then he came nearer to us than ever he could do in the perfection of his Incarnation. I cannot conceive of closer union than that of Christ and souls redeemed by blood. As I look at him in death, I feel forced to cry, "Surely a husband by blood art thou to me, O Jesus! Thou art joined to me by something closer than the one fact that thou art of my nature; for that nature of thine has borne my sin, and suffered the penalty of wrath on my behalf. Now art thou one with me in all things, by a union like to that which links thee with the Father." A wonderful union is thus effected by our Lord's wearing the character of the Lamb.

Once more, *we never feel so one with Jesus as when we see him as the Lamb*. I shall again appeal to your experience. When have you had the sweetest fellowship with Christ in all your lives? I answer on my own account—it has been when I have sung:

> "Oh, how sweet to view the flowing
> Of his soul-redeeming blood,
> With divine assurance knowing
> He hath made my peace with God!"

If I had my choice to-day, while abiding in this present state, to see my Lord in his glory, or on his cross, I should choose the latter. Of course, I would prefer to see his glory, and be away with him; but, while dwelling here surrounded with sin and sorrow, a sight of his griefs has the most effect upon me. "O sacred head once wounded," I long to behold thee! I never feel so close to my Lord as when I survey his wondrous cross, and see him pouring out his blood for me. I have been melted down when we have sung together those sweet lines:

> "See from his head, his hands, his feet,
> Sorrow and love flow mingled down!
> Did e'er such love and sorrow meet?
> Or thorns compose so rich a crown?"

I have almost felt myself in his arms, and like John, I have leaned on his bosom, when I have beheld his passion. I do not wonder, therefore, that since he comes closest to us as the Lamb, and since we come closest to him when we behold him in that character, he is pleased to call his highest eternal union with his church, "the marriage of the Lamb."

And O beloved, when you come to think of it, to be married to him, to be one with him, to have no thought, no object, no desire, no glory but that which dwells in him that liveth and was dead—will not this be heaven indeed, where the Lamb is the light thereof? For ever to contemplate and adore him who offered up himself without spot unto God, as our sacrifice and propitiation; this shall be an endless feast of grateful love. We shall never weary of this subject. If you see the Lord coming from Edom, with dyed garments from Bozrah, from the winepress wherein he has trampled on his foes, you are overawed and overcome by the terror of that dread display of justice; but when you see him clad in a vesture dipped in no blood but his own, you will sing aloud evermore, "Thou wast slain, and hast redeemed us to God by thy blood; to thee be glory for ever and ever." I could go on singing, "Worthy is the Lamb that was slain" throughout all eternity. The theme has an inexhaustible interest about it: there is everything in it: justice, mercy, power, patience, love, condescension, grace and glory. All over glorious is my Lord when I behold him as a Lamb; and this shall make heaven seven times heaven to me to think that even then I shall be joined to him in everlasting bonds as the Lamb. [Here a voice from the gallery cried, "Praise the Lord!"] Yes, my friend, we will praise the Lord. "Praise ye the Lord" is the command which was heard coming out of the throne—"Praise our God, all ye his servants, and ye that fear him, both small and great: for the marriage of the Lamb is come, and his wife hath made herself ready."

IV. Now we come to the last point, THE PREPAREDNESS OF THE BRIDE: "His wife hath made herself ready." Up till now the church has always been spoken of as his bride, now she is "his wife"—that is a deeper, dearer, more-matured word than "bride": "*his wife* hath made herself ready." The church has now come to the fulness of her joy, and has taken possession of her status and dower as "his wife." What does it mean—"hath made herself ready?"

It signifies, first, that *she willingly and of her own accord comes to her Lord*, to be his, and to be with him for ever. This she does with all her heart: "she hath made herself ready." She does not enter into this engagement with reluctance. Some unwisely speak of the grace of God, as though it were a physical force, which sets a constraint upon the will of the quickened man. Beloved, I never preach to you in that fashion. Free will is an unknown thing, except it be wrought in us by grace. Grace is the great liberating force. The will is a slave to evil, till grace comes, and makes it free to choose that which is good. No action of the soul is more free than that by which it quits sin, and closes with Christ. Then the man comes to himself. The heart is free from compulsion, when its love goes forth towards the Lord Jesus. I ask you that love him, do you feel that you are going against your will in so doing? Far from it: you wish to love him more. In the ultimate union of all the chosen with Christ, will you want any forcing to take your part in the marriage of the Lamb? Did not the words I used just now state your longings—"My heart is with him on his throne." Are you not panting to behold his face? Compulsion to a hungry man to eat would seem more likely than compulsion to be joined unto Christ. His wife hath gladly made herself ready: free grace has made her freely choose him.

Does it not mean that *she has put away from herself all evil*, and all connection with the corruptions of the harlot church has been destroyed? She has struggled against error, she has fought against infidelity, and both have been put down by her holy watchfulness and earnest testimony; and so she is ready for her Lord.

Does it not also mean that in the great day of the consummation *the church will be one?* Alas, for the divisions among us! You do not know what denomination my friend belonged to who prayed just now. Well, I shall not tell you. You could not judge from his prayer. "The saints in prayer appear as one." Denomination! A plague upon denominationalism! There should be but one denomination: we should be denominated by the name of Christ, as the wife is named by her husband's name. As long as the church of Christ has to say, "My right arm is Episcopalian, and my left arm is Wesleyan, and my right foot is Baptist, and my left foot is Presbyterian or Congregational," she is not ready for the marriage. She will be ready when she has washed out these stains, when all her members have "one Lord, one faith, one baptism." Unity is a main part of the readiness here spoken of.

I beg you to notice what *the preparation* was. It is described in the eighth verse: "To her was granted." I will go no further. Whatever preparation it was that she made, in whatever apparel she was arrayed, it was granted to her. Observe that the harlot church wore fine linen also, but then she had with it purple, and silk, and scarlet, and precious stones, and pearls. I do not know whence the harlot obtained her apparel, but I know where the true church found her wedding dress, for it is written, "to her was granted." This was a gift of sovereign grace, the free gift of her own Beloved: "To her was granted." She had a grant from the throne, a royal grant, an indisputable right. We also go to heaven by royal grant. We have nothing of our own to carry us there by right, nothing of boasted merit; but to us also is granted acceptance in the Beloved. Oh, it is a glorious thing to hold your own by letters patent, under the Great Seal of heaven! When we shall be united to Jesus, the ever blessed Lamb, in endless wedlock, all our fitness to be there will be ours by free grant.

Look at the apparel of the wife, "To her was granted that she should be arrayed in fine linen, clean and white." How simple her raiment! Only fine linen, clean and white! The more simple our worship, the better. The true church of Christ is content with white linen, and no more. She asked not for those fine things we read about in connection with the harlot. She envied not the unchaste one her harpers, and musicians, and pipers, and trumpeters: she was content with her simple harp and joyful song. She did not need all manner of vessels of ivory, and precious wood, brass and iron, and marble. She did not seek for cinnamon, and odours, and ointments, nor aught else of that finery with which people nowadays try to adorn their worship. The simpler the better. When in worship you cannot hear the voices of the people beyond the noise which might be made by the twitter of half-a-dozen sparrows, because a flood of noise from a huge organ is drowning all the praise—I think we have lost our way. The simpler the worship the better, whether in prayer or praise, or anything else. The harlot church bedecks herself with her architecture, and her millinery, and her perfumery, and her oratory, and her music; but those who would follow the Lamb whithersoever he goeth, will keep their worship, their practice, and their doctrine pure and simple, avoiding all the blandishments of carnal policy and human wisdom, content with the truth as it is in Jesus. What more beautiful than pure white linen?

In the Greek, our text runs thus: "Fine linen, clean and white, for fine linen is *the righteousnesses of the saints.*" Our Revised Version has, in this case, not given us a translation, but an explanation, and that explanation is a contraction of the sense. The revisers word it, "Fine linen is the righteous acts of saints." That word "acts" is of their own insertion. The word "righteousnesses" has a fuller meaning: it is exceeding broad, and they have narrowed it, and misapplied it. We shall have a complete array of righteousnesses in Christ's righteousness, active and passive—a garment for the head, and a garment for the feet, and for the loins. What righteousnesses we have! Righteousness imparted by the power of the Spirit; righteousness imputed by the decree of God. Every form of righteousness will go to make up the believer's outfit; only, all of it is *granted*, and none of it is of our own purchasing. We shall not have Christ's righteousness to cover up our sin, as some blasphemously say—for we shall have no sin to cover. We shall not want Christ's righteousness to make an evil heart seem pure: we shall be as perfect as our Father in heaven is perfect. Washed in the blood of the Lamb, we shall have no spot upon us or within us. We shall have a complete righteousness; and in this arrayed, we shall be covered with the beauty of holiness. This garment is most befitting, for it is "The righteousness of saints." Saints ought to have righteousness. They are themselves made holy, and therefore they ought to be adorned in visible holiness; and so they shall be.

Best of all we shall be arrayed in that day with *that which pleases the Bridegroom.* Do I not remember how he said, "I counsel thee to buy of me white raiment"? Yes, she has remembered his bidding. She has nothing else but that "fine linen" which is the "The righteousness of saints"; and this he delights in. She comes to the Lamb, bearing about her the result of his own passion, and of his own Spirit, and she is well pleasing in his eyes. The Lord sees in her of the travail of his soul, and he is satisfied.

I have done when I have again put this question: Do you trust the Lamb? I warn you, if you have a religion which has no blood of Christ in it, it is not worth a thought: you had better be rid of it, it will be of no use to you. I warn you, also, that unless you love the Lamb you cannot be married to the Lamb; for he will never be married to those who have no love to him. You must take Jesus as a sacrifice, or not at all. It is useless to say, "I will follow Christ's example." You will not do anything of the sort. It is idle to say, "He shall be my teacher." He will not own you for a disciple unless you will own him as a sacrifice. You must take him as the Lamb, or have done with him. If you do despite to the blood of Christ, you do despite to the whole person of Christ. Christ is nothing to you if he is not your atonement. As many of you as hope to be saved by the works of the law, or by anything else apart from his blood and righteousness, you have un-Christianized yourselves; you have no part in Jesus here, and you shall have no part in him hereafter, when he shall take to himself his own redeemed church, to be his spouse for ever and ever. God bless you, for Christ's sake. Amen.

PORTIONS OF SCRIPTURE READ BEFORE SERMON—Revelation xviii. 4—24; xix. 1—9.

HYMNS FROM "OUR OWN HYMN BOOK"—916, 356, 333.

Metropolitan Tabernacle Pulpit.

THE FOLLOWERS OF THE LAMB.

A Sermon

INTENDED FOR READING ON LORD'S-DAY, SEPTEMBER 3RD, 1893,

DELIVERED BY

C. H. SPURGEON,

AT THE METROPOLITAN TABERNACLE, NEWINGTON,

On Lord's-day Evening, August 4th, 1889.

"These are they which follow the Lamb whithersoever he goeth. These were redeemed from among men, being the firstfruits unto God and to the Lamb. And in their mouth was found no guile: for they are without fault before the throne of God."—Revelation xiv. 4, 5.

WHATEVER the saints are in heaven, they began to be on earth. There is, no doubt, a perfection of character in the world to come; but the character must be formed here. In the next world there will be no real change; where the tree falls, there it will lie; he that is filthy will be filthy still, he that is holy will be holy still. I am going to talk to you to-night about those who surround the Lamb, and are with him in the blaze of his glory, singing to his honour. I say that what they were in heaven they were in a measure on earth. The life of glory is the life of grace. That life which men have in heaven comes to them in regeneration on earth. When they are born again, they are born for heaven; then it is that they receive the life which lives on throughout the eternal ages. If you do not have that life here, you will never have it. If you die dead in sin, there is nothing for you for ever but the abode of the dead, "where their worm dieth not, and their fire is not quenched." To-day is the only time which we have for character-forming. Earth is the great place for making instruments of music; here they are tuned and prepared; up there, they play them; but they will never play them there unless they have had them made and tuned here.

The subject of my discourse will be, first, *a survey of the outline of character of those who are to be with Christ hereafter;* and then, secondly, *a contemplation of the perfect picture of the saints with Christ in glory,* where I trust we, too, shall be, in the Lord's good time.

I do not know whether these verses describe all the saints in heaven. If they do, then you must be like them, or you can never be among them. If, however, they describe the elect of the elect, the innermost

No. 2,324.

circle of heaven, if they describe the body-guard of Christ, the immortals that perpetually surround him, nearest to his person, the most divinely like him, if they describe a kind of aristocracy of the skies, the nobility of heaven,—and it seems to me that they do, for they are the firstfruits, and the rest of the righteous may be regarded as the harvest afterwards reaped,—if these words describe some special saints, then we should seek to be like them. I would cultivate a holy ambition to be among the brightest stars of God. Why should we not reach to the highest prize of our high calling? If there be any speciality among the redeemed above, should it not be our earnest desire to attain to that standard?

I. So, first, here is AN OUTLINE OF THE CHARACTER OF THOSE BLESSED ONES WHILE THEY ARE HERE.

And, first, notice *their adherence to the doctrine of sacrifice* while they are here: "These are they which follow *the Lamb*." There are some professing Christians who talk much about the example of Christ, but deny the efficacy of his atoning blood; they are not of those who will be in heaven. There are some who magnify the philosophy of Christ; all his ethical teaching is greatly to their taste; but, as to his being a Substitute offered up as a sacrifice on account of human guilt, they cannot away with it. Very well; they cannot enter heaven, for "these are they which follow *the Lamb;*" not Christ only, mark you, but Christ as the Lamb of God's passover, Christ as the Lamb of God slain before the foundation of the world, Christ as the Lamb of God which taketh away the sin of the world. You cannot be of that blessed number, if you reject Christ as a sacrifice. As for me, and I trust for you also, " God forbid that I should glory, save in the cross of our Lord Jesus Christ!" Christianity without the blood of Christ is a dead Christianity; it has nothing to give life to it, " for the blood is the life thereof." If you take away the doctrine of sacrifice, you have taken away the core, the heart, the pith, the marrow of all Christianity. You have left bones for dogs; but you have not left food for immortal spirits. Whosoever will be saved, before all things it is necessary that he should believe in Jesus Christ, the Lamb of God, who taketh away the sin of the world. "For God so loved the world, that he gave his only begotten Son: that whosoever believeth in him, should not perish, but have everlasting life." Look, look, look unto him, and be ye saved, all ye ends of the earth, for he is God, even the bleeding Saviour, he is God, and beside him there is none else. May it be said of you all, dear friends, that you followed the Lamb by your adherence to his atoning sacrifice!

Many have thus followed the Lamb in spite of fierce persecution. Remember that brave woman, Ann Askew. When they had racked her, and pulled every limb out of its place, so that she ached all over in her exquisitely delicate frame, yet she sat on the stone floor of her cell, and still defended the sacrifice of Christ. When she had an opportunity to write her thoughts, she penned that quaint verse,—

" I am not she that list,
My anchor to let fall,
For every drizzling mist;
My ship's substantial."

She thought that being vexed by Popish priests and torn to pieces on the rack was only a drizzling mist, for which it was not worth while to cast her anchor. She was more than a match for fifty priests. God raise us up a race of such men and women! The devil seems to have taken the backbone out of most people. May we begin to know what we do know, and to believe what we do believe, and to put our foot down, and say, " God helping me, I will not forsake my God, nor turn away from his truth." You remember how Martin Luther, when he stood at the Diet of Worms, closed what he had to say when they bade him recant, and he would not. He said, " Here I stand ; I can do no other, so help me God ; " and thus, invoking the help of his divine Lord, he committed his body to the flames, if need be, sooner than he would renounce a single Word of the Most High, or sin against the light which he had received.

And, next, it is clear of these people that they followed the Lamb by *practically imitating Christ's example,* for it is written, " These are they which follow the Lamb whithersoever he goeth." They so believed in him that—

" They mark'd the footsteps that he trod,
His zeal inspired their breast,
And following their incarnate God,
Possess the promised rest."

You cannot be with Christ unless you are like Christ. If you have really trusted in Jesus, he will transform you, he will take away from you those evil tendencies and vile propensities which are contrary to holiness, he will work in you to will and to do of his own good pleasure. And the highest holiness for you is to be like Christ. The very noblest possible character to which you could ever reach is to follow the Lamb whithersoever he goeth, in obedience to God, in love to man, in self-sacrifice, in humility, in gentleness, in love. You must follow him whithersoever he goeth, and do what he did, so far as your position makes it fit for you to do it. I mean that you cannot do as he did as God, but you can do what he did as man. Try to put your feet down in the footprints that he has left you. Do aim at complete conformity to Christ ; and wherein you fail to reach it, mark that you come so far short of what you ought to be. To be like Christ is that which God intends for you ; and unless you have some measure of it now, you will never be with him, for all they who are with Christ above are the people who were made like to Christ here below. Note that very distinctly, " These are they which follow the Lamb whithersoever he goeth."

Will you, dear friends, labour to take Christ for your pattern ? Do not come and take his name, and then dishonour his character. There are among you some who are very much like your Master ; you are the joy of the church. There are among all the churches some who bear Christ's name, but are not like him. My venerable predecessor, Dr. Rippon, used to say of his church that he had in it some of the best people in England ; and then he used to add in a low voice, *"and some of the worst."* I am afraid that I have to say the same ; but I am very sorry that I should have to say it. The worst people in the world are those who profess most and do least. Do not be among that unhappy number; but do, I pray you, by the blessing of God, and the help of his Spirit, be among those who at least endeavour to "follow the Lamb whithersoever he goeth."

Now, notice in the sketch of these people that *they recognized a special redemption:* "These were redeemed from among men." Christ had done something for them that he had not done for others. They were not redeemed "among men", but "*from among men.*" They recognized the speciality of Christ's sacrifice. They could read, for instance, a passage like this, and understand its meaning, "Christ loved the church, and gave himself for it," for his church, for his body. "These were redeemed from among men." Come, beloved, do you belong to this company of persons who have been fetched out from the rest of mankind by the power of the Spirit of God, and also by the merit of the precious blood? Do you feel that you are marked with the blood as others are not? Do you belong to a people who are not of the world, even as he that bought them was not of the world? Are you henceforth not of the common multitude, but one who has been bought and paid for by that redemptive price which was found in the veins and the heart of the Redeemer, and are you so redeemed as no longer to be one of the great mass of mankind, but fetched out, called out, chosen, "not your own, but bought with a price"? These are they that will be with Christ hereafter, as specially redeemed ones.

And as they recognized a special redemption, you will observe that *they made a full surrender of themselves to God and to the Lamb*: "These were redeemed from among men, being the firstfruits unto God and to the Lamb." On a certain day, when the harvest was getting ripe, a man went down to the fields, and plucked an ear here, a handful there, and another handful further on, and he passed along the field, and gathered ears here and ears there, and when he had collected enough for sheaves, he tied them up, and took them to the temple of God, and presented them to the Lord as an offering, to signify that he owed all the harvest to God, and he brought him the first ripe ears as a sacrifice to him. Now, beloved, has the grace of God plucked you out from among the rest of mankind, and do you feel that now you belong to Christ, that you belong to God, that you are not to be gathered with the mass of men for the great condemnation, but that you are presented unto God, and belong to him altogether? It is a very easy thing for me to talk about this; but, believe me, it is by no means an easy thing to carry it out. I see numbers of people who profess to belong to God; but they live as much for money-making as anybody else, they live quite as much for self-seeking as the world does; and it would be difficult, even if you had microscopes on both your eyes, to see any difference between them and worldlings. This will never do. "Come out from among them, and be ye separate, saith the Lord, and touch not the unclean thing." If you are the firstfruits unto God, be so; if you belong to yourself, serve yourself; but if, by the redemption of Christ, you are not your own, but bought with a price, then live as those who are the King's own, who must serve God, and cannot be content unless their every action shall tend to the divine glory, and to the magnifying of Christ Jesus. Now this is what all of us who are truly the Lord's have in outline. Oh, that the sketch might be properly filled up, that we might become more and more the firstfruits unto God and to the Lamb!

I must take you a little further. These people who are to be with Christ, the nearest to him, are *a people free from falsehood.* "In their mouth was found no guile." Brethren, if we profess to be Christians, we must have done with all craft, policy, double-dealing, and the like. The Christian man should be a plain man, who says what he means, and means what he says. I know of no worse suspicion against any man who professes to be a Christian than the suspicion of not being transparent. It were better for us to be simple as fools than to be cunning as hypocrites, even though our cunning should place us in the front rank of the governors of mankind. The Christian man should scorn to tell a lie; exaggeration and equivocation should be strangers to his lips. "In their mouth was found no guile." The Lord Jesus Christ was a great speaker of plain truth; and those whom he chooses to be near him, to be his personal attendants in heaven, must also be free from guile. With many a mistake, with many a weakness, yet, beloved, the saints are free from falsehood. They are true, whatever may be their mistakes. Look to yourselves, and see whether it is so; as I would look to my own soul, I charge you to look to yours.

And then, once more, it is said that they are *free from blemish*; "they are without fault before the throne of God." "Oh!" says one, "I am not without fault." No, but there is the outline of that character in you if you are, indeed, one of the Lord's people; you have already got rid of many faults, and you are getting rid of more; you grieve over what remains, and you will never rest till every sin is conquered. Is it not so, beloved? Saints are not only men of honour, but men of holiness; we would not tolerate any known sin in ourselves. Whenever we are carried into a fault by temptation or by inbred sin, we feel unhappy; we bow low in the dust, and we cry to God for grace, that we may not commit the like sin again. But God's people are a blameless people, after all. If you are to find pure and right characters, where will you find them but among the followers of the Lamb? You know and I know many believers in Christ whose lives are blameless; we would not say that they are absolutely without fault, but still, the grace of God so works in them that we may safely take them for examples, and do as they have done. It was so in the olden time, and it is so now; and unless your character is such that your children may safely imitate it, and your servants may tread in your footsteps, and your neighbours may act as you do without going wrong, how can you hope to be where Jesus is? Jesus Christ receives sinners, but he makes them saints. The gospel opens a great hospital, not for sick men to lie in it and remain sick, but that there they may recover health, and may be made strong. He that believes in Christ is saved, saved in this sense among others, that he is saved from the power of sin, and turned from an unholy and godless life into a life of purity, honesty, and uprightness. "Be not deceived," any of you, to-night, "God is not mocked; for whatsoever a man soweth that shall he also reap." If there be not about you a likeness to Christ, if there be not at least the sketch which I have tried to depict, then, surely, you are not among those who will be for ever where Jesus is. I have seen an artist make his crayon drawing; he just took a piece of charcoal, and marked out what he was going to draw. I am afraid that is about all that is done with us here. There is an outline made with the charcoal; all the lines of beauty and all the glory of character are yet to be laid on as we grow in grace and in likeness to Christ. But, at least, there must be that sketch. If you have not that, come humbly to the feet of Jesus, and pray that he would begin in you his good work which he will carry on and perfect in the day of his appearing.

Thus much upon the outline of the character of saints while they are upon the earth.

II. Now indulge me for just a few minutes while I try to give you A GLIMPSE OF THE PERFECT PICTURE IN HEAVEN. I cannot really show you the picture; that is in the upper gallery in glory, and you must go up there to see it. I can only tell you my idea of what that picture is like when it is finished.

Well, first, those who are with Christ enjoy *perfect fellowship with him.* Up there, they "follow the Lamb whithersoever he goeth." They are always with him. There were certain young princes chosen in certain courts to attend upon the king. Wherever the king went, they went; where the court was, there was their abode; their one business was to behold the king's face, and to abide near him. That is the business of the glorified ones of whom I am speaking. When will the day arrive that you and I shall enjoy this perfect fellowship with our glorious King, never absent from him, never doubting his love, never cold in our affection towards him, but being—

"For ever with the Lord"?

Shall I go on with the verse?

"Amen! so let it be!
Life from the dead is in that word,
'Tis immortality!"

Some of you have dear children who have outstripped their mother, and are enjoying this felicity even now. Others of us have mothers, brothers, friends who were very dear to us, who follow the Lamb in glory. How many who once sat amongst us here are now up there, following the Lamb, and he leads them unto living fountains of waters, and all tears are wiped away from their eyes! Oh, to think that wherever my Lord shall go I shall go! When he shall descend from heaven with a shout, we shall come with him. When he shall sit upon his throne to judge the world, his saints shall sit with him. When he shall reign amongst his ancients gloriously for a thousand years, we shall reign with him on the earth. When he shall return to the Father's throne,—

"All his work and warfare done,"

we shall partake of his triumph, following the Lamb whithersoever he goeth. I vote to cast in my lot with my Lord in life and in death; what say you? My Master, where thou dwellest, I will dwell; if men put thee to shame, I will be put to shame with thee; if thou diest, I will die with thee, that I may for ever live with thee in thy glory above. Say you not the same, beloved? Say it deep down in your heart to-night.

Well, now, notice in this complete picture, next, that up there *they are perfectly accepted with God:* "These were redeemed from among men, being the firstfruits unto God and to the Lamb." God always accepts them; he always looks upon them as his firstfruits, bought with his Son's blood, and brought by his Son into his heavenly temple, to be his for ever. Sometimes here we mar our service; but they never mar it there. Our songs get out of tune, but theirs never know a discord. We praise the Lord, and yet groan, being burdened; but in heaven there are—

"No groans to mingle with the songs
Which warble from immortal tongues."

We doubt; we fear; we grieve the Holy Spirit; sometimes we get very sadly out of gear with God. It is never so there; fully redeemed from sin, they are accepted in the Beloved, and to the very top of their bent they know it, and enjoy it. Happy day, happy day, when you and I shall be of them and among them!

Observe, also, that *they have perfect truth there in heart and soul:* "In their mouth was found no guile." "No lie," says the Revised Version. Here, dear friends, we do fall into error inadvertently, and sometimes, I fear me, negligently. We say, not knowingly, more than the truth. How often we say much less than the truth, and almost necessarily so when we speak of divine things; but up there they are not only free from wilful guile and deceit, but they are free from all error and mistake. Happy day! Happy day! Do you not long to be there to be rid of every false doctrine, every wrong opinion, every error, every mistake, so that in your mouth there shall never be guile again? This is what they are above, made perfect. He who washed their hearts here has washed their tongues there. As they loved the truth here, they know the truth there. As they sought it here, they have found it there. As they were willing to die for it here, they live in the enjoyment of it there, and shall do so for ever.

One more feature of that perfect picture is this, *they enjoy perfect sinlessness before God:* "They are without fault before the throne of God." That text brings back to my recollection the second sermon I preached to this church, one Sabbath evening, when we were but few: "They are without fault before the throne of God." I had great joy, as a youth, in expatiating upon the perfect blessing of being altogether "without spot, or wrinkle, or any such thing." If there were any fault in them there, they are where it would be seen, for they are before the throne of the all-seeing God; but even there, in that matchless place of light in which there is no darkness at all, they are declared to be without fault, without blemish. Can you think that you will be of that happy number one day? I had to put it very mildly just now when I spoke of saints being without blame here; but you may put it as strongly as you please when you speak of their being without sin there. They were once, perhaps, before conversion, the very chief of sinners; but in heaven there shall be no trace of their sin. They will bless the grace that came to them when they were up to their neck in the filth of sin; but there will be no trace of their filthiness left. There is no blood stain on Manasseh, there is no brand of blasphemy on Saul of Tarsus now; they have washed their robes, and made them white in the blood of the Lamb. Some of these men were by nature and by practice, too, so depraved that it looked as if they could never escape from their evil habits. We might have said of them, "Can the Ethiopian change his skin, or the leopard his spots? Then may these men, who are accustomed to do evil, learn to do well." Yet so has the grace of God changed them, that there is no trace of any evil tendency, no propensity to lust, or lewdness, or blasphemy, or any kind of fault.

What a wonderful change it will be for those who were once great sinners to be found without fault; not only without great crime, not only without gross vice, but without fault, and that, too, as I have said, before the throne of God, where, if there were a fault, it would be seen! They are cleansed from all the guilt of sin, and from all the depravity which the habitude of sin brings to men. "They are without fault before the throne of God." Truly, if you had never heard this before, it might make you laugh for joy to think that it should ever be possible that the very chief of sinners, through faith in Christ, might be made so clean as one day to be without fault before the throne of God. I do think that, when we get there, part of the joy of heaven will be a long surprise, an endless wonder; and if we are permitted there to recollect what we used to be, some of you will recall a night of sin, and say, "And yet I am here." You will recall, perhaps, some dreadful passion, some atrocious outburst of foul language, or some terrible occasion of sin, and you will say, "Yet here am I, clean as the driven snow, washed in the blood of Jesus, and renewed by the Spirit of God." Although they always praise God, I think that they must every now and then have a fresh outburst of hallelujahs when they begin to review the past. One says, "I, even after conversion, was a poor, limping Christian, and I was thrown back once or twice with terrible backslidings. My Christian friends despaired of my ever holding on; and yet here I am, without fault before the throne of God. Hallelujah!" Will not a man be obliged to break out like that, and do you not think that all the saints around him will take up the Hallelujah, too, till it goes in swelling chorus all round the choirs of heaven, "Hallelujah to God and the Lamb"? And another one will say, "And I, after I had long known the Lord, fell, oh, so sadly, so grievously! But he would not give me up, he followed me; and by his mighty grace, I was restored, my broken bones were set again, and I was made to sing of free grace and forgiving love. He created in me a new heart, and renewed a right spirit within me; and now I, even I, am here without fault, without a single fault." You can hardly imagine it, can you? You begin to think, "Well, surely that cannot be," for, if you look within, you see so many faults over which you groan; but you will look without and look within, when you once get there, and neither without nor within, in any respect whatever, will you have any kind of fault; for "they are without blemish before the throne of God."

I do not feel inclined to preach any more, but just to shout, "Hallelujah," again and again, at the very thought that I shall be there. Oh, it is hard to go to heaven from such a place as that which I occupy! Your eyes sometimes startle me in my dreams, these thousands of eyes fixed upon one poor mortal man, who has to try to lead you to Christ, and lead you to heaven. Your eyes at times seem to pierce me like so many daggers. I think, sometimes, "What if I am not faithful, if I do not preach plainly, if I do not warn them, if I do not invite them earnestly, if I do not with all my heart cry, 'Come to Christ'? What shall I do in eternity if six thousand pairs of eyes are for ever seeming to stick, like daggers, into my heart?" Oh, but it will not be so! I believe in him that justifieth the ungodly; and I have fully preached him to you, and all my great congregation. My hope is in the precious blood that cleanseth from all sin; and I have pointed all my hearers to that precious blood; and the day will come when I, with all who believe in Jesus, shall be without fault before the throne of God. The very thought of it makes me cry "Hallelujah," and with that I finish. Hallelujah! Hallelujah! Say "Hallelujah," all of you. ["*Hallelujah*" *from the congregation.*] Hallelujah! Hallelujah to God and the Lamb! The Lord bless you, for Christ's sake! Amen.

Exposition by C. H. Spurgeon.
REVELATION XIV.

Verse 1. *And I looked, and, lo, a Lamb—*
John always writes of Jesus as the "Lamb." His Lord is to him in his sacrificial character always "the Lamb of God which taketh away the sin of the world" by the shedding of his blood. "I looked, and, lo, a Lamb"—

1. *Stood on the mount Sion, and with him an hundred forty and four thousand, having his Father's name written in their foreheads.*

The Revised Version has it, "having his name, and the name of his Father, written on their foreheads." Now they are known to be the Lord's; on earth that fact was questioned, but his name is written on their foreheads now. Sometimes they themselves had to question it, but now it is apparent to all, the distinguishing mark is stamped upon their brow: "having his Father's name written in their foreheads."

2. *And I heard a voice from heaven, as the voice of many waters, and as the voice of a great thunder: and I heard the voice of harpers harping with their harps:*

It was very loud, but very sweet. It is not easy in earthly music to blend the two: but in heaven, all the energies of living men shall be thrown into the song; and yet it shall be sweet as the touch of a minstrel when he lays his fingers gently among the strings of the harp.

3. *And they sung as it were a new song before the throne,*

They could not sing any old song there. The songs of earth, sweet as some of them are, are not good enough to be sung in heaven. With a new experience, new delights, and a clearer vision of their Lord, they must have a new song.

3. *And before the four beasts, and the elders: and no man could learn that song but the hundred and forty and four thousand, which were redeemed from the earth.*

Heaven is not the place to learn that song; it must be learned on the earth.

You must learn here the notes of free grace and dying love; and when you have mastered their melody, you will be able to offer to the Lord the tribute of a grateful heart, even in heaven, and blend it with the harmonies eternal. Suppose, for a moment, that you could go there, and that you were unprepared to sing the new song, you would have to say, "I cannot join in the chorus, for I do not know the tune." You must learn the song now, the new song of praise unto our God, or you cannot be admitted there. I should not expect, if I went down to the Handel Festival, for the conductor to permit me to take a place in the choir. He would ask me, "Can you sing? Have you ever rehearsed the matchless music of Handel?" and when I answered "No," he would tell me to stand aside; so you must learn the music of Calvary, you must learn the music of the name of Jesus, or you cannot sing in heaven. No man could learn the song but the redeemed from the earth; not redeemed, you see, by a general redemption, of which some so loudly talk; but redeemed from among men by a special redemption, which took them out from the rest of mankind, by a price paid for them, so that they were bought as others were not bought, by the precious blood of Jesus, as of a Lamb without blemish and without spot.

4. *These are they which were not defiled with women; for they are virgins.*
They were pure and chaste in the sight of God.

4. *These are they which follow the Lamb whithersoever he goeth.*
His choice attendants, his body-guard.

4, 5. *These were redeemed from among men, being the firstfruits unto God and to the Lamb. And in their mouth was found no guile:*
"No lie." They were truthful, they were truth-speakers.

5. *For they are without fault—*
Or, blemish.

5. *Before the throne of God.*
Like him with whom they associated, the Lamb of God, they were without blemish and without spot.

6. *And I saw—*
What wonderful sights John saw! I do not wonder that he saw them; he had leaned his head on Christ's bosom, and that qualified him to see what you and I cannot see. Near communion to Christ is the best qualification for a vision of mystery. Get thee into the very heart of Christ, and thou shalt see wonderful things: "I saw"—

6, 7. *Another angel fly in the midst of heaven, having the everlasting gospel to preach unto them that dwell on the earth, and to every nation, and kindred, and tongue, and people, saying with a loud voice, Fear God, and give glory to him;*
Is this the gospel? It is one version, evidently, of the everlasting gospel. "The fear of God is the beginning of wisdom." Truly, to worship him as he reveals himself, is true godliness; and in it lies all the gospel: "Having the everlasting gospel to preach unto them that dwell on the earth, and to every nation, and kindred, and tongue, and people, saying with a loud voice, Fear God, and give glory to him."

7, 8. *For the hour of his judgment is come: and worship him that made heaven, and earth, and the sea, and the fountains of waters. And there followed another angel, saying, Babylon is fallen, is fallen,*
This will not happen till the gospel is fully preached. Superstition does not come down unless true religion is set up. One angel proclaims the everlasting gospel; the next declares that the great system of error is fallen: "Babylon is fallen."

8. *That great city, because she made all nations drink of the wine of the wrath of her fornication.*

You know that gigantic system of error which professes to come from God, and to be the only true church; but it must fall.

9, 10. *And the third angel followed them, saying with a loud voice, If any man worship the beast and his image, and receive his mark in his forehead, or in his hand, the same shall drink of the wine of the wrath of God, which is poured out without mixture into the cup of his indignation; and he shall be tormented with fire and brimstone in the presence of the holy angels, and in the presence of the Lamb:*

They sometimes say that we talk very terribly about the world to come. Do we say more than the Scripture says? Do we use more terrific emblems than the Holy Ghost uses when he speaks after this fashion? This is a generation that is not to be pleased, neither do we seek to please it. God's wrath is terrible, and our language cannot be too strong to express the overwhelming power of it.

11. *And the smoke of their torment ascendeth up for ever and ever: and they have no rest day nor night, who worship the beast and his image, and whosoever receiveth the mark of his name.*

Keep you true to Christ; wear his name in your forehead. Follow no system of error; do not be deluded either by Ritualism or Rationalism, by superstition or by unbelief. Keep close to the Word of God, and ask to be taught of the Spirit of God.

12, 13. *Here is the patience of the saints: here are they that keep the commandments of God, and the faith of Jesus. And I heard a voice from heaven, saying unto me, Write, Blessed are the dead which die in the Lord from henceforth: Yea, saith the Spirit, that they may rest from their labours; and their works do follow them.*

Accursed were they who carried the mark of the beast, and went after falsehood; but blessed are they who follow Christ, even though they die. Dying in the Lord, their works survive them, and they themselves live for ever with him.

14. *And I looked, and behold a white cloud,*

One of these days, every eye will look and see what is here described. A little time may elapse, but it will soon be past. How quickly years fly away! Think where you will be in the day when you, too, will say, "I looked, and behold a white cloud."

14—16. *And upon the cloud one sat like unto the Son of man, having on his head a golden crown, and in his hand a sharp sickle. And another angel came out of the temple, crying with a loud voice to him that sat on the cloud, Thrust in thy sickle, and reap: for the time is come for thee to reap; for the harvest of the earth is ripe. And he that sat on the cloud thrust in his sickle on the earth; and the earth was reaped.*

This is the gathering in of the godly, who are Christ's wheat. He himself reaps them; no angel, mark you, but himself, with his own sharp sickle and with his own dear hand. These are his sheaves, he sowed for wheat; he himself was that wheat which fell into the ground and died, and brought forth much fruit. So he, into his own bosom, gathers his own sheaves with his own hand. "May I be among them!" Make that your prayer to-night. "May I be one golden ear in Christ's great harvest!"

17. *And another angel came out of the temple which is in heaven, he also having a sharp sickle.*

Not this time the King, but an angel; not the Son of man that sat on the cloud, but an angel, the servant of God, deputed to execute vengeance.

18, 19. *And another angel came out from the altar, which had power over fire; and cried with a loud cry to him that had the sharp sickle, saying, Thrust in thy sharp sickle, and gather the clusters of the vine of the earth; for her grapes are fully ripe. And the angel thrust in his sickle into the earth, and gathered the vine of the earth,*

This is the gathering together of the ungodly, those wicked clusters that ripen in sin, and that become red with iniquity. Christ does not gather them, you see. That is left to an angel to do; he thrust in his sickle, and gathered the grapes of the earth.

19. *And cast it into the great winepress of the wrath of God.*

Can you see the clusters flung into the winepress? Will you be there? God grant that neither you nor I may, in that terrible day, be among the clusters of the wicked!

20. *And the winepress was trodden without the city, and blood came out of the winepress, even unto the horse bridles, by the space of a thousand and six hundred furlongs.*

So terrible will be even the preliminary destruction of the ungodly. Though they grow in clusters, yet shall they perish. "Though hand join in hand, the wicked shall not be unpunished."

"He that hath ears to hear, let him hear what the Spirit saith" unto each one of us. Amen.

HYMNS FROM "OUR OWN HYMN BOOK"—878, 855.

Metropolitan Tabernacle Pulpit.

A VOICE FROM HEAVEN.

A Sermon

DELIVERED BY

C. H. SPURGEON,

AT THE METROPOLITAN TABERNACLE, NEWINGTON.

"Here is the patience of the saints: here are they that keep the commandments of God, and the faith of Jesus. And I heard a voice from heaven saying unto me, Write, Blessed are the dead which die in the Lord from henceforth: Yea, saith the Spirit, that they may rest from their labours; and their works do follow them."—Revelation xiv. 12, 13.

THE text speaks of a voice from heaven which said, "Blessed are the dead which die in the Lord." The witness of that voice is not needed upon every occasion, for even the commonest observer is compelled to feel concerning many of the righteous that their deaths are blessed. Balaam, with all his moral shortsightedness, could say, "Let me die the death of the righteous, and let my last end be like his." That is the case when death comes in peaceful fashion. The man has lived a calm, godly, consistent life; he has lived as long as he could well have wished to live, and in dying he sees his children and his children's children gathered around his bed. What a fine picture the old man makes, as he sits up with that snowy head supported by snowy pillows. Hear him as he tells his children that goodness and mercy have followed him all the days of his life, and now he is going to dwell in the house of the Lord for ever. See the seraphic smile which lights up his face as he bids them farewell, and assures them that he already hears the harpers harping with their harps,—bids them stay those tears, and weep not for him but for themselves—charges them to follow him so far as he has followed Christ, and to meet him at the right hand of the Judge in the day of his appearing. Then the old man, almost without a sigh, leans back, and is present with the Lord.

"Heaven waits not the last moment; owns her friends
On this side death, and points them out to men;
A lecture silent but of sovereign power!
To vice, confusion—and to virtue peace."

No. 1,219.

Even the blind bat's-eyed worldling can see that "blessed are the dead which die in the Lord" in such a fashion as that, nor is it difficult to perceive that this is the case in many other instances. We have ourselves known several good men and women who were afraid of death, and were much of their lifetime subject to bondage, but they went to bed and fell asleep and never woke again in this world, and as far as appearances go they could never have known so much as one single pang in departure, but fell asleep among mortals to awake amid the angels. Truly, such gentle loosings of the cable, such fordings of Jordan dry shod, such ascents of the celestial hills with music at every step, are beyond measure desirable, and we need no voice out of the excellent glory to proclaim that blessed are the dead who in such a case die in the Lord.

But that was not the picture which John had before his mind. It was quite another—a picture grim and black to mortal eye. The sounds which meet the ear are not those of music, nor the whispered consolations of friends, but quite the reverse; all is painful, terrible, and the very opposite of blessed, so far as strikes the eye and ear. Hence it became needful that there should be a voice from heaven to say, "Blessed are the dead that die in the Lord." I will give you the picture. The man of God is on the rack. They are turning that infernal machine with all their might; they have dragged every bone from its place; they have exercised their tortures till every nerve of his body thrills with agony. He is flung into a dark and loathsome dungeon, and left there to recover strength enough to be led in derision through the streets. Upon his head they have placed a cap painted with devils, and all his garments they have bedizened with the resemblance of fiends and flames of hell. And now, with a shaveling priest on each side holding up before him a superstitious emblem, and bidding him adore the Virgin or worship the cross, the good man, loaded with chains, goes through the street, say of Madrid or Antwerp, to the place prepared for his execution. "An act of faith," they call it—an *auto da fé*—and an act of heroic faith it is indeed when the man of God takes his place at the stake, in his shirt, with an iron chain about his loins, and is fastened to the tree, where he must stand, and burn "quick to the death." Can you see him as they kindle the faggots beneath him, and the flames begin to consume his quivering flesh till he is all ablaze and burning—burning without a cry, though fiercely tormented by the fire? Now assuredly is that voice from heaven wanted, and you can hear it, "Blessed are the dead which die in the Lord,"—blessed even when they die like this. "Here is the patience of the saints," and, in the esteem of angels and of glorified spirits, such a death may under many aspects be adjudged to be more blessed than the peaceful deathbed of the saint who had some fellowship with Jesus, but was not so made to drink of his cup, and to be baptised with his baptism, as to die a painful and ignominious death as a witness for the truth. It must have been a dreadful thing to watch the rabble rout hurrying to Smithfield, to stand there and see the burning of the saints. It would have been a more fearful thing still, if possible, to have been in the dungeons of the Low Countries and seen the Anabaptists put to death in secret. In a dungeon dark and pestilential there is placed a huge vat of water, and the faithful witness to Scriptural baptism is drowned, drowned for following the Lamb whithersoever he goeth, drowned alone where no eye could pity, and no voice from out of the crowd could shout a word of help and comfort. Men hear only the coarse jests of the murderers who have given the dipper his last dip, but the ear of faith can hear ringing through the dungeon the voice, " Blessed are the dead which die in the Lord." True, through the connection of their names with a fanatic band, these holy ancestors of ours have gained scant honour here, yet their record is on high; blessed they are, and blessed they shall be. Wheresoever on this earth, whether among the snows of Piedmont's valleys or in the fair fields of France, saints have died by sword or famine, or fire or massacre, for the testimony of Jesus, because they would not bear the mark of the beast either in their forehead or in their hand, this voice is heard sounding out of the third heavens, " Blessed are the dead which die in the Lord."

It matters not, my brethren, where they die who die in the Lord. It may be that they have not the honour of martyrdom in man's esteem, but yet are witnesses for the Lord in poverty and pain. Here is the patience, and here also is the blessedness of the saints. Yonder poor girl lies in a garret, where the stars look between the tiles, and the moon gleams on the ragged hangings of the pallet where she bravely suffers and, without a murmur, gradually dissolves into death. However obscure and unknown she may be, she has been kept from the great transgression; tempted sorely, she has yet held fast her purity and her integrity; her prayers, unheard by others, have gone up before the Lord, and she dies in the Lord, saved through Jesus Christ. None will preach her funeral sermon, but she shall not miss that voice from heaven, saying, "Write, blessed are the dead which die in the Lord."

We repeat it, it matters not when you die nor in what condition; if you are in the Lord, and die in the Lord, right blessed are ye.

Now, it is quite certain that very soon every one of us must leave this world. We know that we are no more immortal than our fellow men. Though by a sad piece of imposition upon ourselves we count all men mortal but ourselves, right surely mortal we are, and pass away out of this world each one of us shall, in due time. The saints themselves must die, though to them death is far other than to sinners. It is greatly wise to be ready for our undressing, prepared for the sweet sleep in Jesus; and if we are not in Christ, it is all the more imperative upon us to consider our latter end, that we rush not forward in the dark. I therefore want, for a few minutes only, to disengage your mind from the too abundant snares of this world, and the thraldom of human cares, that you may look across the border into the great future so surely yours, perhaps so nearly yours. Oh, that you might be helped to prepare for that future, that by such preparation, through divine grace, you may be numbered among the blessed who die in the Lord.

First, we shall briefly *describe their character*, then mention *the rest* which constitutes their blessedness, and conclude by meditating upon *the reward*, which is a further part of that blessedness.

I. First, then, let us describe THE CHARACTER. " Here is the patience of *the saints.*" To be blessed when we die we must be saints. By nature we are sinners, and by grace we must become saints if we would enter heaven; for it is the land of saints, and none but saints can ever pass its frontiers. Since death does not change character, we must be made saints here below if we are to be saints above. We have come to misuse the term "saint," and apply it only to some few of God's people. What means it but this—holy? Holy men and holy women—these are saints. It is not *Saint* Peter and *Saint* John merely; you are a saint, dear brother, if you live unto the Lord; you are a saint, my sister, however obscure your name, if you keep the Lord's way, and walk before him in sincere obedience. We must be saints, and in order to be this we must be renewed in spirit, for we are sinners by nature; we must, in fact, be born again. All unholy and unclean, we are by nature nothing else but sin; and we must be created anew by the power of the eternal Spirit, or else holiness will never dwell in us. Our loves must be changed, so that we no longer love evil things, but delight only in that which is true, generous, kind, upright, pure, godlike. We must be changed in every faculty and power of our nature by that same hand which first made us, and across our brows must be written these words, "Holiness unto the Lord."

The word saint denotes not merely the pure in character, but those who are set apart unto God, dedicated ones, sanctified by being devoted to holy uses—by being, in fact, consecrated to God alone. My dear hearer, do you belong to God? Do you live to glorify Jesus? Can you honestly put your hand on your heart, and say, "Yes, I belong to him who bought me with his blood, and I endeavour by his grace to live as he would have me live. I am devoted to his honour, loving my fellow-men and loving my Lord, endeavouring to be like unto him in all things"? You must be such, for "without holiness no man shall see the Lord."

"But how am I to attain to holiness?" You cannot rise to it save by divine strength. The Holy Spirit is the Sanctifier. Jesus who is our justifier is also made unto us sanctification, and if we by faith lay hold on him, we shall find in him all that we want. Let this be a searching matter with every one here present, as I desire to make it with myself, and may God grant we may be numbered with the saints!

But the glorified are also described in our text as *patient* ones,— " Here is the patience of the saints," or, if you choose to render it differently, you may lawfully do so—" Here is the endurance of the saints." Those who are to be crowned in heaven must bear the cross on earth. "No cross, no crown," is still most true. Many would be saints if everybody would encourage them; but as soon as a hard word is spoken they are offended. They would go to heaven if they could travel there amidst the hosannas of the multitude, but when they hear the cry of "Crucify him, crucify him," straightway they desert the man of Nazareth, for they have no intention to share his cross, or to be despised and rejected of men. The true saints of God are prepared to endure scoffing, and jeering, and scorning; they accept this cross without murmuring, remembering him who endured such contradiction of sinners against himself. They know that their brethren who went before "resisted unto blood, striving against sin," and as they have not yet come to that point, they count it foul scorn that they should be ashamed or confounded in minor trials, let their adversaries do what they may. Those who are to sing Christ's praise in heaven must first have been willing to bear Christ's shame below. Numbered with him in the humiliation must they be, or they cannot expect to be partakers with him in the glory. And now, dear brethren and sisters, how is it with us? Are we willing to be reproached for Christ's glory? Can we bear the sarcasm of the wise? Can we bear the jest of the witty? Are we willing to be pointed at as Puritanic, punctilious and precise? Do we dare to be singular when to be singular is to be right? If we can do this by God's grace, let us further question ourselves. Could we endure this ordeal if its intensity were increased? Suppose it came to something worse—to the thumbscrew or the rack, could we then bear it? I sometimes fear that many professors would cut a sorry figure if persecuting times should come; for I observe that to be excluded from what is called "society" is a great grievance to many modern Christians. When they settle in any place, their enquiry is not, "Where can I hear the gospel best?" but "Which is the most fashionable place of worship?" And the question with regard to their children is not "Where will they have Christian associations?" but "How can I introduce them to society?" —introduction to society frequently being an introduction to temptation, and the commencement of a life of levity. Oh, that all Christians could scorn the soft witcheries of the world, for, if they cannot, they may be sure that they will not bear its fiery breath when, like an oven, persecution comes forth to try the saints. God grant us grace to have the patience of the saints; that patience of the saints which will cheerfully suffer loss rather than do a wrong thing in business; that patience of the saints which will pine in poverty sooner than yield a principle though a kingdom were at stake; that patience of the saints which dreads not being unfashionable if the right be reckoned so; that patience of the saints which courts no man's smile, and fears no man's frown, but can endure all things for Jesus' sake, and is resolved to do so. "Can you cleave to your Lord when the many turn aside? Can you witness that he hath the living word, and none upon earth beside?" Can you watch with him when all forsake him, and stand by him when he is the butt of ribald jest and scorn, and bear the sneer of science, falsely so called, and the politer sarcasm of those who say they "doubt," but mean that they utterly disbelieve? Blessed is that preacher who shall be true to Christ in these evil days. Blessed is that church-member who shall follow Christ's word through the mire and through the slough, o'er the hill and down the dale, caring nothing so that he can but be true to his Master. This must be our resolve. If we are to win the glory we must be faithful unto death. God make us so! "Here is the patience of the saints"—it cometh not by nature; it is the gift of the grace of God.

Farther on these saints are described as "*they that keep the commandments of God.*" This expression is not intended for a moment to teach us that these people are saved by their own merits. They are saints to begin with, and in Christ to begin with, but they prove that they are in Christ by keeping the commandments of God. Let us search ourselves upon this matter. Brethren and sisters, we cannot hope to reach the end if we do not keep the way. No man is so unwise as to think that he would reach Bristol if he were to take the road to York. He knows that to get to a place he must follow the road which leads thither. There is a way of holiness in which the righteous walk, and this way of obedience to the Lord's commands must and will be trodden by all who truly believe in Jesus, and are justified by faith; for faith works obedience. A good tree brings forth good fruit. If there be no fruit of obedience to God's commands in you, or in me, we may rest assured that the root of genuine faith in Jesus Christ is not in us at all. In this age the keeping of Christ's commandments is thought to be of very little consequence. It is dreadful to think how Christians in the matter of the law of God's house do not even pretend to follow Christ and his appointments. They join a church, and they go by the law of that church, though that church's rule may be clean contrary to the will of Christ; but they answer to everything, "That is our rule, you know." But then who has a right to make rules for you or for me, but Christ Jesus? He is the only legislator in the kingdom of God, and by his commands we ought to be guided. I should not, I could not, feel grieved if brethren arrived at contrary conclusions to mine, I being fallible myself; but I do feel grieved when I see brethren arrive at conclusions, not as the result of investigation, but simply by taking things just as they find them. Too many professors have a happy-go-lucky style of Christianity. Whichever happens to come first they follow. Their fathers and mothers were this or that, or they were brought up in such and such a connection, and that decides them; they do not pray, "Lord, show me what thou wouldst have me to do." Brethren, these things ought not so to be. Has not the Master said, "Whosoever shall break one of the least of these my commandments, and teach men so, the same shall be least in the kingdom of heaven"? I would not stand here to condemn my fellow Christians for a moment; in so doing I should condemn myself also, but I plead with you, if you do indeed believe in Jesus, be careful to observe all things whatsoever he hath commanded you, for he has said, "If ye abide in me, and my words abide in you, ye shall ask what ye will, and it shall be done unto you;" and again, "If ye love me keep my commandments."

A worldling once said to a puritan, "When so many great make rents in their consciences, cannot you make just a little nick in yours, for peace sake?" "No," said he, "I must follow Christ fully." "Ah, well," you say, "these things are non-essential." Nothing is non-essential to complete obedience: it may be non-essential to salvation, but it is selfishness to say, "I will do no more than I know to be absolutely necessary to my salvation." It is essential to a good servant to obey his master in all things, and it is essential for the healthiness of a Christian's soul that he should walk very carefully and prayerfully before the Lord, else otherwise he will miss the blessing of them of whom it is said, "These are they which follow the Lamb whithersoever he goeth." To be blessed in death we must keep the commandments of God.

The next mark of the blessed dead is, that they kept *"the faith of Jesus."* This is another point upon which I would speak thunderbolts, if I could, for to keep the faith of Jesus is an undertaking much ridiculed now-a-days. "Doctrines!" says one, "we are tired of doctrines."

> "For forms and creeds let graceless bigots fight,
> He can't be wrong whose life is in the right."

The opinion is current that to be fluent and original is the main thing in preaching, and provided a man is a *clever* orator it is a proper thing to hear him. The Lord will wither with the breath of his nostrils that cleverness in any man which departs from the simplicity of the truth. There is a gospel, and "there is also another gospel which is not another, but there be some that trouble you." There is a yea yea, and there is a nay nay; and woe unto those whose preaching is yea and nay, for it shall not stand in the great day when the Lord shall try every man's work of what sort it is. Search ye, my brethren, and know what the gospel is, and when you do know it, hold it: hold it as with a hand of iron, and never relax your grasp. Grievous wolves have come in among us, wolves of another sort to what were wont to be in the churches, yet, verily, after the same fashion they come disguised in sheep's clothing. They use our very terms and phrases, meaning all the while something else; they take away the essentials and vitalities of the faith, and replace them with their own inventions, which they brag of as being more consistent with modern thought and with the culture of this very advanced and enlightened age, which seems by degrees to be advancing, half of it to Paganism with the Ritualists, and the other half of it to Atheism with the Rationalists. From such advances may God save us! May we be enabled to keep the faith, and uphold the truth which we know, by which also we are saved. I, for one, cannot desert the grand doctrine of the atoning blood, the substitutionary work of Christ, and the truths which cluster around it. And why can I not desert these things? Because my life, my peace, my hope, hang upon them. I am a lost man if there be no substitutionary sacrifice, and I know it. If the Son of God did not die, "the just for the unjust, to bring us to God," I must be damned; and therefore all the instincts of my nature cling to the faith of Jesus. How can I give up that which has redeemed my soul, and given me joy and peace and a hope hereafter? I beseech you, do not waver in your belief, but keep the faith, lest ye be like some in old time, who "made shipwreck of faith and a good conscience," and were utterly cast away. Woe unto those who keep not the doctrines of the gospel, for in due time they forget its precepts also and become utterly reprobate. In departing from Christ men forsake their own mercies both for life and death. The blessed who die in the Lord are those who "keep the commandments of God and the faith of Jesus."

Notice, that these people *continue faithful till they die.* For it is said, "Blessed are the dead which *die* in the Lord." Final perseverance is the crown of the Christian life. "Ye did run well; what did hinder you that ye should not obey the truth?" Vain is it to begin to build, we must crown the edifice or all men will deride us. Helmet and plume, armour and sword, are all assumed for nothing unless the warrior fights on till he has secured the victory.

Those who thus entered into rest, *exercised themselves in labours for Christ.* For it is said, "They rest from *their labours,* and their works do follow them." The idle Christian can have little hope of a reward; he who serves not his Master can scarcely expect that his Master will at the last gird himself and serve him. If I address any here who are not bringing forth fruit unto God, I can say no less than this, "Every tree that bringeth not forth fruit is hewn down and cast into the fire." "Be not deceived; God is not mocked: whatsoever a man soweth that shall he also reap." The rule is invariable. It must be so. If there be no works and no labours for Christ, no suffering or patient endurance, we lack the main evidence of being the people of God at all.

To close this description of character, these people who die in the Lord *were in the Lord.* That is the great point. They could not have died in the Lord if they had not lived in the Lord. But are we in the Lord? Is the Lord by faith in us? Dear hearer, are you resting upon Jesus Christ only? Is he all your salvation and all your desire? What is your reply to my enquiry? You are not perfect, but Jesus is. Are you hanging upon him as the vessel hangs upon the nail? You cannot expect to stand before God with acceptance in yourself, but are you "accepted in the beloved"? That is the question—"accepted in the beloved." Are you in Christ, and is Christ in you by real vital union, by a faith that is the gift of God and the work of the Holy Spirit in your soul? Answer, I charge you, for if you cannot answer these things before one of your own flesh and blood, how will you answer in your soul when the Lord himself shall come?

II. So much with regard to the character. And now a very few words with regard to THE BLESSEDNESS which is ascribed to those who die in the Lord. "They rest from their labours."

By this is meant that the saints in heaven *rest from such labours as they performed here.* No doubt they fulfil service in heaven. It would be an unhappy heaven in which there should be nothing for our activities to spend themselves upon. But such labours as we can do here, will not fall to our lot there. There we shall not teach the ignorant, or rebuke the erring, or comfort the desponding, or help the needy. There we cannot oppose the teacher of error, or do battle against the tempter of youth. There no little children can be gathered at our knee and trained for Jesus, no sick ones can be visited with the word of comfort, no backsliders led back, no young converts confirmed, no sinners converted. They rest from such labours as these in heaven.

They rest from their labours in the sense that they are no longer subject to the *toil* of labour. Whatever they do in heaven will yield them refreshment and never cause them weariness. As some birds are said to rest upon the wing, so do the saints find in holy activity their serenest repose. They serve him day and night in his temple, and therein they rest. Even as on earth by wearing our Lord's yoke we find rest unto our souls so in the perfect obedience of heaven complete repose is found.

They rest also from the *woe* of labour, for I find the word has been read by some "they rest from their wailing." The original is a word which signifies to beat, and hence, as applied to beating on the breast it indicates sorrow ; but the beating may signify conflict with the world, or labour in any form. The sorrow of work for Jesus is over with all the blessed dead. Naught to that place approacheth their sweet peace to molest ; they shall no more say that they are sick, neither shall adversity afflict them.

Their rest is perfect. I do not know whether the idea of rest is cheering to all of you, but to some of us whose work exceeds our strength it is full of pleasantness. Some have bright thoughts of service hereafter, and I hope we all have, but to those who have more to do for Christ than the weary brain can endure,—the prospect of a bath in the ocean of rest is very pleasant.

They rest from their labours. To the servant of the Lord it is very sweet to think that when we reach our heavenly home we shall rest from the *faults* of our labours. We shall make no mistakes there, never use too strong language or mistaken words, nor err in spirit, nor fail through excess or want of zeal. We shall rest from all that which grieves us in the retrospect of our service. Our holy things up there will not need to be wept over, though now they are daily salted with our tears. We shall there rest from the *discouragements* of our labour. There no cold-hearted brethren will damp our ardour, or accuse us of evil motives ; no desponding brethren will warn us that we are rash when our faith is strong, and obstinate when our confidence is firm. None will pluck us by the sleeve, and hold us back, when we would run the race with all our might. None will chide us because our way is different from theirs, and none will foretel disaster and defeat when we confidently know that God will give us the victory. We shall also rest from the *disappointments* of labour. Dear brother ministers, we shall not have to go home, and tell our Lord that none have believed our report. We shall not go to our beds sleepless because certain of our members are walking inconsistently, and others of them are backsliding, while those that we thought were converted have gone back again to the world. Here we must sow in tears : there we shall reap in joy. There we shall wear the crown, or rather cast it at the Master's feet ; but here we must plunge deep into the sea to fetch up the pearls from the depths that they may be set in the diadem. Here we labour, there we shall enjoy the fruits of toil, where no blight or mildew can endanger the harvest.

It will be a sweet thing to get away to heaven, I am sure, to rest from all *contentions* amongst our fellow Christians. One of the hardest parts of Christ's service is to follow peace, and to maintain truth at the same time. He is a wise chemist who can in due proportions blend the pure and the peaceable ; he is no mean philosopher who can duly balance the duties of affection and faithfulness, and show us how to smite the sin and love the sinner—to denounce the error, and yet to cultivate affection for the brother who has fallen into it. We shall not encounter this difficulty in yon bright world of truth and love, for both we and our brethren shall be fully taught of the Lord in all things. We shall be free from the clouds and mists of doubt which now cover the earth, and clear of the demon spirits which seek to ruin men's souls beneath the shadow of deadly falsehood. Blessed be God for this prospect! It will be joy indeed to meet no one but a saint, to speak with none but those who use the language of Canaan, to commune with none but the sanctified. Truly blessed are the dead which die in the Lord, if they reach to such a rest as this.

"To this our labouring souls aspire,
With ardent pangs of strong desire."

"Our feet shall stand within thy gates, O Jerusalem."

III. The last matter for our consideration is THE REWARD of th blessed dead:—"They rest from their labours, and their works do follow them." They do not go before them, they have a forerunner infinitely superior to their works, for Jesus and his finished work have led the way. "I go," says he, "to prepare a place for you." In effect he says to us, "Not your works, but mine; not your tears, but my blood; not your efforts, but my finished work shall lead the van." Where then do our works come? Do they march at our right hand or our left as subjects of cheering contemplation? No, no, we dare not take them as companions to comfort us: they follow us at our heel; they keep behind us out of sight, and we ourselves in our desires after holiness always outmarch them. The Christian should always keep his best services behind, always going beyond them, and never setting them before his eyes as objects for congratulation. The preacher should labour to preach the best sermons possible, but he must never have them before him so as to cause him, in self-satisfaction, to say, "I have done well;" nor should he have them by his side, as if he rested in them, or leaned upon them, for this were to make antichrists of them. No, let them come behind: that is their proper place. Believers know where to put good works; they do not despise them, they never say a word to depreciate the law, or undervalue the graces of the Holy Spirit, but still they dare not put their holiest endeavours in the room of Christ. Jesus goes before, works follow after.

Note well, that *the works are in existence and are mentioned;* immortality and honour belong to them. The works of godly men are not insignificant or unimportant as some seem to think. They are not forgotten, they are not as the sere leaves of last year's summer; they are full of life, and bloom unfadingly; they follow the saints as they ascend to heaven, even as the silver trail follows in the wake of the vessel. I pictured just now a man burning at the stake; his enemies thought they had destroyed his work, but they only deepened its hold upon the age in which he suffered, and projected his influence into the effect for ages to come. They made a pile of his books, and as they blazed before his eyes they said, "There is an end of you and your heresies." Ah, what fools men have been! Truth is not vanquished with such weapons, nay, nor so much as wounded. Think of the case of Wycliffe, which I need not repeat to you. They threw his ashes into the brook, the brook carried them to the river, and the river to the sea, till every wave bore its portion of the precious relics, just as the influence of his preaching has been felt on every shore. Persecutors concluded beyond all question that they had made an end of a good man's teaching when they had burned him, and thrown away his ashes, but they forgot that truth often gathers a more vigorous life from the death of the man who speaks it, and books once written have an immortality which laughs at fire. Thousands of infidel and heathen works have gone, so that not a copy is to be found: I hope they never may be unearthed from the salutary oblivion which entombs them: but books written for the Master and his truth, though buried in obscurity are sure of a resurrection. Fifty years ago our old Puritan authors, yellow with age, and arrayed in dingy bindings, wandered about in sheep-skins and goat-skins, destitute, afflicted, tormented, but they have been brought forth in new editions, every library is enriched with them, the most powerful religious thought is affected by their utterances, and will be till the end of time. You cannot kill a good man's work, nor a good woman's work either, though it be only the teaching of a few children in the Sunday-school. You do not know to whom you may be teaching Christ, but assuredly you are sowing seed which will blossom and flower in the far off ages. When Mrs. Wesley taught her sons, little did she think what they would become. You do not know who may be in your class, my young friend. You may have there a young Whitfield, and if the Lord enable you to lead him to Jesus, he will bring thousands to decision. Ay, at your breast, good woman, there may be hanging one whom God will make a burning and a shining light; and if you train that little one for Jesus your work will never be lost. No holy tear is forgotten, it is in God's bottle. No desire for another's good is wasted, God has heard it. A word spoken for Jesus, a mite cast into Christ's treasury, a gracious line written to a friend—all these are things which shall last when yonder sun has blackened into a coal, and the moon has curdled into a clot of blood. Deeds done in the power of the Spirit are eternal. Therefore, "Be ye steadfast, unmovable, always abounding in the work of the Lord, forasmuch as ye know that your labour is not in vain in the Lord."

Good works follow Christians, and they will be rewarded. The rewards of heaven will be all of grace; but there will be rewards. You cannot read the Scripture without perceiving that the Lord first gives us good works, and then in his grace rewards us for them. There is a "Well done, good and faithful servant," and there is a proportionate allotment of reward to the man who was faithful with five talents and the man who was faithful with two. You who live for Jesus, may be quite certain that your life will be recompensed in the world to come. I repeat it, the reward will not be of debt, but of grace, but a reward there will be. Oh, the joy of knowing, when you are gone, that the truth you preached is living still! Methinks the apostles since they have been in heaven must often have looked down on the world, and marvelled at the work which God helped twelve poor fishermen to do, and they must have felt a growing blessedness as they have seen nations converted by the truth which they preached in feebleness. What must be the joy of a pastor in glory to find his spiritual children coming in one by one! Methinks, if I may, I shall go down to the gate and linger there to look for some of you. Ay, not a few shall I welcome as my children there, blessed be the name of the Lord; but what a joy it will be! You, teachers—you my good sister, who have brought so many to Christ—I cannot but believe that it shall multiply your heaven to see your dear ones entering it. You will have a heaven in every one of those whose feet you guided thither, you will joy in their joy, and praise the Lord in their praise. No, no, the good old cause shall never die, and the truth shall never perish. As I have lately read many hard things that have been spoken against the gospel, and as in going up and down throughout this land I have seen the nation wholly given to idolatry, I have felt something of the spirit of the Pole who wherever he wanders says to himself, "No, Poland, thou shalt never perish!" Despite the darkness and ill-savour of the times, the gospel nears its triumph. It can never perish. Great men may fall, great reputations may grow obscure, grand philosophies may be cast into the shade, monstrous infidelities may win popularity, and old superstitions may come back again to darken us; but thy cross, Emmanuel, thy pure and simple gospel, the faith our fathers loved and died for, must continue to be earth's brightest light—her day-star, till the day dawn and the shadows flee away. The vessel of the church can never be wrecked; she rocks and reels in the mad tempest, but she is sound from stem to stern, and her pilot steers her with a hand omnipotently wise. Her bow is in the wave, but see she divides the sea, and shakes off the mountainous billows, as a lion shakes the dew from his mane! Fiercer storms than those of the present have beat upon her, and yet she has kept her eye to the wind, and in the very teeth of hell's tremendous tempests she has ploughed her glorious way: and so she will till she reaches her appointed haven. The Lord liveth and the Lord reigneth, and Christ from the tree has gone to the throne—from Gethsemane and Golgotha up to the glory; and all power is given unto him in heaven and in earth. We have nothing to do but to go on preaching the gospel and baptising in his name, according to his bidding; and the day shall come when the might with the right and the truth shall be, and the right hand of Jesus with the iron rod shall break his adversaries, and reward his friends. The Lord own every one of us as being on his side; and if we are not on that side, oh, that we may speedily become so by repentance and faith! May the Lord turn us, and we shall be turned; for if "Blessed are the dead which die in the Lord," depend upon it, cursed are they that die out of Christ—ay, cursed with a curse, and their works shall follow them or go before them, unto judgment, to their condemnation. May infinite mercy save us from being howled at by our works in the next world, save us from being hunted down by the wolves of our past sins, risen from the dead; for, except we are forgiven, our transgressions will rise from the grave of forgetfulness, and gather around us, and tear us in pieces, and there shall be none to deliver.

May we fly even now to Jesus, and through faith in his blood be delivered from all evil that we also may have it said of us, "Blessed are the dead which die in the Lord."

The Lord bless you for Christ's sake. Amen.

PORTION OF SCRIPTURE READ BEFORE SERMON—Revelation xvi.

HYMNS FROM "OUR OWN HYMN BOOK"— 878, 833, 852.

Metropolitan Tabernacle Pulpit.

THE BARRIER.

A Sermon

DELIVERED ON LORD'S-DAY MORNING, MARCH 27TH, 1881, BY

C. H. SPURGEON,

AT THE METROPOLITAN TABERNACLE, NEWINGTON.

"And there shall in no wise enter into it any thing that defileth, neither whatsoever worketh abomination, or maketh a lie: but they which are written in the Lamb's book of life."—Revelation xxi. 27.

THE text refers to the glorified church of our Lord Jesus Christ. That perfected company of the elect and sanctified is set forth in this wonderful chapter under the image of a city descending "from God out of heaven, prepared as a bride adorned for her husband." Her work-day dress all laid aside, the bride appears in garments of needlework and raiment of wrought gold. The militant church, the church of the present day, is comparable to a tent, and is well imaged by the tabernacle in the wilderness: it is lit up within by the glory of God's presence, and covered without by the fiery cloudy pillar of his eternal providence; but yet to the eyes of men it is mean and inconsiderable, for verily it doth not yet appear what it shall be. By-and-by this same church, which to-day is likened unto a structure of curtains readily removed from place to place, shall become a city, fixed, permanent, high-walled, and compact together, a "city which hath foundations, whose builder and maker is God." The discomforts and trials of the desert life shall be exchanged for the quiet and comfort of a city dwelling. There shall be nothing of the wilderness about the church triumphant; it shall be a right royal abode, the metropolis of the universe, the palace of the great King. Everything that is lustrous, pure, precious, majestic shall be there. Rare and priceless things which are now the peculiar treasure of kings shall be the common possession of all the sanctified. The church shall be no longer despised, but shall sit as a queen among the nations, while at her feet they shall heap up all their glory and honour. In that church there shall remain nothing for which men shall reproach her, but everything shall be manifested in her for which they shall do her honour; her very streets to be trodden on shall be of pure gold like unto transparent glass, and her lowest course of stones shall be of jasper. Everything about the perfected church shall be the best of the best: she shall be recognized as being the fairest among women, the bride, the Lamb's wife, the crown and flower of the universe. We read the sparkling

No. 1,590.

figures of John's vision as emblems of moral and spiritual excellence, but we doubt not that, beyond the spiritual riches of the church, all materialism will also be at her disposal, and the restored creation shall bring her choicest beauties to adorn the chosen bride of the Lamb.

We have said that the glorified church will be the crown of the new creation, and it is into the new heavens and the new earth that she is represented as coming down from God. He that sitteth upon the throne said, "Behold, I make all things new." The creation which is round about us at this hour waxeth old, and is ready to vanish away. Wise men tell us that there are evident preparations in the bowels of the earth for a burning up of the earth and of all the works of men that are upon it, for its centre is an ocean of fire. God shall but speak, and as once the waters leaped upon the world and utterly destroyed all things that were upon it, so shall he call to the waves of flame and they shall rise from their hidden furnaces to melt all things with their fervent heat. Nevertheless we, according to his promise, look for new heavens and a new earth, wherein dwelleth righteousness. The former things shall have passed away, and a new creation shall dwell beneath the new heavens, filling up the new earth; and the flower and perfection of the new creation shall be the church of the living God in her full bloom and perfectness. Even now the regenerate are a kind of first fruits of God's creatures, the forerunners of the renewed universe; but then they shall be its centre and glory. The new birth is the beginning of the new creation: we lead the way, even we who are the church of the firstborn, but the whole creation groans to follow us so as to be delivered from the bondage of corruption into the glorious liberty of the children of God.

It is the glorified church, I say, that is here spoken of, and hence the text may be said to refer to heaven, for at the present moment the nucleus of the glorified church is in heaven, and from heaven every defiled thing must be shut out. Hence, too, it may refer to the kingdom of the millennial age, when the saints will reign with Christ upon the earth for a thousand years, when even upon this battle-field our conquering Leader shall be crowned with victory, and where his blood was shed his throne shall be set up, for among the sons of men shall he triumph, even among those that spat in his face. The text may also be read as including the eternal world of future bliss, for of that glorious, endless, undefiled inheritance the church glorified will be the possessor, but out of her shall long before have been gathered all things that offend, and them that do iniquity. From heaven and from all heavenly joys and states sin must be shut out. Into the perfected church there shall never enter anything that defileth, and from all its honours and rewards every polluted person is shut out by immutable decree.

I should like you for a minute or two to think of that perfected church as she is described in this chapter, for it is a description worthy of the profoundest study. What glory will surround the risen saints in their capacity as the city of God: "having the glory of God," saith the eleventh verse. What a glory of glories is this! Even now, my brethren and sisters, you that are in Christ possess the grace of God, but you shall by-and-by conspicuously shine with the glory of God. At present you share in the dishonour which falls to the lot of your Master and his cause among a wicked generation, but then you shall share in the glory which is the reward of the travail of his soul. "Then shall the righteous shine forth as the sun in the kingdom of their Father." How glorious will that church be whose light shall be the presence of God himself,— light in which the nations of them that are saved shall rejoice. O my God, write my name among them! And to that end write me among thy persecuted saints below. Well may we be content to endure what little of shame shall come upon the church militant on earth if we may participate in the honour of the church glorified above, for this is a glory which excelleth, "having the glory of God."

The city is described as exhibiting great massiveness, for the length and the breadth and the height of it are equal. It is a solid square, perfect and compact:

> "Thy walls are made of precious stones,
> Thy bulwarks diamond square."

What a church will the church of God be in those happier days! Now she is as a rolling thing, removed as readily as a shepherd's tent; but then she shall stand firm as a cube which rests upon its base. We watch the church of God sometimes with trepidation and alarm, for though we know that the gates of hell shall not prevail against her, yet her feebleness makes the timid tremble; but in her state after the resurrection there shall remain no signs of feebleness, for that which was sown in weakness shall be raised in power. She shall be a city the like of which hath never been beheld, whose foundation shall be deeper than the depths beneath, and her towers shall reach above the clouds. No institution shall exist so long or flourish so abundantly as the church of the living God. When you think of the massiveness of the church of God, settled in her place by the Almighty himself who hath established her, remember at the same time her vastness, for a multitude that no man can number shall be comprehended among her inhabitants: her census shall prove her citizens to be as the stars of heaven for multitude. Her stones shall not lie cast about as a little heap, but from her vast foundation the living stones shall rise course upon course, twelve foundations of jewels, till "the mountain of the Lord's house shall be exalted above the hills." I say again, write my name down among the dwellers in the great city! What higher honour can I crave than to have it said, "this man was born there"? To be numbered with princes, to be named with emperors, what of it! Your golden fleece, and silken garter, and gilded star are all poor toys; true glory lies in being part and parcel of the church, to-day despised and rejected of men, which shall ere long look forth fair as the sun, and astonish the world with the brightness of her rising. Ambition's self needs ask no more than citizenship in the heavenly Jerusalem.

The perfection of the church is set forth in her being foursquare, her value in the sight of God by her walls being composed of the rarest gems, and her delights in the variety of the sparkling jewels which bedeck her, there being scarcely one precious stone omitted of those that were known to Orientals, while some are mentioned which are scarcely known to us at all. All manner of joys and treasures and pleasures and delights, every form and shade of excellence, virtue, and bliss shall belong to the perfected ones when their number and character shall be complete, and they shall be comparable to the city of God.

The safety and quiet of the church is set forth by her gates for ever open. In times of war the city gates are fast closed, but for the New Jerusalem there will remain no fear of foe, no need to set a watch against an invader. Gog and Magog will be slain, and Armageddon's battle fought and finished, and unbroken rest shall be the portion of the glorified. Write my name among them, O my God, and permit me to enter into thy rest.

Best of all, remark how holy will the church be. She shall have no temple within her walls, for this simple reason, that she shall be all temple; she shall have no spot reserved for sacred uses, because all shall be "holiness unto the Lord." The divine presence shall be in all and over all, and this shall be the joy of her joy, "The glory of God did lighten it, and the Lamb is the light thereof." Brethren, the glory of the church even here below is the presence of God in her midst, but what will that presence be when it shineth forth in noonday brightness? when spirits strengthened for the vision shall endure with transport the full splendour of Jehovah's throne? Tongue cannot tell the glory, for thought cannot conceive it. Write my name among the blessed who shall see Jehovah's face. O thou living God, my soul thirsteth after thee. To dwell in thy presence is the summit of the soul's delight; to be with thee where thou art, and to behold thy glory, is the heaven of heaven. To what beyond this can thoughts aspire?

I. It being declared that the glorified church is to be all this, and a great deal more, of which we cannot now speak particularly, we may well long to enter within her gates of pearl. But what saith the text? I beseech you listen attentively to the solemn sound of THE WORD OF EXCLUSION—"*There shall in no wise enter into it anything that defileth, neither whatever worketh abomination, or maketh a lie.*" Listen, I say, to this word of exclusion, though it sounds like a death-knell in my ears. Learn that it can be abundantly justified to the conscience of all thoughtful men; learn that your own soul, if it be honest, must set its seal to the sentence of exclusion. This is no arbitrary decree, it is a solemn declaration to which all holy spirits give their willing assent and consent; an ordinance of which even the excluded themselves shall admit the justice.

For, first, *it is not meet that so royal and divine a corporation as the glorified church of God should be ruined by defilement.* God forbid that "her light, which is like unto a stone most precious, even like a jasper stone, clear as crystal," should ever be dimmed by the breath of sin. How beautiful was this fair world in the early morning of her creation, when the dew of her youth glistened upon her, and the sunlight of God made her face to shine. Keep watch and ward, ye shining ones, that this beauty be not marred! Let watchers and holy ones fly round the new-made world to drive far hence the apostate spirit and his fellows who kept not their first estate. Sad was the hour when with dragon wing the fallen spirit descended into Eden, advanced to mother Eve, and whispered in her ear the fell temptation. Oh, ye seraphs, would God your fiery swords had kept out the arch-deceiver, that this world might never have fallen, that we might have dwelt here amidst sunny glades, by pure rivers rippling o'er sands of gold, a holy and happy race, making every hill and vale vocal with the praise of God. Now, O earth, thou art a field of blood, but thou mightest have been a garden of delights; now art thou one vast cemetery, where all the dust was once a part of the living fabric of mortal men; but thou mightest have been as the firmament filled with stars, all shining to their Creator's praise. Alas that Eden should now remain only as a name,—gone as a vision of the night! Inasmuch as we could heartily wish that evil had never entered into the primeval world, we earnestly deprecate the idea that it should ever defile the new. Shall those new heavens ever look down with amazement upon the flight of a rebellious spirit, flying, beneath their serene azure, on an errand of destruction? Shall the jewelled walls of the thrice holy city be overleaped by an enemy of the king who is there enthroned? Shall the serpent leave his horrid trail upon the heavenly Eden, twice made of the Lord? God forbid! The purity of a world twice made, the perfection of the church of the regenerate, the majesty of the presence of God, all demand that every sinful thing should be excluded. All heaven and heavenly things cry, "Write the decree and make it sure, there shall in no wise enter into it anything that defileth." Grave it as in eternal brass, and let omnipotence go with the decree to execute it with the utmost rigour, for it would be horrible indeed if a second time evil should destroy the work of God. Into the church of the firstborn above the breath of iniquity must not enter. It cannot be that the work which cost the Redeemer's blood should yet be defiled. The eternal purpose of the Father, and the love of the Spirit, forbid that the Lord's own perfected church should be invaded by any unholy thing.

Brethren, there can be no entrance of evil into the kingdom of God, for *it is the very essence of the bliss of the glorified church that evil should be excluded.* Imagine for a moment that the decree of our text were reversed or suspended, and that it were allowed that a few unregenerate men and women should enter into the glorified church of God. Suppose, in addition, that those few should be of the gentler sort of sinners, not those who would profanely blaspheme the name of God, nor openly break the eternal Sabbath, but a few who are indifferent to God's glory, and cold and formal in his praise. How could heaven bear with these? These who are neither cold nor hot are sickening both to Christ and to his people, and must they endure the nausea of their society? Why, as in a living body the existence of a dead piece of bone breeds fret, and pain, and disease, so would the presence of these few defiling ones cause I know not what of disquietude and sorrow. It must not be. Love to the saints demands that they be no more vexed by sin or sinners. Pity, mercy, yea, even the partiality of kindred love dare not ask that it may be. All heaven is up in arms at the supposition. Holy spirits are alarmed at the idea that they should be again tempted by the presence of evil. Fast bar the gates of pearl and never open them again, ye spirits, rather than that there should come upon that pure street of transparent gold a foot that will not walk in the ways of God's commandments. or the halls of Zion be disgraced by a single spirit that shall refuse to love the holy and exalted name. Heaven were not heaven if it were possible for evil of any sort to enter there. Therefore, stand firm, O dread decree, for it would be cruelty to saints and destruction to heaven that there should in anywise enter into it anything that defileth.

Furthermore, let me beg you to consider that there is an impossibility of any defiled, sinful, unrenewed person ever entering into the body corporate of the glorified church of God—*an impossibility within the persons themselves.* Look, good sirs, the reason why wicked men cannot be happy is not alone because God will not let rebellion and peace dwell together, but because they will not let themselves be happy. The sea cannot rest because it is the sea, and the sinner cannot be quiet because he is a sinner. How could you, O natural, unregenerate man, ever enter into the kingdom of heaven as you are? You are not capable of it; it is not possible to you. Holiness has in it no attractions for you, since you love sin and the wages of it. You do not know God, and cannot see him; for this is the privilege of the pure in heart, and of them alone. You live in a world where everything has been made by the great Lord, and yet you do not perceive his hand, so great is your blindness. Shall blind men grope through the streets of the New Jerusalem? You are unacquainted with the simplest elements of spiritual things; for they can only be spiritually discerned, and you have no spiritual faculty. You are blind and deaf, yea, dead to God and heavenly things:— you know you are. Well, then, of what avail would it be that you should enter the spiritual realm, supposing it to be a place? for if you were admitted into the place called heaven, you would not be a partaker of the state of heaven, and it is the state of mind and character which is, after all, the essence of the joy. To be in a heavenly place and not in a heavenly condition would be worse than hell, if worse can be. What are songs to a sad heart? Such would heaven be to an unrenewed mind. The element of glory would destroy rather than bless an unrenewed mind. It is as though you saw before you a blazing furnace, in which happy creatures disported themselves among the flames, bathing themselves in the white heat, leaping in rapture amid the rising sparks; for they are children of the flame, who drink in fire, and find it life. Imagine yourself to be a poor fly such as you hear buzzing on the window-pane; and you ask to enter into the glow of the furnace, thinking to be as merry as the fire-children. Keep back. Why tempt your doom? You will die soon enough; why ask to perish more quickly? No place would be so dreadful to a sinner as the place where God is most openly manifest. That holy element, which is the habitat of the new-born soul, would be the grave, the everlasting prison-house of an unholy soul could it enter there. To the wicked the day of the Lord is darkness, and not light, and the glory of the Lord is terror, and not bliss. Oh, unconverted hearer, they sing in heaven; but in their songs your ear would find no delight. They worship God in heaven; but as divine worship is irksome to you, even if it be kept up for an hour or so below, what would it be to dwell for ever and ever in the world to come in the midst of hallelujahs? O soul defiled with sin, you are incapable of heaven. The Roman Emperor Caligula, in his madness, made his horse first-consul of Rome; but his horse could not be a magistrate; it could not judge or govern, whatever the emperor might decree; though he fed it upon gilded oats from an ivory manger, it was a horse and nothing more. Even so, if a man be unregenerate, and unbelieving, we may do what we will with him, but he cannot rise to spiritual joys, and if we could even bid him come into heaven, still he would remain what he was, incapable of the joy and bliss which God hath prepared for them that love him. So standeth it a fact in the very essence and nature of things, that there shall in no wise enter into the realm of the spiritual, the kingdom of the true, the land of the blessed, the home of the perfected, anything that defileth. It cannot come there from incapacity within itself.

Let me add that *our own hearts forbid that evil should so enter.* As I mused on this text I supposed myself to be defiled with sin, yet standing outside the pearl gates of heaven. Then I said within myself, "If I might enter there defiled as I am, would I do so?" and my heart answered, "No, I would not if I might. How could I blot such brightness and spoil such happiness?" Suppose myself infected to-day with a deadly fever—an incurable typhus, which would bring death to all that touched me. The blast is pitiless, and the snow is falling, and I stand shivering at the door of one of your houses longing for shelter. I see inside the room your little children, sporting in full health: shall I venture among them? I long to escape from the cold without; but if I should enter your room I should bring to you fever, and death to your innocent little ones and to yourselves, and thus turn your happiness into misery. I would turn away and brave the storm, and sooner die than bring such desolation into a friend's abode. And well might any honest spirit say at sight of the perfect family above, "Nay, if I might, I would not be admitted into a perfect heaven while yet I might defile it, and spread the fell contagion of moral evil." You know, brethren, how a few rags from the East have sometimes carried a plague into a city; and if you were standing at the quay when a plague-laden ship arrived you would cry, "Burn those rags; do anything with them, but do keep them away from the people. Bring not the pest into a vast city, where it may slay its thousands!" So do we cry, "Great God, forbid it that anything that defileth should enter into thy perfected church! We cannot endure the thought thereof." Draw your swords, ye angels; stand in your serried ranks, ye seraphim, and smite every defiled one that would force a passage within the gates of pearl. It must be so: "There shall in no wise enter into it anything that defileth."

The fiat of God has gone forth, and the fiery sword is set at the gate of the new Eden. Into the first paradise there came the serpent; into the second never shall the subtle tempter enter. Into the first paradise there came sin, and God was driven from it as well as man; but into the second there shall never come anything that approximates to sin or falsehood; but the Lord God shall dwell there for ever, and his people shall dwell there with him. Thus much, then, upon the word of exclusion.

II. I desire, as I continue this meditation, in the power of the Holy Spirit, not so much to preach as to think inwardly, and ask you to think with me, of THAT WORD OF EXCLUSION WORKING WITHIN THE SOUL,—within my soul, within yours. It sits in judgment upon me, and it chastens me. It strikes home to my conscience, and rouses me to self-examination. Its voice is solemn, and strikes heavily upon the ear, as we remember its wide sweep and comprehensive breadth—" There shall in no wise enter into it *anything* that defileth." No person who defiles, no fallen spirit, or sinful man can enter. And as no person, so no tendency, leaning, inclination, or will to sin can gain admission. No wish, no desire, no hunger towards that which is unclean shall ever be found in the perfect city of God. Nor even a thought of evil can be conceived there, much less a sinful act performed. Nothing shall ever be done within those gates of pearl contrary to the perfect law, nor anything imagined in opposition to spotless holiness. Consider such purity, and wonder at it: the term "anything that defileth" includes even an idea, a memory, a thought of evil. Thoughts that flit through the mind as birds through the air that never roost or build a nest—even such shall never glance across the skies of the new creation. It is altogether perfect! And, mark well, that no untruth can enter—"neither whatsoever maketh a lie." Nothing can enter heaven which is not real; nothing erroneous, mistaken, conceited, hollow, professional, pretentious, unsubstantial, can be smuggled through the gates. Only truth can dwell with the God of truth. These are sweeping and searching words,—no evil, nothing that works to evil; no falsehood, nothing that works to falsehood, can ever enter into the triumphant church of God. O my soul, my soul, how bears this upon thee? Cuts it not to the very quick? For how art thou to enter, defiled as thou art, and so diseased with falsehood of one sort or another?

Well may we be aroused when we remember what defiled and defiling creatures we have been in the days of our unregeneracy. Brethren, let us not shrink from the humbling contemplation. Come down from your high places and see the horrible pit in which you lie by nature. Think of your past lives, I pray you, of those days in which ye found pleasure in walking after the flesh. I call on you to remember the sins of your youth, and your former transgressions, of thought, word, and deed. If they are shut out who defile, and are defiled, where are you? where are you? For these sins of ours, though they were committed years ago, are none the less sinful to day; they are as fresh to God as if we perpetrated them this very moment. Thou art still red-handed, O sinful man, though thy crime was worked some twenty years ago. Thou art black, O sinner, still, though it be fifty years ago that thy chief sin was committed; for time has no bleaching power upon a crimson sin. The guilt of an old offence is as fresh as though it were wrought but yester-morn. Our sins in themselves make us unclean and unfit for holy company, and, alas, they are many. Our sins have left a second defilement on us, by creating the tendency to do the like again. Is there one among us that has sinned who does not know that he is all the more likely to sin again? Since after once being drawn aside by sin there are stronger draggings in the same way, sin once committed becomes a fountain of defilement. The stream in which the fish has sported will be sought by it again in its season, and the swallow will return to its old nest; even so will the mind return to its folly. Ay, so it is; and if everything that defileth is shut out from the holy city, my God, my God, am not I shut out too?

Bethink you that not only does actual sin shut men out of heaven, but this text goes to the heart by reminding us that we have within us inbred sin, which would defile us speedily, even if we were now clean of positive transgression. The fount from which actual sin comes is within every unrenewed bosom. How can you and I enter heaven while there is unholy anger in us? The best of men are too apt to retain an unhallowed quickness of temper, which under certain circumstances worketh wrath. There shall in no wise enter into heaven a hasty temper, or a quick imperious spirit, or a malicious mind; for these defile. In certain persons there is no quickness of spirit, but there is a cold, chill obstinacy; so that having once resolved, though the resolve be evil, they stand to it doggedly and cannot be moved. Like obstinate mules, they can scarcely be driven; blows cannot stir them from their purpose. Disobedient obstinacy cannot enter the kingdom: my hearers, are you under its dominion? And, oh, there is in all of us a lusting after evil of some sort or other. Only place us in certain conditions, and the flesh longs after forbidden things, and though we chide ourselves and check the longing, yet is there not within us a relish for the sweet stolen morsels of transgression? We could weep our eyes out when we discover what a palate for pleasurable sin our old nature still retains; yea, a longing for the very sin of which we most bitterly repent and from which we most eagerly long to be delivered. How can we hope to enter heaven if there be these appetites in us? They are there, and they defile! What can we do? There, too, is that vile thing called "pride." Why, some of us cannot be trusted with a pennyworth of success, but we are exalted above measure. Some of God's children cannot have ten minutes' fellowship with Christ but they must needs put on their fine feathers and crow right lustily because they feel themselves to be nearing absolute perfection. Alas for the pride of our hearts, and the pollution which comes of it! How can such vain creatures be admitted among the glorified? Nor is this all; for sloth preys on many, and tempts them to shun God's service, and especially to shun the cross of Christ. Sloth is a rust which has a sadly defiling power: we gather moth and mildew from inaction. Never is a man pure who is not zealous in the service of God. We rot to corruption if we lie still; how, then, shall we be admitted within the jewelled city? Ah, look within thy heart, my brother—look steadily beneath the fair film of the surface, and mark the inward evil which it conceals. Judge not thyself alone when at thy best, occupied with thy prayers and praises and almsgivings, but look steadily into thy soul at other times, and thou shalt see a loathsome mass of evil life, a seething corruption moving within thy heart; for evil remaineth even in the regenerate; and this cannot enter heaven. Thank God, it cannot. Even though the word of exclusion staggers me, and sends me back as with a stunning blow, and makes me cry, "Thou shuttest me out, my God, by this thy decree;" yet I feel that if it be so, the decree is right, and just, and good. "There shall in no wise enter into it anything that defileth." Amen and amen.

Now, I ask you whether this word of exclusion does not, in you who know its meaning, slay all hope of self-salvation? For, first, here are our past sins, and they defile, and make us defiling. How are we to get rid of them? How can we wash out these polluting blots? Tears! So much salt water thrown away if looked upon as a bath for sin! Good works performed! They are already due to God. How shall future discharge of debts repay the past? O, my God, if I have ever known what sin means, I have also known that it is impossible that its defiling nature should ever be changed, or that the pollution should ever be removed by any efforts of my own. I spoke with one the other day who said that she was seeking salvation by good works. I knew that she had performed self-denying acts of charity, and I asked her whether she felt nearer to the salvation at which she aimed. I knew that I spoke to a sincere, honest person, and her reply did not surprise me. She answered sadly, "The more I do, the more I feel I ought to do, and I am no nearer to the point I am aiming at." And so it is; the more a sincere heart doth seek to serve God, the more it feels the shortcoming of its service of him; and the more a person seeks after purity by his own efforts, the further he judges himself to be from it. Our standard rises as we rise towards it; our conscience becomes tender in proportion as we obey it; and so, in the nature of things, rest of heart comes not in that manner. Ah, there remaineth not beneath heaven anything that can wash out the defilement of past sin save one only cleansing flood. O sinful man, plunge thy hands into the Atlantic and thou shalt crimson every drop of its tremendous waters, and yet the stain shall be as scarlet as before. No, no, no: it is certain that no man can enter heaven, by reason of his transgression and his sinfulness, except omnipotence shall cleanse him.

But then look at the other part of the difficulty, that is, the making of your own heart pure and clean. How shall this be done? How shall the Ethiopian change his skin and the leopard his spots? Have you tried to master your temper? I hope you have. Have you managed it? Your tendencies this way or that, you have striven against them, I hope, but have you mastered them? I will tell you. You thought you had. You thought you had bound the enemy with strong ropes: you tied him and you fastened him down, and you shut him up in an inner chamber, and you said, "The Philistines be upon thee, Samson." You felt that the champion was vanquished now, but oh how grimly did he laugh at you as the old adversary arose within you, and snapped the bonds, and hurled you to the ground; defeated when you thought that you had won the victory. I cannot overcome myself, nor overcome my sin. I will never cease from the task, God helping me, but apart from the divine Spirit the task is as impossible as to make a world.

III. It seems to me that we may most fitly come to the close of our sermon by thinking of THE WORD OF SALVATION, which just meets the difficulty raised by the sentence,—"There shall in no wise enter into it anything that defileth." But, first, my past sin, what of that? There are many who are even now within the church of God above, and we will ask concerning them, "Who are these arrayed in white robes, and whence came they?" We receive the reply, "These are they that have washed their robes, and made them white in the blood of the Lamb." "In the blood of the Lamb!" I feel as if I could sing those words. What joy that there should be anything that can take all my stains away,—all without exception, and make me whiter than snow. If Christ be God, if it be true that he did within that infant's body contain the fulness of the Deity, and if, being thus God and man, he did take away my sin, and in his own body on the tree did bear it, and suffer its punishment for me, then I can understand how my transgression is forgiven and my sin is covered. Short of this my conscience cannot rest. The misty atonements of modern divines cannot calm my conscience; they are not worth the time spent in listening to them, they are cobwebs of the fancy, altogether insufficient to sustain the strain even of the present conscience, much less of the conscience which shall be aroused by the judgment bar of God. But this truth,—Christ instead of me, God himself the offended one in the offender's place, bowing his august head to vengeance and laying his eternal majesty in the dishonour of a tomb: this is the fulness of consolation. O Lamb of God, my sacrifice, I shall enter heaven now! I shall pass the scrutiny of the infallible watchers. I shall not be afraid of the eyes of fire. I shall be without spot or wrinkle, or any such thing—"Washed in the blood of the Lamb!" This is our first great comfort, brethren—"He that believeth in him is not condemned." He that believeth in him is justified from all things from which he could not be justified by the law of Moses. "There is therefore now no condemnation to them that are in Christ Jesus."

But here is the point, there is still no entrance into the holy city so long as there are any evil tendencies within us. This is the work, this is the difficulty, and since these are to be overcome, how is the work to be done ? Simple believing upon Christ brings you justification, but you want more than that ; you need sanctification, the purgation of your nature, for have we not seen that until our nature itself is purged the enjoyment of heaven must be impossible? There can be no knowledge of God, no communion with God, no delight in God hereafter unless all sin is put away and our fallen nature is entirely changed. Can this be done? It can. Faith in Christ tells us of something else beside the blood. There is a Divine Person,—let us bow our heads and worship him—the Holy Ghost who proceedeth from the Father, and he it is who renews us in the spirit of our minds. When we believe in Jesus, the Spirit enters into the heart, creating within us a new life; that life struggles and contends against the old life, or rather the old death, and as it struggles it gathers strength and grows; it masters the evil, and puts its foot upon the neck of the tendency to sin. Do you feel this Spirit within you? You must be under its power or perish. If any man have not the Spirit of Christ he is none of his. I would not have you imagine that in death everything is to be accomplished for us mysteriously in the last solemn article; we are to look for a work of grace in life, a present work, moulding our character among men. Oh, sirs, the sanctifying work of the Holy Spirit is not a sort of extreme unction reserved for death-beds, it is a matter for the walks of life and the activities of to-day. I do not know how much is done in the saint during the last minute of his lingering here; but this I know, that in a true believer the conquest of sin is a matter to be begun as soon as he is converted and to be carried on throughout life. If the Spirit of God dwells in us, we walk not after the flesh but after the spirit, and we mortify the corruptions and lusts of the old man. There must be now a treading under foot of lust and pride, and every evil thing, or these evils will tread us under foot for ever in the future state where character never changes. There must be *now* a rejection of the lie, a casting out of the false, or we shall be cast out ourselves for ever. There must be *now* a cry, "O Lord, thou desirest truth in the inward parts: and in the hidden part thou shalt make me to know wisdom. Purge me with hyssop, and I shall be clean: wash me, and I shall be whiter than snow." Beloved, it is to this we must come, to be washed in the water which flowed with the blood from Jesus' side, for there must be a purging of nature as well as a removal of actual transgression, or else the inevitable decree, like a fiery sword, will keep the gate of paradise against us. "There shall in no wise enter into it anything that defileth, neither whatsoever worketh abomination, or maketh a lie."

O my hearers, suppose we should never enter there! Nay, start not, for the supposition will soon be a fact with many of you except you repent. Suppose we should be in the next world what some of us are now, defiled and untruthful—what remains? That is an awful text in the parable of the virgins—"And the door was shut." You read of those who said, "Lord, Lord, open to us," to whom he answered, "I know you not." You have read of them, will any one of us be among them? Will anyone of us who has a lamp, and is thought to be a virgin soul, be among the shut out ones, on whose ear shall fall the words, "I know you not whence you are." You see you cannot be anywhere else but *out* unless you are *in*; and you must be shut out if you are defiled and defiling. Dear heart, this is a question I beg you to look to at once. You do not know how short a time you have left to you in which you may look into it. Some who were here but a Sabbath-day or so ago are now gone from us. Eleven deaths reported at one church-meeting among our members! We are a dying people; we shall all be gone within a very short time. I charge you by the living God, and as you are dying men and women, see to it that you are not shut out, so as to hear the fatal cry, "Too late, too late, ye cannot enter now." There shall be no purgation in eternity, and no possible way of entering in among the perfected, for it is written, "There shall in no wise enter into it anything that defileth." No crying, "Lord! Lord!" no striving to enter in, no tears, no, not even the pangs of hell itself, shall ever purge the soul so as to make it fit to join with the holy church above, should it pass into the future state uncleansed. Shut out! shut out! O God, may that never be true of anyone among us, for Christ's dear name's sake. Amen.

PORTION OF SCRIPTURE READ BEFORE SERMON—Revelation xxi.

HYMNS FROM "OUR OWN HYMN BOOK"—855, 867, 51 (Vers. II.)

Metropolitan Tabernacle Pulpit.

EARLY AND LATE, OR HORÆ GRATIÆ.

A Sermon

Delivered on Sunday Morning, December 10th, 1865, by

C. H. SPURGEON,

AT THE METROPOLITAN TABERNACLE, NEWINGTON.

"For the kingdom of heaven is like unto a man that is an householder, which went out early in the morning to hire labourers into his vineyard. . . . And he went out about the third hour, and saw others standing idle in the market-place. . . . Again he went out, about the sixth and ninth hour, and did likewise. And about the eleventh hour he went out, and found others standing idle, and saith unto them, Why stand ye here all the day idle?"—Matthew xx. 1, 3, 5, 6.

We have frequently observed that we do not think it right to neglect the connection of Scripture. We have no right to tear passages of Scripture from their context and make them to mean what they were not intended to teach; and therefore I have in the reading given you, according to my ability, what I think to be the immediate design of the present parable. It is a rebuke to those who fall into a legal spirit and begin calculating as to what their reward ought to be in a kingdom where the legal spirit is entirely out of place, since its reward is not of debt but of grace. I think I may now, without any violation of propriety, dwell upon one very distinct fact in connection with the parable. It is not right to violate the drift of the parable, but having already observed it and made it as clear as we can, we believe that we are now authorized to make use of one of the main circumstances mentioned in it.

This morning I intend to call your attention to the fact that the labourers were hired at different periods of the day, by which doubtless we are taught, that God sends his servants into his vineyard at different times and seasons; that some are called in early youth, and others are not led to enter into the service of the Master until declining years have brought them almost to the eventide of life.

I must, however, ask you to remember that *they were all called:* by the mention of which the Saviour would teach us that no man comes into the kingdom of heaven of himself. Without exception, every labourer for Jesus has been called in one sense or another, and he would not have come without being so called. They are all called. Were a man what he should be he would need no pressing and invitation to come to the gospel of Christ; but since human nature is perverted, and men put bitter for sweet and sweet for bitter, darkness for light and light for darkness, man needs to be called by the outward word·

No. 664.

he needs to be invited, persuaded, and entreated; he needs, to use the strong expression of the apostle Paul, that as though God did beseech him by us we should pray him in Christ's stead to be reconciled to God. Nay, further than this, although some men come to work in a legal spirit in the vineyard through this common call of the gospel, yet no man in spirit and in truth comes to Christ without a further call, namely, the effectual call of God's Holy Spirit. The general call is given by the minister, it is all that he can give. If the preacher attempts to give the particular call as some of my hyper-calvinistic brethren do, confining the gospel command to a certain character and trying to be themselves the discoverers of God's elect, and to make that particular which is always universal; if the preacher acts thus, and virtually endeavours to give the particular call, he makes a sorry mess of it, and usually fails altogether to preach the gospel of glad tidings to the sons of men. But when man is content to do what he can do, namely, preach the commandment "that we believe on the Lord Jesus Christ," and that "God commandeth all men everywhere to repent," then there comes with the general call to the chosen of God a particular and special call which none but the Holy Ghost can give, but which he gives so effectually that all who hear it become willing in the day of God's power, and turn with full purpose of heart unto the Lord. In what sense is it true that many are called but few chosen, if none are to be called by the preaching of the Word but those who are chosen? There are two callings, the one is general to all who hear of Jesus, and many who are thus called are not chosen; the other is personal and peculiar to the elect, "for whom he did predestinate them he also called." To return to our point; all in the vineyard are in some sense called. There is not a solitary exception to this rule in the entire Christian Church. The doctrine of free-will has not a single specimen to show to prove itself. There is not a sheep in all the flock that came back to the shepherd unsought; there is not a single piece of money which leaped again into the woman's purse, she swept the house to find it: nay, I will go further, and say there is not even a single prodigal son in the entire family who did ever say, "I will arise, and go unto my Father," till first the Father's grace, veiling itself in the afflicting providence of a mighty famine, had taught the prodigal the miserable results of sin, as he fed the swine, and fain would have filled his belly with the husks that the swine did eat, but could not do so.

I want you to notice another fact before I come to the subject now in hand, and that is, that *all those who are called are said to have been hired.* Of course in a parable no word is to be construed harshly; we are to give the meaning according to the drift; but still I think we may say that there is this likeness between hiring a servant and the engagement of a soul to Christ, that henceforth a man hired has no right to serve another, he serves the master who has hired him. When a soul is called by grace into the service of the Lord Jesus Christ, he cries, "O Lord, other lords have had dominion over me, but now thee only will I serve." He plucks off the yoke of sin, its pleasure, its custom, and he puts upon him that yoke of which the Master says it is easy, and he bears that burden which Jesus tells us is light. A hired servant must not work for another, he works for his master; and so a man who is called by grace lives not for any sinister object or motive, but to his Master only. A hired servant, again, does not work on his own account, he is not his own master; and "ye are not your own, ye are bought with a price." Henceforth, though he calls no man "Master" on earth, yet he remembers that one is his Master in heaven, to whom all his service is due. There is a compact between the hired man and his master, and there is a solemn compact of spirit between the true believer and his Lord. We have devoted ourselves to his service, we have given up all liberty of self-will, and henceforth our will is at the government of our Lord, and all our powers and passions are to be, we hope will be, through God's grace, obedient to him who has hired us into the vineyard. Now the word "hired" was used in order to bring in the idea of reward. It was used to suit Peter's view of the case; it was used in order that his legal question of "What shall we have therefore?" might be clearly brought out, and its folly shown in the light of that sovereign grace which does as it wills with his own. Yet for all that believers are hired in an evangelical sense, they do not serve God for nought, they shall not work without a reward. "The wages of sin is death, but the gift of God is eternal life." We shall have our reward for what we do for the Master, and though it be not wages in the sense of debt, yet verily I say unto you, there shall not be a single true-hearted worker for God who shall not receive of his Master most blessed wages of grace in the day when he comes to take account of his servants.

Now to the point, *the master calls these hired servants of his at different hours of the day;* and, in the second place, *distinguishing grace shines forth in each case,* and is illustrated and made more manifest in its varieties of glorious compassion and lovingkindness by the different hours at which the chosen ones are called.

I. ALL ARE NOT CALLED BY GRACE AT THE SAME TIME. Some, according to the parable, are called *early in the morning.* Thrice happy are these! The earliest period at which a child may be called by grace it would be difficult for us positively to define, because children are not all of the same age mentally when they are of the same age physically, and even in the matter of mental development we dare not limit the Holy One of Israel as to the chosen period of operation. As far as our observation goes, grace works upon some little ones at the very dawn of moral consciousness. There are, no doubt, precocious children, whose intellect and affections are very much developed, and very deeply sanctified even so early as two or three years of age. Such children usually are intended by the Master to be taken home at once. There are interesting biographies extant, which prove that holiness may bloom and ripen in the youngest heart, and many anecdotes are treasured up in such collections as "Janeway's Token for Children," of children whom I might call infants with strict propriety, out of whose mouth God ordained praise, and did, through them, still the enemy and the avenger. Little prattlers, whose tongues it would have been supposed could only have talked of toys, have been able to speak with an apparent profundity of knowledge of spiritual, and especially of heavenly things. It is certain that some have wrought their day's work for the Master in their mother's arms; they have spoken of the

Saviour in tones which have melted a mother's heart and gone to a father's conscience, and then they have been taken home. "Whom the gods love die young," said the heathen, and doubtless it is no small privilege to be so soon admitted into glory. Only shown on earth, and then snatched away to heaven, too precious to be left below. Precious child, how dear wert thou to the good God who sent thee here and then took thee home! Fair rose bud! yet in the perfection of thy young beauty taken to be worn by the Saviour on his bosom, how can we mourn thy translation to the skies?

> "No bitter tears for thee be shed,
>   Blossom of being seen and gone!
> With flowers alone we strew thy bed,
>   O blest departed one!
> Whose all of life, a rosy ray,
> Blush'd into dawn and pass'd away."

"Early in the morning," would also include those who have passed the first hour of the day, but who have not yet wasted the second opening hour. I mean those hopeful lads and girls who perhaps would rather I should call them youths;—those who have reached their teens, have overleaped infancy and childhood, and are growing up in the heyday and vigour of youth. Youngsters still more at home in the play-ground than in the work-field, fitter, as Satan tells them, to be sporting in the market-place than busy in the vineyard; such as these, to the praise of divine love, are often hired by the householder. It is worth while to warn some of our brethren who seem to be exceedingly dubious of boyish and girlish piety,—to warn them against indulging harsh and suspicious doubts. We have remarked, and I think those who have watched our membership carefully will have remarked it too, that among all the slips and falls which have caused us sorrow, we have had but little sorrow from those who were added to us as boys or girls. There are those preaching the gospel this day with acceptance and power whom these hands baptized into Jesus Christ very early in their boyhood, and there are among us honoured servants of God who have served this Church well, who, while they were yet at school were joyful followers of the Lord Jesus Christ. With our earliest gettings some of us got an understanding of the things of the kingdom; our Bible was our child's primer, our spelling-book, the guide of our youth and the joy of our earliest years. We thank God that there are Timothys still among us, and those not few and far between; and young Samuels, who, being brought as infants to the Lord's house, have from that day forth worn the linen ephod and served after their fashion as priests unto God, serving him with all their hearts. Happy those who are called early in the morning! they have peculiar reasons for blessing and praising God.

> "Grace is a plant, where'er it grows,
>   Of pure and heavenly root;
> But fairest in the youngest shows,
>   And yields the sweetest fruit."

Let us spend a minute in thinking of their happy case who are saved in boyhood. Early in the morning the dew still twinkles on the leaves, the maiden blush of dawn remains and reveals an opening beauty, which is lost to those who rise not to see the birth of day. There is a beauty about early piety which is indescribably charming, and unutterably lovely in freshness and radiance. We remark in childhood an artless simplicity, a child-like confidence, which is seen nowhere else. There may be less of knowing but there is more of loving; there may be less of reasoning, but there is more of simply believing upon the authority of revelation; there may be less of deep-rootedness, but there is certainly more of perfume, beauty, and emerald verdure. If I must choose that part of the Christian life in which there is the most joy, next to the land Beulah, which I must set first and foremost by reason of its lying so near to Canaan, I think I would prefer that tract of Christian experience which lieth toward the sun-rising, which is sown with orient pearls of love, and cheered with the delicious music of the birds of hope.

Early in the morning, when we have just risen from slumber, work is easy; our occupation in the vineyard is a cheerful exercise rather than a toil such as those find it who bear the burden and heat of the day. The young Christian is not oppressed with the cares and troubles of the world as others are; he has nothing else to do but to serve his God. He is free from the embarrassments which surround so many of us, and prevent our doing good when we would consecrate ourselves wholly to it. The lad has nought to think of but his Lord. There are his books and his lessons, but he can be fervent of spirit in the midst of them. There are the companions of his childhood, but in guilelessness and simplicity he may be of service to them and to God through them. Give me, I say, if I would have an auspicious time to work for Jesus, give me the blessed morning hours, when my heart is bounding lightest and joy's pure sunbeams tremble on my path; when my glowing breast lacks no ardour, and my happy spirit wears no chain of care.

One would prefer early conversion because such persons have not learned to stand idle in the market-place. A fellow, you know, who has been for hours standing with his hands in his pocket, talking with drunken men and so on, is not worth much at the eleventh hour, nay even by the middle of the day it has become so natural to him to prop the walls, that he is not likely to take to work very readily. Begin early with your souls, break in the colts while they are young, and they are likely to take well to the collar. There are no workers like those who commenced work while they were yet children. What a promise of a long day there is for young believers; the sun has just risen, and he has to travel to his zenith and to descend again. There is ample room and verge enough though none to spare. If God in his providence permit it so to happen, that youngster yonder has twelve hours' work before him— what may he not accomplish? For a grand and glorious life early piety if not essential, is certainly a very great advantage. To give those first days to Jesus will spare us many sad regrets, prevent us acquiring many evil habits, and enable us to achieve good success through the Holy Spirit's blessing. It is well to begin to fly while yet the wings are strong, for if we live long in sin the wing may be broken and then they will flap wearily through the rest of our days, even when grace shall call us. Let it be the desire of parents here to have their children converted as children! And oh! may God cast that desire into the hearts of some of you young people that are here this morning that before you reach one-and-twenty, before you are called men, you may be perfect men in Christ Jesus, that while you are yet children you may be children of God. May you as "newborn babes receive the sincere milk of the Word," and the Lord grant that you may "grow thereby." Happy, happy, happy souls, whom the Master thus by distinguishing grace brings "early in the morning!"

The householder went out again *at the third hour.* This may represent the period in which we have mounted above being children and youths and are entitled to be called men. Suppose we settle the first hour as extending over the earliest seven or eight years of age; then the second hour runs on from that to twenty-one or thereabouts; and then we have a good length of time between twenty and thirty and onwards to reckon as the third, and fourth, and fifth hours. There are some whom divine grace renews at the third hour. This is late! one-and-twenty is grievously late, when you consider how much of early joy is now impossible, how much of sinful habit has now been acquired, how many opportunities for usefulness are now gone past recall. A quarter of the day has flown away for ever when we reach the third hour. It is the best quarter of the day, too, that has gone past recall. The first meal of the day is over,—that blessed breaking of the fast with Christ is no more possible. A very precious meal is that, when the Saviour gives us the morning portion, the manna which melteth when the sun is up. Blessed is the child's feeding upon Jesus: truly I remember when I was awakened like Elias from under the juniper tree, and fed on such dainty fare that to this day the flavour abideth with me. The man of one-and-twenty has lost that first meal, breakfast is all over; Christ will say to him as he will to some others, "Come and dine," and that is precious; but the daintiest meal is over, the first early enjoyment, the first early rapture can never be known.

I have no doubt there are many here who think that to be converted at one-and-twenty is very soon; but why one-and-twenty years given to Satan? Why a fourth of man's existence devoted to evil? Besides, it may not be a fourth, it may be one half, nay, in how many cases it is the whole of life. The sun goes down ere it is yet noon, and the idler in the market-place has no hope of ever being a worker in the vineyard. Death who comes when God wills, and gives us no notice, may cut down the flower before it has fully opened. "In the morning it is like grass that groweth up, in the evening it is cut down and withereth." It is late, it is sadly late! It is a sad thing to have lost those bright days in which the mind was least engaged, in which it was the most susceptible of forming godly habits. It is a sad thing to have learned so much of sin as one may have learned by one-and-twenty, a sad thing to have seen so much of iniquity, to have treasured up in one's memory so much of defilement. Twenty years with God; one might have been in such a time a good scholar in the kingdom; but twenty years in the world one begins to be like scarlet that has been lying in the dye till it is stained through and through. *It is late, but we thank God that it is not too late.* Nay, it is not too late even for the grandest of purposes. Not only is this period of life not too late for salvation, but it is not too late to do much for Jesus Christ. Some of us when we were one-and-twenty, had finished five years of Christian ministry, and had been the means of bringing many souls to the cross of Christ; but if others are led by grace to begin then, why there is a good period still remaining if God in providence spares our lives. The young man is now in all his strength and vigour, his bones are full of marrow, and his heart is full of fire. He ought to have acquired a good degree of education, and be prepared to acquire more.

Now he is just in the time when he should work. His plans of life are not settled as yet; he is not married yet, probably; as yet there are no children about him to have been injured by his ill example; he has an opportunity of rearing up a household in the fear of God. He is commencing business, he has an opportunity of so conducting that business that there may never need to be a time when he shall have to tack about and steer another course. He may, if called by God's grace at one-and-twenty, begin an honourable career, in which there need not be an angle or a curve, but straight to the harbour's mouth he may steer and mark upon the sea of life one shining furrow which shall reach in a direct line from the present moment straight to the lights of heaven, which he shall reach with his sail full and a priceless cargo on board to the praise of the glory of divine grace. It is late, it is very late in some respects, but oh! it is not too late to serve the Master well, and to win a crown of great reward, the gift of love divine.

There is abundance of work to do for us who are in this third, fourth, and fifth hour of the day. In fact, I suppose the Church must look to us for its most active work. After this period and the next, a man frequently becomes rather a recipient from the Church than a donor to it in the matter of activity. Its fresh blood, its energy, its warmth of heart, its ready action, must to a great extent come from the young men who are converted. Oh, you of one-and-twenty, I would to God that you were all born from heaven! You maidens, in your early beauty may the Master in his infinite mercy bring you in! Oh, could you know the sweetness of his love, you would not need persuading! Could you understand the joy of true religion, you would not want entreating! There is more hallowed mirth enjoyed in secret with the Lord Jesus Christ, than in all the merriment the world can yield. One ounce of Christ's love is better than a ton of the world's flatteries. The world offers bubbles with fair hues, bright to look upon, but vanishing at a breath; but Christ gives real treasure, enduring as eternity. The world's gold is all base money; it glitters, but it is not precious. There may be less glitter about the things of God, but there is a "solid joy and lasting pleasure," which "none but Zion's children know." May the Master come this morning to your hearts, and by my simple words may he call you at the third hour of the day into the vineyard.

The Master's grace was not exhausted, and therefore *he went out at the sixth hour.* We find him going into the market at high noon. Half the day was over. Who is going to employ a man, and give him a whole day's wages when twelve o'clock has come? He will not do too much if you hire him at six, what will he do if you engage him at twelve? Half a day's work! that is a poor thing to seek or to offer. The Master, however, seeks and accepts it. He promises, "Whatsoever is right, I will give you;" and there are some found who at the sixth hour enter into the vineyard and, being saved by grace, begin their work for Jesus. This may represent the period of life in which man is supposed to be in his prime—when he is past forty and onward. *This is sadly late, very sadly late.* Sadly late in a great many respects, not only because there is so little time left, but because so very much of energy, and zeal, and force, which should have been given to God, has been wasted; and has to some extent been used to fight against God. Forty years of hardness of heart! That is a long time for divine patience. Forty years of sin! That is a long season for conscience to mourn over. "Forty years long was I grieved with this generation," said God. In the wilderness they hardened their hearts all that time; and he sware in his wrath that they should not enter into his rest. What a blessing for you of forty and unconverted, that he has not sworn so terrible an oath concerning you, that still his longsuffering lingers, still his patience bears with you, still does he say to you, "Go, work, my son—go work this day in my vineyard." It is sadly late, because it has become so more than natural to you to walk in the way of sin. You will have so much to contend with in future, as the result of the past. Putting the ship of the soul about is not such easy work as turning a vessel by her helm; only a divine hand can steer a soul upon the tack of grace. You will need much grace to conquer those corruptions which have had forty years to take root in. You have a tenant in your house who is in possession, and you will find that possession to be nine points of the law; it will be a hard ejectment for you to effect, so hard indeed, that only a "stronger than he" can cast him out. To your dying day the recollection of evil things which you heard during these forty years of unregeneracy will stick by you; you will hear the echoes of an old song just when you are trying to pray, and some deed which you regret and mourn over, will come to check you just when you are about to say, "Abba Father," with an unstammering tongue. It is late, it is very, very late, this sixth hour, *but it is not too late.* It is not too late for some of the richest enjoyments; you can yet dine with Jesus; he can yet manifest himself unto you, as he doth not unto the world; you can have yet much time to serve him in. It is not too late yet to be distinguished among his servants. Take John Newton's life; he was called in the middle of the day, but John Newton left his mark in God's vineyard, a mark that will never be forgotten. I suppose Paul could not have been much less than of that age when he was called by sovereign grace; nay, the most of the apostles were probably very little short of this age when mercy met with them; still they did a glorious day's work. If saved by grace in middle life, my brother, you must work harder, you must let the time past suffice you to have wrought the will of the flesh, and now you must redeem the time, because the days are evil. Why, a man converted at forty should go double quick march to heaven, there should not be a moment lost now. Work the engine at high pressure, and give two strokes for every one that might be given by younger men and younger minds. Seek in the divine strength to do twice as much in the time, since you have only half the time to do a life's work in. Crowns for Christ, I know you wish to win them; then be up and doing, beloved. You are saved by grace, and by grace alone. You pant to honour Christ, because of his free love to you; cannot you endeavour to honour him as much in the remnant which remains as others do in the whole length of their life? You may by zeal, and prudence, and discretion, and perfect consecration, yet serve the Master well.

The householder *went out at the ninth hour*, at three o'clock in the afternoon. Nobody thinks of engaging day-labourers at three o'clock in the afternoon. A day's work to be done from three till six! It shows you that this gospel hiring is nothing like a legal hiring; it must be all of grace, or a man would not think of doing such a thing. Well now, three o'clock in the afternoon, that is from sixty to seventy. The prime of life has gone. *It is late, it is sadly late, very sadly late.* It is late because all the powers of the man are weak now. His memory begins to fail; he thinks his judgment better than ever it was, but probably that is only his own opinion. Most of the faculties lose their edge in old age. He has acquired experience, but still there is no fool like an old fool; and a man who has not been taught by divine grace learns very little of any value in the school of providence. Sixty thousand years would not make a man wise if grace did not teach him. Now think of it, is it not late? Here is the man: if he be converted now, what is there left of him? He is just a candle end. He may give a little light, but it is almost like a snuff burning in the socket. All those sixty years, seventy years, have been spent, where? Cover it all up. Let us go backward as Noah's sons did, and cover it all up; and oh, may almighty grace cover it too! The fact is terribly appalling—sixty, seventy years spent in the service of Satan! Oh what good the man might have done! Had he but served his God as he served the world, what good he might have done! He has made a fortune, has he! How rich he might have been in faith by this time. He has built a house! Yes, but how he might have helped to build the Church. The man has been playing at card-houses; he has been like boys by the sea-shore building castles of sand, which must all come down, and must come down very soon too, for I hear the surges of the dread tide of death, it is rolling in even now. Those teeth which have fallen out, those pains and rheumatics, and so on, all show that this is not his rest. The tabernacle is beginning to crumble about the man, and the warning is loud which reminds him that he must soon be gone, and leave his wealth and his house; and so if this be all, in the end it will turn out that he has done nothing; he has piled up shadows, heaped together thick clay, and that is all he has done; when he might, if he had believed in Jesus, have done so much for God and for the souls of men. What evil habits he has acquired! What can you ever make of this man? If he be saved, it will be so as by fire. He is called, and he shall enter heaven, but oh! how little can he do for the Master, and what strong corruptions will he have to wrestle with, and what an inward conflict even till he gets to heaven! It is late, it is very late, but oh! blessed be God! *it is not too late.* We have had within these walls persons who have long passed the prime of their days, who have come forward and said, " We will cast in our lot with you because the Lord is with you." We have heard their joyous story of how the old man has become a babe, and how he that was hoary with years has been born again into the kingdom of Christ. It is not too late. Did the devil say so? The gate is shutting; I can hear it grating on the hinges, but it is not shut! The sun is going down, but he is not lost beneath the horizon yet; and if the Master calls thee, only run thou the faster because it is so; and when thou art saved, serve him with all thy might and main, because thou hast so little time to glorify him here on earth, and short space in which to show thy sense of deep indebtedness to his surpassing love.

The day is nearly over, *it has come to the eleventh hour,* five o'clock! The men have been looking at their watches to see whether it will not soon be six; they are longing to hear the clock strike; they hope the day's work will soon close. See; the Master goes out into the market-place among those hulking fellows who are still loitering there, and he pitches upon some and asks them, "Why stand ye here all the day idle? Go and work! and whatsoever is right I will give you." At the eleventh hour they come in—half-ashamed to come I will be bound,—hardly liking the others to see them; ashamed to begin work so late. Still they did steal in somewhere; and there were generous labourers who looked over the tops of the vines, and said to them, "Glad to see you, friends! glad to see you, however late." There were a few, I dare say, among the labourers, at least there are if this be the vineyard, who would even stop their work and begin to sing and praise God to think that their fellows had been brought in at the eleventh hour. Now the eleventh hour must be looked upon as any period of life which is past threescore years and ten; how late it may extend I cannot tell. There is an authentic instance of a man converted to God at the age of a hundred and four, during the last Irish revival, who walked some distance to make a confession of his faith in Jesus Christ; and I recollect a case of one converted in America by a sermon which he had heard, I think, eighty-one years previously. He was fifteen when he heard Mr. Flavell at the end of a discourse, instead of pronouncing the blessing, say, "I cannot bless you. How can I bless those who do not love the Lord Jesus Christ? 'If any man love not the Lord Jesus Christ let him be Anathema Maranatha;'" and eighty-one years or more afterwards that solemn sentence came to the man's recollection when he was living in America, and God blessed it to his conversion. There have been some to whom the eleventh hour has been the very hour of death; some, I say, how many or how few is not for me to know. There is one instance we know in Scripture, it was the dying thief. There is but one; God however, in his abundant mercy can do as he wills to the praise of the glory of his grace, and at the eleventh hour he can call his chosen. It is very late, it is very very, very late, it is sorrowfully late, *it is dolefully late, but it is not too late,* and if the Master call thee, come—though an hundred years of sin should make thy feet heavy to thee, so that thy steps are painfully limping. If he call thee it is late but not too late, and therefore come. Have you ever thought of how the thief worked for his Lord? It was not a fine place for working, hanging on a cross dying, just at the eleventh hour; but he did a deal of work in the few minutes. Observe what he did. First he confessed Christ—he acknowledged him to be Lord, confessed him before men. In the second place he justified Christ—"This man has done nothing amiss." In the next place he worshipped the Lord Jesus, calling him "Lord." He even began to preach, for he rebuked his fellow sinner; he told him that he should not revile one who was so unrighteously condemned. He offered a petition which has become a very model of prayer—"Lord, remember me when thou comest into thy kingdom." At any rate I wish I could say of myself what I can say of the thief, *he did all he could;* I cannot say that of myself, I am afraid I cannot say it of any of you. I do not know anything the thief could have done on the cross which he did not do. As soon as ever he was called, he seems to have worked in the vineyard to the utmost extent of his ability; and so let me say to you, if you should be called at the eleventh hour, my dear hearer, though thou be well stricken in years and aged, yet for Jesus Christ's sake out of great love for all the great things which he hath done for thee, go thy way and praise him with all thy might.

II. My time has gone, and I wanted to have shown that DISTINGUISHING GRACE SHONE RESPLENDENTLY IN EVERY INSTANCE. Those called in the early morning have delightful reason for admiring sovereign grace, for they are spared the ills and sins of life. I must content myself, however, by repeating concerning them the lines of Ralph Erskine.

> "In heavenly choirs a question rose,
> That stirred up strife will never close;
> What rank of all the ransomed race,
> Owes highest praise to sovereign grace.
>
> Babes thither caught from womb and breast,
> Claimed right to sing above the rest;
> Because they found the happy shore,
> They never saw nor sought before."

What distinguishing grace is that which called us when we were young! Herein is electing love. "When Ephraim was a child then I loved him, and called my son out of Egypt." Some of us in time and in eternity will have to utter a special song of thankfulness to the love which took us in our days of folly and simplicity, and conducted us into the family of God. It was not because we were better disposed children than others, or because there was naturally anything good about us; we were wilful, heady, and high-minded, proud, wayward, and disobedient as other children are, and yet mercy separated us from the rest, and we shall never cease to adore its sovereignty.

Look at the grace which calls the man at the age of twenty, when the passions are hot, when there is strong temptation to plunge into the vices and the so-called pleasures of life. To be delivered from the charms of sin, when the world's cheek is ruddy, when it wears its best attire, and to be taught to prefer the reproach of Christ to all the riches of Egypt, this is mighty grace for which God shall have our sweetest song.

To be called of the Lord at forty, in the prime of life. This is a wonderful instance of divine power, for worldliness is hard to overcome, and worldliness is the sin of middle age. With a family about you, with much business, with the world eating into you as doth a canker, it is a wonder that God should in his mercy have visited you then, and made you a regenerate soul. You are a miracle of grace, and you will have to feel it and to praise God for it in time and eternity.

Sixty again. "Can the Ethiopian change his skin, or the leopard his spots? If so, then ye who are accustomed to do evil may learn to do well." And yet you have learned, you have had a blessed schoolmaster who sweetly taught you, and you have learned to do well. Though your vessel had begun to rot in the waters of the Black Sea of sin, you have got a new owner, and you will run up a new flag, and you will sail round the Cape of Good Hope to the Islands of the Blessed, in the Land of the Hereafter.

But what shall I say of you that are called when you are aged? Ah you will have to love much, for you have had much forgiven. I do not know that you may be in thankfulness a whit behind those of us who are called in our early youth; we have much to bless God for, and so have you. We are at one extreme and you are at the other; we would love much because we have been spared much sinning, and you must love much because you have been delivered from much sinning. Not to go through the fire is a theme for song; but to traverse the flame and not be burned, to walk the furnace and to be delivered from its vehement fire, oh! how should you find words with which to express your gratitude! Called early or called late, called at midday or called at early noon, let us together, since we have been called by grace alone, ascribe it all to the Lord Jesus, and moved by the mighty constraints of his love, let us work with body, soul, and spirit—work for him till we can work no longer, and then praise him in the rest of glory.

I pray you, brethren, suffer no idleness to creep over you. If you have sought to extend the Redeemer's kingdom, do it more. Give more, talk more of Christ, pray more, labour more! I often receive the kind advice, "Do less." I cannot do less. Do less! Why, better rot altogether than live the inglorious life of doing less than our utmost for God. We shall none of us, I am afraid, kill ourselves with working too hard for Jesus. It were such a blessed act of suicide that if there be a sin that is venial, it would certainly be that. I am not afraid that you are likely to perpetrate such an enormity. Work for the Master! Labour for the Master! We must spend and be spent, and wear ourselves out for him! Make no reserve for the flesh to fulfil the lusts of it! And oh, how happy shall we be, if we may be privileged to finish the work, and hear him say, "Well done, good and faithful servant, enter thou into the joy of thy Lord." May the Lord bless you for Christ's sake. Amen.

PORTION OF SCRIPTURE READ BEFORE SERMON—Matthew xix. 27 to end of chapter; xx. to end of verse 29.

Metropolitan Tabernacle Pulpit.

NUMBER 2,500; OR, ENTRANCE AND EXCLUSION.

A Sermon

INTENDED FOR READING ON LORD'S-DAY, JANUARY 17TH, 1897,

DELIVERED BY

C. H. SPURGEON,

AT THE METROPOLITAN TABERNACLE, NEWINGTON,

On Thursday Evening, May 21st, 1885.

"And they that were ready went in with him to the marriage: and the door was shut."—Matthew xxv. 10.

DURING the waiting period, the wise and foolish virgins seemed much alike, even as at this day one can hardly discern the false professor from the true. Everything turned upon the coming of the bridegroom. To the ten virgins, that was the chief event of the night. If it had not been for his coming, they would not have gone forth with their lamps. It was because they knew he would surely come that they prepared themselves to join in the marriage procession, and attend him with their songs to the place of his abode. Yet, for a while, he did not come. The sun had gone down, and darkness had stolen over the whole landscape, but the bridegroom did not come. The dews of night were falling fast, yet still he did not come. The hours were long, and slowly passed away one after the other, yet he did not come. It was waxing toward the middle of the night; a few stars were visible, but there was no lingering light of the day remaining. It was the time of darkness, and the eyes of the waiting virgins grew heavy with watching. Why was the bridegroom so long in coming? They had been bidden to look for him, they had fully expected him; yet he had not come. There were whisperings that it was all a delusion, and that he never would come; and then there was that guilty sense of slumber which stole over them. In the case of some of the ten, their spirit was willing, but their flesh was weak; but in the case of the others, both flesh and spirit were perverse, so that their sleep became exceeding deep, as when a man sleepeth even unto death.

But the bridegroom did come, as, brethren, in our case, the Heavenly Bridegroom will come. However long we may have

No. 2,500.

waited for him, let us rest assured that he will come. As surely as he came once, so, "unto them that look for him shall he appear the second time without sin unto salvation." It seems to me that it needs less faith to believe in the second Advent of Christ than in his first Advent. He has been here before, so he knows the way to come again. He has been here before, and wrought a wondrous work; surely, he will come back to receive the reward of his service. The Good Shepherd came to earth once to lay down his life for the sheep; he will surely come again as the Chief Shepherd to recompense the under-shepherds who have faithfully kept the night watches for him. Jesus will come again, as surely as the bridegroom came at the midnight hour.

Yes, the bridegroom did come. Despite the waiting time, he did come; and then came the dreadful separation between those who had been waiting for his appearing. Scarcely by any act of his, the foolish and the wise were parted the one from the other. They were awakened by the sound of his approach; the herald that preceded him cried, "Behold, the bridegroom cometh," and the sleepers were all aroused. Then the true adherents of the bridegroom, the wise virgins, penitent for their guilty sleep, poured the oil into their lamps, which were burning low, and soon they were blazing up clear and bright. As the bridegroom's procession came near, "they that were ready went in with him to the marriage: and the door was shut." But the foolish virgins —those who had despised the secret stores of oil,—those who had never gone to the Divine Spirit for his matchless grace,—were separated from their wiser companions; not, indeed, by any special act of the bridegroom, but as the natural result of their own unprepared condition. They had to go away to buy oil of those that sold it, and when they came back, it was too late for them to go in to the marriage. They came up to the gate of the palace, and found the door fast closed against them, —shut for ever,—and learned that they must abide in the outer darkness, to weep and lament that they were not found worthy to behold the bridegroom's face, or to enter into his joy.

I am going to talk to you, dear friends, as simply as I can, but with deep soul-earnestness, about the two sets of persons mentioned in the text. First, I will speak of *the ready, and their entrance:* "They that were ready went in with him to the marriage." And, secondly, I will say something about *the unready, and their exclusion:* "And the door was shut."

I. First, then, let us think of THE READY, AND THEIR ENTRANCE: "They that were ready went in with him to the marriage."

Let us meditate a little, first, about the entrance itself, and then talk together about the persons who enjoyed it.

Concerning their entrance, note that it was *immediate upon the coming of the bridegroom.* As soon as he appeared, there seems to have been no interval, but, at once, "they that were ready *went in* with him to the marriage." Beloved friends, the manifestation of Christ shall be the glorification of his people. We shall want nothing else but to behold his face, and then our bliss shall be perfect and complete. So each believer says with Job, "I know that my Redeemer liveth, and that he shall stand at the latter day upon the earth: and though after my skin worms destroy this body, yet in my flesh shall I see God, whom I shall see for myself, and mine eyes shall behold, and not another." Never entertain the slightest fear of any such purgatorial state as some have begun to dream of again. That lie, which the Reformers rightly called, "purgatory pick-purse," which filled the pope's treasury, and was a curse to myriads of immortal souls, was exposed in all its naked ugliness by the light which God gave to Luther and Calvin; yet now, amid the abounding scepticism of these evil days, there is coming back this foul night-bird, or rather, this dragon of the dark ages; and sometimes even the children of God feel the influence of its pestilential presence. Dear Christian friends, be not afraid of any purgatory. If you die, you shall be absent from the body and present with the Lord at once, for this shall be your blessed portion in Christ. If you are alive and remain till Jesus comes again, your body shall be changed in a moment, in the twinkling of an eye, and you shall rise to meet your Lord in the air, and so shall be ever with him; but if you have fallen asleep in Jesus, those who are alive at his coming shall have no preference over you, but you shall be raised incorruptible, and in the moment of that rising, when your spirit, by the divine fiat, shall have been re-united with your perfectly purified and glorified body, you shall go in with him to the marriage, and be for ever with him and like him. Do not trouble yourself, therefore, about what is to happen, or what is not to happen. Be you confident of this,—if you sleep, you shall sleep in Jesus, and when you wake up, you shall wake up in his likeness, and you shall never be parted from him whose company even now is your highest source of joy, and whose society shall be your delight for ever and ever.

Notice, next, that the entrance of the wise virgins into the marriage feast was not only immediate, it was also *intimate*. "They that were ready went in *with him* to the marriage." I like that expression "with him." I would go nowhere without him; and if I may go anywhere with him, wherever he shall lead me, it shall be a happy day to me; and so it shall be to all who love his appearing. You know, beloved, that our Lord Jesus left it in his will that we are to be with him in his glory; listen to this clause out of his last will and testament: "Father, I will that they also, whom thou hast given me be with me where I am; that they may behold my glory." O beloved, you who know what it is to be one with Jesus, crucified with him, risen with him, made to sit together with him in the heavenlies, you, I am sure, will find something more heavenly about heaven than otherwise had been there when that sweet sentence is true of you, "They that were ready went in *with him* to the marriage." Our Lord Jesus himself shall escort us to our place in glory, he shall conduct us to the sources of highest blessedness, for as the elder said to John in the Revelation, "The Lamb which is in the midst of the throne shall feed them, and shall lead them unto living fountains of waters." This, it seems to me, is the very centre of the bliss of heaven. Heaven is like the Eshcol cluster of grapes; but the essence, the juice, the sweetness of the cluster, consists in this fact,—that we shall be with Jesus, "for ever with the Lord." Ah, me! my brethren, how else could we ever hope to go in to the marriage, if we did not go in with him,—hidden behind him, covered with his righteousness, washed in his blood? John saw a great multitude, which no man could number, of all nations, and kindreds, and people, and tongues, standing before the throne, and before the Lamb, and it was of them that the elder also said, "These are they which came out of great tribulation, and have washed their robes, and made them white in the blood of the Lamb. Therefore are they before the throne of God, and serve him day and night in his temple: and he that sitteth on the throne shall dwell among them." No one will object to the entrance into glory of those who go in with him. Even the pure and holy God will not raise any question as to our entrance, if we enter with his Son. All the demands of divine justice will be fully met by the fact that we go in with him. Covered with his righteousness, adorned with his beauties, inseparably united to his person, the beloved of his heart, we shall go in with him to the marriage, and none will think of wanting to have us excluded.

I am tempted to linger over such a delightful theme as this; but I must not, and I need not, for you can meditate upon it to your heart's content when you are at home. To my mind, there is indescribable sweetness in these words: "They that were ready went in *with him* to the marriage."

Then, next, notice how exceedingly *joyous* was the entrance: "They that were ready went in with him *to the marriage*." It was not their portion to stand outside the door, to listen to the music and enjoy the light that might come streaming through when it was opened for a few seconds; but they "went in with him to the marriage." It was not the intention of our Lord to tell us in this parable in what capacity the saints shall enter heaven. The parable is meant to teach certain lessons, and it explains them very clearly. If it tried to teach us everything, we might miss the most important lesson of all; but from other passages of Scripture we know that we shall go in with Christ to the marriage, not as mere spectators of his joy, as friends of the Bridegroom who rejoice exceedingly in his gladness; but we shall go in with him to share his bliss. Be it ever remembered that, sinners though we are, and utterly unworthy of so distinguished an honour, the Lord Jesus says to every believing soul, "I have espoused thee unto myself, to be mine for ever and ever." Oh, matchless word! You, believer, shall go in with him to that heavenly marriage feast, as part of that wondrous bride, the Lamb's wife, who is then to find her bliss for ever consummated with her glorious Husband. What a mercy it is to have grace enough to be able to believe this, for it needs much faith to believe that such a distinction shall ever be the lot of those who were once heirs of wrath even as others, and who by their sins have deserved to be cast into the deepest hell! Yet, beloved, there are no heights in heaven which we shall not climb, there are no joys before the throne of which we shall not be partakers, we shall not be present at that wedding feast merely as Christ's servants, or as on-lookers, or as favoured guests; but we shall be there to partake to the full of all the bliss and glory, ourselves all the while the object of that innermost love, that most special, most dear and near and intimate communion with our Beloved. We shall for ever be one with Christ by conjugal bands; nay, more than that, for even conjugal bands are only used as a humble metaphor of the eternal union between our souls and Christ. "This," said the apostle Paul, when referring to marriage, "is a great mystery: but I speak concerning Christ and the church." "They that were ready went in with him to the marriage," right up to the banqueting table, to partake of all the rare dainties gathered from all the ages, brought from all the dominions of the great King, to make high festival for that greatest of all days for which all other days were made, the day of judgment itself included.

Even on earth, we always properly associate the highest degree of joy with a marriage, when it is what it ought to be. If ever there is any joy on earth that belongs naturally to us as beings of flesh and blood, it is upon our marriage day. The wedding of a loving couple is looked forward to with great expectations, and often looked back upon with fond memories. However much of blight and withering blast may in after life fall upon that relationship which is commenced upon the marriage day, yet the day itself is always the figure and emblem of joy. See, then, what heaven is to be to the people of God; it is a marriage, a perpetual festival, a banishment of everything that is dolorous, a gathering together of all that is joyous. A marriage on earth,—well, we know what that is; but a marriage in heaven,—who can describe that? The marriage of men and women,—we are familar enough with that; but this union of which I am trying to speak is the marriage of the Christ of God with his redeemed people. Earthly marriage is contracted between two sinners; but this heavenly wedding is the marriage of One, who is all pure and holy, to another, whom he has purified from every stain, or spot, or wrinkle, or any such thing, and so made ready for this everlasting union.

"They that were ready went in with him to the marriage." These words sound to my ear and heart like the pealing of wedding bells. Listen. These people had been in the battle, fighting as good soldiers of Jesus Christ; but, by-and-by, they "went in with him to the marriage." They had been in their Lord's vineyard, toiling amid the burden and heat of the day; the sun had looked upon them, and they were bronzed and browned with the burning heat; but in due time they "went in with him to the marriage." They had sometimes seen their Lord for a season, and then they had missed him for a while, but they "went in with him to the marriage." They had even wandered from him sometimes, and darkness had surrounded them; ay! and they had wickedly fallen asleep when they ought to have watched; but they "went in with him to the marriage." Oh, the blessedness of being where all evil is for ever ended, and all joy is begun, never to end; all sin and imperfection blotted out by Christ's precious blood, and all holiness and perfection put upon us for ever and ever! All this and more I read in the words, "They that were ready went in with him to the marriage."

Then comes this little sentence, which is so terrible to the ungodly, but, oh! so sweet to the gracious: "And the door was shut." These words show that the entrance of the righteous into heaven is *eternal*. The door was shut for two purposes, but chiefly, as I understand it, to shut in the godly; and before that door can be opened to let in the wicked, it will have to be opened to let out the righteous. These two declarations of our Lord stand side by side: "These shall go away into everlasting punishment: but the righteous into life eternal." If you deny the eternity of the one, you must deny the eternity of the other, for it is the same word in each case. You must break down the door which is the security of the saints within, ere there can be a change for the ungodly who are without; and that can never be. The joy of this marriage feast is eternal joy; this is implied in our Saviour's utterance, "They that were ready went in with him to the marriage: and the door was shut."

I want you, next, to notice who these people were who went in with the Bridegroom. According to the text, they were *a prepared people*, a people that were ready: "They that were ready went in with him to the marriage." There are none among the sons of men who are naturally ready to go in to that marriage feast; before they can enter, they must undergo a wondrous change, they must, in fact, be born again. Think for a moment what creatures we are by nature, quite unfit to go in with Christ to the heavenly marriage. Then think of what Christ is, so bright, so pure, so holy,—who is she who is fit to go into heaven, to be for ever with this glorious Bridegroom? O my soul, thou art but dust and ashes; and thy Lord is the Sun of righteousness! O my soul, thou art, through sin, comparable to a dunghill; and thy Saviour is infinite perfection. Canst thou ever be "ready" to go in with him to the marriage? Not unless that same God, who became man that he might be a fit Husband for thee, shall make thee holy, that thou mayest be meet to be wedded to him for ever.

A great change has to be wrought in you, far beyond any power of yours to accomplish, ere you can go in with Christ to the marriage. You must, first of all, be renewed in your nature, or you will not be ready. You must be washed from your sins, or you will not be ready. You must be justified in Christ's righteousness, and you must put on his wedding dress, or else you will not be ready. You must be reconciled to God, you must be made like to God, or you will not be ready. Or, to come to the parable before us, you must have a lamp, and that lamp must be fed with heavenly oil, and it must continue to burn brightly, or else you will not be ready. No child of darkness can go into that place of light. You must be brought out of nature's darkness into God's marvellous light, or else you will never be ready to go in with Christ to the marriage, and to be for ever with him.

Brethren beloved in the Lord, I pray you often look to your readiness for going in to the marriage. Are you all ready now? If, at this moment, the archangel's trumpet voice should sound, or if now, as lately happened to certain dear friends of ours, you should be struck down with paralysis or apoplexy, and in a moment pass away, are you ready for the great change? Are you quite ready to go in with Christ to the marriage? I would advise you, not only to be ready in all the great things, but to be ready also in the little things, and in everything that concerns yourself in relation to your Lord. Perhaps you have not yet publicly put on Christ in baptism. Then, in that respect, you are not ready. Do not delay obedience to Christ's command, remembering his own words, "He that believeth and is baptized shall be saved." With your mouth confess the Lord Jesus, if with your heart you have believed on him. Disregard no commands of Christ. Perhaps you have never yet been to his table of communion. If that is the case, I do not think you can call yourself "ready" to go in with him to the marriage. Perhaps you call these things little matters, and they are small compared with that greater matter of which I have already spoken. But I would not wish you to die with a single command of Christ's neglected. You have not prayed with your boys and girls yet, have you? Well, then, you are not ready. You have not made your will, you have not set your house in order; I would have you get all such things quite ready, for a little unreadiness may greatly trouble you in your departing moments. You have not yet fulfilled what has been very nearly a vow toward God; you have not yet done what you ought to do of your work for the present generation; you have not yet been to that ungodly friend, and warned him, as your heart a little while ago prompted you to do. I would like to have you, my brother, or sister, in such a state that, if you fell down dead on your way home to-night, others might regret it, but you would be thankful that for you sudden death was sudden glory. Mr. Whitefield used to say that he did not like to go to sleep at night if he had left his gloves out of his hat where he might find them in the morning. It is delightful to feel, "All is right between God and my soul, between myself and my wife and my children and all my surroundings. Now let death come when it will. Let the sweet chariot swing low,—as the Jubilee Singers' song quaintly put it,—and let it bear my soul away up to the heavenly country where I shall go in with him to the marriage."

Be ready, dear friends, be ready; especially be ready in the great matter of salvation; but see that you are ready in everything. You know that when you are going to see a very special friend, or some person of importance, you put on your best coat and everything that will make you ready to see him; but, afterwards, when you get near the friend's door, or the great man's mansion, I notice that you brush off any little dust from the street that may have been blown upon your garments, and so you get quite ready to meet him when he appears. So, in spiritual affairs, even if you have on your best robe, yet still there may be a little brushing needed, and I would have you do it, so that it may be said of you without anything to qualify it, "they that were ready went in with him to the marriage: and the door was shut."

I read, in an American tract, a little sketch written by a gentleman who, having often to cross the great lakes, was in the habit of providing himself with a life-preserving belt in case of need. One night, while he was asleep, an alarm was raised, and he rushed on deck with his life-belt round him, but found that there was no cause for fear. He went downstairs again, and as he lay in bed he had something like a dream, though it was really a waking reverie, and it took this shape. He thought he was on board the great vessel in which all of us are floating on the broad sea of time, and that a great and terrible storm came on. There were some men on deck, with life-preserving belts round them; they had been laughed at while the weather was calm and the sea was smooth; but, as they stood there, with the vessel rocking, and the timbers straining, there were none to mock at them, but many who greatly envied the quiet peacefulness which rested on their countenances. You know who these men are, and what is their protection. Faith in Jesus is the great life-preserving belt; let the tempest come when it may, faith in Christ will enable us to swim through every flood till we reach the happy shores of heaven.

As this gentleman stood on the deck, and looked about him, he heard one man say, "I was going to buy one of those belts; I lived just opposite the shop where they were sold; and I was often told by friends that I had better get one at once, and I meant to; but I put it off, and started just a little too late to get it, so I was obliged to come without it, though I meant to have one." The gentleman saw this man washed overboard, as the others were who had not the life-belt, and his good intention could not save him. No doubt there are many here who have meant to get the spiritual life-belt, and they mean to do so now, so they say. Ah! heaven is being filled with people who have believed in Jesus, and hell is being filled with people who *meant* to believe in Jesus, but did not. That is the difference between the two classes, but what a difference it will make between them when they come to die! These are the people who crowd the corridors of perdition, men and women who *meant* to trust the Saviour, but who never did it. They lived just opposite the places where these life-belts were to be had, and they meant to have had them, but they had them not when the last great storm came on, and so they were lost, and lost for ever!

There was another man who said, "I have been across this sea so often without a belt that I thought I would run the risk once more." He, too, was washed away; and there are some of you, my hearers, who say, "I have lived twenty, thirty, forty, fifty, sixty, or seventy years, and I am not dead yet; I will run the risk for another year." Really, nowadays, nobody seems to grow old. You meet a man of seventy-five or eighty, and he thinks that he will be old some day, but he has known somebody who lived till he was ninety-nine, and he thinks he shall reach the same age. I have heard of an aged farmer who wanted to buy his neighbour's field. He was eighty, and his neighbour was five years younger; so, when his neighbour would not sell him the land, he said to him, "Ah, well! never mind; you are an old man, and I can buy it when you are dead!" That is just the way people talk. "All men think all men mortal but themselves." Here was a man who was five years older than the other, yet he was going to buy the field after the younger man was dead! It is such people who say, "I have been sailing over this sea so long without a life-belt, I will risk it still longer." Thus, they also are lost!

There was another man, who ran to his trunk to get out his life-belt; he pulled up the lid, and took out the belt, but he found it was out of order, and quite useless. The fact was, it was a bad one when he bought it; and after carrying it about with him for a little while, he became weary of such a useless appendage, so he threw it into his trunk, and now that he really needed preservation from the storm, it was of no use to him. You are here, sir, I know you! You used to make a profession of religion; you had a life-belt once, so you thought; but it was not a good one, or you would have it now. It was one that looked like the right thing, and you wore it for a while. You used to be at the prayer-meeting, you even became a member of the church, you carried your religion for a time, but what has become of it now? Where were you last night? I repeat the question,—*Where were you last night?* If the devil had laid hold upon you, and taken you down to his own dominions, there would have been none who would have cried, "Stop, thief!" when he flew away with you, for they would have known that he was only taking his own property, which he had found on his own premises. Yet you did once make a profession of religion, you used to sit at the communion table, possibly you were even baptized; but where is your life-belt now? It is gone! God save you, who have become backsliders, lest you also prove to be apostates! If you have turned back, then return, return, return, while yet there is time, while yet there is hope for you; and if you never were converted, may God begin the gracious work within you even now!

There was another one on board who had a life-belt, and he seemed very pleased when he put it on, but when the waves washed him off the vessel he floated for a few moments, and then down he sank. The fact was, his belt was a counterfeit; somebody had told him that the other sort was so very expensive, and here was one that looked even better. True, there was a whisper that it would not stand the needful tests; but the man did not care much about that, for his belt looked as good as the genuine one, and he had the credit of standing with those sensible people who had the true thing, so it answered very well *until he came into the surging sea.* So there may be some of you here who have counterfeit life-belts. You are members of the church, you come to the communion table, and everybody respects you. Ah! but, with a sham religion, how will you do in the swelling of Jordan? What will you do when heart and flesh fail? Oh! ere it be too late, may God take away from you the sham, and give you genuine godliness,—a new heart and a right spirit!

As the gentleman looked round him, he saw yet another of the passengers,—a young man who was clinging to someone else who had on a life-belt. He was crying to him, "Let me lay hold on you; will not your belt be sufficient to sustain both of us?" But the other answered, "It will only suffice for one; it will only keep one afloat." Then the gentleman thought of our Saviour's parable of the ten virgins, and of what the foolish said unto the wise, "Give us of your oil; for our lamps are gone out." But the wise answered, "Not so; lest there be not enough for us and you." So let us remember that nothing but personal piety will avail, the religion of another can be of no service to you. Our Lord's message to all is, "Ye must be born again," and there is no such thing as being born again by proxy. You must fly to Jesus for refuge, and there is no one who can do this for you. You must, by the Holy Spirit's power, trust in Christ for yourselves; no one can believe for you.

I rejoice that there are so many here who have on the genuine gospel life-belt. Standing in Christ Jesus, they are not afraid.

"No condemnation do they dread,
For Jesus is their all."

They can without a tremor face floods or flames, and the devouring deep; they can even be—

"Fearless of hell and ghastly death,"

knowing that they shall be safely landed on heaven's peaceful shore, to go no more out for ever.

II. I am almost thankful that I have only a few minutes to spend upon the second part of my subject,—THE UNREADY, AND THEIR EXCLUSION. I will try to say much in a few words, and I beg you to let every word abide with you.

What, then, was this exclusion? "The door was shut." It was not ajar, it was shut, and so tightly was it closed that *there was a complete severance* between the guests inside and the too-late foolish virgins outside.

Yet, *this severance was perfectly just.* The foolish virgins ought to have been there in time, they ought to have gone in with the bridegroom; was it not their very office to attend him, and accompany him home? The time for entering in had fully come; it was the right and proper time. The bridegroom had given them all that night to get ready, and they had even complained of the length of the delay before he came; so, when the door was at last shut, it was very late. They had had all that time in which to get the oil, and to trim their lamps. It was not as though the bridegroom had come in the first watch of the night, and they had said, "We had not time to trim our lamps." No, it was not so. So, dear friends, you have had all this life, all these years of your Lord's long-suffering and patient entreaty; and it will be just that the door should be shut when your last hour shall come. Oh, be wise ere it is too late!

When "the door was shut," *the exclusion was final.* In all my searchings of the Word, I have never found any kind of hope that the door, once shut, will ever be opened again. There may be a "larger hope" indulged in by some, but I implore you never to risk your souls upon that rotten plank, for there is no Scripture warrant for it whatsoever. Even if there were, what larger hope do you want than that which the gospel itself affords? Why do you not get ready to enter in with Christ to the marriage? Why be left to tarry outside? What is there in the cold midnight that should tempt you to delay with the risk of never being able to enter the door? If there were any such larger hope as deludes so many, it still must be a desperate risk to trust to it. They also who talk about annihilation, or restitution, at any rate offer you nothing that ought to charm you away from immediate faith in Christ and immediate and everlasting salvation by him. So far as you yourself are concerned, it should cease to be an awful thing that, in the world to come, "There are no acts of pardon passed." Why should you throw away the certainty of a present salvation and immediate deliverance from the curse, which you may have at this moment,—which you shall have at once if you believe in Jesus,—under some foolish dream that perhaps the door of mercy may open after ages of weeping and wailing and gnashing of teeth? Nay, rather, be ready to enter in with Christ to the marriage, for, as the Lord liveth, I cannot clear my soul of all responsibility unless I tell you that, as I read the Bible more and more, I am more and more certain that, when that door has once been shut, it will never again be opened to any living soul. Where death meets you, judgment will find you, and there you will remain to all eternity. I pray you, risk not your eternal destiny, but " Seek ye the Lord while he may be found, call ye upon him while he is near: let the wicked forsake his way, and the unrighteous man his thoughts : and let him return unto the Lord, and he will have mercy upon him; and to our God, for he will abundantly pardon."

Who were these persons who were shut out when the door was closed? *They bore the name of virgins,* yet the door was shut against them. They were not rank outsiders, not mere tramps of the street; not infidels, not agnostics, but members of the church. They were called virgins, yet against them the door was shut; they also had lamps, and lamps that once burned as brightly as others. There was, for a while, no difference between the lustre of their lamps and the lustre of the wisest, yet they were shut out. They had at least some oil, they were for a time companions of the wise virgins, they went out with them to meet the bridegroom, and the wise virgins, probably, never suspected that these others were foolish till, in the middle of the night, they found too late that their lamps were going out. O sirs, O sirs, shall we drink out of the same communion cup, and eat of the same bread at the Lord's table, and be reminded of his broken body and his shed blood, and yet, shall some of us be shut in with God for ever, and shall some of you be shut out for ever because you have not received the Holy Ghost, because you have not the secret inward store of the oil of grace? May God prevent it by his grace!

Notice that *these people acted in much the same way as those acted who went in with the bridegroom.* They went forth to meet the bridegroom, they went on the same road and at the same rate as the others went; they went to sleep, alas! as the others went to sleep; they awoke as the others awoke; and they began to trim their lamps as the others were trimming theirs. Their spot seemed to be the spot of God's children, and they appeared to have many of the marks of the election of grace; yet they were not of it, nor in it, for they had no oil in their vessels with their lamps, no grace, no indwelling of the Holy Ghost, no supernatural operation of him who worketh in the saints to will and to do of his own good pleasure. They were so like the real bride of Christ that only the Bridegroom could tell the difference until the midnight came, and then the difference was apparent to all observers.

It seems to me also that these persons, who were shut out, were *people who knew something about prayer*. They did not, that night, for the first time pick up the agonized cry, "Lord, Lord, open to us." They had probably been *habitués* of prayer-meetings, they had been where people called Christ "Lord," and they used that formula themselves. Perhaps they might have said, "Lord, Lord, have we not prophesied in thy name? and in thy name have cast out devils? and in thy name done many wonderful works?" Yet the door was shut against them, and they, outside, knew something of what was going on inside, and therefore would gnash their teeth all the more because they could not enter. The door was shut against those who had seen the light, but whose lamps had gone out. They had been carrying in their hand the very lamps which entitled them to claim a place in the procession, but those lamps had gone out; and therefore they were not entitled to any such place, and the door was shut against them. O you who are only professors of religion, will you shut yourselves outside the door of mercy? You will do so if you neglect to obtain that secret oil of grace which can only be supplied by the Holy Spirit.

Before another Sabbath comes round, your preacher may be suddenly struck down, as one of our brethren has been; I may never have another opportunity of speaking to you who are professors, and warning you to make sure that you are also possessors, and that you really have the grace of God in your souls. Or, possibly, some of you may be taken away without a moment's warning, as one of our friends has been. Suppose that then you could turn round upon me, in another world, and say, "Preacher, we heard you again and again, we listened to all that came from your lips, we even came out on Thursday nights to listen to you, yet you prophesied smooth things to us, and you said, 'Peace, peace, when there was no peace.'" I pray God that I may have no man's blood upon the skirts of my garments in that last tremendous day, and therefore I bid you now to escape from the wrath to come. Flee to Christ, flee to his dear cross, and look up to his bleeding wounds, for—

"There is life for a look at the Crucified One."

Flee from your sins, flee from yourselves. Flee from any worldly pursuits which entangle you, and put your trust in Jesus Christ and him crucified, and from your heart say,—

"'Jesus, thy blood and righteousness
My beauty are, my glorious dress,'"

"I will go in with thee to the marriage, and when the door is shut, I shall be on the right side of it,—

"'Far from a world of grief and sin,
With God eternally shut in.'"

The Lord save us all, for his name's sake! Amen.

Hymns from "Our Own Hymn Book"—364, 365, 1043.

N.B.—This Sermon is No. 2,500 in the regular weekly issue, which has been continued without intermission for more than forty-two years. It is specially suitable for widespread distribution among the unsaved, and forms a fitting companion to the following discourses previously published in the *Metropolitan Tabernacle Pulpit*,—
    Number 1,000; or, "Bread Enough and to Spare."
    Number 1,500; or, Lifting up the Brazen Serpent.
    Number 2,000; or, Healing by the Stripes of Jesus.
    Number 2,400; or, "Escape for thy Life!"

All these are admirably adapted for circulation at or before evangelistic services, and also for personal presentation to the anxious or the careless.

Messrs. Passmore and Alabaster will be pleased to supply quantities at reduced prices, or they can be obtained through all booksellers.

SCRIPTURE INDEX OF SERMONS

Genesis 3:14,15	13
Genesis 3:15	25
Numbers 21:9	153
1 Kings 5:17	1
Micah 5:2	37
Matthew 1:23	45
Matthew 20:1,3,5,6	401
Matthew 25:10	413
John 1:43-45	93
John 7:38,39	213
John 9:35,36	105
John 13:3-5	189
John 16:7	213
John 16:14,15	225
John 18:37	201
Acts 1:10,11	317
Romans 8:14	237
Romans 7:24,25	273
1 Corinthians 11:26	249
2 Corinthians 4:4	129
Galatians 2:21	117
Philippians 3:13,14	281
1 Timothy 3:16	57
1 Timothy 3:16 (second sermon)	69
Hebrews 7:4	81
Hebrews 12:14,15	261
Hebrews 12:24,25	165
Hebrews 12:24,25 (second sermon)	177
1 John 1:6,7	293
1 John 1:7	305
Jude 3	141
Revelation 5:6,7	329
Revelation 5:8-10	341
Revelation 14:4,5	365
Revelation 14:12,13	377
Revelation 19:7,8	353
Revelation 21:27	389

www.ingramcontent.com/pod-product-compliance
Lightning Source LLC
Chambersburg PA
CBHW050426240426
43661CB00055B/2290